Encyclopedia of
American Forest and Conservation History

Editorial Advisory Board

Encyclopedia of
American Forest
and
Conservation History

RICHARD C. DAVIS

Editor

VOLUME TWO

Macmillan Publishing Company, New York
Collier Macmillan Publishers, London

The Free Press, a division of Macmillan, Inc.
866 Third Avenue, New York , N.Y. 10022

Collier Macmillan Canada, Inc.

Library of Congress Catalog Card Number: 83-811

Printed in the United States of America

printing number
1 2 3 4 5 6 7 8 9 10

Library of Congress Cataloging in Publication Data
Main entry under title:

Encyclopedia of American forest and conservation history.

Includes index.
1. Forests and forestry—United States—History—
Dictionaries.   2. Forest conservation—United States—
History—Dictionaries.   I. Davis, Richard, C., 1939–
SD143.E53   1983   333.75′0973   83-811
ISBN 0-02-907350-2 (set)
ISBN 0-02-907750-8 (v. 1)
ISBN 0-02-907770-2 (v. 2)

We gratefully acknowledge the use of several tables, as specified
in the text.

The preparation of this volume was made possible in part by a
grant from the Program for Research Tools and Reference Works of
the National Endowment for the Humanities, an independent federal
agency.

The Forest History Society is a nonprofit, educational institution
dedicated to the advancement of historical understanding of man's
interaction with the North American forest environment. It was
established in 1946. Interpretations and conclusions in FHS publications are those of the authors; the institution takes responsibility
for the selection of topics, the competence of the authors, and their
freedom of inquiry.

Editorial and Production Staff

Charles E. Smith, *Publisher*
Elly Dickason, *Project Editor*
Morton I. Rosenberg, *Production Manager*
Joan Greenfield, *Designer*

M

MACKAYE, BENTON (1879–1975)

Benton MacKaye is remembered for his pioneering work in regional planning and for being a founding member of the WILDERNESS SOCIETY. In recent years when urban forestry attracted much interest, some saw MacKaye as an early shaper of urban forestry concepts that would not achieve general articulation until later. Obviously, he was a many-faceted man.

MacKaye was born in Stamford, Connecticut, on March 6, 1879. He graduated from Harvard in 1900 and again in 1905 with a master of arts in forestry. He held a research position with the U. S. FOREST SERVICE from 1905 to 1918, when he investigated timber and water resources. He spent a one-year stint with the U. S. Department of Labor, where he specialized in land colonization. Returning to Harvard as an instructor in forestry, MacKaye wrote an article for the October 1921 issue of the *Journal of the American Institute of Architects* entitled, "An Appalachian Trail: A Project in Regional Planning." The proposal and the ultimate completion of the 2,050-mile footpath from Georgia to Maine would earn him the title of Father of the Appalachian Trail.

The following decades, MacKaye served as a planning consultant to public agencies or commissions. In 1928, he accepted an invitation from the Massachusetts Governors Committee on Open Spaces to make a regional survey. Five years later, he studied

Hikers enjoy the portion of the Appalachian Trail that crosses the Jefferson National Forest in Virginia. Forest Service Photo.

Indian reservations in Arizona, New Mexico, and South Dakota for the Bureau of Indian Affairs. In 1934, he began what he would later remember as "the two damndest years of my life" with the Division of Land Planning and Housing of the TENNESSEE VALLEY AUTHORITY. From 1938 to 1941, he was flood-control consultant to the Forest Service; in 1945, he completed a feasibility study for a proposed Missouri Valley Authority. MacKaye officially retired in 1945 but remained active into the 1970s.

MacKaye, Robert MARSHALL, and six others founded the Wilderness Society on January 21, 1935; MacKaye was then fifty-five years old. He served as president of the organization from 1945 to 1950 and as honorary president from 1950 until his death on December 11, 1975.

As an author, MacKaye wrote of subjective, aesthetic topics in clear, lean prose. He also wrote professional papers with technical accuracy. In a memorial issue following his death, *Living Wilderness*, published by the Wilderness Society, listed nearly eighty books, reports, and articles that MacKaye had authored between 1913 and 1973. A seven-part series published in *The Survey* in 1950–1951 entitled "Geography to Geotechnics" offers a good sample of MacKaye's thoughts.

FURTHER READING: Lewis Mumford et al., "Benton MacKaye: A Tribute," *Living Wilderness* 39 (Jan./Mar. 1976): 6-34. Henry J. Vaux, "Bridge to the Profession's Future," *Journal of Forestry* 78 (May 1980): 260-262.

MAINE FORESTS

Maine is the most heavily forested state in the union, with 90 percent of its land covered with trees. This forest began about 12,000 years ago when spruce and fir, along with a few smaller plants such as alders, arctic willows, and some of the heaths, invaded the landscape of rocks, ponds, and bogs left behind when the glacial ice withdrew. Of Maine's 17.7 million wooded acres in 1980, 17 million were commercial forest.

The extensive white pine forest growing in the sandy, well-drained soils of southwestern Maine attracted colonists to the region in 1607 and provided Maine with its nickname—"The Pine Tree State." However, other forest types make up a larger part of Maine's diverse timber growth. The spruce-fir forest predominates in the unorganized northern region, formerly known as Maine's "wild lands." This extensive area covers about 10 million acres. Next in quantity is the maple-beech-birch or northern hardwood type which is concentrated in the south and west but also occurs in patches throughout the state. The white pine-red pine-hemlock forest is the third most prevalent type and can be found mainly in the south and west. There are also areas of oak and a less expansive forest of red maple-elm-ash. Aspen and birch are scattered through the entire region.

To Maine's Indian population, the forest was useful as a habitat for wildlife and a source of forage. Maine and adjoining portions of Canada were among the last regions of the Americas to be populated by Indians; the first tribes probably arrived there 4,000 to 10,000 years ago, largely settling in southern and coastal Maine. They were both hunters and horticulturists. To clear land for crops they burned or girdled the trees. To early European explorers such alterations in the forest were most apparent near the mouth of the Saco River, but they also extended along the coast and far up the major river valleys.

In 1605, Captain George Weymouth returned to England with a sample of Maine white pine. Britain welcomed these magnificent trees as a source of masts for the Royal Navy. In 1607, thirteen years before the Mayflower landed at Plymouth, English colonists settled at Popham, Maine, and in the following year they constructed the first wooden ship launched in the New World, a thirty-ton pinnace built at Sagadahoc (Bath). The Popham colony was abandoned after only two years, but Maine shipbuilding was firmly established when the first commercial shipyard was built on Richmond Island in the Kennebec River in 1632. Shipbuilding was a major industry in Maine during the age of wooden vessels. By 1855, the United States had the world's largest merchant marine fleet, and more than half of its ships came from Maine.

Sawmilling, according to most accounts, got its start in the New World in 1634, when Captain John Mason of London arrived on the ship *Pied Cowe* and began construction of a waterpowered mill on a branch of the Piscataqua River in South Berwick. From these beginnings in Maine, the lumber industry in North America grew rapidly. By 1663, the year the first sawmill was built in England, the New England colonists had nearly 100 sawmills in operation. An extensive river system and ample supply of pine and spruce gave Maine a strong competitive edge in lumber markets throughout the world. In its heyday in the 1840s, Bangor shipped more lumber than any other port in the world. In its peak year, 1909, the Maine lumber industry produced 1.1 billion board feet. Production nearly reached that figure again in 1915, but thereafter it declined to 200 million board feet in 1932. After the Depression, the industry increased again, and in 1970, 634 million board feet of lumber were produced in the state.

A variety of other forest products also contributed to Maine's early economy. Hand-rived barrel staves were shipped to New England and Mediterranean ports for use in the wine and rum trade. Pine and cedar shingles provided a ready cash income in backwoods settlements and even served as a medium of exchange in frontier areas such as Aroostook County. Hemlock was a source of tannin, the valuable bark being peeled in the woods and the logs left to rot. By 1810, there were about 200 small tanneries in Maine, and by 1860 tanning was the state's third largest industry. Shortages of hemlock and new tanning techniques brought about a decline in the industry in Maine after 1900. The wood-turning industry provided a market for Maine's hardwoods. A wide variety of items were produced, such as bobbins and spools, spokes and hubs, shoe pegs, clothespins, and rake, shovel, and hoe handles. Machine manufacture of toothpicks is said to have started in Strong, Maine, about 1860, and is still a part of the state's forest industry. Plywood has been produced in Maine, largely from hardwoods, since 1897.

When the most accessible pine had been cut, Maine lumbermen turned to the abundant stands of spruce. Spruce lumber production surpassed white pine in the 1890s and continued to be Maine's dominant forest product until overshadowed by the burgeoning pulpwood industry. Initially, Maine's pulpwood was shipped to Massachusetts and Pennsylvania papermakers, but Maine's first pulp mill began production in 1868, and before the end of the century the state contained many thriving pulp plants. Huge mills such as Great Northern's Millinocket plant brought about a revolution in timberland harvests. Starting in 1912, more spruce was cut for pulpwood than for lumber, and from 1914 through the 1920s Maine led the United States in pulpwood consumption and pulp production. In 1919 and after, Maine's pulpwood consumption exceeded its total lumber cut. Pulp and paper have remained the state's foremost industry. In 1970, seventeen pulp mills received a total of 3.4 million cords of roundwood. Of this, 3.1 million came from Maine forests. Although the industry uses mainly spruce and fir, new pulping processes more and more use hardwood species and chips salvaged from other wood-using industries.

During the early nineteenth century, Maine viewed her vast public domain as a source of government revenue. By the mid-1870s, the state's remaining wildlands, principally located in the northeast, had been sold to private interests, who typically held their investment in a system of common and undivided ownership. Huge tracts were acquired and many of these properties have remained intact since the 1850s. When wood pulp manufacturers outgrew supplies brought to the mills by local farmers, they began to acquire timberlands as well. Most of Maine's forest has remained in private hands, with forest industries owning approximately 8 million acres and individuals owning about an equal amount. Great Northern Paper Company, founded in 1897, is the largest landowner in Maine, with over 2.1 million acres in the northern counties.

In 1975, the Penobscot and Passamaquoddy Indians sued the state for 12 million acres of these timberlands, alleging that a 1794 treaty that deeded their hunting grounds to the state violated a federal statute of 1790. This statute had stipulated that all transfers of land between Indian tribes and state governments be sanctioned by Congress. Massachusetts, which then owned the District of Maine, failed to clear the 1794 treaty. The Indian claim was settled on October 10, 1980, when President Jimmy Carter signed an act giving the two tribes $54.5 million to buy land from the fourteen major landowning companies in Maine. In addition, the Indians received a $27 million trust fund to be administered by the DEPARTMENT OF THE INTERIOR.

The development of large corporate landownership patterns paved the way for the introduction of sustained-yield management practices. Some of the owners of Maine timberlands introduced professional forest-management techniques at the end of the nineteenth century in order to make their extensive investments a long-term economic resource. The Berlin Mills Company employed Austin CARY as a forester in 1898 and the Great Northern Paper Company used the services of the U. S. Bureau of Forestry in 1901. Cooperation between state and private interests to control fire, disease, and forest pests has been the hallmark of Maine forestry since the creation of the Maine Forestry District in 1909.

Because of its ownership by forest industries and its remoteness from population centers, close to 10 million acres of north Maine woods was never settled. In addition, a sizable portion of southern and coastal Maine reverted to trees in the nineteenth century as farmers abandoned their tilled fields for more productive farmlands in the Midwest. Consequently, of the 18.5 million acres of timberland that originally covered Maine, 17.7 million are today in forest.

Maine forests have survived a number of natural catastrophes. Storms have on occasion destroyed thousands of acres of trees. Since 1634, at least eight major hurricanes have caused damage. The 1938 hurricane alone downed between 89 million and 158 million board feet of timber, mostly in the valuable coastal and southern Maine pine forests. Sawmills operated on the salvage of this wood for years. Northern Maine has been more fortunate in avoiding such winds, although twisters and other freak storms have occasionally downed stands of spruce and fir.

More damaging have been the recurrent epidemics of the native spruce budworm, whose first recorded invasion of Maine took place in 1770. An outbreak between 1910 and 1919 destroyed 27 million cords of spruce and fir—40 percent of the entire spruce and fir stock in Maine. Disastrous fires followed the epidemic. In 1977, another major spruce budworm infestation defoliated the trees on 5 million acres.

Fires have also been a long-standing threat to the Maine forests. In 1796, one near Mount Katahdin burned 150,000 acres of spruce and fir. Widespread blazes in 1903 and 1908 drew public attention to the problem and spurred the creation of the Maine Forestry District. The 1947 fires led to improved fire control in organized towns. Most of Maine's historic fires have been attributed to lightning or land clearing by settlers. Most recently, recreational use of the woods has been another source of forest fires.

Although the state owns relatively little forestland, the Maine State Park Commission manages seventeen units comprising 15,576 acres. Baxter State Park, Maine's largest, is administered separately by the Baxter State Park Authority. This extensive reserve, which surrounds mile-high Mount Katahdin, is named for Governor Percival P. Baxter, who beginning in 1931 donated the land in small parcels to the state as he acquired them. By 1980, Baxter State Park included nearly 200,000 acres, much of it wilderness. Another 400,000 acres of Maine is managed by the State Bureau of Public Lands as "public lots," scattered holdovers from the public domain that were reserved by the state in the unorganized territory in northern and eastern Maine.

Acadia National Park was proclaimed in 1916 as Sieur de Monts National Monument and was established as LaFayette National Park in 1919. It was given its present name in 1929. Built around a 6,000-acre gift from John D. ROCKEFELLER and others, Acadia was the first national park in the East and the nation's first seacoast park. Today Acadia contains 37,930 acres of federal land. Other federally managed lands in Maine include the Moosehorn Wildlife Refuge, established in 1937 for the study and protection of the American woodcock. The refuge contains 22,665 acres. The White Mountain National Forest covers 53,561 acres in Maine, the rest being situated in New Hampshire.

FURTHER READING: Philip T. Coolidge, *History of the Maine Woods* (1963). James Elliott Defebaugh, *History of the Lumbering Industry in America*, vol. 2, chaps. 1-9 (1907). Stewart H. Holbrook, *Yankee Loggers, A Recollection of Woodsmen, Cooks, and River Drivers* (1961). David C. Smith, *A History of Lumbering in Maine 1861–1960* (1972). John S. Springer, *Forest Life and Forest Trees* (1971). Henry David Thoreau, *The Maine Woods* (1864). Austin H. Wilkins, *The Forests of Maine, Their Extent, Character, Ownership and Products*, Maine Forest Service Bulletin No. 8 (1932). Richard G. Wood, *A History of Lumbering in Maine 1820–1861* (1935).

LESTER A. DECOSTER

MAINE STATE FORESTRY

Since its separation from Massachusetts in 1819, Maine has undergone a change in land ownership. Once a vast public domain, Maine's timberlands are today 96 percent private, a transfer virtually completed by 1878. A second shift in land ownership began at the turn of the nineteenth century, when a number of large private family ownerships were acquired by expanding pulp and paper companies. Great Northern Paper Company, for instance, bought nearly 1.4 million acres between 1899 and 1928.

Forestland ownership in Maine in 1980 consisted of 7.2 million acres of scattered small woodlands in 492 organized municipalities and 10.5 million acres of large unbroken timber tracts in the unorganized territory lying mostly in the northern and western parts of the state. Although there are more than 100,000 individual owners, many of the larger tracts are held jointly by several different parties, who share expenses and losses and gains. This unique system of land tenure, descended from Maine's colonial past, is known as "common and undivided ownership."

It was from this background that state forestry in Maine emerged. Maine was among the earliest of the states to implement forestry practices; its history demonstrates the important and largely unappreciated role states have played in the forestry movement. Other than colonial ordinances of limited applicability, the first fire control measure passed in the state came in 1891 at the insistence of Maine's timberland owners. In that year, the Maine legislature created a Forest Commission for the Protection of Forests. This was the origin of the Maine Forest Service, which has continued to the present, although its status was changed in 1973 from a cabinet-level agency to a bureau within the Department of Conservation.

Widespread fires in 1903 burned 269,451 acres and prompted stronger preventive measures. The forest commissioner was empowered to appoint fire wardens within the unorganized townships, an authority previously vested in the county governments. Three fire lookout stations—the first in the nation—were built in 1905 and from them wardens spotted forty-eight blazes in the ensuing season. In 1909, the unique Maine Forestry District (MFD) was created, encompassing 10 million acres of unincorporated wilderness. The MFD was a cooperative effort on behalf of private landowners and the state. Full implementation of Maine's new forestry program was made possible by vesting the MFD with statutory authority to take necessary control or preventive measures whenever required. All early funding was provided by a special tax on timberlands. Later budgets were derived from the General Fund and matching monies under cooperative state and federal programs. In 1972, Maine adopted a Tree Growth Tax Law and became one of the first states in the country to implement a productivity approach to forest TAXATION on a large scale.

The disastrous fires of 1947 in Maine resulted in the creation of the Northeastern Forest Fire Protection Commission, the earliest in coordinated regional efforts to control forest fires. Enactment was authorized by Congress in 1949 and ratified by the New England states and New York in 1950. The provinces of Quebec and New Brunswick entered the commission in 1969 and 1970.

In 1921, following a spruce budworm epidemic that killed 40 percent of its spruce and fir, Maine, in cooperation with the private forest industries, began an intensive study of forest insect pests. During the 1958 epidemic, 302,000 acres of timberland were sprayed with DDT, reducing the budworm population in the northern part of the state by 96 percent. Tree diseases such as the white pine blister rust have also been the object of control measures since 1917. During the 1930s, the CIVILIAN CONSERVATION CORPS (CCC), under the direction of the Maine Forest Service, strung telephone lines, removed slash, constructed campgrounds, built about 400 miles of access roads in the woods, and assisted in forest fire suppression. The CCC helped salvage timber downed in 1938 by a hurricane and worked to control the gypsy moth, spruce saw fly, and white pine blister rust. By the 1950s, Maine forestry had come to full flower, pursuing on-going programs of fire, disease and insect control, forest management, utilization guidelines, and public information and education.

There are about 600 public and private registered professional foresters in Maine who serve the interests of all landowners in the state. Large forest owners, who control 49 percent of the state's commercial forestland, employ sizable staffs of professional foresters. The Maine Forest Service cooperates with them by providing help and leadership in the Tree Farm and Keep Maine Green programs. In addition, the state is responsible for fire protection on all privately owned lands. Today, the state's management programs are primarily focused on the tens of thousands of small woodland owners. The state assists these owners in improving the quality and quantity of wood fiber.

From 1912 to 1975, the state had no lands to manage. Since then, the state has gained management responsibility for approximately 400,000 acres of forestland. The state has not enacted a statewide forest policy, although such a course of legislative action has been recommended. Recently, the Maine Forest Service, after a series of studies and reviews, implemented an internal forest policy plan of goals and objectives as a guideline for its forestry programs.

Although the legislation of 1891 was limited to creation of a state forestry commission for fire protection, it signaled early recognition of a need for public education and training in forestry. By 1903, the first appropriation was made for forestry instruction at the University of Maine. Until 1929, the forestry curriculum was funded through the Maine Forest Service, illustrating the close links between the state university and state forestry agencies. Since 1929, funding of the forestry school has been through the University of Maine budget system.

State forestry in Maine has been a matter of continuing cooperation between state, federal, and private agencies to protect, enhance, and promote the wise use of Maine's valuable forest reserves.

FURTHER READING: Ralph R. Widner, ed., *Forests and Forestry in the American States* (1968). Austin H. Wilkins, *Ten Million Acres of Timber* (1979).

AUSTIN H. WILKINS

MARSH, GEORGE PERKINS (1801–1882)

The son of a successful Vermont attorney, George Perkins Marsh was born on March 15, 1801; he became a scholar, statesman, diplomat, and the author of *Man and Nature: or, Physical Geography as Modified by Human Action* (1864), the first treatise on environmental history.

Marsh's early life provided important influences for developing the perspective which he later defended in *Man and Nature*—that human activities tend to degrade the environment. His childhood home was located at the base of a mountain along the Quechee River at Woodstock, Vermont. The practices of lumbering and sheep grazing caused rapid runoff of the rain water from the mountainside. Consequently, the Quechee flooded in the spring and dried up in the summer. His father explained this situation to him while he was a child.

Marsh obediently followed the example of his father and grandfather in training for the law, but his deepest interests lay in European languages and history. He would have become a college professor if the pay had been adequate for his needs. Instead, he entered the Vermont legislature and later represented his state in Congress. In 1850, Marsh became the American minister to Turkey. While serving there, he traveled around the eastern Mediterranean and became impressed with the evidence of civilization's impact upon the land. He rightly concluded that deforestation and the grazing of goats were major causes of desertification in arid regions. Traveling to France, he witnessed the severe erosion which had followed the deforestation of mountains, and he learned details of reforestation programs.

After five years abroad, Marsh returned to America and wrote a book (1856) on the advantages of introducing camels into the West. In the following year, the governor of Vermont appointed him state fish commissioner, and Marsh used the opportunity to publish a *Report on the Artificial Propagation of Fish* (1857), which explained the impacts upon fish streams from logging, sheep grazing, farming, and industry. This report was a step toward his more comprehensive treatise, *Man and Nature*.

In 1861, President Lincoln appointed Marsh minister to the new kingdom of Italy. He retained this position for the remainder of his life. At the urging of his wife, he had already begun writing *Man and Nature* in Vermont in 1860, but he only completed it in 1863, while residing in France and Italy. His publishers had misgivings about the book, and some of the early reviews were unfavorable. Nevertheless, its acceptance came quickly and several printings were required as well as new editions in English in 1874 and 1885 and in Italian in 1869 and 1872.

Marsh believed that civilizations must learn to manage wisely both their natural and their domesticated resources. Science should provide the guidance. The science which he emphasized was geography as Humboldt had envisioned it. Today, what Marsh had in mind might be called ecology. *Man and Nature* included chapters on wildlife, waters, sands, and the side effects of engineering projects, but the longest chapter was on the ecology of forests and the consequences of deforestation.

In America, the influence of *Man and Nature* helped convince the federal government to establish a forest policy later in the nineteenth century, and in Europe the book exerted significant influence upon such scientists as Charles Lyell and Elisae Reclus. It has been an intellectual foundation stone for the conservation and environmental movements of the twentieth century.

FURTHER READING: David Lowenthal, *George Perkins Marsh, Versatile Vermonter* (1958). George Perkins Marsh, *Man and Nature*, edited by David Lowenthal (1965).

FRANK N. EGERTON

MARSHALL, ROBERT (1901–1939)

Born on January 2, 1901, Robert Marshall was the son of Louis Marshall, a prominent constitutional lawyer, social reformer, and defender of the NEW-YORK STATE FOREST PRESERVE in the Adirondacks. As a youth, Robert Marshall spent his summers at his family's Adirondack estate on Lower Saranac Lake, where he developed both exploration skills and a love of nature. These early adventures were the source for his first published work, *High Peaks of the Adirondacks* (1922). He received the B.S. degree from the New York State College of Forestry, Syracuse, in 1924; the M.F. from Harvard Forest in 1925; and the Ph.D. from Johns Hopkins University's Laboratory of Plant Physiology in 1930.

From 1925 until 1928, when he left for Johns Hopkins, Marshall worked for the U. S. FOREST SERVICE's Northern Rocky Mountain Forest Experiment Station in Missoula, Montana. He worked for the Forest Service again in 1932 and 1933 as a collaborator on the *National Plan for American Forestry*, writing the chapters on forest RECREATION. In 1933, he became director of forestry for the Office of Indian Affairs where he took part in Commissioner John Collier's efforts to increase participation by Indians in the management of the resources on their reservation lands. Marshall also successfully urged the retention of roadless areas on the reservations where Indians could withdraw from contact with whites.

In May 1937, Marshall returned to the Forest Service as chief of the new Division of Recreation and Lands in the Washington office, a mission he filled with vigor until his death from heart failure on November 11, 1939, when not yet thirty-nine years of age. As chief of recreation and lands, Marshall urged greater protection for primitive areas in national forests, and he secured the adoption of the so-called U regulations for wilderness and wild areas in 1939. Marshall recommended that virtually every large roadless tract in a national forest be classified as a primitive area, although he displayed little interest in protecting smaller areas already established. He also monitored proposals for recreational developments to ensure that adequate provision was made for the needs of lower income groups.

Marshall's finest achievements as a writer sprang from his infatuation with the Alaska frontier. He made his first visit there, fulfilling a boyhood dream, in the summer of 1929 with a trip to the upper Koyukuk River drainage in the Central Brooks Range above the Arctic Circle. He returned in 1930–1931, studying tree growth at the Arctic timberline, exploring and mapping the virtually unknown Brooks Range, and observing the life of the Eskimo and sourdough residents of the tiny community of Wiseman in the wilderness. After his return, Marshall published *Arctic Village* (1933), which received praise from both explorers and sociologists and was reprinted as a Literary Guild selection. In 1938 and 1939, he made two more trips to the Brooks Range; his adventures on these journeys provided the subject for *Arctic Wilderness* (1956), published in book form after his death.

One of Marshall's leading concerns was the social management of America's forests. In February 1930, he was the youngest of the six signers of Gifford PIN-CHOT and George P. Ahern's circular, "Letter to Foresters," which blamed the mismanagement of privately owned forestlands for "forest devastation." The needed remedies, the "Letter" said, were increased federal and state regulation of private forestry practices and expanded public ownership of forestlands. During the early Depression years, Marshall expounded upon these themes in a pamphlet, *The Social Management of American Forests* (1930), and in a book, *The People's Forests* (1933).

Marshall's love of outdoor adventure and his concern for social welfare came together in his program for WILDERNESS PRESERVATION. Shortly before his first trip to Alaska, Marshall wrote his chief philosophical statement on this issue, published in *Scientific Monthly* as "The Problem of the Wilderness" (1930). He proposed that even if the general public did not care to engage in wilderness recreation, the preservation of such lands could be justified on the grounds of the rights of a minority. Furthermore, the proportion of wilderness users would increase in the future. Recreational experiences in the wilderness fulfilled a psychological need for adventure, which otherwise might find expression in less socially desirable ways. It would not be necessary to deny the nation the benefit of large economic resources in order to preserve wilderness, he added; scientific management on other forestlands would more than compensate for those resources that remained undeveloped in preserved areas.

Marshall described the specifics of a national wilderness policy in the *National Plan for American Forestry* (1933). He proposed that 45 million acres, or 9 percent of the total commercial forestland in the United States, would be required primarily for recreational use. He described seven distinctive categories of forest recreational areas, ranging from "superlative areas" of national park caliber to developed "roadside areas," "camp-site areas," and "residence areas." He proposed 10 million acres of "wilderness areas," a minimum of 200,000 acres in size and characterized by an absence of permanent inhabitants and mechanical transportation. An additional 11 million acres of "outing areas" would be smaller than wilderness areas and would have fewer restrictions against economic development. His desire for wilderness preservation was not limited to the public lands, however, and he included an inventory of thirty-eight large wilderness tracts totaling nearly 30 million acres (20 million of which were forested) in national forests, national parks, and Indian reservations, and in state and private ownership. Marshall thought livestock grazing and even logging to be permissible uses of wilderness areas. Their primary purpose was "not to make possible contact with the virgin forest but rather to make it possible to retire completely from the modes of transportation and the living conditions of the twentieth century." To provide samples of undisturbed forest growth, Marshall proposed a separate series of tracts over 5,000 acres in size called "primeval areas," whose value would be both scientific and inspirational.

To enable concerned citizens to watch over government protection of preserved areas, Marshall became the principal founder and financial supporter of the WILDERNESS SOCIETY in 1935.

Marshall was famous for hiking prowess, once walking seventy miles in twenty-four hours to make connections for a trip; perhaps such exertions contributed to his early death. Marshall, who never married, left half of his $1.5 million inherited fortune to be used to promote the advancement of an economic system "based on production for use and not for profit." Another quarter of his estate went to promote the advancement of civil liberties, and most of the remainder was left to endow the work of the Wilderness Society in educating American citizens on the importance of wilderness. In 1940, the Forest Service paid tribute to his work by reclassifying three Montana primitive areas as the Bob Marshall Wilderness Area.

FURTHER READING: James P. Gilligan, "The Development of Policy and Administration of Forest Service Primitive and Wilderness Areas in the Western United States," Ph.D. dissertation, University of Michigan (1954), chap. 5. George Marshall, "Robert Marshall as a Writer," *Living Wilderness* 16 (Autumn 1951): 14-20; "Bibliography of Robert Marshall, 1901–1939," *Living Wilderness* 16 (Autumn 1951): 20-23, and "Bibliography of Robert Marshall: Supplement" *Living Wilderness* 19 (Summer 1954): 31-35. Roderick Nash, "The Strenuous Life of Bob Marshall," *Forest History* 10 (Oct. 1966): 18-25, and *Wilderness and the American Mind* (rev. ed., 1982), pp. 200-208.

MARYLAND FORESTS

Maryland's first settlers in 1634 found a land nearly 95 percent forested. In most of the colony, hardwoods were the major species and large trees were common. The great variety of tree species found in the state de-

rives from topographical diversity, ranging from coastal plains on the eastern shore through the piedmont, to mountains up to 3,000 feet elevation in the west. Among the more common hardwoods are the upland oaks, yellow-poplar, red maple, sugar maple, birch, red gum, beech, white ash, black walnut, sycamore, black locust, elm, and black cherry. Chestnut, once one of Maryland's most valuable trees, died off in the early part of the twentieth century, a victim of the chestnut blight. The bald cypress reaches the northern limits of its range in the state. Other common conifers are loblolly pine, shortleaf pine, eastern white pine, Virginia pine, Atlantic white-cedar, eastern redcedar, and eastern hemlock. Loblolly pine, eastern white pine, red pine, and Scotch pine have been planted extensively.

Maryland's total land area is 6,330,200 acres. Forty-two percent, or 2,653,200 acres, was classed as forestland by a 1976 forest survey. Almost all of this (2,522,700 acres) was commercial forest; only 108,900 acres was classed as productive reserved forestland. In 1976, 75 percent of the commercial forest was largely in small private tracts, 10 percent was public, 5 percent belonged to forest industries, and 10 per-

A team of oxen pulls a load of logs carried by a small-scale "big wheel" near Salisbury, Maryland, 1940. American Forest Institute Photo.

cent to other corporations. In 1976, there were an estimated 95,800 forestland owners in the state.

As in other colonies, the early settlers of Maryland looked on the forest as an enemy which not only provided food and shelter for hostile Indians but also had to be laboriously cleared to make way for fields and homes. At the same time, the forest provided building material for the colonists' homes and furniture, fuel for heat, and rails for their fences; but the largest part of the material cleared to make way for agriculture was burned.

Commercial lumbering began about 1629, and the colony developed an export trade in pipe staves and other wood products. In the eighteenth century, NAVAL STORES became the colony's most important forest product export, although Baltimore remained an important lumber export center, partly because of cargoes transshipped from Virginia and North Carolina. Another important industrial use of Maryland timber was for charcoal used in iron works. The first furnace was established in Cecil County in 1721, and by the American Revolution there were eighteen forges in operation.

The economy of the colony and later of the state was primarily agricultural, and the growth of towns and cities provided a stable market for local forest products. During the earlier years, transportation kept stumpage costs low and logging costs high, prompting lumbermen to select only the most valuable trees. In the westernmost and mountainous part of the state, the major logging took place between 1890 and 1920, after railroads could be adapted to steep terrain. The peak production of lumber was in 1909 with 268 million board feet. Hardwood accounted for just over 51 percent of the total. Other important lumber trees were oak (27 percent), chestnut (12 percent), and eastern hemlock (8 percent). Lesser amounts of lumber came from (in descending order of importance) maple, spruce, yellow-poplar, white pine, red gum, hickory, basswood, ash, cypress, birch, elm, sycamore, cherry, walnut, tupelo, and cedar. Lumbering declined thereafter to a low of 68 million board feet in 1917 and fluctuated greatly during the 1920s; in 1933, the annual production was only 80 million board feet, but this figure increased generally until it ran around 200 million board feet a year during the 1950s and 1960s.

Pulpwood, about two-thirds of it from softwood, became a major product of Maryland's forests during the twentieth century. The state has also been a producer of fuelwood, veneer, cooperage logs, poles, and piling. Among specialized products are tobacco hogsheads, sweetgum spoon bolts, and sweetgum shredded bark mulch.

The Maryland General Assembly created a state forestry department in 1906, when Robert and John W. Garrett donated 2,000 acres of forestland to the state. Written by Senator W. McCulloch Brown, the 1906 state forestry act has never required any basic changes and has become a model for other states. The Department of Forests and Parks was created in 1941. Now known as the Maryland Forest Service, it continues to work with the many federal programs to promote private forestry and maintains an adequate forest protection program. It also maintains a system of 144,000 acres in ten state forests for watershed protection, timber production, and outdoor recreation. The service cooperates with the State Wildlife Service on activities in state forests. Since 1967, extensive acquisition of interior holdings in state forests have been made with state open-space funds.

An extensive outdoor recreation program is operated in state parks under the direction of the Maryland Park Service. In 1975, there were forty-eight state parks and recreation areas totaling 62,000 acres. Since the beginning of the 1960s, emphasis has been on the acquisition of lands for urban and suburban parks.

FURTHER READING: F. W. Besley, *The Forests of Maryland* (1916). Benjamin F. G. Kline, Jr., *Tall Pines and Winding Rivers: The Logging Railroads of Maryland* (1976). Ralph R. Widner, ed., *Forests and Forestry in the American States* (1968).

WILLIAM A. PARR

MASON, DAVID TOWNSEND (1883–1973)

Born on March 11, 1883, David T. Mason graduated from Rutgers University with a B. S. degree in civil engineering in 1905 and received an M. F. degree from Yale in 1907. He worked for the U. S. FOREST SERVICE until 1915. During this period, he made a study of the unstable conditions in the lumber industry of the Inland Empire and impressed lumbermen with his understanding of their problems. His *Timber Ownership and Lumber Production in the Inland Empire* was published in 1920. In 1915, Mason left the government to become a professor at the University of California, the training of a new generation of foresters being an important task adopted by many early American professional foresters.

During World War I, Mason was a major in the famed forestry regiment stationed in France. Returning to the United States, he became head of the Bureau of Internal Revenue's timber section in 1919. In this post he was responsible for determining the valuations of timber holdings, decisions upon which federal income tax assessments would be based. Mason earned the respect of industry through his decisions on value, decisions that often corresponded to the figures submitted by lumbermen. Resigning in early 1921, he returned briefly to his teaching duties at Berkeley but soon abandoned the traditional government-university career line.

Mason moved to Portland, Oregon, to begin work as a consulting forester. Several foresters—such as E. T. Allen and C. S. Chapman—had preceded him into private work, and others—notably William B. GREELEY—would follow, but Mason was probably the most admired exemplar in the changing focus of the profession. Soon joined by Carl Stevens, his successor in the timber section, Mason became the leading private forester in the Pacific Northwest, carrying out numerous planning projects for timber companies. From 1931 to 1935, he served as manager of the Western Pine Association (WPA).

Mason was most prominently identified with promotion of the theory of sustained yield, described by him as "the policy of managing . . . lands for permanent timber production." Through restriction of each year's cut to the amount of timber replaced by new growth, the lumber industry would be stabilized in the short run through elimination of overproduction and in the long run through maintenance of timber stands. As consultant, trade association head, and government official, he strived to persuade lumbermen to adopt the concept.

In 1931, Mason served on the Timber Conservation Board of the Hoover Administration, and in 1933 he was closely involved in the writing of the National Recovery Administration lumber code, a New Deal effort to produce economic recovery through the control of production and prices. He was particularly important in the drafting of the code's famous Article X, which required lumbermen to adopt conservation measures. Subsequently, Mason became executive officer of the Lumber Code Authority, the government's supervisory agency, serving in that position until the death of the NRA at the hands of the Supreme Court in 1935.

Mason returned for a short time to his position with the WPA, then resigned to become again a private consultant. He helped draft federal sustained-yield legislation in 1937 and 1944 and continued to work for his prized concept while chairman of the Oregon and California Railroad Revested Lands Advisory Board. As a director of the Forest History Society, Mason was one of the early sponsors of work in the history of forestry.

Mason is an important figure in forest history because of his work on behalf of sustained yield. Of equal importance, he was one of the leading participants in the transformation of the forestry profession, as foresters moved from government and the universities into private industry. Mason died on September 3, 1973.

FURTHER READING: Rodney C. Loehr, ed., *Forests for the Future: The Story of Sustained Yield as Told in the Diaries and Papers of David T. Mason, 1907–1950* (1952).

ROBERT E. FICKEN

MASON, WILLIAM HORATIO (1877–1940)

Inventor of a process for fabricating boards from wood fibers and founder of the Masonite Corporation, William H. Mason was born February 19, 1877, on a farm in Summers County, West Virginia. After attending Greenbriar Military Academy and Washington and Lee University, Mason graduated from Cornell University in 1898 with a degree in civil engineering. Entering the navy after graduation, he served as an engineering officer throughout the Spanish-American war. Returning to civilian life, Mason joined the organization of Thomas A. Edison. In 1902, he became general superintendent of the Edison Portland Cement Company, serving in that capacity until 1915 when he became general engineer in charge of erecting and operating Edison's chemical plants. At the outbreak of World War I, Mason left Edison's employ to construct a shipyard at Bristol, Pennsylvania, for the Emergency Fleet Corporation.

In 1908, Mason married Marian Alexander Dana, daughter of a prominent Wisconsin lumberman, Frank G. Dana. The couple had two daughters, Elizabeth and Jean.

At the close of the war, Mason turned from construction to invention. He spent a year with General Motors attempting unsuccessfully to develop a hydraulic transmission mechanism of his own design. Mason next moved in 1920 to the lumber manufacturing center at Laurel, Mississippi, where he perfected a method of extracting NAVAL STORES from sawn yellow pine lumber by the use of steam. Continuing his experiments with steam, Mason conceived of novel means of cheaply reducing wood into fibers by impregnating wood chips with high-pressure steam and then suddenly relieving the pressure. In 1924, the inventor achieved the desired results by firing wood chips from a steam "cannon." When experiments in manufacturing paper from exploded wood fibers proved disappointing, Mason turned his attention to fabricating insulation from this material. Eventually, by first passing his wood fibers through a papermaker's fourdrinier machine and then compressing the resulting pulp in steam-heated presses, Mason was able to make an efficient insulating board which did not come apart when wet.

Mason's subsequent experiments revealed that a board both hard enough and strong enough to substitute for lumber could be made from his wood fiber if sufficient heat and pressure were applied. The product was a dense mass stronger than the original wood. This hardboard, called Masonite, was put to many uses in the late 1920s and 1930s. During World War II, immense quantities went into the construction of Quonset huts used by the military, making both the inventor and his corporation famous.

Financed by Wisconsin lumbermen, Mason organized the Mason Fiber Company (renamed the Masonite Corporation in 1929) and erected a plant in Laurel during 1926 to manufacture insulation board and hardboard. As executive vice president, Mason directed the manufacturing operations of the firm until 1937. Retiring from management in that year at age sixty, Mason continued to engage in research until his death on August 24, 1940.

Mason deserves to be remembered for his achievement in creating an entirely new forest products industry.

FURTHER READING: John Hebron Moore, "William H. Mason, Southern Industrialist," *Journal of Southern History* 27 (May 1961): 169–183.

JOHN HEBRON MOORE

MASSACHUSETTS FORESTS

Most of the coastal area north and south of Boston was covered with oak, chestnut, and other hardwoods when Puritans established the first towns on Massachusetts Bay. As the settlers moved inland in the 1630s, they encountered a complex hemlock-white pine-hardwood stand that extended west to the spruce-hardwood forests of the Berkshires and north and south beyond the present borders of the state. Swamps were numerous in some coastal and inland regions, and wet soils sometimes nurtured the fragrant and valuable white cedar.

The exploitation of the forest for domestic needs and demands for markets in the West Indies and in the Portuguese and Spanish wine-growing regions became an important activity in the agricultural communities of early Massachusetts. Income from the manufacture of cedar shingles, white pine boards, and oak for construction, shipbuilding, and cooperage stock allowed the purchase of tools and other manufactured goods from England. Small waterpowered sawmills accelerated the depletion of the virgin white pine. Despite many local and royal restrictions on the cutting of this valuable species, rapid population growth and the increasing need for open land for farming prevented the implementation of a rationalized forest policy.

The demand for furs and animal skins in Europe also led to an assault on wildlife. Deer were killed in great numbers while trappers and Indians rapidly exterminated the beaver. Wolves, bears, wildcats, and other predators may have increased during the early years of settlement because of the introduction of domestic animals, but bounties and organized drives soon reversed this trend. Rattlesnakes also were killed systematically, and the blackbirds, crows, and passenger pigeons that plundered the cereal crops in the new settlements were shot or trapped with birdlime.

Boston quickly became the major center for forest-related crafts. In the colonial period, its shipwrights launched more tonnage than did those of any other East Coast port, and its cooperages and tanneries expanded along with the fishing and meat-packing industries. By the early eighteenth century, however, eastern Massachusetts had become open countryside and the wood-based industries of Boston were importing forest supplies from the District of Maine, New Hampshire, and the colonies to the south. Even the firewood burned in Boston and the surrounding towns was brought in by sea from northern New England.

In the years after the French and Indian War, the more than 1 million acres cleared in the Connecticut Valley and eastern Massachusetts were no longer enough to sustain the growing population. Settlers began to open up the previously neglected uplands in the Berkshires and the central section of the colony. Logging and land-clearing for agriculture in this hill country continued on a large scale well into the nineteenth century. In regions where the transportation of bulky forest products was not feasible, the manufacture of many small wooden products, such as bowls, tool handles, and shoe pegs, provided extra income for farmers. Even in the 1840s, when competition from grain producers in the Midwest and the lure of factory employment in the cities led to the abandonment of many marginal farms, sheep raisers were opening up new lands and sawmill operators with access to railroads continued to clear thousands of acres. In 1865, the 1,159 sawmills operating in Massachusetts cut 140 million board feet of timber; less than 30 percent of the state then remained in forest.

Eventually, the decline of sheepherding, the abandonment of farms, and the clearcutting of timber led to new forest successions. In some coastal regions there was regeneration among the oaks, and the chestnut returned until blight virtually destroyed the species in the early twentieth century. Further inland, the light, winged seeds of the white pine found nurture on abandoned logging sites, meadows, and previously cultivated grounds, and between 1900 and 1928, the proportion of the state classified as forestland increased from 39 to 54 percent.

As the second growth of white pine in the state reached maturity at the end of the nineteenth century, it was cut for box and board lumber. Lumbering in Massachusetts reached its peak in 1908, when 384.5 million board feet were produced. By 1920, Massachusetts was no longer a leader in primary forest products. Its forests supplied less than 10 percent of the lumber consumed in the state. During the Great Depression, lumber production declined to 23 million board feet; after World War II, it leveled off around 130 million.

A milestone in forest conservation was the founding of the Massachusetts Forestry Association (MFA) in 1898. It was originally heavily interested in shade trees, and the association's first legislative effort resulted in an 1899 law requiring each town to elect a tree warden. MFA was instrumental in establishing the office of state forester in 1904 and in promoting the subsequent purchase of lands for state forests and parks. Under MFA auspices, the nationwide town forest movement got its start in 1914. MFA was also active in fire, insect, and disease control programs. In 1932, it became the Massachusetts Forest and Park Association.

State ownership of forests began in 1892 when the Trustees of the Public Reservations was created and authorized to purchase lands for the state; by 1900, the state had acquired almost 10,000 acres of beach and inland park lands, including the Middlesex Fells, Blue Hills, and Mount Greylock reservations. In 1914, the State Forest Commission was given the responsibility for buying lands for state forests. This authority was reorganized in 1919 under the Department of Conservation and again in 1953 under the Department of Natural Resources. By 1975, its Division of Forests and Parks administered some 235,000 acres of state land in 126 parks and recreation areas and 240,100 acres of state forests. County and municipal forests, held largely for recreation and educational purposes and watershed protection, totaled 115,700 acres.

Another result of Massachusetts' search for a rational and scientific forest policy was the founding of the Harvard Forestry Department in 1903 and its purchase of 2,000 acres in Petersham for an experimental forest in 1907. Since 1914, both the school and the

forestlands have been known as the Harvard Forest. That institution's concentration on research has left most forestry instruction in the state in the hands of the forestry department established in 1947 at the University of Massachusetts at Amherst.

Although most of the forest regrowth of the twentieth century is too dense and too poorly managed to produce commercial lumber, the state continues to be one of the most heavily forested in the nation. Large amounts of firewood were cut well into the 1930s, but the volume of timber grew steadily after cordwood was replaced by cheap oil. There was a moderate decline in timber acreage during the postwar building boom, but over 3 million of the state's 5 million acres were still classified as woodland in 1980. After the Arab oil embargo of 1973, however, the production of firewood increased. Once again the forests were cleared at a faster pace than the natural process of renewal; even the slash was converted to wood chips used to fire industrial boilers.

FURTHER READING: Charles F. Carroll, *The Timber Economy of Puritan New England* (1973). W. H. Clark, *The First Fifty Years of the Massachusetts Forest and Park Association, 1898–1948* (1948). George B. Emerson, *A Report on the Trees and Shrubs Growing Naturally in the Forests of Massachusetts* (4th ed., 1887). Alfred J. Godin, *Wild Mammals of New England* (1977). Ernest M. Gould, Jr., *Fifty Years of Management at the Harvard Forest*, Harvard Forest Bulletin No. 29 (1960). Howard S. Russell, *A Long, Deep Furrow: Three Centuries of Farming in New England* (1976).

CHARLES F. CARROLL

MATCH SPLINTS

The first commercial friction matches—wooden sticks dipped in potassium chlorate and antimony sulfide, and meant to be scratched on sandpaper—were marketed in the 1820s as "Lucifers" in both England and the United States. Lucifers were safe but not pleasant to use. This drawback was only gradually overcome by experiments with new self-igniting compounds, especially in England and Sweden. In the meantime, the many manufacturers who divided the market devised any number of refinements. The first "safety match" (the phosphorus was impregnated in the sandpaper on the package) was invented in 1845. In 1892, the paper match was invented. Immediately perceiving the possibilities for advertising on the covers of the "books," the largest American match company, Diamond of New Haven, Connecticut, purchased the patent. This jump on the competition not only established Diamond's domination of the industry, but it also inaugurated the American custom, still almost unique, of universally available free matches.

The ubiquitous paper match consumed vast quantities of wood pulp; however, it was the manufacture of wooden matches that moved Diamond and other companies to become their own lumbermen. John K. Robinson of the Barber Match Company patented a diamond-shaped wooden match splint in 1870. When twelve match manufacturers settled a disastrous price war by consolidating in 1880, the new firm took its name from the diamond-shaped splint. Under the leadership of Ohio Columbus Barber, Diamond began the purchase of timberland and sawmills at Ontonagon, Michigan, in 1882. In the following year, the company amended its articles of incorporation to include logging as one of its major concerns.

Diamond eventually almost monopolized the wooden match market as well as that for paper matches because of a fortuitously purchased patent, the match-making machine invented by Ebeneezer Beecher in 1888. When it was perfected, Beecher's machine could produce as many as a million matches per hour. Such an appetite for timber motivated Diamond to secure exclusive contracts with white pine and aspen forests in New England, Minnesota, Idaho, and Washington. In 1902, anticipating the depletion of the white pine at Ontonagon, Diamond began the purchase of a number of logging companies with vast holdings in the Sierra Nevada above Chico, California.

Hoping for a perpetual supply of matchwood, Diamond introduced conservative logging practices to California and, in 1904, hired Harvey C. Styles as land manager, the first professional forester employed by a West Coast lumber company. Diamond constructed a modern mill at Stirling City and a huge factory in Chico in the valley below. The two were connected by flumes and a railway but, by the 1910s, it was clear that Diamond had miscalculated the suitability of the local sugar pine for matches. As a lumber business, however, Diamond's California operation thrived. In 1947, the company's revenues from lumber and building materials exceeded that from matches; soon after, so did revenues from paper products. Diamond became not only the nation's largest match producer but also the maker of such diverse products as lumber, woodenware, and pulp and paperboard, and entered such related fields as printing and advertising.

In the late 1930s, twenty-four firms in the United States produced 368 billion wooden matches annually, a figure which had fallen to 287 billion a decade later (at that time 240 billion paper matches were produced a

This German machine chopped sheets of wood veneer into square match sticks. Forest History Society Lantern Slide Collection.

year). Annual lumber consumption by the match industry was then over 80 million board feet a year. White pine was the preferred wood because its soft texture and resin content made it readily flammable and it did not splinter easily. Western white pine, sugar pine, and eastern white pine all were employed. The principal species used in 1940 were western white pine, 90.5 percent; aspen, 6.9 percent; birch, 2.4 percent; and spruce and maple, 0.1 percent. Twenty to 25 percent of the annual production of western white pine lumber in the 1940s went into match planks. Large kitchen matches were made primarily from western white pine cut in Washington and Idaho and sawed parallel to the grain into 2-inch or 2-1/2-inch planks which, after seasoning, were cut into blocks 2 3/8 inches long. These match blocks were shipped to factories chiefly located in the eastern United States, there to be sliced by machines into "round" grooved splints, forty to a block. Splints for the smaller safety matches were cut square from 1/10-inch aspen or popple veneer from the Lake States. With white pine in demand for lumber, in the later twentieth century aspen veneer from Minnesota and Colorado supplied the splints for both sizes of wooden matches.

FURTHER READING: William Franklin Fleming, *America's Match King: Ohio Columbus Barber, 1841–1920*

(1981). W. H. Hutchinson, *The California Investment: A History of the Diamond Match Company of California* (1957). Kent Stephens, *Matches, Flumes, and Rails: The Diamond Match Company in the High Sierra* (1977).

MATHER, STEPHEN TYNG (1867–1930)

Stephen T. Mather, who became the first director of the NATIONAL PARK SERVICE, was born on July 4, 1867, in San Francisco, California. Following his graduation from the University of California in 1887, he joined the *New York Sun* as a reporter, stayed five years, then left the paper for the New York City office of the Pacific Coast Borax Company. By 1894, he was manager of the company's Chicago distribution facilities, which he planned; in 1903, he helped organize the Thorkildsen-Mather Borax Company of Chicago, whose operations earned him a modest fortune.

Mather's love of the outdoors attracted him to the ranks of the SIERRA CLUB as early as 1905. Nine years later, following a camping trip into the High Sierra, Mather wrote to Secretary of the Interior Franklin K. Lane to protest the deterioration and improper management of the region's national parks. Coincidentally, Lane was looking for someone of Mather's wealth and background to put the national parks in order. Thus Lane replied: "Dear Steve, If you don't like the way the national parks are being run, come on down to Washington and run them yourself." Mather finally accepted the challenge on Lane's assurance that a young lawyer in the Interior Department, Horace M. ALBRIGHT, would handle any legal questions and red tape.

Mather, appointed assistant to the secretary of the interior in January 1915, first worked to put the national parks on a sound political and financial footing. Foremost among his priorities was formation of the National Park Service, which Congress finally approved on August 25, 1916. With the official inauguration of the agency early in 1917, Mather was appointed director while Horace Albright became assistant director. A letter of instruction, probably prepared by Mather for Lane's signature early in 1918, succinctly stated the three principles that were to underlie the policies of the new agency: "First, that the national parks must be maintained in absolutely unimpaired form for the use of future generations as well as those of our own time; second, that they are set apart for the use, observation, health, and pleasure of the people; and third, that the national interest must dictate all decisions affecting public or private enterprise in the parks."

In practice, Mather's task was challenging. Existing and future national parks had to be secured against crippling commercial invasions such as the Hetch Hetchy dam, which, despite its intrusion within YOSEMITE NATIONAL PARK, had been approved by Congress and the president in 1913. It was clear that without greater public support for the national parks, none might survive; publicity and better tourist facilities were needed to attract more visitors, whose numbers, in turn, would serve as additional justification for the national park idea. Furthermore, it was imperative to increase funding for both the National Park Service and the park system, for without larger appropriations there could be none of the necessary improvements in roads, parking lots, and overnight accommodations. Finally, there remained the need to expand the national park system into areas of unique scenic quality not yet represented by the park idea, including the deserts of the Southwest and the forest-clad mountains of the eastern United States.

In each of these endeavors Mather was eminently successful. Congressmen, struck by his warmth, sincerity, and hospitality, increased funding for the Park Service and its charges, just as railroad executives responded to his calls for more trains to the national park approaches and better advertising and tourist accommodations. Meanwhile, Mather fought off schemes which, among other examples, would have turned Yellowstone Lake into a huge irrigation reservoir for neighboring agricultural interests in Idaho. Instead, Mather was able to preserve the National Park System intact while winning such noted additions as the Grand Canyon, Zion, and Bryce Canyon in the Southwest, and Acadia, Shenandoah, and Great Smoky Mountains in the East.

Although his most important role was in the preservation of the most outstanding scenic wonders in the National Park System, Mather was also instrumental in advancing a state park movement to protect lesser natural landmarks and outdoor recreation areas. In 1921, he arranged a conference in Des Moines which led to the creation of the NATIONAL CONFERENCE ON STATE PARKS, a permanent organization.

Growing health problems forced Mather's retirement in 1929; he died in Brookline, Massachusetts, on January 22, 1930. Seeking a suitable epitaph for his many achievements, his friends conceived a memorial plaque bearing the inscription: "There will never come an end to the good that he has done."

FURTHER READING: Alfred Runte, *National Parks: The American Experience* (1979). Robert Shankland, *Steve Mather of the National Parks* (1951). Donald C. Swain, *Wilderness Defender: Horace M. Albright and Conservation* (1970).

ALFRED RUNTE

MCARDLE, RICHARD EDWIN (1899–   )

Richard E. McArdle was born February 25, 1899, in Lexington, Kentucky. He earned B.S. and M.S. degrees in forestry at the University of Michigan in 1923 and 1924, then entered the U. S. FOREST SERVICE as a silviculturist working out of the Pacific Northwest Forest and Range Experiment Station's new headquarters in Portland, Oregon. In 1927 he took a three-year leave of absence for graduate study and teaching to earn his Ph.D., returning to Portland to become a leader in fire research. He left the service again in 1934 to serve for a year as dean of the School of Forestry, University of Idaho, then resigned to become director of the new Rocky Mountain Forest and Range Experiment Station at Fort Collins, Colorado. After three years there, he took the same post at the Appalachian (now Southeastern) Station in Asheville, North Carolina. In 1944, he served as assistant chief for state and private forestry cooperative programs in Washington, D.C. He served as chief from July 1, 1952 to March 17, 1962.

During his regime, McArdle pressed for a congressional mandate for balanced management and long-range plans for the national forests and for research. He also pushed for accelerated recreation development, intensified timber management with adequate reforestation, curbing of mining and grazing abuses, more aid for state and private forestry, and increased professionalization and upgrading of personnel. Some results were the Multiple-Use Mining Law of 1955, the MULTIPLE USE-SUSTAINED YIELD ACT of 1960, a substantial increase and better balance in funds for the agency, continued improvement in conditions of its grazing lands, new responsibility for 7 million acres of Great Plains grasslands, and higher service grades for rangers and other field personnel in crucial positions.

McArdle abandoned as impractical and self-defeating the long intermittent attempt to get federal regulation of timber-harvesting practices on private lands. He thereby improved relations with the timber industry and was able to prevent the granting of vested grazing rights to livestock men in national forests.

He was active in INTERNATIONAL FORESTRY and was a founder of the North American Forestry Commission of the United Nations Food and Agriculture Organization. He helped organize, and served as president of, the Fifth World Forestry Congress held in Seattle, Washington, in 1960. After retirement he was executive director of the National Institute of Public Affairs, lectured at various colleges, and was an official of a forest industry group. He served on the boards of various forestry organizations and received numerous awards, including the Department of Agriculture Distinguished Service Award, 1957; the President's Gold Medal for Distinguished Federal Civilian Service, 1961; the Society of American Foresters' Sir William Schlich Memorial Medal, 1962; and the American Forestry Association's John Aston Warder Medal, 1978. In addition, he received the Knight Commander Order of Merit from the government of West Germany, 1962, and the Order of Merit for Forestry from the government of Mexico, 1961. He has been the recipient of honorary degrees from the University of Michigan, Syracuse University, and the University of Maine.

FRANK J. HARMON

MCFARLAND, JOHN HORACE (1859–1948)

J. Horace McFarland, a Harrisburg, Pennsylvania, business and civic leader, rose to prominence as one of America's leading proponents of urban beautification and scenic preservation. Born September 24, 1859, in McAlisterville, Pennsylvania, McFarland was the beneficiary of a family newspaper publishing business, whose wealth and security freed him for the philanthropy and civic activism he loved. The absence of financial worries also compensated for his lack of a formal education, although he more than made up for this deficiency by mastering the printer's craft.

A specialist on horticulture and the propagation of roses, McFarland won the editorship of the "Beautiful America" column of the *Ladies' Home Journal* in 1904. That same year, he was elected president of the new American Civic Association. He immediately used both posts as springboards for a vigorous, outspoken crusade against the disfigurement of NIAGARA FALLS by commercial power interests, which were preparing to divert the flow of the Niagara River around the cataract to turbines set downstream in the Niagara Gorge. If approved, McFarland bitterly concluded, the project would stand as "The Monument of America's shame and greed."

McFarland was thus intellectually and emotionally prepared to support the SIERRA CLUB between 1908 and 1913 in its battle against the Hetch Hetchy Valley dam, approval of which would mar the heart of YOSEMITE NATIONAL PARK. Accordingly, as president of the American Civic Association, McFarland joined the Sierra Club in lashing out against what preservationists had termed "the Hetch Hetchy Steal."

Convinced that only a separate government agency committed to protecting the national parks could save them from similar encroachments in the future, McFarland was instrumental in calling for the NA-

TIONAL PARK SERVICE and in lobbying for its creation. The bill, first introduced to Congress in 1911, required five more years of intensive effort to win approval, but finally, on August 25, 1916, preservationists had their National Park Service Act.

Meanwhile, McFarland continued to speak out on behalf of Niagara Falls and on issues such as urban beautification and billboard control. These campaigns, although only qualified successes, nonetheless propelled him to the forefront of American conservation. Honors and accolades poured in, including the vice presidency of the Municipal League (1912–1928) and the office of secretary of the Harrisburg Municipal League (1907–1945). Both posts were in addition to the presidency of the American Civic Association, which he held until 1924. Simultaneously, McFarland involved himself in a host of additional campaigns on behalf of scenic preservation, including calls for the creation of Shenandoah, Everglades, and Grand Teton national parks.

A Progressive in the classic sense of the term, McFarland firmly believed that city, state, and national parks were the foundation for human health, patriotism, and worker productivity. "The park," he once observed, "is the closest competitor, in the United States, of the courts, of the jail, of the cemetery, and a very efficient competitor with all of them." Calm and dignified in appearance, he nonetheless became impassioned and aroused whenever he faced ugliness in the human environment. As a result, he was still of the opinion that his battle for beauty had only just begun when death came on October 2, 1948.

FURTHER READING: Alfred Runte, *National Parks: The American Experience* (1979). William H. Wilson, "Harrisburg's Successful City Beautiful Movement, 1900–1915," *Pennsylvania History* 47 (July 1980): 213-233.

ALFRED RUNTE

MCGUIRE, JOHN RICHARD (1916–   )

John McGuire was born on April 20, 1916, in Milwaukee, Wisconsin. After his graduation in forestry from the University of Minnesota, he obtained a part-time research position with the U. S. FOREST SERVICE in Columbus, Ohio.

McGuire won a scholarship to Yale, where he earned his M.F. in 1941 and worked at the Forest Service research facility on the campus. For the next four war years, he served with the army in the Pacific, rising to major in command of the Eighth Engineering Battalion. In 1945, he returned to New Haven to work for the Forest Service's newly consolidated

Northeastern Forest Experiment Station. In 1950, he was transferred to the station's Upper Darby, Pennsylvania, headquarters where he did forestry economics research while earning his M.A. in economics at the University of Pennsylvania. In 1953, he became the station's chief of forest economics and for the next four years commuted to Washington, D.C., to help in the preparation of *Timber Resources for America's Future* (1958).

In 1957, he became a division director of the service's Pacific Southwest Forest and Range Experiment Station in Berkeley, California. One of his more interesting tasks was to establish a program of forest research in Hawaii.

By 1962, McGuire was staff assistant to the deputy chief of the Forest Service for research, but after eighteen months he returned to Berkeley as station director. During the next four years, he rapidly increased the use of computers in research, started programs in remote sensing and the development of safer pesticides, and established one of the Forest Service's major fire laboratories in Riverside, California.

McGuire's transfer in 1967 to Washington as deputy chief for programs and legislation moved him into the agency's leadership, where his duties included liaison with the DEPARTMENT OF AGRICULTURE and with Congress. In 1971, McGuire became associate chief and one year later the tenth head of the service. He served as chief until mid-1979. During his tenure the service modified and integrated its methods of land management, weathered the attacks of some environmental critics, and avoided the imposition of legislative controls on national forest timber harvesting when the NATIONAL FOREST MANAGEMENT ACT was passed in 1976. In addition, the service became heavily involved in national renewable resource planning under the terms of the FOREST AND RANGELAND RENEWABLE RESOURCES PLANNING ACT of 1974 and engaged in a successful program to involve the public in establishing additional wilderness areas within the national forests.

DENNIS M. ROTH

MCNARY, CHARLES LINZA (1874–1944)

Charles L. McNary, United States senator from Oregon between 1917 and 1944, sponsored a number of the most important pieces of forestry legislation in American history. Born on a farm near Salem, Oregon, on June 12, 1874, McNary attended Stanford University and then became a lawyer in Salem, Oregon's capital. He served as prosecuting attorney, dean of the Willamette University law school, and state supreme court justice before becoming chairman of the state Republican party in 1916. The following year, McNary was appointed to a United States Senate vacancy. Elected and re-elected, he served in that body for the remainder of his life. He became Republican Senate leader in 1933 and received his greatest national attention in 1940, when he was nominated as Wendell Willkie's running mate.

Throughout his long Senate career, McNary was noted for his efforts on behalf of Oregon's principal economic activities, agriculture and lumbering. His work in the latter area accounts for his importance in forest history. In the early years of the twentieth century, American forestry stressed fire protection and alterations in the system of TAXATION to enable private interests to manage their timber properly. Many lumbermen cooperated in these efforts. After 1910, however, Gifford PINCHOT and his followers, impatient with the progress of voluntary conservation, increasingly called for federal regulation of private logging practices. Many foresters, especially those moving into industry, continued to advocate government–business cooperation, and the great debate over forestry policy commenced. McNary became a leading spokesman for the views of conservative foresters.

The CLARKE-MCNARY ACT of 1924 provided federal funds for cooperative efforts against forest fires and for a study of the impact of tax laws on reforestation. These were the two main areas where industry and conservative foresters desired governmental assistance. The MCSWEENEY-MCNARY ACT of 1928 created a federal forestry research program and mandated a survey of forest conditions in the United States. The day after the senator's death on February 25, 1944, Congress approved the McNary-sponsored Sustained-Yield Forest Management Act. The legislation allowed the FOREST SERVICE and the DEPARTMENT OF THE INTERIOR to create cooperative sustained-yield units with private timber owners. Under such units, government timber would make possible the stabilization of industry and of small towns dependent upon logging and milling operations.

The Clarke-McNary, McSweeney-McNary, and Sustained-Yield Forest Management Acts represented the conservative view of forestry: federal government should aid private enterprise with money and research and public timber but should stop short of forcing industry to conduct itself in the public interest. Government should cooperate, not regulate. With such actions, Congress catered to special interest groups and slanted the direction of forestry in the

United States. McNary's career illustrates the role of politics in determining forestry policies.

While in the Senate, McNary also sponsored legislation for federal aid to state parks, to encourage the preservation of roadside timber along scenic highways, and to aid agriculture (the McNary-Haugen Farm Relief bills of 1926–1928). As a farmer, he introduced the filbert into the United States from Spain.

ROBERT E. FICKEN

MCSWEENEY-MCNARY ACT, 1928

Even the most desirable policy cannot be effectively applied without adequate knowledge. Therefore, when Congress passed the McSweeney-McNary Act on May 22, 1928, greatly expanding forestry research capability, it provided substantial and significant support for the conservation movement. The act is named for Senator Charles L. MCNARY of Oregon and Congressman John W. McSweeney of Ohio.

The U. S. FOREST SERVICE had given research high priority from the beginning. Associate Chief Earle H. CLAPP was unofficial author of this legislation which authorized the Forest Service to establish eleven regional experiment stations. The results were on-the-ground, practical studies of reforestation, timber growing, protection, utilization, economics, and similar topics and a nationwide inventory of timber resources.

MEAD, ELWOOD (1858–1936)

Elwood Mead was born January 16, 1858, on an Indiana farm and was educated at Purdue University and Iowa State College. He won acclaim for his work in irrigation engineering while on the faculty of Colorado State Agricultural College in the 1880s. Mead left Colorado in 1888 to become territorial engineer for Wyoming. He drafted the 1890 constitutional provisions on water rights that made Wyoming an exemplar of western water development.

Mead joined the DEPARTMENT OF AGRICULTURE in 1899 as head of the Office of Irrigation Investigations. During the eight years of Mead's leadership, this office initiated cooperative programs with state engineers and agricultural experiment stations to achieve water-law reform using the "Wyoming Idea" as a model and to educate farmers in irrigation practices. Mead also wrote extensively on these subjects; his principal publication was *Irrigation Institutions* (1903). In 1907, Mead assumed the directorship of a huge Australian water conservation and land settlement program, the Victoria State Rivers and Water Commission, encompassing thirty-two irrigation projects. He returned to the United States in 1915 to join the University of California faculty and head the state's Land Settlement Board. Mead's experiences in Australia and California shaped his philosophy of government-sponsored settlement and local autonomy. He upheld the value of the small family farm and proposed that planned development, combining social and public works engineering, would enhance the quality of rural life.

Although the model colonies Mead started in California would not prove to be successful in the long run, the Coolidge administration in 1923 appointed him to its Fact Finders Committee to investigate the BUREAU OF RECLAMATION. To bring about the reorganization he recommended, Mead became the agency's commissioner in 1924 and served in that capacity until his death. His reforms in the 1920s strengthened the economic position of settlers and reaffirmed social benefits. He was the first director of the bureau to end reclamation project debt, but the Great Depression interrupted his work. His initiative in creating the National Reclamation Association in 1932 brought congressional support for project development. During the Depression, Mead guided his bureau's evolution from a builder of irrigation works into a multiple-purpose water resource agency. He was a leading advocate of the Boulder Canyon Project and administered a huge construction program undertaken to relieve unemployment and restore economic stability. When Mead died on January 26, 1936, Franklin D. ROOSEVELT acclaimed him as a "builder with vision."

FURTHER READING: Paul K. Conkin, "The Vision of Elwood Mead," *Agricultural History* 34 (Apr. 1960): 88-97. James R. Kluger, "Elwood Mead: Irrigation Engineer and Social Planner," Ph.D. dissertation, University of Arizona (1970). Michael C. Robinson, "Elwood Mead," *APWA Reporter* 44 (June 1977): 6-7.

MICHAEL C. ROBINSON

MEDICINAL PRODUCTS

When the early colonists came to what is now the continental United States, they found vast forests containing many species of hardwoods and conifers. There was an even larger number of small trees and shrubs growing in thickets at the forest edge or in natural clearings. Finally, on the forest floor, there was a third, distinct flora composed principally of small perennials. Taken together, these three ecologically interrelated floras provided food, medicine, and other economically

important products to the American Indians. Most of the New World species were unknown to the colonists, though with generations of experience in the utilization of forest products, they correctly detected a resemblance to the European species of oak, beech, pine, and larch. These similarities suggested their medicinal uses in treating aches, fevers, wounds, and bites, as well as their common names.

After peaceful relations were established with local Indian tribes, a second source of information became available regarding the medicinal uses of forest trees and plants. For example, Indians taught settlers the medicinal uses of American beech (*Fagus grandifolia*) for frostbite, yaupon (*Ilex vomitoria*) for anemia, and sweetbay magnolia (*Magnolia virginiana*) for chills and fever. Medicinal use of many other forest species followed, some of which continue today in the Appalachians and Ozarks: steam inhalation of eastern redcedar (*Juniperus virginiana*), witch hazel (*Hamamelis virginiana*) as a lotion for bruises, wintergreen (*Gaultheria procumbens*) as a tea, and pipsissewa (*Chimaphila umbellata*) as a tonic.

As succeeding generations of settlers moved westward, more new forest species were encountered that would enter folk *materia medica*. Hackberry (*Celtis occidentalis*) with edible fruit and roots used for dye, wahoo or spindle tree (*Euonymus atropurpureus*) of which the root bark was used as a purgative, Kentucky coffeetree (*Gymnocladus dioicus*) from which the green fruit was made into a pulp for medicine, and butternut (*Juglans cinerea*), a favorite for toothaches and rheumatism, are among the most common. Although their medicinal properties were not always confirmed by later investigators, these and other forest products were used for two reasons: the virtual absence of trained physicians and the lack of pure, commercially prepared substances. Under these circumstances, the settlers and their families treated their complaints and injuries with locally available, inexpensive, and easily obtainable substances, such as the resinous exudation of *Populus balsamifera*, commonly known as Balm of Gilead used as cough medicine, the bark of wild black cherry (*Prunus serotina*) for fever, leaves of slippery elm (*Ulmus rubra*) for poultices, and the bark of cascara buckthorn (*Rhamnus purshiana*) as a popular laxative.

Ginseng (*Panax quinquefolium*) has been a highly prized medicinal herb for centuries. Users believe in its many restorative properties, and much of the American root has been sold in China; in 1841, $437,245 worth was shipped to the Orient. Ginseng commanded 52 cents per pound in 1858; by 1897, the

This portable still produced oil of eucalyptus, to be used for medicinal purposes. Forest History Society Lantern Slide Collection.

price had risen to $4.71, and by 1919, the best grades brought $12 per pound. By 1972, 168,835 pounds of ginseng, valued at $5.8 million, were exported; 97 percent of the total was shipped to China.

Throughout the first half of the nineteenth century, the medicinal uses of most of the forest species had become common knowledge. The claims made on their behalf, though sometimes exaggerated, could not be ignored; consequently, many of the old-time favorites entered into proprietory drugs. Owing largely to their predictability and demonstrable physiological action, principally as cathartics, emetics, diuretics, and counterirritants, some species such as dogwood (*Cornus florida*), fringetree (*Chionanthus virginicus*), prickly-ash (*Zanthoxylum americanum*), spikenard (*Aralia racemosa*), and sweet gum (*Liquidambar styraciflua*) became officially recognized by the *U.S. Pharmacopoeia* and *National Formulary*, where they remained for varying periods of time. Whether or not the various forest species were officially recognized, their role in folk medicine continued. In some areas, the collection of various portions of local species became a sizable and lucrative business.

The commercial exploitation of the forests and their products was already underway by the early eighteenth century. Although the principal products were large timbers, barrel staves, and wainscoting, medicinal products were both sold and bartered. Especially at the local level, Indian contacts were essential. In fact, one of the first forest industries was the frantic but short-lived search for sassafras (*Sassafras albidum*). Early in the seventeenth century, English ships were dispatched to the colonies for the purpose of transporting many tons of the loose root bark. Sassafras was regarded as a virtual panacea and, as such, commanded an exorbitant price in England. Tea made from its root bark was popular among herbal tea drinkers until the 1960s, when it was discovered to contain safrole, a weak carcinogen, and the Food and Drug Administration banned it from the marketplace.

NAVAL STORES, another forest industry, was destined to outlast the sassafras industry. Although medicinal uses of turpentine, pitch, and rosin were secondary, these products of pine trees were among the most common ingredients in domestic medicine in the nineteenth century. Another forest species, wintergreen, served as a tea substitute, a decoction for various internal complaints, and as a flavoring agent in medicaments, cosmetics, and tobacco.

The small, independent "herb and root houses" in the Southeast still continue to do a thriving business. A 1976 western North Carolina price list mentions seventy-two species, the majority of which are forest species. They are collected by the hill people and sold, usually in the crude, partially dried state, to the local "herb house." They are then mechanically cleaned, sorted, and sold to the larger wholesaler. In turn, the wholesaler processes the materials, packages, and distributes the dried bark, leaves, seeds, and root slices to health food stores throughout the United States.

FURTHER READING: Arnold Krochmal and Connie Krochmal, *A Guide to the Medicinal Plants of the United States* (1973). Hu Maxwell, "Indian Medicines Made from Trees," *American Forests* 24 (Apr. 1918): 205-211. Clarence Meyer, *American Folk Medicine* (1975). Louise Veninga, *The Ginseng Book* (1973).

JERRY STANNARD

MERRIAM, JOHN CAMPBELL (1869–1945)

John Campbell Merriam's career epitomizes the role that some natural scientists played in the early park preservation movement. Born in Iowa on October 20, 1869, Merriam received his doctorate in vertebrate paleontology from the University of Munich in 1893. He was professor of paleontology and historical geography at the University of California, Berkeley (1894–1920), and president of the Carnegie Institution of Washington, D.C. (1920–1938). His numerous papers described the fossil reptiles and fossil mammals of western North America and the historical geology of the Pacific Basin. In his books *The Living Past* (1926) and *The Garment of God: The Influence of Nature in Human Experience* (1943), Merriam interpreted the philosophical and religious import of Darwin's theory of evolution. Active in scenic preservation, Merriam served as an officer in several national conservation organizations. He was president of the SAVE-THE-REDWOODS LEAGUE (1920–1945) and a leader on the advisory board of the NATIONAL PARK SERVICE (1920–1933).

Merriam believed that national and state parks could serve as laboratories essential to future scientists as well as places where laymen might study and draw inspiration from the earth's biological and geological past. He wrote widely about the parks and personally developed the observation station for visitor education at Yavapai Point on the rim of the Grand Canyon. A purist, Merriam advocated severe limitations on recreational development of the national parks.

He was active in international scientific and preservation organizations including the Commission du Parc National Albert in Zaire and La Asociacion Conservadoro de los Monumentos Arquelogicos de Yucatán. He died on October 30, 1945.

FURTHER READING: *Published Papers and Addresses of John Campbell Merriam*, Carnegie Institution of Washington Publication 500 (1938). Susan R. Schrepfer, "A Conservative Reform: Saving the Redwoods, 1917 to 1940," Ph.D. dissertation, University of California, Riverside (1971).

SUSAN R. SCHREPFER

MICHAUX, ANDRE (1746–1802) AND FRANÇOIS ANDRE MICHAUX (1770–1855)

Two of the most astute observers of the forest flora of North America in the late eighteenth and early nineteenth centuries were the French botanists and silviculturists André Michaux and François André Michaux. The elder Michaux was the son of the manager of the royal farm at Satory near Versailles. At the age of twenty-one, André became supervisor of this 500-acre estate. Despondent over the death of his wife during the birth of their son in 1770, André sought to alleviate his anguish by the diligent study of botany. He studied at the Trianon and the Jardin des Plantes and came under the guidance of Bernard de Jussieu. After traveling and collecting seeds in England, he worked with Jean Lamarck in the Auvergne and Pyrenees. Seeking to establish himself as a botanical explorer, he used his appointment as secretary to the French consul at Isfahan, Persia, as an opportunity to botanize in Mesopotamia, where he studied the flora from 1782 to 1785.

Upon his return to France, the government of Louis XVI sent him to America to determine which of this continent's trees, in particular the oaks, could be profitably grown in France. Generations of neglect and unrestricted cutting had seriously depleted the forests and its future as a naval power could not be assured until it had adequate stands of trees to provide ship timbers. From the fall of 1785 to the fall of 1787, André Michaux and his son, François André, collected seeds and seedlings and established a nursery at Hackensack, New Jersey. In 1787, another nursery was established in Charleston, South Carolina. With Charleston as a base, the Michaux botanized in the Carolina mountains, southern Appalachians, Spanish Florida, and the Bahamas. In addition to exporting American seedlings to Europe, André Michaux introduced into the United States the camellia, mimosa, ginko, tallow tree, sweet olive, and Grecian laurel. As the turmoil of revolution swept across France, the 60,000 trees which he had carefully collected and shipped to France were neglected. He nevertheless persisted in his efforts and in 1792 he made an eight-month trip north to Hudson Bay.

The following year, he sought to embark upon an expedition across the continent to the Pacific. Although initially supported by the American Philosophical Society and by President Washington and Thomas Jefferson, authorization for this trip was canceled when Washington learned of Michaux's involvement with the schemings of the French minister against Spanish Louisiana. Thwarted in his attempts to travel into the Far West, Michaux nevertheless made a three-month trip to Kentucky. In the next year, 1794, he collected in the Appalachians and then traveled west to Illinois.

Lacking support from his government and exhausting his own resources, he returned to France in the late summer of 1796. Misfortune continued to plague him. Shipwrecked off the coast of Holland, he lost portions of his journals and herbarium. A penurious French government refused to indemnify him or to support future American investigations. After preparing his American studies for publication, he joined Captain Nicolas Baudin's Australian Expedition in 1800. Wishing to botanize on the island of Madagascar, he landed there in 1802. Before any extensive work was completed, he contracted a tropical fever and died in November of that year.

André Michaux's contributions to American forest history were substantial, for he was a meticulous field naturalist. His beautifully illustrated *Histoire des Chênes de l'Amérique* (1801) was the first significant study of the American oaks. With its exquisite drawings prepared by Pierre Joseph Rédouté, one of the masters of botanical illustration, it is one of the most handsome works in American silviculture. With the posthumous publication of Michaux's *Flora Boreali-Americana* (1803), also illustrated by Rédouté, the first systematic study of the flora of North America was available to botanists.

François André Michaux inherited his father's interest in silviculture and continued his father's work. An active supporter of the French Revolution, he was charged by his government in 1801 to return to America and to investigate, as his father had, those trees which might profitably be used to reforest French lands. In June 1802, after having visited his father's nurseries at Hackensack and Charleston, he set forth for a journey to Ohio, Kentucky, and Tennessee. Whereas his father's field notes are concerned primarily with the varieties of plant life, François André's journals contain not only comments upon the objects of natural history that intrigued him but also substantial observations upon the life of the frontier.

Returning to France in 1803, he quickly published *Voyage à l' Ouest des Monts Alléghanys dans les Etats de l'Ohio, et du Kentucky, et du Tennessée, et retour à Charleston par les Hautes-Carolines* (1804) and presented his report to his government. The latter was titled, *Sur la Naturalisation des Arbres Forestiers de l'Amérique du Nord* (1804).

In 1806, François André Michaux returned to America and for the next three years continued to study the eastern forests. In August 1807, he was one of the two passengers on the maiden voyage of Robert Fulton's steamboat. Encouraged by American scientists, he continued to collect materials for an inventory of this nation's forest resources. In his writings he sought to convince the citizens of the United States of the immediate need for proper forest management. He suggested that the American government should play an active role in the preservation of its forests.

Upon the conclusion of his last American trip, he began publication of the *Histoire des Arbres Forestiers de l'Amérique Septentrionale* (1810–1813), known in its English translation as *The North American Sylva; or, a Description of the Forest Trees of the United States, Canada, and Nova Scotia, Considered Particularly with Respect to their Uses in the Arts and their Introduction into Commerce* (1818–1819). *The North American Sylva* not only was a carefully arranged assessment of American forests east of the Mississippi River but it was also a plea for conservation and a condemnation of the prodigal use of America's timber resources. Until the middle of the nineteenth century, this work was the most valuable and comprehensive study of American forests. Thomas NUTTALL later prepared a three-volume supplement. When François André Michaux died in 1855, he left a bequest to the American Philosophical Society to promote silviculture in America.

FURTHER READING: J. P. F. Deleuze, "Notice historique sur André Michaux," *Annales du Museum national d'histoire naturelle* 3 (1804): 191-227. Elias Durand, "Biographical Memoir of the Late François André Michaux," *American Journal of Science* 74 (1857): 161-177. Joseph Ewan, "André Michaux," *Dictionary of Scientific Biography* 9 (1974): 365-366. André Michaux, "Portions of the Journal of André Michaux, Botanist, Written during His Travels in the United States and Canada, 1785–1796," introduction and explanatory notes by Charles S. Sargent, *Proceedings of the American Philosophical Society* 26 (1889): 1-145. Jacob Richard Schramm, "Influence—Past and Present—of François André Michaux on Forestry and Forest Research in America," *Proceedings of the American Philosophical Society* 101 (Aug. 1957): 336-343. Rodney H. True, "François André Michaux, the Botanist and Explorer," *Proceedings of the American Philosophical Society* 78 (1937): 313-327.

PHILLIP DRENNON THOMAS

MICHIGAN FORESTS

Some 35.2 million acres, or 96 percent of Michigan's total land area, was at one time covered with a diversified forest ranging from the oak openings in the south to pure stands of white pine in the Saginaw Valley, and from jack pine on the sand hills bordering Lake Superior to pure stands of beech on Grand Island and tamarack in swampy regions throughout the state. A diversity of soils, drainage, and topography accounts for this variety. Generally speaking, surveyors found three forest belts in the state. The area south of a line from Bay City to Muskegon was largely forested with hardwoods such as oak, basswood, elm, maple, cherry, and beech. To the north, conifers prevailed, mostly white pine and hemlock, with some yellow birch, beech, elm, and basswood intermixed. The Upper Peninsula generally grew a northern hardwood forest of poplar, white and yellow birch, and maple mixed with pine, white and black spruce, balsam, and tamarack; there were also some pure stands of white and Norway pine.

The forest was intensively used by the Indians and the early white settlers. From cedar, birch bark, and spruce roots the Indians built canoes that were well adapted for their seasonal migrations. They occupied maple sugar groves for a month or so each spring for processing sugar and syrup. A variety of types of shelters were made from wood and the bark of cedar and birch. Europeans exploited the fur-bearing animals of Michigan forests early in the seventeenth century, and frontier settlers employed wood for dwellings, tools, and fuel.

Federal lands in Michigan were opened to settlement in 1814, and from then until the middle of the century, farmers cleared substantial areas in the southern part of the state. Completion of the Erie Canal in 1823 opened a northern settlement route that directly aided Michigan's population growth. Commercial lumbering of the white pine and hardwoods in the Lower Peninsula began during this period; by 1837, 435 sawmills were in operation, all but 83 of them in the south. By 1873, the state contained 1,600 mills, and more than half of these were in the northern pineries in and above the Saginaw Valley. Only after the 1870s did lumbering for the domestic market develop on the Upper Peninsula; before then, logging there was largely confined to hardwoods used for charcoal by the mining industry and squared white pine timbers for the Canadian market. The white pine industry that grew in northern Michigan was based on export to the urbanizing East and the spreading settlements on the prairies.

The Great Lakes offered cheap, direct transportation for such bulky cargoes as logs and lumber. When in the 1850s Michigan began to export timber to the East, the Erie Canal served as a highway to connect the lakes with the older regions of the country. Extensive river systems, such as the Manistee and Muskegon flowing into Lake Michigan, the Saginaw, Au

Sable, and Thunder rivers flowing into Lake Huron, and the Tehquamenon, Manistique, and Sturgeon draining the Upper Peninsula, provided potential highways for logs cut in the interior regions of the state. Lumbermen and lumbermen's associations spent decades dredging, straightening, and clearing these streams.

Michigan timberlands were easily acquired. Large federal land grants were made to railroads and to the state when it joined the Union in 1837. These grants in turn were sold to private parties; by the end of the century, all but a half million acres of Michigan's onetime public domain was in private hands. Timber investors from Detroit and Chicago and from the East scrambled for the best white pine stands. Speculation was particularly intense during the 1850s when the state forestlands sold for an average price of $1.50 an acre. Lands assigned under military bounty warrants could be had even more cheaply. Values boomed, and by the 1880s prime pineland might go for $125 an acre.

In the 1850s, Michigan residents considered it no crime to steal timber off government lands, and federal agents learned to distinguish between innocent and felony trespassers. When discovered, the former might escape by paying on the basis of mill scale or might be forced to purchase the violated land. For more serious cases, the government sporadically embarked upon campaigns of seizing the cut logs, and relations between frontier loggers and federal timber agents were often warlike. Once most of the land had left federal ownership, loggers became more circumspect, but still lawsuits for even minor trespasses on private lands were common.

The development of high-speed milling, involving changes from muley to circular saws in the 1860s and to band saws late in the 1880s, called for better harvesting techniques. In the late 1870s, the introduction of the logging railroad permitted lumbermen to haul greater loads and to harvest timber on a year-round basis. Standard-gauge lines were also extended into the lumbering districts, facilitating the movement of lumber to markets such as Chicago and Albany. These innovations freed lumbermen from the vicissitudes of weather, permitted enormous increases in the yearly cut, and paved the way for the destructive clearcutting practices that, along with seasonal forest fires, leveled Michigan's pineries between 1870 and 1910.

The proportion of the desired white pine in Michigan's annual timber cut gradually increased to about 90 percent in the early 1880s. Total timber production peaked at 5.48 billion board feet in 1889 (64 percent white pine, 23 percent hardwood, and 11 percent hemlock). As early as 1890, wholesale dealers complained

This state forest nursery at Higgins Lake in north-central Michigan provided planting stock to reforest logged areas, c. 1925. Forest Service Photo.

about the inferior quality of pine coming from Michigan forests. For some time thereafter, sawmills maintained production by rafting logs from the Ontario forests across the lakes, but the industry was clearly declining. Production remained over a billion board feet annually until 1917. With the depletion of the white pine, hemlock and maple were the leading lumber species. Hardwoods supplied more than half the lumber produced after 1912. The lowest annual total came in 1932, when fifty-three mills reported a production of only 111,000 board feet, 73 percent of it hardwood. Michigan's annual lumber production never again reached 500 million board feet. As a lumber manufacturer, the state ranked only twenty-second in the nation in 1960. In 1977, the total forestland area had been reduced to 53 percent of the state. Of 19.27 million forested acres, 18.78 million were of commercial value and were available for utilization. Of the remaining commercial forest, 10.1 million acres were privately owned, forest industries holding 2.26 million acres.

In addition to lumber, Michigan produced a number of other forest products. Hemlock bark was used by tanneries, 240,652 tons (93,808 cords) of it in 1905. Changes in tanning techniques brought about a decline in the hemlock bark industry, but with the pine depleted, hemlock itself became a valuable source of lumber, surpassing white pine in board feet of annual production by 1904.

Mining of copper and iron developed in the Upper Peninsula beginning in the mid-1840s; hardwood was consumed as charcoal to stoke the kilns, and thousands of feet of white pine were used for timbering the copper mines. The 2 million tons of pig iron produced in the Upper Peninsula before 1902 required a total of 5 million cords of wood for charcoal, representing some 166,666 acres of hardwood forest, while mine shafting consumed another 12 million board feet of lumber.

As early as 1839, coopers had used Michigan white pine for barrels at the Isle Royale posts of the American Fur Company. For a time, Michigan led the nation in the production of slack cooperage. In 1908, the state produced about 42 percent of the nation's elm staves and 38 percent of its maple staves, but only seventeen years later the COOPERAGE INDUSTRY had declined to insignificance.

The FURNITURE INDUSTRY, which developed in the nineteenth century around Grand Rapids in the southern part of the state, became an important consumer of hardwoods. Sugar maple was the principal native wood used in the furniture industry, and in much of the twentieth century more sugar maple was harvested in Michigan than any other species except hemlock. In 1963, furniture manufacture ranked second only to pulp and paper in importance among Michigan's forest industries, although much of the wood used was imported from other states.

Pulp and paper production in Michigan began in the late 1800s and became an increasingly important part of the state's forest products industry. In 1899, 34,300 cords of pulpwood were consumed; in 1978, consumption had reached nearly 1.8 million cords, 95 percent of it harvested within the state. About 8 percent of Michigan's pulpwood in that year came from mill residues; 72 percent of the total was hardwood.

As privately owned timberlands were exhausted, they were allowed to revert to the state for nonpayment of taxes. In the Upper Peninsula, CUTOVER LANDS were promoted and sold as farmland, but the sandy soil that supported the great white pine stands proved unsuitable for agriculture. The farms failed and these lands too reverted to the state. In 1893, the state opened its lands to homesteading and in 1899 it provided for their direct sale; this disposal policy lasted until 1913. Sale and reversion of individual tracts sometimes occurred several times in succession.

The change from exploitation to forestland management began slowly in the late nineteenth century. In 1899, the legislature authorized a forestry commission and a forestry warden, a post first filled in 1902 by Filibert Roth. The University of Michigan founded a forestry school in 1902 and Michigan State University followed a year later. Under leaders like Filibert Roth and P. S. Lovejoy, these schools preached the gospel of sustained yield and multiple use, gained the cooperation of progressive lumbermen like William Marshon and William C. Mather, and worked with the state forestry commission, organized in 1903. Supported by sportsmen concerned with saving game habitats, the commission and the universities began developing a state forest system starting with the Au Sable and Houghton Lake units of 35,000 acres in 1903; game and forest conservation were to go hand in hand in Michigan. To provide planting stock for reforestation of the state forests, Roth started the Higgins Lake nursery in 1905 and established experimental plantations elsewhere in the ensuing years. In 1909, the state formed a Public Domain Commission to govern the tax reverted lands, and in 1910 it appointed its first full-time forester. The state reorganized its apparatus for administering natural resources in 1921 when it established the Department of Conservation, which incorporated the Public Domain Commission, the State Board of Fish Commissioners, the Board of Geological Survey, and the state park, forest, and game commissions. The new agency was renamed the Department of Natural Resources in 1968.

Concern about what to do with the cutover and repeatedly burned-over lands led to the Land Economic Survey, administered by the State Department of Conservation and conducted between 1922 and 1933. Instigated by P. S. Lovejoy, longtime advocate of reforestation, the survey studied soil, forestry, wildlife, and recreation potential in the northern counties. Although dropped from the budget before completion, the studies resulted in sound land-management policies and provided information about which lands the state should keep and which should be returned to private hands.

A state game refuge program was initiated in 1924; in 1931, purchases were authorized for expansion of the system. In 1946, the sixteen existing refuges were absorbed into the state forest system, essentially completing that system. By 1980, it included over 3.76 million acres, 20 percent of Michigan's forest area. Eighty-three percent of the state forestland had been acquired through tax reversion.

Michigan created its first state parks, among the earliest in the United States, in 1895 when it accepted the transfer of Mackinac Island and Fort Michilimackinac, former federal military reservations. The state established a park commission in 1919 but absorbed it into the new Department of Conservation two years later. Nevertheless, additional parks were added to the system, such as the Porcupine Mountains in the Upper Peninsula in the 1940s and the Hartwick Pines in lower Michigan. Small vestiges of the original forests were added from enclaves, mostly in the Upper Peninsula, which lumbermen had reserved as pleasure grounds for themselves and their families as they swept through the country. In 1975, Michigan had ninety-three state park and recreation areas with 224,000 acres; together with the twenty-three forests, they made up one of the largest state park and forest systems in the country.

The U. S. FOREST SERVICE has undertaken major programs in Michigan. Gifford PINCHOT in 1898 offered cooperation to private timber owners with the Division of Forestry's Circular 21, *Practical Assistance to Farmers, Lumbermen, and Others in Handling Forest Lands*. This policy struck a responsive chord in the farmers from New England who had settled southern Michigan and were accustomed to woodlot management. Some of the more progressive timberland owners, such as the Cleveland Cliffs Iron Company, obtained working plans from the service and began managing their tracts on a sustained-yield basis, while owners of estates and parks asked for advice on preserving the forest for amenity values. As in other areas, federal, state, and private owners cooperated against their common enemy, fire. Forest Service and state authorities together encouraged the development of industrial forestry on private lands. P. S. Lovejoy, who promoted sound woodlot management, and Bruce G. Buell, who helped put these precepts into practice, pioneered in this movement during the 1930s. The Forest Service's North Central Region developed the Continuous Forest Inventory in the hardwood areas under the direction of Calvin Stott.

Two national forests, the Marquette and Michigan, were established in the state in 1909. Additional lands were acquired for these, new units were designated, and the system was reorganized several times so that by 1980 there were four national forests in Michigan, including over 2.7 million acres of federally owned land.

The National Park Service also controls a sizable area in Michigan, chiefly in Isle Royale National Park, famous for its wolf and moose populations. Isle Royale, on an island in Lake Superior, was authorized in 1931, although it was not established until 1940. Originally comprising 133,405 acres, it had a total of 571,796 acres by 1979. Michigan's two national lakeshores have a combined total land area of 121,595 acres; one of them, Pictured Rocks, was America's first national lakeshore when it was authorized in 1966.

There are also two national wildlife refuges in Michigan, the Seney and the Shiawassee, which cover 104,400 acres. The Seney's 95,500 acres were completely cut over in the late 1870s and 1880s, but now they contain stands of red and jack pine amid the sand ridges and freshwater marshes and ponds.

FURTHER READING: Philip P. Mason, *Lumbering Era in Michigan History, 1860–1900* (1956), and Rolland H. M. Maybee, *Michigan's White Pine Era, 1840–1900* (1960), cover the great logging era, but George W. Hotchkiss, *History of the Lumber and Forest Industry of the Northwest* (1898) is still the most detailed source on Michigan's lumber industry. More specialized studies include George Blackburn and Sherman L. Ricards, Jr., "The Timber Industry in Manistee County, Michigan: A Case History in Local Control," *Journal of Forest History* 18 (Apr. 1974): 14-21; Ruth Birgitta Bordin, "A Michigan Lumbering Family," *Business History Review* 34 (Spring 1960): 64-76; Anita Shafer Goodstein, "Labor Relations in the Saginaw Valley Lumber Industry, 1865–1885," *Bulletin of the Business Historical Society* 27 (Dec. 1953): 193-221; and Lucile M. Kane, "Feder-

al Protection of Public Timber in the Upper Great Lakes States," *Agricultural History* 23 (Apr. 1949): 135–139. George Irving Quimby, *Indian Culture and European Trade Goods* (1966) is excellent on Indian use of the forest. Norman J. Schmaltz's doctoral dissertation, "Cutover Land Crusade: The Michigan Forest Conservation Movement, 1899–1931" (University of Michigan, 1972) and his "P. S. Lovejoy: Michigan's Cantankerous Conservationist," *Journal of Forest History* (Apr. 1975): 72-81, give a good summary of the conservation movement in Michigan. State policy is outlined in David D. Olson, "The Development of the Michigan State Forest System," *Timber Producer* (Mar. 1980): 14, 44. On the development of industrial forestry, George B. Amidon, *The Development of Industrial Forestry in the Lake States* (1961), has some material on Michigan, as does Henry Clepper, *Professional Forestry in the United States* (1971). Stewart Edward White, *The Blazed Trail* (1902), is an adventure novel that portrays life in Michigan logging camps and mill towns in remarkably vivid and realistic detail. William N. Sparhawk and Warren D. Brush, *Economic Aspects of Forest Destruction in Northern Michigan*, U. S. Department of Agriculture Technical Bulletin No. 92 (1929), includes some incidental history.

LAWRENCE RAKESTRAW

MILLWORK INDUSTRY

Millwork is wood shaped by machine in a mill or factory for use in buildings. It is an often ambiguous term at times used as a synonym for all woodwork, at times for the machines in a mill. It includes those products of a mill used in buildings, such as sashes and doors, moldings, blinds and shutters, stairwork, mantels, and built-in cabinets of all kinds—in short, architectural elements, mass-produced in factories.

Shaping of wood by machine is very ancient. Waterpowered sawmills date from Roman times and were common in the Middle Ages throughout Europe. These early sawmills were adaptations of the pit saw, in which a vertical blade in a wood frame was worked against a horizontal log by a sawyer at the top and a man in a pit at the bottom. A thirteenth-century French manuscript describes a waterpowered vertical sawmill, and such mills were in use at Augsburg in 1322. As early as 1575, a mill at Regensburg was sawing several boards at once with a vertical gang saw powered by the Danube River.

Colonists built sawmills in North America almost as soon as they arrived. The abundant forests of the Eastern Seaboard supplied material for building, and lumber was sent back to England on some of the earliest returning ships. As a historian has pointed out, the American sawmill originated in continental Europe rather than in England, where sawyers fearful of their jobs had resorted to violence to delay the building of very many before the middle of the eighteenth century. Technicians from Hamburg had sawmills in operation on the James River in Virginia in the summer of 1611, and the Dutch built many mills along the Hudson River soon after. A windmill was powering a sawmill on an island in New York harbor as early as 1623. Other early mills recorded include York, Maine, 1623; Portsmouth, New Hampshire, 1631; Scituate, Massachusetts, 1640; and Silvermine, Connecticut, 1688. There were probably more than 100 others in operation before 1700.

Later technical advances in sawmilling included circular saws for special purposes, such as shingles, which became common after 1820. Band saws began to see wide usage after about 1870, when improved technology in the steel industry made them practical. A steam-powered sawmill on the Delaware River in 1802 has been noted, but not until after the Civil War did steam seriously compete with waterpower. Even after steam engines were in wide use, the westward spread of sawmills closely followed water courses, still the easiest way to transport the logs to the mills.

The end of the eighteenth century saw the invention of many specialized machines for millwork. Sir Samuel Bentham (brother of Jeremy Bentham, the Utilitarian philosopher) is pre-eminent among the inventors of WOODWORKING MACHINES. He perfected more than twenty new devices before 1800, including machines for planing, molding, dove-tailing, mortising, boring, rabbeting, and screw threading. Lathes for turning irregular forms have been described by eighteenth-century French writers Condamine, De la Hire, and Plumier. Bentham patented a similar device in 1793. Isambard Kingdom Brunel, British engineer and naval architect, perfected a lathe for shaping ships' blocks, but it was Thomas Blanchard of Philadelphia whose lathe, patented September 6, 1819, had the greatest impact on later wooden manufacture. A British parliamentary committee that visited the United States in 1854 was impressed by a Blanchard lathe it observed making gunstocks at the Springfield Armory. Whereas a skilled man could make two gunstocks per day before, Blanchard's lathe, and variations on the principle, made it possible to produce irregular shapes of any kind in a fraction of the time—and all exactly alike. The principle employed was the use of a model and a blank, the contours of the model guiding the cutting tool to produce a duplicate from the blank.

The parliamentary committee of 1854 reported that specialized machines in American factories were producing wooden elements for buildings for much less than the cost of making them by hand. They visited a factory where 20 men were making 100 paneled doors a day. A Cohoes, New York, plant reported in 1847 that six to eight men could make the sash for fifty windows in one day.

The United States Census of 1850 listed 433 sash and blind factories. There were 1,605 in 1870, and 1,288 in 1880. Although the number of factories decreased in the 1870s, total millwork production did not. The development of canals and railroads and a population that had tripled between 1830 and 1860 made possible vast new markets for millwork factories, which now began to sell their wares outside their own neighborhoods.

White pine was the standard wood used in American building until about 1850. The industry centered in Maine before shifting to upstate New York, which then produced about 8 billion board feet per year. By 1860, Pennsylvania was the center. The forests of Michigan and Wisconsin followed but were much depleted by 1900, when the South and Pacific Northwest took over the lead. At this point, eastern white pine production was surpassed by southern yellow pine and by Douglas-fir, ponderosa pine, and western white pine. Redwood was an important millwork and construction species in California and was also exported to other markets.

While the pine forests of the Great Lakes region were being harvested, lumber was shipped east by lake steamer and down the Mississippi by raft to Iowa and Illinois, where a great millwork industry was centered after the Civil War. The spread of the railroad network during this same period gave these Midwest mills a national market.

Many other species of wood were processed in millwork factories, including oak, ash, walnut, and cherry. Although little publicized, due to widespread prejudice against it, poplar was a very important wood in the East after 1880, when white pine became scarce. A writer of the day noted that poplar had almost entirely superseded pine for architectural trim, especially moldings. It was also widely used in furniture, under veneers, and was successfully stained to imitate cherry.

The trade catalog became a new force in American building after 1850. Pattern books had served country carpenters well, earlier in the century, when houses and their components were fashioned by hand. The catalog, containing standardized millwork, now made architectural construction in much larger degree a process of assembly. Builders and their clients could order doors, windows, complete porches, staircases, mantelpieces, and all interior and exterior moldings and finish from an illustrated catalog.

In a few short years, there was a greater standard-

Western hemlock has been transformed into interlocking pieces of tongue-and-groove flooring. Forest History Society Photo.

ization of American architectural styles. The same wooden elements were used on houses from coast to coast for two basic reasons: they were cheaper than could be made by hand locally, and they often represented the latest in architectural fashion. Standardization of designs for moldings reduced costs for stock items, and even though all factories advertised that they could make to order anything a customer wanted, the stock patterns prevailed.

Newly formed manufacturers' associations published books of these standard moldings. The Wholesale Sash, Door and Blind Manufacturers Association of the Northwest was organized in the 1880s, with headquarters in Chicago. In 1896, this Midwest group joined the Eastern Sash, Door and Blind Manufacturers Association in the publication of a *Universal Molding Book* and in the adoption of a standard price list. Members could be fined heavily for price cutting or other practices in violation of association rules. Although federal law later made price-fixing illegal, manufacturers' associations have continued to set national standards for millwork. The National Door Manufacturers Association was formed in 1933 and later became the National Woodwork Manufacturers Association. Its seal of approval was inaugurated in 1938 and became the recognized standard for woodwork treated against decay with water-repellent preservatives. In 1957, the stock millwork industry also organized to promote its products more effectively.

Numerous other regional and specialized associations are active in the industry.

FURTHER READING: James Elliott Defebaugh, *History of the Lumber Industry of America* (1907). Brooke Hindle, ed., *America's Wooden Age: Aspects of Its Early Technology* (1975). William B. Lloyd, *Millwork, Principles and Practices: Manufacture, Distribution, Use* (1966).

ARTHUR A. HART

MINE TIMBER

Underground mines have been major consumers of timber. When excavating beneath the surface of the ground, miners erected artificial supports, ordinarily made of timber in either round or square-sawed lengths, to shore up the roof and sides of the mine. Although subject to decay and insect damage, timber mine props proved for their day to be economical, versatile, and strong. They also failed gradually, their creaking and popping noises giving warning to miners of an impending collapse. The sounds of timber under pressure may account for the mythical creatures called "Tommyknockers," who looked after the safety of deep-level miners. Elsewhere, mine operators relied on timber for constructing surface buildings, lining hoist shafts, making crossties for tramways, and as a fuel.

The size and depth of a mine, along with the nature of the mineral being removed and the stability of the adjacent ground, determined how miners used tim-

Interior of a mine shows the large amount of timber needed to shore ceilings and walls. Forest History Society Lantern Slide Collection.

bering. In horizontal veins, they generally set vertical props topped by wooden caps to secure the sides and back of the mine, while narrow, steeply inclined veins required "stulls" wedged into place horizontally. Many variations on these conventional methods were possible. When digging through loose material, for instance, a crib built out of timbers laid log cabin style would support the sides and keep the workings free of debris.

The soft, heavy ground encountered by miners on the rich Comstock silver lode at Virginia City, Nevada, defied traditional timbering systems. At the Ophir mine, an able, young engineer named Philip Deidesheimer found an immense ore body surrounded by weak walls which forced him to devise a new timbering technique. His efforts in 1860 resulted in a major engineering innovation called the square-set. Deidesheimer replaced the ore as it was removed with interlocked sets of rectangular framed timbers, similar to building a house room by room in all directions. Many mining regions subsequently adopted this system, particularly in the West where ore bodies occurred in large masses. In developing the valuable copper properties near Butte, Montana, the Anaconda Company extensively employed the square-set method with good results. Yet the square-set was not risk-free. In time, engineers recognized the hazards in constructing the cubes too high, failing to brace the sets sufficiently, or not filling in the spaces between the timbers with waste rock. Furthermore, this man-made forest invited fast-spreading fires.

A timber-intensive method, the square-set system often depleted nearby forests. Between 1860 and 1880, Comstock mines are thought to have consumed about 600 million board feet of timber. That was enough, said one expert, to construct a town of six-room houses for 150,000 people, and the Comstock reputedly left treeless a 100-mile stretch of the neighboring Sierra Nevada. Miles of V-shaped flume, made of wood and running down the mountainsides, fed enormous quantities of timber to the valley below for delivery to the mines. Comstock became known as the "tomb of the Sierra."

Typically, miners drew their timber supplies from local sources, often initiating the rise of logging and milling industries in a new area. In some instances, however, prospectors thoughtlessly destroyed the trees in their search for outcroppings of ore. The U. S. Commissioner of Mining Statistics in 1870 decried the "wanton destruction of timber" in Colorado through accidental fires, waste, and "criminal design," leading him to propose measures safeguarding timber re-

sources in mining regions. Mine operators preferred the hardness and durability of oak and chestnut trees for the round timber used in sets and employed softer varieties, such as southern pine, for sawing. For the most part, however, miners took what was available, even resorting to mesquite and yucca in the deserts.

The exhaustion of nearby wood supplies meant hauling timber from greater distances at higher cost. Virtually every mining district in the United States had to import timber at some stage in its development. Within ten years of its discovery in 1891, the Cripple Creek gold district in Colorado had denuded adjacent hillsides and began shipping in timber from mills located 100 miles away and buying heavy timbers from Oregon. The combined effects of great depth, very thick coal beds, and the presence of water underground accounted for the extensive use of timber in the anthracite mines of northeastern Pennsylvania. In that district, mine timber soon had to be imported from neighboring states, from the loblolly pine lands of the South, and even from the Pacific Northwest by way of the Panama Canal.

This increasing cost of transportation encouraged efforts to find suitable replacements for timber or to

Worker in West Virginia stacks beech and black gum "washers" which are used to reinforce bolted mine timber joints. American Forest Institute Photo.

Props are stacked near the entrance of a Kentucky clay mine. American Forest Institute Photo.

extend the life of timber placed underground. Metal supports were introduced, but their weight, expense, tendency to buckle suddenly, and corrodibility limited widespread adoption. More successful were techniques to pressure-treat timber with creosote to preserve the wood, particularly those timbers used in the more permanent parts of a mine. Together with these developments came new mining procedures that reduced timber consumption. Block caving, for example, involved undercutting large ore deposits, permitting them to fall, then recovering the broken material. Cheaper methodologies also evolved in the twentieth century, including the open pit system used in the low-grade copper mines of the Southwest and the strip-mining of coal, both of which employed power shovels to excavate at the surface.

Despite the scarcity of reliable data, it is clear that the mining industry has depended on an uninterrupt-ed supply of timber. During the 1880s, the Anaconda copper mines used about 40,000 board feet of timber per day. Colorado mines in 1911 consumed approximately 23 percent of all timber produced in that state for the year; Illinois coal mines utilized nearly 20 million cubic feet of mine timber in 1921; and the anthracite mines of Pennsylvania alone used 66 million cubic feet of timber in an average year of the 1930s. Deep-level mining continues to be a substantial market for timber products, with each mine owner setting his own specifications for timber and contracting with sawmill operators or brokers to supply his needs. The observation made by Gifford PINCHOT in 1901 that "prosperous mining is impossible without prosperous forests" remains true.

FURTHER READING: Nelson C. Brown, *Timber Products and Industries* (1937). John D. Galloway, *Early Engineering Works Contributory to the Comstock* (1947). R. R.

Hornor and Harry W. Tuffts, *Mine Timber: Its Selection, Storage, Treatment, and Use* (1925). William H. Storms, *Methods of Mine Timbering* (1894).

JOSEPH E. KING

MINING CLAIMS ON NATIONAL FORESTS AND NATIONAL PARKS

Catching up with a lot of neglected problems after the Civil War, Congress passed a series of acts intended to establish some order among miners in the generally lawless West. The first was the Lode Law of 1866; the second, the Placer Act of 1870. These acts merely legalized what had been going on following the Gold Rush to California in 1849 and the later, turbulent rushes caused by discoveries of gold in the Colorado, Nevada, Idaho, and Montana territories. The General Mining Law of 1872 consolidated the two earlier acts and confirmed the principle that gold, silver, or other minerals in the public domain belonged to the person who found it.

The 1872 act spelled out the claim-patent system by which the prospector "staked his claim" with a minimum of paper work. Then, for a fee of $2.50 per acre for a placer claim or $5.00 per acre for lode, he could become the outright owner not only of the minerals, but also of the surface of the land, with no obligation to pay royalties on production. It established the claim area at approximately twenty acres and set no limit on the number of claims one person or company could file. The prospector, who might be a corporation, had no need to hurry to mine or seek patent; he could hold his claim indefinitely by performing $100 worth of work each year—his annual assessment—usually affirmed by affidavit, seldom by on-site inspection.

Although Congress has since placed fossil fuels and certain other minerals under lease or sales systems, and has tightened procedures, the heart of the 1872 mining law—claim-patent system, low fees for patenting, no royalties—remains intact for the so-called hardrock minerals on the public lands. The law applies to the national forests that were withdrawn (reserved) from the public domain.

In 1920, Congress passed the Mineral Leasing Act, putting oil and natural gas, oil shale, phosphate deposits, sulfates, carbonites, and certain other "soft" materials under a system that requires the lessee to pay rental and royalty fees while the government retains ownership of the land. In the Materials Disposal Act of 1947, as amended in 1955, Congress allowed the government to sell sand, gravel, stone, clay, pumice, pumicite, and cinders from federal lands. In both, the secretary of the interior (or agriculture) has discretion to permit or to deny development in any particular area and to require competitive bidding. The 1872 mining law grants no such discretion.

In the early 1950s, the U. S. FOREST SERVICE and allies, such as the AMERICAN FORESTRY ASSOCIATION and the IZAAK WALTON LEAGUE, launched a campaign to expose widespread abuses under the mining law. Newspapers and journals assigned investigative reporters and publicized such examples as mining claims never mined but used instead as homesites, fishing and hunting camps, saloons, and other commercial enterprises, even for trash dumps. Even worse for the purposes of the national forests, mining claims were being "mined" of their valuable timber, particularly in the rich West Coast stands of Douglas-fir. Some companies had blocked in hundreds of claims, preventing timber sales by the Forest Service and thwarting other management plans. The situation took on the aspects of scandal, and Congress responded by passing an important reform, the Multiple-Use Mining Act of 1955. This act made it clear that prior to patent, the surface and vegetative resources of a claim remained under the jurisdiction of the government and could be used by the claimant only for purposes incidental to mining.

Another reform was written into the FEDERAL LAND POLICY AND MANAGEMENT ACT of 1976. Previously, claims were filed only in the local county courthouse—no copies went to federal agencies—and it was impracticable for them—or anybody—to know how many claims encumbered the public lands or where they were. The 1976 law requires claims to be filed with a state office of the BUREAU OF LAND MANAGEMENT. Old claims had to be refiled under the new system by October 22, 1979, or become invalid. Thus, for the first time an accurate count of claims was possible. The total reported by the 1979 deadline was in excess of 1.1 million claims.

Recent environmental laws also have enabled both the Forest Service and the Bureau of Land Management to require prefiled mining plans and to tighten regulations concerning access roads, surface management, and reclamation after mining. Access to a mining claim, however, cannot be denied. Patents (deeds) are issued upon proof of a "valuable mineral deposit," and for nearly a century the judgment of "valuable" was based on whether a "prudent man" would proceed with mining. In 1968, in *United States* v. *Coleman*, the Supreme Court added a test of "marketability," proof that the mine could be operated at a profit.

With a few exceptions, national parks and monuments in the West were withdrawn from mining loca-

Prospector pans for gold on Alaska's Tongass National Forest, 1930. Forest Service Photo.

tion by the acts of Congress or executive orders that created them. One of the exceptions was Death Valley National Monument, where expanded strip mining for borates and talc in 1975 caused a public outcry and prompted Congress to pass the National Park System-Mining Activity Act of 1976. This act closed out application of the mining law in the six national park units where it had remained in effect. In addition to Death Valley, these were Mount McKinley and Crater Lake national parks, Glacier Bay and Organ Pipe Cactus national monuments, and Coronado National Memorial. The act also set up a process for appraising existing claims and mining operations, so that Congress could decide whether they should be bought out—by condemnation if necessary.

In addition to the existing unpatented claims (thousands of new ones are filed every year), both the national forests and many national parks in the West are dotted with patented claims, many used minimally for mining, if at all. These privately held tracts constitute nuisance in-holdings that complicate administration of the areas, unless and until they can be acquired. The unpatented claims themselves are legal encumbrances that complicate other public land programs such as range and timber management or improvements for wildlife and recreation. Claims have snarled federal efforts to block up holdings and improve administration by selling or exchanging lands.

Federal land agencies and private conservation groups have long advocated, as a basic reform, repeal of the claim-patent system and substituting for it a lease-royalty system. The mining industry has successfully blocked such legislation in Congress.

FURTHER READING: DeWitt Nelson and Lowell Besley, "The First Step toward Correcting Abuses of Mining Laws," *American Forests* 5 (May 1955): 18–19, 44. Cleveland Van Dresser, "Abuses under the Mining Laws," *American Forests*, six-part article, 58 (Jan. 1952): 6-9; 58 (Feb. 1952): 20-22, 49-52; 58 (Mar. 1952): 20-22, 42-44; 59 (Jan. 1953): 18–19, 42; 59 (Feb. 1953): 20-22; 59 (Mar. 1953): 8-9, 30-31; and "The Mining of America's Parks," *National Parks & Conservation Magazine* 50 (Jan. 1976): 18-20.

CHARLES H. CALLISON

MINNESOTA FORESTS

Forests originally covered two-thirds of Minnesota's total land area of nearly 51 million acres. Vegetation patterns reflected the intergrading of several distinct communities, including the tall-grass prairies, the "Big Woods" of mesic deciduous forests, the mixed forests of hardwoods and conifers, and the boreal forests characterized by balsam fir, black spruce, and tamarack. One hundred and fifty years of settlement, agricultural land-clearing, logging, forest fires, and forest management have radically altered the original forest, leaving only remnant stands in state parks and state and national forests.

The "Big Woods," a dense mesic deciduous forest that included basswood, sugar maple, and red oaks, with some black walnut, butternut, and hickory, were confined to several large blocks in southeastern, south-central, and west-central Minnesota, while smaller isolated stands mixed with the oak savannas and the northern conifer forests. The "Big Woods" were especially attractive to settlers because of their deep rich soils. The region also supplied ash, hickory, oak, and maple for wagons, tools, and barrels. Along the Mississippi and other Minnesota rivers, men called wood hawks felled the elm, ash, willow, and cottonwood for steamboat fuel.

Red, white, and jack pines, black spruce, balsam fir, white birch, and quaking aspen distinguished the forests of northern Minnesota. Unlike the pure white pine stands of New England, Michigan, and Wisconsin, those in Minnesota contained mixtures of red and white pines with an understory of balsam fir, black spruce, white cedar, or sugar maple. Jack pine predominated on dry sandy plains or in the thin soils overlying bedrock. In the bogs and muskegs, the forest was balsam fir, black spruce, white cedar, and tamarack, with an undergrowth of heath. Although aspen and birch with an understory of conifers covered extensive areas of the original forest, this was a successional type that followed forest fires and other disturbances.

Little is known about the ethnohistory of Minnesota's forests but it is thought that Indians favored the reproduction and survival of useful species such as sugar maple, basswood, and birch. The treaties that ceded the pineries to the United States often explicitly reserved sugar maples for Indian use. The Sioux, who once held title to about half the state, were transferred to Dakota after an 1862 uprising and now hold only about 3,000 acres in southern Minnesota. The Chippewas have about 754,999 acres scattered throughout seven reservations in the northern part of the state.

The lumber industry in Minnesota was influenced by lumbermen from Maine and later from Michigan. Maine loggers began cutting along the St. Croix River in 1837 and had erected sawmills at Stillwater on the St. Croix and St. Anthony Falls (Minneapolis) on the Mississippi by 1847. Until the late 1870s, most of Minnesota's logs and lumber were rafted down the Mississippi River to Winona, Dubuque, St. Louis, and other railheads for shipment west. Cutting proceeded up the Mississippi and St. Croix rivers and their tributaries. In the 1870s, completion of the Northern Pacific Railroad to Duluth opened the Lake Superior basin as well.

Logging entered its heyday during the 1880s with the arrival of Michigan lumbermen such as Thomas Shevlin, Henry C. Akeley, and C. S. Smith. By pooling capital, Michigan men bought much of the 2 million acres of land offered in the Duluth Land District in 1882. These men transformed the state's lumbering industry by infusing it with capital, consolidating smaller companies, moving the sawmills closer to the forests, and introducing technical innovations such as logging railroads and steam jammers. Minnesota pine was shipped to eastern markets, particularly Cleveland, Ohio, and Tonawanda, New York. As Minneapolis gained importance as a regional rail and shipping center sending Minnesota pine eastward, the flow of lumber down the Mississippi dwindled. In 1890, Frederick Weyerhaeuser (*see* WEYERHAEUSER FAMILY) of Rock Island, Illinois, bought the stumpage on the Northern Pacific Railroad line, moved his opera-

tions to Minnesota, and by 1900 dominated the industry.

In their turn, Stillwater, Minneapolis, and Duluth flourished briefly as the state's white pine lumber capital. In 1876, the Minneapolis mills sawed 193 million board feet of pine and in 1890 increased production to 500 million board feet. At their peak in 1902, Minnesota's mills produced more than 2.5 billion board feet of lumber yearly. By 1914, the state's lumber output had dropped to 1 billion board feet, and by 1918 production slipped to 400 million board feet. Winona's last mill closed in 1909, Minneapolis's in 1922, Duluth's in 1924, and Virginia's in 1929. Reported production reached a low of 48.7 million board feet in 1933 (with white pine still providing over 90 percent). When the best stands of white pine had been logged, small operators cleaned up the remnants overlooked in the great cut. Widespread fires and land-clearing eliminated much of the remaining pine and other conifers that might have provided seed sources for reforestation. Because of its fire tolerance and reproduction from root stock, aspen supplanted other species as the most characteristic tree across northern Minnesota.

The end of the pine logging era coincided with the beginning of the PULP AND PAPER INDUSTRY, which initially used spruce and balsam fir. Mills were established at Cloquet in 1898 and at International Falls in 1914. Minnesota pulp mills consumed only 30,000 cords in 1905; by 1965, the state's annual pulpwood production amounted to a million cords, with Minnesota mills consuming about 80 percent of the harvest.

As lumber companies abandoned CUTOVER LANDS to avoid taxes, state and county governments actively induced farm settlement. Cutover farming boomed in the northern counties until 1919, when nearby logging operations began shutting down, depriving settlers of the local markets provided by lumber camps. A rural depression followed, and farmers forfeited their lands as had the lumbermen. Many counties, such as Lake of the Woods, went into debt draining lands for farming and were saved from bankruptcy only when the state assumed the debts. Between 1925 and 1950, more than 9 million acres became tax delinquent. Of these, nearly 8 million were acquired by federal, state, and county governments for forestry purposes.

Forestry in Minnesota began in 1871 with a pioneering tree-bounty act designed to encourage afforestation of the prairies. Five years later, following John Warder's call for a national forestry organization, a group of citizens organized the Minnesota State Forestry Association. At the association's urging, the legislature established ARBOR DAY in 1876 and provided funds to pay tree-planting bounties. During the 1890s and early 1900s, forestry concerns shifted to protecting standing timber from logging and fires. Minnesota's proximity to the dry plains resulted in disastrous forest fires during the droughts of 1894, 1908, 1910, 1922, and 1936. The Hinckley fire of 1894 and the Cloquet fire of 1918 each took more than 400 lives. After the Hinckley fire, the legislature established a state fire warden force modeled on similar organizations in New York and New Hampshire, and in 1911 the system of volunteer fire wardens was replaced by a professional Minnesota Forest Service.

Christopher C. Andrews, who served as Minnesota's chief fire warden and forestry commissioner between 1895 and 1911, learned about forestry while serving as ambassador to Sweden and Norway during the 1870s. Andrews publicized forestry, promoted fire prevention, and secured the first forest reserves in the state, including the Minnesota National Forest in 1908 (which twenty years later would become the Chippewa National Forest) and the Superior National Forest in 1909. In 1880, Andrews proposed a school of forestry, an idea finally realized by the University of Minnesota in 1903.

Minnesota's state forests began in 1899 with the creation of the Minnesota State Forestry Board, a committee chartered by the legislature to receive and manage lands donated to the state as forest reserves. In 1902, former governor John S. Pillsbury donated the first tract—Pillsbury Forest Reserve—to the state, and in 1903 the federal government ceded lands to the state for the Burntside Forest Reserve. State legislation passed in 1939 authorized the counties to zone their lands for agricultural or forestry purposes. In 1977, of the 16 million acres of commercial forestland in the state, about 2 million acres were in national forests, 6.4 million acres were owned by other state, county, and federal agencies, only 814,000 acres were owned by the forest industry, and 6.8 million acres were in other private ownerships.

Until the creation of the Department of Conservation in 1931, forest policy was divided between the state forester, who was authorized to protect and manage state timber, and the state auditor, who, as land commissioner, was empowered to sell it. The new department consolidated these functions into the Division of Forestry and opened the way for coordinated forest management. During the 1930s, the CIVILIAN CONSERVATION CORPS (CCC) aided the state in fire protection, forest management, disease control, nursery work, and other related projects. In eight years, the CCC planted 25 million trees, strung 1,635 miles of telephone lines, and built 330 miles of firebreaks and 1,380 miles of truck trails. The legislature of 1943 codified Minnesota's forest laws and promulgated the state's first cutting regulations. In 1954, the state completed its first timber inventory.

Since 1956, the state forestry agencies have cooperated with private forest landowners to increase wood production. After World War II, private woodland companies, such as Blandin Paper, retained their cutover lands and began to manage them for sustained yields of cordwood. Through Keep Minnesota Green, established in 1944, and the Tree Farm programs inaugurated in 1943, the state has attempted to involve private landowners in state forest policy.

Minnesota began designating parklands in 1891 when the legislature established Itasca State Park at the headwaters of the Mississippi River for watershed protection. Other units established in the 1890s to commemorate historical events and protect unusual geological features set the pattern for subsequent additions. Creation of the Division of State Parks in 1935, when there were ten units in the system, the availability of tax-forfeited land, and the manpower of the CCC and the Works Progress Administration brought major expansion and development. By 1979, Minnesota had sixty-six major state parks, twenty-two state monuments and wayside parks, eight state trails, five state wild rivers. This system represented the major ecological, geological, and historical features of the state and offered a wide range of recreational opportunities.

Park development followed national trends. Between the 1930s and the late 1960s, Minnesota's parks catered to motorists by providing elaborately constructed commissaries, bath houses, trails, and golf courses. As public interest in primitive camping increased in the early 1970s, the parks embarked upon nature interpretation projects and restoration of native flora, adding tracts with ecological rather than recreational significance. Until the advent of comprehensive planning in the early 1970s, additions to the state park system depended upon local interest or gifts of land from private citizens. The Minnesota Outdoor Recreation Act of 1973 established a framework for parks, scientific and natural areas, wild rivers, and state trails. Patterned after federal legislation, the state wild rivers and trails acts provided for zoning in concert with county governments and acquisition of rights-of-way across county, state, federal, and private lands. County parks complement the state system; Hennepin County's park areas, dedicated primarily to wildlife protection and nature interpretation, form the largest county system.

One-quarter of a million cords of pulpwood in the yard of the Minnesota and Ontario Paper Company, 1937. Forest Service Photo.

Federal parklands in Minnesota began with Pipestone National Monument, which preserves an aboriginal quarry of catlinite, the source of Indian pipe bowls. A 1858 federal treaty reserved the site to the Yankton Sioux. The tract was purchased in 1928 and made a national monument in 1937. Grand Portage National Monument, which preserves a historic nine-mile fur trade portage between Lake Superior and the Upper Pigeon River, as well as the sites of Fort Charlotte and the Grand Portage post, was named a national historic site in 1931 and redesignated as a monument in 1958. Voyageurs National Park protects 138,828 acres of wooded lakeland similar to the Boundary Waters Canoe Area Wilderness. Minnesota citizens proposed the park in 1964, Congress authorized it in 1971, and it was formally established in 1975. Recreational use of the St. Croix River began when Northern States Power Company donated to public use its surplus flowage lands above Taylor's Falls. The river, famous as an explorer's highway and later as a log-driving river, was

among those originally protected in the federal Wild and Scenic Rivers Act of 1968. Despite dense settlement at its lower end, the upper river remains pristine and an important habitat for bald eagles.

The best known federal recreational land in Minnesota, however, is the Boundary Waters Canoe Area Wilderness, a part of the Superior National Forest along the Canadian border. The area was first retained by the U. S. FOREST SERVICE under various protective classifications beginning in 1922 and has figured prominently in debates over national wilderness policy thereafter.

FURTHER READING: Elizabeth Bachmann, *A History of Forestry in Minnesota, with Particular Reference to Forestry Legislation* (1969). Samuel T. Dana, John H. Allison, and Russell N. Cunningham, *Minnesota Lands: Ownership, Use, and Management of Forest and Related Lands* (1960). Ralph W. Hidy, Frank Ernest Hill, and Allan Nevins, *Timber and Men: The Weyerhaeuser Story* (1963). Agnes M. Larson, *History of the White Pine Industry in*

Minnesota (1949). Roy W. Meyer, "Forestville: The Making of a State Park," *Minnesota History* 44 (Fall 1974): 82-95. R. Newell Searle, "Minnesota Forestry Comes of Age: Christopher C. Andrews, 1895–1911," *Forest History* 17 (July 1973): 14-25; "Minnesota National Forest: The Politics of Compromise, 1898–1908," *Minnesota History* 42 (Fall 1971): 242-257; and Minnesota State Forestry Association: Seedbed of Forest Conservation," *Minnesota History* 44 (Spring 1974): 16-29.

R. NEWELL SEARLE

MISSISSIPPI FORESTS

Mississippi might have been called the forest state rather than the magnolia state, for the region was originally almost totally forested. In 1977, 16.9 million acres, or nearly 56 percent of the state's total land area, was still wooded. Nearly all of this was commercial forestland, and 90 percent of it was in private ownership.

Mississippi contains two main land areas. The Mississippi alluvial plain is in the western part of the state along the Mississippi River. This lowland region is called the delta by most Mississippians, and although it is primarily cotton and soybean country it also supports a significant hardwood industry. East of the alluvial plain is the east gulf coastal plain which covers the rest of the state. This region contains enormous areas of forested hills.

Although some 120 varieties of trees grow in Mississippi, the most important commercially are the softwood species. These include the loblolly, slash, and longleaf pines in the southern part of the east gulf coastal plain and the shortleaf pines of the state's central and northern portions. Also commercially important are the hardwoods, including gum, hickory, poplar, and willow, in the delta and hilly areas along the western perimeter of the east gulf coastal plain.

French, Spanish, and English colonists sought ship timbers and NAVAL STORES along the Gulf Coast, and similar activities were carried on in the early American period. One Natchez lumber manufacturing firm traces its foundation back to the 1820s. Stimulated by the rise of New Orleans and the extension of that city's overseas trade routes, steam sawmills began appearing along the Gulf in the late 1830s. By 1860, lumbering was the state's largest industry, but the real boom was yet to come.

As the Lake States forest was cut out in the post-Civil War era, many northern lumbermen began to move their operations to the South. In the 1880s, hardwood producers from Indiana, Michigan, and other states established offices and mills in Memphis, soon to become the self-proclaimed "hardwood capital of the world." From Memphis, logging and mill operations reached down the delta into the hardwood stands of Mississippi. Northern speculators and lumber companies sent timber cruisers into the vast pine regions, and the Illinois Central Railroad ran special trains into the piney woods for prospective timberland owners. Beginning in the 1880s, acquisition of enormous timber holdings and the establishment of large mill operations became standard in the Mississippi industry.

Early hardwood log transportation was hampered by lack of buoyancy in oak, hickory, and gum timber, which prevented log drives, and by the difficulty of extending roads into the heavily watered region. In the 1890s, narrow-gauge logging railroads began to replace earlier ox-powered tram roads. Coupled with steam-powered cable skidders, the hastily constructed, accident-prone logging railroads made large-scale hardwood operations feasible.

Between 1889 and 1899, annual lumber production in Mississippi increased from 460 million board feet to 1.2 billion board feet. By 1908, the state ranked third in the nation in lumber production. In 1925, Mississippi's reported lumber production peaked at over 3.1 billion board feet, 82 percent of it yellow pine and only 17 percent hardwood. Already the industry was changing; fewer large mills were being established, and by 1930, production was shifting toward smaller operations as some of the larger concerns followed the usual industry practice of migrating to untapped forest stands in other regions. By 1932, at the low point in the Depression, Mississippi manufactured only 531 million board feet annually.

Mississippi's lumbering boom left the state with millions of acres of CUTOVER LANDS that most lumbermen considered either worthless or suitable primarily for agriculture. As agriculture on the cutover areas foundered, some Mississippians moved toward reforestation and sustained yield. In 1926, the state established a forestry commission, provided funds for a modest fire protection program, and launched an educational campaign to reduce incendiarism, which accounted for more than half of the fires in Mississippi. By the late 1930s, as a result of these beginnings, the activities of the National Recovery Administration's Lumber Code Authority, the work of the CIVILIAN CONSERVATION CORPS, and other federal, state, and private endeavors, the greening of Mississippi's cutover lands was well under way. The tree farm movement, begun in 1941 in Washington State, gave Mississippi more tree farms than any other state in the nation.

By the 1950s, Mississippi's major forest crop was

Mule teams haul loads of red gum logs across the muddy Mississippi Yazoo Delta. Forest History Society Photo.

still sawlogs, which accounted for about half the wood taken from the forests. Woodpulp was the fastest growing forest industry, however, and it consumed an increasing amount of hardwood as well as much yellow pine mill waste. Fuelwood also remained an important product. Plywood and veneer, poles and piling, and cooperage were also significant. In the following decade, the state could count over 1,000 saw and planing mills, 45 furniture factories, and 20 pulp mills. The latter consumed more than 2 million cords of wood annually.

Mississippi saw the establishment of four national forest units in 1936, one more in 1959, and another in 1961. By 1980, federal land acquisitions within these forests passed 1.14 million acres. Another 73,000 acres of federal land in Mississippi comprises four national wildlife refuges. The State Game and Fish Commission, created in 1932, administers twenty-five wildlife management areas covering 1.3 million acres, mostly leased from private landowners. Many privately owned forests are also open to hunters and other recreational users. In 1956, the Mississippi legislature created a park commission, which by 1975 administered twenty-four park and recreation areas totaling 17,000 acres.

In the course of roughly a century, Mississippi has evolved from a state with large virgin forests supporting wildlife and a fledgling timber products industry, through the development of a large exploitative industry which devoured the timberlands and the wildlife habitat, to restored and protected wildlife areas and a forest industry based on sustained yield, reforestation, and scientific forestry.

FURTHER READING: Nollie W. Hickman, *Mississippi*

Harvest: Lumbering in the Longleaf Pine Belt, 1840–1915
(1962), and "Mississippi Forests," in Richard Aubrey McLemore, ed., *A History of Mississippi* (1973).

JAMES E. FICKLE

MISSOURI FORESTS

Missouri includes three major physiographic provinces and vegetation regions: (1) the plains including the glacial plains north of the Missouri River and an extension of the Great Plains in the western counties south of the river, both of which were originally bluestem prairie with scattered oak-hickory woodland and, along rivers and streams, elm, ash, and cottonwood; (2) the Ozark highlands south of the Missouri River and characterized by steep, chert-mantled slopes with thin soils of low fertility supporting predominantly oak forest, formerly with admixture of shortleaf pine on about 5 million acres in the St. Francois Mountains at the geologic core of the southeastern Ozarks, together with extensive cedar glades in the south-central counties along the Arkansas border; (3) the southeastern lowlands, which are part of the Mississippi embayment, with rich alluvial soils originally almost entirely forested with baldcypress, tupelo gum, and other swamp hardwoods, and, on sand ridges, the westernmost extension of American beech and holly. About 31 million acres, or 70 percent of Missouri's 44 million acres were forested before white settlement, but by 1980, the state was less than 30 percent forested. The state's 15 million acres of prairie have been reduced by 99.5 percent.

The French began trading with the Osage and other Indians for furs in the late 1600s and by the 1720s mined lead in the eastern Ozarks, using wood to smelt the ore. French culture predominated in communities along the Mississippi River until about 1800, when Anglo-American settlers moved up the Mississippi and Missouri rivers and their tributaries, clearing wooded loessial soils for agriculture and, at first, avoiding open prairies. Several outlying settlements developed in the lead and iron mining areas of the southeastern Ozarks, where pine and hardwoods were available for charcoal for smelting. Major migration during the 1830s and 1840s continued to follow river systems, until the Graduation Act of 1854 encouraged settlement of more remote lands in the northern counties and in the Ozarks. The poorly drained soils of the southeastern lowlands and the most remote and infertile soils of the Ozarks were filled in gradually during the remainder of the nineteenth century and the first two decades of the twentieth.

Land clearance for agriculture and local milling of timber proceeded gradually in most areas of the state, but except for the mining areas and some cutting along the Gasconade River for the St. Louis market, a lumber industry did not flourish in Missouri until the extension of railroads into the Ozarks and the southeastern lowlands beginning in the 1870s. Outside capital found Missouri's low stumpage rates attractive; pine stumpage in 1899 averaged $1.22 per 1,000 board feet, compared with the national average of $1.89 and $3.00 for white pine in Wisconsin and Michigan. That same year, Missouri lumber production peaked at 723 million board feet.

The Missouri Lumber and Mining Company, largest of many firms operating in the area, had financing from western Pennsylvania. Under the management of John Barber White, the firm bought tax-reverted shortleaf pine lands in Carter, Ripley, and Shannon counties and established sawmills at Grandin and West Eminence that for some years were rated the largest in the nation. Each day, the Grandin mill sawed the timber logged from sixty to seventy acres of land, and it had an annual capacity of 15 million board feet. Outside the pine area, white oak crossties were a major forest product, cut by lumber firms such as the Hobart-Lee Tie and Timber Company at Springfield or by local farmers and floated down the Niangua and other Ozark streams to railhead. Redcedar was extensively harvested in the White River drainage basin near the Arkansas border, while in the southeastern lowlands, a thriving hardwood trade and cooperage industry developed under the aegis of the American Sugar Refining Company, International Harvester, and the Himmelberger-Harrison Lumber Company. Kansas City was a major transshipper of lumber, and Robert A. Long, one of its leading citizens, would be elected president of the NATIONAL LUMBER MANUFACTURERS ASSOCIATION.

In the aftermath of logging, around 1910–1920, the lumber companies dismantled the mills, took up the rails, abandoned the lumber towns, and sold the cutover lands for agriculture. The rich alluvial soils of the southeastern lowlands, drained and planted to cotton and later to soybeans, became the most valuable agricultural lands of the state. Only about 5 percent of the area remains in forest, including the 22,000-acre Mingo National Wildlife Refuge, established and reflooded in 1943. On the thin, stony soil of the Ozarks, however, agriculture in most areas was not profitable, and large acreages went tax delinquent. The Ozark tradition of open range and of firing the woods each spring to encourage grass for livestock prevented regeneration of forests and led to severe erosion. Such trees as

This stand of large red gum was found in the southeast corner of Missouri. Forest History Society Photo.

remained were subject to timber poaching, or "grand-mawing." The region was severely depressed even before the Great Depression of the 1930s.

The federal government established eight national forest purchase units that could potentially add three million acres in Missouri in 1934-1935. In 1939, the

U. S. FOREST SERVICE established the Mark Twain and Clark national forests, which after several years of designation as the National Forests of Missouri were merged in 1976 as the Mark Twain, totaling 1.4 million acres. At the state level, conservation activity was spurred primarily by hunting and fishing interests. Missouri had a state fish commission as early as 1878, and in 1905 it passed a state game law, including a license and warden system that was advanced for its day. Legislative diversion of hunting and fishing license money for state park purposes, beginning in 1917, resulted in acquisition of considerable state park acreage in the 1920s. By 1928, there were twelve state parks containing nearly 37,000 acres.

Sportsmen, concerned about the continued decimation of wildlife, fisheries, and forests and the diversion of the license money, formed the Restoration and Conservation Federation of Missouri in 1935 (now the Conservation Federation). They also mounted a campaign for a constitutional amendment to create an independent bipartisan state conservation commission. Widely supported by other groups, including the Missouri Farmers Association and Kansas City political boss Tom Pendergast, the amendment was approved more than 2:1 by the voters in 1936; the Missouri Conservation Commission was established in July 1937, with responsibility for wildlife, fisheries, and forestry activities. Also in 1937, the legislature created a separate board to administer the state park system. The system in 1982 had sixty-six parks and historic sites embracing about 100,000 acres; since 1974, it has been administered by the Division of Parks and Historic Preservation of the Missouri Department of Natural Resources.

The state also supported forestry education; the forestry program at the University of Missouri which was reestablished in 1936 was expanded to a full School of Forestry in 1957.

Together, the Forest Service and the Missouri Conservation Commission mounted an educational campaign against the damaging traditions of woods burning and open range and began the restoration of forests, fisheries, and wildlife. In 1946, the State Forestry Act was passed, permitting classification of forest crop lands, which could be taxed at a lower rate. The state legislature finally repealed local-option stock laws in 1969, and fire protection, extended to more than half of the forested acreage by 1958, was by 1980 virtually complete. The Conservation Commission achieved national recognition for its success in restoring thriving populations of wild turkey, beaver, and deer.

As another aspect of recovery, the U. S. Congress authorized more than thirty hydroelectric and flood-control dams on the Missouri River system in the 1930s and 1940s, following the spectacular recreational boom at previously constructed reservoirs (Lake Taneycomo, 1913; Lake of the Ozarks, 1931). The U. S. ARMY CORPS OF ENGINEERS completed several new dams in the succeeding decades, but by the 1960s public opposition to the damming of free-flowing streams and flooding of farmland began to mount. This opposition resulted in designation in 1964 of the Current River as the nation's first National Scenic Riverway. In 1978, there was an overwhelming public referendum against the proposed Meramec Park Dam in eastern Missouri.

Four decades after creation of the Conservation Commission, Missouri citizens voted in 1976 for another pathbreaking constitutional amendment to levy a one-eighth of one percent sales tax in support of the commission's "Design for Conservation." This was a nationally significant program to provide support from general fund revenue for forest and wildlife conservation efforts benefiting the general public. The tax, producing about $30 million per year, has made Missouri a leader in management of nongame wildlife and wildlife and forestry research and education. It is also allowing the state to more than double its state-owned forests and wildlife lands (starting from a low 275,000 acres in 1975) and to enhance the state's great river borders. (Channelization of the Missouri River by the Corps of Engineers for flood control and commercial barge navigation had reduced the total water surface area of the river by 50 percent between 1879 and 1972, reduced island area by 98 percent, and decimated fish and wildlife habitat.)

Despite continuing state and federal purchase of forestlands, about 84 percent of forests in Missouri in 1980 belonged to individuals or nontimber-related corporations. Missouri forests, though still of relatively low quality, produce a significant portion of the nation's oak hardwood flooring, redcedar novelties and closet lining, charcoal, pallet lumber, railroad ties, walnut gunstocks and veneer, and white oak staves for whiskey barrels. In 1969, Missouri led the nation in cooperage and charcoal production.

The greatest consumer of forests is land conversion. In the 1960s and 1970s, over two million acres of Missouri forest were cleared for pasture or cropland, with the greatest losses occurring in the southeastern Ozarks and in the prairie regions. Erosion from such converted lands and farmlands elsewhere in the state is severe—Missouri in 1980 was second in the nation in soil degradation, losing an average of twelve tons of soil per acre annually. Thus the state continues to be plagued by massive land use problems, a heritage of physiography and centuries of abuse, even as its citizens and public agencies have achieved national stature as leaders in conservation.

FURTHER READING: Charles H. Callison, *Man and Wildlife in Missouri: The History of One State's Treatment of Its Natural Resources* (1953). Dan McKinley and Philip

Howell, "Missouri's Wildlife Trail, 1700–1976," *Missouri Conservationist* 37 (July 1976): 1-61. Werner O. Nagel, ed., *Conservation Contrasts: Three Decades of Non-Political Management of Wildlife and Forests in Missouri* (1970). Milton D. Rafferty, *The Ozarks: Land and Life* (1980). John C. Spencer, Jr., and Burton L. Essex, *Timber in Missouri* (1976). Julian A. Steyermark, *Vegetational History of the Ozark Forest* (1959).

SUSAN L. FLADER

MONTANA FORESTS

Montana's forests cover about 35,000 square miles (25 percent of the state), of which approximately 70 percent are commercial. Along with a variety of local factors, including stand history, landform, and soil, Montana's forest distribution is largely a response to altitude. Foothill bunchgrass intermingles with the ponderosa pine forest at lowest elevations. Next in elevation is the Douglas-fir–western larch forest, and above this to the timberline (7,500 feet on the Canadian border to 8,500 feet in the south) is the Engelmann spruce forest. Lodgepole pine occurs erratically in stagnant stands throughout the Douglas-fir and Engelmann spruce forests. Moisture is also an important determinant of forest distribution. Precipitation in Montana is generally higher in the northwest, where valley floors are dominated by species found only on intermediate slopes in central Montana. Consequently, the most productive forests are concentrated in the western and northwestern parts of the state.

The ratio of public to private forest ownership is roughly four to one. With eleven national forests, two national parks, and ten wilderness and primitive areas, the U. S. FOREST SERVICE and the BUREAU OF LAND MANAGEMENT have jurisdiction over 8,635,000 acres of commercial forestland. Indian reservations, notably the Flathead, include 554,242 acres of commercial forestland. In addition, the state owns about 608,000 acres of forest gained through congressional grants, of which roughly a third is concentrated in seven state forests. The more than 14,000 private forest owners include mostly small ownerships. A few large companies, notably railroad and forest products concerns, hold extensive tracts of forestlands. Checkerboard landownership patterns originated in congressional land grants for railroad construction, beginning in 1881.

Isolation from markets, sparse local population, and rugged terrain slowed the development of forest industries in Montana. Heavy timber cutting in the 1860s supplied charcoal for smelting and construction material for a growing mining industry. Montana's first mill was constructed in 1863 in present-day Madison County; purchases from the lumber yard were payable in gold dust. In the 1870s, railroad construction also required extensive timber operations. Creation of the Montana Improvement Company in 1882 to supply lumber, ties, and timber to the Northern Pacific Railroad marked the beginning of organized, well-financed lumbering in the state. Responding to mining and railroad booms in the 1880s and 1890s, annual lumber production in Montana increased from 12.5 million board feet in 1869 to 93.6 million board feet in 1899. By 1910, Anaconda Copper Company owned 1.2 million acres of timberland in Montana and the company's operations, centered around Bonner, east of Missoula, were the largest in the state.

Completion of the Great Northern Railroad system in the 1890s gave Montana lumbermen access to markets in the Midwest and East. Lumber output rose to 255.7 million board feet in 1899 and remained between 300 and 400 million feet yearly through the 1920s. Production dropped to a Depression low of 111 million in 1932 but increased dramatically during the post-World War II construction boom. In 1956, output levels reached 883 million board feet, and in 1973, 1.4 billion board feet were produced. The present forest products industry is located around Missoula, the Kalispell-Columbia Falls-Whitefish, and the Libby-Troy districts. The diversified industry, which includes rough and finished lumber, pulp, plywood, poles, and posts, accounts for about 35 percent of Montana's manufacturing employment. About half of Montana's forest products are used within the state, and the rest is exported, mainly to the north central states. Christmas trees and prefabricated log houses provide other important forest industries.

About one-half of Montana's forest acreage is grazed by sheep and cattle during four to six months of the year; grasslands at lower and intermediate elevations provide spring and fall forage. Other forest uses include big game hunting, fishing, camping, hiking, and, more recently, snowmobiling, Nordic skiing, and backpacking. Controlling conflicts among various recreational groups and between recreational and commercial users is becoming a major management concern.

The adoption of forestry methods gained support in Montana when widespread fires along the Idaho-Montana border consumed 3 million acres of timber and killed eighty firefighters in 1909 and 1910. In 1909, Montana's first state forester was appointed, and a ranger school was established at the University of Montana at Missoula. The university's school of forestry was founded five years later. Between 1910

Unpacking equipment on the Beaverhead National Forest, 1945. Forest Service Photo.

and 1918, Montana acquired two state forests—Stillwater and Swan—by trading lands with the federal government. Donations by Anaconda Copper Company in 1937 and by Northern Pacific Railway in 1939 provided land for the Lubrecht Experimental Forest, associated with the University of Montana. The Pattee Canyon Fire near Missoula destroyed 1,200 acres and six homes in July 1977, and brought to public attention the need for better fire control. Private landowners created the Northern Montana Forestry Association in Kalispell to provide protection for the 1.1 million acres of private and state lands in northwestern Montana.

In addition to fires, insects and diseases have significantly damaged Montana's forests. Spruce bark beetle, spruce budworm, and mountain pine beetle have been the major insect pests, and white pine blister rust, dwarf mistletoe, and needle blight the major diseases. The attempt to SALVAGE spruce damaged by spruce bark beetle infestation following heavy wind damage in 1949 helped to make spruce one of Montana's most important commercial species. Since the early 1950s, spruce budworm epidemics have damaged more than 5 million acres in predominantly Douglas-fir forests across the state.

Montana's state park system was conceived in the early 1920s but received no legislative support until 1929, when the state forester was designated state park director and the State Board of Land Commissioners was authorized to establish a park system.

State Forester Rutledge Parker, a park advocate, began gathering public and legislative support for a few model parks. The Depression slowed park development until the arrival of the CIVILIAN CONSERVATION CORPS (CCC) in 1933. Stimulated by CCC activity, Montana created the State Recreation Committee to prepare a recreation inventory. In 1935, with CCC help, the state developed facilities at Morrison Cave (then designated as Lewis and Clark National Monument).

Despite early enthusiasm, no comprehensive plan for a park system was conceived until 1937, and only in 1947 did the legislature appropriate funds for the system. At that time, there were five state parks, located in the northwestern and southwestern part of the state. Because of fiscal difficulties in the 1950s, the State Park Commission was abolished and its functions were transferred to the State Highway Commission. In 1964, parks jurisdiction was given to the Division of Recreation and Lands Development under the Fish and Game Commission. Funding during the 1960s came from participation in federal programs under the Land and Water Conservation Fund Act, and from state fuel taxes and park fees. Between 1965 and 1975, sixty-two new sites were added and $3 million was spent to provide basic facilities such as roads, parking, and toilets. In 1978, Montana's state park system consisted of 250 areas, totaling over 94,000 acres.

FURTHER READING: G. Wesley Burnett, David G. Conklin, and Paul R. Saunders, "Montana Forests: A Synthesis," *Western Wildlands* 7 (Fall 1981): 32-37. David G. Conklin, "The Long Road to Riches: The Development of Montana's State Park System," *Montana Outdoors* 9 (1978): 2-8. Ralph R. Widner, ed., *Forests and Forestry in the American States* (1968).

G. WESLEY BURNETT

MOUNT RAINIER NATIONAL PARK

The largest single-peak glacier system in the United States radiates from the summit of Mount Rainier, an inactive volcano. The lower slopes are cloaked in dense forests and subalpine flowered meadows. The massive landmark (summit elevation 14,410 feet) had attracted explorers, climbers, and early settlers who publicized its spectacular beauty while issuing warnings that the natural setting was in danger of exploitation by such interests as railroads, graziers, and timber and mining companies. Coinciding with the preservation sentiment was the potential for commercial tourism seen by the business communities of nearby Tacoma and Seattle. As a result, strong support emerged for national park status, and on March 2, 1899, Congress established Mount Rainier as the nation's fifth national park, incorporating some 200,000 acres taken from the Pacific Forest Reserve. The Northern Pacific Railroad was allowed under this legislation to exchange any of its land grant included in either the forest reserve or in the new park for an equal area of any public domain lands, surveyed or unsurveyed, anywhere in the states through which its lines ran. This provision was criticized as being even more generous than the FOREST MANAGEMENT ACT of 1897, used by the Northern Pacific to exchange barren mountainside for valuable timberland in Oregon. Although the Mount Rainier Act allowed mining and prospecting to continue within the park, lack of mineral resources kept this clause from presenting a serious problem to park administrators. (The clause was repealed in 1908.)

During Mount Rainier National Park's formative years, development and management were poorly funded, a situation shared by other national parks before Congress created the NATIONAL PARK SERVICE in 1916. Between 1903 and 1915, local interests were able to have a road constructed to Paradise Valley, to complete the Wonderland Trail around the mountain for ninety miles, and to provide basic fire protection. Aiding this effort were increased federal appropriations made possible in part by the lobbying of the Seattle-Tacoma Rainier National Park Committee representing commercial organizations in the two cities.

The first tourist facilities within the park area were established by the Longmire family at Longmire Springs in 1884. By 1915, other concessionaires were operating in the southwestern part of the park. Other parks during this period had similarly uncoordinated and individual visitor services. Stephen T. MATHER, the first director of the National Park Service, formulated a new concessions policy, consolidating independent operations in each park under one private company wherever possible. In 1916, the Rainier National Park Company was thus organized. Its contract was renewable under specific terms. The major development in visitor accommodations during the Mather period was the construction of Paradise Inn in 1917 at a cost of $100,000. This historic landmark continues to operate as a high-elevation hotel in Paradise Valley.

A number of projects in road and trail building, visitor services, and park management continued into the 1920s and 1930s, with the work of the CIVILIAN CONSERVATION CORPS, the construction of the fifteen-mile West Side Road, and an ambitious but short-lived attempt at winter sports development being the most important. World War II severely curtailed park operations, but afterward public demands to improve facilities led to the designation of Mount Rainier as a pilot park for Mission 66, the ten-year development program launched by the National Park Service in 1956. Although it attempted to strike a balance between public use and preservation, the Rainier plan was the focus of considerable local controversy. The major contributions were the linking of the east and west sides by completion of the Stevens Canyon Road in 1957, campground expansion, the relocation of administrative headquarters outside park boundaries, and construction of new visitor centers. Since the 1960s, major developments have been halted to emphasize wilderness protection and use, reflecting the adoption of stronger preservationist policies by the National Park Service.

FURTHER READING: Aubrey L. Haines, *Mountain Fever* (1962). Arthur D. Martinson, "Mount Rainier National Park: First Years," *Forest History* 10 (Oct. 1966): 26-33. Edmond S. Meany, *Mount Rainier: A Record of Explorations* (1916). Robert Shankland, *Steve Mather of the National Parks* (1970).

ARTHUR D. MARTINSON

MUIR, JOHN (1838–1914)

Born on April 21, 1838, John Muir left his native Scotland in 1849 with his family for a farm on the Wisconsin frontier. Escaping a life of drudgery under his father's domination, Muir in his mid-twenties attended the University of Wisconsin where he studied the literary works of Emerson and Thoreau and the scientific theories of Agassiz, Gray, and others. Although exhibiting a genius for invention that could have become his life's work, Muir chose to explore the plant life in parts of the Midwest and Canada before embarking on a 1,000-mile walk from Indiana to the Gulf of Mexico.

Following passage by ship to California in 1868, Muir lived intermittently in Yosemite Valley for several years, climbing the highest peaks in the Sierra Nevada and studying its geology and botany. In 1871, he launched his literary and scientific career, writing an article for the *New York Tribune* in which he argued that glaciers had carved the valley of the Yosemite. Muir soon became alarmed at the deforestation and erosion that resulted from the inroads of lumbermen and sheepherders into the forests and meadowlands of the Sierra. He wrote and spoke actively in defense of forest preservation, both because of the dependence of California's farmers on the Sierra watershed and because of the scenic beauty of the mountains.

After marriage in 1880 and several years in which he applied his horticultural and business skills to become a successful farmer, Muir returned to his life's work, writing and working for the preservation of wilderness. At the urging of Robert Underwood Johnson, editor of *Century Magazine*, Muir wrote two articles and contacted many influential people in support of the creation of YOSEMITE NATIONAL PARK, which was established in 1890. Two years later, he helped to organize and became the first president of the SIERRA CLUB, a California environmental organization dedicated to the enjoyment and preservation of the Sierra Nevada. Under Muir's leadership, the club gained national recognition. Although he was instrumental in early efforts to establish forest reserves and national parks, Muir met bitter defeat in the major environmental battle of his life, the effort to prevent authorization of a large reservoir in Hetch Hetchy Valley within Yosemite National Park.

In order to reach an influential and national audience, Muir wrote for leading national magazines of the period, such as *Harper's Monthly, Scribner's Monthly, Atlantic Monthly, Century,* and *Overland Monthly,* as well as for major newspapers. His books —*The Mountains of California* (1894), *Our National Parks* (1901), *My First Summer in the Sierra* (1911), and others—also gained national acclaim. His literary work combined his enthusiasm and religious fervor for all living things, his skills of observation of nature, and his accounts of personal adventures in the out-of-doors.

Throughout his career as a naturalist, Muir attacked the orthodox Christian idea that the earth had been made for man and that its resources had value only as commodities for man's use. He regarded all living things as equally important parts of the unity of the universe. Muir aroused a concern and appreciation for wilderness that has been reflected in the creation of an American wilderness system and the spread of national parks throughout the world. He died on December 24, 1914.

FURTHER READING: William Frederic Badé, *The Life and Letters of John Muir* (1924). Holway R. Jones, *John Muir and the Sierra Club: The Battle for Yosemite* (1965). William F. Kimes and Maymie B. Kimes, *John Muir: A Reading Bibliography* (1977). Herbert F. Smith, *John Muir* (1965). Linnie Marsh Wolfe, *Son of the Wilderness: The Life of John Muir* (1945).

DOUGLAS H. STRONG

MULTINATIONAL CORPORATIONS

Since the colonial era, foreign investors have participated in America's forest products industries. German-born, British-financed Peter Hasenclever, for example, in the 1760s developed and exported American potash. American producers of forest products often exported, but they rarely set up sizable international organizations before the twentieth century. An exception was the Diamond Match Company, which developed a vast international business in the late nineteenth and early twentieth centuries. However, facing competition from the firms which became Swedish Match, Diamond sharply curtailed its worldwide endeavors. Other companies established export organizations for joint lumber sales abroad, and by 1928 some American lumber mills had established branch selling and distributing offices overseas.

The main foreign investments of United States forest products companies before World War II were in Canada. These stakes began in the late nineteenth century, when, with the frontier closing, American businesses invested in Canadian timberland; later, Americans began to build lumber and paper and pulp mills in Canada where the water resources offered low-cost power. Canadian dominion and provincial governments encouraged processing in that country. So did the United States when in 1911 it admitted Canadian newsprint duty-free. By 1914, American firms had invested $74 million in Canadian paper and pulp—a third of the total American investment in Canadian manufacturing.

World War I saw an expansion of American paper and pulp interests in Canada; in 1915, the average cost of manufacturing a ton of newsprint in Canada was $26.38, compared with $30.52 in the United States. Lower Canadian costs persisted, and through the

TABLE 1. Percentage of Output in Seven Locales Accounted for by U. S. Forest Products Companies and by All U. S. Manufacturing Firms That Rank in the Top 300 of U. S.-Based Multinational Companies—1970

	Canada	U.K.	Belgium-Luxembourg	France	West Germany	Mexico	Brazil
Paper	39	5	19	8	2	13	23
Lumber, Wood, and Furniture	50	1	0	0	1	1	1
All Manufacturing	52	16	16	6	8	18	25

SOURCE: U. S. Tariff Commission, *Report on Implications of Multinational Firms* (1973), chap. 7.

1920s and 1930s American business expanded over the northern border. By 1940, Americans had invested $308 million in Canadian paper and pulp, still a third of the total American investment in manufacturing in Canada. The dollar value of U. S. investment in paper and pulp in Canada was larger than in any other single type of manufacturing in the dominion, but when measured by percentage of output controlled it was far less than in electrical equipment, automobiles, rubber tires, or aluminum.

A 1973 U. S. Tariff Commission report indicated the persisting importance of Canadian investment to American forest products companies as well as the role that U. S. paper companies were playing in other countries. Table 1, summarizing data from that report, shows the percentage of output in Canada, the United Kingdom, Belgium-Luxembourg, France, West Germany, Mexico, and Brazil attributable to American paper companies and American lumber, wood, and furniture companies. For purposes of comparison, the percentage of output controlled in these locales by the top 300 American-based multinational

manufacturing companies is also included. Only in Belgium-Luxembourg and France did U. S. paper companies control a higher than average (for all manufacturing) percentage of output. The general case, including Canada, was that the forest products industries controlled a lesser percentage than did other U. S. manufacturers. It is, however, notable that in 1970 American lumber, wood, and furniture companies controlled 50 percent of Canadian output, while American paper companies controlled 39 percent of Canadian output, 23 percent of Brazilian output, and 19 percent of Belgium-Luxembourg output in their respective industries.

In the world's 100 largest industrial companies (ranked by sales at year's end, 1976), no forest products company is included. In the next 225 companies, however, nine United States-headquartered firms appear. Table 2 indicates their multinational involvement at the end of 1976. The table reveals that the largest of these enterprises, International Paper, had 20 percent of its total assets and 21 percent of its total employees abroad. Scott Paper, with its advertised, differentiated

TABLE 2. U. S. Paper Companies' Involvement in International Business—Year-End, 1976

		Foreign Sales			Foreign Assets as % of Total Assets	Foreign Earnings as % of Total Earnings	Foreign Employees as % of Total Employees
Rank[a]	Company	Exports from U.S.	As percentage of total sales	Sales of Foreign Affiliates to Third Parties			
104	International Paper	7		23	20		21
132	Georgia-Pacific		8				
140	Champion International	[b]		22[c]	28	3	30
143	Weyerhaeuser	24		7[d]	4	7	
192	Crown Zellerbach		15			20	22
249	St. Regis Paper	5		13	28	24	14[c]
262	Mead		5			12	
264	Kimberly-Clark		34		39	18	53
306	Scott Paper		45		15	18	

[a]Ranked by sales of largest enterprises worldwide, year-end 1976.
[b]Less than 5%.
[c]Estimated.
[d]Excluding Canada.
SOURCE: United Nations Economic and Social Council, *Transnational Corporations in World Development* (1978), pp. 294–304.

products, ranks first among such companies in foreign sales as a percentage of total sales. Fully 45 percent of its sales were outside the United States. Kimberly-Clark, another company with trademarked, specialized products, had 39 percent of its total assets and, even more impressively, 53 percent of its employees in foreign countries. In 1976, no United States-headquartered forest product company depended for more than a quarter of its profits on international business; nonetheless, such companies were very much involved as multinational corporations.

While American-based firms were acquiring interests abroad, foreign companies were investing in the United States forest products industries. These enterprises were no less multinational than the American businesses that went to foreign lands. In the 1880s, Canadian and British firms invested in American forest products industries on a small scale. Foreign brokers established branches in the United States and invested in timberlands, sawmills, and ships. In 1928, several large sawmills on the Gulf Coast were said to be owned and operated by foreign lumber merchants. The Seattle branch of Mitsubishi Trading Company dealt in lumber exports in the interwar years, as did the Seattle branch of Mitsui and Company. These Japanese interests terminated with World War II, but they would be resumed in the postwar years. For the most part, foreign investments in American forest products companies in the pre-World War II years were intended to provide imports to supply the home market.

Investments in American forest products by foreign firms expanded substantially after World War II. By 1976, some twenty foreign-owned companies had operations in the American forest industry, primarily in processing. Three Canadian firms (MacMillan Bloedel Ltd., Abitibi Paper Co., Ltd., and Irvine Pulp and Paper Co.), one British (Bowater Ltd.), and one Japanese (Mitsui and Company) reportedly owned or controlled through leases about 1.75 million acres of private timberland in the United States.

Relative to American producers, the foreign presence in the United States forest products industries during the 1970s was quite small, totaling less than 3 percent of production, capacity, or employment. Japanese investors seemed to be seeking resources in the Pacific Northwest and Alaska for export to Japan, whereas British and Canadian investors looked to the North American market for their output.

Of the U. S. lumber producers, the first twenty-eight by rank are American-owned, but the twenty-ninth, the Wrangell Lumber Company, is a subsidiary of the Japanese-owned Alaska Pulp Company, Ltd. The Canadian-owned MacMillan Bloedel is an important lumber, particle board, and plywood producer in Alabama; it owns Blanchard Lumber Company, which is the largest United States wholesaler of lumber (with 1974 sales of $177 million). Abitibi Paper in 1974 had seven plants in the United States producing building materials; it reported U. S. building products sales of over $61 million in that year. Abitibi Paper is also a sizable U. S. producer of newsprint. Mitsui and Company owns a plywood company in Long Beach, California, while the British-owned Bowater Corporation is the second largest producer of newsprint in the United States. MacMillan Bloedel, Bowater, and other foreign multinational enterprises also participate in the manufacture of a variety of miscellaneous forest products.

FURTHER READING: There is no book focusing on international business in the forest products industries, but among works useful on American-headquartered multinational corporations are two volumes by Mira Wilkins, *The Emergence of Multinational Enterprise: American Business Abroad from the Colonial Era to 1914* (1970) and *The Maturing of Multinational Enterprise: American Business Abroad from 1914 to 1970* (1974). See also U. S. Tariff Commission, Report on Implications of Multinational Firms (1973) and United Nations Economic and Social Council, *Transnational Corporations in World Development* (1978). On foreign enterprise in America, see U. S. Department of Commerce, *Foreign Direct Investment in the United States* (1976), vols. 3 and 4, and William J. Reader, *Bowater* (1981).

MIRA WILKINS

MULTIPLE USE-SUSTAINED YIELD ACT, 1960

The Multiple Use-Sustained Yield Act of June 12, 1960, was congressional codification of seventy-five years of FOREST SERVICE tradition and policy. The act defined multiple use to include outdoor recreation, range, timber, watershed, and wildlife and fish resources. Wilderness is compatible with multiple use, as are mineral resources. The law was considered to be supplemental to the 1897 FOREST MANAGEMENT ACT.

Multiple use means giving equal consideration to the various uses; management is to use combinations of resources "that will best meet the needs of the American people," without impairment of productivity and not necessarily measured in economic terms. Resources are to be managed on a sustained-yield basis, which is defined as "maintenance in perpetuity of a high-level . . . output of the various renewable resources of the national forests."

On this section of the Cherokee National Forest, timber harvest and recreation are compatible. Forest Service Photo.

The Forest Service strongly supported the multiple-use bill during the legislative process. With skill, the agency reduced opposition and gained support from an initially reluctant forest industry and conservation community. The agency viewed the act as a vital balancing mechanism to reduce the problem of increasing demands for all resources.

Assessment of the Multiple Use Act is made difficult by the environmental disruptions of the 1960s and early 1970s, when, for example, original opponents of the act now acted as its champions and filed suit against the Forest Service for alleged violations. Nonetheless, the basic purposes of the act seem to have been fulfilled by establishing a workable framework for modern decision making. The NATIONAL FOREST MANAGEMENT ACT of 1976 and the FEDERAL LAND POLICY AND MANAGEMENT ACT of 1976 reaffirmed the concept of multiple use, broadened its definition, and applied it to other federal agencies, such as the BUREAU OF LAND MANAGEMENT.

FURTHER READING: Edward C. Crafts, "The Saga of a Law," *American Forests* 76 (June 1970): 12–19, 52-54, and 76 (July 1970): 28-35. J. Michael McCloskey, "Natural Resources—National Forests—The Multiple Use-Sustained Yield Act of 1960," *Oregon Law Review* 41 (Dec. 1961): 49-78.

MUNICIPAL PARKS AND URBAN FORESTRY

Urban parks have passed through three revolutions of thought and use. Until about 1840, practically no one considered reserving open space in cities, beyond the few squares dotting the more enlightened townsite plats, such as Philadelphia (1682). There were objections to splurging municipal funds on parks, apart from considerations of cost and the loss of potentially valuable land. Colonists detested the wilderness, a sanctuary for beasts and savages. That idea died hard. Besides, there was plenty of nature nearby. As late as the 1840s, fields and woods rimmed the compact eastern cities, well within what was then regarded as easy walking distance. Until then, and in interior cities until the late nineteenth century, there were "groves," vacant lots, and open waterfronts to compensate for the lack of parks.

Developments beginning in the 1840s radically altered the urban scene. Open spaces surrendered to commercial, industrial, and residential use in the city core. Orchards and woodlands fell before suburbs made possible by streetcars. A heightened appreciation of these nonurban scenes accompanied their retreat. The writings of Emerson and Thoreau and the landscape paintings of the Hudson River School evoked the pastoral-romantic ideal. Beginning in the 1850s, middle class people vacationed in the midst of picturesque natural surroundings. Meanwhile, the middle class became aware of the plight of the industrial workers: the discipline of the machine, the fatigue, and the deprivation of natural settings.

These developments promoted a Manichaean view of nature, salubrious and beneficial, versus the city, with its artificial and corrupting environment. Little wonder that reformers bent on improving the surroundings and behavior of the urban masses hit upon introducing the natural landscape into the city. To understand this revolution, it is necessary to remember two things: first, early landscape architects' ideas about the role of parks were radically different from later notions, and second, the landscape architects did not always practice what they preached.

Frederick Law OLMSTED, the dean of landscape architects, saw his first creation, New York City's Central Park (1858), as an alternative to the city. In Central Park, the "tired worker" would recuperate morally, mentally, and physically from the city's assaults. Central Park was an alternative but not a pastoral-romantic one. Olmsted rejected the romantic parks of his day as being too fussy and contrived. The phrase "naturalistic constructivist" would better describe Olmsted's creations. For one thing, they were massive public works that significantly reshaped and replanted an expanse of ground to *look* natural. What Olmsted and his followers desired was a "middle landscape," nature tamed but not refined. For another, Olmsted from the beginning introduced unromantic, nonpastoral designs in his parks. Formal malls, promenades, and grounds for active recreation competed with naturalistic elements.

This departure from romanticism demonstrates the divergence between the rhetoric of landscape architects and what they built. Landscape architects preached passive recreation and psychic restoration amid tranquil natural scenes. They practiced construction techniques that brought about the visual and aural interpenetration of city and park. This second revolutionary change comprised three elements. First, landscape parks increasingly included concessions to active public use, as opposed to the passively restorative. Zoos and tennis courts scarcely were havens for romantic contemplation. Landscape architects paid growing attention to the role of stairs, walks, and plantings in guiding park visitors from one area or activity to another. Second, beginning with Olmsted's Buffalo park and boulevard system (1871), design efforts moved from single parks to complex systems planned to give cities unity and definition. Third, about 1900, landscape architects surrendered the idea of the park as a refuge from the irredeemable city. Instead, they claimed for parks and parkways the ability to conquer the cities in the name of beauty.

If acceptance of the municipal park was the first revolution, and the changed relationship between park and city the second, the third involved the special interests' demands for park space. Beginning in the late nineteenth century, various groups viewed parks as free sites for their pet projects. The first museums, schools, and playgrounds usually were small, bearable intrusions on the landscape. Institutional growth and the proliferation of the car changed all that. After 1915, the ubiquitous automobile devoured parkland for roads and parking lots. The limited access highways of the mid-1950s and after did the worst damage. A Cabrillo Freeway interchange gobbled up forty acres of Balboa Park in San Diego. The West Sixth Avenue Freeway crashed through the middle of Barnum Park in Denver, and freeway construction altered the slopes of Kansas City's West Terrace Park. The third revolution continues, but with opposition. Park lovers who desire an evocation of nature in their reservations have battled institutional and highway encroachments. They have fought street and parking lot expansions. These struggles emphasize the continuing importance of municipal parks to the populations they serve.

Urban forestry partook of the two most recent park revolutions. City officials discovered a need to study trees under urban conditions of soil compaction, damage from animals, and air pollution. Park departments added specialists to cope with these problems and with those of insects and disease. There were, however, thousands of trees beyond the parks and parkways, indifferently planted and maintained along the median strips or side parkings of ordinary streets.

The planted street was potentially a vital extension of the park and parkway ambiance. Arboriculture could spread trees' shading and cooling effects around the city. A city tree warden could conduct a tree inventory, save trees from mutilation, and direct plantings along the streets. Street tree commissions appeared in the 1890s, an early response to these opportunities.

Since the late nineteenth century, urban forestry has become a widespread municipal function. By the 1960s, urban forestry had become a rapidly growing specialty. Urban foresters actively circulate lists of trees suited and unsuited to adverse urban situations. They combat inadequate soil, wind buffeting, and dryness with special tree maintenance programs. Their profession has induced debates about the methods and extent of urban arborists' control. Conflicts over administrative structure, tree management, and planting design continue. Like the arguments over park use, these debates reflect the vitality of their subject.

FURTHER READING: Gene W. Grey and Frederick J. Deneke, *Urban Forestry* (1978). August Heckscher, *Open Spaces: The Life of American Cities* (1977). Leonard J. Simutis, "Frederick Law Olmsted, Sr.: A Reassessment," *Journal of the American Institute of Planners* 38 (1972): 276-284.

WILLIAM H. WILSON

MURIE, OLAUS JOHAN (1889–1963)

The son of Norwegian immigrants, Olaus Murie was born in Moorhead, Minnesota, on March 1, 1889. Raised in that rural environment, he developed an ever deepening interest in the natural world. For Murie, nature was at once a source of spiritual and aesthetic appreciation and an object for scientific inquiry. This perceptual unity was to characterize Murie's thinking and writing throughout his career of thirty years as a wildlife field biologist and eighteen years as a political spokesman for WILDERNESS PRESERVATION.

Murie's interest in nature led him to the study of biology at Fargo College, North Dakota, and Pacific University, Oregon, where he received an A.B. degree in 1912. His early work, first as field mammal curator for Pittsburgh's Carnegie museum and from 1920 to 1927 as field biologist for the U. S. Bureau of BIOLOGICAL SURVEY, allowed him to live in the northern reaches of Hudson's Bay and the interior of Alaska. There Murie studied extensively a variety of wildlife, such as caribou, bear, and waterfowl, in their natural habitats. This experience enabled him to witness firsthand the fragile web of interdependence that bound together wilderness, wildlife, and human culture in that harsh environment. His early writings for scientific and popular journals pointed out the links between wildlife and wildland habitats and what he saw as growing threats to this way of life from a quickly modernizing world.

In 1927, a new assignment, a major study of North American elk, brought Murie to Jackson Hole, Wyoming, which was to be his home for the remainder of his life. Here, his concern for wildlife habitat grew into a desire to preserve and maintain remaining examples of wildlands on a continent no longer uncharted or untrammeled. This concern led Murie into a fertile exchange of ideas with colleagues of like views, notably Robert MARSHALL, Aldo LEOPOLD, and Benton MAC-KAYE. Their relationship culminated in the formation of the WILDERNESS SOCIETY in 1935. Murie was elected to the council of the society in 1937 and remained on that body until his death. In 1945, Murie became a director of the society. During these years, Murie was a key figure in the wilderness movement's efforts to define substantive goals, to develop an effective program, and to build a broad base of support. These efforts ultimately resulted in passage of the Wilderness Act of 1964.

Murie believed the long-term success of the wilderness movement would ultimately depend upon the degree of support it received from American citizens. Consequently, he spent much time promoting the organizational sophistication, communications skills, political adroitness, and leadership continuity of citizen groups throughout the country. Murie's efforts materially increased the numerical and geographical base of the wilderness movement in the United States. Murie died on October 21, 1963, and did not live to see final passage of the Wilderness Act, in 1964 but this legislation was in large measure a reflection of his lifelong beliefs and actions.

For his contributions to WILDLIFE CONSERVATION, Murie received the Aldo Leopold Memorial Medal of the WILDLIFE SOCIETY in 1952. In 1954, he received the Cornelius Armory Pugsley Bronze Medal of the American Scenic and Historic Preservation Society and the Conservation Award of the AMERICAN FORESTRY ASSOCIATION. Other recognition came to Murie as the Audubon Medal of the NATIONAL AUDUBON SOCIETY (1959) and the John Muir Award of the SIERRA CLUB (1963). He held various offices in these and other conservation organizations. His most important book, *The Elk of North America* (1951), received the Wildlife Society's award for an outstanding ecological publication in 1961. The last of his seven books, *Wapiti Wilderness* (1966), was published posthumously, having been completed by his wife, Margaret E. Thomas Murie.

CRANDALL BAY

MUSEUMS OF FOREST HISTORY

Museums exist for reasons of both education and inspiration, using iconic objects to make their messages known. Icons of forest history, ranging from axes to restored sawmills, inform viewers of forest technology, life in the logging camps, and other historical stories. Equally important, forest history museums convey a philosophy about resource use and management. Few museums glorify the waste of timber, which pioneer woodsmen unleashed on the white oak in the eighteenth century or on the longleaf pine in the nineteenth. The theme of saving the forest for future generations through good management, reforestation, conservation, and fire fighting, by contrast, is amplified for inspirational purposes.

More than seventy museums in the United States and Canada are devoted entirely or in large part to forest history. Perhaps the oldest of these is the Fisher Museum of Forestry, established in 1908 by Harvard University. Its diorama series depicts New England forestry from the seventeenth century to the present. The Lumberman's Museum (Patten, Maine), the Pennsylvania Lumber Museum (Galeton, Pennsylvania), the Texas Forestry Museum (Lufkin, Texas), and the Western Forestry Center (Portland, Oregon) tell local or regional stories of men and trees.

A good many general history museums have forestry exhibits or collections among their holdings. In New York, the American Museum of Natural History's Hall of North American Forests is devoted to a conservation theme. In Washington, D.C., the Smithsonian's National Museum of American History contains several thousand artifacts of forestry and wood technology, though they are not on permanent exhibit. Old Sturbridge Village (Sturbridge, Massachusetts), Upper Canada Village (Morrisburg, Ontario), and the Shelburne Museum (Shelburne, Vermont) exhibit working sawmills of the eighteenth and nineteenth centuries. The Lycoming County Historical Society and Museum (Williamsport, Pennsylvania) has a lumbering exhibit. Most states in which forestry was or remains a prominent economic activity have museums telling some aspect of this story. In addition, historic houses occasionally have related forestry interpretations. George Washington, for example, was a fairly sophisticated amateur forester, as the restoration of the grounds at the Mount Vernon Mansion Farm indicates.

Besides their exhibits, museums often contain important research materials in their objects, books, manuscripts, and photographs. The Tongass Historical Society Museum (Ketchikan, Alaska) maintains records of the Ketchikan Spruce Mills. The Pensacola Historical Museum has descriptions and photographs of northern Florida and southern Alabama dating from the late nineteenth century. In Augusta, the Maine State Museum contains the records of three companies. Museums usually make their study collections and libraries available to scholars and hobbyists. Working exhibits, such as the Georgia Agrirama's 1880 turpentine mill (Tifton, Georgia) are based on a body of historical research with great emphasis on detail.

The FOREST HISTORY SOCIETY has published *Forest History Museums of the World* (1983), listing nearly 350 museums around the world that contain significant collections. The American Association of Museums' annual *Official Museum Directory* details the nature of collections and facilities.

ROBERT G. WALTHER

N

NATIONAL ASSOCIATION OF STATE FORESTERS

The National Association of State Foresters (NASF) is composed of "state foresters whose agencies are the legally constituted authorities for conducting public forestry work within the state." NASF began informally in 1908 at a New York City meeting of six foresters. An outbreak of white pine blister rust in 1909 prompted the Association of Eastern Foresters to stage a conference to determine the best course of action. In 1911, the small group adopted a constitution and began maintaining more formal proceedings but still as the Association of Eastern Foresters.

In 1920, Gifford PINCHOT, at that time chief of the Pennsylvania Department of Forestry, invited all state foresters to a meeting in Harrisburg. The group organized as the State Foresters Association, and William T. Cox of Minnesota was elected president. At its 1964 meeting in Alaska, its present name was adopted. In 1980, NASF had fifty members.

The NASF meets annually and has worked closely with the U. S. FOREST SERVICE and other national forestry organizations. It has not itself been an innovative association, but in its annual policy statements it has reflected the major trends in American forestry. In 1979, the NASF adopted a five-year legislative program calling on the federal and state governments to adopt tax credits, low-interest loan projects, and amendments of inheritance tax laws that could promote reforestation and, especially, retention of forest stands to maturity by private landowners.

NATIONAL AUDUBON SOCIETY

The National Audubon Society, a citizen environmental organization which in 1980 had over 400,000 members in some 440 chapters, began in the late nineteenth century as an association for the protection of wild birds from market hunters, eggers, and the millinery trade. Named for John James Audubon, famed naturalist and painter of birds, the initial Audubon Society was founded by George Bird GRINNELL in 1886 through *Forest and Stream* magazine; it grew quickly to 39,000 members before Grinnell disbanded the organization. In 1896, the Massachusetts Audubon Society was founded, followed by societies in more than thirty-five other states. State representatives in 1901 created a loose federation, the National Committee of Audubon Societies, incorporated in 1905 in New York as the National Association of Audubon Societies.

The association established a corps of wardens to patrol key nesting colonies of wildfowl, promoted legislation to protect wildlife and wildlife habitat, developed an educational program in natural history, and in the 1920s began establishing a system of wildlife sanctuaries that has become the largest privately maintained system of wildlife preserves in the world, embracing some seventy-six areas totaling about 250,000 acres in 1980. Beginning the the 1930s, the association developed its own scientific research program, originally focused on endangered species of birds; it also pioneered in operating a system of four summer nature study camps and six nature centers around the country and encouraged the establishment of hundreds of others. Its sponsorship of wildlife film series encouraged production of hundreds of natural history films long before the popularity of such films on television.

The name of the organization was changed in 1940 to the National Audubon Society (NAS), and the title of its official organ, *Bird-Lore* (owned and edited by Frank M. Chapman from 1899 to 1935) was changed in 1941 to *Audubon Magazine* and in 1961 to *Audubon*. Edited since 1966 by Les Line, the magazine has won numerous awards for design and reporting. The society has also published *American Birds* magazine since 1947, *Audubon Leader* newsletter since 1973, educational materials, and scientific research reports. Chief executives of the organization have been William Dutcher (1901–1910), T. Gilbert Pearson (1910–1934), John H. Baker (1934–1959), Carl W. Buchheister (1959–1969), Elvis J. Stahr (1969–1979), and Russell W. Peterson (1979–   ). Individual membership declined to a low of 3,500 in 1934, then rose to about 30,000 members by 1960, 100,000 in 1970, and over 400,000 in 1980. The society organized nine regional offices in the 1960s and encouraged the formation of hundreds of new local chapters. Several state Audubon societies, especially in the East (for example, those in Massachusetts, Maine, Connecticut, and Florida) have remained pre-eminent in their areas and are only loosely allied with the national organization.

Once focused primarily on birds and habitat, the scientific, educational, and legislative activities of NAS by the 1960s and 1970s spanned the entire spectrum of environmental concern, including wildlife, energy, pollution, land and water policy, population, and international problems. NAS established a reputation for responsible, scientifically grounded positions on controversial issues and for effectively monitoring and influencing legislative and executive affairs of government. National headquarters are in New York City.

FURTHER READING: Carl W. Buchheister and Frank Graham, Jr., "From the Swamps and Back: A Concise and Candid History of the Audubon Movement," *Audubon* 75 (Jan. 1973): 4-45. William Dutcher, "In the Beginning: An Early History of Our Origin and Growth," *Audubon* 57-58 (Mar. 1955-July 1956), is a series of short articles on the period 1883–1895, reprinted from *Bird-Lore* (1905). Frank Graham, Jr., "The Audubon Ark," *Audubon* 80 (Jan. 1978), is a special issue on the sanctuary system. T. Gilbert Pearson, *Adventures in Bird Protection* (1937).

SUSAN L. FLADER

NATIONAL CONFERENCE ON OUTDOOR RECREATION

In the years after World War I, Americans experienced a general reduction in the hours of their labor, an increase in their standard of living, and an increase in their mobility as a result of widespread automobile ownership. All of these changes contributed to a rapid expansion of the use of the out-of-doors for leisure purposes.

Henry S. GRAVES in 1920 wrote an article for *American Forestry* in which he pointed out that the lack of a national policy on RECREATION uses on federal lands had led to undesirable competition between the Forest Service and the National Park Service.

The impetus for developing such a policy, which would affect the programs of federal, state, and local governments and private agencies, came from upper class sportsmen in the Coolidge administration. Largely at the behest of Undersecretary of the Navy Theodore Roosevelt, Jr., Coolidge issued an atypically powerful statement on April 14, 1924, calling for "a national policy which should not merely coordinate under federal guidance all activities in behalf of outdoor recreation, but also formulate a program to serve as a guide for future action." In May, over 300 delegates representing 128 national organizations (ranging from conservation associations to athletic clubs) gathered in Washington, D. C., to form the National Conference on Outdoor Recreation (NCOR).

NCOR was administrated through liaison between the President's Committee on Outdoor Recreation, comprised of five cabinet members, and an executive committee, representing the member organizations. An advisory council (later called the general council) composed of delegates from the organizations served as a policymaking body. As executive secretary, the NCOR had the services of two foresters, first Leon F. Kneipp (1924–1925) and later Arthur Ringland (1925–1928). However, NCOR was not supported by the public treasury. Its finances depended on contributions from participating organizations, private gifts, and a large grant from the Laura Spelman Rockefeller Memorial Foundation. NCOR defined itself not as a governmental agency but as an association of organizations "interested in the promotion and development of one or more kinds of recreation, in the use of which the land, water, forest, plant, scenic, or wild life resources of the United States are essential." It set as its first task the compilation of an inventory of these resources.

One successful contribution made by the conference was a recommendation for the creation of a Coordinating Committee on National Parks and Forests to include within its membership the heads of both services and to advise on all proposed transfers of lands between the two agencies. Also important to the future development of federal land policies was the report (compiled in 1924–1926 and published in 1928) of the Joint Committee on Recreational Survey of the Federal Lands, sponsored by the AMERICAN FORESTRY ASSOCIATION and the National Parks Association under NCOR auspices. NCOR also cooperated in recreational surveys made by such organizations as the Playground and Recreation Association of America, the Bureau of Labor Statistics, the Russell Sage Foundation, the NATIONAL CONFERENCE ON STATE PARKS, and the American Association of Museums. In addition to the inventories prepared under its sponsorship, NCOR held general meetings in 1924 and 1926 which publicized the importance of outdoor recreation and urged continued planning on all levels.

In his final report to President Herbert Hoover on May 29, 1929, Chairman Chauncey Hamlin called for the creation of a permanent Joint Board on Federal Land Planning "as a practical step looking to the coordination of measures for the productive management of the Federal Lands." Soon distracted by the stock market crash and the Depression, Hoover never really responded to NCOR's recommendations. Nevertheless, in broaching the subject of the federal government's role in outdoor recreation, the work of the conference (like other social and resource inventories of the 1920s) marked an important precedent for New Deal activities in the field and, through its surveys, contributed some of the raw material with which the New Deal reformers worked.

FURTHER READING: *National Conference on Outdoor Recreation: A Report Epitomizing the Results of Major Fact-Finding Surveys and Projects Which Have Been Undertaken Under the Auspices of the National Conference on Outdoor Recreation,* 70th Congress, 1st session, Senate Document 158 (1928). *Proceedings of the National Conference on Outdoor Recreation,* 68th Congress, 1st session, Senate Document 151 (1924). *Proceedings of the Second National Conference on Outdoor Recreation,* 69th Congress, 1st session, Senate Document 117 (1926).

NATIONAL CONFERENCE ON STATE PARKS

In 1921, Stephen T. MATHER, the first director of the NATIONAL PARK SERVICE, called a conference in Des Moines, Iowa, to discuss the expansion of the state park systems into areas suitable to parks but not sufficiently outstanding to be brought into the national park system. About 200 persons attended. Only a minority were employees of state park systems; others represented conservation, outing, and recreation organizations. In order to have a national voice encouraging the establishment, growth, and proper administration of state park systems, the delegates voted to make their organization permanent. John Barton Payne served as chairman until 1927.

Within a few years, the National Conference on State Parks (NCSP) evolved into a quasi-professional association. As state park systems grew, park managers and other employees gradually came to constitute a majority of NCSP membership. To this extent, its functions paralleled those of the older American Institute of Park Executives, although NCSP's emphasis on state institutions provided a unique service. The conference met annually and published a number of standard books in the field of forestry, including Raymond H. Torrey, *State Parks and Recreational Uses of State Forests in the United States* (1926), and Beatrice Ward Nelson, *State Recreation: Parks, Forests, and Game Preserves* (1928). Both of these volumes were the result of national surveys and both remain valuable sources for information on contemporary park facilities and systems. The NCSP also published a quarterly magazine, *State Recreation.* By the end of the 1950s, it became obvious that several organizations in the field of recreation were duplicating the functions of others, and as a result, the membership of none was completely representative of the profession. In 1965, the NCSP joined with four other organizations to form the NATIONAL RECREATION AND PARK ASSOCIATION.

NATIONAL ENVIRONMENTAL POLICY ACT, 1969

On January 1, 1970, President Richard M. Nixon signed the National Environmental Policy Act of 1969 (NEPA). In his public statement, the president gave credit to the law's authors, Senator Henry M. Jackson and Congressman John D. Dingle, and observed, "It is particularly fitting that my first official act of the new decade is to approve the National Environmental Policy Act—the 1970's absolutely must be the years when

America pays its debt to the past by reclaiming the purity of the air, its waters and our living environment. It is literally now or never." The bill had not evoked controversy, and its enactment received only perfunctory notice in professional and conservation journals. Within a few years, however, the section requiring the preparation of an environmental impact statement by any agency proposing "major federal action significantly affecting the quality of human environment" had proved to be very controversial.

NEPA established a three-member Council on Environmental Quality (CEQ) to report directly to the president. Mr. Nixon appointed Russell Train to head CEQ, which began with an initial appropriation of $300,000; by 1976, the CEQ budget was $2.7 million. NEPA required that CEQ prepare an annual assessment of environmental quality and review all federal programs and "to use all practical means—to create and maintain conditions under which man and nature can exist in productive harmony and fulfill the social, economic and other requirements of present and future generations of Americans."

NEPA's requirement for environmental impact statements proved to be a powerful tool, or weapon, depending upon one's point of view. CEQ established guidelines for the impact statements and from time to time did battle with various federal agencies over proposed projects. Outside of government, environmental groups skillfully manipulated the impact statement requirement to cause or to threaten costly delays in federal projects, as a means to attain changes favorable to their point of view.

FURTHER READING: Samuel T. Dana and Sally K. Fairfax, *Forest and Range Policy* (2nd ed., 1980). John C. Whitaker, *Striking a Balance: Environmental and National Resources Policy in the Nixon-Ford Years* (1976).

NATIONAL FOREST MANAGEMENT ACT, 1976

The National Forest Management Act was approved on October 22, 1976, following a lengthy and heated controversy that grew out of a lawsuit against FOREST SERVICE logging practices in West Virginia. The court agreed with the IZAAK WALTON LEAGUE OF AMERICA contention that clearcutting, in this case on the Monongahela National Forest, violated the FOREST MANAGEMENT ACT of 1897. Therefore, new legislation was required if the Forest Service wished to have the option of clearcutting.

The law amends the FOREST AND RANGELAND RENEWABLE RESOURCES PLANNING ACT (RPA) of 1974 and provides a comprehensive blueprint for the management of national forests. Throughout, the act reaffirms the intent of RPA, that is, the idea of assessing long-term national needs for forest products and planning to meet those needs. A dominant requirement is to assure public involvement in the assessment and planning process. The concept of multiple use is endorsed and its definition expanded to include maintenance of a diversity of plant and animal species. The redefinition of sustained yield caused considerable controversy, which now includes the concept of nondeclining yield, with specified exceptions, for each national forest. Another controversial issue concerned clearcutting, which the act defines as an acceptable silvicultural practice. The act also gave statutory status to the national forest system, which had largely existed since 1891 under a series of presidential proclamations.

FURTHER READING: Dennis C. LeMaster and Luke Popovich, "Development of the National Forest Management Act," *Journal of Forestry* 74 (Dec. 1976): 806-808.

NATIONAL FOREST PRODUCTS ASSOCIATION

From its founding in 1902 until 1965, the National Forest Products Association (NFPA) was known as the NATIONAL LUMBER MANUFACTURERS ASSOCIATION (NLMA). The name change reflected the growth of the association's interests beyond lumber manufacturing, particularly in resource management and in the increasing diversity of wood products made by association members. However, NFPA remained a federation of other associations until 1975 when a by-law revision made it possible for individual companies to join directly. Subsequently, a special dues rate encouraged the participation of wood pulp producers. By 1981, NFPA membership had grown to include thirty-one federated associations, three contributing associations (nonmembers which helped support NFPA programs), and nineteen companies.

Under the executive leadership of Mortimer B. Doyle (1957–1968), Henry Bahr (1968–1969), and James R. Turnbull (1969–1971), NFPA enjoyed growth in the number of member associations, staff capabilities, program effectiveness, and reputation. Governmental relations activities were extended, particularly in the areas of timber-supply and land-management issues. Under Ralph D. Hodges, Jr., who became executive vice- president in 1971 and was the first permanent leader to have arisen from within the organization, NFPA confronted the new challenges posed by the ENVIRONMENTAL MOVEMENT.

During the post-World War II decades, competitive

and sometimes innovative building materials made severe inroads into lumber's traditional markets. In 1958, NLMA launched the National Wood Promotion Program (NWPP) to popularize the use of wood as a generic product without regard to species or regional differences, recover lumber's lost markets, and expand opportunities for new uses. The NWPP sponsored the National Wood Council, representing about thirty organizations. Among other accomplishments, the council won congressional designation of the third week in each October as National Forest Products Week. On the local level, the council activated more than seventy-five community wood promotion groups. In 1965, NWPP separated from NLMA to become Wood Marketing, Inc. (known as the American Wood Council after 1968).

The NWPP was backed by scientific research activities demonstrating the virtues of wood in many applications. Large-scale comparative fire tests of steel and heavy-timber roof systems at Southwest Research Institute in 1960 did much to support building code provisions favorable to wood, a goal of NLMA activity since 1918. The fight against wood restrictions was unending and during the 1970s NFPA undertook to support a consultant at the National Bureau of Standards who would carry out research on the feasibility of code provisions for building materials on the basis of rate-of-heat release in a fire.

NLMA-NFPA also provided leadership for continuing efforts to overcome the confusing multiplicity of grades and related terminology in the various softwood-producing regions. The NLMA Special Committee on Grade Simplification and Standardization, authorized in 1960, developed a program for softwood lumber standards which included grades for species used in residential and light frame construction, uniform grade requirements between species, and standard sizes for seasoned and unseasoned lumber. However, these proposals, submitted to the American Lumber Standards Committee (ALSC) of the Department of Commerce in 1962, met vigorous opposition from producers and distributors of green lumber. Not until 1970, after ALSC polls of distributors, consumers, users, and producers showed 87 percent approval, did the proposed standard go into effect.

Also during the 1960s, NFPA pioneered in a new wood construction concept called the UNICOM modular system for housing and light frame construction. UNICOM's speed and economy made it a norm for house construction and afforded a uniform basis for wood framing whether the units were site-built or prefabricated.

A task even more important for NLMA than lumber trade promotion after World War II was that of assuring that federal forestlands contributed their share toward meeting the nation's wood needs. Postwar housing construction, following upon wartime lumber demands, increased Western dependency upon the national forests and other federal lands. Whereas NLMA had formerly been heavily concerned with warding off federal attempts to regulate private forests, in the 1950s and after, it saw its prime mission as the safeguarding of the industrial values of commercial forests on public lands against withdrawal from timber management for such single-purpose uses as recreation, wilderness, and wildlife. NLMA fought the multiple-use legislation of 1960 until a clause had been added containing assurances that the bill would not contravene the FOREST MANAGEMENT ACT of 1897, which specified timber supply and water flow as national forest purposes. NLMA was concerned that U. S. FOREST SERVICE timber sales and appraisal practices increased costs and lowered profits, that too little attention was given to the need to harvest the full allowable cut, that the appeals procedure was weighted against industry, and that too many provisions in timber sale contracts were discretionary with the Forest Service. To remedy these problems, NLMA in 1962 presented to Secretary of Agriculture Orville Freeman a "Four Point Program" calling for revisions in performance standards, appraisal methods, appeals procedures, and contracts. To support these reforms, NLMA organized the Federal and Community Timber Supply Program (FACTS), composed of local and regional committees of leading citizens from timber-dependent districts in California, Oregon, Washington, Montana, Michigan, Louisiana, and Mississippi, who sought federal policies productive of jobs, income, and community stability.

After receiving assurances from Freeman, industry perceived its relations with the Forest Service as improving. Still, the continuing timber supply problem had by 1969 led to recommendations by the President's Task Force on Softwood Lumber and Plywood for a National Timber Supply Bill which would establish a fund from national forest timber sale receipts to support timber management on national forests in order to increase yield. Opposed by preservationists and by the Nixon administration, which disliked legislative earmarking of any funds, the bill was shelved pending the 1970 report of the PUBLIC LAND LAW REVIEW COMMISSION (PLLRC). The PLLRC report in turn failed to be implemented after it provoked controversy between industry and environmentalists over the principle of land allocation on the basis of dominant use.

Another governmental relations problem which NLMA-NFPA faced concerned recurring government efforts to control access to private lands intermingled with public lands. Beginning in the 1940s during the federal regulation controversy, the problem of access persisted at intervals thereafter. By 1961, Forest Service and industry representatives had agreed in principle on needed right-of-way legislation, but proposed regulations issued by the secretary of agriculture in 1962 were greeted with industry dismay; NLMA contended that the proposed regulations could deny access rights to private owners and their effect would be equivalent to federal confiscation of private property without fair compensation. NLMA thereupon sought amendment to pending access legislation, and in 1964, after the issue had been thoroughly aired in House and Senate committees, Congress authorized the secretary of agriculture to issue easements across national forest lands. This statute afforded a basis for cooperative development of regulations, which were agreed upon by both the Forest Service and NFPA in 1966.

From the point of view of the forest products industry, federal policies with respect to land use generally deteriorated, however, particularly after the passage of the Wilderness Act of 1964. NFPA launched a major campaign to make certain that product needs were considered and decisions on land allocation would be reached in a timely fashion in the Forest Service review process which began in 1971–1972 as the Roadless Area Review and Evaluation (RARE I) and resumed in 1977 as RARE II. NFPA intervened in the wilderness lawsuits brought by environmentalist groups and made its influence felt in the legislative and administrative battles.

Disturbed not only by increasing wilderness classification but also by the "legislative taking" of private lands for a public purpose such as occurred in the establishment and enlargement of REDWOOD NATIONAL PARK in 1968 and 1978 and in the creation of the Voyageurs National Park in 1971, NFPA sought a rational policy that would clarify the status of lands needed to meet commodity requirements. In 1968, it sponsored a "Land and the American People" seminar in Washington, D.C., to explore the implications of this continual removal of productive lands for public, noneconomic purposes. NFPA favored the "dominant use" principle advanced by the PLLRC in 1970.

Through the FOREST INDUSTRIES COUNCIL (FIC), NFPA cooperated with the AMERICAN PAPER INSTITUTE and the AMERICAN FOREST INSTITUTE in the publication of *A Handbook on Environmental Information for the Forest Industry* in response to the environmentalists' "Earth Day" in 1971. Aimed at plant managers, information specialists, and other spokesmen, the *Handbook* began a sustained cooperative effort to achieve public understanding of industry's concern with environmental responsibility, a program followed up by FIC establishment of an Environment and Health Council.

The environmental movement's allegations of abuses perpetrated by the forest industries posed one of the major problems for NFPA during the 1970s. Because of the unsightliness of the terrain for years following harvest, environmentalists objected to "clearcutting" or "block cutting," a management technique widely applied in regions where predominant tree species required direct sunlight for regeneration. Despite approval of clearcutting as a sound silvicultural tool by the U. S. Senate Subcommittee on Public Lands, which in 1971 held extensive hearings on the subject under its chairman, Frank E. Church of Idaho, the Council on Environmental Quality recommended that the president limit clearcutting in the national forests. NFPA, which had opposed legislative prescription of silvicultural practices, equally opposed their prescription by executive order. When the administration decided not to issue such an order, critics cried that there must have been "blatant collusion" between government officials and the timber industry.

The IZAAK WALTON LEAGUE thereupon brought a federal district court suit against the secretary of agriculture aimed at outlawing the practice of clearcutting in the Monongahela National Forest of West Virginia. NFPA intervened in the case as *amicus curiae*. The court's decision in 1973 for the plaintiff involved a momentous interpretation of the Forest Management Act of 1897 which, if applied nationally, would adversely affect management practices essential to the regeneration of the Douglas-fir forests of the western states and a number of species elsewhere. In 1975, the U. S. Appellate Court upheld the decision and the government declined to seek Supreme Court review. Recognizing the far-reaching consequences for timber availability, NFPA organized a Monongahela Task Force to develop and oversee a plan to create public awareness of the decision and the need for corrective legislation. The NFPA also briefed congressmen on the relations between the Monongahela decision and the interests of their constituents. But in late 1975, a U. S. District Court in Alaska agreed with the decision, thus halting a large timber sale in the Tongass National Forest; it appeared that Forest Service annual timber sales might soon be reduced from a 12 billion board feet allowable cut to 3 billion.

Considering these court decisions to be the gravest

threat ever faced by the forest industries, NFPA supported a bill offered by Senator Hubert Humphrey of Minnesota which would amend the Forest Management Act of 1897 and strengthen the FOREST AND RANGELANDS RENEWABLE RESOURCES PLANNING ACT of 1974 by increasing the productivity of the national forests for all their benefits, including timber. Although the House passed a version of this bill satisfactory to the industry, the Senate added amendments insisting on a nondeclining-yield policy and providing economic criteria that would restrict lumber production in many areas. The final measure adopted in conference as the NATIONAL FOREST MANAGEMENT ACT of 1976 was an acceptable compromise giving the Forest Service greater flexibility to determine harvest levels consistent with multiple use and sustained yield. NFPA President Thomas M. Orth called it "likely the most constructive forest legislation in history." The Public Relations Society of America recognized the forest industry's effective participation in this outcome with presentation of its "Silver Anvil Award" to the FIC.

The inflationary trend of the economy of the 1970s posed a different kind of challenge to the forest industries. NFPA applauded the president's temporary 1971 freeze on wage and price increases and pledged the lumber and plywood industry's cooperation. NFPA submitted proposals for Phase II economic controls to the Office of Emergency Preparedness and warned that unless high levels of production for wood products were maintained, shortages would result by the end of the freeze period, thus leading to further inflation of prices; the effective way to limit prices would be to stabilize demand and avoid raw material scarcity. When these warnings were ignored, restriction of timber supply from the national forests combined with unprecedented housing activity (stimulated by the National Housing Policy Act of 1968) led to a situation in late 1972 in which prices for wood building materials were in the forefront of major rises. In response, NFPA joined a new alliance with the National Association of Home Builders and the National Lumber and Building Materials Dealers Association to press Congress to alter national forest policies.

The three groups also sought to reduce home building costs by increasing efficiency in the use of wood in construction. Technical studies begun during the NWPP in the 1960s were updated. Influential advances included an all-weather wood foundation, the plenum floor system, and new framing methods which improved insulation qualities. Through its Special Committee on Wood Products Markets, NFPA devel-oped a constructive relationship with the concerned governmental agencies to stimulate improved housing in rural areas and offer a range of economical small home plans.

Throughout the 1970s, the NFPA technical staff assumed increasing responsibilities because of the multitude of federal regulations and environmental activities. New obligations were imposed by the Occupational Safety and Health Act of 1970, the Clean Air Act of 1970, the Water Pollution Act of 1975, and the Clean Water Act of 1977. NFPA represented the industry on such diverse matters as issues relating to wood dust, radio equipment, and formaldehyde; herbicides, pesticides, and fungicides; controlled burning; dredge and fill operations and their effect on soils and water; the environmental effects of roadbuilding; Alaska lands disposition; and the release of roadless areas in national forests for multiple-use purposes. NFPA, on behalf of the FIC, conducted a comprehensive forest productivity study as the basis for reforestation and management aimed at doubling timber production by the year 2030. In 1980, NFPA added to its resource and product program areas an international trade program.

HAROLD P. NEWSON

NATIONAL FOREST RESERVATION COMMISSION

Established in 1911 under the WEEKS ACT, the National Forest Reservation Commission (NFRC) was made up of the secretaries of agriculture, interior, and war, plus two senators and two members of the House. NFRC's first chairman was Secretary of War Henry L. Stimson. Throughout its sixty-five-year history, Stimson's successors in the war and later army departments continued to head the commission.

The function of NFRC was to recommend lands for acquisition for the national forests. The U. S. FOREST SERVICE identified possible additions which the U. S. GEOLOGICAL SURVEY evaluated according to the Weeks Act requirement that reserves be vital to the maintenance of navigable waterways. Then NFRC screened these findings and reported to the president.

NFRC's first two years were its busiest. It oversaw the addition of 700,000 acres to established national forests in the East. By 1920, 2 million acres had been acquired upon its recommendation. During this period and into the 1920s, NFRC directed most of its attention to the South. Most of the fifty new national forests whose creation and enlargement it oversaw were located there. By 1961, the total number of acres of national forest additions recommended by NFRC had passed 20 million.

In the revision of national land policy that took place during the 1960s and 1970s, the commission appeared to be redundant and was abolished by the NATIONAL FOREST MANAGEMENT ACT of 1976. Its functions were absorbed by the office of the secretary of agriculture.

NATIONAL FORESTRY PROGRAM COMMITTEE

In December 1919, the SOCIETY OF AMERICAN FORESTERS published Gifford PINCHOT's most scathing attack to date on "the continued misuse of forestry lands privately owned." Declaring "the lines are drawn," Pinchot called for massive federal regulation of logging practices and protection of forestlands. There was an uproar. For a year, the manifesto was hotly debated in the *Journal of Forestry*. A referendum indicated that 60 percent of the Society's members supported Pinchot's call, but the large minority and especially the leaders of the wood-using industries were not cowed.

They formed the National Forestry Program Committee (NFPC) for the purpose of "presenting a united front in support of a forward-looking forest policy in the United States." It was a diverse collection of groups, including representatives of the AMERICAN FORESTRY ASSOCIATION, the WESTERN FORESTRY AND CONSERVATION ASSOCIATION, the AMERICAN TREE ASSOCIATION, the Society for the Protection of New Hampshire Forests, the U. S. Chamber of Commerce, the American Newspaper Publishers Association, the Association of Wood Using Industries, the American Pulp and Paper Association, the National Wholesale Lumber Dealers Association, and other local and regional groups. Royal S. Kellogg, secretary of the Newsprint Service Bureau, was chairman of the NFPC for the eight years of its existence. NFPC inveighed against the "socialist features" of the Pinchot program and called for "encouragement of local initiative" rather than federal regulation.

When Senator Arthur Capper introduced Pinchot's formula as a bill in Congress in May 1920, the Committee responded by drafting an alternative sponsored by Representative Bertrand H. Snell of New York. Somewhat ironically, for the Snell Bill emphasized state action, both bills were criticized by states-rights congressmen and unceremoniously died.

Although Pinchot himself eased his demands in the face of this opposition, the National Forestry Program Committee remained in existence, urging reforesta-

tion and fire prevention as an alternative to regulatory action. Representatives of the committee helped draft the CLARKE-MCNARY ACT and the MCSWEENEY-MCNARY ACT which, temporarily, mollified both sides. In 1928, NFPC dissolved.

FURTHER READING: Harold K. Steen, *The U. S. Forest Service: A History* (1976).

NATIONAL HARDWOOD LUMBER ASSOCIATION

At the invitation of a committee of the Chicago Hardwood Lumber Exchange, representatives of thirty-seven firms assembled in Chicago on April 8, 1898. By that afternoon, the group had formed the National Hardwood Lumber Association (NHLA) and elected William A. Bennett of Cincinnati as its first president. By the 1960s, NHLA could boast of more than 1,600 members, with 42 having maintained an uninterrupted membership for over fifty years.

The organization aimed "to protect the interests of the hardwood trade; to establish, maintain and apply a uniform system for the inspection and measurement of hardwood lumber," and to maintain training schools for inspectors. In 1901, NHLA established its Inspection Bureau, its nine members appointed by the president. Bureau expenses were defrayed by fees for service. The system was revamped in 1906 with the use of salaried inspectors who were more closely monitored by NHLA than their predecessors. By the 1960s, there were more than 100 inspectors for the United States and Canada.

To assure the quality of its inspectors, NHLA established a permanent grading school in Memphis, Tennessee, in 1949. By 1972, more than 2,500 had completed the five-month course in hardwood grading, measuring, and tallying. In 1971, the course was shortened to four months. Many graduates are not inspectors, but their knowledge of basic grading rules is of utility throughout the hardwood industry.

Standards for length, thickness, and grade for hardwood lumber and veneer are contained in the NHLA *Rules Book*. Published in English and French, many thousands of copies have been distributed worldwide. Differences of opinion about standards prompted factions split along geographic lines, between wholesale and retail, and between competitive species. The factions rallied around "good face" and "poor face" inspections. Advocates of good face insisted that the manufacturer could set standards, and since ordinarily hardwood was used with only one face exposed, the better face should be used to determine grade. The poor facers insisted that the consumer had to be involved in rule preparation, and the consumer would be interested in the quality of both sides. Following a generation of debate, modern rules were adopted in 1931 which took into account scientific tests, consultations with consumers, and the advice of experienced inspectors. Since 1931, the hardwood grading rules have attained a long-lived consistency.

FURTHER READING: M. B. Pendelton, "A Short History of the National Hardwood Lumber Association," *Southern Lumberman* 193 (Dec. 15, 1956): 127–130. *The People, Policies, and Progress of the National Hardwood Lumber Association* (1972).

NATIONAL LUMBER MANUFACTURERS ASSOCIATION

At the end of the nineteenth century, businessmen, learning the limitations of regional trade groups, sought organization on a national scale to resolve overlapping jurisdictions and to provide strong voices for the collective views of each industry in a national government policy. Led by white pine manufacturers from the Lake States, lumbermen began working in concert on a broader scale beginning in 1897 when groups from various parts of the country met to discuss political strategy to restore the tariff on lumber. The two regional bodies chiefly responsible for the formation of a national lumber trade association over the next five years were the Southern Lumber Manufacturers Association and the Mississippi Valley Lumbermen's Association. In 1902, representatives of these and other groups met in St. Louis, Missouri, to organize the National Lumber Manufacturers Association (NLMA). The association continued to operate as the NLMA until 1965, when, reflecting the increasingly integrated character of major forest industry firms, it became the NATIONAL FOREST PRODUCTS ASSOCIATION. By 1906, when the Western Pine Manufacturers Association joined, NLMA included eleven regional and specialty trade groups who represented nearly 1,500 company members. NLMA was headquartered in St. Louis until 1913 when it relocated to Chicago, where it remained through World War I.

The association's activities during its first years of operation embraced most of the perennial chores of typical manufacturing trade groups of the period, such as compiling statistics, underwriting insurance, providing credit ratings, sponsoring tariff legislation, monitoring raw material costs, and sponsoring tax reforms. A primary need was the development of standard sizes and grades to replace the multitude of designations which had evolved in the principal lumber markets. An NLMA committee issued recommendations for grades of greater uniformity at the association's first annual meeting in 1903, but it was not until after World War I that real progress was made. Turn-of-the-century lumbermen also had numerous and long-standing complaints about problems with railroad car equipment, car shortages, demurrage, and the promptness of shipments. In one of its early attempts to flex its muscles, NLMA invited railroad managers from across the country to attend its second annual meeting in St. Louis in 1904. Nevertheless, the new association was unable to prevent railroad-related issues from continuing to be a cause of aggravation to the industry for many years. More successful cooperation occurred between NLMA and the U. S. Bureau of Forestry (U. S. FOREST SERVICE after 1905) in the compilation of statistics and in otherwise providing both government and industry with data on the production and handling of lumber and lumber products. NLMA supported federal and state legislation designed to alleviate the prolonged strains of depression in the lumber industry which began in 1907 and continued well after the outbreak of war in Europe. During the same years the association defended its regional affiliates against charges of antitrust violations when the Bureau of Corporations conducted an investigation of the lumber industry. NLMA sought an equitable tariff on imported lumber, increased support for fire protection, and adjustments in state timber taxes so that owners would not be forced to liquidate their stands at low prices to meet carrying charges.

An NLMA subsidiary, the National Lumber Manufacturers Credit Corporation, was authorized in 1903 with the same board of directors as the parent organization. This corporation became the Lumbermans Blue Book, Inc., in 1932, and in the following year merged with Clancy's Red Book, a privately operated service, to form the Lumberman's Credit Association. Another subsidiary, the Inter-Insurance Exchange, which existed between 1915 and 1933 under an advisory committee, was composed predominantly of NLMA members. Ultimately it was absorbed into the Lumbermen's Underwriting Alliance, an independent company.

World War I gave a great boost to the influence and prestige of NLMA as it did to that of trade associations generally. NLMA officials served as government production and distribution managers and coordinated the allocation of war purchases from the various regional affiliates. The war experience also revealed some of the structural weaknesses of NLMA, and as a result, the association underwent a thorough reorganization, enforced more efficient and equitable dues-collecting procedures, and created the influential position of secretary-manager. In 1918, Wilson COMPTON was appointed as the first secretary-manager, a post he held for the next twenty-six years. The increasing importance of national affairs in the industry's policies and practices dictated NLMA's move to Washington, D. C., in 1921. Auspiciously for the lumber industry, the shift to the nation's capital occurred at a time when the trade association movement was achieving significant influence under Secretary of Commerce Herbert Hoover.

Throughout the 1920s, NLMA enjoyed considerable influence in both legislative and executive branches. Cooperative programs between government and industry proved fruitful. A program for the development of lumber standards adopted by the American Lumber Congress in 1919 led, two years later, to the establishment of the Central Committee on Lumber Standards in cooperation with the United States Department of Commerce. Secretary Hoover praised NLMA for its effort to rationalize and make more efficient the industry's business relationships; NLMA, he once remarked, was "Exhibit A" of government–industry cooperation. Hoover drew attention specifically to the industry's efforts to implement standardization and to promote the more efficient use of wood. NLMA also did yeoman work in getting through Congress the CLARKE-MCNARY ACT of 1924.

The Great Depression had a mixed influence on NLMA. Because the lumber market had experienced a steady decline beginning in 1925, the Depression came to the lumber industry well before the stock market collapse in 1929. To counter the vexing problem of a productive capacity that continued to exceed demand, a few members of NLMA suggested a drastic reorganization of the industry and the appointment of a "Lumber Czar" to dictate production controls and provide a central, coordinated authority for the industry. Compton and the established leadership of NLMA survived this threat and the association muddled through the hard times of the early 1930s. Hoover, then president of the United States, worked with Compton and NLMA to establish the Timber Conservation Board, which between 1931 and 1933 made strenuous efforts to achieve voluntary cutbacks of lumber production in the midst of a rapidly deteriorating market. Thereafter, NLMA periodically suggested that Congress relax the antitrust laws to permit price agreements and production controls and that the industry be allowed to speed up the process of merging and consolidating the smaller, less efficient operating units into larger ones.

Most lumbermen greeted Franklin D. ROOSEVELT'S

National Recovery Administration (NRA) with great enthusiasm, and the Code of Fair Competition for the Lumber and Timber Products Industries, which set up new machinery for business cooperation with the government to speed economic recovery, was approved in August 1933. Compton and other NLMA officials, together with representatives from the regional affiliates, served in influential positions in administering the Lumber Code. When the Supreme Court found the NRA unconstitutional in the spring of 1935, NLMA members greeted the decision with mixed emotions. Most of the NLMA leadership liked the production control mechanism of the Lumber Code and were chagrined that the government did not enforce the provisions. NLMA also charged that the federal government had failed to provide lumbermen with the necessary assistance to make compliance with the code possible—increased support for fire protection, the extension of increased appropriations for forest research, and relief from excessive timberland TAXATION.

Between the demise of the NRA and the outbreak of World War II, NLMA successfully fought a concentrated Forest Service attempt to impose federal regulation on private timberlands. NLMA probably directed more criticism at Chief of the Forest Service Ferdinand A. SILCOX and his successor, Acting Chief Earle CLAPP, than at any of their predecessors. NLMA hopes for cooperation with the federal government declined. Nevertheless, NLMA continued to press for federal policies that would help the industry recover from the Depression.

During the 1930s, NLMA expanded its participation in lumber trade promotion, a responsibility it had taken up soon after World War I when a rash of restrictive building codes sought to limit wood construction. In 1932, Compton organized an NLMA affiliate, the American Forest Products Industries, Inc. (AFPI), to administer trade promotion programs and stimulate new markets. One of AFPI's early actions was to establish the Timber Engineering Company (TECO) to encourage the use of lumber in construction, primarily through promotion and sale of a variety of timber connectors. AFPI was a "special account" under the control of the NLMA board of directors, an arrangement that enabled it to solicit support from forest products companies, such as pulp and paper firms, which could not be members of the solid wood products associations represented in NLMA. The feeling of such firms that this arrangement did not allow them to exert influence commensurate with their financial support, together with a shift of AFPI responsibilities into public relations work, led to the separation of AFPI from NLMA in 1946. (At that time, TECO was transferred to

NLMA, but it, too, became an entirely independent organization in 1969.) NLMA also promoted the use of wood as a building material by providing architects and engineers with technical data enabling wood to compete with steel and concrete. *National Design Specification* (1934) guided the use of lumber as an engineering material and provided the basis for code acceptance of softwood grades and species conforming to the requirements of the American Lumber Standards Committee, while *Wood Structural Design Data* (1934) offered the first comprehensive tabular presentation of the load-carrying capacity of all commercial sizes of framing lumber, posts, and timbers.

World War II proved to be a great boon to the lumber industry and to the effective influence of NLMA. Association officials again served the federal government as coordinators of lumber manufacturing and distribution. At the same time, NLMA gained congressional approval of much of the program it had sought since the early New Deal years. A major legislative success was the encouragement to reforestation of private lands offered by the Internal Revenue Code of 1944, which granted capital gains tax treatment for timber. This reform was largely the work of the Forest Industries Committee on Timber Valuation and Taxation (FICTVT), like AFPI a "special account" of NLMA, established in 1942 under the chairmanship of Charles W. Briggs. FICTVT, like AFPI, later became an independent organization.

Wilson Compton resigned as secretary-manager of NLMA in 1944; in the decades following, NLMA's top executive post passed through the hands of a number of individuals whose tenures were relatively brief, but whose backgrounds in forestry, lumbering, or trade association work had prepared them well for leadership roles. Richard A. Colgan (1944–1950) came from the Diamond Match Company, while Harry T. Kendall (1950–1952) and Leo V. Bodine (1952–1957) had previously served with the Weyerhaeuser Company. Their experience in woods operations, lumber manufacturing and distribution, and corporate public relations was expected to be helpful in opposing the anticipated renewal of federal attempts to regulate private timberlands, in pursuing opportunities in new tax legislation, and later in Korean War governmental-relations matters such as wage and price stabilization and defense mobilization. In 1957, Mortimer B. Doyle left the National Association of Manufacturers to become executive vice-president of NLMA. He undertook basic staff reorganizations to concentrate on governmental affairs and product promotion. During his term, NLMA became the National Forest Products

Association (in 1965), a change in name which recognized the expansion of the organization's scope beyond the limits of strictly lumber manufacturing interests.

NATIONAL MONUMENTS

National monuments are areas of federal land set aside by presidential proclamation to protect historic landmarks, historic or prehistoric structures, and other objects of historic or scientific interest. They are established under authority of the American Antiquities Act of June 8, 1906.

This act was passed because of wholesale vandalism in areas of historic, scientific, and scenic importance. Near the end of the nineteenth century, there came an upsurge of protest against vandalism from scientific and educational groups such as the Smithsonian Institution, citizens' groups such as the Colorado Cliff Dwellers Association, public officials, and members of Congress. The Antiquities Act was largely the work of Representative John F. LACEY of Iowa, who worked closely with Land Office Commissioner W. A. Richards and with Edgar I. Hewett of the U. S. Bureau of Ethnology. The act established penalties for destroying, injuring, or excavating any historic or prehistoric ruin or object of antiquity located on federal lands and authorized the president to set aside by proclamation national monuments and to accept gifts of land. Permits for examination of ruins were to be given by the secretary having jurisdiction over the lands—Interior for the unreserved public domain, Agriculture for the forest reserves, and War for land controlled by the military. These agencies generally cleared such requests with the Smithsonian Institution.

With passage of the act, a large number of national monuments were established. Gifford PINCHOT issued an order to all U. S. FOREST SERVICE field officers requesting that they report on potential areas of monument status within national forests. Chief Inspector Frederick Erskine OLMSTED screened these reports and made many recommendations. Other recommendations came from field officers of the DEPARTMENT OF THE INTERIOR. Many originated in the proposals of groups such as the Alaska Cruise Club and the Mountaineers. The reserved areas protected a large and miscellaneous group of phenomena including elk, cactus, cliff dwellings, missions, totem poles, fur trading posts, and geological formations. The Antiquities Act was a convenient device for reserving land pending final classification, and presidents from Theodore ROOSEVELT to Jimmy Carter have used it for this pur-

Remnant snow lying in deep crevices forms a cross in Colorado's Holy Cross National Monument, 1919. Subsequent erosion has diminished the likeness. Forest Service Photo.

pose. Thus, many areas once established as national monuments later became or were incorporated into national parks. Among them were Cinder Cone and Lassen Peak, reserved in 1906 and included in Lassen Volcanic National Park in 1915; Grand Canyon, reserved as a monument in 1908 and upgraded to park status in 1919; Mount Olympus, which was reserved in 1909 and became OLYMPIC NATIONAL PARK in 1938; and Jackson Hole, reserved in 1943 and incorporated in GRAND TETON NATIONAL PARK in 1950.

The monuments at first were administered by the agencies having control of the land. The quality of administration varied a great deal, depending partly on funding, partly on the interest of the officers in charge. Support was often given by local or state agencies. The Alaska Road Commission, for example, provided most of the maintenance for Sitka National Monument. Local historical societies helped with interpretation in some areas. Two federal agencies played an important part in national monument re-

search and preservation. The Smithsonian Institution made a great many studies of individual monuments. The Forest Products Laboratory developed a variety of preservatives designed to stabilize stone or adobe foundations and to protect wooden structures from the ravages of time.

All national monuments were transferred to NATIONAL PARK SERVICE jurisdiction in 1933. These included sixteen which were formerly under Forest Service jurisdiction and a number which were under the army. The major reason for the transfer was a desire for uniformity of administration. In 1978, however, President Carter created a number of national monuments in Alaska to protect certain areas pending passage of an Alaskan land bill. Two of these new monuments were administered by the U. S. FISH AND WILDLIFE SERVICE, and two by the Forest Service. After passage of the Historic Sites Act of 1936, some of the smaller national monuments, such as Whitman Mission and Fort Vancouver, were reclassified as historic sites.

National parks and national monuments are similar in administrative goals and objectives. The main difference is that national parks are created by an act of Congress, and monuments are created by presidential proclamation following guidelines set up under the Antiquities Act. There is no complete separation of powers, however. Congress can exercise authority over the monuments. Congress may recommend creation of monuments. It may change the status of reserved federal lands; for example, Custer Battlefield National Cemetery was changed to Custer Battlefield National Monument, and Grand Portage National Historic Site was changed to Grand Portage National Monument, both by act of Congress. Congress appropriates money for the management of monuments and may open monuments to commercial activities such as mining; and Congress may place portions of monuments under the wilderness system.

Like national parks, national monuments embrace large tracts of land and frequently have been involved in land use conflicts. Some conflicts of historical importance have involved game management and commercial timber in the Olympic National Monument, grazing in Grand Teton, and mining in Glacier Bay, Death Valley, and Misty Fiords. The unrestricted power of the president to create national monuments has been a subject of political debate and occasionally of congressional efforts to abolish or curtail his power in this direction. The latest manifestation of this spirit came with President Carter's 1978 proclamation of monuments in Alaska.

FURTHER READING: Jenks Cameron, *The National Park Service, Its History, Activities and Organization* (1923). John Ise, *Our National Park Policy: A Critical History* (1961).

LAWRENCE RAKESTRAW

NATIONAL PARKS AND CONSERVATION ASSOCIATION

The National Parks Association was founded in 1919 by Stepen T. MATHER, first director of the NATIONAL PARK SERVICE, and Robert Sterling YARD, one of Mather's chief assistants in establishing an effective parks administration. Mather provided financial assistance and personal encouragement to launch the organization, which Yard, its first executive officer, intended to become the private watchdog of the park system.

Yard's uncompromising, often dictatorial style and the association's opposition to growing commercial attacks against the national park system immersed the new organization in controversy. The association effectively fought such schemes as the attempt to raise the water level in Yellowstone Lake and transform it into an irrigation reservoir. On the other hand, Yard's insistence on absolute purity for the national park system soured him against such noteworthy projects as Shenandoah, the Everglades, and Grand Teton national parks. The Everglades he dismissed as "a promoters' proposition." Jackson Hole, he argued, only "borrowed its grandeur" from the Teton mountains and was not worthy in its own right to be included in the system.

Yard retired as the National Parks Association secretary in 1934 and as its editor in 1936. With the waning of his influence, the association assumed a more professional and credible tone. By 1960, its journal, *National Parks Magazine*, was a recognized leader in the field. Memberships continued to increase, from roughly 5,000 in 1960 to 55,000 in 1972. The ENVIRONMENTAL MOVEMENT of the 1960s in large part contributed to this upsurge; still, the willingness of the association to broaden its mission to ecological preservation as a whole was also an important milestone on the road to its maturity. This expanded mission was reflected in the changing of the group's name to the National Parks and Conservation Association in 1970.

Foremost among the association's achievements during the 1960s and 1970s were blockage of the Grand Canyon dams and Everglades jetport, the establishment of REDWOOD NATIONAL PARK, and the preservation of huge portions of the public domain in Alaska. Similarly, as a reflection of its broader role, the association has taken such positions as support for more public transportation, pollution abatement, and control of human overpopulation. On an even more controversial note, the association closed ranks during the 1970s with organizations seeking the cutoff of all types of illegal immigration, especially from Latin American countries.

Each of these new missions has reflected the association's conviction that the survival of national parks is no longer a regional or national question, but perhaps even an international problem. In this regard, the National Parks and Conservation Association, much like the SIERRA CLUB, the NATIONAL AUDUBON SOCIETY, and the WILDERNESS SOCIETY, has become a far different organization indeed than its founders envisioned.

FURTHER READING: Alfred Runte, *National Parks: The American Experience* (1979). Robert Shankland, *Steve Mather of the National Parks* (1951).

ALFRED RUNTE

NATIONAL PARKS AND NATIONAL PARK SERVICE

Among the institutions of conservation in the United States, the national park system has stood apart. The national park idea is an American original, whereas national forests, wildlife refuges, and city parks by way of comparison, all can be traced to roots in the ancient world and modern Europe. National parks have also represented the conservation movement's spirit of idealism and altruism. Without the national park idea, the intellectual basis for the conservation movement would have been far less diverse. Warding off the possibility of running out of natural resources was only common sense, after all.

The National Park Service, established by Congress on August 25, 1916, has shared the aura of its holdings. Initially, the Park Service openly promoted tourism to insure the protection of the parks against logging, mining, grazing, and hydroelectric power projects. By the 1930s, however, biologists, wildlife managers, and wilderness enthusiasts openly challenged the service not to compromise the ecological resources of the parks for greater visitation alone. This debate about the proper balance between preservation and use still continues, exacerbated by charges that the service has lost its control over large concessionaires and that too many parks have been opened to public whims not in keeping with the complex needs of natural environments.

Two major forces, westward expansion and American nationalism, combined during the nineteenth century to lay the foundations of the national park idea. Well into the 1830s and 1840s, Europeans accused the United States of cultural inferiority. The English clergyman Sir Sydney Smith asked derisively in 1820: "In the four quarters of the globe, who reads an American book? or goes to an American play? or looks at an American picture or statue?" The commercialization of America's unique scenic marvels of the period, especially NIAGARA FALLS, only added to the nation's growing sensitivity to such accusations of callousness. By 1860, the famous cataract was entirely in private hands, forcing all visitors, European and American alike, to pay handsomely for the privilege of viewing nature's beauty.

The westward movement provided the United States with new opportunities to prove that its citizens were in fact worthy custodians of great natural scenery. As early as 1832, the artist and explorer George Catlin proposed "a *nation's* Park, containing man and beast, in all the wild and freshness of their nature's beauty!" But Catlin, who envisaged a reserve of Indians, buffalo, and prairie topography, was still far ahead of his time. Indians and wildlife were to be subdued rather than preserved; meanwhile, the grasslands of North America suffered from the common perception that landscapes without mountains were "monotonous." Spectacular scenery had the strongest popular appeal; Catlin's revolutionary thought of a *National* park thus awaited the discovery of a much more suitable environment.

The opening of Yosemite Valley, California, in 1851 provided a setting beyond America's most enthusiastic expectations. The following year, the giant sequoias, or Sierra redwoods, likewise were revealed to the world. Yet no amount of cultural pride in both wonders could mask the nation's failure to protect either of them from abuse. In 1854, the "Mother of the Forest," a sequoia thirty-one feet in diameter in the Calaveras Grove, was stripped of its bark to a height of 116 feet. Promoters then cut the bark into sections and shipped them east for reassembly and display in New York and London. Shortly afterward the first party of tourists entered Yosemite Valley, and attempts to preempt the gorge for private profit were also under way.

The pending private exploitation of Yosemite and its nearby stands of giant sequoias led in 1864 to a campaign to preserve the valley and the Mariposa Grove of big trees. During the winter, a small group of Californians asked their junior U. S. senator, John Conness, to sponsor a bill granting to the State of California the Yosemite Valley and the Mariposa Grove "for public use, resort, and recreation" and requiring both properties to be held by the state inalienable for all time." Senator Conness agreed, and in May 1864, he introduced his bill to the Senate with a strong reminder that the British, upon hearing the first reports of the big trees, had debunked them as nothing but "a Yankee invention." Similar appeals to national pride won passage of the legislation in the House, and on June 30, 1864, President Abraham Lincoln signed the Yosemite Park Act into law.

Because Congress turned the valley and big trees over to California to be managed, there has long been a lively debate about the significance of this piece of legislation with regard to the origins of national parks. It is fair to say that the Yosemite grant marks the realization of the national park *idea*, though not the national park *system*. The legislation was both passed by Congress and conceived in the national interest. The stipulation that California must hold the grant "inalienable" was a precondition with strong nationalistic overtones, for without continuity, Yosemite's value as a symbol of national pride would be meaningless. But because Yellowstone, set aside eight years later, remained in federal control, the origins of the national park idea in Yosemite often have been discounted or overlooked.

Yellowstone, like Yosemite, provided the United States with still another unparalleled opportunity to enhance national pride through the dramatic landscapes of the West. The surveyors, adventurers, artists, and photographers who explored Yellowstone between 1869 and 1871 also wrote in glowing terms about its cultural possibilities. In this vein, Yellowstone's great rock formations were compared favorably to the castles, ruins, and Gothic cathedrals of western Europe. Similarly, the explorers took heart in the knowledge that not even Iceland or New Zealand could boast of geysers on the order of Old Faithful.

As the reports about Yellowstone's wonders were confirmed and publicized in the East, officials of the Northern Pacific Railroad extension project were among the first to call for protection of the region. Congress proved supportive, provided the explorers could show that Yellowstone was "worthless" for mining, agriculture, grazing, lumbering, and settlement, uses still closer to the nation's heart than preservation for the sake of tourists. Finally, on March 1, 1872, President Ulysses S. Grant signed the Yellowstone Park Act into law.

Because Yellowstone, unlike Yosemite, was part of a territory rather than a state, Congress had no choice but to keep the reserve under federal jurisdiction. In this manner, largely accidental, Yellowstone became the first national park in name as well as in fact. Uncertain that there were no additional geyser basins in Yellowstone, Congress established a park encompassing more than 3,300 square miles, far larger than the Yosemite Grant. Congress's reluctance to fund scenic preservation had not been overcome, however; five more years alapsed before $10,000 was appropriated to begin management of the new reserve.

Yet even with this appropriation, YELLOWSTONE NATIONAL PARK was often in serious jeopardy. Souvenir hunters and vandals carried off or destroyed many of its attractions during these early years, and poachers shot wildlife with abandon. Not until 1883 did Congress authorize patrol of the park by the United States Cavalry; even then, it was three more years before the troopers entered the reserve and provided some semblance of protection.

With these meager improvements, both the pattern of park creation and administration were established well into the twentieth century. Parks were to be composed of "monumental" scenery and to include only lands surrounding the primary attractions themselves. For all intents and purposes, parklands were to be useless from the standpoint of sustained economic development other than tourism.

Even so, it was 1890 before Congress once more responded to appeals to protect the nation's "wonderlands" with the creation of Yosemite, Sequoia, and General Grant national parks, all in California's High Sierra. At roughly 1,500 square miles, Yosemite, with its heart still in state ownership, was by far the largest of the three. Nevertheless, its size was due as much to growing concern about protecting the watersheds of the San Joaquin Valley as it was to support for scenic protection. At the request of the secretary of the interior, the United States Cavalry patrolled the new parks against poaching, vandalism, and illegal grazing, although it had no legal authority to do so.

In subsequent years, Congress added other areas of obvious scenic merit to the national park system, including Mount Rainier, Washington (1899), Crater Lake, Oregon (1902), Mesa Verde, Colorado (1906), Glacier, Montana (1910), Rocky Mountain, Colorado (1915), and Mount Lassen, California (1916). Passage of the Antiquities Act of 1906, which empowered the president to set aside "objects of historic or scientific interest" on the public domain as NATIONAL MONUMENTS, foreshadowed other parks, including the Grand Canyon of Arizona. The Grand Canyon, proclaimed a national monument in 1908 by President Theodore ROOSEVELT, was elevated to national park status by Congress in 1919. Neither in the Grand Canyon, however, nor in the other parks established during this period, had Congress relaxed its implicit precondition that the lands set aside must be worthless for all but RECREATION. Rather, in keeping with a precedent as old as Yellowstone, the national parks that came easiest into the fold encompassed only the leftovers of the public domain.

Two major reversals of the national park idea, both affecting Yosemite, underscored the strength and persistence of this crippling precondition. In 1905, Congress deleted 542 square miles from YOSEMITE NATIONAL PARK; the lost territory, transferred to the adjacent Sierra Forest Reserve, was deemed too valuable for lumbering, mining, and grazing to remain in a national park. Shortly afterward, the city of San Francisco launched a vigorous campaign to lease the Hetch Hetchy Valley portion of Yosemite National Park for use as a municipal water supply reservoir. Despite the claim that Hetch Hetchy was a second

Yosemite and over the strong objections of emerging preservation groups, Congress approved the request. In December 1913, the right to dam Hetch Hetchy Valley passed into the hands of San Francisco and its engineers.

By January 1915, when Stephen T. MATHER became assistant to the secretary of the interior, the department had jurisdiction over thirteen national parks and eighteen national monuments. These reservations covered over 4,750,000 acres in fourteen states, all west of the Mississippi River, and in the Territory of Alaska. Only a strong governing agency specifically dedicated to the defense and administration of these reserves, preservationists firmly believed, could withstand further raids against what little resources the parks and monuments might contain. Thus, the preservationist response to the loss of Hetch Hetchy was a redoubling of efforts to win congressional approval of a National Park Service. To this end, preservation groups such as the American Civic Association sought alliances with the large western railroads, all of which looked to the national parks as wise investments in tourism and public relations. Every patriotic citizen, the railroads trumpeted in their advertisements, would want to visit his own country before spending his money abroad. In a similar vein, preservationists found the "See America First" campaign a fitting departure for their own attempts to broaden the base of the national park idea to include worker efficiency, public health, and similar themes. If it could be shown that the national parks were not luxuries but the key to improving industrial output through the encouragement of physical and moral fitness among the working classes, Congress would have a stronger incentive for adding to the system rather than dismantling it.

The strategy worked superbly, and on August 25, 1916, Congress authorized the National Park Service. Under Stephen T. Mather and Horace M. ALBRIGHT, respectively its first director and assistant director, the National Park Service achieved a distinguished record of accomplishment between 1916 and 1933. Following Mather's retirement in 1929, Albright, then superintendent at Yellowstone, became director. Albright carried on the Mather tradition for the next four years, when he, too, resigned from the National Park Service. In a very real sense, the Mather-Albright era never quite lost its influence on the National Park Service and its policies. It was under their administrations, for instance, that the national park idea gained its first recognition in the East, most notably in Acadia, Shenandoah, Great Smoky Mountains, and Everglades national parks. Similarly, the park system

in the West obtained new wonderlands of great distinction, including Zion, Bryce, and Grand Teton national parks. Finally, and perhaps of even greater significance, the national park idea matured to recognize the distinctiveness of wilderness areas and wildlife as well as spectacular scenery. In no region was the emerging standard more evident than the Everglades of southern Florida, whose level, so-called monotonous wetlands seemed a far cry from the magnificent landforms of the American West.

This record of accomplishment was marred only by the continuing complexities of balancing the mission to both preserve and use the national parks. According to the Organic Act of 1916, the fundamental purpose of the national parks "is to conserve the scenery and the natural and historic objects and the wild life therein and to provide for the enjoyment of the same in such manner and by such means as will leave them unimpaired for the enjoyment of future generations." But precisely what was meant by "unimpaired?" Did the word make allowances for roads and parking lots, for example? In either case, who was to determine such standards in the first place? The euphoria of having won approval of the National Park Service Act deflected the consideration of such questions during the early years of the agency.

Yet such issues only increased in importance. Following brief respites from growing visitation during World War II, overcrowding soared during the following decades. Initially, the Park Service still greeted the tourists with open arms, seeing in greater popularity for the parks the major prerequisite for their long-term survival against far more damaging forms of use. Accordingly, the Park Service proposed major programs leading to the construction of better roads, visitor accommodations, visitor centers, and camping sites.

Construction in the parks culminated in the Mission 66 program, a massive effort to improve the parks for the fiftieth anniversary of the National Park Service in 1966, when, it was estimated, 80 million auto vacationers would crowd the reserves. By comparison, the debate about whether or not to open the parks to automobiles after the turn of the century paled to insignificance. Nationwide, preservation groups challenged the wisdom of forfeiting the national parks to the automobile, especially in an era of dwindling energy resources and open spaces. Similarly, biologists and botanists, by restating criticisms first voiced during the 1930s, joined wildlife experts of every persuasion in attacking the Park Service for succumbing to "carnivalism." Needed instead, these scientists agreed, were standards of usage in keeping with environmental limitations such as the carrying capacity of each particular park.

Other preservationists accused Congress and the Park Service of broadening the mission of the national park system at the expense of its unique primeval holdings, specifically of including recreation areas whose management needs drained away funds urgently required for rounding out existing units. Regardless, during the 1960s and 1970s the holdings of the National Park Service dramatically increased as Congress mandated new directions for the agency. Included were urban parks, parkways, and national recreation areas, which, it could still be argued, were better left to state acquisition and management.

National parks closed out the 1970s under a cloud of controversies that were even more bitter. The most notable of these disputes concerned the future of parklands in Alaska. Seeking parks of truly unquestionable ecological significance, preservationists looked to the forty-ninth state as the one last hope to redress the imbalance dating from the era of "monumentalism" when scenery alone was the basic criterion in selecting national parks. Controversy also arose over the older parks, especially Yosemite, where rejection of a development-oriented master plan in 1974 led to the first major attempt to assess public opinion in park history.

Assaults against the national parks during the past three decades left ecologists little reason for optimism on the basis of historical precedent. Proposals during the 1950s and early 1960s calling for dams in Dinosaur National Monument and Grand Canyon National Park, although defeated, merely underscored the vulnerability of even existing parks to massive development. REDWOOD NATIONAL PARK, conceived as an integral biological unit with a complete watershed, instead entered the system in 1968 as a piecemeal series of California state parks, cutover land, and redwood "corridors" that included only the "monumental" trees. Expansion of Redwood National Park in 1978 also appeared anticlimactic, inasmuch as 39,000 of the 48,000 acres added to the park already had been logged.

And yet, the world still looked to the United States, as the inventor of the national park idea, for guidance and inspiration. The First World Conference on National Parks, convened in 1962 in Seattle, Washington, was followed in 1972 by an even more elaborate gathering to celebrate the Yellowstone centennial. At this Second World Conference, delegates from more than eighty nations discussed the role of national parks from an environmental perspective. Eight years later, 110 nations listed upward of 1,200 national parks and "equivalent" reserves, proof that America's national park system, despite its limitations, was still the standard for global preservation. In this spirit, environmentalists entered the 1980s with a renewed determination to round out the national park system of the United States to encompass fitting examples of the totality of the American land, not merely its spectacular masterpieces.

The national park system includes national parks established by act of Congress, national monuments proclaimed by the president under the Antiquities Act, and many lesser reservations designated as national preserves, national lakeshores and seashores, national rivers, national historic sites and historic parks, national memorials, national recreation areas, national parkways, and a variety of other classifications. In 1979, the service administered 320 separate areas of which 39 were national parks and 92 national monuments. The units of the system were located in 49 states, the District of Columbia, Guam, Puerto Rico, Saipan, and the Virgin Islands. The total acreage was 76.7 million, and of this, 16 million acres were in national parks.

FURTHER READING: William C. Everhart, *The National Park Service* (1972). John Ise, *Our National Park Policy: A Critical History* (1961). Alfred Runte, *National Parks: The American Experience* (1979). Conrad Wirth, *Parks, Politics, and the People* (1980).

ALFRED RUNTE

NATIONAL PLAN FOR AMERICAN FORESTRY

See Copeland Report

NATIONAL RECREATION AND PARK ASSOCIATION

In 1965, five national organizations of park administrators and recreation experts joined to form the National Recreation and Park Association (NRPA). Laurance S. ROCKEFELLER was the first president of the new organization. The merging groups included the American Association of Zoological Parks and Aquariums, the American Institute of Park Executives (founded 1898), the American Recreation Society (1938), the NATIONAL CONFERENCE ON STATE PARKS (1921), and the National Recreation Association (1906). By 1971, it was obvious that the preponderance of members had common interests in kinds of parks and recreation at odds with those of the zoo and aquarium administrators, and the first of the constituent groups amicably left NRPA to resume its independent status.

With headquarters located in Arlington, Virginia, NRPA had about 22,000 members in 1980, organized in fifty-eight chapters. The majority of members are administrators and other professionals concerned with park and recreation management. NRPA is principally concerned with sports programs and recreational programs in urban areas, but a significant minority of the membership consists of state park administrators, including foresters.

NRPA has an extensive publishing program. In addition to books, it publishes the monthly *Parks & Recreation* magazine (which deals with problems of forest management as well as other topics), the scholarly quarterlies *Journal of Leisure Research* and *Therapeutic Recreation Journal*, the *Washington Action Report - Dateline: NRPA*, and an annual *Guide to Books on Parks and Recreation*.

FURTHER READING: Richard F. Knapp and Charles E. Hartsoe, *Play for America: The National Recreation Association, 1906–1965* (1979), chap. 9, "The Merger of National Recreation and Park Organizations."

NATIONAL WILDLIFE FEDERATION

The National Wildlife Federation (NWF) was established in 1935 as the General Wildlife Federation with Jay "Ding" DARLING as its first president. It incorporated as the National Wildlife Federation in 1938. The federation idea came from Darling who, at a meeting he organized in 1934 with leading industrialists and munitions makers, asked for subscriptions to a national consortium of organized sportsmen. The federation, with local, county, and state groups as members, was to act as a clearinghouse of information and also as a lobby on wildlife- and conservation-related legislation. Not wanting to ask for a membership fee, the federation created the wildlife stamp as a fund-raising device. The first stamps were drawn by Darling in 1938.

After Darling resigned the presidency in 1939, the National Wildlife Federation lost its sense of mission. In 1946, when its debts were dissolved by the American Wildlife Institute, the federation was reactivated and eventually became the largest membership conservation organization in America. In 1947, NWF started the *Conservation Report*, which showed the status of conservation legislation pending in Congress.

The NWF sponsors National Wildlife Week, the Backyard Wildlife Habitat program, and Ranger Rick's Nature Club. It publishes the annual *Conservation Directory* and the periodicals *National Wildlife, International Wildlife, Ranger Rick's Nature Magazine*, and the *Conservation Report*.

FURTHER READING: David L. Lindt, *Ding: The Life of Jay Norwood Darling* (1979). Carl D. Shoemaker, *The Stories Behind the Organization of the National Wildlife Federation and Its Early Struggles for Survival* (1960). Ernest F. Swift, *A Conservation Saga* (1967).

NATURAL AREAS

Programs to designate and protect natural areas in the United States are related to the serious study of ecology, which began about a century ago. In 1917, the ECOLOGICAL SOCIETY OF AMERICA established a Committee for the Preservation of Natural Conditions. This committee became the Ecologists' Union in 1946 and in 1950 was renamed NATURE CONSERVANCY. Nature Conservancy is a national conservation organization, receiving its support from the public and devoting its resources to the protection of natural areas and the diversity of life they support. First priority is given to preserving those areas that safeguard rare or endangered plants, animals, and other natural features. As of March 29, 1980, the organization had been involved in 2,332 projects and had saved 1,625,519 acres of natural areas. It manages over 700 preserves by using volunteer land stewards and staff to encourage compatible use by researchers, students, and the public.

Inherent to the concept of wilderness is the need for natural conditions. Since YELLOWSTONE NATIONAL PARK was established in 1872, wilderness protection has undergirded the management of the National Park System. Thus, the parks provide a series of natural areas. Although the FOREST SERVICE set aside the Gila Wilderness Area as early as 1924, the concept was not legally recognized until the passage of the Wilderness Act of 1964. From the beginning, the agency saw these areas as providing "ecological benchmarks" that could be used by natural scientists. As of January 1, 1980, it had preserved 19,336,980 acres within 190 units, of which 110 were administered by the Forest Service, 25 by the National Park Service, 52 by the FISH AND WILDLIFE SERVICE, and 3 by the BUREAU OF LAND MANAGEMENT.

The SOCIETY OF AMERICAN FORESTERS (SAF) in 1946 formed a Committee on Natural Areas. The committee was charged with the identification of areas of forestland to be preserved permanently in unmodified condition as representative units of virgin forest types. The committee set a minimum size of twenty acres for a single area, within which the virgin type could be as small as ten acres. In order to insure permanency, it required sponsoring agencies to demonstrate how the natural area would be preserved, such as through an act of legislation, regulation, will, or recorded instrument of intent. Finally, the committee set as a national policy that several representatives of each virgin type would be sought throughout the known range of the type, not only on a geographic basis but also on environmental factors such as altitude and climate. The committee urged SAF to recognize the need for a complete natural area system, because only by reference to recorded data could foresters view a managed forest in its proper perspective. As of January 1, 1980, SAF had registered nearly 300 areas located in forty-two states and Puerto Rico.

The Federal Committee on Research of Natural Areas was informally established in 1966. This led in 1974, with the assistance and leadership of the National Science Foundation and the Council on Environmental Quality, to the formation of the Federal Committee on Ecological Reserves, involving some nineteen federal agencies as charter members. As of 1980, the committee had reported the establishment of 389 research natural areas, with a total area of approximately 4.4 million acres in forty-six states and one territory. These areas represent important resources for investigators requiring natural areas unaltered by human intervention. In addition, they present vital repositories of genetic information and invaluable components of America's natural heritage.

In 1963, the secretary of the interior established the National Natural Landmarks Program to designate true and representative examples of the nation's natural history and to encourage the preservation of areas that illustrate the ecological and geological character of the United States. Also, the program is designed to enhance the educational and scientific values of the areas thus preserved, to strengthen cultural appreciation of natural history, and to foster a wider interest and concern in the conservation of the nation's natural heritage. By the end of 1979, 460 Natural Landmarks had been designated, of which 46 had been identified as threatened.

FURTHER READING: Robert M. Romancier, "Natural Area Programs," *Journal of Forestry* 72 (Jan. 1974): 37-42.

JOHN F. SHANKLIN

NATURAL RESOURCES COUNCIL OF AMERICA

Soon after the close of World War II, executives of several conservation associations realized a need for a forum where they could meet for discussion and coop-

eration in the attainment of common goals. In 1946, a group of these executives created the Natural Resources Council of America (NRCA). From the original nucleus of nineteen member organizations, the number had grown to forty-seven by 1980.

NRCA is a private, nonprofit group of national and regional organizations concerned with the conservation of natural resources and the environment. In addition to providing a forum for discussion of conservation issues, NRCA gathers and disseminates to its members information about these issues, including information on actions by Congress, the chief executive, and the federal administrative agencies. NRCA does not attempt to influence the policies or activities of its members.

Membership is by written invitation, following an affirmative vote of the members. Each member organization has but one vote. Those eligible for membership qualify as recognized conservation bodies, scientific societies in natural resource fields, and branches or committees of national organizations whose major activities are in conservation.

Since 1948, NRCA has been holding frequent consultations with cabinet secretaries, bureau chiefs, administrators of federal agencies, and legislative branches of government. These consultations are not for lobbying purposes but rather for the free exchange of information and opinion between government officials and council members for mutual understanding and cooperation.

FURTHER READING: Clinton R. Gutermuth, "Origins of the Natural Resource Council of America: A Personal View," *Forest History* 17 (Jan. 1974): 4–17.

HENRY CLEPPER

NATURE CONSERVANCY

Nature Conservancy is a private, nonprofit conservation organization dedicated to protecting the diversity of life on this planet through the preservation of critical habitats and the variety of life they shelter. The organization is an outgrowth of the Committee for the Preservation of Natural Conditions, established in 1917 by the ECOLOGICAL SOCIETY OF AMERICA. The parent body was an organization of scientists interested in the study of plants and animals in relation to their environment. In 1946, this original group and its companion Committee for the Study of Plant and Animal Communities merged to form the Ecologists' Union. The Ecologists' Union became Nature Conservancy in 1950 and was incorporated the following year.

In 1953, after experiments with various methods of natural area preservation, Nature Conservancy un-

Preservation of North Carolina's Great Dismal Swamp was one of Nature Conservancy's major projects. Forest Service Photo.

dertook its first acquisition project. A group of residents of Mianus River Gorge in Westchester County, New York, asked it for affiliation in order to raise money to purchase and manage the gorge. Their local fund-raising efforts repaid a loan from Nature Conservancy's central fund.

Since that first step, the organization has been involved in 3,000 projects, comprising about 1.8 million acres of land located in every state, Canada, the Caribbean, and Latin America. Major conservancy projects have included the Virginia Coast Reserve, Santa Cruz Island, the Ordway Prairie System, the Great Dismal Swamp, and Mashomack Forest. Forest areas protected by the Conservancy range from the white spruce forests in Maine to koa-ohia forests in Hawaii to Lignum Vitae Key in Florida. In 1981, Nature Conservancy received $31.2 million in contributions and completed 226 land conservation projects that included 86,612 acres in thirty-six states.

Nature Conservancy works by three basic means: (1) identifying the land that contains the best examples of all the components of the natural world; (2) protecting natural areas, usually through acquisition by gift or purchase or by assisting and advising gov-ernment or other conservation organizations. The organization is able to purchase land to be held in trust for a public conservation agency. Its protection of natural areas also involves increasing public awareness of the need to safeguard these areas; and (3) managing the largest private sanctuary system in the world (with over 700 Nature Conservancy-owned preserves), using volunteer land stewards and staff.

Nature Conservancy is a membership organization with an elected board of governors. It has a paid professional staff, with national headquarters in Washington, D. C., regional offices in San Francisco, Minneapolis, Boston, and Leesburg, Virginia, and branch offices in twenty-six states. Thirty-four volunteer chapters and one committee are at work in twenty-nine states. By 1981, the organization had 128,529 members.

FURTHER READING: Anne M. Byers, ''The Nature Conservancy: Preserving the Wetlands,'' *Ducks Unlimited* 40 (May/June 1976): 10–15. Robert E. Jenkins, ''International Heritage Programs?,'' *The Nature Conservancy News* 29 (July/Aug. 1979): 24-25. Peter Wood, ''Business-suited Saviors of Nation's Vanishing Birds,'' *Smithsonian* 9 (Dec. 1978): 76-85.

PATRICK F. NOONAN

NAVAL LIVE OAK RESERVES

Except for a small area in Cuba, the natural range of eastern live oak (*Quercus virginiana*) is confined to a narrow coastal belt extending from southern Virginia through the Carolinas and Georgia, where it widens to include all of Florida and then continues as a narrow belt along the Gulf of Mexico into Texas. Part of this natural range lies within the original thirteen states; all of the remainder, except Cuba, came under the United States flag with the Louisiana Purchase (1803), the purchase of Florida (1819), and the annexation of Texas (1845).

Live oak was highly prized for ship construction, particularly naval vessels. A Navy report in 1832 stated that it was "superior in strength, resistance, and hardness, to the celebrated British oak which forms 'the wooden walls' of England. It is, when used for frames, much more durable than that, or even cedar, which the ancients called 'the everlasting wood,' and in some qualities surpasses the teak of India, which is confessedly the best timber for the greatest number of variety of naval purposes that the research of man has yet discovered."

In 1799, Congress appropriated $200,000 for the purchase of live oak lands, but only two small tracts in Georgia were acquired. The Act of March 1, 1817, authorized the secretary of the navy, with approval of the president, to explore the unappropriated lands of the United States that produced live oak and redcedar timber and to select such tracts as he deemed necessary for the Navy. Despite monumental difficulties, these selections were accomplished with reasonable success. Fourteen presidential orders, from October 23, 1830, to December 19, 1860, set aside more than 200,000 acres as timber reserves, which were administered by the Navy.

In 1828, Navy Secretary Southard appointed Henry M. Brackenridge to be superintendent of the Santa Rosa Reserve near Pensacola, Florida. An important assignment was experimentation with methods of propagating live oak. Success could assure future supplies of this vital naval resource. Political shifts altered priorities, and Brackenridge was relieved as superintendent in 1832. The first federal forestry effort was allowed to languish.

Trespass cutting of live oak on public lands became so widespread as to threaten the supply of trees required to assure future needs of the Navy. Accordingly, by a resolution passed February 25, 1832, the House of Representatives asked the secretary of the navy to report on the situation. The report was submitted December 14, 1832, as *Historical Statement of the Use of Live Oak Timber for the Construction of Vessels of the Navy, and Vessels Built with It;— the Quantity on Lands Reserved from Sale by the United States and on Private Lands, and the Necessity for Its Preservation for Future Use*. The report included a tabulated estimate of the number and location of live oak trees of suitable quality and accessibility for naval use. It stressed the probability of large errors in the estimate but nevertheless used the data in detailed calculations to determine whether the indicated supply was sufficient for the Navy's current and future needs. Legislation was recommended to provide more effective enforcement of existing timber trespass laws. Live oak plantations were discussed, and the report recommended that, if such plantations became necessary to provide adequate supplies, "the expense of the kind of cultivation . . . ought not to be permitted to deter us from undertaking it." In conclusion, the secretary predicted "no occasion at this time either to make further purchases on private lands on which this tree grows, or to carry the artificial cultivation of it, on any of the public lands, beyond what has already been attempted."

On March 8–9, 1862, the Merrimac and the Monitor quickly demonstrated that ships of the future would be ships of steel, and the demand for live oak declined abruptly. The secretary of the navy issued a directive on March 21, 1878, revoking most of the live oak reserves, which were returned to the public domain. The last remnant—3,000 acres in Louisiana—was abolished in 1923.

FURTHER READING: Samuel Trask Dana, *Forest and Range Policy* (1956). William F. Keller, "Henry Marie Brackenridge—First United States Forester," *Forest History* 15 (Jan. 1972): 12-23. George S. Kephart, "Live Oak—The Tree with a Past," *American Forests* 77 (June 1972): 36-39, 58-61. Virginia Steele Wood, *Live Oaking: Southern Timber for Tall Ships* (1981).

GEORGE S. KEPHART

NAVAL STORES

The production of naval stores, an industry based on the exploitation of the pine woods for their resinous juices, is one of the oldest industries in North America. English settlers in Virginia made their first exports of tar and pitch to England in 1608. Wooden sailing vessels used large quantities of tar and pitch for waterproofing hulls and decks and preserving the rigging, and the name naval stores has persisted even though current usage has little to do with ships. Through the eighteenth century, naval stores included masts,

Worker dips resin in a Georgia turpentine still, early twentieth century. Forest Service Photo.

spars, hemp, and other articles necessary to shipbuilding, but since the American Revolution the term has applied only to oleoresin and its derivatives. Oleoresin from living pines and its derivatives are called gum naval stores; similar products derived by steam or destructive distillation from lightwood and stumps are known as wood naval stores; and turpentine and rosin by-products of the sulfate process of manufacturing wood pulp are called sulfate naval stores. Tar and pitch are viscous substances obtained from destructive distillation of wood or of crude gum derived from wood, pitch tending to be more or less solid, while tar is relatively fluid. Crude gum (until the twentieth century also referred to as crude turpentine or gum turpentine) is a semifluid oleoresin traditionally bled from living trees. Crude gum may be distilled into liquid spirits of turpentine, leaving a solid residue called rosin. Turpentine and rosin are also produced, together with a mixture of fatty and resin acids known as tall oil, as a by-product of sulfate pulping. The term tall oil derives from the Swedish word *tallolja*, "pine oil." In the United States, however, the name pine oil usually has been reserved for mixtures of terpene alcohols synthesized from turpentine or found as a minor by-product of steam wood distillation. Before the rise of the wood naval stores industry, pine oil referred to pine needle oil, an aromatic product of the steam distillation of needles and young twigs from various conifers.

Gum Naval Stores

Naval stores were produced in all of the original thirteen colonies, but their chief source in the seventeenth century was New England pitch pine *(Pinus rigida)*. After 1700, as the Southern colonies became more settled, production centered on longleaf pine *(Pinus palustris)*, the most prolific yielder of oleoresin. From the southern border of Virginia to Texas in a coastal belt approximately 100 to 150 miles wide, longleaf forests cover more than 130 million acres. After 1925, the industry had to rely more often on second-growth slash pine *(Pinus elliottii)*, which covers a narrower zone from South Carolina to Louisiana.

In the colonial period, the phrase "tar, pitch, and turpentine" indicated the relative importance of naval stores products. Tar was made by burning dead pine wood in an earthen kiln. "Lightwood," downed timber from which the sapwood had rotted away leaving the resin-rich heartwood, was gathered from the ground, laid in a circle ten to thirty feet in diameter and eight to ten feet high, covered with pine boughs and earth, and held in place with a wooden log frame. After the wood was ignited, air holes in the sides of the kiln controlled the draft and permitted the fire to smolder. The heat forced out the resinous matter, which drained through a trench into a pit outside the kiln. There it was dipped and barreled for market. A kiln of sufficient size to produce 100 to 125 barrels of tar required from four to ten days to "run." Pitch was a concentration of tar, obtained by boiling in large kettles.

Crude gum was obtained from the living tree by removing a section of bark, wounding the tree, and collecting the secreted gum for distillation into spirits of turpentine and rosin. Trees were "boxed" by cutting an elliptical hole about eight to twelve inches wide and four to five inches deep in the base of the trunk, thus forming a cavity to receive the resin. The box was "cornered" by taking off the bark in a triangular pattern on each side of the top of the box, creating a "face." The laborer returned once in ten days to cut a new streak on the face with a tool called a hack and to dip the resin from the boxes and pour it into barrels stationed at intervals in the woods. A worker usually chipped and dipped a "crop" of 10,000 faces during a season, with each crop yielding about 150 barrels of gum turpentine. The tree was cultivated in this fashion from April to October and the face advanced up the tree about two feet per year until it reached a height of seven or eight feet. Crude gum obtained from the first year's dipping was called "virgin dip" and yielded the maximum amount of spirits of turpentine and made the finest quality of transparent rosin, called "water white." Gum from the second and later years' dippings yielded less spirits and more rosin, but the latter was of a darker and lower quality. "Scrape," or gum that had adhered to the face of the tree, was removed at the end of the season and was valuable primarily for its rosin content.

In 1705, the British government, eager to free the Royal Navy from dependence on Baltic sources of naval stores, encouraged colonial production with bounties of 4 pounds per ton for tar and pitch and 3 pounds for turpentine—roughly equal to the cost of transpor-

Pine resin can be processed into many useful products, as this photograph taken in the 1930s clearly shows. Forest Service Photo.

tation from America to England. Thus encouraged, Southern colonists increased production. The industry centered first in South Carolina and later in North Carolina, in part due to the availability of the longleaf pine. Naval stores provided a livelihood and a cash crop for small farmers who lived in the pine forests. By the end of the colonial period, North Carolina produced 70 percent of the tar, 20 percent of the pitch, and over 50 percent of the turpentine used in Great Britain—in value 60 percent of all naval stores shipped from the continental colonies.

Deprived of the British bounty after the Revolution, naval stores production in North Carolina declined. The trade was disrupted further by the embargo of 1807 and the protracted wars of the Napoleonic era. The introduction of iron anchor chains during the War of 1812 eliminated much roping and thus required less tar for preservation. Between 1815 and 1830, exports of tar and pitch gradually decreased in comparison with exports of crude gum, spirits of turpentine, and rosin.

During the period 1835 to 1860, new uses for the products brought a major change and expansion of the naval stores industry. Spirits of turpentine became the leading product, widely used as a solvent for caoutchouc in the developing rubber industry. Camphine, a mixture of spirits of turpentine and alcohol, was used extensively in lamps as a more economical substitute for dwindling supplies of whale oil. Rosin, the by-product of the distillation of turpentine, was used in the manufacture of soap and ink and in the sizing of paper for printing. Rosin oils were used in illuminants and lubricants and a wide variety of other products.

Also contributing to the expansion of the industry was the introduction in 1834 of the copper still with an improved coil or worm, which made distilling of crude turpentine a simpler and more profitable undertaking. In colonial times, barrels of crude gum had been floated down the rivers on rafts and exported to England for distillation; after 1835, distillation was conducted in the port towns along the American coast and after 1845 often at forest distilleries. The crude gum was transported by cart to a distillery and heated with a small amount of water in the copper retort in much the same manner in which whiskey was distilled. The volatile vapor passed through the copper worm, which was chilled with cool water from a stream or well, and condensed into spirits of turpentine. The molten rosin left as residue in the bottom of the still was drained into a vat, strained, and barreled for market. The distiller determined when his brew needed additional water or more heat by listening at the worm tail pipe to the sound made by the boiling gum. There was little change in the process until the first decades of the twentieth century.

Near the distillery stood the cooper's shop, where barrels were made for the products. Barrel staves and heading were usually made from white oak and bound with split hickory saplings. Spirits of turpentine barrels, because of the volatile nature of the fluid, had to

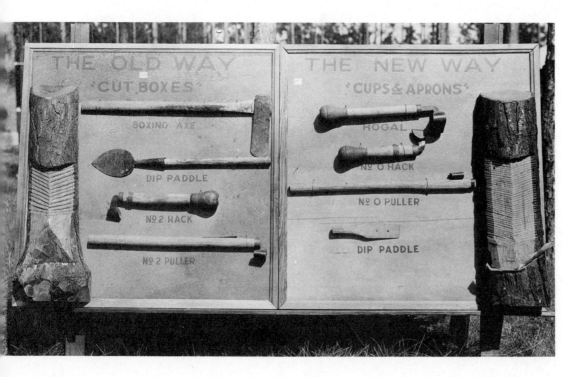

The Forest Service included this photograph in a 1937 report on naval stores. It contrasts the "old" and "new" ways to extract resin from southern pine; the deeper and wider "old" cuts reduced a tree's productive life. Forest Service Photo.

be made with great care, and in the antebellum period they were often purchased in the North as rejected whiskey barrels. Each barrel had to be glued inside to prevent leakage.

The relative weight and bulk of naval stores in proportion to the prices obtained made cheap transportation a necessity if the industry was to return a profit. Wilmington, North Carolina, the chief naval stores port in the antebellum period, after 1836 sponsored railroads radiating north, south, and west, each of which opened up new pinelands. The census of 1840 reported a total production of 619,106 barrels of naval stores in the United States. North Carolina produced over 95 percent of this. No other state supplied even 1 percent of the total.

From its base in the central coastal area around New Bern and Washington, the industry in the 1840s expanded inland along the Cape Fear River. In 1841, Wilmington had only two distilleries; four years later, there were eleven, operating thirty-four stills. The repeal of the British tariff on naval stores in 1845 gave another lift to the industry. The price of turpentine soared from $2.40 to $5.00 per barrel and led many farmers momentarily to abandon agriculture "to get turpentine." Speculation was followed by a market collapse in 1846 and 1847, but expansion continued.

In the 1850s, the naval stores industry was extended to the very limits of North Carolina's pine forests by means of improvements on the Cape Fear River and its tributaries, and by a system of plank roads radiating in all directions from Fayetteville, the head of navigation on the Cape Fear. Many planters moved into the region, purchased or leased timber, and developed large-scale operations employing slave labor. They also transferred the distilling process from the port towns to the forests so that when rosin was depressed in price only the spirits need be shipped.

The North Carolina industry reached its peak around 1855. It was migratory by nature, for the raw material was exhausted after ten or twelve years of exploitation and could not be replaced in a lifetime. The crude and wasteful methods employed by turpentine producers of this period contributed to an early exhaustion of the available naval stores areas in North Carolina and to continued migration of the industry southward. The turpentine woods were also victims of frequent fires as the faces of the chipped trees were easily ignited in an age when light burning of the woods each spring was a common practice. Moreover, a severe pine borer epidemic in the state in 1848 and 1849 destroyed hundreds of thousands of longleaf pines. Even when timber bled for naval stores escaped decay, fire, and insects, nineteenth-century lumbermen considered it worthless for lumber and billions of board feet were allowed to waste on the stump.

There were sporadic efforts at turpentine production in South Carolina and along the Savannah and Altamaha rivers of Georgia and the Palatka and Apalachicola regions of Florida, but the lower South did not become actively interested in turpentine production until the middle 1850s, when the chief development was around Mobile, Alabama. Throughout the antebellum period, North Carolina—the "Tar Heel State"—remained the largest producer of naval stores. The census of 1860 reported the total value of crude and distilled turpentine produced in the South as $7,409,745. Of this value, over 70 percent was produced in North Carolina, with South Carolina second and Alabama third. Counting naval stores products of all types, the total value of the industry in 1860 was approximately $12,000,000—nearly three-quarters the value of the lumber produced in the South.

The Civil War had a disastrous effect on the industry in North Carolina, and although it revived after the war, the main development was in states farther south. Many Carolinians migrated to Georgia, Florida, and Alabama and opened turpentine plantations in the virtually untouched stands of longleaf pine. During this relocation, the industry underwent a major change. Instead of production essentially by small farmers as in North Carolina, factorage houses were formed in the port towns of Savannah, Brunswick, Jacksonville, Pensacola, and later Mobile and New Orleans. These firms acquired control of large tracts of timber, either by lease or purchase, and controlled the naval stores industry from the top. The timber tracts were then subleased to individual operators and all the necessary equipment and supplies provided on credit.

Experienced operators migrated south, often bringing with them the necessary labor force. They established new communities in the pinewoods, complete with commissary, church, and school, all centered around the distillery. The naval stores products were forwarded to the factor to repay debts incurred during the year. North Carolina methods of boxing, chipping, dipping, and distilling prevailed for the next generation. During the half-century from 1870 to 1920, the industry relentlessly exploited the pine region of the lower South until the virgin stands of longleaf were consumed. South Carolina became the leading state in reported production in 1879; Georgia in 1889; and Florida in 1909.

Seeking to avoid the destruction of the Southern pine forest by the turpentine farmers, the U. S. Division of Forestry in 1892 sponsored a study of European and American naval stores practices, conducted by

Charles Mohr. In the mid-1890s, William Willard Ashe of the North Carolina Geological Survey, among others, carried out experiments with adaptations of French cup-and-gutter systems to replace the traditional American boxing methods of gathering oleoresin. The industry itself underwent no change, however, until after 1901 when Charles H. HERTY, working under the sponsorship of the U. S. Division of Forestry, developed a clay cup with a metal trough or apron to guide the resin from the face into the cup. Later, metal cups (and, many years later, plastic ones) were substituted for clay. Use of the Herty cup system did not predominate until 1908 and 1909, and then only because the factors who controlled the trade forced it upon the operators. The cup was a mixed blessing. It provided more oleoresin of finer quality, with less damage to the tree, but it did not diminish damage by facing and deep chipping. It also led producers, eager to extract maximum profit from their three- or four-year lease, to tap every tree capable of holding a cup, a practice that increased the number of young trees destroyed by exhaustion, wind, and fire. Ultimately, cupping led to overproduction with a corresponding decline in price. The peak year of gum naval stores production in the United States, 1908 to 1909, saw a total of 750,000 50-gallon barrels of spirits of turpentine and 2.5 million 500-pound barrels of rosin produced.

Further experiments by Herty led to standards for the depth and width of the gash on the tree and a limit of one cup per tree ten inches in diameter or above. The result was increased yield and a corresponding reduction in loss of timber. This naval stores "revolution" was continued by Fletcher P. Veitch of the Bureau of Chemistry of the DEPARTMENT OF AGRICULTURE. By 1911, Veitch had standardized methods for testing turpentine and had developed standards for using colored glass to grade rosin. Nevertheless, operators were slow to adopt these demonstrated improvements in methods and products except when forced to do so. The inefficient and destructive practices of the pioneer woodsmen continued to threaten the ultimate extinction of the industry. The decline in the southern pine available for turpentining led the U. S. FOREST SERVICE to experiment with the production of naval stores from ponderosa and other western pines in 1911 and 1912. About 1914, Eloise Gerry, a scientist studying microscopic wood structure at the Forest Products Laboratory, began research on oleoresin production. Gerry's investigations were to culminate eventually in the publication of the comprehensive *Naval Stores Handbook* (1935).

World War I delayed reform, and in the aftermath of the war and the economic recession of 1919 the gum naval stores industry faced a number of serious challenges: a rapidly dwindling supply of raw material, inefficient methods of gathering and distilling, unstable markets, increasing competition from thinners and dryers in the developing petroleum and coal tar industries, and competition from wood naval stores produced by steam distillation of old longleaf pine stumps.

The SOUTHERN FORESTRY CONGRESS, organized in 1917 by two North Carolinians, Joseph Hyde Pratt, state geologist, and John S. Holmes, state forester, attempted to solve some of these problems. The congress met annually through the 1920s and slowly awakened the government, the public, and especially turpentine and timber operators to the hazards which careless methods of naval stores and lumber operations posed to the longevity of the industry. The congress devoted its attention to obtaining a national forest policy, the creation of additional national forests, reforestation, elimination of annual woods burnings, more scientific methods of naval stores production, the creation of a Pine Institute, and increased federal appropriations for these purposes. It also helped achieve passage of the CLARKE-MCNARY ACT of 1924.

In 1936, the small producers formed the American Turpentine Farmers Association (ATFA). Judge Harley Langdale, gum producer of Valdosta, Georgia, served as ATFA's president until 1966. The organization provided information on prices, production, and improved methods, and lobbied in the national capital on behalf of producers. Under ATFA prodding, Congress in 1936 established a Naval Stores Conservation Program administered by the Forest Service for the Department of Agriculture. Under this program, cost-sharing payments were made to producers of gum naval stores who voluntarily followed specified improved woods practices.

Federal naval stores research was expanded by the establishment in 1932 at Olustee, Florida, of the Naval Stores Research Station under the Bureau of Chemistry and Soils of the Department of Agriculture. This facility sought new processes, products, and outlets for naval stores. It continued under the Agricultural Research Service after 1953 until it was terminated for economic reasons twenty years later. The Forest Service operated an experimental forest at Olustee after 1933 and in 1963 established a Naval Stores and Timber Production Laboratory there.

When the Olustee Naval Stores Research Station opened, about 1,300 small backwoods fire stills were operating with the time-honored method of "sounding the still." The Olustee Station built a model still and promoted the use of controlled temperatures developed by S. Neal in 1906. The improved fire stills were replaced eventually by the so-called Olustee Process, wherein crude gum was brought to central distilleries and washed and cleaned before distillation. The Glidden Company built the first central processing and distillation plant in 1936 in Jacksonville, Florida. By 1948, thirty such plants strategically placed through the naval stores region processed 80 percent of the crude gum. Central distillation also fostered a cleaner, more uniform product, better packaging, and more economical and convenient distribution. It ended a century of domination by the large-scale operators who had dispersed distilling to the woods after 1840. With the growth of central distilleries, the independent turpentine farmer again became an important source of crude gum. In 1947, of 10,000 producers of gum turpentine, more than 7,000 were small farmers who worked less than one crop of turpentine faces, although more than half the gum still came from large producers.

Immediately after World War II, the scarcity and high cost of labor encouraged operators to adopt the practice of chipping shallow, narrow faces treated with chemicals to stimulate the flow of gum. The Olustee Station, following the lead of researchers in Germany and Russia, had been experimenting with this technique since 1936. By removing the bark and a very light portion of the wood and spraying the exposed surface with a solution of sulfuric acid, a 50 to 100 percent increase in resin yield was obtained during the first week after chipping and an above average yield for the next two weeks. Faces chipped and treated at biweekly intervals cut labor costs in half while increasing yield. The process prolonged the life of the face, causing less damage to the tree, and left the timber "in the round" for later use as lumber. This method helped extend the life of the gum naval stores industry for another twenty-five years. During the 1950s, there were further improvements in tools, cups, and aprons; the introduction of doubleheaded nails for hanging and raising cups; and eventually the stapling of cups to the tree. Nevertheless, labor costs remained excessive, and gradually many of the larger producers were eliminated. By 1952, their contribution had declined from three-fourths of total production to only one-third. Naval stores had again become the domain of the part-time farmer. Of 8,863 producers in 1952, 89 percent worked only one crop of faces.

Despite efforts at a more scientific approach, mechanization, and improved forest practices, the gum naval stores industry waned after 1962. Following World War I, it had encountered competition from wood naval stores; after World War II, it had to compete against sulfate naval stores, produced inexpensively as a by-product from the manufacture of paper. From a postwar production peak of 50 million pounds in 1962, gum naval stores declined to only 2.5 million pounds in 1977. In the two decades from 1952 to 1972, the production of naval stores in fact became an adjunct of the chemical industry. In this environment, gum naval stores was a "horse-and-buggy" industry trying to survive in the space age. Recognition of this fundamental change was evidenced when the government liquidated its stocks of naval stores over a five-year period beginning in 1967, terminated the Naval Stores Conservation Program in 1972, and closed the Agricultural Research Service's Olustee Station in 1973.

Wood Naval Stores

The production of wood naval stores is actually the oldest aspect of the industry. Originally, tar was extracted by heating wood in earthen kilns. Since the late nineteenth century, southern pine wood has been destructively distilled in iron or concrete retorts for the manufacture of tar, turpentine, and CHARCOAL, all often low in quality.

Interest in wood distillation revived when gum naval stores production peaked and producers saw an alternate source in the millions of longleaf pine stumps left from logging operations. After the non-resinous sapwood had rotted away from old-growth stumps, the remaining heartwood yielded up to 25 percent oleoresin (compared with less than 10 percent oleoesin in pine logs). The steam distillation process first developed by Homer T. Yaryan has been much more important for the naval stores industry than dry distillation. Yaryan, a colorful former Treasury agent and the inventor of steam central heating, built the earliest steam-and-solvent wood extraction plant in Gulfport, Mississippi, in 1909. At first, the products were deemed inferior to gum naval stores in quality, color, and odor, but chemical research and improvements in processing after World War I enabled distilled wood products to compete successfully with gum products. Stumps originally were blasted from the ground but later extracted by pullers mounted on crawler tractors. Fields were leased for clearing by companies with trained crews. The stumps were transported on railroad cars to processing plants where they were put through a shredder. The resulting chips were placed in a vertical steel tank holding from ten to thirty tons. Originally, the chips were steamed to drive off the volatile oils and then treated with a solvent of hot petroleum naptha to extract the rosin. In the 1950s, the steam process was eliminated and the turpentine, rosin, and pine oils were extracted simultaneously by a solvent. The product was then fractionally distilled to separate the turpentine from other terpenes and from pine oil, leaving a residue of crude rosin. By 1950, there were fourteen steam-and-solvent extraction plants operating in five southern states from Georgia to Louisiana. One of the largest operators was the Hercules Powder Company, which had acquired the Yaryan Company in 1920. Production reached a post-World War II peak in 1959–1960, with 62 million pounds of turpentine and 640 million pounds of resin. Subsequently, the dwindling supply of old-growth longleaf pine stumps and the growing competition from sulfate naval stores caused a steady decline in production. Only four extraction plants remained in the late 1970s.

About that time, the wood naval stores industry showed new signs of life. Stumps from longleaf and slash pines less than 100 years of age ordinarily do not contain enough resin to make extraction economical, but in 1973 the Forest Service's Naval Stores and Timber Production Laboratory discovered a chemical process to stimulate oleoresin production. Subsequently developed and marketed by Hercules under the name Pinex, this treatment made it commercially practical to extract naval stores from freshly cut second-growth stumps which had been injected with a dilute solution of the herbicide paraquat two years before timber harvest. The process may be used with any species of conifer.

Sulfate Naval Stores

The manufacture of sulfate naval stores is a recent development in the centuries-old naval stores industry. The source is various species of pine including jack pine and eastern white pine but principally southern yellow pine used in the sulfate (sometimes called kraft) process of manufacturing wood pulp. When a mass of wood chips is in the process of being cooked to extract the cellulose for paper, the pressure on the cooking vessel must be relieved at intervals by drawing off the volatile gases. When condensed, these gases become sulfate turpentine. Because sulfate turpentine has a disagreeable odor, it must be refined further to remove the sulfurous compounds, but because it is produced as a by-product of paper manufacturing, it can be sold more cheaply than gum turpentine.

The more valuable product, however, is the crude tall oil or liquid rosin occurring as a sodium "soap," a frothy mass floating on top of the spent cooking liquor. Acidification of the soap releases fatty and resinous acids which constitute the bulk of the original crude. Tall oil fatty acids are used in a variety of industrial processes. Solid rosin and pitch are also obtained from crude tall oil.

Tall oil was first produced in Skutskar, Sweden, in 1901, but it was not until 1949 that Arizona Chemical Company, a subsidiary of American Cyanamid Company and International Paper Company, after more than a decade of research, achieved a fractional distillation process for separating crude tall oil into its components. With this development the naval stores industry entered a new phase. In the next two decades, it evolved from an industry producing primarily turpentine and rosin into a multifaceted branch of the chemical industry extracting chemicals from pine wood for a wide variety of industrial uses. The fatty acids separated are used in alkyd paints, varnishes, textiles, detergents, and soaps. The tall oil rosin has been used in paints, adhesives, linoleum and oil cloth, printing inks and paper size, metallic dryers, disinfectants and cleansers, and rubber chemicals and waterproofing agents.

Eight other companies entered the field in the years following, and in the peak year of 1973, tall oil rosin equaled 440 million pounds. Crude sulfate turpentine reached a peak of 170 million pounds in 1969. The gum naval stores industry and the wood naval stores industry were unable to compete. Total production of all forms of naval stores reached a post-World War II peak for rosin in 1963 with 1.14 billion pounds, and for turpentine in 1965 with 250 million pounds. Since 1973, production of naval stores has declined. The United States remains, however, the world's largest producer.

The Marketing of Naval Stores

In colonial times and until about 1835, naval stores were exported through commission merchants for processing and use abroad. From 1835 until the Civil War, naval stores were more often distilled locally and the spirits and various grades of rosin were marketed through factors and commission merchants in port towns or shipped to northern ports, principally New York, for export abroad. New York and London merchants controlled the prices. From the Civil War until 1936, the trade was controlled by the factors in Savannah and other southern coastal cities, who financed operations in the woods and received produce in payment for credit extended. Savannah was the pre-eminent naval stores market from 1880 until about 1920. From its formation in 1882 as the Savannah Cotton and Naval Stores Exchange, the Savannah Board of Trade established the daily price of naval stores until 1950 when the government intervened and prohibited it from announcing prices. Thereafter, the Department of Agriculture collected and reported statistics and prices on naval stores. The government had previously intervened in 1934 when it recognized processed naval stores as a commodity and provided a support price. From 1946 to 1972 under the Agricultural Marketing Act, the government purchased and stored naval stores products. While the support price initially benefited the gum producers, it ultimately encouraged the search for cheaper products through the development of wood and sulfate naval stores, which eventually almost eliminated gum naval stores from the market.

Various levels of government also played a role in quality control. The New York Port Authority established standards for rosin grades after 1869 for all ports other than southern ports. These standards were superseded by federal government standards after 1911. The Savannah Board of Trade established the office of supervising inspector of naval stores in 1894 and the states of Florida and Georgia established state supervising inspectors in 1903. The federal government began testing naval stores products under the authority of the Pure Food and Drug Act of 1906 and then developed standards for rosin grading. The Naval Stores Inspection Act of 1923 again specified minimum standards and required federal inspection of all naval stores exported.

FURTHER READING: Thomas Gamble, ed., *Naval Stores: History, Production, Distribution, and Consumption* (1921), includes essays on many aspects of its subject. Exports during the colonial period are covered in Joseph J. Malone, *Pine Trees and Politics* (1963). For the antebellum South, see Percival Perry, "The Naval Stores Industry in the Old South, 1790–1860," *Journal of Southern History* 34 (Nov. 1968): 509-526. Among studies limited to particular states are C. C. Crittenden, *The Commerce of North Carolina, 1763–1789* (1936); G. Melvin Herndon, "Naval Stores in Colonial Georgia," *Georgia Historical Quarterly* 52 (Dec. 1968): 426-433; Clifton Paisley, "Wade Leonard, Florida Naval Stores Operator," *Florida Historical Quarterly* 51 (Apr. 1973): 381-400; Jeffrey R. Dobson and Roy Doyon, "Expansion of the Pine Oleoresin Industry in Georgia, 1842 to ca. 1900," *Western Georgia College Studies in the Social Sciences* 18 (June 1979): 43-57; and Nollie Hickman, *Mississippi Harvest* (1962), pp. 330-358. Statements influential in the history of the industry include U.S. Department of Agriculture, *Report of the Chief of the Division of Forestry for 1892* (1893), pp. 330-358; Charles H. Herty, *A New Method of Turpentine Orcharding*, U. S. Bureau of Forestry, Bulletin No. 40 (1903); and A. W. Schorger and H. S. Betts, *The Naval Stores Industry*, U. S. Department of Agriculture, Bulletin No. 229 (1915). Recent developments are examined in Peter Koch, *Utilization of the Southern Pines*, Agriculture Handbook No. 420, vol. 2 (1972), pp. 1476–1492, and Duane F. Zinkel, "Turpentine,

Rosin, and Fatty Acids from Conifers," in I. S. Goldstein, ed., *Organic Chemicals from Biomass* (1981). Articles of historical value frequently appear in *Naval Stores Review*, published since 1890.

PERCIVAL PERRY

NEBRASKA FORESTS

Located in a transitional area of prairie-plains, Nebraska has two native forest types. Along the Missouri River in eastern Nebraska and along the Platte and other rivers traversing the state are woodlands of cottonwood, elm, ash, oak, and other eastern hardwoods. On the Pine Ridge in the northwest, in a separate tract along the Niobrara, and in the semimountainous southwest are stands of ponderosa pine.

Settlement in the nineteenth century eliminated much wood and wildlife, but Nebraskans came to pride themselves on tree-planting efforts. The first ARBOR DAY was proclaimed in Nebraska in 1872. However, the state's first major afforestation project dates from 1902 with the federal designation of forest reserves in the sandhills of central Nebraska. In 1908, these lands became the Nebraska National Forest, the only wholly man-made woodland in the national forest system. The U. S. FOREST SERVICE eventually planted 300,000 acres of trees, although a 1965 fire destroyed over one-third of them. The Nebraska and the Samuel R. McKelvie National Forest, which was separated from the Nebraska in 1971, include 275,021 acres of federal land. The most successful aspect of the national forests has been the Bessey Nursery, which carried on planting experiments and provided seedlings for tree-planting projects on the Great Plains.

Starting in 1910, the private Fontenelle Forest Association preserved some wooded tracts along the Missouri River. Not until 1921, with the first state park at Chadron, was any protection afforded the Pine Ridge, which had been cut over between the 1870s and 1890s. During the Depression, the CIVILIAN CONSERVATION CORPS carried out the Shelterbelt Project headquartered in Lincoln, Nebraska, and planted 4,168 miles of windbreaks on nearly 7,000 farms. Private and federal efforts also resulted in saving whooping crane habitats in the Platte Valley.

The Game, Forestation, and Parks Commission, which dates from 1929, has been the major state agency concerned with conservation. By 1980, the state parks and recreation areas included 11,500 acres of commercially valuable forestlands.

In 1977, about 28.7 million board feet of lumber was being produced annually in Nebraska. Seventy-five

Farmers in Johnson County, Nebraska, are cutting firewood with a circular saw that is powered by the automobile, 1935. American Forest Institute Photo.

percent of it was cottonwood, followed by ponderosa pine (15 percent) and mixed hardwoods (10 percent). The main product of the larger mills was pallet stock and crating material. These goods accounted for 65 percent of the lumber sawed.

Throughout Nebraska's history, water, wood, and wildlife resources have been secondary to farming and grazing interests. As a result, wooded and wildlife areas continue to decrease as more land is cultivated and irrigation increases with little public regulation. A 1955 survey found 1,072,800 acres of forestland of which 1,050,400 ranked as commercially valuable. By 1977, the total forestland had declined slightly to 1,029,000 acres, or about 2 percent of the land area of the state, while land classified as commercial forest measured only 789,000 acres.

FURTHER READING: James C. Olson, "Arbor Day: A Pioneer Expression of Concern for the Environment," *Nebraska History* 53 (Spring 1972): 1-13. Richard A. Overfield, "Trees for the Great Plains: Charles E. Bessey and Forestry," *Journal of Forest History* 23 (Jan. 1979): 18-31. Raymond J. Pool, "Fifty Years on the Nebraska National Forest," *Nebraska History* 34 (Sept. 1953): 138–179. Burton J. Williams, "Trees But No Timber: The Nebraska Prelude to the Timber Culture Act," *Nebraska History* 53 (Spring 1972): 77-86.

RICHARD A. OVERFIELD

NEVADA FORESTS

Nevada's mountains and valleys alternate to form a rugged washboard topography. Although the valleys are mainly desert rangelands, many of the state's 314 mountain ranges support tree cover. Although 17 percent (12 million acres) of the state is classified as forestland, most is noncommercial and better termed as woodland. Singleleaf pinyon and Utah juniper, either singly or in combination, cover 99 percent of the forestlands and are characteristic of the Great Basin. In the extreme western part of the state, the Sierran forest extends into Nevada. This commercial forest consists mainly of Jeffrey and ponderosa pines and, at higher elevations, of red and white fir. Further east, both north and south, there are high-elevation stands of limber, bristlecone, and whitebark pines, white and subalpine firs, as well as Douglas-fir and Engelmann spruce. Throughout the state, pinyon-juniper woodlands occur at intermediate elevations. Mountain streams are often bordered by alder, aspen, willow, or cottonwood; the latter two species extend into the valley floors along the larger streams.

Although a waterpowered sawmill was established at Genoa in the Carson Valley in the early 1850s, large-scale exploitation of Nevada's forests came only after discovery of gold in the Comstock Lode in 1859. By the late 1870s, accessible nearby forests had been practically exhausted for mine timbers, lumber, and smelter fuel. Sawmilling started at Lake Tahoe in 1861. Supplying Carson City and Virginia City through a system of railroads and flumes, the Bliss mill at Lake Tahoe continued operation as Nevada's largest lumber producer until the end of the century. The mining boom also resulted in the extensive cutting of the pinyon-juniper woodlands, which were used to provide fuelwood and to make CHARCOAL for use in smelters as late as the 1920s.

In 1869, Nevada had eighteen mills sawing 35 million board feet of timber annually. Ten years later, the state's nine mills cut less than 22 million board feet. After reaching a low of less than 300,000 board feet in 1946, annual lumber production in Nevada returned in 1960 to 33 million board feet, most of the lumber being sawn from second-growth timber. Whereas lumber production reported in the nineteenth century had come almost entirely from Jeffrey and ponderosa pines, over half of the 1960 figure was comprised of white and red fir.

About 86 percent of Nevada's lands are federally owned. Between 1906 and 1911, extensive areas were withdrawn as national forests. National forests in the state in 1980 totaled over 5.1 million acres of federal land and seven federal wildlife refuges and game ranges cover another 2.85 million acres. There are more than 6 million acres of pinyon-juniper woodlands administered by the BUREAU OF LAND MANAGEMENT.

In 1871, the state legislature passed an act to provide protection to timbered lands. The surveyor-general was designated in 1932 by the state legislature to secure federal fire protection funds for Nevada's forest and watershed areas under the 1924 CLARKE-MCNARY ACT. In 1955, Nevada passed a forest practices act to regulate the cutting of timber and CHRISTMAS TREES, and a year later the state established the State Tree Nursery. In 1957, the legislature provided for a Department of Conservation and Natural Resources and, within it, the Division of Forestry.

During the 1920s, Nevada began acquiring a state park system. In 1957, the state established the Sand Harbor Park, the first park on the Nevada side of Lake Tahoe. Ten years later, 13,000 acres were purchased from a private landowner to give further protection to the forests surrounding Lake Tahoe.

FURTHER READING: Donald J. Pisani, "Lost Park Land: Lumbering and Park Proposals in the Tahoe-Truckee Basin," *Journal of Forest History* 21 (Jan. 1977): 5–17. Douglas H. Strong, "Preservation Efforts at Lake Tahoe, 1880 to 1980," *Journal of Forest History* 25 (Apr. 1981): 78-97. James A. Young and Jerry D. Budy, "Historical Use of Nevada's Pinyon-Juniper Woodlands," *Journal of Forest History* 23 (July 1979): 112–131.

JERRY D. BUDY

NEWELL, FREDERICK HAYNES
(1862–1932)

Born in Bradford, Pennsylvania, on March 5, 1862, Frederick Newell was educated in engineering at the Massachusetts Institute of Technology and spent his early career in petroleum work. In 1888, he joined the U.S. GEOLOGICAL SURVEY (USGS) and became a protégé of the agency's director, John Wesley Powell. At the age of twenty-seven, Newell was appointed chief of USGS's Hydrographic Branch which conducted surveys of the water resources in the western United States.

Newell and his colleagues helped to fashion a multi-ple-purpose philosophy of water conservation and utilization—the coordination of all uses, including navigation, irrigation, power, and flood control. In the 1890s, he worked closely with Congressman (later Senator) Francis G. Newlands of Nevada, George H. Maxwell of the National Reclamation Association, and other conservationists to promote a federal reclamation program that was put into effect by Newlands's 1902 Reclamation Act. Newell was then selected to head the newly created Reclamation Service.

Under Newell's leadership, the service became the world's foremost designer and builder of water storage and transmission structures. By 1914, its programs consisted of 100 dams, 25 miles of tunnels, 13,000 miles of canals, and other facilities that served 20,000 farms. The service Newell led was dedicated to agricultural settlement and enforcement of the family farm limitation in reclamation law. Despite the nonpareil success of reclamation engineering, many of the project settlers experienced great hardships due to speculation, poor planning, soaring construction costs, and low crop prices. Complaints about these problems led Secretary of the Interior Franklin K. Lane to relieve Newell of the position of director in 1914 and dismiss him from the service in 1915. Between 1915 and 1919, Newell served as chairman of the civil engineering department of the University of Illinois. From 1924 until his death in 1932, he was engaged in consulting engineering work.

Newell was a strong upholder of conservation ideals and his professional concerns were virtually boundless. He was the first secretary of the National Geographic Society and the first corresponding secretary of the AMERICAN FORESTRY ASSOCIATION. Throughout his life, he worked tirelessly to arouse public interest in the conservation of water and other natural resources. He was a prolific author and published ten books on water-related topics. He died on July 5, 1932.

FURTHER READING: Michael C. Robinson, "Frederick Haynes Newell," *APWA Reporter* 47 (Mar. 1980): 6-7.

MICHAEL C. ROBINSON

NEW HAMPSHIRE FORESTS

The precolonial forests of New Hampshire were the result of invasion and succession following the Ice Age. Reforestation was more rapid and complete on the fertile glacial tills and loams and less advanced on sandy plains and steep mountain slopes. New Hampshire was entirely forested aside from openings caused by bogs, sand deposits near the coast, fires, windfall, and burns made by Indians to improve hunting. The southern two-thirds of the state was covered with a mixture of hardwoods (such as oak, ash, beech, and maple) and hemlock, with an occasional white pine. In the north, hardwoods consisted of beech, birch, and maple, while the hemlock was replaced by red spruce. Higher elevations were occupied by spruce, balsam fir, and birch.

The first European to see the New Hampshire coast was Captain John Smith. Soon after Smith's arrival in 1614, settlements were established near the mouth of the Piscataqua River. Since lands in New Hampshire were less suitable for farming, particularly in the mountainous northern region, settlers turned to logging, along with trapping and fishing. Colonists exported timber as well as finished products such as tools, furniture, and woodenware. In the seventeenth and eighteenth centuries, white pine, used in the shipbuilding industry, was the colony's greatest resource.

During the nineteenth century, extensive lumbering operations developed in the state. Huge rafts carried pine and later spruce down the Connecticut and Androscoggin rivers. White pine, which had been reserved during the colonial period for the Royal Navy, was rapidly depleted by the large sawmills, and lumbermen turned to the virgin spruce in the White Mountains. Lumber production in New Hampshire peaked in 1900, when the mills sawed 526 million board feet. Over half of it was white pine, about a third was spruce.

In the northern river valleys, fires often followed the cutting, and hardwoods invaded the cleared areas. While hardwoods thus replaced pine in the north, the reverse was happening in the more extensively cleared southern region of the state. As farmlands were abandoned because of western competition, the fields and pastures seeded in to white pine and occasionally spruce, while grazing kept hardwoods in check. This "pasture pine" encroached where the original forest had been hardwood. Hardwood seedlings, however, found a congenial habitat beneath the maturing pine and when the pine crop was clearcut, mostly by hundreds of small steam mills moving from one lot to another, the hardwoods reoccupied their ancestral home. The forest cover, which had been reduced to 50 percent of New Hampshire's almost 5.8 million land acres in 1850, by the 1970s occupied 88 percent of the state.

Toward the end of the nineteenth century, the PULP AND PAPER INDUSTRY dominated the north. Initially, the paper companies used exclusively spruce and fir and some larch. Not until the 1920s did hardwoods become a raw material for pulp. Other New Hampshire forest industries included shingles, cooperage, bobbin stock, lath, woodenware, and agricultural implements. More recently, veneer has been made from yellow birch and other hardwoods.

At the end of the nineteenth century, concentration of landownership, forest depletion through wasteful cutting, and disastrous forest fires in cutover areas spurred a movement toward conservation. A number of farsighted pioneers saw the need to control forest fires, restrain wasteful cutting, establish forest reserves, and preserve New Hampshire's scenic natural features. Federal and state programs, along with private efforts, accomplished these results.

Although not the first voice to be heard, Joseph B. Walker deserves the title of "father of forestry" in New Hampshire. Walker's efforts resulted in the creation of a forestry commission in the spring of 1881. Walker, who frequently served as chairman, wrote most of the commission's reports. His son, Joseph T. Walker, became the first secretary of the Society for the Protection of New Hampshire Forests, founded in 1901 by Governor Frank W. Rollins. Philip W. Ayres, the society's first forester, played an important role in securing congressional enactment of the WEEKS ACT in 1911, which authorized the purchase of lands for national forests in the East, provided that they protect navigable streams. The act's author was another New Hampshire native, John W. Weeks, a representative (and later senator) from Massachusetts. Under the Weeks Act, the government began an acquisition program that made it the largest single landowner in New Hampshire. The White Mountain National Forest, established in 1918, and the White Mountain Purchase Unit together covered 814,387 acres in 1979, and 694,169 acres of the total were federally owned.

The society's greatest contribution to state forestry was the promotion of an act of 1909 that established the State Forestry Department, designated a state forester, and created a system of fire wardens. The Forestry Department fell under the supervision of the Forestry Commission, a volunteer citizen organization. The department received cooperation from the New Hampshire Timberland Owners Association, a private group of large holders founded in 1910 with W. R. Brown, chairman of the Forestry Commission, as its president.

Gifts of land to the State of New Hampshire for parks and forestry purposes began early in the twentieth century. The state, aided by private and federal funds, began purchasing the great notches and steep valleys of the local mountains. Philip Ayres mounted a nationwide campaign to raise money to match state appropriations for acquisition of Franconia Notch, which became New Hampshire's first state park in 1925. Later, Crawford and Dixville Notches, Mount Monadnock, Mount Kearsarge, and Sandwich Notch were added to the public trust. The Society for the Protection of New Hampshire Forests and its advocate Ayres were instrumental in each of these state purchases, as well as in federal forestland acquisitions.

As in much of the East, the pattern of private ownership in New Hampshire consists of thousands of small woodlots, a few large holdings by paper companies, and a few sizable tracts held for purposes other than forest production. The traditional farm woodlot provides firewood, timber, maple sugar and syrup, Christmas trees, and many other economic benefits. A revival of interest in woodlots has been stimulated by the Tree Farm Program, the county foresters, and a number of experienced consulting foresters who coordinate timber sales for small landowners. The forest industries during the 1970s controlled 947,000 acres of commercial forest. A total of 3.2 million acres was held by private owners of less than 5,000 acres each.

Animal populations have been affected by the changing uses and composition of the forests. The reduction of dense virgin forests has aided many species of wildlife which find more food on CUTOVER LANDS. Hence deer, once scarce in the north because of wolves and limited forage, have become common. Snowshoe hare and raccoon have also become more abundant, but mammals such as the wolf, cougar, lynx, marten, and woodland caribou are believed extinct in the state. Until recently, the state offered a $20 bounty on bobcat, which has now become an endangered species. Moose and fisher, which were once eliminated from the forests of New Hampshire, have returned. Beaver are now so numerous that their dams destroy much timber and rare plants. Black bear, which carried a $5 bounty for many decades, is now considered a game animal. Ruffed grouse and migratory ducks are common game birds, and wild turkey has been introduced. Brook, rainbow, and lake trout and landlocked salmon are found in cold lakes and brooks. Bass and pickerel flourish in warmer waters.

FURTHER READING: H. I. Baldwin, *Forestry in New England* (1942). W. R. Brown, *Our Forest Heritage: A History of Forestry and Recreation in New Hampshire* (1958). P. E. Bruns, *A New Hampshire Everlasting and Unfallen* (1969) gives the history of the Society for Protection of New Hampshire Forests. Stewart H. Holbrook, *Yankee Loggers: A Recollection of Woodsmen, Cooks, and River Drivers* (1961). Robert E. Pike, *Tall Trees, Tough Men* (1967). David E. Van Deventer, *Emergence of Provincial New Hampshire, 1623–1741* (1976).

HENRY IVES BALDWIN

NEW HAMPSHIRE STATE FORESTRY

Viewing the forest as an obstacle to settlement, the New Hampshire legislature in 1831 began selling the state's timberlands for as little as six cents per acre. In 1867, all the state's public lands had been sold. By that time, agriculture had begun to decline, and a growing forest industry was looked to as a means of mitigating some of the economic losses. Soon, an emerging landscape scalped of its vegetation and scarred by fire provoked a shift in public attitude from exploitation of the forest to conservation.

The legislature cautiously responded by authorizing a temporary commission of inquiry in 1881. The life of this commission was extended in 1883, 1885, and 1891. Its report for 1891 highlighted three major areas of both immediate and long-range concern to the protection of New Hampshire's forests: fire protection, landownership, and taxation. Based on this report, the legislature in 1893 appointed the permanent New Hampshire Forestry Commission and charged it with guiding the development of forest policy, institutions, and regulations. In the same year, the legislature authorized the appointment of town selectmen or county commissioners as fire wardens. Although this action recognized the need for fire protection, its effect was limited; towns were still responsible for all costs, and no attempt was made to identify and eliminate the cause of fires.

In the private sector, response to fire devastation was not so cautious. In 1901, the Society for the Protection of New Hampshire Forests was organized to encourage the conservation efforts of the state. The society promoted legislation relating to improvements in fire detection and extinguishing techniques and to cost sharing between local and state governments. The Forestry Act of 1909, the most significant development in the history of New Hampshire state forestry institutions, took great strides toward accomplishing fire protection. It provided for a state forester to act as chief fire warden, required spark controls for portable sawmills, and increased the number of fire wardens and lookout towers. It created a forestry department for education, research, and public information, and a state nursery to provide stock for planting. Forest research was launched by private gifts to the state of a $200,000 trust fund and a 370-acre tract of woodland. In 1910, a group of landowners in the northern part of the state organized the New Hampshire Timberland Owners Association in order to augment the efforts of the state in fire protection. Finally, with the passage of the Slash Removal Law in 1915, the threat of forest fire as a major destructive force was significantly reduced.

Many individuals feared that the forests would be adequately protected only under public ownership, however. The Society for the Protection of New Hampshire Forests pressed for the creation of a federal forest reservation in the White Mountains. In

Franconia Notch, with its famous rock outcrop, Old Man of the Mountains, became New Hampshire's first state park in 1925. American Forest Institute Photo.

1903, the legislature responded with an enabling act, but a bill to create a national reservation there failed in the United States Congress. Finally, in 1911, the society's efforts led in part to passage of the federal WEEKS ACT, which authorized funds for the creation of the White Mountain National Forest. The society continued to campaign for state land acquisition, and its work eventually led to the establishment of state parks at Franconia Notch, Kearsarge, and Mount Sunapee.

In 1908, a report to the state forestry commission singled out the policy of levying an annual tax on timber growth as the primary cause of clearcutting practices. To change this policy required an amendment to the state constitution, which for property tax purposes did not distinguish between timber and the land on which it grew. Not until 1942 could such an amendment be adopted, and the eventual result was the passage of the Forest and Conservation Law of 1949. This law provided for a yield tax, levied as a percentage of the stumpage value, and a separate tax on the land. In 1973, the Current Use Law was passed, allowing land to be assessed according to its use rather than its potential market value.

New Hampshire's state forestry institutions were designed to assure the long-range protection of the forest resource. They have accomplished this end through fire protection, appropriate public landownership, equitable taxation of private timberlands, and expanded educational services to landowners.

PAUL O. BOFINGER

NEW JERSEY FORESTS

At the time of first European contact, New Jersey was generally forested land; 93 percent of the state is estimated to have originally been forested. The northern highlands supported oak-chestnut forests with a mixture of yellow poplar, ash, maple, and hickory; the coastal plains, comprising the area known as the Pine Barrens, were composed of pine, oak, and white-cedar, while on the piedmont plateau throve a variety of hardwoods such as oak, birch, maple, gum, and poplar. Some areas, such as the Raritan Valley, were open country with groves of trees here and there. Periodic burning by the Lenape or Delaware Indians is generally credited with providing a parklike landscape in places and the relative lack of understory. This supposition has recently been challenged. Actual clearance by the Indians for agricultural purposes was minimal, perhaps a maximum of only 4,000 acres in any one year, or less than one-tenth of 1 percent of the total land area.

By about 1700, the central portion of the state, stretching from the Delaware River to Raritan Bay, had been settled. The Swedish botanist Pehr Kalm in 1748 reported that between Trenton and New Brunswick "by far the greater part of the country was without woods." Tax records from the 1780s reveal that the piedmont soils in central New Jersey were cleared and only 20 percent or so of the land in many townships was "unimproved," probably largely in woodlots.

At that time, many sawmills flourished, producing lumber for the construction of dwellings, fencing, and the like. Kalm observed that wood products were being sent to New York from New Brunswick on a daily basis, especially "boards, timber, wooden vessels and all sorts of carpenters' work." Contemporaneous newspaper advertisements also indicated a brisk trade in firewood from New York and Philadelphia.

In the better agricultural areas, woodland had become scarce by the end of the eighteenth century, forcing farmers to purchase woodlots lying at a distance to provide for heating, fencing, and lumber. But a hundred years later, marginal land was being abandoned to woodland due to increasing competition from midwestern produce. Woodland continued to lose ground in other places in New Jersey, however, due to the introduction of the portable steam-powered sawmill around 1840, which encouraged the cutting of timber remote from waterpower. From the mid-

nineteenth century on, urban and suburban growth absorbed both farmland and woodland in the northeastern quadrant of the state. Perhaps only one small area of sixty-five acres in the piedmont remained uncut down to the present—the Hutcheson Memorial Forest near New Brunswick, administered by Rutgers University.

The outer coastal plain of the southeast, with its poor soils, and the highland northwest, with its relative inaccessibility, were settled later than the piedmont and inner coastal plain. By 1765, there were only islands of settlement in these districts, several of them associated with lumbering activity. The highlands forests were often clearcut to provide CHARCOAL which was used to reduce iron ore. Vast areas were deforested, often illegally. Deforestation on better soils was often followed by agricultural settlement, not allowing forest regeneration. Depletion of the forests of the northern highlands by the iron industry continued until about 1850, when anthracite replaced charcoal as fuel.

In the outer coastal plain, with poor soils and relative inaccessibility from urban centers, the oak and pine forested area (popularly known as the Pine Barrens) in 1980 still extended for some 1.4 million acres and comprised about 70 percent of New Jersey's wooded land. The first settlement of the area by Europeans may well have been by Swedes and Finns in the 1680s. Ruinous use of the Pine Barrens often was the rule before the nineteenth century. Sawmills were established by 1704 and the Atlantic white-cedar (*Chamaecyparis thyoides*) was widely exploited for shingles, which were shipped to New York, Philadelphia, and the Caribbean. In 1799, a Polish visitor estimated that over 11 million board feet per year of lumber was being carried to Philadelphia or New York from the Great Egg Harbor hinterland alone.

Owners of sawmills often owned only the land upon which the mill was located and simply appropriated whatever timber stood near the millsite. As the land was not permanently occupied by farmers and as landownership was in dispute or held by distant absentees, this situation prevailed for many years. Indeed, a cavalier attitude toward forest resources as well as simple thievery was widespread in New Jersey, often perpetrated even by those responsible for enforcing the colonial laws.

After the Revolution, large tracts in the Pine Barrens were purchased cheaply by the iron manufacturers and the unoccupied forest was allowed to regenerate. Shortly after 1800, the glass industry joined iron as a user of the woodlands for charcoal. The impact of both industries on the forest was alleviated when anthracite superseded charcoal after 1840. The great-

A load of cedar logs in New Jersey, 1897. Forest Service Photo.

est single industrial impact on the forest in the nineteenth century was for fuelwood. Steamboats especially used huge quantities of pine. Other impacts came from the exploitation of inexpensive waterpower created by damming the abundant streams of the region, real estate development, and farming. The latter two especially affected the boundaries of the forested area.

Fire, often set deliberately, has without question had the greatest impact on the Pine Barrens. In 1755, for example, a newspaper published an account of a vast fire "which rendered desolate Lands to the Extent of near thirty Miles." During the nineteenth century, it was not unusual for 100,000 acres to burn in a year, and as late as 1963 over 200,000 acres in New Jersey burned, mostly in the Pine Barrens.

In comparison with other states, New Jersey has never ranked as a major lumber manufacturer. Its greatest production came during the 1870s, with 111 million board feet cut in 1879 alone. Yellow pine was the most abundant single type, supplying 45 percent of the total; hardwoods together provided 44 percent. Lumber production fell off abruptly thereafter, with hardwoods predominating from the early 1900s onward.

Conservation efforts began in 1894 when Essex County dedicated the state's first recreational parks. Other counties soon created park systems, and in 1905 the State Forest Park Reservation Committee was established and began purchasing lands for state forests. In 1915, the Forest Park Reservation Committee, the State Geological Survey, and the various park commissions were combined into the Department of Conservation and Development. New Jersey at that point had six state parks. By 1927, the department also managed over 21,000 acres in state forests, which were partially self-supporting through sale of wood. By 1970, the Department of Conservation was reorganized and titled the Department of Environmental Protection, with a Division of Parks, Forestry, and Recreation. In 1975, there were twenty-four state parks totaling almost 48,000 acres, and ten state forests comprising 175,500 acres.

Five of the state forests were within the Pine Barrens. In June 1979, Governor Brendan T. Byrne signed the Pinelands Protection Act, which imposed controls on development in this unique ecosystem in order to protect land, water, and wildlife resources. A Pinelands Commission was created to plan and implement the provisions of the act. The protected area falls under section 502 of the National Parks and Recreation Act of 1978, which provided for federal, state, and local cooperation to protect the Barrens and its water resources and allocated funds to acquire lands and create a management program. Other forestry efforts in the state have included tree planting, initiated on a large scale in 1923; state tree nurseries, first established in 1926; the extension of forestry services to private landowners; and fire control, which continues to constitute New Jersey's most pressing forestry concern.

By 1977, the New Jersey forests, in addition to the Pine Barrens, existed in protected areas or in locations that discouraged permanent clearance. The major forests, which had all regenerated since their maximum clearance in the mid-nineteenth century, were on northern highlands, the Kittatinny Ridge, and the series of swamps in the Passaic River drainage basin. Of New Jersey's more than 4.8 million acres, 1,928,000 (or 40 percent) were covered by forests. Ninety-six percent of the state's forestland had commercial value, and of this 83 percent was in private hands. Some three-quarters of it was in industrial or other nonfarm ownership.

FURTHER READING: Theodore W. Kury, "Historical Geography of the Iron Industry in the New York-New Jersey Highlands," Ph.D. dissertation, Louisiana State University (1968). Jack McCormick and Richard T. T. Forman, "Location and Boundaries of the New Jersey Pine Barrens," in Richard T. T. Forman, ed., *Pine Barrens: Ecosystem and Landscape* (1979). A. Philip Muntz, "The Changing Geography of the New Jersey Woodlands, 1600–1900," Ph.D. dissertation, University of Wisconsin (1959), and "Forests and Iron: The Charcoal Iron Industry of the New Jersey Highlands," *Geografiska Annaler* 42 (1960): 315-323. Beryl Robichaud and Murray Buell, *Vegetation of New Jersey* (1973). Peter O. Wacker, *The Musconetcong Valley of New Jersey: A Historical Geography* (1968); *Land and People: A Cultural Geography of New Jersey* (1975); and "Human Exploitation of the New Jersey Pine Barrens Before 1900," in Richard T. T. Forman, ed., *Pine Barrens: Ecosystem and Landscape* (1979).

PETER O. WACKER

NEW MEXICO FORESTS

Forests in New Mexico occur only in the mountains and high plateaus located mostly in the northern and western parts of the state. Adequate moisture for forest growth is not available elsewhere. The commercial forests cover 5.7 million acres at elevations from 7,000 to 11,500 feet where annual rainfall ranges from nineteen to twenty-five inches. Ponderosa pine predominates at the lower elevations of the commercial forest while Douglas-fir, white fir, and spruce replace pine in that order as altitudes increase. Quaking aspen occurs

in small, pure stands in the spruce-fir areas. Timber volumes in the pine zone range from 5,000 to 15,000 board feet per acre, while in the spruce-fir stands volumes as much as 25,000 board feet are not uncommon. A second forest type, the extensive noncommercial pinyon-juniper woodland, extends over 15.6 million acres below the commercial forest down to the lower limits of the tree zone at elevations of about 5,000 feet, where precipitation is only twelve to fourteen inches annually. Wood volume runs from three or four cords per acre at the desert fringe to twenty-five cords in the better watered sites. The 21 million acres of total forested area equal about 27 percent of New Mexico's land area.

Forest protection and management in New Mexico began when the Pecos River Forest Reserve was established in 1892. By the mid-twentieth century, five national forests comprised 52 percent of New Mexico's commercial forestland while 30 percent was in private ownership (mostly on farms), 3 percent was owned by state or other local government, 12 percent was located on Indian reservations, and the remainder was in the public domain and other ownerships. Not until 1957 was a state forestry organization established to administer the state forests and enforce the forest practice laws on private land.

The pinyon-juniper woodland provided fuelwood, fencing material, pinyon nuts, and housing logs to the Indians for centuries. New Mexico produced lumber valued at $20,000 in 1849. Commercial forest exploitation received a boost with the production of ties and other material required in the construction of the Santa Fe Railroad in the 1880s. A century later, production of forest products was estimated to use 288 million board feet of timber annually. It provided over 10 percent of the manufacturing employment in the state. Over 60 percent of the lumber produced was ponderosa pine. Since the 1960s, Navajo tribal lands have contributed in a major way to the state's lumber production. With the energy shortages of the 1970s, demand for fuelwood accelerated.

Beyond their value for the production of wood products, other uses of the forests have been extremely important in this semiarid state. Forests provide the habitat for a major portion of New Mexico's wildlife species, and forest streams and nearby lakes support cool-water fisheries. Hunting and fishing are popular and of economic importance. Virtually all forested areas are grazed in summer by domestic cattle and sheep, an industry vital to the state. The function of the forests in protecting the state's primary watersheds and regulating streamflow is of inestimable value. Much of the public and private forestland in

New Mexico is accessible by automobile and is subjected to heavy use both summer and winter by state residents and visitors. Developed winter sports constitute a large business. Under the influence of Aldo LEOPOLD, then a U. S. FOREST SERVICE employee, the nation's first wilderness area, the Gila, was established in 1924 by the district forester. Since then, several additional wilderness areas have been set aside in the national forests of the state.

DAHL J. KIRKPATRICK

NEW YORK FORESTS

Geographically, New York state can be divided into four distinct regions: the Adirondacks, the Tug Hill Plateau, and the St. Lawrence Valley in the northern part of the state; the Erie-Ontario Lake Plain and the Mohawk Valley in the central part of the state; the Southern Tier and Allegheny Plateau stretching across the southern part of upstate New York from Lake Erie to the Catskill Mountains; and the Hudson Valley with the New York Metropolitan region and Long Island to the south. In 1980, forests covered 61 percent of the state, or 18.5 million of its 30.5 million acres. Commercial forests totaled 15.4 million acres, with 979,000 acres in public ownership and 14.4 million acres owned privately. About 44 percent of the state's forestland is found in the northern region, 23 percent in the Allegheny Plateau, 11 percent in the Erie-Ontario Lake plain, and 22 percent in the Hudson Valley-Catskill region.

The original forest of New York consisted mostly of white pine, spruce, hemlock, and northern hardwoods. White pine, the most valuable commercial timber, was distributed throughout the state, and spruce and white-cedar grew in the Adirondacks. The hardwoods—white oak, ash, cherry, black walnut, maple, beech, and birch—thrived in the river valleys. Since the beginning of the twentieth century, hardwoods have predominated, and in 1980 they comprised 80 percent of the state's forests, with sugar maple the dominant species. Beech-birch-maple forest covered most of the state, with oak-hickory growing in the Hudson Valley and the lower Erie-Ontario Lake Plain, and elm-ash-maple in the upper Erie-Ontario Lake Plain and along the northern border. The red-white pine forest existed only in remnant stands, most of which were scattered among the spruce-fir forest in the eastern Adirondacks. Much of the white pine in New York had been damaged by white pine weevil and was of little commercial value.

The early Dutch and English settlers found largely unbroken forest throughout the state. The Iroquois nation made only small clearings for corn and for hunting. White settlement began in 1614 on Manhattan Island and moved up the Hudson and Mohawk valleys and across the Allegheny Plateau. Sawmills were first built at New Amsterdam and Fort Orange (Albany) around 1623, and by 1701, there were about forty sawmills in the province. Early mills produced mainly for nearby villages and farms, but as early as 1675, shipments of lumber were sent to England and Holland.

As domestic markets increased in importance, lumbering operations spread up the Hudson River. Eventually, all of New York's rivers served as thoroughfares for logs and lumber. On Lake Champlain, squared timbers were rafted down the Sorel River to Canada and exported to England in the eighteenth and early nineteenth centuries. On the Hudson River, rafts were piloted to Albany, where lumber was loaded on vessels and carried to New York. After 1813, logs on the upper Hudson were driven loose and milled at Glens Falls. Some timber was shipped from western New York down the Susquehanna and Allegheny rivers to Pennsylvania mills before 1825, but the completion of the Erie Canal in that year opened this magnificent timberland to Albany's mills. By the 1840s, Albany received shipments of white pine from Michigan through the Erie Canal. In addition to Albany, Buffalo, Tonawanda, and New York City served as important markets for western lumber in the second half of the nineteenth century. In northern New York, the interior of the Adirondacks remained inaccessible to lumbermen until the 1870s, when railroads reached into the remote mountain valleys.

Early settlers derived a cash income not only from pine timber but also from the manufacture of cooperage, furniture, maple sugar and syrup, and agricultural implements. In the Catskills, the harvest of hemlock bark for tanning was a major enterprise. A single tannery could use up to 6,000 cords of bark—equal to 6 million board feet of hemlock—each year. Until hemlock lumber became valuable in the mid-nineteenth century, the wood itself was generally left in the forest to rot. By 1870, bark peeling had ceased in the Catskills due to lack of bark.

Lumber production in the state peaked in 1850 at 1.6 billion board feet. Between 1850 and 1860, New York led the nation in production of lumber. By 1860, however, two-thirds of New York's forests had been logged for softwoods. Lumber production declined until 1928, when 364 sawmills produced 157 million board feet. As lumber output declined, pulpwood production emerged as the state's primary wood-using industry. Wood pulp production had an early start in New York. The first mill was established in 1866, and by 1910 New York had ninety-eight pulp mills, leading the nation in pulp production. International Paper Company and St. Regis Paper Company were among those that originated in New York. Early pulpwood was made from poplar, spruce, hemlock, and the less valuable pine, but new chemical processes developed at the College of Forestry at the State University of New York, Syracuse, in the early 1950s enabled a wide range of hardwoods, including maple, beech, cherry, and birch, to be used for paper production. Between 1952 and 1967, softwood declined from 85 percent to 29 percent of the total pulpwood harvest.

Concern was voiced in the late 1800s over what appeared to be indiscriminate logging practices and a lack of good forestry. In 1873, the State Park Commission was appointed to address the question of creating a public forest park from the remaining state-owned Adirondack lands. The commission recommended that logging be restricted and the land be retained by the state. Although nothing was done in response to the report, it did stimulate further public discussion. In 1885, a legislative act created a 715,269-acre forest preserve in the Adirondacks and Catskills and dedicated the commission to the "care, custody, control, and superintendence" of the preserve. The commission was also empowered to employ a state forest warden, along with inspectors and assistants and to appoint town fire wardens in the forest preserve counties. In response to fires in 1903 and 1908 that burned about 868,000 acres

in the Adirondacks, a law was passed in 1909 requiring railroads to burn oil, establishing patrols along railroad lands, authorizing construction of fire towers, and improving the system of payment for fire-fighting personnel. In 1895, the commission, renamed the New York Fisheries, Game, and Forest Commission, was expanded to include new responsibilities, including all state-run forestry programs. In 1971, the commission's name was changed to the Department of Environmental Conservation.

A tree nursery and reforestation program was initiated in New York in 1899 at the Axton Plantation in the Adirondacks. The program was placed under the direction of Bernhard E. FERNOW, the first director of the New York State College of Forestry at Cornell, established in 1898. Unfortunately, Fernow's experimental cutting and tree regeneration studies were misunderstood by the influential and wealthy neighbors of the plantation, and the school was closed in 1902 because of political pressure. Reforestation received support in 1908 when Commissioner Gurth Whipple obtained authority from the legislature to distribute nursery stock to private owners at cost. Between 1902 and 1928, in addition to trees planted on private lands, 57 million trees were planted on forest preserve lands, completely reforesting the preserve. In 1911, the New York State College of Forestry was created at Syracuse. Cornell's program, re-established in 1910, ended in 1937 when the state deter-

A pine forest follows fire in New York, 1900. Forest Service Photo.

mined that it could not afford to support two graduate forestry programs.

Competition from agriculture in the western United States and rising employment possibilities in the state's developing urban areas led to abandonment of the small hill farms of New York. Farm abandonment began about 1830, accelerated after the Civil War, then slowed until the Great Depression. Ironically, new farm land in New York in the fertile valleys was still being cleared as some of the most remote hill farms were being abandoned. Total farm acreage actually increased until 1880, when 24 million acres were cleared for crops and pasturage. By 1969, however, only 10 million acres remained in farm. Farm abandonment, particularly during the Great Depression and in the uplands of the Southern Tier and Adirondack Foothills, depopulated rural communities and undermined their property tax base. In 1929, the County Reforestation Area law was passed, authorizing the state to help counties acquire and reforest abandoned farms that were smaller than 500 acres and contained at least 50 percent open land. Abandoned farms were thereby "put back to work." Land acquisition and reforestation were carried out by the Conservation Department. Under the guidance of Milton Hick and Charles Baker, foresters were employed, plans drawn up for planting, and crews hired to plant trees and construct access roads.

The legislature in 1931 appropriated funds for state acquisition and reforestation of a million or more acres of land idle for fifteen or more years. By the end of 1932, the state had purchased 173,681 acres, of which 61,348 acres had been replanted. Depression-era budgets for forestry were reduced, but the work of the CIVILIAN CONSERVATION CORPS (CCC) helped make up the difference. The CCC planted 222 million trees; developed recreational sites; initiated fire, insect, and disease control projects; and built roads. The reforestation program ushered in a new era for public forestry in the state, providing the basis for virtually all of the Conservation Department's forestry activities after World War II.

As of the early 1980s, state forests, of which over 600,000 acres owned by New York state were lying outside the Forest Preserve of the Adirondack and Catskill Parks, were managed under a multiple-use concept by the Department of Environmental Conservation. They produced merchantable timber both from the trees that were planted and from natural hardwood and softwood stands. Road building and wildlife habitat improvement brought the lands into heavy use by hunters, picnickers, and nature lovers. An additional 110,000 acres were in wildlife management areas, on which timber production is of second-

ary importance. New York state parks, encompassing only a little more than 200,000 acres, are among the most heavily used recreation areas in New York. They number nearly 100 and range in size from the 65,000-acre heavily forested Allegheny State Park in the southwestern Southern Tier to a few tiny, strategic patches of ground along the St. Lawrence River. Finally, there were 125,000 acres of forestland held by counties and municipalities.

During World War II, lumber and pulpwood production rose somewhat from Depression lows, and land use remained stable as agricultural price supports and increased demands for food kept many small hill farms in production. During the later stages of World War II, national concern over the actions of private forestland owners brought forth arguments for federal regulation of private forestry. In New York, where over 80 percent of the forestland was in private ownership, such talk was viewed with alarm. In 1946, partly to stem possible federal regulation and partly to provide assistance to private forest owners, the New York State Forest Practice Act (FPA) was passed. Under this law, the Conservation Department foresters provided on-the-ground free technical forestry advice and assistance to private forest owners, primarily the small nonindustrial owners. The FPA program preceded the federal Cooperative Forest Management Act by four years. The federal program, however, enabled New York to expand its own. In 1980, the cooperative forestry assistance program of the Department of Environmental Conservation annually rendered assistance to about 6,000 forestland owners, involving over 200,000 acres and marking over 30 million board feet of timber for commercial harvest.

By 1980, between 350 and 500 million board feet of sawlogs and 600,000 cords of pulpwood were being harvested annually from New York's forests. This wood supplied about 450 sawmills and nine wood pulp and paper mills within the state. About 3,100 people were employed in the sawmill industry, and annual payrolls amounted to about $29 million. An additional 1,000 people were engaged full time in timber harvesting, with payrolls of about $5 million. In addition, about 10,000 people were employed in the wood pulp and paper industry within the state, with a payroll of about $156 million. In the 1980s, the heaviest concentrations of sawmills and the most intensive sawlog harvesting occurs in the foothills of the Adirondacks and in the eastern and far southwestern parts of the Allegheny Plateau. Softwood lumber production is concentrated in the southeastern Adirondacks. Eight of the nine wood pulp and paper mills operating in New York are located on the eastern and western fringes of the Adirondacks and are supplied mainly from the Adirondack counties. The wood pulp and paper industry also imports substantial amounts of wood and semifinished pulp from other states. Canada, once a major supplier of pulpwood, now exports little to the United States; instead, finished paper (largely newsprint) is exported.

In summary, the long-term trend in wood use in New York has two outstanding characteristics. The first is a long decline in lumber production from 1850 to 1932, followed by a rise during the 1940s and early 1950s, and stable output since then. The second is a continual shift from softwoods to hardwoods, occurring in both lumber and pulpwood. Since the turn of the century, softwood lumber output has drastically fallen, but hardwood lumber production shows a virtually level output.

Land use since the 1950s has been altered by further concentration of farming in more productive areas and increased participation in outdoor recreation by urban dwellers. Farm abandonment on the hills, which slowed in the 1940s and 1950s, again accelerated in the 1960s and 1970s. These lands were sold for amenity values, recreational use, and, in some cases, timber production. In the late 1970s, fuelwood became an important consideration.

The increased demand for outdoor recreation has led to changes in public forestry programs in the state. Although natural forests and earlier conifer plantings are yielding products, the public is pressuring for horse trails, more wildlife habitat, hunting access, and camping and hiking areas. New York's forest environment is thus an increasingly important recreational resource. Campgrounds are located throughout New York but are concentrated in the Adirondacks, Catskills, Allegheny Plateau, and St. Lawrence Valley—the more heavily forested areas of the state. In addition to campgrounds, the Department of Environmental Conservation maintains over 1,000 miles of foot trails, almost all of which are in the Adirondacks and Catskills. Major trails are being developed in the Finger Lakes between Allegheny State Park and Buffalo, and north from New York City to the Catskills.

Wildlife is another major forest product in New York, with bear and wild turkey found mainly in the Adirondacks and Catskills, and white-tailed deer, ruffed grouse, and varying hare occurring throughout the state. Other notable forest uses include Christmas trees, maple syrup, fence posts, utility poles, cabin logs, and firewood.

FURTHER READING: Eleanor Amigo and Mark Neuffer, *Beyond the Adirondacks: The Story of the St. Regis Paper Company* (1980). G. R. Armstrong and M. W. Kranz, eds., *Forestry College: Essays on the Growth and Develop-*

ment of New York State's College of Forestry, 1911–1961 (1961). P. W. Fosburgh, *The Natural Thing: The Land and Its Citizens* (1959). William F. Fox, *History of the Lumber Industry in the State of New York* (1902; reprinted 1976). Ralph S. Hosmer, *Forestry at Cornell, 1898 to 1948* (1950). N. J. Stout, *Atlas of Forestry in New York (1958)*. Gurth Whipple, *Fifty Years of Conservation in New York State, 1885–1935* (1935).

HUGH O. CANHAM

NEW YORK STATE FOREST PRESERVE

The forest preserve of New York State consists of nearly all the state-owned lands lying within the twelve Adirondack counties of northern New York and the four Catskill counties in the east-central portion of the state. Since the state constitutional convention of 1894, all such lands have been subject to a constitutional provision providing that "the lands of the state, now owned or hereafter acquired, constituting the forest preserve as fixed by law, shall be forever kept as wild forest lands. They shall not be leased, sold, or exchanged, or be taken by any corporation, public or private, nor shall the timber thereon be sold, removed, or destroyed." Forest preserve holdings are concentrated within the boundaries of the ADIRONDACK PARK; some are to be found within the CATSKILL PARK; and the balance lies outside the two park areas but within the sixteen forest preserve counties.

The forest preserve was established by law in 1885 as the expression of rising conservation sentiment and a reaction against wasteful logging practices. At that time, the preserve consisted of the state-owned lands within eleven of the northern counties (681,374 acres) and three of the Catskill counties (33,893 acres). Oneida County in the Adirondacks and Delaware County in the Catskills were added as forest preserve counties in 1887 and 1888, respectively.

The same law that established the forest preserve also created a Forest Commission which, among other forestry responsibilities, was given custody over the Forest Preserve. The commission is the predecessor of the present Department of Environmental Conservation. In 1886, the legislature provided that forest preserve lands were to be assessed and taxed at valuations and rates comparable to private lands, an important factor in making the forest preserve concept more palatable locally.

During the century that preceded the establishment of the forest preserve, the attitude of the state government toward the vast forested regions of the Adirondacks and the Catskills had been ambivalent. The state had assumed title as early as 1779 to crown lands, including an estimated 7 million acres in northern New York. Following the American Revolution, many of these lands were sold to speculators to encourage the settlement of undeveloped lands. During the 1830s, principally as a result of a statewide Natural History Survey, the sources of the Hudson River were first explored, bringing the high mountains of northern New York, designated "the Adirondack group," to public attention. While settlement of many of the backwoods areas of both the Adirondacks and the Catskills continued with the establishment of small farms, the development of mining operations, and an ever increasing extension of softwood logging, artists, writers, and sportsmen were discovering these remote areas and beginning to raise questions about their future.

In 1873, a temporary group called the Commissioners of State Parks recommended that protection of the forests of the Adirondacks was justified in the interests of future forest use, RECREATION, and public health. Little action was taken for some years, however. Between 1872 and 1900, the commission secretary, Verplanck Colvin, oversaw a comprehensive topographical survey of the Adirondacks which repeatedly stressed the desirability of creating a park or timber reserve in the Adirondacks. An important part of Colvin's argument was the necessity of preserving the high mountain watersheds of the state, a theme that Colvin probably derived from George Perkins MARSH's *Man and Nature* (1864).

In 1883, such lands as remained in state ownership in ten of the northern New York counties were withdrawn from further public sale, and Colvin was directed to initiate a survey of their boundaries. Meanwhile, the legislature created a committee under the chairmanship of Charles Sprague SARGENT "to investigate and report on a system of forest preservation." It was on the basis of the Sargent committee's report of January 23, 1885, that both a Forest Commission and the forest preserve were created and that protection of the forest preserve was drawn up under terms similar to those included in the state constitution nine years later.

Despite the seeming stringency of the 1894 constitutional provision, some flexibility in the management of the forest preserve has been adopted over the years, including the creation of public camping facilities on forest preserve lands, the construction of foot trails, and the establishment of fire-protection systems. Nevertheless, most substantive issues have been dealt with by constitutional amendment. Of the more than 130 amendments proposed to the forest preserve provision since 1894, relatively few have survived passage at two consecutive sessions of the legislature and approval by voter referendum. Successful amendments included a 1913 provision for the use of up to 3 percent of the forest preserve for the construction and maintenance of municipal water supplies, for the needs of canals, and for stream regulation; various highway construction authorizations, including the use of forest preserve land for the Adirondack Northway in 1959; the creation of ski developments at Whiteface Mountain and Gore Mountain in the Adirondacks and at Belleayre Mountain in the Catskills; permission to sell off detached parcels of land of under ten acres each, lying outside of the Adirondack and Catskill Parks; and exchanges of land between the state, local governments, and, in one case, a private corporation. In 1953, the wording pertaining to the regulation of streamflow was rescinded following a lengthy dispute over a proposal to build dams in the southwestern Adirondacks.

The most important constitutional test of the forest preserve took place in 1929 and 1930 in connection with a proposal to construct a bobsled run on state lands in preparation for the third Olympic Winter Games that were to be held at Lake Placid in 1932. A law authorizing such construction was struck down by both the appellate division and the court of appeals on the grounds that such a project would entail the cutting and removal of trees and timber "to a substantial extent" and would be detrimental to the "wild and natural state" of the preserve. The bobsled run was ultimately built on private lands.

Over the years, the forest preserve has grown from its original 715,269 acres to nearly 2.5 million acres. As in the past, the pattern of ownership continues to resemble a gigantic patchwork, although under a state land master plan drawn up for the Adirondacks in 1972, fifteen areas of 10,000 acres or more have been formally designated as wilderness areas.

During its long history, the forest preserve of New York State has meant many things to many people. It is intimately associated with the beginnings of active conservation and preservation at the state level. It has been closely identified with public perceptions of watershed, forest, and recreational values and has been seen as either the bane or the bulwark of conservation within the state, depending upon the viewpoint of the observer. The example of the New York State Forest Preserve also played a role in the creation of the federal Wilderness Act of 1964, serving as an example of successful wildland preservation and as an entity somewhat removed from what some groups have perceived as the whims of legislative and administrative bodies.

FURTHER READING: Commissioners of State Parks of the State of New York, *First Annual Report*, Senate Document No. 102 (1873). Alfred L. Donaldson, *A History of the*

Adirondacks, 2 vols. (1921). Frank Graham, Jr., *The Adirondack Park: A Political History* (1978). Marvin W. Kranz, "Pioneering in Conservation: A History of the Conservation Movement in New York State, 1865–1903," Ph.D. dissertation, Syracuse University (1961). Dorothy Plum, ed., *Adirondack Bibliography* (1958), and *Adirondack Bibliography Supplement* (1973). Roger C. Thompson, "The Doctrine of Wilderness: A Study of the Policy and Politics of the Adirondack Preserve-Park," Ph.D. dissertation, State University College of Forestry at Syracuse (1962). Norman J. Van Valkenburgh, *The Adirondack Forest Preserve: A Narrative of the Evolution of the Adirondack Forest Preserve of New York State* (1979). Gurth Whipple, *Fifty Years of Conservation in New York State, 1885–1935* (1935). William Chapman White, *Adirondack Country* (1967).

WILLIAM K. VERNER

NIAGARA FALLS

The first great natural wonder to capture the American imagination was Niagara Falls; more than three hundred years after its discovery by Father Louis Hennepin in 1678, it remained third behind only the Grand Canyon and Yellowstone in visual appeal to American tourists.

Concern about the fate of Niagara Falls began as early as 1830, when European visitors in particular started calling attention to the despoilation of its environs by commercial interests and developers. By 1860, private individuals owned all of the primary observation sites. In this regard, the cataract served as a catalyst leading to the government preservation of scenery in the United States. Proponents of the Yellowstone Park Act of 1872 especially took pains to refer to the despoilation of Niagara Falls as justification for their own fears that Yellowstone would suffer a similar fate if not withdrawn from the public domain.

Niagara itself did not win salvation until 1883 when the New York State legislature, acting under growing pressure from both domestic and world opinion, approved the purchase of private lands rimming the cataract and the removal of the eyesores and commercial enterprises they supported. As early as 1879, the landscape architect Frederick Law OLMSTED had prepared a report calling for these steps; finally, on July 15, 1885, New York officially dedicated the Niagara Falls State Reservation. In keeping with the convictions of Olmsted that the park should be kept entirely free of ornamentation, the reserve remains to this day a remarkable contrast to the Canadian side of the cataract, which became a provincial park after New York's example in 1888.

Niagara's "salvation" proved premature, however. By the turn of the century, commercial waterpower interests were seeking to circumvent the park acts by locating electrical generating stations below the cataract in the Niagara Gorge. Huge conduits above the cataract threatened to suck the river dry by diverting the flow of the Niagara River around the falls.

The second battle of Niagara accordingly focused on limiting these diversions to amounts consistent with maintenance of the Niagara Falls spectacle. The Burton Act, passed by Congress on June 29, 1906, provided for a complete study of the river, the falls, and the Niagara Gorge to determine how much water could be diverted without jeopardizing scenic values.

Over the years, however, the power companies won major concessions. As a result, although treaties between the United States and Canada limit the diversions during peak viewing hours, as much as one-half of the flow of the Niagara River still bypasses the cataract during the tourist season. A concrete jetty upstream mitigates these huge diversions by spreading the flow of the river evenly over the brink of the falls; nevertheless, the experience of Niagara is testimony to the fate of great natural wonders whose scenery has commercial value.

FURTHER READING: Alfred Runte, "Beyond the Spectacular: The Niagara Falls Preservation Campaign," *New York Historical Society Quarterly* 57 (Jan. 1973): 30-50, and *National Parks: The American Experience* (1979).

ALFRED RUNTE

NORTH AMERICAN FOREST FIRE MEDAL BOARD

In 1938, five associations jointly formed and subsequently financed the American Forest Fire Foundation for the purpose of honoring Canadians, Americans, and Mexicans who displayed heroic personal bravery while fighting forest fires. The Board struck a medal, originally called the Forest Fire Medal, which would be presented variously at the annual meetings of the five supporting groups. These were the SOCIETY OF AMERICAN FORESTERS, AMERICAN FORESTRY ASSOCIATION, CHARLES LATHROP PACK FORESTRY FOUNDATION, Association of State Foresters (now NATIONAL ASSOCIATION OF STATE FORESTERS), and National Lumber Manufacturers Association (now NATIONAL FOREST PRODUCTS ASSOCIATION). The board awarded its first medals in 1939 and, by 1956, had awarded a total of thirteen, four posthumously.

After 1956, with the forest fire campaign taking different directions, the original organization was inactive for twenty years. Reorganized in the mid-1970s as the North American Forest Fire Medal Board (NAFFMB), it made three awards in 1976 and another the next year. The NAFFMB presently includes a representative of the original five associations as well as of the Canadian Institute of Forestry and the Mexican Segretaria de Agricultura.

FURTHER READING: Henry Clepper, *Crusade for Conservation: The Centennial History of the American Forestry Association* (1975), pp. 69-70.

NORTH CAROLINA FORESTS

"Pocosins," "pine barrens," "laurel hells," and "balds"—these colloquial expressions bring to mind the varied flora encompassed by North Carolina's 20 million acres of forestland. The state's 196 tree species, covering 64 percent of the total land area, demonstrate more variety than the combined forests of Europe. Originally, longleaf pine dominated North Carolina's coastal plain, supplemented by loblolly pine, particularly above the Roanoke, and by pond pine, cypress, cedar, gum, and oak. The adjacent piedmont stood heavy with mixed hardwoods, with chestnut the most prominent, followed by yellow-poplar, oak, maple, black cherry, and black walnut; as well as conifers such as Virginia pine, hemlock, and white pine. Red spruce and Fraser firs, remnants of an alpine forest, haunted the higher elevations.

For centuries prior to the arrival of Europeans, the Carolina forest provided sustenance for a number of Indian tribes. Although their use of the forest was limited largely to its natural abundance, the Indians did use fire to create agricultural clearings and improve wildlife habitat. The region's first Europeans were awed by the forests. Verrazano, in 1520, reported a "mightie great woods . . . with divers sorts of trees," and in 1584, Raleigh's scout, Arthur Barlowe, spoke excitedly of oaks and cedars that far surpassed anything in Europe. Three centuries later, Gifford PINCHOT remarked that "the forest flora of no other State is more varied . . . [nor] the forests so glorious [or] trees so huge!"

The Europeans who succeeded the Indians were less sparing in their use of the forest. Trees supplied building and fence materials, fuelwood, and stock for vehicles, furniture, and an almost endless range of household items. In addition to cutting timber and clearing agricultural land, early settlers ran their cattle and pigs into the forest to forage. The colony exported lumber, oak staves, and sassafras to England and the West Indies. By 1770, the colony ranked seventh in the export of boards, shingles, and staves, and pro-

duced about 20 percent of the 100,000 barrels of tar and pitch shipped annually from the American colonies. Until as late as 1870, the state, drawing upon an abundant supply of longleaf pine, remained the world's greatest producer of NAVAL STORES, thereby earning the nickname of Tar Heel State.

During the nineteenth century, the lumber and naval stores industries spread from the coastal plain up the Tar, Nense, and particularly the Cape Fear rivers into the mountainous interior. In succession, the magnificent longleaf and loblolly pine gave way to the ax, and what the avid timber cutter missed, the farmer removed seeking new ground to replace exhausted fields. Shortleaf pine, with its preponderant sapwood, found only local markets until improved dry kilns made the lumber more suitable for building purposes in the late 1870s. As the better grades of spruce and white pine were depleted in the Northeast, North Carolina shortleaf pine found a ready market in the cities of that region, where the light, kiln-dried sapwood was marketed as "North Carolina pine."

Northern capital, coupled with post-Civil War industrialization, laid the basis for the large-scale exploitation of the Carolina forest that took place in the last decades of the nineteenth century. Splash dams, log flumes, and railroads extended logging operations into the more remote mountains, and steam engines, circular saws, and later band saws accelerated the processing of felled timber. Small portable mills followed the railroads into the interior mountains. By 1909, the stationary mills cut only 16 percent of the lumber in the western part of the state, portable mills manufactured 78 percent, and a scattering of small waterpowered mills produced the rest.

By the 1880s, North Carolina's lumber boom was well under way, with the mountain hardwoods under siege as well. Between 1889 and 1911, annual lumber production increased from 554 million board feet to a record 2.25 billion board feet. Tanneries added to the pressures upon the forest after 1890, as did a growing pulpwood industry. Shortly after the turn of the century, the state's first pulp mill, Champion Fiber Company, built a plant in Canton. North Carolina's FURNITURE INDUSTRY, which developed in the early twentieth century, also used quantities of oak, cherry, yellow-poplar, and walnut. By the 1920s, such pressures had reduced the "mightie great woods" mostly to cull stands of second- and third-growth timber.

Even before lumber production began to fall off in 1915, there occurred a series of events that promised to renew North Carolina forestlands. In the process, the state established several forestry landmarks. In the late 1880s, New Yorker George W. Vanderbilt created the magnificent Biltmore Estate near Asheville. Upon the advice of his landscape architect, Frederick Law OLMSTED, Vanderbilt initiated the first major reforestation program in the United States. To supervise the project, Vanderbilt employed Gifford Pinchot, fresh from French forestry school. Impressed with the challenge of forestry in North Carolina, Pinchot encouraged Vanderbilt to purchase additional forestland, including Pisgah Forest, for the estate. Pin-

chot carried the Biltmore story to the 1893 Columbian Exposition in Chicago, winning publicity for Vanderbilt, for forestry, and for North Carolina. In 1895, he resigned and was replaced by German forester Carl A. SCHENCK. Determined to place the Vanderbilt forest on a profit-making basis, Schenck pioneered forest economics, declaring that "forestry is common sense applied to woodlands." In 1898, Schenck established the Biltmore Forestry School, a one-year academy that

A pine forest establishes itself in an abandoned field in North Carolina, 1900. Forest Service Photo.

was the first of its kind in the United States. Although Schenck severed his relations with Vanderbilt in 1909 and with the school in 1913, his impact upon American forestry has been incalculable; the Biltmore forest is still a mecca for foresters from all over the world.

During the same period in Asheville, Dr. Chase P. Ambler began a movement to establish a national park in western North Carolina. Ambler founded the Appalachian National Park Association in 1899 and for a decade lobbied for his cause. Opposition from lumber interests and others opposed to federal ownership of forestlands cut short Ambler's park plans, but the efforts of his association triggered a federal study of the mountain forests. Agitation for the park and the resulting forest survey contributed to the passage of the WEEKS ACT in 1911, which in turn facilitated development of national forests in the East. Appropriately, the first purchase under the Weeks Act was a tract on Curtis Creek, near Old Fort, North Carolina.

In 1916, George Vanderbilt's widow sold Pisgah Forest to the federal government, and the area was dedicated Pisgah National Forest. Since then, the forest has been expanded to 491,000 acres, and three other national forests have been created in the state—the Nantahala, in 1920; the Croatan, in 1936; and the Uwharrie, in 1961—bringing the total national forest lands to more than a million acres. In 1979, the four national forests hosted 17.9 million recreational visits, supplied over 65 million board feet of timber, and provided game harvests that included deer, boar, turkey, and black bear. The national forests encompass the Joyce Kilmer Memorial Forest, the Linville Gorge and Shining Rock Wilderness areas, and Pisgah Forest's Cradle of Forestry, commemorating the birth of scientific forestry in America. The forests also encompass watersheds for ten North Carolina communities.

State efforts supplemented federal forestry measures. In 1891, the North Carolina Geological Survey was established, with Joseph A. Holmes, the country's first state geologist, at its head. Holmes was directed to conduct forestry investigations and prepare timber inventories for the state. In 1908, the state created a forestry division within the renamed Geological and Economic Survey, and in the following year it placed the division under the direction of graduate forester John Simcox Holmes (not to be confused with Joseph A. Holmes). North Carolina State University at Raleigh established a forestry school in 1929, and ten years later Duke University founded a graduate school of forestry. (In the 1980s, the respective schools manage 82,000 acres and 7,000 acres of experimental forest.) During the 1930s, the CIVILIAN CONSERVATION CORPS worked with state foresters planting trees, checking erosion, building fire roads and towers, and providing numerous recreational sites throughout the state.

The state employs not only a state forester but also regional and local foresters. Along with several seedling nurseries, the state forest system includes the 32,000-acre Bladen Lakes forest and four "mini-forests," which primarily serve educational purposes. In addition, North Carolina annually plants nearly 60 million seedlings.

North Carolina's state park system began in 1915 with the acquisition of the remnant balsam fir forest on Mount Mitchell. By 1975, the system included thirty-four park and recreation areas totaling 69,000 acres. The GREAT SMOKY MOUNTAINS NATIONAL PARK, authorized in 1926 and established in 1930, includes a total of 515,000 acres of federal lands, of which 273 acres are in North Carolina. The Blue Ridge Parkway in 1933 became the nation's first federally owned scenic road system and covers 76,476 acres, of which 45,474 acres are in North Carolina. Situated in beautiful forest settings, these two units have become the most heavily visited areas in the national park system.

By the late 1970s, North Carolina's 19,562,000 acres of commercial forest supplied $5.5 billion worth of forest products annually, including 886 million board feet of lumber—enough to build more than 88,000 five-room homes. The state led the nation in production of hardwood veneer and wooden furniture and ranked fourth in the total number of commercial forest acres. The home of champion trees such as giant basswoods, sourwoods, and hemlocks, the Tar Heel state once again may boast of "mightie great woods" and "forests so glorious."

FURTHER READING: O. C. Goodwing, *Eight Decades of Forestry Firsts: A History of Forestry in North Carolina* (1969). Kenneth B. Pomeroy and James G. Yoho, *North Carolina Lands: Ownership, Use, and Management of Forest and Related Lands* (1964). Carl A. Schenck, *The Birth of Forestry in America: The Biltmore Forest School, 1898–1913* (1974). Ralph R. Widner, ed., *Forests and Forestry in the American States* (1968).

HARLEY E. JOLLEY

NORTH CASCADES NATIONAL PARK

After more than a century and a half of recorded history, much pristine land in the north-central part of Washington State remains. Preservation was assured when on October 2, 1968, Congress created a national park complex of two separate units of the park proper (totaling almost 505,000 acres) and two recreation areas. The park units preserve an extended wilderness landscape where, as the act establishing the park described it, there is "an unmatched array of jagged peaks, majestic mountains, over 300 glaciers, and alpine meadows." Ross Lake National Recreation Area (105,000 acres), which divides the park into two units, was excluded because it contained the route of the North Cascades Highway and hydroelectric-power development on the Skagit River. Lake Chelan National Recreation Area (62,000 acres) in the Stehekin Valley was kept out of the park because of the existence of private holdings in the valley dating from the 1880s.

The Skagit Indians on the west and the Chelans and Wenatchees on the semiarid east side made seasonal use of the North Cascades. Probably other tribes were travelers in the area. Alexander Ross of the British Northwest Company crossed the mountains from east to west in 1814. More systematic exploration was carried out by the federal government through special commissions and the U. S. Army. Notable among these explorers were Henry Custer of the Northwest Boundary Survey in the late 1850s and Lieutenant Henry Pierce who crossed the range from Fort Okanogan by way of the Stehekin Valley and Cascade Pass in 1882.

For a half-century beginning in the 1870s, miners, loggers, homesteaders, graziers, and hotel operators pursued their dreams along the Skagit River and its tributaries, and along the shores of Lake Chelan as far as the Stehekin Valley. As a result, a railroad was constructed a short distance up the Skagit River in the 1920s, and steamboats began to make the fifty-five-mile run up Lake Chelan to Stehekin as early as 1889. Isolated from an outside road connection, Stehekin (1974 estimated population, 75) has been able to preserve historic structures and ways of life. The largest and most important economic development in the history of the region was carried out by Seattle City Light between 1924 and 1949 with the construction of three dams on the Skagit River. Ross Dam, 540 feet high, is one of the tallest in the world, and its reservoir stretches north into British Columbia. All three man-made lakes provide recreational opportunities.

Private property, including patented and unpatented mining claims, although accounting for less than 1 percent of the 1,053 square miles within the complex, has influenced the pattern of federal management. In the 1890s, an attempt to create a national park in the North Cascades gained little support. The area was included in the Washington Forest Reserve in 1897, but there was virtually no government control of utilization until 1905 when all forest reserves were transferred to the jurisdiction of the U. S. FOREST SERVICE under the DEPARTMENT OF AGRICULTURE. Between 1908 and 1924, the Washington Forest Reserve was divided and redivided into new administrative units, the Wenatchee, Chelan, Snoqualmie, and Mt. Baker national forests. During the following decades, the Forest Service gave some measure of protection to the scenic resources of the region by establishment of the North Cascades Primitive Area along the Canadian boundary. When, in the late 1950s, the service proposed establishing nearby Glacier Park as a wilderness, organizations such as the SIERRA CLUB and the Mountaineers and local conservationists united as the North Cascades Conservation Council. Fearing that scenic timbered tracts would be left out, the council renewed the old proposal for a national park. At the direction of President John F. Kennedy, a joint committee of the departments of the Interior and Agriculture studied the North Cascades from 1962 to 1965. The resulting recommendations, after further compromises, became the basis for formation of the North Cascades National Park complex in 1968 out of parts of the Mt. Baker and Wenatchee national forests.

FURTHER READING: Paul Brooks, "A Copper Company vs. the North Cascades: How Responsible is a Corporation to the Public?", *Harper's Magazine* 235 (Sept. 1967): 48-50. Allan May, *Up and Down the North Cascades National Park* (1973). Harvey Manning and Bob and Ira Spring, *The North Cascades National Park* (1969). Alan R. Sommarstrom, "Wild Land Preservation Crisis: The North Cascades Controversy," Ph.D. dissertation, University of Washington (1970).

ARTHUR D. MARTINSON

NORTH DAKOTA FORESTS

Covered by part of the "sea of grass," which lies between the woodlands of eastern and central North America and the Rocky Mountains, North Dakota is estimated to have had a forested area of only 700,000 acres when white settlement began. In 1979, native forests covered but 518,000 acres, or 0.1 percent of the state's total land area. Commercial timber could be grown on 343,000 of these acres, but commercial forestland was decreasing due to clearing for agriculture and flooding for irrigation projects. Sixteen tree species are common to the state and fifteen others occur less frequently. More than half the native forests are in the Turtle Mountains and the Pembina Hills, both near the Canadian border. Most of the other forest areas are along riverbanks and lakeshores. Six principal forest types occur in the state: ash-elm, oak, aspen, and cottonwood in the north and east and along streams elsewhere, and ponderosa pine and juniper in the Kildeer Mountains and badlands of the western part of the state and along the Little Missouri River. Widely dispersed patches of trees are found on land classified as nonforest. Wooded draws providing wildlife habitat total 18,300 acres.

A major portion of forestry activity in North Dakota has always concerned the planting and care of SHELTERBELTS, a practice initiated by early settlers and encouraged by law incentives offered by territorial and state law since 1869. In 1913, the state established a tree nursery at Bottineau and the U. S. FOREST SERVICE started its Northern Great Plains Field Station at Mandan, which soon became a center of afforestation research. The Prairie States Forestry Project of the 1930s planted 36,000 acres of shelterbelts in North Dakota. By 1979, the state's shelterbelts covered 217,400 acres.

Norwegian immigrant Simon Benson became a prominent lumberman in the Pacific Northwest. He used these ocean-going, cigar-shaped rafts to transport logs from Oregon to southern California. Forest History Society Photo.

The North Dakota School of Forestry at Bottineau was authorized in the state's original constitution in 1889 and offered instruction in farm forestry and horticulture; in 1925, it became a junior college with a pre-forestry program. The president of the School of Forestry became state forester in 1913. State forestry has largely involved farm extension. Since 1955, it has also included fire protection.

ANN M. RATHKE

NORWEGIAN IMMIGRANTS AND AMERICAN FORESTS

Norwegian immigration to the United States was directed first to western New York and after 1825 spread to La Salle County, Illinois, which rapidly developed into an established Norwegian community. In 1838, Norwegian immigrants funneled northward

from this settlement into Wisconsin, beginning a sixty-year migration into an area sometimes referred to as "New Norway," which included the states of Michigan, Wisconsin, and Minnesota, the eastern part of the Dakotas, and the northern rim of Iowa and Illinois. Nearly a million Norwegians immigrated to the United States, and perhaps 80 percent of them settled in "New Norway." The eastern portion of this region, site of the great northern pinery, was where Norwegians initially entered the lumber industry in the United States.

Although nearly all Norwegian immigrants came from agricultural backgrounds, many also had experience in lumbering, as it was common for them to work seasonally in their native forests. They did the same in their new locale, and an increasing number of Norwegians entered the lumber industry in the years following the Civil War, working as lumberjacks, in sawmills, and as log drivers. Norwegian settlers also moved into both logging and sawmill operations as entrepreneurs, generally on a small scale. There were no lumber barons among the Norwegian settlers in the Great Lakes region, but by 1890 Norwegian loggers had become a major force in the forests of Wisconsin and Minnesota.

As the lumbering frontier moved into the Far West, Norwegian immigrants moved with it. A relatively small number settled in Montana, and a high proportion of them again took work in the lumber industry or became small-scale entrepreneurs in sawmills or logging. One of them, Anton M. Holter, who settled in Helena, expanded into widespread lumbering activities and became perhaps the first Norwegian-American lumber baron in the United States.

Large-scale Norwegian migration to the Pacific Coast came late in the nineteenth century. Many of these Norwegians were second-stage immigrants, moving on from the Great Lakes region, and they shared experience in the forest industries with first-stage Norwegian settlers. Both groups worked in logging camps and sawmills, particularly during summer months, and some Norwegians moved into business on their own. One was Simon Benson, an immigrant from Norway who had worked as a laborer in the pineries of Wisconsin but then developed large-scale logging operations in both Washington and Oregon in the 1880s. Benson was an innovator in the use of steam-powered logging equipment and pioneered the use of ocean-going log rafts, which he delivered to markets as far away as San Diego.

In addition to these activities, Norwegians frequently served with lumber fleets on the Great Lakes and along the Pacific Coast. After 1860, heavy coastal trade developed between San Francisco and the redwood country of northern California which eventually included as many as 400 schooners. Sometimes referred to as "the Scandinavian Navy," the fleet was crewed and skippered largely by Scandinavians, including many Norwegians. Norwegian skippers were a colorful lot, earning a reputation for skill and daring in plying the dangerous coastal waters.

FURTHER READING: Kenneth O. Bjork, *West of the Great Divide: Norwegian Migration to the Pacific Coast, 1847–1893* (1958). Theodore C. Blegen, *Norwegian Migration to the United States: The American Transition* (1940). Agnes N. Larson, *History of the White Pine Industry in Minnesota* (1949). Carlton C. Qualey, *Norwegian Settlement in the United States* (1938).

DENNIS E. BERGE

NUTTALL, THOMAS (1786–1859)

For almost three and a half decades, Thomas Nuttall carefully studied the flora of North America. Born in England on January 5, 1786, into a family of limited means, he was apprenticed to a printer at the age of fourteen. Seeking to pursue his interests in natural history, he sailed for America in 1808. In Philadelphia he won the friendship and patronage of Benjamin Smith Barton who employed him as a plant collector. In 1810, Barton sent him west to Indian country. When he was unable to follow Barton's itinerary, Nuttall joined a contingent of John Jacob Astor's Pacific Fur Company and traveled up the Missouri River. John Bradbury, an English botanist, was also a member of this group.

In the fall of 1811, Nuttall returned to England where he completed the work resulting from his American travels, *The Genera of North American Plants and a Catalogue of the Species Through 1817* (1818). This was America's first comprehensive flora to be published in the United States and in the English language. Although he used the Linnaean system of classification, Nuttall included a discussion which provided American naturalists with their introduction to A. L. de Jussieu's natural system.

From 1815 to 1820, Nuttall was once more in America, and from 1818 to 1820 he collected along the Arkansas River in Indian Territory where he discovered many new species. From 1823 to 1833, he was curator of the botanic garden in Cambridge, Massachusetts, and lecturer in natural history at Harvard. While there, he published *An Introduction to Systematic and Physiological Botany* (1827, rev. 1830). He also developed an interest in ornithology and published in 1832 and 1834 *A Manual of the Ornithology of the U. S. and Canada,* an inexpensive two-volume guide. When the lure of field work grew too strong, Nuttall resigned his position at Harvard in 1834 and journeyed west once more. He joined Nathaniel Jarvis

Wyeth's second expedition to Oregon. Nuttall invited the ornithologist John Kirk Townsend to accompany him. Upon his arrival on the Pacific coast, Nuttall became the first skilled botanist to have crossed the continent collecting specimens. He returned to Boston in the fall of 1836 after two years of collecting in Hawaii. For the next five years, Nuttall worked on his western collections in Philadelphia. Some of his descriptions of new species were incorporated into Torrey and Gray's *Flora of North America*. Before he returned to England in 1842, he had begun work on a three-volume appendix to François André MICHAUX'S *North American Sylva* (1842–1849) which included the results of his western investigations.

With the exception of a six-month visit to America in 1847–1848, the balance of Nuttall's life was spent in England, where he died on September 10, 1859.

FURTHER READING: Richard G. Beidleman, "Some Biological Sidelights of Thomas Nuttall, 1786–1859," *Proceedings of the American Philosophical Society* 104 (Feb. 1960): 86–100. Jeannette E. Graustein, *Thomas Nuttall, Naturalist* (1967), and "Nuttall's Travels into the Old Northwest, An Unpublished 1810 Diary," *Chronica Botanica* 14 (1951): 1-88. Francis W. Pennell, "Travels and Scientific Collections of Thomas Nuttall," *Bartonia* 18 (1936): 1-51.

PHILLIP DRENNON THOMAS

O & C LANDS

The O & C lands—more formally the Oregon and California Railroad Revested Lands and Coos Bay Wagon Road Reconveyed Lands—comprise over 2.5 million acres in eighteen counties of western Oregon. Intermingled in checkerboard fashion with private and other public lands, the O & C properties contain some 40 billion board feet of timber in the world's richest stand of Douglas-fir. Their history includes both a unique episode in the use of land grants for Western railroad development and a significant example of the development of forest management practices.

In July 1866, Congress made provision for a grant of 3.7 million acres along a projected rail route from Portland, Oregon, to the Oregon-California border. As with other railroad grants, the lands were presumably to be sold to finance construction and insure development along the rail line. Conditions of the grant included limitations on the size of tracts the railroad could sell (160 acres) and on the price for which it might sell them ($2.50 per acre) and a requirement that all buyers be bona fide settlers. Because the recipient of the grant, the Oregon and California Railroad Company (an eventual subsidiary of the Southern Pacific), violated these and other provisions, a federal court ruled in 1913 that remaining unsold grant lands were forfeit. On appeal, the U. S. Supreme Court ruled that formal congressional action would be required to recover the lands, and in 1916 the Chamberlain-Ferris Act revested title with the federal government.

That law also required that revenue from the lands, which were placed under the administration of the GENERAL LAND OFFICE (GLO) in the DEPARTMENT OF THE INTERIOR, be used to pay the railroad $2.50 per acre; to reimburse the federal treasury for monies it had paid to the eighteen counties to cover taxes owed by the railroad between 1913 and 1916 on the lands; and to divide remaining revenues among the counties (in lieu of taxes), the state, and the federal government according to a 25-25-50 percent formula. Revenues were insufficient to meet all these requirements, in part because of lack of either a market for the timber or a program for developing access to it. In 1926, legislation was passed in Congress to provide federal funds to the counties equivalent to taxes that would have been paid had the lands been in private hands from 1916 to 1926. Meanwhile, in 1919, a portion of the lands granted in 1869 to support construction of the Coos Bay Wagon Road between Roseburg, Oregon, and the Pacific were reconveyed to the federal government and thereafter administered jointly with the O & C lands.

The assumption in 1916 was that the O & C lands,

501

Forester employed by the Bureau of Land Management measures the diameter of a Douglas-fir tree growing on the O & C lands of western Oregon, 1965. Bureau of Land Management Photo.

when cleared of timber, would be opened for homesteading. Most of the lands proved not suitable for farming, however. In 1937, they were placed under sustained-yield management on the recommendation of Oregonians led by the chief proponent of the concept of sustained yield, David T. MASON, who became a member of the O & C Advisory Board established the next year. Thus the federal government committed itself to permanent management of lands as timberlands and in so doing began the first large-scale use of sustained-yield management. The new legislation also provided for cooperative agreements with other public agencies (notably the U. S. FOREST SERVICE and with private landowners so that lands intermingled with the O & C checkerboard might be

effectively managed. The 1937 law specified that 50 percent of revenues would go to the O & C counties at the outset. After the federal treasury had been reimbursed for payments to the counties and other expenses, the amount would increase to 75 percent. These larger payments began in 1951. Thereafter, the counties returned a third of their share to the federal government for reinvestment in the sustained-yield management program.

The cooperative agreements encouraged under this legislation proved a source of trouble for O & C administrators. In 1946 and 1947, twelve master units were established, together covering about 60 percent of the O & C lands; in each unit, continual production within the limits of the allowable cut would be assured.

The master units were relatively uncontroversial, but the next phase, subdivision of master units into areas for cooperative agreements, faced serious challenges. In 1948, the BUREAU OF LAND MANAGEMENT (BLM), successor to the GLO, held hearings on its proposed Mohawk Cooperative Unit in Lane and Linn counties, no doubt encouraged by the decrease in timber on private holdings as a result of the post-World War II housing boom. The Mohawk proposal would have given one middle-sized lumber company all the allowable cut of federal timber for 100 years on 76,000 acres, 45 percent of it federal, 25 percent belonging to the company, and the remainder in other private, county, or state hands. Small independent timber operators and spokesmen for labor unions, the Grange, and the IZAAK WALTON LEAGUE, among others, testified against such agreements, charging that they would establish monopolies impervious to competition and insensitive to the public's needs. In particular, small operators, dependent on access to federal timber, feared that their livelihood would be destroyed.

Following the Mohawk hearing, the Department of the Interior announced a revised management policy for the O & C lands: potential cooperators (who might be groups of small operators) would be granted the privilege of bidding for timber in cooperative units on an open-auction rather than a sealed-bid basis, and the cooperative agreements would be mutually reviewed and adjusted at more frequent intervals. This new policy made clear BLM's continued preference for controlling production through access and management.

The issue of timber access has also created tensions. The land-grant pattern of alternate sections resulted in a checkerboard of O & C and private holdings. Access roads constructed by private operators often effectively precluded other operators from bidding on O & C timber because they could not get to the timber without using such roads. The policy statement of 1948 allowed the sale of timber only to operators who agreed to permit use of their roads by others, charging tolls to be established by BLM. Road planning and maintenance would be mutually worked out.

The O & C administration has also had to deal with conflicts over jurisdiction on public lands. Almost half a million acres of the O & C lands were "indemnity lands," included in the original grants to make up for other tracts that had passed out of federal hands before the grants were made in 1866. These indemnity lands were on the fringes of the O & C checkerboard, intermingled with national forest lands, and were in fact managed by the Forest Service in the DEPARTMENT OF AGRICULTURE. Tensions over management and sales practices on indemnity lands erupted in the early 1940s and were exacerbated by contemporary proposals to realign or merge the Interior and Agriculture departments. In 1954, the immediate problem of the management of indemnity lands was resolved with the Forest Service continuing to administer them, while indemnity lands timber-sale receipts (about one-fifth of all O & C timber receipts) were to be distributed following the formula established in 1937, a formula more beneficial to local governments than usual Forest Service practice. Meanwhile, exchanges were sought to "block up" each federal agency's holdings.

BLM's responsibility for the O & C lands has been made more complex by concerns for environmental issues, by the enormous increase in timber market prices (from approximately $34 per thousand board feet in 1965 to $160 per thousand board feet in 1975), and by limitations on the allowable cut. The O & C lands had annual sales of well over 1 billion board feet in 1970; as prices for stumpage increased, by the end of the decade the local counties received about $100 million in O & C payments annually—a substantial portion of their income. Furthermore, BLM's sustained-yield management of the O & C lands remained a model for federal management of timber resources.

FURTHER READING: David Maldwyn Ellis, "The Oregon and California Railroad Land Grant, 1866–1945," *Pacific Northwest Quarterly* 39 (Oct. 1948): 253-283. Jerry A. O'Callaghan, *The Disposition of the Public Domain in Oregon* (1960). Elmo Richardson, *BLM's Billion-Dollar Checkerboard: Managing the O & C Lands* (1980).

JUDITH AUSTIN

OBERHOLTZER, ERNEST CARL (1884–1977)

A landscape architect and conservationist who pioneered WILDERNESS PRESERVATION and land use planning, Ernest Oberholtzer proposed international protection of the Rainy Lake and Pigeon River watersheds along the Minnesota-Ontario border, from Lake Superior to Rainy Lake. In 1927, he proposed that the 14,500-square-mile area be protected by treaty and dedicated to wilderness RECREATION, wildlife protection, and forestry in carefully coordinated and compatible uses. Oberholtzer spent his life championing the plan but it was never fully realized. Present protection of wilderness areas in Quetico Provincial Park, the Boundary Waters Canoe Area Wilderness, Voyageurs National Park, and Grand Portage National Monument can be traced to his original vision.

Born in Davenport, Iowa, on February 6, 1884, Oberholtzer studied at Harvard under Frederick Law OLMSTED, Jr., and graduated in 1908. To recover from the effects of rheumatic fever, he canoed the Minnesota-Ontario border lakes with local Indians in 1908, 1909, and 1910. In 1912, Oberholtzer and an Indian companion were the first to reach Hudson Bay by canoe across a section of the Canadian barrens uncrossed by any European since the 1770s. After the trip he settled at Ranier on Rainy Lake to study Indians and their way of life.

He entered the conservation cause in 1925 when the Minnesota and Ontario Paper Company proposed to construct power dams along the border and then log the forests for pulpwood. The plan threatened the local Indians' way of life. Between 1925 and 1934, Oberholtzer proposed and championed his plan for an international wilderness. Through nearly single-handed effort he persuaded Congress to pass the Shipstead-Nolan Act in 1930. In 1935, Oberholtzer was one of eleven men, including Robert MARSHALL and Aldo LEOPOLD, who founded the WILDERNESS SOCIETY. He served on its council until 1968 and as honorary vice-president until his death on June 6, 1977.

FURTHER READING: R. Newell Searle, *Saving Quetico-Superior: A Land Set Apart* (1977).

R. NEWELL SEARLE

OHIO FORESTS

At the beginning of settlement in the eighteenth century, forests covered nearly 95 percent of the 26.3 million acres of land which later constituted the state of Ohio. Prairies, bogs, and marshes covered the nonforested land. Ohio's original forests contained about 150 tree species and probably averaged between 12,000 and 14,000 board feet per acre. Three forest types were important. The beech-maple type occupied more area than any other, forming in general a broad band northeast to southwest across the state. A mixed-oak and hickory forest covered nearly as much land in the hills of the eastern and southern counties. Smaller in extent was the swamp and bottomland forest which covered the Great Black Swamp—an area 40 miles wide and 120 miles long in northwestern Ohio—and poorly drained upland flats and valley flood plains throughout the state. The swamp forest's dominant trees were elm, ash, and soft maple.

By 1940, agricultural clearing and heavy grazing had reduced Ohio's forests to 14 percent of its land area. Virtually all of the original forest had been removed at one time or another; very few virgin trees remained. Farm abandonment, natural timber re-

growth, and some reforestation thereafter brought total forest acreage in the late 1970s up to 6.8 million acres or 26 percent of the original timberland. Most of this growth occurred in the hill counties of southern and eastern Ohio, which then contained 70 percent of the state's timberland. In western Ohio, however, forest decline had never stopped, although that portion of the state still held the best of the remaining timber. More than half of the Ohio forest in the middle of the twentieth century was in small farm woodlots interspersed with cropland and pasture. The state's woodland was shared by 150,000 landowners, and the average holding was something over 30 acres.

About thirty-five species of trees native to Ohio have commercial value. The state ranked as an important lumber producer in the 1840s and 1850s, trailing only New York, Pennsylvania, Maine, and later Michigan. Output of lumber in Ohio fluctuated widely in the latter part of the nineteenth century, hitting peaks of 911 million board feet in 1879 and almost 990.5 million in 1899, when the state ranked thirteenth. Thereafter, Ohio's lumber industry fell into a long decline, dropping below 100 million board feet during the 1930s. After World War II, annual production averaged about 250 million board feet. In the year of peak output, 1899, 96 percent of the lumber produced in Ohio was hardwood. Oak provided 62 percent, elm 9 percent, and poplar slightly less than that. Smaller amounts of lumber came from ash, maple, hickory, basswood, chestnut, walnut, sycamore, and cottonwood.

At various times in its history, Ohio produced many other forest products. The census of 1840 ranked the state second after North Carolina in the production of NAVAL STORES and second after New York in the production of potash. By 1870, Ohio was an important producer of wood furniture, wood carriages and wagons, millwork, and cooperage. By the early twentieth century, a wide variety of wooden products industries continued to be important in Ohio, but while continuing to utilize local forests heavily, most of these industries depended largely upon wood imported from other states—more than 75 percent of the wood used in Ohio in 1910 was imported. Only such specialized industries as tool handle manufacturing (using mostly white ash) and chair making and machine construction (employing largely white oak) got half or more of their raw material from Ohio forests. Considerable quantities of primary forest products such as fuelwood, posts, MINE TIMBER, pulpwood, hewn ties, and cooperage staves continued to be produced locally, often providing important supplementary farm income. In 1937, Ohio ranked as the third state in maple syrup production. By the 1950s, although Ohio

Much of the raw material used in the manufacture of tool handles comes from Ohio forests. American Forest Institute Photo.

ranked seventh among the states in consumption of lumber, veneer, and bolts, less than 5 percent of the wood used by industry there came from local woodlands. The state's PULP AND PAPER INDUSTRY, too, depended upon imports until the 1950s when some plants converted to use domestic hardwoods. In 1952, less than one-third of the pulpwood consumed in Ohio had been grown there, but by 1959 the domestic harvest had jumped from 32,000 to 165,000 cords, and the latter figure provided 90 percent of the state's pulpwood consumption in that year. In 1973, the state's pulpwood production was 369,000 cords.

John Aston Warder, an Ohio resident, was instrumental in founding the AMERICAN FORESTRY ASSOCIATION in 1875, and in 1882 he and others convened the first American Forestry Congress in Cincinnati. A year later, Warder formed the Ohio Forestry Association, which successfully lobbied for creation of a state Bureau of Forestry in 1885—making Ohio one of the first four states to have a forestry agency. Nevertheless,

early forestry efforts in Ohio did not draw public support and died before the end of the nineteenth century.

State forestry was revived in 1906 when the legislature established a Department of Forestry at the Ohio Agricultural Experiment Station in Wooster. The new agency set about addressing the problems of the state's scattered woodlots and the need for widespread reforestation. In 1912, the state amended its constitution to provide for forest tax laws, state forests, and forest conservation districts. The forester of the Agricultural Experiment Station both conducted research and administered fire control, land acquisition, and management of state forests and nurseries until 1949 when administrative functions were transferred to a new Department of Natural Resources in Columbus.

In 1915, Ohio began purchasing tracts where tree planting could be undertaken. These state forests were considerably expanded in 1939 when the U. S. Resettlement Administration turned 40,000 acres of submarginal farmland over to the state. By 1980, the State Division of Forestry administered eighteen state forests with a total of 163,972 acres, two reclamation areas totaling 5,911 acres, and three tree nurseries. The division maintained a staff of service foresters to assist private landowners. In 1971, it initiated an urban forestry program.

Ohio State University at Columbus offered forestry courses as early as 1891. A school of forestry was begun, but after World War I its curriculum was reduced to only two years. The modern School of Natural Resources dates from 1969.

The only national forest in Ohio is the Wayne, established in three separate units in the southern hills by the U. S. secretary of agriculture in 1951, largely for the reclamation of land which had been stripped of its forest for farms and surface mining. By 1974, only 175,097 out of 833,000 acres within the Wayne National Forest boundaries had passed into federal hands, although almost two-thirds of the annual WEEKS ACT purchase allocation for the U. S. FOREST SERVICE'S Region 9 (Lake and Central States and New England) was being spent there.

Of the 6,422,000 acres of commercially productive timberland in Ohio in 1977, over 94 percent was privately owned, less than 4 percent belonged to state or local government, and a little over 2 percent was federally owned.

Many species of Ohio wildlife, such as wild turkey, passenger pigeon, and timber wolf, were exterminated as a result of changes in land use, among other factors. With the re-establishment of forests in the south and east, there have been upswings in the populations of white-tailed deer, ruffed grouse, and gray squirrels, and the wild turkey has been successfully reintroduced.

OLIVER D. DILLER

OKLAHOMA FORESTS

The commercial forests of Oklahoma are concentrated in the eastern third of the state, where shortleaf and loblolly pine mix with upland hardwoods, primarily of the oak-hickory type. Central Oklahoma consists of oak and oak-hickory savannah, and the western third of the state is grassland. The river bottoms of the east were also lined with oak-gum-cypress forest.

After the Civil War, lumbermen encroached upon the Indian timberlands of eastern Oklahoma, exporting prized walnut logs out of Indian jurisdiction by floating them down the Arkansas River and its tributaries. The Indian Nations tried to control this traffic, with varying degrees of success, but depredations continued until after the end of tribal government in 1906.

Lumber production in Oklahoma increased from an earliest reported figure of 11 million board feet in 1889 to a reported peak in 1916 of 232 million board feet cut by ninety-one mills. Eighty-nine percent of that figure was supplied by southern yellow pine. Oklahoma forests were logged by mules and oxen with eight-wheel wagons that pulled the logs to railroad spurs. During the industry's brief heyday, clearcutting was practiced extensively, and abundant pine forests in nearby Arkansas, Louisiana, and eastern Texas gave lumbermen no reason to consider reforestation in Oklahoma. CUTOVER LANDS were sold to settlers cheaply. By the 1920s, intensive cutting and unchecked fires had depleted the state's best commercial forests and reduced lumber production to between 100 and 150 million board feet yearly.

Growing interest in forest conservation coincided with the drop in lumber production. In 1925, the new Oklahoma State Forestry Commission established a program of fire prevention, forestry education, and tree planting. During the mid-1930s, the work of the commission was continued under the Forestry Division of the state Planning and Resources Board. Working with the CIVILIAN CONSERVATION CORPS, the state forester initiated a program that resulted in 2,900 miles of SHELTERBELTS, 823 miles of farmstead windbreaks, and 500 acres of reforested lands by the 1950s. Oklahoma forestry gained additional support with the establishment of a department of forestry at Oklahoma State University at Stillwater in 1946.

Better forestry practices and more diverse markets reinvigorated Oklahoma forest industries after World War II. During the 1950s and 1960s, the eastern section of the state was harvested not only for sawlogs but also

Three teams are needed to pull this wagon loaded with a single red gum in the southeastern corner of Oklahoma. Forest History Lantern Slide Collection.

for posts, poles, pulpwood, and hardwood ties. In 1969, the Weyerhaeuser Company purchased approximately 900,000 acres of eastern Oklahoma timberland from Dierks Forests, Inc., and began a program of site improvement by clearcutting and reforesting with selected pine seedlings. By 1975, Oklahoma produced almost 200 million board feet of lumber annually. In addition, the forest industries of the state included pulpwood, pine and hardwood veneer logs, fiber and particleboard, kraft liner board and corrugated medium, paper, posts, poles, and handle stock. Oklahoma in 1977 contained 8.5 million acres of forest, or a little over 19 percent of the state's land area. Only 4.3 million forest acres were classified as commercial, all in the eastern counties. Despite increased interest in conservation, Oklahoma's commercial forestlands had continued to diminish during the 1950s and 1960s, mostly because of clearing for pastureland to support a rising cattle industry.

Oklahoma's seventy-four state parks and recreation areas, managed by the state Division of Parks, totaled 90,000 acres in 1975. Oklahoma also contains the 9,112-acre Chickasaw National Recreation Area, authorized as the Sulphur Springs Reservation in 1902, rededicated as the Platt National Park in 1906, and finally given its present name in 1976. A strip of Oklahoma land along the Arkansas boundary was added to the Ouachita National Forest in 1931. In 1979, the Ouachita included 247,000 federally owned acres in Oklahoma.

FURTHER READING: Leon Rice Elroy and William T. Penfound, "The Upland Forests of Oklahoma," *Ecology* 40 (Oct. 1959): 594-608. A. N. Emmerling, "Forests of Oklahoma," *American Forests* 54 (Dec. 1948): 554-555, 574. Ed R. Linn, *A Forest Industries Survey of Oklahoma* (1948).

DALE C. CAMPBELL

OLMSTED, FREDERICK ERSKINE
(1872-1925)

Born November 8, 1872, in Hartford, Connecticut, F. E. ("Fritz") Olmsted was a cousin of Frederick Law OLMSTED, Jr. He graduated from Sheffield Scientific School of Yale University in 1894 and then joined the U.S. GEOLOGICAL SURVEY. While working for the survey in North Carolina, he met Gifford PINCHOT, who was then at the Biltmore Estate near Asheville, Pinchot persuaded Olmsted to take up forestry as a career. Olmsted studied forestry at the Biltmore Forest School under C. A. SCHENCK and in Germany under Dietrich Brandis, receiving his diploma from the University of Munich in 1899. He worked under Pinchot

in the Bureau of Forestry, developing working plans between 1898 and 1902 for a number of timberland owners in New York, Tennessee, Georgia, Arkansas, and North Carolina, and for a time heading the Timber Physics Section. From 1902 to 1905, he directed boundary surveys on forest reserves in the West. With the establishment of the U. S. FOREST SERVICE, Olmsted became chief inspector of the field service. In this position he strengthened administrative standards in the field, recommended new national forests, examined areas recommended for NATIONAL MONUMENTS, and explained the national forests to the public. In 1907, he became chief inspector of the California district, and with decentralization of the service in 1908, he became district forester in California.

In 1911, Olmsted resigned from the Forest Service and became a consulting forester with the firm of Fisher and Bryant in Boston. He moved to California in 1914. There he organized and headed the Tamalpais Fire Protective Association in Marin County, the first such organization in California. He also worked in California for the Diamond Match Company, developing conservative cutting practices and management plans.

In 1919, he became president of the SOCIETY OF AMERICAN FORESTERS. He was active in the controversy over public regulation of private cutting, siding with Pinchot in favoring federal regulation. He died on February 19, 1925.

Olmsted was an active, athletic man. His writings and reports are characterized by a vivid prose style, a gift for description of nature, a keen interest in human nature, and a liberal, idealistic viewpoint. He made major contributions to both public and private forestry.

FURTHER READING: Coert duBois, "Frederick Erskine Olmsted," *American Forests and Forest Life* 31 (1925): 234. Carl A. Schenck, ed., *The Biltmore Immortals* (1953).

LAWRENCE RAKESTRAW

OLMSTED, FREDERICK LAW, SR.
(1822-1903), AND OLMSTED, FREDERICK LAW, JR. (1870-1957)

Frederick Law Olmsted and his son, Frederick, Jr., dominated the field of landscape architecture from the mid-nineteenth until well into the twentieth centuries. Born into a prosperous Connecticut family at Hartford, on April 26, 1822, Frederick, Sr., was to begin study at Yale University in 1837, but a bout with poison sumac affected his eyes and cost him a sustained formal education. This deficiency did nothing to inhibit his growth and maturity as a writer, however; following a tour of Europe and Britain in 1850, he composed the first of several books, *Walks and Talks of an American Farmer in England* (1852). By 1861, he was also renowned for his lengthy series of articles about the antebellum South and slavery, which he had prepared as a traveling correspondent for the *New York Times*. These works, collected and condensed as *The Cotton Kingdom* (2 vols., 1861), revealed Olmsted's keen sense of observation and political astuteness.

Olmsted's greatest reputation, of course, was still to be linked with the rising field of landscape architecture. As early as 1850, he had praised the city parks of London and Liverpool in England as a noble experiment in democracy. Regarding Birkenhead Park in Liverpool, for example, he exclaimed: "The poorest British peasant is as free to enjoy it in all its parts as the British queen. . . . Is it not a grand, good thing?" That England had beaten its young rival, the United States, to the invention of parklands for the common man did not escape the attention of American nationalists, who themselves had long argued for city parks as a means of protecting the quality of urban surroundings for both the working and the leisure classes. Thus, Olmsted was philosophically prepared when an opportunity presented itself for him to become superintendent of Central Park in New York City in 1857. Shortly afterward, he and his partner, Calvert Vaux, entered the competition to draw up a new design for the preserve, which the two men won under the title of "Greensward." Accordingly, on May 17, 1858, Olmsted was appointed architect-in-chief of Central Park in addition to superintendent.

With the outbreak of the Civil War, Olmsted resigned as head of Central Park to become general secretary of the United States Sanitary Commission. Then, in 1863, he moved to California to become superintendent of the Mariposa Mining Estate in the Sierra Nevada foothills at Bear Valley. To the east lay Yosemite Valley, which Olmsted and his family first visited in August of 1864. Two months earlier, on June 30, 1864, Congress had set aside the valley and the nearby Mariposa Grove of giant sequoias and had presented both areas to California to be managed as a state park "for public use, resort, and recreation." The state was further required to protect the park "inalienable for all time."

Some accounts link Olmsted's name with the park campaign itself, although there is no direct evidence of his participation in the initial movement to preserve the valley. Rather, Olmsted's major contribution came as head of the Yosemite Park Commission, for which he prepared a detailed assessment of the valley. This report, presented to the commissioners in 1865, outlined steps to mitigate the inevitable conflicts that would arise between the desire to protect the park and that to open it to visitors. Unfortunately, after Olmsted left California his fellow commissioners failed to present the report to the legislature, and the text of the document was lost until 1952. By that time, the worst of Olmsted's fears about Yosemite Valley being overrun with tourists and resort facilities had come true.

While in California, Olmsted also sketched out some ideas for the campus of the University of California at Berkeley and Golden Gate Park in San Francisco. Meanwhile, however, he and Calvert Vaux had been reappointed as landscape architects to the commissioners of Central Park, so Olmsted returned east in 1865 to pick up where he had left off in New York City. For the next decade and a half, the firm of Olmsted and Vaux laid out a great variety of projects, including Prospect Park in Brooklyn, the Boston city parks system, and the suburban community of Riverside near Chicago. In 1874, Olmsted was commissioned to design the grounds of the United States Capitol Building in Washington, D.C. Five years later, he once more turned seriously to scenic preservation by immersing himself in the campaign to restore NIAGARA FALLS to its natural condition and protect the environs of the cataract as a free public park. In 1885, he realized these goals with the dedication of the Niagara Falls State Reservation; in 1888, Ontario followed New York State's example with the opening of its own provincial park on the Canadian side of the falls.

Final highlights of the older Olmsted's career included his design of the grounds for the Chicago Columbian Exposition of 1893; Stanford University in Palo Alto, California; and George W. Vanderbilt's Biltmore estate near Asheville, North Carolina. Olmsted spent his declining years in ill health and growing senility and died on August 28, 1903, in Waverly, Massachusetts.

It remained for his son, Frederick, Jr., to bring the family tradition full circle. Fortunately, young Frederick was prepared to follow in his father's footsteps. Biltmore and the Chicago Columbian Exposition had provided superb opportunities to learn the older man's techniques, and in 1894 Frederick, Jr., had obtained his B.A. degree from Harvard University.

With the death of Frederick, Sr., in 1903, Frederick, Jr., and his half-brother, John, found themselves in command of the largest landscape architecture firm in the United States. Great responsibilities and opportunities followed. As early as 1900, young Frederick began the first curriculum in landscape architecture in the United States at Harvard University and served on its faculty until 1914. In 1901, President Theodore

Frederick Law Olmsted, Sr., helped George Vanderbilt plan his baronial Biltmore Estate near Asheville, North Carolina. Forest Service Photo.

ROOSEVELT appointed him to the Senate Park Commission to assist in restoring and developing the L'Enfant plan for Washington, D.C., in light of modern needs. As a result, Olmsted assumed responsibility, in whole or in part, for such projects as the White House grounds, Lafayette Park, the Jefferson Memorial, the National Arboretum, and portions of Rock Creek Park. He was also instrumental in founding the Fine Arts Commission, on which he served from 1910 to 1918. Between 1926 and 1932, he served as a member of the National Capital Park and Planning Commission. Thus was his father's work on the Capitol grounds given even wider and more lasting significance.

So, too, in the field of scenic preservation, Frederick, Jr., added to the Olmsted tradition. In one notable instance, preservationists seeking to establish a NATIONAL PARK SERVICE turned to him for suggestions regarding key passages of the proposed enabling act. Time and again, his drafts of the bill passed back and forth between him and its chief proponents, until finally the language was acceptable to everyone. Specifically, the National Park Service Act, approved August 25, 1916, stated that the fundamental purpose of the national parks "is to conserve the scenery and the natural and historic objects and the wild life therein and to provide for the enjoyment of the same in

such manner and by such means as will leave them unimpaired for the enjoyment of future generations."

Similar projects further underscored the concern of the Olmsted family for the physical environment. Proposed diversions of water from the Niagara River between 1906 and 1913 brought Frederick, Jr., back to the scene of his father's earlier accomplishments, this time to assess whether or not the falls themselves could survive such dramatic attempts to siphon off their flow. Olmsted, who maintained a part-time residence in California, conducted a survey of potential park sites there in 1928; his report laid the basis for the elaborate state park system developed by California during the following decades. In 1932, Olmsted headed a special investigation to assess the suitability of the Everglades of southern Florida for national park status. Largely on the basis of his report, preservationists opposing the park because it was a swamp came to agree that its uniqueness lay in its sense of wildness and remoteness and that these features, coupled with wildlife, justified creating a park so dramatically different in physical structure from the wonderlands of the West.

Olmsted retired to California in 1950, where he continued his lifelong campaigns to protect noted features of the Golden State, especially the coast redwoods. He was also active in plans to realize his father's hopes for better management in Yosemite Valley when death came on Christmas Day of 1957.

FURTHER READING: Laura Wood Roper, *FLO: A Biography of Frederick Law Olmsted* (1973). Alfred Runte, *National Parks: The American Experience* (1979), and "Beyond the Spectacular: The Niagara Falls Preservation Campaign," *New-York Historical Society Quarterly* 57 (Jan. 1973): 30-50. Elizabeth Stevenson, *Park Maker: A Life of Frederick Law Olmsted* (1977).

ALFRED RUNTE

OLSON, SIGURD FERDINAND (1899–1982)

A conservationist, author, and teacher, Sigurd Olson drew upon the science of ecology, classical learning, and personal experience for his philosophy that mankind needs contact with nature and wildness to retain its humanity and that protection of wilderness is preservation of the human spirit. Olson's experiences teaching biology at Ely Junior College, Minnesota, and as a guide and canoe outfitter prepared him for his later active role in securing wilderness protection for the border lakes. After 1946, Olson dedicated himself to full-time efforts to protect the QUETICO-SUPERIOR wilderness and later devoted his energies to the protection of other wild areas, notably in Alaska. His fame as a writer and his wilderness philosophy are an integral part of his preservation efforts.

Sigurd Olson was born in Chicago on April 4, 1899, and raised in northern Wisconsin. His father, a Swedish Baptist minister, influenced him with his belief that only farming, the ministry, or teaching were occupations worthy of pursuit. Olson chose teaching and graduated from the University of Wisconsin School of Agriculture in 1920. He taught biology and agriculture at Nashawk, Minnesota, and explored the Quetico-Superior region. He moved to Ely, Minnesota, in 1922 to teach at a junior college. His first canoe party was in 1923 and he operated an outfitting business until he entered full-time conservation work and writing in 1947.

Beginning in 1925, Olson wrote scores of pieces on hunting, fishing, and camping based on his first-hand experiences. His interest in science and ecology found its outlet in graduate study at the University of Illinois where he earned an M.S. in 1931 with a pioneering study of the ecology of timber wolves. Although he published his first philosophical essay in 1932, such pieces were not a large part of Olson's writings until after 1947. Later works, especially his books, interpret nature and develop a philosophy of wilderness and its relationship to culture, society, and individuals.

Singing Wilderness (1956), Olson's first book, is a collection of nature essays organized around a progression of seasonal themes. *Listening Point* (1958) follows the same format and explores the history and ecology of the Quetico-Superior country by focusing on features found on a point of land owned by Olson. Other works include *Lonely Land* (1961), *Runes of the North* (1963), *Hidden Forest* (1969), *Open Horizons* (1969), *Wilderness Days* (1972), and *Reflections from the North Country* (1978). These works expand upon and round out his philosophy of wilderness and its affirmation of civilized values. Olson received numerous awards for writing and conservation work, including the SIERRA CLUB'S John Muir Award in 1967 and the John Burroughs Memorial Association's John Burroughs Medal in 1973.

As a conservationist, Olson was effective through active membership in and leadership of many national organizations, including the National Parks Association (president, 1954–1959), the WILDERNESS SOCIETY (council member since 1956; vice-president, 1963–1968; and president, 1968–1972), the IZAAK WALTON LEAGUE (wilderness ecologist since 1947), and the President's Quetico-Superior Committee (wilderness consultant, 1947–1965). He was a consultant to the secretary of the interior (1960–1966); a member of the Department of Interior's Committee on Wilderness Preservation, Wildlife Refuges, National Parks, and Archeological and Historic Sites (1960–1968); and a consultant to the director of National Parks (1960–1973). He died January 13, 1982.

FURTHER READING: R. Newell Searle, *Saving Quetico-Superior: A Land Set Apart* (1977).

R. NEWELL SEARLE

OLYMPIC NATIONAL PARK

The creation of Olympic National Park in 1938 marked the climax of one of the great environmental battles in American history, pitting state against federal government, Forest Service against Interior Department, and industry against conservationists. In the far northwestern corner of the United States, the Olympic Peninsula presents wonderful scenery: mountains, herds of elk, and murky rain forest stretching its moss-covered fingers down to the Pacific shore. A million-and-a-half acres of this land was given forest reserve status by President Grover Cleveland in 1897. Subsequently, under Theodore ROOSEVELT, the rugged central portion became Mount Olympus National Monument. Reduced in size during World War I, the monument eventually passed under jurisdiction of the DEPARTMENT OF THE INTERIOR.

Early in the New Deal years, Interior Secretary Harold ICKES, backed by eastern conservationist groups and wilderness advocates in the Pacific Northwest, began a campaign for creation of a national park on the peninsula, combining extensive national forest scenic areas with the monument. Opposition quickly developed from the U. S. FOREST SERVICE and from the PULP AND PAPER INDUSTRY, both having plans for the use of hemlock on the western slopes of the Olympics for expansion of manufacturing on the peninsula. In addition, the Forest Service opposed the surrender of a portion of its holdings to the Interior Department. Joining the opposition was the State of Washington, as Governor Clarence Martin and other officials feared the impact of the proposed park on economic growth. Emotions were high and neither side in the conflict was willing to concede that its opponent had legitimate motives.

The real dispute was not over creation of a park but over the size of the eventual park. Proponents favored as large a park as possible, including ocean beaches and the rain forest valleys. Opponents argued for restriction of the park to the interior region and retention of the western lands by the Forest Service, allowing that agency to sell timber to pulp and paper mills on Grays Harbor and the Strait of Juan de Fuca. A series of bills introduced by Congressman Monrad Wallgren of Washington between 1935 and 1938 favored first one and then the other group, depending upon the pressure each was able to bring to bear in the nation's capital.

Finally, President Franklin D. ROOSEVELT entered the dispute, mandating a compromise that seemed to offer, in classic Roosevelt fashion, something for both opponents and proponents. In the fall of 1937, Roosevelt visited the peninsula. Early in 1938, he conferred with Governor Martin, promising to consult with the state about the final size of the park. Compromise legislation passed in June 1938 created a "small" Olympic National Park of 648,000 acres but authorized the president—after consultation with the state of Washington—to increase the park by an additional 250,000 acres. To supporters of a large park, Roosevelt let it be known that he would use this procedure to add the rain forests of the Bogachiel, Hoh, and Queets valleys, left outside the initial boundaries.

Under the terms of the legislation, Roosevelt and his successor, Harry Truman, expanded the park to its maximum limit. Pulp and paper interests failed in the late 1940s and again in the mid-1950s to secure major reductions in the park boundaries, reductions that would enable them to acquire timber. These failures hampered expansion of the industry in the region, as

park opponents had predicted. However, all but the most ardent advocates of growth have conceded that preservation of the scenic wonders of the Olympic Peninsula has largely compensated for any retardation of industry.

FURTHER READING: Ruby El Hult, *The Untamed Olympics: The Story of a Peninsula* (1954). Murray Morgan, *The Last Wilderness* (1955). Elmo R. Richardson, "Olympic National Park: Twenty Years of Controversy," *Forest History* 12 (Apr. 1968): 6–15. Ben W. Twight, "The Tenacity of Value Commitment: The Forest Service and the Olympic National Park," Ph.D. dissertation, University of Washington (1971).

ROBERT E. FICKEN

ONTHANK, KARL WILLIAM (1890–1967)

Karl Onthank was an educational administrator active in a number of conservation, civic, and professional organizations. Born on August 7, 1890, in New Jersey, Onthank earned B.S. (1913) and M.S. (1915) degrees from the University of Oregon and did additional graduate work at Columbia and Stanford universities. He began his professional career as a public school administrator in Oregon. From 1916 until his retirement in 1956, he served in various administrative capacities at the University of Oregon.

Always an avid hiker, Onthank played a leading role in conservation groups in the West from about 1948 until his death on October 27, 1967. He was an important participant in controversies over plans for construction of hydroelectric power facilities at Beaver Marsh on the upper McKenzie River in Oregon; over the proposed Oregon Dunes National Seashore; over the proposed exclusion of prime timberland from the Three Sisters Wilderness Area in the Cascade Ranges of Oregon; and over limitations to development around huge, pristine Waldo Lake, also in the Cascades.

Onthank was the first to advocate the ambitious Willamette River Greenway project, begun under Oregon's Governor Tom Lawson McCall and continued since. Onthank called for the establishment of rigid controls to clean up the Willamette and for the creation of a belt of interconnected park and wild lands along both sides of the stream through the length of the valley, a distance of over 100 miles. The project, he argued, would restore one of the nation's major rivers while making unparalleled recreational facilities available in the most densely populated part of the state.

Onthank served as president of the FEDERATION OF WESTERN OUTDOOR CLUBS from 1955 to 1957 and of the Oregon County Parks Association. He chaired the

Oregon Water Resources Board; was an organizer and officer of the Friends of the Three Sisters Wilderness after 1955 and of the Save the McKenzie River Association; and he was active in the Columbia Basin Inter-Agency Committee, the SIERRA CLUB, and other groups concerned with natural resources. While he was its president, the Federation of Western Outdoor Clubs sponsored the first Northwest Wilderness Conference. Michael McCloskey, executive director of the Sierra Club, described Onthank as "a truly catholic conservationist" primarily interested in parks and wilderness but also "deeply involved in the problems of water, reclamation, and forestry." To McCloskey, however, Onthank's greatest contribution lay in the host of young people in whom he instilled a lifelong commitment to conservation; McCloskey numbered himself in that group.

THOMAS R. COX

OREGON FORESTS

Of Oregon's 61,587,460 land acres, nearly half (30,023,000) were forested in 1977, and 39.6 percent (24.4 million) were capable of and available for growing timber for commercial harvest. Oregon trailed only Alaska among the states in acreage of commercial forest. Of this, the federal government held 14,193,000 acres including Indian lands, private owners held 9,345,000 acres, and state and local governments owned 997,000 acres.

Oregon's commercial forest may be classified as two distinct zones: the Douglas-fir region of 13.9 million acres between the Pacific Ocean and the Cascade crest and the western pine region of 10.6 million acres east of the crest. More than twelve tree species have commercial importance. The most prominent of these is the Douglas-fir, which grows from the western slope of the Cascades to the Pacific Ocean and on the Blue and Wallowa mountains of northeastern Oregon. Western hemlock of commercial quality is found almost exclusively on the western slopes of the Cascades and in the Coast Range. Ponderosa pine predominates in the drier eastern part of the state, grows widely in the Cascades, and occurs mixed with Douglas-fir in the southwest. There is also an extensive noncommercial woodland of western juniper in eastern Oregon. With control of range fires and overgrazing beginning in the late nineteenth century, juniper has invaded large areas that were formerly grassland, reducing their grazing potential.

The sparse Indian population of the Pacific Northwest used wood and bark from the forests sparingly, largely for plank houses, canoes, fuel, clothing, and some implements. The Indians regarded the forests less as a source of raw materials than as a home of spirits and animals significant to their culture. For the most part, Indians did little to alter or manage the vast tracts of timber on whose margins they lived. In the Willamette Valley, however, up to the 1830s when their population was reduced by epidemics, the Kalapuya (or Calapooya) annually burned the tall grass of the savannahs to aid in food gathering and maintain open vistas to allow detection of the approach of their enemies. Early white observers reported that such fires often destroyed large amounts of timber.

The arrival of white men in significant numbers early in the nineteenth century changed man's relationship to Oregon's forests. Although the original interests of the British, French Canadians, and Americans who came to the new land were in furs and farming, it was not long before the forests and their wood resources were exploited. In the earliest stages of settlement, timber had little monetary value, but it was important to the lives of the new farmers. Homes, furniture, implements, utensils, vehicles, machinery, and heat came from wood. Settlers in the Willamette Valley took up residence on the edge of the prairies to avoid much arduous clearing of cropland while still having a supply of wood close at hand. Sawmilling within the boundaries of the present-day state began at the Falls of the Willamette in Oregon City in 1842.

The California gold rush and the explosive growth of San Francisco made lumbering Oregon's leading industry. In 1849, thirty sawmills were operating there, mostly along the lower Columbia and Willamette rivers. That year, 16,853,000 board feet of lumber were manufactured south of the Columbia, four times the production in what would become the Territory of Washington north of the river. Although Oregon's lumber output soon fell behind that of its northern neighbor, it continued to expand through the remainder of the century, supplying materials for construction locally, in California, and around the Pacific Basin. Despite the opening of a direct transcontinental rail link in 1883, high freight rates kept midwestern markets from contributing much to this growth for at least a decade. Not until 1906 would as much lumber be exported from the Pacific Northwest by rail as by sea. In the nineteenth century, railroads were most important in opening up some of the remote forests to the loggers who previously had been tied to navigable bodies of water. After the Oregon and California Railroad was completed between Portland and Sacramento in 1887, lumbermen in southwestern Oregon provided new

The awesome Tillamook Burn devastated over a third of a million acres in western Oregon during the 1930s and 1940s. The rehabilitation of this vast area into productive land is one of forestry's great success stories. American Forest Institute Photo.

competition to the cargo mills which depended upon the sea routes.

As the century drew to a close, the depletion of the timber stands of the Lake States and the East brought more lumbermen and timberland investors into the Pacific Northwest, where the Homestead Act and the Timber and Stone Act both proved more useful in transferring lands to loggers than to farmers. Over 3 million acres in Oregon were purchased as Timber and Stone claims between 1900 and 1909. But it was federal railroad and wagon road grants that concentrated timberland ownership in the hands of relatively few large owners. When the U. S. Bureau of Corporations investigated the lumber industry in 1911 and 1912, it found that 264,520 acres in Oregon had been taken up through the use of Northern Pacific lieu scrip issued to compensate the railroad for its lands that had been absorbed into MOUNT RAINIER NATIONAL PARK and the Pacific Forest Reserve. The Weyerhaeuser Timber Company alone had acquired 160,043 of these Oregon forest acres. The holdings of the state's two largest private landowners—Weyerhaeuser and the Southern Pacific (which had absorbed the Oregon and California and its large land grant)—comprised 22.7 percent of the timberland in Oregon.

Oregon's reported annual lumber production passed 3 billion board feet in 1920, when the state passed Louisiana to rank second, behind only Washington. Oregon peaked just under 4.9 billion board feet in 1929, dropping to a Depression era low of 1.6 billion feet in 1932. By 1938, Oregon's lumber production had grown again to almost 3.8 billion board feet, and in that year Oregon passed Washington to become the largest lumber-producing state, a position it has held ever since. Douglas-fir alone provided over 62 percent of

Oregon's 1938 lumber output, while ponderosa pine accounted for 31 percent. Other significant lumber species in descending order were hemlock, sugar pine, cedar, and spruce. Very minor amounts of lumber (aggregating to about two-thirds of 1 percent of the total) came from white pine, white fir, larch, lodgepole pine, redwood, and hardwoods. Oregon's lumber production continued upward through World War II and after, peaking at over 9 billion board feet in 1953. The harvests have been mostly of old-growth timber, but since 1950 an increasing percentage has come from second-growth trees. This trend is particularly notable in the northwestern part of the state, the area first settled by whites, where the earliest logging occurred. By 1972, only one-half the cut in that part of Oregon was old-growth timber.

The use of wood pulp for papermaking in Oregon dates from the opening of a mill on Young's River near Astoria in 1884. Unlike neighboring Washington, Oregon was slow to become a major provider of wood pulp, ranking in twelfth place in 1955. Hemlock and spruce were the principal species used. By the 1950s, half of the wood consumed by Oregon pulpmills came from lumber and veneer residues; in 1980, this proportion stood at 85 percent. The state's annual pulp production reached almost 2.7 million tons in 1979. Another significant Oregon product, which depended heavily on lumber and veneer leftovers, was composition board. Oregon's board output rose from 650 million square feet in 1960, when the state manufactured over a quarter of the total United States supply, to 1.1 billion square feet in 1979.

Oregon did not become a major producer of plywood until 1950, when its output passed 1 billion square feet (calculated on a 3/8- inch basis). It ranked first in the nation after 1953 and in that year provided half the United States supply of softwood plywood. Unlike lumber production, Oregon's plywood manufacture continued to expand and passed 7.9 billion square feet in 1979. Other important forest products of Oregon were shingles and shakes, panel doors, poles and piling, and Christmas trees and greens. At that time, the state's forest industries directly employed 95,500 persons, or 44 percent of the total manufacturing employment.

Federal forestry activity in Oregon began with the proclamation by President Benjamin Harrison in 1892 and 1893 of the Bull Run, Ashland, and Cascade Range forest reserves, covering 4.7 million acres of public domain and intermingled private lands. Between 1904 and 1907, President Theodore ROOSEVELT designated over 7.1 million acres as twelve additional reserves. By the middle of the twentieth century, these tracts had been reorganized as fourteen national forests covering over 12 million acres of federal land. The last to be established was the Winema National Forest, which in 1961 was designated on land purchased from the Klamath Indians after the remainder of their reservation had been allotted. In 1924, the U. S. FOREST SERVICE established in Portland the Pacific Northwest Forest and Range Experiment Station, its administrative center for research in Oregon and Washington.

A significant development of the Progressive period was the return to the federal government in 1916 of nearly 3 million acres of some of the best timberland in the state when the Southern Pacific failed to comply with the provisions it had inherited from the Oregon and California Railroad (O & C) land grant. Under an act of Congress in 1937, the GENERAL LAND OFFICE (later BUREAU OF LAND MANAGEMENT) administered the revested O & C LANDS for sustained yield. Cooperative sustained-yield units comprising O & C and interspersed private lands, while not fully successful, were used as a model after 1944 for similar units on some national forest lands.

Another federal land-managing agency operating in the state was the NATIONAL PARK SERVICE, which administered only one primary natural unit in Oregon, Crater Lake National Park. In response to efforts by local citizens, Congress designated this park on 160,290 acres of forest reserve land in 1902.

Fires led to state interest in forestry. At least 1,580,000 acres of Oregon timber burned between 1848 and 1864. The Yaquina fire in 1853 burned 480,000 acres, destroying more than 25 billion board feet of timber. Such devastation led to passage of the state's first fire law in 1864. Designed largely to protect settlements, it outlawed arson or allowing a fire to spread from the property of one owner to that of another. Nevertheless, the State of Oregon was slow in becoming involved in the protection and administration of forest resources. Another round of ruinous fires in 1902 prompted the enactment of the forerunner of a forestry code, the fire patrol law of 1905. This measure marked progress made cooperatively by conservationists, lumber interests, and state officials, and the forest industries rapidly established their own fire-protection organizations. Nevertheless, Oregon did not establish a Board of Forestry until 1909. The state's park system also began slowly as an adjunct of the highway commission in the 1920s. In 1933, 1939, and 1945, fire burned and reburned some half million acres of the best timberland in the state. The blackened area, known as the Tillamook Burn and located in the Coast Range of northwestern Oregon, became a symbol of the danger to the state's primary economic asset. Government, industry, and private groups united to reforest the area and prevent further destruction. In 1948, the voters of Oregon approved the issuance of bonds to finance fire protection and reforestation on the Tillamook, a task completed in 1973.

Oregon State University in Corvallis established a forestry department in 1910. Three years later, it became the School of Forestry. In 1961, the school immensely expanded its research facilities with the acquisition of the Oregon Forest Research Center, which had formerly been a separate state agency. The research facility continued to be financed through a severance tax on timber.

The national housing boom from the 1950s through the 1970s and the demand for a variety of new wood products developed by industry strained the relations between state and federal agencies and the lumber companies. A powerful lobby of conservationists and environmentalists sought restrictions upon timber harvesting. An ongoing controversy was the "evenflow" debate, which centered on the need of the federal government to harvest its old-growth timber in the southwestern part of the state before it could rot, while receiving assurance that private enterprise would not cut its second-growth wood prematurely, thus damaging the marketability of lumber and reducing potential for future harvest. A second continuing problem was the argument among environmentalists, industry, and public officials over the amount of federal land that should be set aside as inviolate wilderness. By 1980, designated wilderness in Oregon totaled 1.2 million acres of federal land and another 800,000 acres were under consideration for wilderness designation or further planning.

FURTHER READING: Thomas R. Cox, *Mills and Markets: A History of the Pacific Coast Lumber Industry to 1900* (1974). Stephen D. Beckham, "Asa Mead Simpson: Lumberman and Shipbuilder," *Oregon Historical Quarterly* 68 (Sept. 1967): 259-273. Lawrence Rakestraw, A History of Forest Conservation in the Pacific Northwest, 1891-1913," Ph.D. dissertation, University of Washington (1955, reprinted 1979).

CRAIG E. WOLLNER

OREGON STATE FORESTRY

Serious attempts to start a forestry program in Oregon began after the devastating fires of 1902. In 1904, the Booth-Kelly Timber Company in Lane County started a cooperative fire patrol with adjoining landowners, and in the following year the state legislature authorized counties to appoint fire wardens and imposed a closed season on burning. With the support of the timber industry, a state Board of Forestry was formed in 1907 to investigate forest conditions, but funds were appropriated only to cover office expenses. In response to the White House CONFERENCE OF GOVERNORS convened by President Theodore ROOSEVELT, Oregon in 1909 created a Conservation Commission to re-evaluate its forestry program. The commission's recommendations, combined with the disastrous 1910 fire season, led the legislature to enact laws in 1911 to re-establish the Board of Forestry, authorize a state forester and a state Forestry Department, and appropriate $60,000 for a two-year period. F. A. Elliott was appointed Oregon's first state forester.

Under the Compulsory Fire Control Act of 1911, fire protection became the primary responsibility of the new department. This law required landowners to either protect their lands according to state standards or pay an assessment to the state forester who would provide this protection. In 1920, the Board of Forestry adopted policies calling for increased fire protection, a forest nursery, insect- control efforts, and formation of state forests. A Pine Beetle Control Law was passed the following year. Over 1 million acres were declared a zone of infestation under this act and were eventually treated for pine beetles. Oregon's first state forest nursery was established in 1925. By the time this nursery was replaced with a new one in 1964, it had produced over 100 million seedlings. Private landowners were encouraged by a 1929 law to reforest cutover lands for future timber crops. The law deferred forest TAXATION until timber was harvested.

Forest management was added to departmental responsibilities in 1929, when Oregon consolidated a state forest of 70,000 acres by exchanging scattered lands which had been obtained from the federal government upon statehood in 1859.

After the first of three Tillamook fires burned 250,-000 acres of virgin timber in northwest Oregon in 1933, the state forester was given authority to require permits for operating power-driven machinery in forest areas. The state's regulation of private forestry increased with the Oregon Forest Conservation Act of 1941, the first law in the nation requiring that private logged-over lands be reforested, either by leaving a seed source or by artificial restocking. In the mid-1940s, the department began forestry assistance for private nonindustrial woodland owners. Portions of the Tillamook burned again in 1939 and in 1945 until some 350,000 acres had been covered. Most of these lands were acquired by counties because of delinquent taxes, and ownership was transferred to the department under legislation of the late 1930s.

Oregonians approved a major rehabilitation program for the Tillamook Burn in a constitutional amendment of 1948. The next quarter century saw $12 million invested in SALVAGE, reforestation, and fire protection there. In 1973, twenty-four years to the day after the Tillamook rehabilitation program had begun, the project was completed and the area dedicated as the Tillamook State Forest. Altogether, state-owned forests managed by the department extended to over 786,000 acres. The state's forest nursery by 1980 produced 25 million seedlings annually.

The impact of the new ENVIRONMENTAL MOVEMENT was reflected in the passage of Oregon's 1971 Forest Practices Act which became a model for other states. This act emphasized educational programs for landowners and forest operators. Close cooperation by the forest industry and natural resource agencies contributed to the act's success. It required reforestation and protection of water quality, and regulated road construction and maintenance, timber harvesting, use of chemicals, and slash disposal. The year 1969 saw the beginning of the Oregon Smoke Management Plan, which regulated the burning of slash on public and private forests to allow reduction of hazards and preparation of planting sites while keeping smoke from population areas. Improved fire protection came after 1975 with the "closest man" plan, which eliminated traditional boundaries among protection agencies in favor of initial attack by the nearest available forces.

In 1977, the Board of Forestry developed a program outlining specific actions to avoid projected timber supply shortages in the next twenty years. By that time the policymaking board had grown from five members to eighteen, representing forest industry, agriculture, farming, labor, and the public. In 1980, over 600 full- time personnel and 1,000 seasonal employees worked for the Department of Forestry.

FURTHER READING: Gordon B. Anderson, Jr., "Oregon's Forest Conservation Laws," *American Forests* 83 (Mar. 1977): 16–19, 52-56; (Apr. 1977): 19-21, 41-44. Oregon State Forestry Department, *Forest, People & Oregon: A History of Forestry in Oregon* (1978). Ralph R. Widner, ed., *Forests and Forestry in the American States: A Reference Anthology* (1968), pp. 165–171, 276-291.

JAMES G. FISHER

OREGON STATE PARKS

In 1919, Robert W. Sawyer, editor of the *Bend Bulletin*, was urged by Stephen T. MATHER of the NATIONAL PARK SERVICE and Madison Grant of the New York Zoological Society to undertake a campaign to save roadside beauty in Oregon. Sawyer set to work,

arranging for the reservation from logging of timber along the highway south of Bend and for the donation of park sites to the state. Sawyer joined forces with Governor Ben Olcott, who was calling on Oregonians to keep their state the "most livable," and a major campaign was soon under way.

Olcott proposed a package of laws for the preservation of scenic beauty. Only his bill allowing the State Highway Commission to acquire roadside parks passed the legislature, but with Sawyer on the Highway Commission this was sufficient to ensure action even after Olcott was defeated in the gubernatorial election of 1922.

In 1919, Oregon had pioneered gasoline taxes earmarked for highways. Such taxes meant that parks under the Highway Department would have an assured source of funding. Officials of the NATIONAL CONFERENCE ON STATE PARKS (NCSP) disliked this approach and urged a separate State Parks Department for Oregon. Sawyer and fellow commissioner Henry B. Van Duzer, believing that public support for parks was as yet too limited to make such a department secure during the biennial scramble for legislative appropriations, successfully squelched the NCSP proposal and kept parks under the Highway Department, where they have remained ever since.

Sawyer then persuaded his fellow commissioners to hire a state parks superintendent, Samuel H. Boardman, who remained in the position from 1929 to 1950. Boardman built up one of the nation's premier systems of state parks. He emphasized acquisition while land was still relatively inexpensive; development could come later. Wanting to keep the parks natural, he opposed overnight camping, trailer facilities, commercial development, and extensive recreational facilities. To Boardman, parks were "sermonettes" bringing visitors closer to the divine; the artificial should intrude as little as possible.

Sawyer was removed from the Highway Commission in 1930 but even though subsequent commissioners showed little interest in parks, growth of the system continued. Boardman's enthusiasm, his ability to rally community support, his doggedness, and his persuasive arguments for prompt action resulted in a steady stream of acquisitions.

Boardman emphasized acquisitions in western Oregon. He described how, coming across the Cascades from the arid eastern part of the state, he had thought that everything from the mountains to the sea ought to be one giant park. He was especially active in obtaining sites along the coast, but his greatest scheme there came to naught. In the 1930s, he proposed a state bond issue for the purchase of all the land between U. S.

Highway 101 and the coastline wherever the two were closely parallel; never again would the land be so cheap, he said. In the face of depression-spawned problems, his proposal received no serious attention in spite of his argument, successful on other occasions, that Oregon should learn from California's sad example and acquire parkland before prices had skyrocketed and many sites were permanently developed.

Both circumstances and Boardman gradually changed during his tenure. The small roadside parks acquired during the system's first years became less important as modern highways replaced earlier roads with their slow speeds and more frequent stops. A handful of large parks came to receive most of the attention and most of the visitors. Fortunately, a number of early acquisitions fit the new needs, although highway relocation bypassed some of the old parks and timbered roadside strips that Boardman and others had saved during his earlier years. Meanwhile, Boardman's tastes in scenery broadened, and he acquired parks in the rugged Deschutes River canyon at The Cove, in the John Day Fossil Beds (which became John Day Fossil Beds National Monument in 1974), and in other places east of the Cascades that once would not have appealed to him.

At the time of Boardman's retirement, postwar tourism was booming. It had become the state's third largest industry, and pressure for overnight camping and recreational facilities was immense. The state's travel promotion agency, like parks a division of the Highway Department, joined many others in advocating expanded facilities. Responding, the Highway Commission selected Chester H. Armstrong as Boardman's replacement. Armstrong emphasized development rather than acquisition. He opened parks to camping, put in trailer and recreational facilities, and when he did add new parks, he generally obtained sites valued for their recreational rather than scenic potential. Armstrong called his tenure the "construction period."

Following Armstrong's retirement in 1960, a more balanced program emerged, especially under David G. Talbot, who assumed the superintendency in 1964. State parks had become a familiar and accepted part of the Oregon scene, though they were seldom in the public eye.

Then, under Governor Tom Lawson McCall (1967–1975), parks were pushed to center stage. Echoing Governor Olcott of forty years before, McCall campaigned to keep Oregon the most livable of states. Picking up a proposal made by Karl W. ONTHANK, McCall urged creation of a Willamette River Greenway, a series of parklands bordering the Willamette River for the length of its valley. With strict pollution controls along the river, McCall argued that the greenway could become one of the great scenic and recreational sites in the United States. Unlike most large parks, it would be located in the state's densely populated heartland. As grandiose as Boardman's dreams for the Oregon coast, this proposal came at a more propitious time. Carried along by rising public concern for the environment and by the support of McCall and his successor, Robert Straub, the Willamette River Greenway moved bit by bit toward becoming a reality.

Under Talbot, Oregon's parks have been less isolated from activities elsewhere than they were in the time of Sawyer and Boardman. Still, Oregonians maintain their tradition of independence on environmental matters, as their pioneering bottle bill and the recent ban on fluorocarbon sprays demonstrate. It has been a constructive independence. As McCall told Secretary of the Interior Stewart UDALL during a disagreement over park policy, "in Oregon . . . the quality and number of parks is legendary"; therefore, Udall ought not to approach McCall's administration —or Oregon—as an adversary. McCall's point was well taken. Oregon was among the leading states in per capita acreage and expenditures for parks. By the late 1970s, Oregon's system totaled over 90,000 acres in more than 230 units.

FURTHER READING: Chester H. Armstrong, *History of the Oregon State Parks, 1917–1963* (1965). Thomas R. Cox, "Conservation by Subterfuge: Robert W. Sawyer and the Birth of the Oregon State Parks," *Pacific Northwest Quarterly* 64 (Jan. 1973): 21-29.

THOMAS R. COX

ORNAMENTAL PLANTS

Generally thought of as a nursery product, a large number of ornamental plants were harvested from the forest as late as the 1950s.

Park landscapers in the nineteenth century drew upon the forests for their trees, plants, and shrubs. With the growth of cities, it became fashionable for the well-to-do to obtain landscaping materials from the woods and, in the age of Victorian bric-a-brac, to keep plants in their homes.

At first, securing these plants was an informal affair. However, by the early twentieth century, a minor industry to fill growing urban and suburban needs had developed. In addition to raising house and landscape plants from seed or cuttings, nurserymen arranged for the harvesting of trees and shrubs from privately owned or state and national forests. The various forest services cooperated both as a means of thinning out azaleas, rhododendrons, holly, leucothoe, and laurel in order to encourage the growth of more valuable species and as a means of generating a modest income.

The practice of collecting ornamental plants grew with the expansion of suburbia during the 1920s. Nelson Courtlandt Brown wrote in *Timber Products* (1937) that "from the mountain forests of the southern Appalachians, many carloads of rhododendrons, azaleas, mountain laurel, and other ericaceous plants are obtained." At that time private forestland owners in New York State were digging, potting, and shipping thousands of forest plants and trees to East Coast cities most weeks of the late winter and spring.

The U. S. FOREST SERVICE maintained a program from the 1930s into the 1950s under which 17,000 leucothoe plants and 37,000 rhododendrons and mountain laurels were annually removed from the Unaka National Forest in Tennessee.

Several national forests in Colorado and elsewhere in the West sold rooted stock of blue spruce, ponderosa pine, and Rocky Mountain cedar to plant wholesalers. Many of the larger trees sold as late as the 1970s originated in state or local forests.

OUTDOOR RECREATION RESOURCES REVIEW COMMISSION

On June 28, 1958, President Dwight D. Eisenhower signed an act creating a high-level commission "to determine the outdoor recreation wants and needs of the American people now and what they will be in the years 1976 and 2000; to determine the recreation resources of the Nation available to satisfy those needs . . . ; and to determine what policies and programs should be recommended to ensure that the needs of the present and future are adequately and efficiently met." The enabling legislation was largely drafted by Joseph W. PENFOLD of the IZAAK WALTON LEAGUE and Edward C. Crafts, assistant chief of the U. S. FOREST SERVICE. Both men subsequently worked closely with the Outdoor Recreation Resources Review Commission (ORRRC) and its chairman, Laurance S. ROCKEFELLER.

Composed of four senators, four representatives, and seven presidential appointees, the ORRRC was advised by a council of fifteen government bureaucrats and twenty-five representatives of a variety of economic and recreational interests. Although little attention was given to urban facilities such as city playgrounds, golf courses, and zoos, the ORRRC surveyed almost every other aspect of American recreation out of doors. The work of the ORRRC was thus in many respects a parallel for its time to the work of the NATIONAL CONFERENCE ON OUTDOOR RECREATION in the 1920s. However, reluctant to establish another permanent agency of government, Congress directed the ORRRC to dissolve within seven months of submitting its final report on January 31, 1962.

The commission made fifty-two highly specific recommendations, some of which profoundly influenced government programs and popular attitudes toward forests. The ORRRC discovered that simple activities, especially walking and hiking, were the most popular forms of forest recreation. Although ORRRC favored multiple use of forestlands, it also called for congressional action to ensure the permanent protection of wilderness on federal lands as well as "natural environment" areas where only limited developments would be allowed. ORRRC also recommended a comprehensive national program of public land acquisition and recreational development, to be supported by federal and state funds in matching shares.

In deference to state sensibilities, the commission assigned the states a "key role" in carrying out its recommendations but tacitly gave the federal government chief responsibility. It evaded its own prescribed termination by calling for the establishment of a permanent bureau which would prepare a comprehensive plan to serve the country's recreational needs until the year 2000. Tacitly critical of the NATIONAL PARK SERVICE, the commission's recommendations resulted in the establishment of the Bureau of Outdoor Recreation in 1962 and the passage in 1964 of the Land and Water Conservation Fund Act. Its reports influenced other federal recreation legislation of the 1960s, much of which had been delayed pending the completion of the ORRRC report.

FURTHER READING: Edwin M. Fitch and John F. Shanklin, *The Bureau of Outdoor Recreation* (1970). *Outdoor Recreation for America: A Report to the President and to the Congress by the Outdoor Recreation Resources Review Commission* (1962).

OWNERSHIP

See Forest Ownership

P

PACK, CHARLES LATHROP (1857–1937)

Charles Lathrop Pack, the son of a lumberman, was born May 7, 1857, in Lexington, Michigan, and educated at Brooks School in Cleveland, Ohio. While visiting Germany, Pack was impressed by the scientific forest management practiced in the Black Forest. After two years in the Michigan lumber industry, Pack invested profitably in southern pine timber. He also had interests in numerous other businesses, such as the Cleveland Trust Company.

Pack was a delegate and speaker at the American Forest Congress sponsored by the AMERICAN FORESTRY ASSOCIATION (AFA) in Washington, D.C., in 1905, a forestry adviser at the White House CONFERENCE OF GOVERNORS in 1908, a member of the National Conservation Commission the same year, and president of the National Conservation Congress in 1913. Pack served as a director of AFA after 1911 and as president from 1916 to 1922. During World War I, Pack organized the National War Garden Commission to promote home gardens and extend America's food supplies.

In 1920, Pack conceived of and financed gifts of tree seeds to Belgium, France, and Italy to reforest war-devastated lands. In 1922, 100 million Douglas-fir seeds were sent to Great Britain and France to rehabilitate forests whose wood had been cut for war use.

That year, with his son Arthur Newton Pack (1893–1975), Pack founded two organizations headquartered in Washington, D.C.: the AMERICAN TREE ASSOCIATION and the AMERICAN NATURE ASSOCIATION, the first to advance public awareness of forests as economic resources and the second intended to address a broader range of conservation problems. Pack also started a current awareness magazine in 1923, *Forestry News Digest,* distributed free to foresters and others. Circulation eventually reached 55,000 copies. In 1924, he endowed scholarships at seven schools of forestry. The awards were to be made to students who wrote essays presenting the ideals and principles of forestry "in a way that will appeal to the general public and help enlist public cooperation." Pack subsidized the first demonstration forests at Lake George in the Adirondacks (operated by the New York State College of Forestry) and at La Grande on the Mount Rainier Highway (operated by the University of Washington). Pack also endowed a chair of forest soils and two fellowships at Cornell University. He made numerous other endowments to support forestry education and increase the understanding of forestry principles among the public. These activities culminated in 1930 in the creation of the CHARLES LATHROP PACK FORESTRY FOUNDATION.

In recognition of his contributions to forestry, the

SOCIETY OF AMERICAN FORESTERS elected Pack an honorary member, and four institutions awarded him honorary degrees: Trinity College (LL.D., 1918), Syracuse University (D.Bus.A., 1925), Oberlin College (LL.D., 1926), and Rutgers University (Sc.D., 1930).

Pack was the author of *Schoolbook of Forestry* (1922), *Trees as Good Citizens* (1923), and *Forestry Primer* (1926). He coauthored with Thomas Harvey Gill two other works, *Forests and Mankind* (1929) and *Forest Facts for Schools* (1931).

Charles Lathrop Pack died June 14, 1937.

HENRY CLEPPER

PATHOLOGY

See Forest Pathology

PENFOLD, JOSEPH WELLER (1907–1973)

Man and organization united for more than twenty years of fruitful conservation effort when Joe Penfold worked for the IZAAK WALTON LEAGUE OF AMERICA (IWLA), first as its western representative in Denver (1949–1957) and thereafter as its conservation director in Washington, D.C., and Arlington, Virginia.

Born in Marinette, Wisconsin, on November 18, 1907, Penfold took his time in finding the career road he would travel to conservation accomplishment. In the Great Depression years, he directed conservation activities of the National Youth Administration in Ohio, where he was strongly influenced by the philosophy of Bryce R. Browning, executive of the Muskingum Watershed Conservancy District. After World War II, Penfold witnessed scars on the people and the earth of China while he was a field man for two years with the United Nations Relief and Rehabilitation Administration.

Penfold's return to the United States and employment by the IWLA in 1949 at the age of forty-two came at the close of the "Great Land Grab" attempt of certain livestock interests and during early stages of the effort by the same group to curtail the authority of the U. S. FOREST SERVICE over its rangelands. It was a challenge that Penfold met well. About the same time he became aware of BUREAU OF RECLAMATION plans for two high dams—Echo Park and Split Mountain—in Dinosaur National Monument in Colorado and Utah. He took steps that proved to be among the most effective in defeating the plan, and this success had significance toward safeguarding the entire National Park System from similar invasions. In 1952, Penfold arranged and took part in a floating and camping trip in

the threatened area with Congressman Wayne N. Aspinall, subsequently chairman of the House Interior and Insular Affairs Committee, and Congressman John P. Saylor, the committee's ranking minority member; both later acted to kill the dams plan.

After his transfer to Washington, Penfold was often asked by other conservationists, and even members of Congress, to intercede with Aspinall on critical resource issues. Once, when Minnesota supporters of Voyageurs National Park had offended Aspinall, Penfold talked with the congressman and spent midnight hours on the telephone and rewriting the bill to please all parties. In 1978, Aspinall wrote that "as Joe worked so hard during his last years and months (under physical conditions which have destroyed others) my admiration for this man developed to a degree very few others have ever had in my life." Their mutual respect led to many beneficial enactments and to the elimination of harmful passages in other legislation.

Penfold crystallized thoughts he had evolved in exchanges with others and wrote the act that established the OUTDOOR RECREATION RESOURCES REVIEW COMMISSION (ORRRC) in 1958. He served on ORRRC as a presidential appointee. Its report, completed in 1962, led to creation of the Bureau of Outdoor Recreation (BOR), the Land and Water Conservation Fund, and a score or more of national recreation areas as well as the BOR-directed development of comprehensive outdoor recreation plans for all states. Penfold gave the IWLA all credit for the ORRRC success. As Margaret E. Murie has said, Penfold was "self-effacing," although "strong and fearless in standing for what had to be done."

Penfold also worked in support of stronger antipollution measures, the MULTIPLE USE-SUSTAINED YIELD ACT of 1960, the Wilderness Act of 1964, the Wild and Scenic Rivers Act of 1968, legislation strengthening the BUREAU OF LAND MANAGEMENT, and higher fees for livestock grazing on public ranges. He did not live to see the creation after 1975 of a system of wilderness areas in eastern national forests, a program which he had initiated.

He was secretary of the NATURAL RESOURCES COUNCIL OF AMERICA from 1957 to 1965, vice chairman in 1966, and chairman from 1967 to 1969. Near the end of his career, Penfold earnestly tried to bring about an IWLA-led crusade for environmental betterment in large cities, but this effort died in 1977.

Penfold's part in initiating ORRRC earned him the DEPARTMENT OF THE INTERIOR's Conservation Service Award in 1962. In 1969, the AMERICAN FORESTRY ASSOCIATION created a special award to honor him, and at the 1973 North American Wildlife and Natural Resources Conference, less than three months before his death on May 25, Penfold was the honored guest at a surprise luncheon in which representatives of the entire conservation community took part, with many of its leaders and high governmental officials rising in turn to pay him tribute.

WILLIAM VOIGT, JR.

PENNSYLVANIA FORESTS

The name given in 1681 to the territory granted by Charles II to William Penn recognized that these lands were a heavily forested domain. About 98 percent of the 28 million acres of Pennsylvania was originally tree-covered. Pine and hemlock cloaked the higher portions of the Alleghenies, with hardwoods increasing in prominence at lower elevations on either slope. Below the mountains in the southwest, the forest consisted almost entirely of hardwoods. In 1977, after centuries of land clearing and logging, 17,832,000 acres, or almost 64 percent of the state, were in forests, with nearly 17.5 million acres classed as commercial. Four forest types comprised 91 percent of the commercial forest. The most extensive was oak-hickory (almost half of the commercial forest), dominating the southern and central areas of the state. The maple-beech-birch type (another quarter of the commercial forest) covered the Allegheny Plateau and formed a belt along the state's northern boundary. There are also significant areas of elm-ash-red maple and of aspen-birch forest. White pine, once the most valued timber, by 1975 predominated only in small areas.

Swedish settlers along the Delaware River in 1638 began the clearing for farming of the fertile piedmont in the southeast. Eventually, farmers cleared the long, narrow valleys lying between the eastern and central Appalachian ranges, while the forests of the mountain ridges and portions of the Pocono Plateau of the east central and northeastern portions of the state were cut to provide CHARCOAL for the iron industry and, when anthracite coal was exploited after 1840, for mine props and timbers. As early as 1830, farmers brought rafts of white pine, cut square or as rough-sawed lumber, down the Delaware and Susquehanna rivers to provide building and shipbuilding materials in Philadelphia and Baltimore. Others brought similar rafts down the Allegheny.

In 1850, John Leighton and James H. Perkins of Maine, in partnership with John DUBOIS and other local lumbermen, constructed a boom across the West Branch of the Susquehanna at Williamsport. The Williamsport boom and those which soon followed on that and other principal rivers of Pennsylvania introduced a new, mass-production phase to the lumber industry. The log-driving practices imported from the rivers of Maine provided the raw material to sustain huge sawmills and prompted the acquisition of large tracts of timberland under common ownerships. Harvesting of the forests on the mountain and plateau lands of the northern, central, and southwestern areas followed, and by 1860, Pennsylvania led the nation in lumber production. It remained one of the leaders, surpassed only by the Lake States, through the rest of the nineteenth century.

Introduced into the state in 1864, the logging railroad opened areas remote from streams. By the 1880s, railroads had become the chief means of log transportation. Pennsylvania's principal forest products during this period were white pine and hardwood lumber, chemical wood, and hemlock bark for a vast tanning industry. Lumber production reached a peak of almost 2.5 billion board feet in 1890, nearly four-fifths of it pine and hemlock. For nearly three decades beginning in 1889, Pennsylvania also ranked as one of the top five states in pulpwood production.

The supply of available softwoods declined so rapidly, however, that by 1900 Pennsylvania was a net importer of lumber and by 1915 the state was producing more hardwood lumber than softwood. Pennsylvania's lumbermen looked elsewhere for timber. Frank H. and Charles W. GOODYEAR, for example, having depleted their hemlock stands in north-central Pennsylvania, invested in the yellow pine of Louisiana and Mississippi. In 1911, the Goodyears closed their Galeton and Austin sawmills, which had been the two largest lumber producers in Pennsylvania. By 1930, land clearing, logging, and fire had reduced Pennsylvania's forested area to about 13 million acres, 46 percent of the surface of the state.

The harvesting of the remaining old-growth timber continued into the twentieth century, ending about 1935. Thereafter, forest utilization declined until the end of World War II. Only small sawmills (producing mine timber, railroad ties, and rough lumber) and a few small pulp mills comprised the forest industry. In the next decade, the state forestry program coupled with extensive farmland abandonment began to increase the acreage of forests and the volume and quality of the timber. A survey of 1955 found 15 million acres, or 54 percent of the state, forested. In the next two decades, despite growing urban sprawl, forests gained over 1.8 million acres and covered 58 percent of Pennsylvania. In 1980, important forest products were lumber, pulp and paper, CHRISTMAS

TREES, hardwood furniture, and a wide variety of other items, including mine and railroad timber.

The agreement made in 1681 between Penn and the purchasers of lands provided "that, in clearing the ground, care be taken to leave one acre of trees for every five acres cleared, especially to preserve oak and mulberries for silk and shipping." In a number of acts beginning in 1683, the colonial assembly and later the state legislature limited to certain seasons (and in 1794 outlawed) the burning of the woods and proscribed the unauthorized cutting of timber. In 1874, Governor John Hartranft called for conservation of Pennsylvania's forests, and in 1887 the legislature attempted to encourage widespread reforestation. These early measures were not successful in protecting the forests of the state, however.

Joseph T. ROTHROCK and other citizens, concerned about the devastation of the forested mountain areas through logging and fires resulting from slash accumulations, joined in 1886 to found the Pennsylvania Forestry Association. This group was not the first such state group to be founded in the nation, but eventually it would become the oldest one with an unbroken record of activity. The association was the major force responsible for the establishment of an effective state forestry program and for the development of that program over its initial two decades. In 1893, the legislature authorized the governor to appoint a committee to report on the forest resources of the state. As a result of that report, largely written by Rothrock, the state in 1895 created a Department of Agriculture with a Bureau of Forestry. Rothrock became the first commissioner of forestry. Legislation of 1897 authorized the state to assume responsibility for forest fire control and to purchase land for state forest reservations which would serve to demonstrate good practices. The first units of what would eventually become a state forest system of 2 million acres were established on abandoned tax-delinquent land in 1898. In 1901, Rothrock became secretary of the new Department of Forestry, and in the same year the state hired its first professional forester, George H. Wirt, a graduate of Carl A. SCHENCK's Biltmore Forest School in North Carolina. A state tree nursery began operation in 1902. It supplied stock for planting on both the state forests and private lands. Initial work of the state forest service included the development of the state forests, reforestation, and fire control. Between 1900 and 1910, the state acquired nearly a million acres of logged and burned-over land in order to protect the watersheds of the Susquehanna, Allegheny, Delaware, and Potomac rivers. Pennsylvania launched its efforts in

forestry research in 1911 when it became the first state to appropriate major funds for investigation of chestnut blight.

As state forest commissioner after 1920, Gifford PINCHOT divided the state into forest districts, expanded forestry programs on private lands, and had steel fire towers and other new facilities constructed. In 1923, state forestry in Pennsylvania was reorganized as a bureau of the new Department of Forests and Waters. The advent of the CIVILIAN CONSERVATION CORPS in 1933 tremendously expanded work in the state forests and a growing forest park system. Nevertheless, Pinchot's term as commissioner (1920–1922) and two terms as governor (1923–1927 and 1931-1935) disappointed Pennsylvania foresters such as George Wirt, who felt that forestry had made few advances under Pinchot and that the state service had become riddled with politics.

During the two decades following World War II, the Bureau of Forestry modernized its protection plans for fire, insects, and disease, and initiated the use of aircraft. Management plans for state forests completed in 1955 and 1970 provided for resources in timber, water, wildlife, RECREATION, and wild and natural areas. Starting in 1956, revenues from oil and gas underlying state forests helped support flood control and state park development. Reforestation of Pennsylvania's nearly 1 million acres of strip-mined coal lands became an important state activity after 1957. The state parks were bureaus within a new Department of Environmental Resources. Forestry programs since then have placed particular emphasis on recreation and the development of wood as an energy resource.

The shortage of professional foresters in America had hindered Rothrock's early reforms. In 1903, Pennsylvania became the first state to train its own foresters when the Department of Forestry established the Forest Academy at Mont Alto, with Wirt as director. In 1924, this academy became the Pennsylvania State Forestry School. Pennsylvania State College inaugurated a department of forestry in 1906, and absorbed the State Forestry School in 1929. The combined institution, now known as the Pennsylvania State University School of Forest Resources, offers degrees in a variety of forestry and wildlife specialties. Williamsport Community College also offers training in forest technology.

Federal forestry activity in Pennsylvania began in 1921 with purchase under the WEEKS ACT of lands that became the basis of the Allegheny National Forest in the northwestern part of the state. Following passage of the CLARKE-MCNARY ACT in 1924 and subsequent cooperative program legislation, strong working relationships developed between the State Bureau of Forestry and the U. S. FOREST SERVICE State and Private Forestry Section in fire prevention and control, tree nursery programs, insect and disease control, personnel training, administration and management, and urban forestry. The first Forest Service research unit in Pennsylvania was the Allegheny Forest Experiment Station headquartered in Philadelphia in 1927 which in 1945 merged into the Northeastern Forest Experiment Station, later located in Upper Darby.

Of the nearly 17.5 million acres of commercial forestland in Pennsylvania in 1977, over 14 million (80 percent) was in private ownership. State and local governments owned about 2.9 million acres and the federal government held 515,000.

FURTHER READING: Henry Clepper, "Rise of the Forest Conservation Movement in Pennsylvania," *Pennsylvania History* 12 (June 1945): 200-216, and "Forest Conservation in Pennsylvania: The Pioneer Period, from Rothrock to Pinchot," *Pennsylvania History* 48 (Jan. 1981): 41-50. Thomas R. Cox, "Transition in the Woods: Log Drivers, Raftsmen, and the Emergence of Modern Lumbering in Pennsylvania," *Pennsylvania Magazine of History and Biography* 104 (July 1980): 345-364. James Elloitt Defebaugh, History of the Lumber Industry of America 2 (1907): 517-655. Benjamin F. G. Kline, Jr., Walter C. Casler, and Thomas T. Taber III, *Logging Railroad Era of Lumbering in Pennsylvania* (13 vols., 1971-1973). Susan R. Schrepfer, Edwin vH. Larson, and Elwood R. Maunder, *A History of the Northeastern Forest Experiment Station, 1923 to 1973*, U. S. Forest Service General Technical Report ME-7 (1973). Ralph R. Widner, ed., *Forests and Forestry in the American States: A Reference Anthology* (1968).

SAMUEL S. COBB

PESTICIDES AND BIOLOGICAL CONTROL

Attempts to wring maximum yields from farm, forest, and range require the suppression of competing species, whether plants or insects. Pest problems are most acute in annual crops, where cultivation creates an artificial, short-lived monoculture, open to invasion by plants that flourish on disturbed ground and attractive to insects that prey on the particular crop. However, such pests exist in all areas where humans attempt to bias a complex system toward the production of a single product. People have developed both direct methods of dealing with pests—weeding, gathering insects by hand, using chemical poisons or biological agents—and indirect means or manipulation of the environment to hinder the reproduction or survival of pests, such as destroying favored breeding or resting places, changing farming practices to minimize contact with the pest, and introducing or favoring predators or parasites.

Economic entomology developed along with modern methods of insect control in post-Civil War America, in response to the insect problems farmers faced. The appointment of Charles V. Riley as head of the Department of Agriculture's Division of Entomology in 1878 marked the beginning of serious federal commitment to research in this area. The Hatch Act of 1887 gave funding for state agricultural experiment stations and established the network of research institutions that would nourish the discipline of economic entomology. The Division of Entomology became a bureau in 1904 and merged into the Bureau of Entomology and Plant Quarantine in 1934. A section on FOREST ENTOMOLOGY was established in 1904. When the bureau was abolished fifty years later, forest entomology went to the U. S. FOREST SERVICE as the Division of Forest Insect Research, but most of the bureau's other work went to the Agricultural Research Service.

Chemicals were long the most common means of pest control; Paris green (copper aceto-arsenite) and other arsenicals were in use since the late 1860s. Biological control, the use of a pest's natural enemies such as insects, viruses, and fungal and bacterial agents, dated from 1889, when a vedalia beetle from Australia was turned loose on the cottony-cushion scale in California orchards. Chemicals, however, dominated insect pest control and pest control research by the 1920s. Farmers preferred chemicals because they did not require changes in farm practices, and they offered immediate aid against insect irruptions. Economic entomologists also found chemicals ideal, because they often gave visible and even spectacular results, impressing both farmers and appropriations committees.

Indirect controls, particularly biological controls, depended on a more sophisticated knowledge of the ecology of pests and their enemies than was available. The difficulties became apparent in the Bureau of Entomology's campaign against the gypsy moth, one of the largest attempts to control an imported pest by establishing its natural enemies in this country. In 1905, Leland Howard, chief of the bureau, had been confident that natural enemies would end the problem, and he predicted success in three to five years. By 1911, after the attempted establishment of some three dozen predators and parasites which preyed on the moth in Europe, entomologists were beginning to think that the eventual control might require the es-

A predator wasp attacks a bark beetle, one of the most destructive forest pests. Forest Service Photo.

tablishment of a whole complex of insects to attack the moth in all phases of its life, from egg to adult. Federal and state enthusiasm and funding for the project fell off sharply. Only in a few places did entomologists continue to use biological control as more than a specialized method.

Forest entomologists, for both ecological and economic reasons, followed a different path than their colleagues in agriculture. In particular, forest entomologists relied less on chemicals. Forests are relatively stable ecosystems with a variety of natural mechanisms which control insect populations, and there was no great influx of forest pests in the nineteenth century. These circumstances encouraged forest entomologists to depend on indirect controls and to strengthen the existing system of checks. In addition, timber was too low in value, too generally available, and its growth cycle too long to allow the economical treatment of large areas with arsenicals, the most prevalent insecticides before DDT. The arsenicals, also, were too obviously poisonous to be used heavily around fish and wildlife.

The discovery in the 1940s of several synthetic organic chemicals that killed insects or plants marked the beginning of a new phase in almost all fields of pest control. The new compounds, of which the insecticide DDT and the herbicide 2,4-D were the most conspicuous, had many qualities their predecessors lacked. They were effective against many pests, relatively nontoxic to other forms of life, suitable for aerial sprays, and cheap enough to use in many areas where cost had previously barred direct controls. They replaced older poisons in economic entomology, allowed direct controls in forest entomology, and helped launch many new projects in range weed control.

Although aerial spraying of forests had been tried in the early 1920s, only with the introduction of DDT did it become economically feasible. By 1950, five years after DDT's release for civilian use, forest managers were treating several million acres each year to curb defoliating insects (particularly such epidemic species as the gypsy moth and spruce budworm) and other pests. In 1956, they launched a cooperative project to eradicate the gypsy moth from North America. Forest entomologists did not become total converts to the new compounds—there remained too many pests which could not effectively be treated by spraying—but there was a greater emphasis on direct controls and a general slighting of the indirect methods which had been the core of forest entomology before 1945. The profession as a whole paid little attention to the few warnings that pesticide sprays might upset biotic balances or have long-term effects on nontarget species.

The effects of the new chemicals on people and the environment, discovered only after they had been in use for some time, brought into existence a determined opposition which sought to ban some persistent chemicals. Biological control specialists had warned in the late 1940s that DDT upset natural systems of pest control, and medical scientists had become concerned about the accumulating residues in human body fat in the early 1950s. However, public opposition did not begin until the latter part of that decade. Several visible and damaging control programs during this period helped mobilize public and scientific opposition. DDT spraying on Long Island in the summer of 1957, part of the gypsy moth eradication campaign, caused a storm of public protest, and a conservation group brought suit, seeking to halt the spraying. The next year, the spreading of poisoned bait for fire ants in several Southern states brought further objections from scientists, citizens, and local officials. Sprays to kill the insect vector of Dutch elm disease left dead robins on lawns and caused citizens to protest in town council chambers across the East and Midwest.

In 1962, Rachel CARSON published *Silent Spring*, making the effects of pesticide residues a public and political issue. *Silent Spring* made many people aware of problems with chemical insect control which scientists had privately discussed for years. It encouraged public discussion of alternative methods of insect control and of the statutory apparatus of pesticide regulation. Indirectly, *Silent Spring* made it easier to obtain funding for work on the environmental effects of pesticides. The Environmental Defense Fund, organized in 1967 to fight environmental pollution through legal action, offered a forum for scientists who accumulated an even larger volume of evidence implicating pesticide residues as the cause of environmental problems in fish, birds, and other forms of life. The fund's successful suits against DDT use helped open the regulatory process to the concerned public and set a precedent for action against the use of other pesticides.

Public pressure and lawsuits changed the legal structure of pesticide regulation. As late as 1967, the DEPARTMENT OF AGRICULTURE had claimed that only manufacturers and formulators of pesticides had standing to contest decisions on registration made under the 1947 Federal Insecticide, Fungicide, and Rodenticide Act (FIFRA). However, in 1970 a three-judge panel of the District of Columbia Court of Appeals ruled that all affected citizens had standing under FIFRA to participate in registration decisions. The NATIONAL ENVIRONMENTAL POLICY ACT of 1969 provided another legal avenue for public participation by requiring an environmental impact statement for major fed-

eral projects, including, environmentalists asserted, campaigns against insects involving chemicals that contaminated the ecosystem. A few months later, Congress transferred enforcement of pesticide registration from the Department of Agriculture to the new Environmental Protection Agency.

Environmental opposition ended the use of some pesticides and influenced the direction of research. The EPA banned DDT in 1972 except for emergency use, and heptachlor, chlordane, dieldrin, and aldrin (all persistent chlorinated pesticides) in 1975. Mirex, used against the fire ant, was also banned, although congressional pressure still threatens to bring it back. Concern about environmental effects and possible carcinogenicity in humans has led researchers away from the chlorinated aromatic hydrocarbons, encouraged work on more specific and less persistent compounds, nonchemical methods, and the integration of new chemicals with other means, a system called Integrated Pest Management.

Forest entomology suffered some, but not all, of the shocks which agricultural entomology endured. By the time the campaign against DDT had begun in earnest in the late 1960s, forest managers had cut back on or abandoned many of their massive spraying campaigns; problems with the gypsy moth and the effects of spraying done in Canada to control the spruce budworm had already convinced many that large-scale use of persistent pesticides was hazardous to wildlife and fish and unacceptable to the public. In 1964, the Forest Service had abandoned the use of DDT, its primary defense against forest insects since the late 1940s. Then, in 1974, the service challenged public opposition by obtaining a special permit to use DDT against a tussock moth outbreak in eastern Oregon forests, as it believed there was no other effective agent available. Generally, however, the separation of forest entomology from agriculture and the Agricultural Research Service's responsibility for pesticide registration meant that environmentalists concentrated their fire there; forest entomology was largely ignored.

The herbicide 2,4-D caused changes in weed control similar to those DDT brought to insect control; it offered the chance to use direct methods against unwanted species. In situations where the goal was eradication of plant life (as along power lines and railroads) 2,4-D seemed ideal, and it often replaced mechanical methods. But when the goal was to kill one species, and not the rest, the lack of selectivity of the early synthetic organic herbicides prevented a complete adoption of chemical controls, although more selective compounds were introduced in the 1960s.

Weed control suffered less from the reaction against the synthetic organic chemicals than had insect control. Public interest and alarm centered around one compound, 2,4,5-T, and its effects on humans, and this issue arose in the wake of military use of defoliants in Vietnam. The problem, it appeared, was contamination of the 2,4,5-T in Agent Orange by dioxin (a powerful teratogen). Former soldiers filed suits against the Veterans' Administration, seeking compensation for injuries alleged to have been caused by 2,4,5-T, and Congress considered bills to make veterans exposed to the chemical eligible for compensation for their illnesses. Other suits were filed against companies using 2,4,5-T in the United States, alleging that the chemical is responsible for abortions and miscarriages. The reaction, though, did not generally affect herbicide use.

By the end of the 1970s, pest control experts were becoming more concerned about side effects in the ecosystem, and controls were based more and more on biological study. Although chemicals, even persistent ones, continue to have a place in pest control, a return to the chemical era of the immediate post-World War II period remains unlikely, although increasing needs for food and fiber make pest control even more urgent.

FURTHER READING: Thomas R. Dunlap, *DDT: Scientists, Citizens, and Public Policy* (1981). Frank Graham, Jr., *Since Silent Spring* (1970). John H. Perkins, *Insects, Experts, and the Insecticide Crisis* (1982).

THOMAS R. DUNLAP

PETERSON, RALPH MAX (1927–   )

When R. Max Peterson, holder of B.S. and M.P.A. degrees in engineering and public administration, was named eleventh chief of the U. S. FOREST SERVICE on June 27, 1979, he was the first nonforestry graduate to head the agency since Gifford PINCHOT. Peterson had, however, a thorough knowledge of forestry gained from experience in all phases of Forest Service work.

Peterson was born on July 25, 1927, near Doniphan, Missouri, within the Clark (now Mark Twain) National Forest. South-central Missouri had become an area of cutover forests, with poor soil for farming and very little wildlife. Two of Peterson's uncles went to work for the Forest Service, and many local residents found employment at the CIVILIAN CONSERVATION CORPS (CCC) camp administered by the service.

During World War II, Peterson served in naval aviation, and as a partial result of his military training he received a bachelor's degree in civil engineering in 1949 after completing three years at the University of Mis-

souri. Since the Forest Service had impressed him in his youth, Peterson accepted a position as engineer in the Plumas National Forest in California. During the next nine years, he worked on the Cleveland and San Bernardino national forests in California. In 1958, he was awarded a Rockefeller Foundation fellowship in the Water Resources and Land Use Planning Program at Harvard University, where he received a master's degree in public administration in 1959.

Peterson returned to the Forest Service to work at the Northern Region headquarters in Missoula, Montana, in 1959, and two years later he was shifted to the Washington Office for a variety of administrative and engineering assignments. In 1966, he returned to California as regional engineer, and in 1971 he was appointed deputy regional forester for the Southern Region in Atlanta, Georgia. The following year, he was named regional forester for the thirteen-state Southern Region. In 1974, he returned to Washington as deputy chief for programs and legislation where he was deeply involved in working on the NATIONAL FOREST MANAGEMENT ACT of 1976. He also directed the national assessment required by the FOREST AND RANGELAND RENEWABLE RESOURCES PLANNING ACT of 1974 and was responsible for program and budget formulation.

DENNIS M. ROTH

PHILOSOPHY, RELIGION, AND AMERICAN FORESTS

American philosophical and religious attitudes toward the forest were initially derivative of European attitudes. Celtic and Germanic peoples had profound religious respect for trees in pre-Christian times. From a Christian standpoint, however, trees were not sacred, and, with the spread of Christianity, tree spirits and other supernatural beings of the forest were relegated to mythology and folk tales. This desacralization of the forest prepared the way for secular exploitation.

In the late Middle Ages, the forest was not aesthetically appreciated. Pictures of forests, mostly hunting scenes, depict dark, gloomy, sinister places. Loving appreciation of forests and of nature in general was considered by the Christian church to be in conflict with the love of God. In the early modern period following the Middle Ages, this enmity was gradually resolved with Europeans coming to see God through nature rather than by looking beyond it. This new religious view is most strongly expressed in nineteenth-century American landscape painting, where the forest gloom is replaced by intense light signifying the presence of God, as well as in American transcendental philosophy, especially the writings of Emerson.

At the beginning of the American colonial period, most Europeans considered travel in forests both unpleasant and dangerous. Poor roads made travel uncomfortable and, moreover, there were the dangers, real and imaginary, of robbers, beasts, and monsters. Part 3 of the René Descartes's *Discourse on Method* (1637) reflects the general aversion for forests. While illustrating his code of morals, Descartes uses an analogy about travelers lost in a forest. According to Descartes, they should "walk as straight as they can in one direction, not diverging for any reason, even though it was possibly chance alone that first determined them in their choice. By this means if they do not go exactly where they wish, they will at least arrive somewhere at the end, where probably they will be better off than in the middle of the forest."

The single most important philosophical influence on American attitudes toward the forest from this period is Locke's theory of property in *Two Treatises of Government* (1690). Forests (wildernesses) are depicted as being of little value until they have been improved through human labor. Even then the labor itself constitutes most of the value present and is the basis for personal ownership. Locke repeatedly cites the forests of inland North America as examples of worthless areas to which human labor has not yet been applied.

Distinctively American philosophical and religious attitudes toward the forest first took form in New England. Early Puritan settlers regarded the forest both as an enemy and as a resource. Clearing the forest away provided a foothold for civilization in the wilderness and also established property rights to the newly enclosed land. At the same time, however, Puritans regarded the forest wilderness as an appropriate place for religious contemplation. It is largely from this additional use of the forest that modern American religious and aesthetic feeling for the forest is derived.

The aesthetic appreciation of forests in general can be traced to the picturesque movement in Europe. This movement was concerned with the development of taste for scenery. Although falling under the heading of philosophical criticism and preceding the establishment of aesthetics as a field of philosophy, these discussions retrospectively are not considered part of the formal history of philosophy, but they are nevertheless important in the study of philosophical attitudes toward forests. The need for the picturesque as an aesthetic category arose out of discussions about the beautiful and the sublime. William Gilpin, who established the picturesque as a subcategory of the

Totem Bight, north of Ketchikan, Alaska, 1958. Forest Service Photo.

beautiful, was influential in America in connection with American taste for scenery. Thoreau's early writings are modeled to some degree on Gilpin's writing style.

The strong American appreciation and love for the forest was already fully developed in Emerson's *Nature* (1836) and reflects both the Puritan religious experience and the picturesque taste for scenery. Strictly speaking, the American transcendental philosophy, which Emerson's writings exemplify, was derived from a European idealism which did not recognize the physical existence of the world. This American idealism, however, maintained a connection with physical nature, not characteristic of its European predecessor. While European philosophers spoke of nature as human nature, transcendentalists like Emerson cited rocks, trees, plants, and animals. In the writings of Thoreau and John MUIR, who also considered themselves transcendentalists and followers of Emerson, the inconsistent presence of physical nature is even more strongly evident.

A special American contribution to nature aesthetics was the elevation of wildness to the status of a major aesthetic category. Wildness had always been an element of physical beauty, but it became a matter of national pride when Americans found themselves forced to defend the beauty of their forest landscapes on the grounds that their wildness compensated for the lack of picturesque castles and ruins.

At the end of the nineteenth century, William James discussed the conflict of aesthetic and instrumental uses of the forest in "On a Certain Blindness in Human Beings" (1899). James claimed that "the beauties and commodities of the American forest gained by the centuries are sacred. They are our heritage and birthright." Although in general the forest played no fundamental role in James's philosophy, it was sometimes an inspiration, as, for instance, in his famous example about a squirrel hiding behind a tree in "What Pragmatism Means" (1907).

The most philosophically and theologically significant discussions of the forest in the twentieth century occur in the writings of Alfred North Whitehead in connection with his theory of organism. In the last chapter of *Science and the Modern World* (1925), Whitehead states, for example, that "a forest is the triumph of the organisation of mutually dependent species." Whitehead's "process philosophy" continues to be important today, theologically, especially in the writings of John B. Cobb, Jr., and, philosophically, in the writings of Charles Hartshorne, both of whom have included an environmentalist dimension in their thought.

Since the mid-1970s, philosophers and theologians have begun writing on philosophical issues relating to wilderness and nature generally in professional publications. Much of this material can also be applied to the study of forests.

FURTHER READING: Kenneth Clark, *Landscape into Art* (1949). Ralph Waldo Emerson, *Nature* (1836), and "The American Scholar" (1837). Christopher Hussey, *The Picturesque* (1967). Hans Huth, *Nature and the American: Three Centuries of Changing Attitudes* (1957). Roderick Nash, *Wilderness and the American Mind* (rev. ed., 1982). Marjorie Hope Nicolson, *Mountain Gloom and Mountain Glory: The Development of the Aesthetics of the Infinite* (1959). Barbara Novak, *American Painting of the Nineteenth Century: Realism, Idealism, and the American Experience* (1969). Alfred North Whitehead, "Requisites for Social Progress," in *Science and the Modern World, Lowell Lectures, 1925.*

EUGENE C. HARGROVE

PILING INDUSTRY

See Poles and Piling Industry

PINCHOT, GIFFORD (1865–1946)

The oldest son of James W. Pinchot, a wealthy manufacturer in New York and Pennsylvania, and his wife Mary Eno Pinchot, Gifford Pinchot was born on August 11, 1865, in Simsbury, Connecticut. He received most of his early education in private schools in Paris and New York City and later attended Phillips Exeter Academy in New Hampshire. Before his graduation from Yale University in 1889, Gifford Pinchot decided to enter the profession of forestry, then little known in the United States. He studied at the French Forest School in Nancy, examined model forests in France, Switzerland, and Germany, and returned to the United States in December 1890.

Pinchot began the first systematic forest management in America in February 1892 at Biltmore, North Carolina, on the estate of George W. Vanderbilt. In December 1893, he opened an office in New York City as a consulting forester and during the next four years prepared management plans for extensive privately owned forestlands in the Adirondacks and central Pennsylvania, examined the principal forest districts of New Jersey, and developed outlines for academic forestry instruction. In 1896, he was appointed a member of the National Forestry Commission, which was created by the National Academy of Sciences to recommend a national forest policy, and during the following year he continued his study of public forests as a special agent for the DEPARTMENT OF THE INTERIOR.

A major phase of Pinchot's forestry career began in July 1898 when he was appointed chief of the Division of Forestry (later called the Bureau of Forestry and since 1905 called the FOREST SERVICE) in the U. S. DEPARTMENT OF AGRICULTURE. As chief, Pinchot inaugurated a government cooperative forest management program to assist private forest owners, successfully led efforts to transfer control of federal forest reserves from the Department of the Interior to his own bureau, established the foundation of the present National Forest System, conducted an extensive publicity program to acquaint Americans with the need for forest conservation, and introduced policies of conservative and regulated use of national forest resources that have influenced federal management of other natural resources. Much of his success in these efforts was due to ardent support from President Theodore ROOSEVELT. Meanwhile, Pinchot was the leader of a conservation crusade that climaxed at a White House conference in 1908, which was a landmark in efforts to stimulate the conservation of the nation's natural resources. The conference led to the appointment of the NATIONAL CONSERVATION COMMISSION under Pinchot's chairmanship and the preparation by this group of the first comprehensive inventory of the country's natural resources. Pinchot's service as a federal government Scientific Work (1903), PUBLIC LANDS COMMISSION (1903), Committee on Department Methods ernment Scientific Work (1903), Public Lands Commission (1903), Committee on Department Methods (1905–1909), Inland Waterways Commission (1907), and Commission on Country Life (1908). In a disagreement on conservation policy with Secretary of the Interior Richard A. Ballinger, Pinchot was removed from office by President William H. Taft in 1910 (see BALLINGER-PINCHOT CONTROVERSY).

His interest in forestry and conservation continued strongly after his departure from federal government service, although it was mixed with unsuccessful strivings as a candidate for United States senator from Pennsylvania (1920 and 1926) and service as governor of Pennsylvania for two terms (1923–1927 and 1931–1935). He was active in the SOCIETY OF AMERICAN FORESTERS organized under his leadership in 1900. He was a professor of forestry from 1903 to 1936 at the Yale University School of Forestry, which he had helped to establish in 1900. He organized the National Conservation Association in 1909 as a pressure group to promote his views on national conservation policies. From 1920 to 1922, he served as commissioner of forestry for Pennsylvania and established a forest program

characterized by the strong leadership, dynamic public relations, and diversified work reminiscent of his direction of the Forest Service. After 1910, he was also active in efforts to secure federal regulation of private forestry and to prevent transfer of the Forest Service from the Department of Agriculture to the Department of the Interior or a proposed Department of Conservation.

Pinchot was the author of numerous publications on forestry and conservation. The most important were *Biltmore Forest* (1893), *The Adirondack Spruce* (1898), *A Primer of Forestry* (Part I, 1899; Part II, 1905), *The Fight for Conservation* (1909), *The Training of a Forester* (1914, 1937), and his autobiography, *Breaking New Ground* (1947). For his achievements in forestry and conservation he received honorary degrees from Yale University (1901 and 1925), Princeton University (1904), Michigan Agricultural College (1907), McGill University (1909), and Temple University (1931). The Society of American Foresters in 1940 awarded him the Sir William Schlich Memorial Medal for distinguished service to American forestry.

Pinchot once declared: "I have been a Governor every now and then, but I am a forester all the time—have been, and shall be to my dying day." The statement was remarkably true. A few days before his death on October 4, 1946, he had been working on a revised forest management plan for his estate at Milford, Pennsylvania. His long, persistent, and successful promotion of forestry practice on private and public timberlands of the United States and his dramatic awakening of Americans to the importance of regulated use of natural resources were the chief contributions of his career in forestry and conservation.

FURTHER READING: The principal publications focusing on Pinchot's work in forestry and conservation are his autobiography, *Breaking New Ground* (1947), and Harold T. Pinkett, *Gifford Pinchot, Private and Public Forester* (1970). *The U. S. Forest Service: A History* (1976) by Harold K. Steen provides a useful account of Pinchot's administration of the Forest Service. M. Nelson McGeary's *Gifford Pinchot, Forester-Politician* (1960) is the principal publication on his general career.

HAROLD T. PINKETT

PIONEER FARM LIFE AND FOREST USE

For almost three centuries, from about 1610 to 1910, the pioneer farmer cleared the forests of the eastern half of the country and the Pacific Northwest to create new farmland and to supply towns and industry with fuel and raw materials. Much of what happened to the forest was unrecorded because it was but an incidental accompaniment to farming and hence of little concern to the contemporary observer. Nevertheless, the farmers' enormous impact on the forest provided an epic experience shared by millions of Americans before the twentieth century.

Clearing the Forest

In contrast to the European practice of felling the trees and grubbing out the roots so that the ground could be plowed and seeds sown, the American pioneer avoided much arduous and time-consuming labor by seeking out abandoned Indian clearings in which to start his farming. He copied or adapted many of the Indian uses of the forest, gathering wild berries and nuts, hunting game, girdling the trees, and planting quick-maturing crops like squash, pumpkins, corn, and beans, which grew easily in small mounds or in patches of irregularly cleared ground. In the Indian system of hoe agriculture, stumps could be avoided, the fields did not have to be large or regular, and a varied and bountiful supply of food could be harvested without heavy equipment, draft animals, or large inputs of labor. In time, however, the trend was to clearcutting, especially in New England and Pennsylvania and places subsequently populated from those regions, such as western New York, Ohio, Tennessee, and Kentucky. In the South, girdling continued to be more common, although it was by no means absent in the northern colonies.

When forestland was cleared, the undergrowth and small trees were first grubbed out, piled up, and burned, and then the larger trees were chopped down. The best logs were snaked out of the debris and reserved for house building and other construction. The rest were burned on the spot, the ash making a useful fertilizer or being sold to a manufacturer of potash. Since relatively few pioneer farmers possessed oxen, the larger logs could be moved only with the cooperation of neighbors who gathered for logging bees to clear a few acres of ground and to construct a cabin, the task lightened by the distribution of copious quantities of rum and by games and talk afterward.

When land was cleared the stumps remained, and their removal was more arduous than the felling of the trees. Farmers soon learned that the stumps could be left in the ground until they rotted in perhaps five or ten years, after which they were easier to lever out or drag out with oxen. Provided the crop to be sown was grass, which would be harvested with a scythe, or tobacco, flax, potatoes, or corn, which could all be planted and harvested by hand, the stumps were merely a nuisance. Where some stumps had been removed the ground could be opened up with a plow and crops planted. The first crops were usually prolific, reaching forty to fifty bushels an acre for wheat and thirty to forty bushels for corn in good river-valley locations, and half those amounts on the hillsides. Farmers near markets, such as in much of New England, dispensed with crops and sowed grasses on which cattle could be grazed.

Compared to clearcutting, girdling was more economical in labor. The farmer merely cleared the undergrowth and planted corn between the skeletons of the deadened trees. The standing trunks were burned once they had dried out. This system produced less ash than did clearcutting, and no construction timber, but it was a good pioneer expedient that solved many of the problems of rationing the limited amounts of time and energy available during the early years of pioneering.

In the South, the commonly planted crops such as tobacco and cotton led, within a few years, to soil toxicity and nutrient exhaustion. The fields were thereafter abandoned for another twenty to thirty years. In these circumstances, to clearcut the forest was a waste of energy for the smallholder and a waste of money for the large plantation owner with slave labor.

Clearing was long, hard, and gradual. A wide range of samples indicates that in the eighteenth century clearing cost between five and six dollars an acre. The cost rose in the early nineteenth century, to a little over ten dollars where it stayed stable for many years. As for the number of "man days" it took to clear an acre of forest, nineteen estimates between 1800 and 1890 range from thirteen to thirty-six days. After they had rotted, stumps took a further twelve days to clear, making a mean total of about thirty-two man-days per acre. At such a rate, one man could clear a little over ten acres in a year. Of course, the rate of clearing depended upon many variables, such as the density and size of the trees, the hardness of the timber, the thoroughness of the clearing, and the other tasks that the farmer needed to accomplish, which ranged from the construction of houses and roads to the making of furniture. However, unless there was a readily accessible market for produce, the pioneer found little point in clearing more ground than needed to feed his family. Nor was there any reason to clear more land than could be worked by members of the family. Twenty-five acres was often enough.

From 1850 onward, various machines were invented to aid in stump pulling, most of them little better than the traditional tools of ax, lever, spade, and chain, and the help of an ox. However, the farmer could reduce his labor by about half by using dynamite for blasting, a

A forest homestead near Grays Harbor, Washington. University of Washington Photo.

method which became common in the late 1880s in the cutover lands of the Lake States and the Pacific Northwest.

The Forest Edge

Those pioneers from Kentucky and Tennessee who pressed northwestward via the river valleys into southern Illinois and Indiana came to the edge of the forest as early as 1815. Others reached the southern Michigan prairies by about 1820. This was a critical point in the use of the forest for agriculture. After an initial period of prejudice and technical inability to farm the prairie, it became evident that far less labor was needed to convert grassland to farmland than was needed to make a farm out of forest. On the average, it took only a day and a half to prepare an acre for agriculture in the prairie, compared to thirty-two days per acre in the forest, and in the twentieth century even that day and a half was reduced to half a day with improved plowing equip-

ment. As a consequence, the number of improved acres in the nonforested areas of the country increased rapidly, not only because settlement was pressing westward into the prairie but also because open grasslands were perceived as more desirable.

The Amount of Land Cleared

Although there can be no truly accurate measurement of the amount of land cleared for agricultural purposes, a fair estimate may be derived from the census records of improved land, which in the East must have borne a close relationship to cleared land. The predominantly forested counties of the United States in 1850 reported approximately 113 million acres of improved land in farms. Between 1850 and 1859, a further 39.7 million acres of forestland were cleared compared with 9.1 million acres of nonforested land settled during the same period on the prairies. By 1909, an estimated total of over 300 million acres had been cleared and

Improved Land in Farms in Forested and Nonforested Counties (in millions of acres)

	Forested Areas	Nonforested Areas
Before 1850	113.7	—
1850–1859	39.7	9.1
1860–1869	20.2	19.4
1870–1879	49.3	44.7
1880–1889	28.6	55.7
1890–1899	31.0	41.1
1900–1909	22.4	51.6

SOURCE: Martin L. Primack, "Land Clearing under Nineteenth Century Techniques: Some Preliminary Calculations," *Journal of Economic History* 22 (Dec. 1962): 484–497.

farmed. This figure may be compared with an estimated original forest area of 822 million acres, or roughly half the area in the contiguous United States.

Stock in the Forest

The use of the forest did not end with the making of farmland. Uncleared and unfenced tracts were used as grazing for herds of razorback hogs that ran at large, foraging on the nuts, young shoots, and roots of the trees and multiplying rapidly. The swine provided an inexpensive form of protein for the pioneers, and pork was the most widely consumed meat until the latter part of the nineteenth century. The system of open grazing worked, provided that there was enough unfenced woodland for the herds to roam, but depredations against crops by wild stock eventually led to efforts for regulation. The problem was particularly acute in the South, where the marauding herds were largest. By various stages, control went from rounding up and branding cattle and notching the ears of swine to the erection of town pounds (especially in New England) and fencing of cultivated land.

Fencing

Once trees were felled, material for FENCING was available. Crude, makeshift fences of tangled branches, rolled logs, and piled-up stumps eventually gave way to more permanent and elaborate structures. The Virginia fence, also called the worm or snake fence, was the form used almost universally in the East. It consisted of slender logs or split rails laid in a zigzag pattern and intersecting with one another at right angles. With six to ten rails in each segment of the fence and sometimes with heavy bracing logs at the intersections, the zigzag fence required enormous amounts of timber and took up large areas of land. The advantages of the Virginia fence were that it required no postholes, pegs, notches, or ties, and it was easy to repair and to

move to new locations, an important point in the incremental enlargement of the clearings, or the shifting tobacco cultivation in the South. Because it did not need posts with one end embedded in the ground, the Virginia fence did not rot easily and was said to last for twenty to thirty years. From the colonial period, responsibility for the protection of crops from wild stock lay with the cultivator. A Virginia act of 1632 required that every man "shall enclose his ground with sufficient fences or else plant upon their own perill." This was the basic principle of fencing for the next 250 years.

Post-and-rail fencing was more economical in its use of timber and ground than the zigzag fence, but it meant more labor for the farmer who had to dig the holes as well as split the rails. The invention of the spiral auger for posthole digging after 1800 caused a great rise in the popularity of the post-and-rail fence. Although the farmer had to be more selective in the wood used, because of the rotting of the post feet, the post-and-rail fence used relatively little wood, a great advantage on farms near the prairie edge.

Housing

Pioneers making a new farm in the forest had an urgent need to provide shelter for their families. The log cabin, symbol of American pioneer farming life, was probably introduced into the Delaware region by the Swedes during the late seventeenth century, and its use became universal in timbered areas of the country. It had much in common with the zigzag fence: it was extravagant in its use of wood, but because it required no nails, holes, or shaping, it was easy to construct. With about eighty logs of between twenty and thirty feet in length and a few helpful neighbors, a cabin could be erected in three days.

The details of corner notching and stone chimney style varied from region to region, but the basic plan of one large room, perhaps with a division for sleeping quarters, was general. Only floorboards, doors, and furniture consisted of sawn or, more likely, hewn timber. Later, as the region became more settled, water-powered sawmills were located on suitable sites and sawn timber became available in sufficient quantities for the method of construction of farmhouses to change. Then the more elaborate and elegant clapboard houses built around carefully stressed timber frames became more common and the log cabin was abandoned, or, sometimes, built over and incorporated within a clapboard house.

Fuelwood

The use of wood for fuel has probably exceeded all other demands on the American forests. The cold winters made cheap and abundant fuel indispensable for settlement in the northern two-thirds of the United States, and even in the South the winters were cold enough for houses and huts to require heating. Fortunately, the forests were at hand to supply the wood for fuel and, as one early settler said, the remedy for cold winters was "not to spare the wood of which there is enough." Great blazing fires halfway up the chimney were a common sight in pioneer cabins.

Fuel was the incidental by-product of clearing a field or building a cabin. Consequently, there is little statistical evidence of how much wood was cut, gathered, or burned. Probably the average pioneer farmer devoted between one-eighth and one-fifth of his time to chopping, splitting, and stacking cords of wood. Twenty to thirty cords of annual consumption was common for a rural household, and larger farms used double that. Benjamin Franklin thought that a large house with several fireplaces needed one man full time to cut, split, and haul firewood.

Fuelwood could also be an important source of cash for the pioneer farmer. Even if he did not live near a large town, such rural industries as blacksmith shops, tanneries, and iron manufactories might provide a market. All the larger towns on the eastern seaboard were short of fuel from the early seventeenth century onward, and land haulage was found practical for up to twenty-five or thirty miles. During the colonial period, firewood was moved beyond that distance only if water transport was available, either by river or along the coast. Wood for New York City came from Maine and New Jersey. Merchants who cornered this lucrative coastal trade relied on the farmers sending their cordwood downstream from the interior. After the Revolution, the scarcity of fuelwood became even more of a problem in the older settled regions and prices rose, making it profitable for farmers to haul cordwood greater distances than ever before. Statistics from the census of 1840 indicate very close relationships between cordwood cutting and dense urban populations as well as areas of recent settlement. The fuel needs of steamboats plying the inland waterways caused the Mississippi and Ohio rivers to be lined with counties recording higher than average sales, most of which must have come from pioneer farms.

Potash and Pearlash

Wood ashes could be leached to produce potash and the somewhat purer pearlash, both raw materials in the making of soap and glass and in bleaching, calico-printing, and other chemical operations where potassium hydroxide was needed. Like fuelwood, POTASH AND PEARLASH were valuable commodities which the pio-

neer farmer could sell for cash. During the early nineteenth century, potash sold for between $160 and $250 a ton and was so important that in 1822 Governor DeWitt Clinton listed it along with wheat as one of the two leading export commodities of New York State. The only requirement for successful production was that the pioneer farmer should be within a reasonable distance of his market, which meant that production tended to be concentrated in New England and New York. Often, potash was produced on farms as part of the clearing process, but soon enterprising individuals set up "asheries," which were manufacturing and collecting centers located near areas of new farm clearing and on major transport routes to the industrial centers.

In the census of 1840, the bulk of reported potash and pearlash production came from the newly settled counties of western New York and those bordering Lake Erie in Ohio. These areas produced 87 percent of the national total of 16,550 tons. Production of ashes remained high until the mid-1840s when the discovery of potash and soda salts in mineral waters reduced its importance in international trade, although ashes remained of local significance in the self-sufficient economies of pioneering regions.

Lumber

After and sometimes even during the initial years of pioneering, the farmer participated in the lumber trade. He cut timber on his farm for sale directly to consumers or more likely to small local mills; he sold others cutting rights on his land; and he sometimes found seasonal employment working in the woods or mills owned by lumbermen. Where large rivers such as the Hudson, Delaware, Susquehanna, or Savannah and their tributaries flowed past an area of pioneer farming and on to a market, many farmers cut timber and rafted the logs downstream, returning with essential supplies bought from the proceeds of the sale.

At least until the mid-nineteenth century, the distribution of lumber activity in the United States and the distribution of agricultural settlement were almost coincident, the establishment of a mill usually coming a few years after the first pioneers. The number of mills in any particular location was a reflection of the length of time since settlement and the density of the population. A gristmill and sawmill formed the first local industry to be established in the semisubsistence, self-sufficient economy of the new pioneer areas. As new ground was cleared, timber would be sent to the mill to be made into clapboards, floorboards, beams, and other lumber. Smaller pieces were rived with axes and wedges and made into shingles, staves, and rails. During this period, it was only after agriculture failed, as in the upland and steep-sloped areas of New England and New York after the middle of the nineteenth century, that lumbering developed as a specialized industry.

To think of the pioneer farmer as only an agriculturist is a mistake. Similarly, any account of forest utilization before about 1850 must give a pre-eminent place to the activities of the pioneer farm families that adapted their skills and strength to make use of the resources available to them.

FURTHER READING: Clarence H. Danhof, *Change in Agriculture: The Northern United States, 1820–1870* (1969). Brooke Hindle, *America's Wooden Age: Aspects of Its Early Technology* (1975). Richard G. Lillard, *The Great Forest* (1948). Martin L. Primack, "Land Clearing Under Nineteenth Century Techniques: Some Preliminary Calculations," *Journal of Economic History* 22 (Dec. 1962): 484-497. Philip L. White, *Beekmantown, New York: Forest Frontier to Farm Community* (1979). Michael Williams, "Products of the Forest: Mapping the Census of 1840," *Journal of Forest History* 24 (Jan. 1980): 4-23.

MICHAEL WILLIAMS

PLANK ROADS AND WOOD BLOCK PAVEMENTS

The use of wood for surfacing rural highways in the United States had its antecedents in the improvised corduroy roads of the eastern forests. In most cases the corduroy road was little more than a causeway of logs laid across swampy ground transversely to the line of the road. In slightly more elaborate form, the surface might be leveled up by wedging the gaps with triangular sections split from other logs. When used as military or lumbering roads through new territory, necessary timber for corduroying could usually be secured from the clearance of the roadbed. The name was taken from the new variety of cotton cloth introduced in England around 1780 and applied by analogy to roads in North America in the early 1800s.

The residents of Upper Canada were the first North Americans to extend the idea of corduroy roads to experiments with surfaces made from sawed planks. The earliest reported plank road in North America was finished near Toronto in 1836. The provincial Board of Works followed in 1839 with a program of construction that eventually totaled 200 miles of plank road. Four years later, interest in plank roads spread to the south side of Lake Ontario, with a series of articles in the *Rochester Democrat* and a short communication "On Plank Roads in Canada" appended to the annual report of the U. S. Commissioner of Patents.

New York's first planked highway opened near Syracuse in July 1846. Within a year, the increase of applications for charters caused the legislature to enact a general incorporation law for private plank road companies. Fifty-two companies organized under this act in 1848, 80 in 1849, and about 200 more in the 1850s. The enthusiasm spread to Pennsylvania, which passed a general plank road act in 1849, and to New Jersey, where the innovation was especially popular in the isolated Pine Barrens. Throughout the Mid-Atlantic states, some 700 companies were chartered and about 7,000 miles of plank highways completed before 1857.

Since transcontinental expansion brought the need for thousands of miles of new country roads each year, it is no surprise that national publications were fascinated by an innovation that promised to lift the United States out of the mud. *Niles' Register* and the *New York Tribune* praised plank roads for their ease of construction. *Scientific American* wrote that plank roads would completely change the rural transportation of the country. *Hunt's Merchants' Magazine* recommended their general use and claimed that "the plank road is of the class of canals and railways. They are the three great inscriptions graven on the earth by the hand of modern science." A report by the New York Senate's Committee on Roads and Bridges gave Americans their first detailed instruction on building and operation in 1847. George Geddes, the engineer of the first New York road, published his *Observations on Plank Roads* in 1850, and another New York engineer, William Kingsford, brought out his *History, Structure, and Statistics of Plank Roads in the United States and Canada* in 1851. Other widely used sources were *A Manual of the Principles and Practice of Road Making* by William Gillespie of Union College (first published in 1847) and the *Brief Practical Treatise on the Construction and Management of Plank-Roads* by Robert Dale Owen of Indiana (1850).

In describing the essentials of plank road construction, these writers followed closely the methods worked out in Canada. Few engineers would have disagreed with the following summary by Gillespie: "In the most generally approved system, two parallel rows of small sticks of timber (called indifferently *sleepers*, *stringers*, or *sills)* are imbedded in the road, three or four feet apart. Planks eight feet long and three or four inches thick, are laid upon these sticks, across them, at right angles to their direction. A side track of earth, to turn out upon, is carefully graded. Deep ditches are dug on each side, to ensure perfect drainage; and thus is formed a Plank Road." In addition,

Plank road in North Carolina. Forest Service Photo.

the surface of the road was often covered with fine gravel or sand to protect it from horseshoes and steel rims. The planks were held in place with spikes or by dirt heaped over their ends. Except for heavily traveled roads, it was thought sufficient to lay a single track of eight-foot planks paralleled by a dirt track on which vehicles could turn out to pass. Heavily loaded vehicles bound toward urban centers had the right of way. Experts also stressed that the planks should lie directly on the surface of the ground to avoid rot from air spaces below.

The plank road mania spread rapidly from the Atlantic states to the new farmlands across the Appalachians. Abundant forests supplied the materials for numerous plank roads in Alabama, Mississippi, Tennessee, and other Southeastern states. Even more, the plank road found its home in the upper Middle West. During 1847, favorable articles appeared in newspapers from Indiana to Iowa and in the widely read *Prairie Farmer* of Chicago, and the region's first planked highway was finished from Milwaukee to Watertown, Wisconsin. Within a year, there were companies that hoped to make a profit from plank roads in every state of the Old Northwest. Most of the roads were financed by local subscriptions and designed to funnel trade into farm market towns. Chicago, Cleveland, and Milwaukee simultaneously experimented with plank pavements on city streets. Standardized procedures for the incorporation of plank roads usually included schedules of maximum tolls for vehicles, horsemen, and animals.

The hope that plank roads would produce a profit for their builders was predicated on their low initial cost and the belief that the surface would last for a number of years. Early writers asserted, with little direct evidence, that pine planks would last seven years and oak would last ten to twelve. As the plank road companies discovered, however, planks decayed with unexpected speed. On the soggy lands around the Great Lakes, where the roads were most popular, it was difficult to secure decent drainage. When the rains abated, the sun warped the planks and made the roads unusable. Many plank pavements disintegrated in two years. No new plank roads were started after 1854 in Ohio, Indiana, Illinois, Missouri, or Iowa, and most of the existing roads were abandoned by 1856 or 1857.

Use of planking as a temporary pavement survived the wave of enthusiasm and disillusionment only in lumbering regions such as upper New England, the upper Great Lakes states, and the Pacific Northwest. As Q. A. Gillmore wrote in his *Practical Treatise on Roads, Streets, and Pavements* (1876), "the ease and rapidity with which they can be constructed renders them a popular and even desirable make-shift in newly-settled districts and towns where lumber can be procured at low cost." Although farming counties around Detroit and Milwaukee abandoned plank roads in the 1850s, they remained in use in the pineries of northern Wisconsin and Michigan for several decades. The Willamette Valley of Oregon had similarly gone through the cycle of enthusiasm for plank roads in the 1850s, but sections of planked pavement remained in use in the Cascades into the automobile era. Ten miles of plank road also survived near Albany, New York, at the start of the twentieth century, and plank pavements were occasionally used elsewhere on an experimental basis in the early years of the automobile.

The surfacing of city streets posed as many problems as did rural roads. The growth of urban population from 300,000 to 30 million during the nineteenth century demanded cheap pavements capable of sustaining the constant traffic of wagons, cabs, carriages, omnibuses, and horsecars. With stone block pavements noisy and expensive and planking discredited, engineers after mid-century tried wooden blocks. Two decades of experiments in eastern cities led to a presumed breakthrough when Samuel Nicholson laid the first of his patented wood block pavements in Boston in 1866. The Nicholson pavement consisted of rectangular, creosote-impregnated pine blocks three to four inches wide, six to fourteen inches long, and six inches deep. With their end grain exposed to the surface, the blocks were set on a foundation of pine boards. Cracks between the blocks were filled with a mixture of tar and gravel to fix them in place and to provide traction for horseshoes.

In its first five years, the Nicholson pavement and its imitators (differing slightly in the treatment of joints and foundations) spread quickly to New York, Newark, Cleveland, Detroit, and other northern cities. E. S. Chesbrough, the city engineer of Chicago, reported that his city's cheap lumber market made wooden pavements especially popular with property owners. Unfortunately, a complexity of problems largely discredited the Nicholson pavement during the 1870s. Wood blocks were slippery when wet or fouled by mud from unpaved streets and offered poor traction on steep grades. The wood absorbed horse urine and excrement and sweated putrid fluid in hot weather. The blocks rotted rapidly as well, with a normal maximum use of six years and a reported life of only two years in Washington, D.C. In the Chicago fire of 1871, creosoted pavements burned along with the adjacent buildings.

From the 1880s into the new century, the attractions of quietness and cheapness brought one more round of experimentation with wood block pavements in the United States, Australia, and western Europe. Toronto, Chicago, Duluth, Minneapolis, Milwaukee, Indianapolis, and smaller midwestern cities turned to round cedar blocks as a quick, cheap pavement that might last five or six years. Chicago counted 880 miles of such pavement in 1900. In the usual construction, the blocks were set on a foundation of planking, the interstices filled with gravel, and the surface coated with coal tar and gravel. Other treated woods were used on concrete foundations—mesquite in San Antonio, tamarack in Montreal, redwood in San Francisco, pine in Galveston. Different styles of wood block pavements were used in Sydney, Melbourne, Paris, and London and other British cities in the same decades.

In the cases of both plank roads and wood pavements, the attractiveness of cheap materials and the desperate need for hard surfaces combined to generate enthusiasms without adequate testing. The experiments solved some immediate problems but probably added to total cost and effort in the long run. Since both surfaces were designed for horse-drawn transportation systems, their abandonment was related to the development of new technologies. During the second half of the nineteenth century, the construction of 250,000 miles of railroad absorbed public and private capital and entrepreneurial talent that might otherwise have been devoted to road improvements. In the early twentieth century, the volume and weight of automobile traffic and the traction characteristics of rubber tires required smooth, seamless pavements and ended the use of gravel, stone blocks, and wood blocks on heavily traveled city streets in favor of macadam and concrete.

FURTHER READING: Carl Abbott, "The Plank Road Enthusiasm in the Antebellum Middle West," *Indiana Magazine of History* 63 (June 1971): 95–116, Joseph Durrenberger, *Turnpikes: A Study of the Toll Road Movement in the Middle Atlantic States and Maryland* (1968). Q. A. Gillmore, *A Practical Treatise on Roads, Streets, and Pavements* (1876). Edwin C. Guillet, *The Story of Canadian Roads* (1966). William Kingsford, *History, Structure and Statistics of Plank Roads in the United States and Canada* (1851).

CARL ABBOTT

PLYWOOD AND VENEER INDUSTRIES

Plywood is made of three, five, or more thin sheets of wood, called veneer, glued together with the grain direction alternating. Some plywood is also made with lumber cores or center plies or, since the 1970s, with particle board cores. The softwood industry has in recent years introduced the concept of "layers" made up of parallel-laminated veneers. (For example, there is substantial production of a four-ply, three-layer panel of one-half inch thickness.) Sometimes other materials, such as plastics or metal, are used in the lay-up of plywood. Veneer has been widely used separately for containers (wirebound boxes, hampers, baskets) and for decorative surfacing material in furniture and art work. Veneering, or gluing veneers to other surfaces, was practiced for decorative purposes by the ancient Egyptians.

Modern veneer was first made on circular saws, then on band saws. Still later, saws were replaced by veneer slicers (using a knife instead of a saw); these are known to have been in use before 1875 and have remained in use for hardwood plywood. The workhorse of the softwood veneer industry has been the lathe, on which the log is rotated against a knife edge.

High-grade Douglas-fir log spins in a huge lathe that peels long sheets of veneer. Three to five layers of veneer are criss-crossed and glued to form plywood. American Forest Institute Photo.

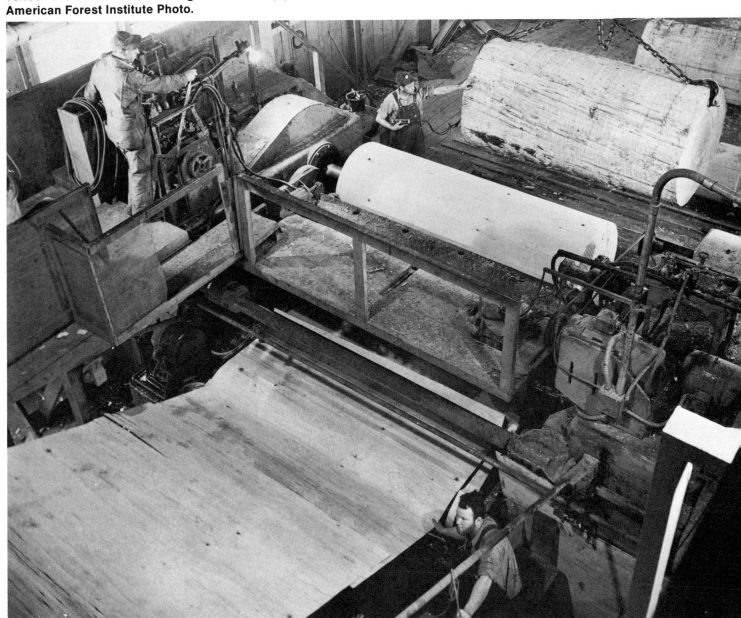

Veneer is also produced by slicing with long knives, as shown here. American Forest Institute Photo.

A hand-cranked veneer lathe was patented in 1840 by John Dresser of Stockbridge, Massachusetts, but veneer lathes were not in practical use until about 1870.

Early hardwood plywood products were curved sewing machine cabinets, introduced in 1867, to be followed before 1875 by flat or curved chair and bench seats, often perforated. Furniture uses developed rapidly after the early 1880s. Flat plywood door panels, curved S-shaped sleigh bodies, and barrel-top trunks were known to be made of plywood by 1890.

Early centers of hardwood plywood manufacture were Louisville, Kentucky; Sheboygan and Two Rivers, Wisconsin; Grand Rapids, Michigan; and Newport, Vermont. The species used were birch, poplar, maple, basswood, elm, walnut, and oak from local forests, and mahogany imported for decorative face veneers. In the 1890s, new hardwood plywood factories opened in Jamestown, New York; Portsmouth, Ohio; Algoma, Wausau, and Marshfield, Wisconsin; and northern New England. Arkansas, Missouri, and other states on the lower Mississippi were producers of red gum veneer. In Kentucky, Tennessee, West Virginia, and North Carolina, yellow-poplar and chestnut were the principal veneer species.

On the West Coast, softwood veneers were in use in 1901 by the Portland Manufacturing Company for baskets, boxes, and crates. Having brought in a veneer and plywood expert from Michigan, the Portland company produced the first large plywood panels of western woods, both softwoods and hardwoods, rotary-cut and hand-glued, for exhibit at the Lewis and Clark Centennial Exposition in Portland in 1905. The firm soon began producing three-ply, 3/8-inch-thick Douglas-fir plywood to order for door manufacturers and for trunk stock and drawer bottoms. Other companies, mostly in Washington, soon joined in. The Long-Bell Lumber Company box-shook plant at Weed, California, began the manufacture of ponderosa pine plywood for doors in 1911. By 1920, Douglas-fir plywood was an important structural material and had found use in automobile bodies.

The term "plywood" and the standard, stock-panel type of product that it connotes did not come into common use until World War I. The softwood plywood industry did not participate in World War I military production as did the hardwood industry. Hardwood plywood found extensive wartime use for such products as containers, furniture, and parts for aircraft.

World War I glue research resulted in improvements in the starch and casein glues previously in use and in the introduction of water-resistant blood-albumin glue, cured in the hot press. Soybean glue, then under research, did not reach commercial application until 1923, when it became a staple glue for "interior type" softwood plywood.

The principal regional association of hardwood plywood manufacturers was the Plywood Manufacturers Association started in Chicago in 1921. It was called the Plywood Manufacturing Institute after 1938 and later the Hardwood Plywood Institute (HPI). This group strove to promote product standardization and developed a commercial standard for hardwood plywood, CS-35 (now "Product Standard PS-51" for hardwood and decorative plywood). In 1953, the HPI amalgamated with the Southern Plywood Manufacturers Association of Atlanta and in 1964 it became the Hardwood Plywood Manufacturers Association, which maintains offices and a testing laboratory in Reston, Virginia.

The West Coast softwood industry expanded in more homogeneous fashion. It was composed of seventeen plants in 1929 when it produced 358 million square feet of panels (3/8-inch thickness basis). Its trade organization was the Douglas Fir Plywood Association, formed in 1933 and later renamed the American Plywood Association. The commercial standard for Douglas-fir plywood, CS-45, was promulgated in 1933. Revised, it still serves for all softwood and construction plywood as "Product Standard PS-1."

Synthetic resin adhesives, imported from Germany in 1933 and manufactured in the United States after 1937, made truly waterproof plywood. Urea formaldehyde glue, for use at room temperatures or in hot presses, found application in the hardwood industry. Phenol formaldehyde glue, requiring hot-pressing and forming a completely waterproof glue line, was introduced by the Harbor Plywood Company for its Douglas-fir "exterior type" plywood. Synthetic glues are used in more than 90 percent of softwood plywood production.

Both hardwood and softwood plywood found a great many uses during World War II, such as in aircraft nacelles, wings and fuselages, boat hulls, communications equipment, surgical appliances, prefabricated structures, and shipping containers. "Double curvature" structural parts were molded in complicated fluid pressure devices. A famous British aircraft, the Mosquito, was made of balsa wood sandwiched between two layers of very thin aircraft-quality plywood derived from American and Canadian yellow birch.

Growth of softwood plywood production following World War II has been phenomenal. Production had just reached 1 billion square feet (annual rate, 3/8 inch basis) at the start of the war, chiefly of interior type. By 1977, production stood at over 19 billion square feet of which most was bonded with exterior-type adhesives. Tremendous markets in construction, especially for sheathing buildings, had been developed, as had other uses in industry and on the farm. Southern pine plywood came onto the market on a large scale in the mid-1960s, having been made possible by an abundant supply of small southern pine logs and technical developments in the efficient cutting of small logs. Over a dozen species of trees, including hardwoods, came into regular use in the manufacture of construction and general utility plywood.

In the early 1950s, about 50 percent of hardwood plywood was used in the manufacture of furniture. Thin paneling, suitable for doors as well as walls, followed shortly thereafter. By 1964, two-thirds of hardwood plywood consumption was in wall paneling, much of it grooved and prefinished, and most of it imported from Southeast Asia and other foreign areas.

Between 1952 and 1962, hardwood plywood consumption increased by well over 1 billion square feet (surface measure), whereas domestic production increased by only about 300 million square feet. In 1977, domestic production was over 1.3 billion square feet, but over 4 billion square feet were imported. During the 1970s, mobile home manufacturers offered an important new market for plywood, although a large part of their panel consumption has been of particle board.

Other technical developments during and after World War II included the manufacture of plywood treated with preservatives (such as Douglas-fir exterior type for marine applications and, more recently, building foundations) and fire retardants (such as decorative hardwood wall paneling for public buildings and offices); the manufacture of very large panels, made by scarf-joining panels end to end or side to side; and structural components such as stressed-skin panels and plywood box and I-beams. The 1970s saw the use of panels made of wood fibers or flakes as cores in plywood, or, with suitable factory-finishing systems, as substitutes for plywood.

FURTHER READING: Thomas D. Perry, *Modern Plywood* (2nd ed., 1948), and "Plywood Is Engineered Wood," in Timber Engineering Company, *Proceedings of Wood Symposium* (1952), pp. 57-65, describe the history of plywood manufacturing processes. Robert M. Cour, *The Plywood Age: A History of the Fir Plywood Industry's First Fifty Years* (1955), focuses on people and institutions. Richard F. Baldwin, *Plywood Manufacturing Processes* (1975), concentrates on softwood plywood. *Plywood in Retrospect* (sixteen issues, 1967-1976), published by the Plywood Pioneers Association, is a series of articles on the history of West Coast plywood plants.

HERBERT O. FLEISCHER

POLES AND PILING INDUSTRY

Poles and piles have been used in North America since prehistoric times. Klamath Indians erected dwellings on piles driven into lake bottoms, while others used long poles to support their teepees and form their travois. From the beginning, European settlers in the New World used poles to form defensive palisades, as had various Indians before them. But these uses of logs in the round involved few commercial transactions and no ongoing production. The pole and piling industry of North America can more appropriately be dated as beginning with the construction of the first large bridge built on a pile trestle, a 270-foot span over the York River in Maine designed by Samuel Sewell and erected in 1761. Piles were also used at an early date in building wharfs and bulkheads, although the dates of the first such structures built in North America are not clear.

Piles could be used to produce docking facilities quickly and cheaply. Thus, when San Francisco boomed following the discovery of gold in California in 1848 and ships began to jam its waterfront, entrepreneurs erected pile-supported docks to accommodate them and end the need for expensive lightering of goods and passengers to shore. One wharf, built by Henry Meiggs, was 2,000 feet long. Such construction generated a demand that helped bring commercial timber harvesting to Puget Sound. By 1850, cargoes of piles were being dispatched from the sound to San Francisco by Captain Lafayette Balch and others. The trees awaited; all one needed to engage in this trade were access to a vessel and a few willing laborers. By advertising the quality of the area's timber stands, the pile trade helped to pave the way for more capital-intensive operations such as sawmills, which followed in due course. San Francisco may have been the most spectacular of the nineteenth-century markets for piles, but similar demands also developed in Chicago and other centers where water-borne commerce loomed large.

Initially, poles and piles used in the United States were untreated. As a result, they needed frequent replacement, for marine borers, decay, and other enemies soon attacked untreated wood. Europeans developed methods of treating wood with preservatives to slow this destruction. In 1838, John Bethell of England patented a system of impregnating wood with preservatives by using a vacuum followed by pressure. Americans adopted this and other European techniques, but the relative cheapness and availability of wood in the United States kept them from turning rapidly to the use of treated poles and piles. The first Bethell process plant in the United States was built by the Old Colony Railroad at Somerset, Massachusetts, in 1865 to treat bridge timbers. In 1872, also in Massachusetts, the navy built the second successful vacuum-process plant in the United States.

Methods of treatment gradually improved and costs fell. A practical method of manufacturing creosote from coal tar was developed in 1850. For many years, creosote remained the main treatment for poles and piles. Zinc chloride, copper sulphate, copper arsenate, pentachlorophenol, and other chemicals have been used when conditions have warranted, but most of these are water-soluble formulations and thus appropriate for such things as mine props but ineffectual for piles or poles that were to have ground contact.

Initially, most of the treated wood used in the country was sawn rather than left in the round, and used in structures that were more sophisticated and less easily repaired than docks and bridges, which were long the main uses for piles. As technology improved, the use of treated poles and piles increased. In Seattle, Washington, piles used in docks and other harbor facilities had an average life of thirty or more years in spite of severe infestations of marine borers in local waters. As word of this and other early successes spread, more and more builders turned to treated wood and the modern pole and piling industry gradually emerged.

Pole yard in Alabama. Dark poles at right have been treated with creosote to retard rot and insect attacks. Light-colored poles in the background are air-seasoning prior to treatment. American Forest Institute Photo.

Developments during the late nineteenth and early twentieth centuries heightened demand for poles and piles and hastened development of the industry. American railroads used large quantities of piles in building trestles and bridges, unlike those in Europe which normally used masonry in such structures. The ready availability of wood in the United States, the development of the steam-powered pile driver in the nineteenth century, and bridge-building techniques perfected during the Civil War by Herman Haupt to meet Union military needs made the American approach practical. Following the war, Haupt's methods were used to extend rail lines quickly and cheaply, especially across the midwestern prairies during the 1870s. The lightly built lines that resulted were rebuilt as traffic and income mounted. Both initial construction and subsequent upgrading consumed enormous quantities of wood, including unprecedented numbers of piles. During the rebuilding, if not initially, much of the piling was treated. Here as in harbor facilities, treated piles proved their durability, lasting three to five times as long as did untreated piles. The railroad trestle across Lake Pontchartrain, Louisiana, provides an extreme example. Built in 1883 using piles of southern pine that had been pressure-treated with creosote, it remained sound and in daily use over seventy years later.

Expanding telegraph, telephone, and electric power-distribution systems created a new demand for poles. At first, the poles used either were entirely untreated or were given only a butt treatment. However, fully treated poles proved more durable and thus cheaper in the long run for some uses. By 1929, 47.3 percent of the poles sold in the United States were pressure-treated; by 1934, the figure had risen to 92.7 percent. As in subsequent years, most were of southern pine.

The twentieth century also saw greatly increased use of piles to provide a solid base on which to erect large buildings. Treated piles, driven into the ground, could last almost indefinitely and made the construction of major buildings possible on hitherto unsuitable sites. Modern skyscrapers made the use of piles necessary where extra support had not been required

A New Orleans hospital was constructed on a foundation of 9,600 piles. Forest History Society Photo, Robert K. Winters Collection.

for lower, less heavy structures. By 1936, buildings erected on piling included what was then the world's largest grain elevator, located in Albany, New York; the U. S. FOREST SERVICE's regional headquarters buildings in Ogden, Utah; and various federal buildings on Government Island in Alameda, California. In subsequent years, piles of concrete and other substances were increasingly substituted for wood for such purposes, but the use of timber piles did not cease.

The Great Depression reduced demand for poles and piles, as it did that for other forest products. In 1929, major consumers had purchased over 4.5 million poles; by 1931, consumption was down 46.9 percent. Many treatment plants were idle. Demand gradually recovered beginning in 1932, but not until 1941 was the record set in 1929 broken.

Demand has remained generally high since 1941, although rising costs and scarcity of good stands of pole trees have encouraged the use of substitutes for wooden poles, and increased placement of telephone and electric power lines underground has undercut demand. In 1946, a shortage of creosote caused temporary problems, and the Columbus Day storm of 1962 destroyed many stands in the Pacific Northwest. Japanese buying and the use by sawmills of smaller

sizes of logs have also increased competition for the pole and piling industry's raw materials. For a time during the 1950s and 1960s, poles were popular as inexpensive structural members for barns and storage buildings. Subsequently, much of this market has gone to solid sawn material—normally in 6 by 6 or 8 by 8 sizes—for this material is easier for carpenters to work with.

Many species of trees have been used for poles and piles. Southern pine has been the most commonly used for as long as statistics have been kept, although before the rise of railroads, species growing nearer Northern and midwestern population centers no doubt dominated. Chestnut was used for early pole lines because of its durability, but the chestnut blight gradually wiped out this source of poles as it spread following its accidental introduction into the United States in 1904. Before World War II, most western utility requirements were satisfied with western redcedar, mostly procured in Washington and British Columbia and transported to California by ships owned by such firms as J. H. Baxter & Company. During the 1940s, Douglas-fir and lodgepole pine rose to importance, over 100,000 of each being sold in 1945 for the first time (lodgepole pine for poles only, not for piling).

Western redcedar, Douglas-fir, and lodgepole pine

have continued to be major pole species since World War II, even though there are many alternative uses for Douglas-fir and western redcedar, and even lodgepole pine—long despised as a "weed" tree—has now found a market in sawmills. Their high value makes poles a preferred use for trees. Those of pole quality often bring 50 percent or more above what they would if used for sawlogs. Historically, piles were less valuable, but during the 1960s and 1970s, Douglas-fir piles rose in cost until by 1980 they were only slightly less valuable than poles of the same species (and in some sizes even more valuable).

Some plants, especially smaller ones, cut most of their poles to order. Most try to balance procurement with estimates of sales, build up stocks of poles fifty feet and shorter, and sell out of that inventory. With longer sizes, such as transmission poles, firms have longer lead times for delivery, so even the larger companies usually aim their procurement to fit their order file.

Southern pine was traditionally peeled in the woods with a long-handled spud while the bark was still tight. At the plants, pole-peeling machines completed the job and shaved off irregularities prior to treatment. In the West, by contrast, most poles have long been shipped to plants and poleyards with their bark intact. There they have been debarked, smoothed, incised to aid the penetration of preservatives, air-dried, and treated. Since about 1960, Southern producers have applied these same techniques.

Standards for the quality of wood are set by the American National Standards Institute, while treatment standards are set by the American Wood-Preservers' Association. The latter organization has met in annual conventions since 1904 and cooperates with the Forest Service and others in gathering and disseminating information on the pole and piling industry as well as on railroad crossties and other treated wood products.

FURTHER READING: The poles and piling industry has been little studied by historians; however, useful material may be gleaned from issues of *Wood Preserving News* and from the following: Robert D. Graham, "History of Wood Preservation," in *Wood Deterioration and Its Prevention by Preservative Treatments*, ed. by Darrel D. Nicholas (1973). W. F. Goltra, "History of Wood Preservation," *Proceedings of the American Wood-Preservers' Association* 58 (1913): 178-202. American Creosoting Co., *Pioneer Work in Modern Wood Preservation: Bethel, Bouton, Chanute* (1929). Centennial of Engineering Convocation, *Proceedings of Wood Symposium: One Hundred Years of Engineering Progress with Wood* (1952).

THOMAS R. COX

POLISH IMMIGRANTS AND AMERICAN FORESTS

The first products of American industry shipped out of the Jamestown settlement were pitch, tar, and lumber manufactured and produced primarily by the colony's Polish settlers. Poland in the seventeenth century had a monopoly on the world's tar and pitch industry. Captain John Smith welcomed Polish immigrants who were skilled in the processes of producing forest products. Admired by Smith as "the only ones who knew what work was," the Poles produced pitch and cut Virginia's pine trees. Long before discovery of the staple tobacco crop, Polish indentured servants in the forest-related industries provided Jamestown with its initial exports.

In the Maine lumbering district, Polish workers drifted into the northern forest late in the nineteenth century. While never large in numbers, the Polish lumberjacks were hired, as were other "Boston men" or immigrant laborers, to replace the native sons and Canadian workers who had moved westward.

It was not until the logging frontier had reached the Great Lakes states that large numbers of Polish immigrants became employed in the lumber trades. In 1870, 200 Polish families migrated from New York, Chicago, and Detroit to take up residence in the booming mill town of Bay City, Michigan. By 1885, approximately 11 percent of the labor force in the Michigan and Wisconsin lumber mills was Polish. In the early 1880s, additional Polish immigrants were recruited to serve as strikebreakers in the Michigan and Wisconsin mills. However, large families, low pay, and long hours created a militant labor consciousness among the Poles. During the famous "Ten Hours or No Sawdust" strike in the Saginaw Valley in 1885, the leaders of the strike were mostly "Polanders." The following year, after the strikers were defeated, mill owners let it be known in the newspapers that they would not hire Polish mill hands.

The year 1885 was the peak year in Great Lakes lumber production, and, as the business declined, many Poles followed the migration westward. Some worked in Wisconsin and Minnesota, but many trekked to the far Northwest. In the mills of Washington and California, approximately 5 percent of the work force was described as either "South European-Slavic" or Polish. As the Lake States lumber business declined in the late nineteenth and early twentieth centuries, Polish laborers took up farming in several midwestern Polish communities or drifted into industrial occupations in the larger urban areas.

FURTHER READING: Alvin Duke Chandler, "The Poles at Jamestown," *The Polish Review* 2 (Autumn 1957): 3. Vernon H. Jensen, *Lumber and Labor* (1945). Joseph A. Wytrwal, *America's Polish Heritage: A Social History of the Poles in America* (1961).

JEREMY KILAR

POTASH AND PEARLASH

Potash, consisting of a mixture of potassium salts, was originally obtained by leaching wood ashes and evaporating the resultant solution. It was a significant product of North American hardwood forests, from New York to Maine and westward to the trans-Mississippi grasslands, during the late eighteenth and early nineteenth centuries. Pearlash is refined potash, produced by redissolving potash in water, removing the undissolved matter (principally potassium sulphate), and evaporating the solution that contains primarily potassium carbonate. Depending on the particular woods from which the original potash was made, varying amounts of potassium chloride are present.

In the eighteenth century, potash constituted the most important industrial chemical of the day, being essential in the manufacture of glass, soap, various drugs and dyes, and saltpeter. It was practically the only alkali used in the textile industries for bleaching linens, scouring woolens, and printing calicoes. Its only competitors were barilla, made from the ashes of certain mosses that grow in Spain and Sicily, and kelp, a derivative of burnt seaweed. Both of these substances contain much less alkali than potash, hence their use was generally confined to making hard soap and hard glass. No use was made of potash in agriculture until the middle of the nineteenth century, when the work of Justus von Liebig on plant nutrition became known. By that time, the first mineral sources of potash, which were more economical than wood ashes, had been discovered at Stassfurt, Germany, and they quickly captured the world market.

Potash became increasingly vital to Great Britain as its industries grew and diversified. However, it was unable to secure significant amounts of the product from its North American colonies until shortly before the American Revolution, despite efforts by colonial governments, Parliament, the Crown, and the Royal Society of Arts to encourage potash manufacture. The slow growth of the American potash industry was the result of technological underdevelopment. The history of the industry is marked by a decade and a half of intensive experimentation beginning in 1750, which simplified the production process by reducing the heavy initial investment that had characterized earlier methods. The first experimenters had built complicated leaching vats, large furnaces, and complex equipment designed for continuous production rather than a simple batch process. The limited ability of local foundries to produce thick-walled vessels capable of withstanding prolonged high heats was also a factor in early failures. By 1765, these problems were solved; in that year, North America supplied 37 percent of Britain's total potash import. Ten years later, the figure had risen to 66 percent.

The new technology, sufficiently uncomplicated to allow any pioneer farmer to make potash, was widely disseminated during the American Revolution in an effort to improve supplies of saltpeter for making gunpowder. Anyone possessing the equipment for making maple sugar could make crude potash. Needed was a leaching hopper, four or five feet high, with sloping sides and perforated bottom, made from virtually any available wood or bark. Dampened wood ashes were packed into the hopper and water was poured through them to dissolve the potassium salts, producing lye. The collected liquid was then boiled in a thin-walled cast-iron kettle about two feet in diameter, as was generally used in boiling maple syrup. Crude potash, commonly called "black salts," resulted when the lye boiled down to a dark syrupy consistency.

The next step required a larger, thick-walled vessel, generally known as a "potash kettle," which could sustain a prolonged red heat. Such kettles were costly and relatively scarce and were more likely to be owned by a local general store merchant or a potash dealer rather than a farmer. The crude salts were boiled in the large kettle until its bottom reached a red heat; the temperature was maintained until all the charcoal and organic debris were burned out of the salts. Inorganic contaminants were skimmed off the top of the molten potash. The process was complete when the molten mass became quiescent. The commercial grade potash could then be ladled into smaller vessels for cooling. The potash would solidify into a hard, stonelike substance, gray on the outside, pink on the inside, which was broken up with an ax or sledge hammer, packed into barrels or casks, and tightly sealed to prevent moisture absorption.

The economics of the industry became evident as soon as the simpler technology emerged. Farmers sold wood ashes or crude potash to local storekeepers, as they would any other cash crop. The storekeeper then processed the material in his own kettle or used the services of a local "potashery" to obtain the finished product. He could trade potash, along with other country produce, for merchandise from export-import merchants in the major coastal port towns of the Middle Atlantic and New England regions. These merchants were eager to obtain potash, because it was one of the few products of the area that enjoyed a ready market in Great Britain and could therefore be used in direct payment for purchases of British manufactured goods. The trade did not develop further to the south, because the soft and resinous woods of southern forests yield very little potash. Massachusetts was the early center of the industry and the leader in technological innovation. The first patent issued by the Federal Patent Office was to Samuel Hopkins of Boston, for an improvement in potash manufacture. From Massachusetts, the industry spread northward into Canada and westward through New York and Ontario into the Great Lakes states.

In the 1790s, potash ranked seventh by value among American exports, surpassed only by lumber (including masts, staves, and headings) among forest products. It retained its relative rank throughout the first quarter of the nineteenth century, despite violent fluctuations due to embargo, war, and the growing pains of the British Industrial Revolution. Normally, potash production was a by-product of clearing land for farming. Occasionally, when the price spurted upward, trees were cut and burned solely for their potash content. As the trade moved westward with the advance of the frontier following the War of 1812, an increasing percentage of American potash exports went to Great Britain by way of Canada in order to take advantage of the British tariff preference in favor of Canadian potash. In 1828, the Canadian preference was reduced to a negligible figure, and Canada lost the American potash trade.

American potash production peaked in the 1840s, then declined precipitously. By that time, only a third of the total production was exported, the balance being consumed in America's growing industries. The decline, which also affected Canadian production, can be attributed to two factors. First, the adoption of chlorine bleaching by the British cotton textile industry and the development of the Le Blanc soda ash industry in England provided alternative alkalis which were cheaper and quicker than potash. The North American potash industry not only lost its principal overseas market but also suffered domestic competition. Imports of English soda ash began about 1830 and increased exponentially until imports of German mineral potash began after the Civil War; the first American ammonia process soda plant was built in 1882. The second factor was the advent of cheaper transportation in the form of canals and railways, which made it economical for farmers to ship bulkier commodities, such as lumber and foodstuffs, to urban markets. Pioneer farmers no longer had to burn the timber they cut in order to obtain a product sufficiently valuable in proportion to bulk to sustain transportation costs.

American potash production never exhausted timber resources. Census figures show that a small amount of potash, chiefly to supply local industries such as leather tanneries, continued to be manufactured in the hardwood belt until the twentieth century.

FURTHER READING: Theodore J. Kreps, "Vicissitudes of the American Potash Industry," *Journal of Economics and Business History* 3 (1930): 630-666. Harry Miller, *Canada's Historic First Iron Castings* (1968). William I. Roberts, III, "American Potash Manufacture before the American Revolution," *Proceedings of the American Philosophical Society* 116 (Oct. 1972).

WILLIAM I. ROBERTS, III

POTTER, ALBERT FRANKLIN (1859–1944)

Albert F. Potter was a down-to-earth pioneer livestock man from the Southwest. He was the first Westerner to hold a high post in the U. S. FOREST SERVICE. He organized the service's grazing policies and remained in charge of this vital work for nineteen years. Grazing was the most important first use made of the federal forest reserves, and it remained the most controversial for the longest time.

Potter was born on November 14, 1859, in the Sierra foothills of California; he moved to eastern Arizona for his health at the age of twenty-four. Potter started in the cattle business near Holbrook but by 1896 had switched to sheep raising and was soon a leader among sheepmen, probably the best organized livestock interest in the West in the 1890s. Their ire was aroused by a ban on sheep grazing on the forest reserves in the dry Southwest, issued by the secretary of the interior in 1898. Potter led a delegation to Washington seeking postponement of the ban.

Early in 1900, the secretary of the interior sent out an inspection party which included Gifford PINCHOT, head of the Division of Forestry in the DEPARTMENT OF AGRICULTURE. Albert Potter, as secretary of the eastern division of the Arizona Woolgrowers' Association, conducted Pinchot's party around Arizona and adjacent New Mexico on a three-week horseback trip. This tour was the beginning of constructive cooperative grazing control and management on public lands. Grazing by sheep, as well as cattle, was to be permitted in limited numbers whenever it would not seriously damage the range. Pinchot decided that Potter was the ideal man to carry out such a policy. The forester was tremendously impressed with the sheepman. As Pinchot recalled many years later in his autobiography, *Breaking New Ground (1947)*, Potter's "thorough mastery of his business, his intimate acquaintance with the country and its people, his quiet, persistent steadiness, his complete fearlessness and fairness, gave him a standing and influence that were remarkable." Potter's position in the Southwest would prove to be a tremendous asset to the Forest Service, and he would become, as Pinchot said, "the cornerstone upon which we built the entire structure of grazing control."

Potter became an assistant forester early in 1907 and associate forester in 1910 after Pinchot left; he might have been the forester but for Pinchot's successful efforts to put Henry S. GRAVES in that post. Potter did become acting forester during World War I, from June 1917 to February 1918, when Graves was with the army in France, but his fight to establish the power of government to maintain its rules and regulations, including reasonable fees and reasonable numbers, against stubborn and persistent challenges was his most important contribution to grazing in the national forests. By the spring of 1920 when Graves resigned, Potter concluded that his mission had been accomplished and others should take over his duties. He retired to southern California where he enjoyed many years of deep-sea fishing. He died on January 1, 1944.

JEAN PABLO

PREDATOR AND RODENT CONTROL

Americans have generally treated predatory mammals as menaces and rodents as nuisances and have killed these animals wherever they interfered with human activities. Early settlers relied on shooting, snaring, or the use of pits and deadfalls. Strychnine came into common use just after the Civil War and was the major weapon against western predators until late in the nineteenth century when steel leg-hold traps became generally available. Poisonous gases were used to kill western rodents during this period, but they were never widely employed. Hunting for furs or bounties wiped out large predators in the East by the late nineteenth century and severely reduced populations of both burrowing rodents and predators in the West. Poisons changed in the twentieth century, with thallium compounds coming into use in the 1920s and Compound 1080 (sodium fluoroacetate) in 1945. In the 1930s, the cyanide gun and aerial hunting were developed to kill western coyotes.

Government involvement in predator control be-gan in the 1630s, when Massachusetts Bay and Virginia placed bounties on wolves. Other colonies followed suit, and the bounty system, usually at the state but sometimes at the county level, was virtually universal in America until well into the twentieth century and was the primary policy of state governments with regard to such animals. Federal work began when large tracts of game lands were reserved permanently in government ownership. After 1905, the U. S. FOREST SERVICE hired trappers to kill wolves on national forest grazing land. Congress appropriated funds for the Bureau of BIOLOGICAL SURVEY to undertake "experiments and demonstrations" relating to the control of "noxious animals" in 1910. In 1915, Congress directed the agency to undertake predator control in the West. It employed hunters, took over the Forest Service's program, and by 1918 had begun to organize its efforts on the basis of cooperative agreements with states, counties, or local associations of stock raisers. The aim of control work, which was funded jointly by the government and the cooperating groups, was to reduce stock losses and damage to grazing lands by reducing rodent and predator populations. Although bureau officials stoutly denied it, eradication seemed to be the goal, and both ranchers and state officials openly called for an end to predators. Despite protests by various scientists and members of the public, the program grew steadily. By the 1930s, government hunters were each year killing over 10,000 coyotes, the only predators, aside from remnant populations, left in the western grazing areas. Congress provided clearer statutory authority for the work in 1931, and although a reorganization in 1939 shifted the program—then called Predator and Rodent Control (PARC)—from the Department of Agriculture to that of the Interior, it left the legal organization and operation unchanged. The program's name was changed to Wildlife Services in 1966 and to Animal Damage Control in 1974.

In the 1960s and 1970s, scientific understanding of the role of predators in healthy ecosystems, changes in public attitudes toward predators, and concern about the effects of poisons on nontarget species, particularly on endangered species, changed predator-control policy and law. Widespread use of Compound 1080 had caused protests as early as the 1950s. Its extreme toxicity and the possibilities of accidents and secondary poisoning (death to animals eating the carcasses of 1080-killed animals) alarmed the public and scientists. The public, too, was coming to value predators for their aesthetic and spiritual value as symbols of wilderness and for their role in the wild. The report of Secretary of the Interior Stewart L. UDALL's Advisory Board of

Wildlife Management (headed by A. Starker Leopold) in 1964 helped focus public attention on the issue; the board said that PARC's program was economically unjustified and biologically unsound. In 1971, a second advisory committee, headed by Stanley Cain, reached essentially the same conclusions. These reports and the rising pressure from environmentalists forced changes. In February 1972, President Nixon issued Executive Order 11642 banning the use of 1080, strychnine, thallium, and cyanide compounds on public lands, and a month later the Environmental Protection Agency suspended and canceled registration of these substances for predator control. The Federal Environmental Pesticide Control Act, passed on October 21, 1972, extended federal authority to intrastate uses. The use of cyanide guns was still allowed by the end of the 1970s, but research was to be directed toward nonlethal or selectively lethal methods which remove only the offending animal.

THOMAS R. DUNLAP

PRICE, OVERTON WESTFELDT
(1873–1914)

The son of American parents who moved from North Carolina to England just after the Civil War, Price was born in Liverpool on January 27, 1873. He came to the United States and attended high school in Virginia. After a year's study at the University of Virginia, Price went to work as a forestry apprentice under Carl A. SCHENCK at the Biltmore Estate of George W. Vanderbilt, near Asheville, North Carolina. There he made the acquaintance of Gifford PINCHOT who had overall charge of Vanderbilt's forest holdings. Price decided to make forestry his life's work. To secure a thorough technical background he went to Germany and studied for two years at the University of Munich. He followed this by a year of practical experience in European forests under the guidance of Sir Dietrich Brandis. After returning to America, Price worked again on the forest of the Biltmore Estate and at lumber camps in the Great Lakes region.

In June 1899, Price accepted the invitation to again become assistant to Gifford Pinchot, who by then was the forester of the United States Division of Forestry. Over the next two years, Division of Forestry personnel increased from 11 to 179 and the division was raised to the status of a bureau. Price, now with the title of associate forester, was given the task of organizing this group into an efficient unit, and Pinchot came to value him highly and rely on him heavily. In February 1905, the work of the bureau, renamed the FOREST SERVICE, was greatly enlarged by transfer of the federal forest reserves from the GENERAL LAND OFFICE of the DEPARTMENT OF THE INTERIOR. Price remained in charge of and largely responsible for executive management policies and organizational methods which made the Forest Service a model of efficiency in the federal government and permanently established federal forestry in the United States.

In January 1910, Price's employment with the Forest Service was terminated as a result of the BALLINGER-PINCHOT CONTROVERSY over coal leases on federal lands in Alaska. The sudden separation from a career to which he had given so much was keenly felt by Price and affected his health. He was pessimistic about his chances of again having the opportunity to use his abilities to the full in his chosen career, although he did some writing, worked as a forestry consultant, and served as the principal active official of the National Conservation Association, founded by Pinchot. Four years later, on June 11, 1914, he ended his life at age forty-one at his summer home near Asheville. Price had married Alice V. Lindsey in 1903 and had four children. He was one of the seven charter members of the SOCIETY OF AMERICAN FORESTERS.

JEAN PABLO

PRICES

See Lumber, Plywood, and Paper Prices

PUBLICATIONS

See Forest and Conservation Publications

PUBLIC LAND COMMISSION, 1879

Congress established the first Public Land Commission on March 3, 1879, with the same act that also created the U.S. GEOLOGICAL SURVEY. Approximately 3,500 federal statutes dealing with public and private lands had been enacted since 1785, and codification was sorely needed. There was also a need to reexamine the rectangular survey system, which had limitations in the mountainous and arid West. The commission made an extensive visit to the western lands. However, their investigation did not offer a balanced view; California consumed a full third of the 673 pages of testimony, but Kansas and Minnesota, which led the nation in homestead applications in 1879, were not represented. Nonetheless, the report contains a wealth of historical information.

The commission recommended that Congress establish a classification for forestlands as well as for mineral and varieties of agricultural lands. The commission also recommended that public forestlands be withdrawn from sale or entry, and the timber be sold under the supervision of the secretary of the interior. Of great potential consequence, the commission further recommended that the government and land grant railroads be allowed to exchange lands in order to consolidate ownerships. Congress did not respond to these recommendations, but historians suspect that the FOREST RESERVE ACT of 1891 passed more easily because of the commission's efforts.

Directly attributable to the commission and of considerable historical value, however, is the work of commission member Thomas Donaldson. His 1,343-page *The Public Domain: Its History with Statistics* (1884; reprint 1970), although biased and dated, remains an important reference work for nineteenth-century public land history. His outspoken criticism of public land policy was unusual for an official document. Also, his prejudices against immigrants with "almost unpronounceable names" of "appalling length and queerness" caused unfortunate distortion of a land policy that had been designed specifically to accommodate newcomers. Nonetheless, *The Public Domain* is a treasure trove of data and perceptions that are central to understanding American land policy.

FURTHER READING: Thomas Donaldson, *The Public Domain: Its History with Statistics* (1884, 1970). Paul W. Gates, *History of Public Land Law Development* (1968), pp. 422-434.

PUBLIC LAND LAW REVIEW COMMISSION

Meeting between 1965 and 1969, the Public Land Law Review Commission (PLLRC) was established as part of a compromise between the preservationist lobby and the House Interior and Insular Affairs Committee, especially its chairman at the time, Congressman Wayne Aspinall of Colorado. In 1961, 1962, and 1963, the Senate passed wilderness preservation bills that were then killed by the House. Sensitive to the wishes of mining interests, Aspinall was opposed to a number of antidevelopment provisions in the bills, particularly those that forbade mineral prospecting in wilderness areas.

In 1964, a compromise was worked out. In return for a nineteen-year allowance of prospecting in wilderness areas and the establishment of a commission that would thoroughly examine American public land policy, Aspinall delivered the wilderness bill to the House floor, where it passed with only one dissenting vote.

The PLLRC was composed of nineteen members, including six senators, six congressmen, six presidential appointees, and the chairman selected by the members, Aspinall. An advisory council consisted of liaison officers from departments and agencies concerned with public land law, twenty-five other people representing citizens' groups, and one representative of each state governor. The commission was authorized to examine federal laws, rules, and regulations as they applied to the public domain, reserves (except for Indian reservations), national parks and forests, and wildlife refuges and ranges. It received testimony from over 900 witnesses at ten regional hearings held between 1966 and 1968.

The PLLRC authorized the preparation of thirty-three written studies on selected aspects of the public land laws by its own staff and by private contractors under staff supervision. These detailed reports contain a wealth of information on the various land problems the government agencies and Congress faced in the 1960s. Two of them were published by the Government Printing Office: *Digest of Public Land Laws* (1968) and *History of Public Land Law Development*, by Paul W. Gates and Robert W. Swenson (1968). In 1970, the commission issued its final report, *One Third of a Nation's Land*.

The commission made several dozen general recommendations and 137 specific ones. Reflecting the Western, commodity-oriented values held by its chairman and most of its members, the PLLRC called for revision of the laws governing disposal of public lands. Its recommendations asserted congressional authority over the executive branch in establishing policies for the public lands: all reservations established by the executive (such as national forests and NATIONAL MONUMENTS), as well as lands of the public domain, were to be reviewed for disposal to state and private hands. Insensitive to the environmentalist sentiments then at a high level in the nation and ambivalent toward the concept of multiple use, the PLLRC suggested in place of the latter that "the highest and best use of particular areas" should be recognized as "dominant over other authorized uses."

Such propositions were at odds with the widespread environmentalist sentiments of the period, and consequently the PLLRC recommendations had little immediate influence on legislation and policymaking. However, despite Aspinall's defeat in his attempt at re-election in 1972, the point of view represented in the PLLRC influenced such federal legislation as the FEDERAL LAND POLICY AND MANAGEMENT ACT, the act providing federal grants in lieu of taxes in public land states, and the NATIONAL FOREST MANAGEMENT ACT, both passed in 1976.

FURTHER READING: Samuel Trask Dana and Sally K. Fairfax, *Forest and Range Management: Its Development in the United States* (2nd ed., 1980). Paul W. Gates, "Pressure Groups and Recent American Land Policies," *Agricultural History* 55 (Apr. 1981): 103–127.

PUBLIC LANDS COMMISSION, 1903

In response to a recommendation from Gifford PINCHOT, President Theodore ROOSEVELT on October 2, 1903, appointed the nation's second Public Lands Commission. Roosevelt directed the commission "to report upon the condition, operation, and effect of the present land laws, and to recommend such changes as are needed." The president appointed Pinchot, chief forester of the Bureau of Forestry (since 1905, the FOREST SERVICE), W. A. Richards, commissioner of the GENERAL LAND OFFICE, and Frederick H. NEWELL, chief engineer of the Reclamation Service. Richards was chairman.

The commissioners held hearings and gave special attention to the views of stockmen, attending meetings of the National Livestock and the National Wool Growers associations. The commissioners reported that "the present laws are not suited to meet the conditions of the remaining public domain." However, they adhered to the traditional principle that the remaining land should be disposed of in small parcels for farming, an idealistic recommendation that in retrospect seems rather unrealistic, even naïve, for so-called experts to have made.

The commissioners carefully scrutinized the 1878 Timber and Stone Act and found blatant abuse in three Oregon and Washington test counties. For example, under the law designed to aid actual settlers obtain needed wood, 50 percent of the 160-acre parcels had been sold to timber firms for as much as $3,000.

Fourteen hundred stockmen returned the commission's questionnaire on grazing conditions. Numbers and kinds of livestock on public range were determined with improved precision, as was the condition of the range itself. Perhaps not surprising, considering the commission's membership, the report stated that "forest-reserve regulations have resulted in an improvement in the conditions of summer grazing lands" by limiting both numbers of stock and the duration of their stay. This limitation of numbers was important, because "overstocking has undoubtedly been by far the greatest cause of range destruction and decrease in its carrying capacity." Some stock-

men insisted that grazing controls and fees would put them out of business.

The report's 373-page appendix contains a wealth of historical data. However, the commission made only two forestry-related recommendations: enactment of a forest homestead law and repeal of the so-called lieu-land provisions of the 1897 FOREST MANAGEMENT ACT which encouraged fraud. The Forest Homestead Act became law on June 11, 1906; Congress had repealed the lieu-land provision in 1905, but Gates (1968) believes that this repeal would have occurred without the commission's recommendation. The much abused Timber and Stone Act was not repealed until 1955.

FURTHER READING: Paul W. Gates, *History of Public Land Law Development* (1968). *Report of the Public Lands Commission, with Appendix* (1905, 1972 reprint).

PUERTO RICO AND AMERICAN VIRGIN ISLANDS FORESTS

With a total land area of 2.32 million acres, Puerto Rico and the American Virgin Islands evidently were entirely forested at the time of their discovery by Columbus in 1493. Elevations ranging to 4,000 feet, precipitation varying from 30 to 180 inches, and a variety of soil conditions provided the islands with a complex forest distribution, including some 550 native tree species of which about 26 are endemic.

The immediate coastal vegetation was generally shrubby, due to salt spray, and yielded to mangrove in lagoons and bays. However, in more protected coastal areas, particularly along the north coast of Puerto Rico, there grew stands of valuable timber-producing trees such as *Palo de Maria, Ausubo, Roble*, and *Tortugo amarillo*. Further inland along the coastal plain to elevations of 500 feet or more, the forest was largely evergreen, containing two or three stories each with distinct tree species. Forest types in this region depended upon soil and precipitation and were classified as moist coast, moist limestone, dry coast, and dry limestone forests. Mountain forests were found mainly in Puerto Rico on the Luquillo Mountains in the east and on the central cordillera. Trees have reached heights of 110 feet, some with 8-foot diameters. At elevations above 2,000 or 3,000 feet, forest growth was stunted to under 60 feet by heavy rains (100 to 180 inches a year) that leached the soil and created boggy ground.

Despite the crucial contribution of the forests to primitive life on these islands, there is little evidence that significant areas of forest were removed or modified before the arrival of the Europeans. Then, although the better timbers were used for construction, boat building, furniture, posts, and fuel, most of the forests were either burned or left to decay as land was cleared for agriculture.

During the seventeenth and eighteenth centuries, agricultural settlement, chiefly for sugar production, almost completely cleared the original forest on Saint John and Saint Croix, and to a lesser extent on Saint Thomas. On Puerto Rico, widespread land clearing began with the liberalization of Spanish colonization and trade policies in 1815. In 1828, about 72 percent of the island was in timber and brush, whereas by 1912, less than 25 percent of this cover remained. In 1980, only about 1 percent of the forestland remained in virgin condition.

Deforestation, burning, cultivation, and grazing of land better suited for forest have nearly run their course in these islands. Most such lands have been abandoned and have returned or are returning to forest. In 1980, at least 1.1 million acres, about half of the land area of the islands, was considered forestland. Of this, about 88 percent was tree covered, including coffee plantations, of which most had been abandoned. Since the mid-1950s, forested acreage had increased almost 60 percent, largely due to land abandonment.

The beginnings of forestry are best documented for Puerto Rico. The Spanish government as early as 1513 passed laws to protect the trees of Puerto Rico. Local concern with watershed protection was first recorded in a government circular of 1824, and the first forestry budget was issued in 1860. Between 1860 and 1898, the Spanish government established a forestry organization and regulated cutting and the sale of timber in two forest regions in eastern and central Puerto Rico.

The United States took possession of Puerto Rico in 1898 following the Spanish-American War, and five years later the federal government established the Luquillo National Forest on the eastern end of the island. However, no supervisor was assigned to the 12,400-acre forest until 1917. In 1935, the Luquillo was renamed the Caribbean National Forest, and by 1980, the forest's area included 27,846 acres of federal land. Puerto Rico authorized an insular forest service in 1917 and in 1917 and 1919 reserved seven public forests covering 34,000 acres. No appropriations were made for the Puerto Rico Forest Service until 1919. In that year, under a cooperative agreement, the officer in charge of the Luquillo National Forest was also employed as chief of the insular service.

Since 1920, the U. S. FOREST SERVICE has sponsored a continuous program of information, technical assistance, free planting stock, and, more recently, cost-sharing incentives for reforestation of private lands. Tree planting during the past fifty years has been attempted on some 125,000 acres of private lands and public forest, although tree plantations have not been successful in many cases. Research to improve reforestation efforts began in the early 1920s, were formalized in 1939, and have been gradually extended ever since.

In the Virgin Islands, the end of slavery in the early nineteenth century marked the beginning of the decline of sugar production and the return of brush and finally forests to the dry rocky hillsides. West Indies mahogany, apparently introduced in the 1700s, became a common tree on roadsides and abandoned lands in Saint Thomas and Saint Croix, eventually covering nearly 400 acres as an almost pure forest in central Saint Croix.

The United States purchased the Virgin Islands from Denmark in 1917, and efforts to reforest the territory began between 1930 and 1932, under the auspices of the U. S. Bureau of Efficiency (discontinued in 1933) and the Navy Department. The Forest Service staff in Puerto Rico made occasional investigations in the Virgin Islands thereafter, but a continuous forestry program was not begun by the Virgin Islands Corporation and the Forest Service until 1953. By 1980, some 370 acres, mostly mahogany, had been planted in Saint Croix. In 1956, about 60 percent of Saint John—7,660 acres—was set aside as the Virgin Islands National Park. By 1980, the park encompassed 12,678 acres. The Buck Island Reef National Monument was created on St. Croix in 1961 and in 1980 included 800 acres of federal land. By 1963, the 147-acre Estate Thomas Experimental Forest was established on the Island of St. Thomas.

FURTHER READING: William P. Kramer, "Forestry Work in the Island of Puerto Rico," *Journal of Forestry* 24 (Apr. 1926): 419-425. Louis A. Murphy, *Forests of Puerto Rico: Past, Present, and Future, and Their Physical and Economic Environment* (1916). Robert W. Nobles, "Forestry in the U. S. Virgin Islands," *Journal of Forestry* 58 (July 1960): 524-527.

FRANK H. WADSWORTH

PULP AND PAPER INDUSTRY

Paper is manufactured from cellulose fibers by separating them into a pulp, suspending them in water, and distributing them on a screen to form a sheet, which is then drained, pressed, and dried. Until the nineteenth century, most of the pulp used for paper was made from linen or cotton rags. Matthew Lyon of Fair Haven, Vermont, is said to have published a newspaper on paper manufactured from pulp made from basswood bark and rags in 1794. The growth of population, increased literacy, and the mechanization of the papermaking process prompted an interest in making pulp from wood as a substitute both cheaper than cloth and available in larger quantities. The endless-web papermaking machine, later known as the fourdrinier, was first patented in France in 1799 and imported to America in 1827; the cylinder machine, invented in England in 1809, was separately developed in the United States in 1817. As these machines drove out handmade paper, the demand for pulp outstripped the supply of rags and the price of paper began a long-term growth. The Civil War and the accompanying growth of government bureaucracy particularly increased paper demand, and the following years saw processes of pulping wood become both technologically possible and financially profitable.

The mechanical and alkaline (soda) wood-pulping processes originated in Europe and were imported into the United States beginning in the 1860s. Mechanical or groundwood pulp is produced by forcing bolts against rapidly revolving grindstones, while water is flooded over the grinding surface to prevent burning of the wood. Mechanical pulp is the lowest grade and cheapest form of pulp used in papermaking, as it retains all the lignin and hemicelluloses and consists of bundles of fibers and fragments of fibers instead of individual fibers. The presence of the impurities and the structural weakness of the fibers means that paper made from mechanical wood pulp lacks strength, permanence, and durability. Mechanical pulping processes are high in energy consumption, but they have the advantage of yielding 90 percent of the dry weight of the wood in pulp—far more than any chemical pulp. Mechanical pulp also makes paper of high printing quality. In the 1970s, the use of disk refiners to fiberize wood chips at atmospheric or elevated steam pressure produced mechanical pulp with improved properties.

Manufacture of mechanical wood pulp in the United States began in Lucerne, New York, in 1865 with an American-invented grinding machine, and in Interlaken, Massachusetts, the following year with imported German machines. It was first manufactured largely from poplar and used mainly as a filler to provide opacity to paper made with stronger chemical fibers. Subsequently, spruce and balsam fir became the dominant species used for mechanical wood pulp. Aspen has been used in this process, but hardwood fibers are usually too short to make an adequately strong paper. About 1884, newsprint made of mechanical pulp began to come into general use, and subsequently in the United States, most mechanical pulp (most often mixed with about 20 percent sulfite pulp or 25 to 30 percent sulfate pulp) has gone into newsprint. In 1980, about 9 percent of the wood pulp produced in the United States was mechanical pulp.

By dissolving the nonfibrous part of wood in a solution, chemical pulp-making processes leave the cellulose fiber in a purer form than that resulting from mechanical processes. The oldest chemical pulp-making technique is the soda process, which began producing wood pulp in the United States under a British patent in 1866 at Manayunk, near Philadelphia. Caustic soda (NaOH), a strong alkali, is the active ingredient. The process is capable of pulping most species of wood, but it was most often applied to nonresinous hardwoods. Originally, soda pulp was made largely from poplar wood; later, yellow-poplar and hemlock came into use, and in the twentieth century aspen has been the principal species employed. Until chestnut trees succumbed to blight, the soda process was used with chestnut pulp after extraction of the tannin. These short-fibered hardwood soda pulps were used, after bleaching, as a filler in printing and writing papers made from softwood sulfite pulps. In 1980, soda pulp remained in production in only one mill in the United States; the wood used was mostly oak.

In 1866, Benjamin Tilghman of Manayunk, Pennsylvania, obtained an English patent for the manufacture of wood pulp from chips cooked with sulphurous acid. This sulfite process first gained commercial success in Sweden and Germany, however, and was reintroduced in the United States in the 1880s, when production was started in Providence, Rhode Island, by Charles S. Wheelwright and at Alpena, Michigan, by Albert Pack and George N. Fletcher, lumbermen seeking a profitable means to dispose of mill waste. By the second decade of the twentieth century, the production of sulfite pulp in the United States exceeded that of mechanical wood pulp and remained the largest consumer of pulpwood until after the introduction of the sulfate process; by 1980, however, only 5 percent of the wood pulp produced resulted from the sulfite process. It was originally applied to spruce chips, and spruce and balsam continued to supply the bulk of the raw material, although hemlock furnished a substantial amount and some hardwoods such as aspen were used. Resinous woods like pine required special treatment for removal of pitch before use in the sulfite process. Sulfite pulp has been generally used to provide strength in mixtures with either soda or mechanical pulp; it is also bleached for use in writing and printing papers.

The sulfate (or kraft) process, a development of the

soda process, was employed in Germany in the 1880s but was not applied in the Western Hemisphere until 1907, and then first in Quebec. The process was used in 1909 at Roanoke Rapids, North Carolina, and in 1911 in Wisconsin and Texas, but it did not become important in the United States until around 1920 when commercial production was undertaken in the Lake States, New England, and the South. It involves treating wood chips under high temperature and pressure in a caustic soda solution containing one-third sodium sulfide, which dissolves lignin rapidly but with less destruction to the cellulose than any other cooking liquor. The pulp can be used in strong, tough paper. It was originally restricted to applications where color was unimportant, such as in wrapping and bag paper. Since the 1930s, bleached sulfate pulp has found its way into fine papers. The sulfate process can handle almost any wood, including resinous woods which posed difficulties for other chemical processes. It has been used mostly on southern pine. It often uses sawmill waste formerly discarded. In 1980, the sulfate process supplied over 76 percent of the wood pulp produced in the United States.

Chemical processes produce less than one-half the original weight of wood as pulp. To increase yield, wood chips softened by a mild chemical process are then ground to a fibrous mass called semichemical pulp. This pulp was developed by the Forest Products Laboratory about 1925, and in the 1940s and 1950s it was introduced commercially. It has primarily been used in corrugating medium. It has usually been made from hardwoods, often from chestnut wood in connection with the extraction of tannin. Semichemical pulp, however, contains more lignin than chemical pulp. In 1980, it constituted about 8 percent of American-made wood pulp.

As these processes of manufacturing pulp from wood were perfected, the price of paper dropped while the number of mills grew. Competition became very strong throughout the industry. During the first twenty-five years of wood pulping, 1867 to 1892, mills were located primarily in the older lumbering areas of New England and New York. Where pulp mills had already been established they often were able to shift to the new processes, but the timing of the shift was critical as the price drop came very abruptly.

Older rag mills that introduced the new machinery at the right time and prospered in this boom period included S. D. Warren of Westbrook, Maine; many mills in Holyoke, Massachusetts; and Knowlton Brothers in Watertown, New York. As early as 1875, some paper companies began to purchase woodlands. The trees providing the new source of fibers tended to be second- and third-growth trees the lumbermen had passed over. In many areas, environmental problems of overcutting became prominent, and by the 1880s public interest in forest conservation and replanting trees was widespread. Several of the paper companies in Maine and New York, particularly the Great Northern Paper Company after 1901, were leaders in the effort to institute forest-management programs.

The problems and opportunities posed by the expansion of production and the lower paper prices which followed the introduction of wood pulp affected especially the newsprint industry just when newspapers were competing for the enlarged readership resulting from increased public education. Prices for newsprint dropped from as high as twelve to twenty cents per pound during the Civil War to one cent per pound at the height of the competition. The late nineteenth century, while offering prosperity to some papermakers, drove other firms out of business. The American Paper and Pulp Association (APPA) was founded in 1884 to deal with the problems of unrestrained competition. To some extent, the founding of labor unions in the paper industry was also an indirect result of competition, since some companies sought to extend hours or lower wages; but other firms went to eight-hour shifts and provided more benefits to workers.

The first large combination formed to control the competition was the International Paper Company, created in 1898 from many small papermakers in New England and New York. International Paper soon branched out to purchase woodlands and began to concern itself with distribution. A second large company was the Great Northern Paper Company, incorporated in 1899. Great Northern purchased large amounts of woodland and power sources and built dams, mills, and whole towns, such as Millinocket, Maine. Other large efforts at consolidation were less successful. In the early 1900s, a number of Wisconsin paper firms considered merging into a new giant able to compete with International Paper. The effort failed, but it stirred the interest of the U. S. Congress to inquire into trust activities in the industry in 1909. Merger efforts in Ohio, which concerned mostly converting plants (those using paper to produce final products), were more successful. In Holyoke and other older centers, closeness of interest and family ownership tended to solve the competitive problems. The formation of an association of newsprint producers in 1915 attracted another congressional inquiry and an extensive Federal Trade Commission (FTC) investigation. The result was the creation under FTC aegis of the Newsprint Service Bureau for the collection and dissemination of statistical information.

Also in 1915, the APPA formed a section to coordinate research, disseminate results, and administer a code of ethics for chemists in the industry. This group later became the Technical Association of the Pulp and Paper Industry.

By World War I, the paper industry had weathered a number of storms. The wood-pulp processes were well established. Large consolidation had occurred in the older areas of the industry. Colleges of forestry and of chemical engineering were producing trained personnel. Land-use plans and controlled cutting of company timber were accepted in the older areas. A trade press was active and widely used. Small mills were operating on the West Coast and in the South, but the industry was centered in a belt from Maine through New England and New York, Pennsylvania, Ohio, and Wisconsin. Most manufacturers produced book paper and newsprint, although some demand continued for items such as paper collars, wallpaper, and boxes. The Underwood Tariff of 1913 placed newsprint on the free list, and subsequently a number of United States firms built mills in Canada, which became the major supplier of American newsprint.

The next twenty years saw major changes in the industry, both in geographical location and in the products manufactured. In 1912, the kraft process was perfected to the point where southern and western trees could be used to manufacture such products as heavy paper boxes. Although common carriers were resistant to the new paper boxes, a decision by the FTC forced their use after 1914. During the war, the use of paper boxes was also encouraged by the military forces.

These forces tended to work together during the 1920s to create another great flurry of activity. Pulpwood plantations were established in many areas of the South, often on land which had fallen into disuse because of the boll weevil, changed consumer demands for cotton, and the growth of cotton agriculture on the irrigated lands of the Southwest. Many northern companies expanded to the South to take advantage of the possibilities of inexpensive land, cheap labor, and a favorable tax base. Other firms were created there as well. A major publicity effort was initiated by Charles H. HERTY of Savannah, Georgia, to entice both companies and investors to the South for paper manufacturing. The kraft paper industry gradually moved southward during the 1920s and 1930s. Herty demonstrated that newsprint could be successfully manufac-

tured from southern pine, which previously had been thought too resinous, and in 1938 Ernest L. Kurth founded the first Southern newsprint plant, Southland Paper Mills of Lufkin, Texas.

On the West Coast, small mills manufactured paper from local materials in the 1860s and imported wood chips and wood pulp from the East. Once the sulfite process allowed the use of western evergreens, the largest western paper firm, the California Paper Company, imported eastern money and technology and during the 1880s established the Willamette mill in Oregon. By 1914, a series of mergers produced the Crown-Willamette Company, then the second largest paper manufacturer in the country. The opening of the Panama Canal facilitated the movement of goods, people, and ideas, and Western lumbermen welcomed the expansion of the pulp industry as providing a market for their hemlock. The number of pulp and paper mills in the Pacific Northwest grew rapidly in the late 1920s; then, beginning in 1928, most of them merged to form the Crown Zellerbach Company, which, together with the closely related group of firms that became Rayonier, Inc., dominated the industry on the West Coast. These firms relied for their wood supply on logs purchased from independent timber operators. After World War II, Rayonier undertook a timber purchase program, obtaining ownership of some 350,000 acres, or nearly 5 billion board feet, in the Pacific Northwest. Another large Western landholder, the Weyerhaeuser Timber Company (see WEYERHAEUSER FAMILY), had already made its entry into the Pacific Coast pulp and paper industry in 1931 when it opened a large new mill at Longview, Washington, for the exploitation of hemlock mill waste. Within thirty years, pulp and paper products would account for half of Weyerhaeuser's total sales. Unlike most Eastern companies, Western pulp and paper companies could also obtain timber from federal lands.

Although paper production sank to 9.2 million tons in 1933, or only 67 percent of mill capacity, the Depression had less disastrous effects on pulp and paper than on many other branches of American industry. Most paper firms continued to pay dividends except in 1932 and 1933. Newsprint, the weakest segment of the industry, saw continued consolidation. The National Industrial Recovery Act codes of industrial behavior were worked out and, until they were set aside as unconstitutional, helped to solve problems of overproduction. The APPA and its president, David Clark Everest, provided leadership in weathering the storm of the Depression.

Pulped wood fibers pass over a fast-moving wire screen that allows water to drain, leaving a mat of wet paper. The paper is then squeezed to remove still more water and dried and placed on large rolls. Forest History Society Photo.

The New Deal era witnessed expansion of reforestation programs and the adoption of continuous forest-management policies and improved land use patterns. These conservation efforts occurred in all regions, particularly in the South. U. S. FOREST SERVICE personnel such as Austin CARY and Inman F. ("Cap") Eldridge carried the gospel of better cutting and planting to Southern timberland owners. Many of the older firms also adopted these techniques. By the end of the 1930s, the South had witnessed the growth of an entirely new pulp and paper industry and thereby found profitable new uses for its lands.

The development of new consumer products, results of the research technology of the 1920s and 1930s, aided the prosperity of the industry. The Kimberly-Clark Corporation, headquartered at Neenah, Wisconsin, pioneered in the manufacture of sanitary napkins, paper towels, and facial tissues. Early in the 1930s, a number of sulfite pulp mills on the Olympic Peninsula in Washington began manufacturing dissolving pulp for use in rayon; these firms merged into Rayonier, Incorporated, in 1937.

The New Deal fostered labor growth through the National Industrial Recovery Act Section 7a, and new unions sprang up in the mills throughout the industry in the 1930s. In the woods, contract labor was ordinarily used, even on company-owned lands, or wood was purchased from independent loggers or landowners. With the introduction of truck hauling and the availability of the private motor car, crews in the woods tended to be less tied to the companies and more to their middlemen contractors. This general pattern of unionized mill operations and nonunion woods operations was still true in 1980. Exceptions may be found: woods operations are generally unionized in the West, but on the whole a major portion of the wood and wood chips delivered to pulp mills is produced by independent loggers or by other forest-land owners.

Mechanization in the pulp and papermaking industry increased enormously during the period between World Wars I and II. Machines became much larger and many more were introduced into plants, especially as electric power became available. These plants tended to be larger, the machines faster, and the technology more complicated. The small motor truck, the power-driven loading machinery, and the development of better sales and office techniques also modified those aspects of the industry greatly. Many firms in the 1920s introduced company periodicals, stock purchase options, and other amenities to aid in personnel management. The papermaker had traditionally been a peripatetic individual, but by the end of the 1930s this stereotype was disappearing.

Professional education in papermaking began at the University of Maine in 1913. A number of other institutions followed in offering higher education in the field, including the Institute of Paper Chemistry at Lawrence College in Wisconsin in 1929 and the Crown Zellerbach Corporation, which in 1933 initiated a course at Camas, Washington, that in the 1950s grew into a degree-conferring school. By 1970, half a dozen American colleges and universities offered degrees in pulp and paper technology.

During World War II, the industry experienced tremendous growth. The uses for paper were to expand ever more with wartime bureaucratic and military requirements. Papers that would withstand great colds, tropical damps, and molds and paper that would repel water all were demanded immediately, and a major research program was organized. The production of gunpowder, made from wood pulp in a process similar to

that used for rayon, placed additional burdens upon many mills.

Labor in the pulp mills was given some preferential selective service treatment, but not that in the woods. Women were widely used in the mills and in the Southern woods, where the use of black labor expanded. The mills in the Northeast attempted to hire the French of Quebec and New Brunswick, a traditional labor source in hard times. This led to difficulties with the Canadian government and American labor unions. By the end of the war, much of the pulpwood cutting east of the Mississippi was being done by prisoners of war.

Wartime supplies of equipment and material, including truck tires, gasoline, and sulphuric acid, became inadequate for industry's needs. The War Production Board (WPB) appointed an Owens-Corning Glass executive, Harold Boeschenstein, as coordinator for the pulp and paper industry. Heavy pulpwood cutting led to temporary abandonment of some land use plans, farmers were encouraged to cut wood on their lands, and wastepaper was collected for recycling. Although not a paper man by background, Boeschenstein was a driving force in the WPB Forest Products Bureau, and his leadership enabled the industry to finish the war in good shape.

After the war, consumer demand increased dramatically for a wider variety of paper and paper products than ever before. Paper and cardboard cartons dominated the field of shipping boxes and containers. New papers were developed for reproduction, photography, and tissue products. The industry experienced a surge of growth, nearly as great as the expansion which had followed the introduction of wood pulp. New mills were very large, and their machinery was huge and very fast. Most of the financing for these new large mills, many of them located in the South, had come from outside the industry. The need for an acceptable return on investment prompted a new wave of consolidation. By 1970, many of the smaller firms, especially those manufacturing a single line of products, had disappeared. In their place were a number of very large industrywide, vertically organized firms, many of them older companies which had branched out both into new areas of the country and into new areas of production and sales.

Since the 1930s, there were concurrent developments in harvesting, wood preparation, pulping, bleaching, and stock preparation, all of which followed from the need for ever increasing amounts of high-quality pulp to feed faster and wider paper machines. These developments included the chain saw, feller-buncher, and whole-tree chipper in the woods; the drum and ring debarkers, multiknife chippers, and chip washer in wood preparation; the continuous digester, chemical recovery, and disk fiberizers in pulping; multistage bleaching with chlorine, chlorine dioxide, and oxygen in bleaching; centrifugal screens and cleaners, and disk refiners in stock preparation; and twin-wires, double headboxes, and plastic wires and foils in papermaking.

New England remained a major producer of specialty papers and newsprint for local consumption, but many of the small mills there did not survive the competitive stress of the postwar period. Those with woodlands have tended to survive, although usually through mergers into nationwide firms. Much of the same can be said of mills in the Middle West, where the diversity is greater and the spread into other products most pronounced. These regions in 1979 supplied 49 percent of total United States paper production; Wisconsin and Maine were the two leading paper-producing states.

In the South and West, the pulp and paper industry has grown rapidly since World War II. In 1979, the South supplied 37 percent of the national paper production (including 40 percent of the newsprint) and 63 percent of the paperboard production. Very large mills and woods operations on company-owned or leased land, with detailed land use plans usually involving tree planting from genetically selected stock, dominate the Southern and Western industry. The computer plays a very large role in running the mills. The personnel are highly trained. Competition is still great,

A seven-ton roll of paper forms at the end of the drying process. Forest History Society Photo.

U. S. Production and Consumption of Paper Products (in tons of 2,000 pounds)

	Total Paper and Paperboard			Apparent Consumption	
	Production	Imports	Exports	Tons	Lbs./ Capita
1899	2,167,593	—	—	2,167,593	57.9
1909	4,121,495	55,962	74,764	4,102,693	90.8
1919	5,966,076	707,548	420,540	6,253,084	119.6
1929	11,140,235	2,533,603	262,383	13,411,455	220.3
1939	13,509,642	2,687,494	248,569	15,948,567	243.7
1949	20,315,436	4,751,810	372,277	24,694,969	331.0
1959	34,014,825	5,622,175	911,917	38,725,083	435.5
1969	53,489,052	7,493,492	2,765,631	58,216,913	572.9
1979	64,881,000	9,125,000	3,672,000	70,334,000	638.0

and the sales techniques in the industry have received much attention. The American pulp and paper industry is beginning to branch out into other areas of the world and also into the production of chemicals and other forest products. Yet the United States continues to be an importer of paper: in 1979, 63 percent of American newsprint needs were met by Canada.

Since much of the pulp and paper industry was founded as a conservation measure to reduce wastage of timber resources, it was ironical that the industry became widely regarded as a conservation menace because of air and water pollution in the environmentally conscious 1960s and 1970s. Compliance with federal and state regulations regarding effluents, air emissions, and solid wastes has cost the industry as much as 38 percent of its total capital investment (in 1972), over $600 million in one year (1975). Some older mills have closed because they could not justify such expenditures. Energy shortages starting in the early 1970s induced the pulp and paper industry to reduce its energy expenditures through improved efficiency and by substituting bark and wood-waste fuel and coal for oil and natural gas. Fossil fuel consumption per ton of product decreased 21 percent between 1972 and 1980. Another conservation development of the 1970s was an increased use of wastepaper, particularly in the recycling of newsprint. Overall, wastepaper provided the raw material for 22 to 24 percent of paper and paperboard production during the decade. Lumber mill residues also increased in importance as a source of fiber; in 1979, sawmill waste provided 38 percent of the total pulp-wood supply. The increased importance of sawmill waste for pulp production has emerged as an important consideration in the planning of fully integrated forest products manufacturing facilities.

FURTHER READING: L. Ethan Ellis, *Newsprint: Producers, Publishers, Political Pressures* (1960), and *Print Paper Pendulum* (1948). John A. Guthrie, *The Newsprint Paper Industry: An Economic Analysis* (1941). Dard Hunter, *Papermaking: The History and Technique of an Ancient Craft* (rev. ed., 1947). Royal S. Kellogg, *Newsprint Paper in North America* (1948). Mary Claire McCauley, *Pulp and Paper Policies of the War Production Board and Predecessor Agencies, May 1940 to January 1944*, Historical Reports on War Administration, War Production Board Special Study No. 7 (1944). Newsprint Service Bureau, *Bulletin* (1922–1950). Jack P. Oden, "Charles Holmes Herty and the Birth of the Southern Newsprint Paper Industry, 1927–1940," *Journal of Forest History* 21 (Apr. 1977): 76-89. David C. Smith, *History of Papermaking in the United States, 1691-1969* (1970); "Wood Pulp Paper Comes to the Northeast, 1865–1900," *Forest History* 10 (Apr. 1966): 12-25; "The California Paper Industry to 1900," *Southern California Quarterly* 57 (Summer 1975): 129–146; "Pulp, Paper, and Alaska," *Pacific Northwest Quarterly* 66 (Apr. 1975): 61-70; and "Wood Pulp and Newspapers, 1867–1900," *Business History Review* 38 (Autumn 1964): 328-345. John G. Strange, *The Paper Industry: A Clinical Study* (1977). U. S. Congress, House, Pulp and Paper Investigation Select Committee, *Pulp and Paper Investigation Hearings*, House Document 1502, 60th Congress, 2nd session (1909). Lyman H. Weeks, *A History of Paper-Manufacturing in the United States, 1690–1916* (1916).

DAVID C. SMITH

QUETICO-SUPERIOR

Adjacent areas of Minnesota and Ontario lying between Lake Superior and Rainy Lake and famous for wilderness canoeing were established as Quetico Provincial Park and Superior National Forest in 1909. Efforts to protect the wilderness qualities of the region began in the 1920s and have resulted in landmark legislation and court decisions.

The region is characterized by the Laurentian Shield, a plate of ancient granitic rocks and thin glacial soils, dotted with thousands of interconnected lakes and rivers. Most of the area is covered by boreal conifers dominated by spruce, fir, and jackpine and by mixed forests of birch, aspen, and pines. Superior National Forest has the largest population of eastern timber wolves in the lower forty-eight states. Other significant wildlife includes moose, pine marten, beaver, bald eagles, and osprey.

Ojibway tribes occupied and resided in the area at the time of the first explorers. In 1732, La Vérendrye explored a water route that is now the international boundary and opened the way to the fur grounds to the northwest. Until the 1840s, the border lakes were an international highway for fur brigades. Later, short-lived gold, silver, and iron rushes opened the area, particularly after discovery of the Mesabi Iron Range in 1884. Loggers cut over much of the Min-

nesota side during the 1890s and early 1900s and similarly exploited the Ontario woods until the 1930s.

Wilderness protection began in 1922 when Arthur Carhart completed a recreation plan for the Superior National Forest that emphasized canoeing. When the Minnesota Highway Department planned roads through the forest in 1923, the IZAAK WALTON LEAGUE protested. In 1926, the secretary of agriculture rejected the proposed roads and set aside 1,000 square miles of forest as one of the nation's first wilderness areas.

Meanwhile, west of the national forest, the Minnesota and Ontario Paper Company at International Falls, Minnesota, proposed construction of power dams on the border lakes. Canadian and American governments referred the proposal to the International Joint Commission (IJC) in 1925 for study and recommendations. The IJC completed its report in 1934 and recommended that no dams be built.

Opponents of the dams formed the Quetico-Superior Council in 1928 and endorsed a plan for an international wilderness to be established by treaty. This Quetico-Superior wilderness would be devoted to recreation and wildlife and dedicated as a memorial to the Canadian and American veterans of World War I. Logging within the area would be limited to tracts out of sight of waterways.

The Quetico-Superior Council persuaded Congress

Canoeists enjoy Lac La Croix in the Boundary Waters Canoe Area of northern Minnesota. Forest Service Photo.

to pass the Shipstead-Nolan Act in 1930 to protect in their natural states the shorelines, waterfalls, rapids, and riparian timber on federal lands in northeastern Minnesota. Minnesota passed a similar act pertaining to state lands in 1933. The federal statute was the first act specifically intended to protect wilderness.

Between 1928 and 1936, the U. S. FOREST SERVICE enlarged Superior National Forest from 857,000 to 2,871,000 acres by acquiring cutover and tax-forfeited lands. Parcels of private lands were included within the enlarged wilderness area, and during the 1940s the private landowners developed resorts serviced by hydroplanes. Resorts and aircraft undercut the wilderness

policies established in 1926. Attempts to purchase the resorts with funds raised by the Izaak Walton League were partially successful. Congress responded in 1948 with the Thye-Blatnik Act and authorized the Forest Service to purchase the resorts and private lands within the wilderness and compensate the respective counties for lost tax revenues. For the first time in its history, the Forest Service could purchase land for recreational rather than forest protection, timber, or watershed purposes. This act foreshadowed similar provisions of the Land and Water Conservation Fund Act of 1965.

The Thye-Blatnik Act did not affect aircraft,

however, and in 1949 President Harry S Truman established an airspace reservation over the wilderness that banned low-level flights and landings after January 1, 1952. Three resort owners defied the ban and defended their acts in court by challenging the constitutionality of the president's order and the legality of maintaining wilderness as a public policy or public use. In *United States* v. *Perko*, the federal district and appeals courts and the Supreme Court all upheld the president's order and recognized wilderness as a legal public purpose of federal land.

After World War II, the conservationists attempted to interest Canadians in the proposed treaty for the international wilderness but failed because of official opposition from Ontario officials. In 1959, the provincial government exchanged letters with the United States, each party pledging to consult regularly with the other before changing policies to assure a coordinated and harmonious administration of the Quetico-Superior.

The federal Wilderness Act of 1964 included the Minnesota area as the Boundary Waters Canoe Area (BWCA) but sections of the act allowed continued logging, motorboats, and snowmachines within parts of the wilderness. Between 1965 and 1978, the exceptions led to a series of complicated court suits and controversies about the intent of the law. In 1969, a private individual attempted to explore for copper and nickel deposits on federal lands within the BWCA but was halted by a suit filed by the Izaak Walton League and the State of Minnesota. In 1972, the SIERRA CLUB and the Minnesota Public Interest Research Group temporarily halted logging in the BWCA by filing a suit under provisions of the Wilderness and National Environmental Policy acts. Congress resolved the controversies in 1978 by passing the Boundary Waters Canoe Area Wilderness Act. This statute enlarged the wilderness area to approximately 1.1 million acres, banned logging and mining, sharply curtailed motorboat and snowmachine uses, and provided funds to purchase resorts adjacent to the wilderness.

FURTHER READING: R. Newell Searle, *Saving Quetico-Superior: A Land Set Apart* (1977).

R. NEWELL SEARLE

R

RAILROADS AND FORESTS

Throughout their histories in the United States, the railroad and forest products industries have been closely related. Each influenced markedly the geographical configuration of the other. Railroads have been both major transporters of timber products and important consumers of lumber. Some rail carriers were, and a few continue to be, owners of large tracts of timberlands. Some of them have maintained developmental programs in forestry.

Timber Transportation

Railroads had a significant impact on the development and location of the lumber industry. In the Lake States, lumbering was well established by the time of the Civil War, but the role of railroads in its subsequent evolution there was great. Railway construction in northern Michigan, Wisconsin, and Minnesota permitted the establishment of lumbering in those areas, while the extension of rail lines west of Mississippi River points created huge farm markets for the lumber produced.

In the South, rail transportation was essential in the development of the lumber industry. The first railroads in the region were built to move cotton to river or coastal ports, but they also made possible the beginning of commercial lumbering in the interior of the pine belt. After the Civil War, enterprising railroad men led in promoting large-scale production. A freight agent of the Illinois Central sent the first carload of yellow pine north of the Ohio River in the 1870s. Soon, other rails carried southern pine and cypress to the growing markets of the North, while many miles of line were built for no other immediate purpose than to open timberlands.

Railroads played a similar role in the development of lumbering in the Pacific Northwest. The lumber industry there predated the arrival of railroads, but it was dependent upon local markets and those that could be reached by water transport. The building of the transcontinentals created new demands for lumber. The Central Pacific, which used 65 million board feet of lumber to build thirty-seven miles of snowsheds in the Sierra Nevada, consumed huge amounts of Puget Sound timber, and each of the transcontinentals that followed stimulated the lumber industry. More important in the long run were the markets opened by these lines. The completion of the Southern Pacific to Portland strengthened the position of Northwestern lumber in California, while the extension of the Union Pacific to Oregon permitted the sale of Pacific Northwest lumber in the Denver area. The completion of the Northern Pacific in 1883 made it possible to ship some Northwestern lumber to the upper Middle West, al-

563

though the great bulk of the lumber for the settlement of the Northern Plains continued to come from Minnesota. A decade later, after the Great Northern had reached Puget Sound and James J. Hill had slashed rates, greater penetration of midwestern markets occurred. The real boom, however, came after the turn of the century. In 1905, railroads hauled 65,000 carloads of lumber out of Washington State alone, and lumbermen were already complaining of car shortages. When Washington millmen won a favorable ruling on freight rates in the Portland Gateway Case in 1908, their shipments rose even further.

Lumber traffic, actual or potential, was often one of the factors shaping railroad strategy. A few examples from the twentieth century will suffice. In 1901, the Great Northern and the Northern Pacific purchased the Chicago, Burlington & Quincy, which served the major centers of the Middle West and owned subsidiary lines extending from Colorado to the Gulf Coast. Motives of the purchasers were mixed, but company executives were well aware that the northern transcontinentals served the lumber-producing areas of the Northwest and that the Burlington reached the major lumber-consuming region in the country. Early in the 1920s, the Southern Pacific built its Natron Cutoff through Klamath Falls, a town in southern Oregon that promised to become the center of a new lumber empire. Great Northern's extension into southern Oregon and northern California a few years later was inspired in part by the desire to tap the standing timber there.

Forest products have always bulked large in the traffic mix of railroads, although they were relatively more important in the nineteenth century, when it was common for logs and lumber to make up 30 percent or more of a line's total freight. In the early years of the twentieth century, products of forests amounted to roughly 11 percent of all originated revenue freight. This percentage drifted downward after 1910, although tonnage did not reach a peak figure until 1923. In the 1920s, traffic in forest products was 8.2 percent of the total; during the Depression, this figure dropped to 5.2 percent. It has gradually increased in each decade since then. Aggregate tonnage in 1960, however, was only 69 percent that of 1923. During the years 1964–1978, forest industries (including primary forest products, lumber, and lumber products except furniture) gave railroads 6.9 percent of their total freight revenue.

Lumber traffic was generally more important to railroads in the South and West than to those in the East. In 1910, for example, about 21 percent of all carload traffic in the South and 17 percent in the West, as compared to only 5 percent in the East, was forest products. By mid-century, forests were generating 7.6 percent of all tonnage in the South, 10.6 percent in the West, and 2.8 percent in the East.

Until recent decades, railroads hauled a substantial volume of logs to mills. Logging roads, often of narrow gauge and lightweight construction, came into their own in the late nineteenth century, when many were built in Pennsylvania and the Great Lakes states. Later, they were common in the South and Pacific Northwest where they once aggregated some 6,000 miles of line. Standard practice was to run a logging road into a forest area, perhaps as far as thirty miles, and to build from it as many as six temporary spurs per mile. Logging roads tended to concentrate lumbering in fewer hands since only owners of large tracts of timberlands could afford the investment required.

The first logging roads were primitive in construction and operation. Rails were often logs or sawed stringers, and motive power consisted of animals or geared locomotives capable of handling steep grades and sharp curves. Later, builders used secondhand rails and antiquated standard engines. Cars were generally ordinary flats or skeleton types with steel bunks. Some logging roads were upgraded and became parts of major systems and a few became independent common carriers, but most were abandoned or replaced by trucks and Caterpillar tractors. By 1977, only a handful of logging roads continued in service in the Pacific Northwest.

The rise of the PULP AND PAPER INDUSTRY in the South since the 1930s generated important new business for railroads there. In the 1960s, about 60 percent of the pulpwood arrived at mills by rail. Within a radius of fifty miles of a mill, trucks generally provided transportation; at greater distances, they hauled pulpwood to yards which were supplied with rail connections.

Rolling stock used in the transport of forest products underwent change, especially after World War II. Rising labor costs and growing intermodal competition rendered obsolete the old method of transporting lumber in ordinary boxcars. To permit mechanical loading, railroads acquired boxcars with wider openings and later, when the shipping of packaged lumber became feasible, bulkhead flatcars, which were also used for the transport of pulpwood logs. In the 1960s and later, various types of specialized cars replaced ordinary boxcars and gondolas for the hauling of wood chips.

Timber Consumption

The railroad has been known as the iron road, but it would be equally as appropriate to label it the wooden road. Pioneer railroads were built largely of wood, beginning with the crossties and going on to cars, stations, telegraph and other poles, fences, and miscellaneous structures. Trestles and bridges were generally of wood, tunnels were lined with wood, and passenger cars, stations, and engines were fueled with wood.

Railroad use of timber, expressed in relative terms, reached a peak in the 1880s when the industry consumed some 25 percent of the total timber cut. After 1900, use fell off, but in the 1920s railroads still consumed over 15 percent of the national output of forest products. Consumption declined dramatically in the 1930s and later. The Great Depression had a marked impact; construction of new lines ceased and steel replaced wood in cars and structures. By the 1960s, railroad use of lumber equaled perhaps 3 percent of the nation's output. Still, purchases in 1969 amounted to $123 million, mainly for crossties, piling, and similar items.

During the first forty years of railroad history in the United States, wood was the primary locomotive fuel. Engines consumed 3.7 million cords in 1860. As a fuel, wood offered a number of advantages which explained its almost universal use. It burned evenly, cleanly, and rapidly, and it was generally available. Railroads could contract with farmers to supply wood at designated points. Some varieties of wood, including hardwoods and pitch pine, were favored, while green or rotten wood was avoided.

The rising cost of wood, its scarcity in some areas, and the increasing output of soft coal caused railroads to begin to shift from wood in the 1850s. Studies by the Burlington in 1859–1860 showed that fuel costs per engine mile were ten cents for coal and nineteen cents for wood. The change in fuel came first in the Middle Atlantic states and on the prairies of the Middle West, more slowly in the South. In 1859, the Philadelphia & Reading was using nothing but coal. The Illinois Central acquired its first coal-burner in the 1850s, and by 1870 it was for all practical purposes a coal-burning road. Even Southern railroads such as the Louisville & Nashville bought no wood-burners after the Civil War. By 1900, except for a handful of minor roads, wood was used mainly for kindling.

As early as the 1840s, inventors had produced metal cars, but their work inspired little interest in the railroad industry until after 1900. The Pennsylvania Railroad led the way to steel cars in 1906, followed closely by the Pullman Company and other carriers. Although a steel coach cost twice as much as a good quality wooden one, the change to steel was rapid. Only 25 percent of the passenger car orders in 1909 were for wooden cars, and the last all-wood car for domestic service was manufactured in 1913. However, many wooden cars remained in service for a quarter of a century or more, and they required substantial amounts of wood for repairs.

The shift to steel in freight car manufacturing came earlier than in the case of passenger equipment, but the change took longer to complete. The first all-metal hopper and gondola cars appeared in the 1880s, but as late as 1919 only 57 percent of the nation's open-top cars and 2 percent of its boxcars were

Most ties were sawn or hewn, but sometimes conveniently sized logs were used. Forest History Society Photo, Robert K. Winters Collection.

of steel. Some railroad companies continued to acquire wooden boxcars because they wanted to avoid antagonizing shippers of lumber and because wooden cars were easier to repair. Nevertheless, steel obviously had many advantages, and the trend was toward its use. In the 1920s and 1930s, many wooden cars were provided with metal roofs, ends, and body framing, and all-steel cars increased in popularity. By 1949, 87 percent of the open-top and 67 percent of the boxcars were of all-steel construction.

The largest single use of wood by railroads has been as cross, switch, and bridge ties. Crossties, by far the most common, average 3,000 per mile of track and are described as "transverse beams set in the roadbed to position and support railroad rails." Early attempts to use stones as foundations for rails proved unsuccessful, and the T-rail on wooden crossties bedded in ballast came to be the standard structure. It had the advantage of resiliency, strength, elasticity, and resistance to shock.

So successful has been the wooden crosstie that its use has never been successfully challenged in the United States, although some 2,500 patented ties have been introduced. In 1959, when major (Class I) railroads had 965 million crossties in their tracks, only 81,000 were of a material other than wood. Nonwood ties have constituted an insignificant percentage of ties laid since then, although a few railroads have experimented with prestressed concrete ties.

Wooden crossties have not changed much in form. Early ties were smaller than those in use later, but the Central Pacific, completed in 1869, employed ties measuring six by eight inches by eight feet. In the 1930s, the standard tie was from eight to eight and a half feet in length and measured seven by nine inches in cross section. Several railroads began using nine-foot ties after World War II. In the nineteenth century, ties were generally hewed, sometimes on only two faces, but after 1900 sawed ties gradually increased in popularity, especially on the Pacific Coast. By the 1970s, practically all ties were the products of sawmills.

Hewed ties were generally produced from farm woodlots within one to six miles of railroads, from scattered remote timber stands, and from cull trees and tops left after logging operations. Farmers often used tie-making as winter employment. Trees from ten to seventeen inches in diameter at breast height were generally used. Ties were hewed in the woods and often sold to tie producers, who supplied railroads and often owned timberlands. Hewed ties wasted much wood in chips, but the sidings and slabs removed during the manufacture of sawed ties were useful as lumber. Because sawed ties were more uniform in size, they could more conveniently be subjected to preservation treatments.

In selecting wood for tie use, railroad men look for straight-grained timber that will hold a spike well and that is resistant to mechanical wear and physical damage. Splitting, checking, and rail cutting and crushing can be reduced by installing antichecking irons and tie plates and by using larger and harder ties. Spike killing can be minimized by boring spike holes and by using screw spikes. Timber for untreated crossties needs to be selected for resistance to termites and decay. If treatment is planned, a capacity to absorb preservatives is more important.

Early railroads tended to use those varieties of wood that were available locally, but some are much more serviceable as ties than others. Hardwoods headed the list because they are heavy, close-grained, and less susceptible to decay and physical damage. White oak, with an average untreated tie life of eleven years, traditionally has been considered the best, followed by other oaks and mixed hardwoods. The softwoods, including the cedars, pines, cypress, and redwood, were widely used in the early years of railroading because of their availability. Some of them are resistant to decay, but they crush and rail-cut easily. Cottonwood is one of the least desirable varieties. In 1958, of the ties given preservative treatment, 53 percent were oak and another 19 percent were mixed hardwoods. Ten percent were Douglas-fir, the leader of the softwoods.

Regardless of the type of wood, the service life of ties is influenced by seasoning, climate, volume of traffic, and the use of preservatives. In the nineteenth century, ties were preferably cut in winter and the best ones came entirely from heartwood. Like other timber, ties needed seasoning to develop mechanical strength and stability. Modern wood preservation plants often use kiln drying and chemical drying agents to shorten and control the seasoning process. A cold, dry climate permits longer tie life than does a warm, damp one. A heavy volume of traffic generally shortens tie life, but the use of diesel power lengthens it, since the pounding effect of steam locomotives is eliminated.

The extensive use of wood, especially as crossties, caused railroads to be pioneers in developing and using wood preservatives. In 1873, the Louisville & Nashville Railroad built a creosote pressure plant at Pascagoula, Mississippi, to treat pine timbers used in bridge construction. Three similar plants were at work in the South by 1880, and five years later the

Wooden trestles and bridges spanned ravines and rivers throughout the mountainous West, consuming huge quantities of high-quality timber as railroads expanded into remote areas. Forest History Society Photo.

Santa Fe began treating pine ties in New Mexico. Other railroads displayed little interest until the late 1890s when the price of lumber began to rise and the cost of tie renewals became a matter of concern. The Burlington established a tie-treating plant in South Dakota in 1899 and later added others in Wyoming and Illinois. Soon, that railroad was treating not only ties but also some of its bridge and car lumber. By 1920, the practice of treating at least some ties had become general in the industry (see WOOD PRESERVATION).

In the first years of the twentieth century, most railroads treated ties with zinc chloride, but by 1910 creosote was gaining in popularity, partly because its cost fell as a by-product of the growing steel industry. Both treatments continued in use, but creosote came to be the most common. Zinc chloride, being water soluble, gave satisfactory results only in dry climates. Creosote was always preferred in damp climates and sites. Pentachlorphenol is also used for treating much railroad lumber.

Treatment greatly increased the life of a tie, extending it to an average of thirty years. The saving thus provided was a powerful catalyst; in the 1930s, about 80 percent of all renewals were with treated ties; thirty years later, practically all ties in the tracks of major carriers had been treated. This development sharply reduced the number of new ties required by the industry. In 1921, major carriers installed in their tracks 87 million ties, but three decades later annual replacements averaged only 24 million. In 1979, railroads installed 27 million new ties, an unusually large number that reflected substantial delayed maintenance.

Despite the decline in numbers of new ties needed, tie-replacement costs in the 1970s averaged more than $100 million annually and were still an important item in maintenance expenses. Tie prices have increased dramatically in recent years. In the 1850s, they cost no more than 25 cents, and as late as 1929 the average was 93 cents for untreated and $1.46 for treated ties. By 1972, prices for treated ties ranged from $5 to $6, and they doubled in the next four years. With shipping expenses and cost of installation added, the total outlay for putting a tie into a track amounted to as much as $18.

Timberland Management

Some railroads, especially those carriers that received huge land grants, became owners of valuable timberlands. The policy of the land-grant roads, beginning with the Illinois Central, was to sell their granted lands to actual settlers. Timberlands were at first handled in about the same manner, but later some carriers resolved to retain title. In the early years, much land was sold. Land-grant roads in Wisconsin and Minnesota, for example, sold considerable acreage to lumbermen, and one of the largest sales came in 1900 when the Northern Pacific sold 900,000 acres in Washington to the Weyerhaeuser interests (see WEYERHAEUSER FAMILY). Other sales came later.

Railroads without granted lands found it advisable to buy timberlands for later sale or lease to customers. Several roads in Arkansas, Louisiana, and east Texas did so, but perhaps the largest railroad purchaser was the Milwaukee, which acquired sizable acreages in the Pacific Northwest to generate traffic for its Pacific Extension, completed in 1909.

The decision to retain title to or purchase timberlands meant that several railroads were major landholders in the twentieth century. In 1913, the Southern Pacific had huge holdings in Oregon, and the Northern Pacific still owned about 9 percent of the privately owned standing timber in Washington and 32 percent in Montana. Half a century later, the latter road (now the Burlington Northern) owned 1.4 million acres of timber-growing lands.

Ownership of such acreages, combined with the desire to maximize over time the flow of traffic from them, took railroads into the field of modern forest management. As early as the 1920s, the Missouri Pacific turned over management of about 100,000 acres in Arkansas to a timberland firm. After World War II, the Milwaukee began a reforestation program on its Western timberlands using aerial reseeding, and the Southern Pacific employed a corps of foresters to institute proper management practices on its properties. By the 1960s, the Northern Pacific owned fourteen certified TREE FARMS, and the Southern had one in South Carolina.

Forestry Promotion

Recognizing the importance of timber to the railroad industry, both as freight and to meet its own needs, the carriers instituted at various times promotional programs in forestry. In the late nineteenth century, some railroads west of the Mississippi River took up forestry promotion as part of their efforts to lure settlers to the prairies. Several set out trees, hoping to demonstrate how the comfort and attractiveness of prairie homesteads could be enhanced. A new surge of activity came in the early years of the twentieth century. Railroad men became caught up in the conservation movement, and many were convinced that the industry would soon face a severe shortage of timber. Several companies established forestry plots along their lines, primarily in an effort to assure a future supply of ties and other timbers. A few railroads combined their interests in their own needs with a concern for control of erosion, general conservation, and beautification of railway property. Some carriers established nurseries to supply seedlings, and in 1906 the Pennsylvania employed a professional forester.

In the 1930s, railroad activities shifted more to educational work, the goal being the long-term generation of traffic. Southern railroads were especially active. The Seaboard Air Line established a distinct forestry department, and in the 1940s the Illinois Central maintained the largest such office in the country. Agents staged demonstrations in the countryside, operated educational trains, cooperated with public and private agencies interested in forestry, worked with rural youth, and led in the development of a mechanical tree planter suitable for use by small farmers.

These activities reached something of a peak in the 1950s. They declined in the next decade, and by the 1970s railroads had for all practical purposes abandoned their educational and promotional work, leaving such activities to public agencies and the timber companies.

FURTHER READING: Thomas R. Cox, *Mills and Markets: A History of the Pacific Coast Lumber Industry to 1900* (1974). Nollie Hickman, *Mississippi Harvest: Lumbering in the Longleaf Pine Belt, 1840–1915* (1962). Ralph W. Hidy et al., *Timber and Men: The Weyerhaeuser Story* (1963). Sherry H. Olson, *The Depletion Myth: A History of Railroad Use of Timber* (1971). Richard C. Overton, *Burlington Route: A History of the Burlington Lines* (1965). Julius H. Parmelee, *The Modern Railway* (1940). Roy V. Scott, "American Railroads and the Promotion of Forestry," *Journal of Forest History* 23 (Apr. 1979): 72-81. John F. Stover, *History of the Illinois Central Railroad* (1975). Thurman W. Van Metre, *Trains, Track, and Travel* (1950). John H. White, *The American Railroad Passenger Car* (1978).

ROY V. SCOTT

RECLAMATION AND WATERPOWER DEMANDS ON FORESTS

The national CONSERVATION MOVEMENT fostered from its beginnings the twin injunctions of "Save the Forests and Store the Floods." The slogan first appeared in the successful nationwide campaign leading to passage of the federal Reclamation Act in 1902. Two of the most important proponents of this legislation, which promised a new homestead frontier through federally financed irrigation projects, were Gifford PINCHOT, chief of the Bureau of Forestry, and Frederick H. NEWELL, chief hydrographer of the U.S. GEOLOGICAL SURVEY and future director of the Reclamation Service. Their partnership signaled a long-standing and continuing cooperation between two groups, one seeking reservation of the public domain for national forests, the other advocating arid-land reclamation projects. Reservation of public lands was to be a feature of natural resource administration central to the conservation movement which culminated in the administration of President Theodore ROOSEVELT between 1901 and 1909. It closed the era of exploitation which had lasted from the colonial period to the 1890s and had been based upon the principle of alienation or disposal of public lands to private parties under the prevailing individualistic ethos fostering settlement and rapid, often wasteful, development of the nation's resources.

The speeches, lectures, and press interviews of Pinchot's and Newell's Western tours during the years 1899 through 1901 reiterated the "streamflow" theme that forest reservations at the headwaters of streams were catchment basins or natural reservoirs that broke the force of storms, diminished soil erosion, and permitted the gradual runoff of silt-free surface water into man-made reservoirs. Forest reserves also enabled the national government to retain future reservoir sites. In this connection the national conservation movement's multiple-purpose concept was prefigured in constant references to the advantages found in conserving formerly wasted winter flood waters behind federal dams. The reservoirs held water for irrigation, the generation of hydroelectric power, municipal and domestic water supplies, and flood control. Here was an example of scientific planning and systematic resource use. When this approach was combined with the principle of sustained yield in the national forests and controlled grazing and mineral exploitation of public lands through leasing, the essentials of the Pinchot-inspired Roosevelt administration's conservation policy would be in place. This program, based on the field surveys of government scientists and engineers, was institutionalized by the Reclamation Act (1902) and the Forest Transfer Act (1905). It was administered with surprising freedom from congressional control by Newell and the Reclamation Service, Pinchot and the U. S. FOREST SERVICE, and Secretary of the Interior James Garfield until the advent of the Taft administration and the BALLINGER-PINCHOT CONTROVERSY over national conservation policy. Left intact in the reversal of conservation advances that followed were the federal programs of reclaiming arid lands and protecting the water and timber resources in the national forests.

The Reclamation Service's physical and institutional structures survived primarily because they met the developmental needs of the West as a section. The people in the Western states and territories measured the Reclamation Act by the result of its implementation, which was a marked increase in population and economic growth. Western irrigationists accepted the intimate relationship between expanding national forests and reclamation policies. They had supported the creation of forest reserves under the FOREST RESERVE ACT of 1891, and they worked for passage of the FOREST MANAGEMENT ACT of 1897 which included watershed protection as one of its objectives.

During the Reclamation Service's vital planning and preliminary construction years, Director Newell and Chief Engineer Arthur Powell Davis reiterated at every opportunity the basic dependence of each reclamation project on the expansion of national forests. Public relations releases from the infant service combined with the promotional endeavors of George H. Maxwell's National Irrigation Association were influential in the campaign for congressional adoption of the Forest Transfer Act of 1905. At last, Newell and Pinchot were each to share a wide latitude of power in administering closely related scientific water and forest management policies. Newell located reclamation projects at sites dictated by predominant economic interests. Pinchot won the support of large timber and grazing interests for his sustained-yield principle of national forest use. Both reclamation projects and streams in the national forests were subject to state water-rights law, and both administrators operated within these constrictions. Finally, Newell cooperated with Gifford Pinchot and Garfield to achieve reservation of waterpower sites on the public domain in 1909. This action helped precipitate the Ballinger-Pinchot imbroglio.

To the surprise of some, the West found that the federal reclamation program encouraged a boom in commercial and state-sponsored irrigation projects which lasted to about 1915. Developmental forces in Western states and territories were stimulated by the rise in property values in regions adjacent to reclamation projects, the increase in population, and the release of purchasing power during construction operations. The Reclamation Service soon became world famous for the innovative design and monumental scale of construction in its numerous dams, tunnels, and canals at twenty-five project sites in arid America.

Some of the projects took over the unfinished works of commercial enterprises that were stalled for lack of funds. The sale of hydroelectric power and surplus water to neighboring municipalities came to be a feature of project operations which were ratified by congressional statute of 1906.

The efficiency of the engineers responsible for the triumphs of public waterworks construction, however, was not followed by successful management of the projects as business propositions. Nevertheless, even the discouraging reports of poorly sited projects, interminable construction delays, distress of settlers who were ill-equipped as irrigation farmers on sites that were eventually abandoned for lack of fertile soil and proper drainage did not destroy Western faith in irrigation as the stimulus for economic growth. The fact that countless numbers of settlers could not pay off construction costs during the mandatory ten-year period or meet their operation and maintenance charges was taken in stride, for Western political leaders knew the federal government eventually would be forced to grant extended payout periods and even a moratorium on payments. Some asked why the marginal producer in reclamation projects should have to carry the full burden of capital costs when the entire Western economy benefited from the projects. Solvency would come after Elwood MEAD, commissioner of reclamation from 1924 to 1936, improved agricultural practices and applied hydroelectric power revenues to the reduction of debt. In the meantime, during the 1920s, almost 10 million acre feet of stored water attributable in large measure to national forest collection basins irrigated over a million and a quarter acres on 32,385 farms in Reclamation Service projects.

Other watercourses in the national forests directed their spring floods toward privately built reservoirs destined to drive turbines and electric power generators for utility companies' customers many miles distant. When Gifford Pinchot adopted a policy of granting permits for private companies who wished to generate electricity at waterpower sites in the national forests in 1907, he set a precedent that would be followed by the Theodore Roosevelt administration elsewhere. Most of the undeveloped waterpower of the nation was under the control of the federal government and half was located on the forest reserves and public domain. Permits for harnessing falling water on these lands had been granted under the Right-of-Way Act of 1901 without limit as to time and without compensation to the government before 1905 when the forest reserves were brought under the forester's jurisdiction. The companies received free water rights under state law and assumed that Forest Service management would continue the practice of granting free perpetual site leases. However, Pinchot knew that the 1901 law allowed him to revoke these licenses at will. Since he had already adopted the practice of issuing annually renewable fee permits to grazing and timber companies in the forest reserves, he determined also to assess a waterpower rental against utility companies. The fee was based upon the reservoir function of forest cover along the headwaters of the streams in combination with the special topographic feature that provided a valuable drop of water. Speculation was eliminated by requiring development of the site and rates were fixed according to the size of area taken up with generating plant and right-of-way. Instead of annual permits, the secretary of agriculture suggested a fifty-year nonrevocable lease for waterpower facilities. Although the industry protested these terms and challenged the system in the courts, the Forest Service design for waterpower regulation won.

The national forests contributed substantially to hydroelectric power generation in the West. O. C. Merrill, chief engineer of the Forest Service, reported in 1916 that national forests held a third of the potential waterpower resource of the West and actually provided 42 percent of the developed waterpower in the country. The national forest regulatory pattern offered a model for federal government control of waterpower on the public domain generally and along navigable streams elsewhere in the nation, but the Taft administration, the ARMY CORPS OF ENGINEERS, and Congress delayed full implementation of these measures until passage of the Water Power Act of 1920.

Even though water development was compatible with multiple-use management of the national forests, it was branded as an anticonservationist intrusion when proposed within national parks and monuments. Most of the national park enabling acts passed in the two decades following the Right-of-Way Act of 1901 included provisions allowing for water development; this was true of the acts establishing Glacier, Grand Canyon, Rocky Mountain, Lassen Volcanic, Hawaii, and Mount McKinley national parks. Nor were older parks secure. The legislation permitting private water and power development within YOSEMITE NATIONAL PARK in 1913 marked the culmination of the first virulent clash between the aesthetic and the utilitarian branches of the conservation movement. YELLOWSTONE NATIONAL PARK was also subject to repeated attempts by private and state reclamationists to develop water supplies within its borders. The Water Power Act of 1920 authorized the new Federal Power Commission to permit projects inside parks and monuments as well as elsewhere on federal lands and reservations. However, pressed by NATIONAL PARK SERVICE Director Stephen MATHER and Secretary of the Interior Franklin K. Lane, President Woodrow Wilson threatened to veto the bill unless its backers promised to have it amended to curtail the commission's jurisdiction over existing parks and monuments. They carried this promise out in 1921. Nevertheless, the BUREAU OF RECLAMATION (as the Reclamation Service was known after 1923) and the Army Corps of Engineers plagued the National Park Service with plans for water projects incompatible with the latter agency's objectives. Following World War II, dam-building proposals threatened to undo decades of progress by park and wilderness enthusiasts. From the late 1940s through the 1960s, the successful political struggles against planned dams in such places as Dinosaur National Monument and Grand Canyon, Glacier, and other national parks, although not always directly involving forested lands, were milestones in the broadening of the relatively narrow wilderness movement into the environmental crusade of the 1970s.

FURTHER READING: Paul W. Gates, *History of Public Land Law Development* (1968). Samuel P. Hays, *Conservation and the Gospel of Efficiency: The Progressive Conservation Movement, 1890–1920* (1959). Jerome G. Kerwin, *Federal Water Power Legislation* (1926). Lawrence B. Lee, *Reclaiming the American West: An Historiography and Guide* (1980). Grant McConnell, "The Multiple-Use Concept in Forest Service Policy," *Sierra Club Bulletin* 44 (Oct. 1959): 14-28. E. Louise Peffer, *The Closing of the Public Domain; Disposal and Reservation Policies, 1900-1950* (1951). Gifford Pinchot, "The Long Struggle for Effective Federal Water Power Legislation," *George Washington Law Review* 9 (1945): 9-20.

LAWRENCE B. LEE

RECREATION

For this essay, forest is defined as a community of trees and its related environment, where recreation, a chosen nonwork experience, takes place. A forest in the United States can cover millions of acres.

In Western civilization, the recorded use of forests for recreational purposes goes back to the early use by royalty. A specific case is the New Forest in England, established by William the Conqueror in 1087, primarily as a place for the royal hunt and protection of the king's deer. In general, a forester, or forest surveyor, looked after the preserve for the king, and commoners were given rights to graze animals on the land and to obtain wood and forest litter.

When the concept of forest as an entity was transferred to the North American colonies, it was expressed in a broader public use context. An early manifestation was the creation in 1710 of a 110-acre community forest in Newington, New Hampshire. Although it primarily provided wood and other useful products, this forest was open for walks and other leisurely pursuits. Previously, in 1641, the Great Ponds Act passed by the Massachusetts Bay Colony reserved bodies of water as a public resource for fishing and hunting, setting a precedent for recreational use of public places.

The forest has long been thought to have qualities for renewing the human spirit. In his essay on nature, Ralph Waldo Emerson spoke of people entering the forest and throwing off the burdens of society, suggesting a concern for forest protection and recreational use.

Recognizing the limits of simplification, one could say that policy on forest recreational use and management in the United States has evolved along three general paths. The first of these is the path of the public forest as a park, in which the forest is an amenity backdrop for various kinds of activities and experiences, exemplified by our present national and state parks. The second path evolved from the practice of public forestry as espoused by Gifford PINCHOT, where all the assets of the forest are for use. Recreation is one of many forest uses. The national forests, and most of the state forests, fall into this category. The third avenue is that of the private commercial forests. In earlier years, most private owners were concerned simply with the harvest. Recreation was not a consideration, except for some hunting or fishing on cutover lands.

Development of these three paths reveals the challenges, complexities, and problems of forest recreation in the United States. As professional land managers, foresters have been involved with all three approaches.

Early events along the park path included establishment of the unique Yosemite Valley as a California state park in 1864. Later, it was revested back to the federal government (1906) and became part of a national park. In 1872, Yellowstone was created as a national park and public pleasuring ground. The emphasis in Yellowstone was on a spectacular tourist attraction, in which the resources were preserved for viewing and amenity. In the 1870s, pressure for protection came primarily from people in the eastern United States, who had seen the development and exploitation of forests in their region. Western settlers, on the other hand, were largely interested in getting tangible supplies and resources from the forest rather than the less tangible benefits from preserving parks.

Early developments on the second path included establishment in 1881 of the Division of Forestry in the DEPARTMENT OF AGRICULTURE. There was interest in scientific management of forests, perhaps best expressed by Pinchot, who became chief of the Division of Forestry in 1898. The agency was reorganized in 1905 as the U. S. FOREST SERVICE, responsible for millions of acres of public forest. Pinchot stressed management of forest resources to meet public needs on a renewable basis, which would overcome the exploitation of the past. Recreation was considered to be a secondary aspect; a 1907 Forest Service book on the use of the national forests stated that, quite incidentally, forests served a good purpose as playgrounds for the American people, particularly for local townspeople. Local people were viewed as being most important to national forest management, and still are. But forests primarily were for sustained timber production and not preserved from use, as the 1891 FOREST RESERVE ACT had suggested.

On the third or private forest path, recreation was of lesser importance initially. Recreational activities were believed to be adequately taken care of on public lands. Occasionally, however, large private forest tracts were given or sold for park purposes, as in the redwood region of California. Yet, it was not until the 1950s that recreation became a major concern of large private forest owners.

Conflicts occurred with overlapping interests. One of the first of these confrontations was the debate over construction of the Hetch Hetchy Dam on the forested Tuolumne River in YOSEMITE NATIONAL PARK. This issue pitted John MUIR, the founder of the SIERRA CLUB, a great naturalist and park protector, against forester Gifford Pinchot. Pinchot sided with San Francisco to build the dam for its water supply, and the dam was built. The extent of Pinchot's influence on the specific outcome is not clear, but the conflict identified and expanded the schism between use and preservation that still exists.

The National Park Act of 1916, which many historians believe resulted from the Muir–Pinchot dispute, together with the designation of Stephen T. MATHER as first Director of the NATIONAL PARK SERVICE (NPS), saw an orientation toward a national view of parks and their development. Early policy statements made it clear that parks, mostly forested natural areas, were to be preserved in perpetuity but also to be developed for public sightseeing, education, and related use. Mather stressed the importance of park roads, the automobile, and suitable visitor facilities.

In 1918, Frank A. Waugh, a Forest Service landscape architect, reported on recreational use of the national forests (some 3 million recreation visitors each year). Visitor activity locations were discussed, including summer homes, municipal playgrounds, and camping and picnic areas. Picnickers and campers were seen as potential fire fighters for the nearby forests. Although Waugh did not address winter sports, skiing on the national forests started in the early 1900s in the Northeast. By 1914, the Sierra Club was conducting ski outings on California's Tahoe National Forest.

Waugh suggested that on some national forests there were areas that had potential for national parks (at that time, the Grand Canyon was under the Forest Service jurisdiction as a national monument). On the other hand, some national forests had potential for major recreational use. He stressed harmony between the federal park and forest agencies, with respect to recreation, but rivalry prevailed.

In 1921, at the first NATIONAL CONFERENCE ON STATE PARKS, Arthur Carhart, Forest Service landscape architect discussing national forest recreational uses, was immediately challenged by NPS director Mather. When Mather stated that recreation was the purview of the national parks and not the Forest Service, he voiced a difference in viewpoint that has long been a source of conflict between the two agencies as they have striven to demonstrate their leadership role in recreation. When the NATIONAL CONFERENCE ON OUTDOOR RECREATION, convened by President Coolidge in 1924, reported on the two agencies' recreation programs, it criticized both for overdevelopment. In fact, it accused the Park Service of swapping the concept of natural wonders for the more popular "people's playground."

Although there have been exceptions, most of the programs for recreation on the public forests have emanated either from the federal government or from citizen groups, like the Sierra Club, advocating specific programs. Because of federal aid and funds, states often have followed the federal lead on park and forest matters.

In the private forest sector, there have been opportunities for cooperation in forest park protection. For example, the SAVE-THE-REDWOODS LEAGUE and private timber owners in California agreed on the protection of certain areas for parks, subject to purchase by the league and the state.

During the 1920s and 1930s, many state park and forest organizations made forest areas available for recreational use, often with federal aid and advice. Conflict continued between the Forest Service and the Park Service over the creation of new parks involving national forestland, such as the OLYMPIC NATIONAL PARK in Washington. Within the Forest Service there was a belief that lands should be set aside for wilder-

ness where naturalness and solitude were emphasized. Two of the principal proponents were Aldo LEOPOLD and Robert MARSHALL. As early as 1921, Leopold had written of the need for forest areas where the emphasis was on protection of the primitive rather than the production of timber.

In 1929, the secretary of agriculture issued regulation L-20, which set aside primitive areas on national forests. The regulation provided for minimal development and opportunity for trail access, horse camping, hunting, and fishing. The possibility of timber production, grazing, or mining were not excluded. Later, under Marshall's tutelage, restrictive wilderness regulations were set up to reclassify primitive areas to reduce development and resource production.

During the Great Depression, there was much federal public works activity on federal lands and state forests and parks. Programs of the CIVILIAN CONSERVATION CORPS were often directed at the provision of recreational facilities on forestlands, including trails, picnic areas, and public and group camps. The depressed lumber industry had limited pressure for recreation on its land. An exception was the Weyerhaeuser Timber Company, which in the 1930s allowed people to camp on some of its lands in Washington's Spirit Lake area.

Also during the 1930s, skiing became popular at developed forest and park locations. A number of the big ski hills on the national forests and the national parks, such as Mount Hood in Oregon and Badger Pass in Yosemite Park in California, were among the more important.

Some of the recreational uses in national parks seem to be inconsistent with the forest-natural areas preservation policy. From the beginning, fishing was allowed in the national parks but not hunting, which was felt to be contrary to protection of the game for public view. Also, predators were controlled up to the 1950s, a practice that conflicted with the concept of a "natural" system.

Summer homes on the national forests were very important in the early 1900s. The state forests allowed home leases, too. In later years, home leases became an embarrassment, because Forest Service general policy favored the use of lands for the benefit of large public groups rather than exclusive individual benefits.

Trail location in the forested parks is different from that in the national forests. Trail development in the parks was for access but also for scenic views. In the national forests, the trails generally were built mainly for fire protection in particular and rapid access in general.

After World War II, many things came together to

Campers on Montana's Lolo National Forest, 1920. Forest Service Photo.

bring the three forest use paths into rather sharp focus and conflict. The federal conservation programs of the Depression were terminated, generally constraining recreational maintenance and development on forestlands. At the same time, there was increased demand for timber, particularly on public lands, caused by an expanding population and economy, with coincidental increases in demand for housing and improved forest access. The public, now working only forty hours per week, sought recreation on all kinds of forestland for developed camping, picnicking, water access areas, and also for use of wilderness and remote trail areas. Forest harvest increased on private lands and even more so on public lands, particularly on national forests, where private timber companies could supplement their operations through purchase of public timber.

Some of the areas that had been protected or preserved for wilderness under the Forest Service wilderness and primitive area regulations included valuable timber stands. Confrontation soon developed between the wilderness preservation groups and those who wanted development and production. This conflict added to the pressure for federal wilderness legislation to cover not only national forests but also national parks, refuges of the FISH AND WILDLIFE SERVICE, and, later, BUREAU OF LAND MANAGEMENT lands.

In response to a national concern about recreation, Congress in 1958 created the OUTDOOR RECREATION RESOURCES REVIEW COMMISSION (ORRRC) to review the overall outdoor recreation picture in the United States, to gauge resources and needs of the American people, and to project ahead to 1976 and 2000, respectively, with recommendations on policies and programs. In 1961, ORRRC made a number of recommendations affecting forest recreation. Suggesting that some of the best opportunities for recreation in the United States were on forests and related lands, it recommended passage of wilderness legislation, which passed in 1964. In order to resolve the conflicts between different kinds of uses and overlapping agency policies, as well as to coordinate federal recreation programs, ORRRC recommended the creation of the BUREAU OF OUTDOOR RECREATION (BOR) in the Department of the Interior. Secretary of the Interior Stewart L. UDALL established BOR in 1961 and named former Forest Service Assistant Chief Edward C. Crafts as the agency's first director.

The Wilderness Act of 1964 focused attention on a critical problem in recreational land use policy for forests; it also encouraged increased public involvement in decisions on the use of public lands. This act, and subsequent federal and state legislation concerning forests and recreation, brought the problem of local interests versus state and federal agencies and the national interest to the surface. In general, local people feel that they lose recreation and commercial opportunities when big reserves are created, particularly those by the federal government. Each activity and interest has come to be represented by organizations, from the snowmobile clubs to the Sierra Club and the AMERICAN FOREST INSTITUTE.

In 1975, Congress passed the Eastern Wilderness Act covering national forest wilderness lands east of the 100th Meridian, where most of the population is and which possesses the fewest and smallest wilderness reserves. Earlier, in 1960, the MULTIPLE USE-SUSTAINED YIELD ACT had dealt with national forests; for the first time, recreation officially took its place with timber, water, range, and wildlife as a major forest use. Subsequently, some states passed similar legislation.

The NATIONAL FOREST MANAGEMENT ACT of 1976 broadened recreational, wilderness, and other uses. Also in 1976, the FEDERAL LAND POLICY AND MANAGEMENT ACT made important provisions for forest recreation on lands administered by the Bureau of Land Management.

Over the years, recreational use of national forestlands has greatly increased, from about 3 million people visiting the national forests in 1918 to over 204,700,000 visitor days in 1977. In 1974, forested, nonurban, natural areas of the national park system received some 55 million users.

In recent years, the emphasis on forest recreation has shifted from activities to opportunities, including their social and environmental characteristics. For example, fishing in a crowded forest stream near the city would be much different from fishing as a solitary person in the million-acre Bob Marshall Wilderness in Montana. Also, on many forests at the national as well as the state level, recreation has centered more on dispersed use on trails, rivers, and nondeveloped forest areas. River running in rafts or canoe, for example, is an activity that has become popular, with the added impetus of the Wild and Scenic Rivers Act of 1968. Winter activities have become increasingly important. The big alpine ski areas on private and public forestlands have expanded greatly since World War II. Since 1970, cross-country skiing, which predates alpine skiing, along with snowmobiling, has become the fastest growing winter forest recreation activity.

Private forestlands have been made available for snowmobiling and cross-country skiing trails. In general, the private forest path has evolved to greater public recreational use. It is good for the private sector's public relations if dispersed recreation can be integrated with forest harvest in many areas. Some southern timber companies are even providing small wilderness tracts.

The development of U. S. forest recreation has evolved along three main paths. Use as well as public interest in recreational areas and activities have increased. Public and private jurisdictions, somewhat separated in the past, now are pitted together on the same lands without new territory. Some old conflicts have been resolved, but more can be expected as concerned citizen groups become involved for their locality or activities. Energy limitations have entered the discussion, also, as people avoid remote areas in favor of opportunities closer to home. Certainly, land management in the future will become more complex rather than less as the attempt is made to serve more people and more diverse uses than early proponents foresaw.

FURTHER READING: C. F. Brockman and L. C. Merriam, Jr., *Recreational Use of Wildlands* (1979). Arthur H. Carhart, "Historical Development of Outdoor Recreation," in *Outdoor Recreation Literature: A Survey*, ORRRC Study Report 27 (1962), pp. 99–129. Russell Lord, ed., *Forest Outings by Thirty Foresters* (1940). Frank A. Waugh, *Recreation Use on the National Forests* (1918).

L. C. MERRIAM, JR.

RECREATION AND HERITAGE CONSERVATION AND RECREATION SERVICE

See Bureau of Outdoor Recreation

REDWOOD NATIONAL PARK

Between 1852 and World War II, eight serious proposals for a redwood national park were advanced. They failed because the *Sequoia sempervirens* of northern California was commercially valuable and quickly passed into private ownership in the nineteenth century. Large federal park land purchases were unprecedented. Between 1901 and World War II, however, the Sempervirens Club and the SAVE-THE-REDWOODS LEAGUE raised state and private funds for the establishment of redwood state parks.

Influenced by accelerated redwood logging, the Save-the-Redwoods League, the SIERRA CLUB, and the National Geographic Society began agitating for a national Park in 1960. In 1964, the NATIONAL PARK SERVICE reported that only 300,000 acres of the original 2 million acres of redwoods remained unlogged, and only 50,000 of these were in public parks. Encouraged by the passage of the Land and Water Conservation Fund Act, the service recommended that a national park be established in Humboldt County on Redwood Creek,

site of the tallest measured tree in the world (367.8 feet in 1963).

The Sierra Club campaigned vigorously for a 90,000-acre Redwood Creek park with newspaper advertisements and *The Last Redwoods* (1964) by Francois Leydet. The league recommended a park of 45,000 acres on Mill Creek in Del Norte County. In 1964, Senator Lee Metcalf sponsored the club's ambitious legislation. The league's plan was embodied in the bill introduced by Senator Thomas Kuchel during President Johnson's administration. All bills were opposed by the industry, loggers, and Humboldt and Del Norte County residents who feared the loss of tax revenues and jobs.

In October 1967, Senators Kuchel and Henry Jackson advanced a compromise to placate the club and the league and to divide the park's economic impact between two counties and four lumber companies. Passed by the Senate, their bill provided for a 64,000-acre park, with a northern unit on Mill Creek and a southern unit on Redwood Creek. Under the influence of Wayne Aspinall of the House Interior and Insular Affairs Committee, the House also passed a two-unit park bill, but one for only 26,888 acres. A compromise was worked out in conference and signed by President Johnson on October 2, 1968. The act provided for a two-unit park of 58,000 acres, of which 27,500 acres represented the projected inclusion of state park lands. The southern unit comprised Prairie Creek Redwoods State Park, a large tract along lower Redwood Creek, and a corridor, one-half mile wide and six miles long, up Redwood Creek to the so-called Tall Trees Grove. The northern unit included Jedediah Smith and Del Norte Coast Redwoods state parks, some private land on Mill Creek, and several coastal strips. The federal government took title to the private lands effective with the act's passage. The act appropriated $92 million for land purchases, but compensation set by the U. S. Court of Claims eventually reached a quarter of a billion dollars.

Citizen groups soon charged that logging on lumber company lands in the Redwood Creek watershed was causing erosion that threatened the park. The lumber companies countered that erosion was minimal and unrelated to current operations. Nonetheless, in response to a suit filed by the Sierra Club in 1973, U. S. District Court Judge William Sweigert found the DEPARTMENT OF THE INTERIOR negligent in protecting the park against logging damage. In 1976, however, he ruled that Interior had done all that it could and that park protection demanded financial commitment from Congress.

Before 1977, the House Committee on Interior and Insular Affairs, as well as the Nixon and Ford administrations, blocked federal regulation of private forestry and additional land acquisitions in Redwood Creek. That year, Jimmy Carter assumed the presidency and Phillip Burton of San Francisco became chairman of the House Subcommittee on National Parks and Insular Affairs. With administration support and Burton's sponsorship, a Redwood National Park expansion bill passed Congress in March 1978.

The act provided $359 million for acquisition of 48,000 acres in the Redwood Creek watershed, with exact property values to be established by fair market appraisal in the U. S. District Court in San Francisco.

Since 39,010 of these acres were cut over, the act appropriated $33 million for reforestation and rehabilitation and authorized Interior to purchase, if necessary, a 30,000-acre buffer zone. Due to intense union opposition, the act provided $40 million in unprecedented compensation for lumber workers who would lose their jobs due to park expansion.

As of 1980, there were 75,500 acres in the Redwood National Park, but the 30,000 acres in state parks had not yet been transferred to federal jurisdiction. Of the federal lands, only 19,900 acres protected old-growth

President Richard M. Nixon dedicates Lady Bird Johnson Grove in newly created Redwood National Park on August 27, 1969. Flanking the president are Secretary of the Interior Walter J. Hickel, the Reverend Billy Graham, Mrs. Nixon, Mrs. Johnson, California Governor Ronald Reagan, former President Lyndon B. Johnson, and Congressman Donald H. Clausen of California. Nixon Library Photo.

redwoods. Pending reforestation, much of the park remained vulnerable to erosion. When rehabilitation is complete, the park will extend from ocean bluffs up through the dense forests lining Redwood and Mill creeks into the meadows of the coastal range.

SUSAN R. SCHREPFER

REGULATION OF FOREST PRACTICES

Recommendations and proposals for the regulation of private forestry in the United States have been presented frequently during the twentieth century. They have been stimulated mainly by the belief that regulation is necessary to prevent a major depletion of the forest resources of the country. At the famous White House conference on conservation in 1908, President Theodore ROOSEVELT declared: "We are over the verge of a timber famine in this country, and it is unpardonable for the Nation or the States to permit any further cutting of our timber save in accordance with a system which will provide that the next generation shall see the timber increased instead of diminished." The necessary corrective system, in the view of conservation leader Gifford PINCHOT, needed to be based upon legislation that would control private forest management. Thus, as early as 1909, Pinchot called for state laws that would restrict private forest owners in the use of their property if such use tended to impair or destroy the productivity of the forests.

In 1919, Pinchot was appointed chairman of a committee of the SOCIETY OF AMERICAN FORESTERS (SAF) which was asked "to recommend action for the prevention of forest devastation of privately owned timberlands in the United States." Contending that within less than fifty years the nation's timber shortage would become a "blighting timber famine," the committee recommended that the federal government be authorized to fix standards and promulgate rules to prevent forest devastation and to promote the productivity of forest crops on privately owned commercial timberlands. The report thus advocated federal control of cutting practices. It was not approved by SAF, however, because many of its members believed that if regulation of cutting was necessary it should be exercised by state governments rather than by the federal government. This position was adopted by William B. GREELEY, who became chief of the U. S. FOREST SERVICE in 1920.

The Pinchot committee report became the basis of a bill introduced in the senate by Arthur Capper of Kansas in May 1920, while Greeley's views were presented in a bill introduced by Congressman Bertrand H. Snell of New York in December 1920. The Snell bill proposed federal assistance to the states in the exercise of their police power over private lands. Both bills were debated widely and heatedly. Opponents of the Snell bill believed that even if the federal government gave financial assistance to the states to keep private forestlands productive, the state laws would be weak in language or execution because powerful lumber interests would control the legislatures. Those who opposed the Capper bill argued that the federal government's role in keeping forestlands productive should be through cooperative relations with the states and not through the use of federal police powers to regulate private forest management, which many commercial owners maintained was unconstitutional. Both measures included provisions relating to cooperation of the federal government with the states for protection against forest fires. A compromise on this basis was reached with the passage of the CLARKE-MCNARY ACT of 1924, which broadened the fire-protection cooperation of the WEEKS ACT of 1911 and omitted authorization for public regulation of private forestry.

A modified form of public regulation was proposed and briefly implemented under the National Industrial Recovery Act of 1933 (NIRA). The idea for this development was suggested to President Franklin D. ROOSEVELT by Ward Shepard, a former Forest Service official, who had studied the administration of forest regulatory laws in Austria, Czechoslovakia, and Germany. Shepard urged Roosevelt to use the authority for industrial production control under NIRA as a means for preventing forest destruction on private lands and keeping them productive through sustained-yield management. Roosevelt approved this idea and ordered its implementation in a Code of Fair Competition for the Lumber and Timber Products Industries prepared under NIRA. Under the code, forest-practice rules, formulated by forest industry leaders and Forest Service representatives, established minimum standards of forest management. The rules covered fire, insect, and disease protection; reproduction of forests; seed supply; slash disposal; economic selective logging; and sustained yield. Rules developed for each forest region were to be binding on the logging operators in that region. In short, operators complying with the Code of Fair Competition agreed to a form of industry self-regulation. The forest-practice rules adopted under the Code were in force less than a year when on May 27, 1935, the Supreme Court ruled that NIRA was an unconstitutional delegation of legislative authority. Thus a short-lived effort in the regulation of private forestry ended, although some forest conservation practices stimulated by NIRA were kept alive voluntarily by industrial associations and individual operators.

Regulation again became a prominent issue with its

advocacy by the Forest Service during the late 1930s and the 1940s. Chief Ferdinand A. SILCOX in 1935 declared: "Public control over the use of private forest lands, which will insure sustained yield, is essential to stabilize forest industries and forest communities." Even before the demise of the Lumber Code under NIRA, Silcox contended that the application of the required practices on private forestlands must be supervised by public agencies and not left to the forest industry. He helped influence President Roosevelt in 1938 to recommend an inquiry into public regulatory controls that would adequately protect private and public interests on all forestlands. Congress responded to the recommendation with the creation of the Joint Committee on Forestry, which held hearings and focused public attention on action to prevent destructive timber cutting on private lands. In its report of 1941, the joint committee recommended various cooperative aids to private forest owners and a federal–state system of regulation of forest practices. These recommendations were included in the Omnibus Forestry Bill introduced in November 1941 by Senator John H. Bankhead of Alabama. The Forest Service considered the bill a step in the right direction, but it failed to receive any attention, probably due to the nation's entry into World War II the next month.

During the war, however, regulation continued to be advocated by the leadership of the Forest Service. Forest Service Acting Chief Earle H. CLAPP supported an effort in 1942 to obtain legislation empowering the secretary of agriculture to administer federal regulatory control of timber cutting on private lands. After this effort was disapproved by the Budget Bureau and President Roosevelt, Clapp attempted to induce the president to require compliance with timber-cutting regulations that the Forest Service would develop under the president's emergency war powers. The War Production Board opposed this and the idea was abandoned. However, the fact that regulation remained a goal of the Forest Service was evident when Lyle F. WATTS became chief in January 1943. Early in his administration, Watts declared that "nation-wide regulation of cutting practices on private forest lands under strong federal leadership is absolutely essential, if needless destruction of productive growing stock is to be stopped."

Meanwhile, some support for the idea of public regulation began to be provided by a number of lumbermen, professional foresters, and public officials outside the Forest Service, although most forest industry leaders continued to oppose the idea. In a broad study of private forest management in the United States published in 1944, Clarence F. Korstian, dean of the Duke University School of Forestry, concluded: "Public control of forest cutting practices on private lands in the United States now appears inevitable.... The American public and industry itself will not long tolerate the mistreatment of forest lands even by any minority of owners and operators." Korstian's study also presented two model bills for state regulation that had been prepared by foresters and legal officers associated with the Eastern States Council of State Governments. Both bills provided for the formulation of minimum cutting-practice rules by a state board of forestry and they probably influenced legislation regulating cutting practices adopted in several states during the 1940s.

The regulation issue during Lyle Watts's term as chief focused on proposals for federal guidelines for state forestry administration. This approach was taken in a bill introduced by Senator Clinton P. Anderson of New Mexico in 1949. Opposition came from SAF and from the forest industries which were well organized under the leadership of the American Forest Products Industries, Inc., for the defense of private enterprise management against proposals regarded as socialistic. By the time the Eisenhower administration came into office in 1953, the Forest Service had turned its attention away from the regulation issue, and since then no serious efforts have been made to enact federal legislation for regulation of private forest management.

The earlier attempts, though unsuccessful in their primary purpose, have had significant results. Forest industry operators, criticized for destructive practices and threatened by possible federal regulation, have striven to improve their public image and to make regulation seem unnecessary. Many have adopted scientific forest-management methods, employed professional foresters, established TREE FARMS, and supported public information campaigns designed to show that industry is concerned with growing and protecting timber for permanent yield. They have stressed recent advances in the management of industrial forests that have occurred without federal regulation. Moreover, the pressure for federal regulation influenced some states to become more responsive to the need for better protection and management of forest resources. Hence, by 1950 most states had created forestry departments to encourage cooperation between the federal and state governments and private owners in forest protection and reforestation. A few years earlier, the Forestry Committee of the Council of State Governments had recommended enactment of state regulatory legislation to counteract the demand for federal legislation. Such state enactments have been less stringent than proposed federal laws, but they were indicative of a recognition of need for improvement in private forest management. That the issue of federal regulation is not entirely dead, however, was evidenced during the 1970s when one effort was made to pass federal legislation to authorize a broad range of regulatory practices, including compulsory licensing of foresters and preparation of mandatory harvesting plans for private forest owners.

FURTHER READING: Henry Clepper, *Professional Forestry in the United States* (1971). William B. Greeley, *Forests and Man* (1951). Clarence F. Korstian, *Forestry on Private Lands in the United States* (1944). *Report of the Chief of the Forest Service* (1935–1950). Harold K. Steen, *The U. S. Forest Service: A History* (1976).

HAROLD T. PINKETT

REID, KENNETH ALEXANDER (1895–1956)

Born in Connellsville, Pennsylvania, on April 14, 1895, Ken Reid attended Phillips Andover and earned a Ph.B. degree from Yale University in 1917. He served as a flight instructor, Army Air Service, in World War I. For the next twenty years, he worked as a sales executive.

Reid joined the IZAAK WALTON LEAGUE OF AMERICA (IWLA) in the late 1920s and was its executive director from January 1938 until March 1949. He made the IWLA a vehicle for implementing his philosophy on the management of national forests and other federal lands. The essence of this philosophy is found in his terse 1945 declaration: "No use shall be made of [public lands] that will establish any right superior to that of the public or the Government." In support of this creed, Reid fought the timber industry, mineral interests, livestock permittees, and even fishing, hunting, and outdoor recreation seekers when he thought them in the wrong. Usually quiet and reserved, Reid was no fireball at the lectern; he persuaded through knowledge of his subject instead of hortatory exercises. He had been an avid angler since childhood and he was dismayed by water pollution from municipalities and industry, including acid from coal mines near his Connellsville home. He had a leading role in initiating and conducting the IWLA's fourteen-year crusade that culminated in the passage of the Water Pollution Control Act in October 1948. The act was weak, but it would become the forerunner of the potent federal laws of 1972 and later years. Exhausted from that long struggle and from the seemingly endless campaigning on a wide range of issues, World War II exigencies, and administrative and other problems, Reid suffered a severe stroke and resigned shortly after passage of the 1948 act.

After a period of recuperation, Reid established a sound forestry program for the C. V. Whitney holdings in the Adirondacks before retiring in 1955 to Reidmore, his Connellsville family home. He died on May 21, 1956.

Reid lifted the IWLA from its Great Depression nadir to relative strength by the end of World War II, and he led it to a high place in conservation councils. U. S. FOREST SERVICE Chief Lyle F. WATTS once said of the Reid era: "When the League spoke, we listened."

Reid helped found the NATURAL RESOURCES COUNCIL OF AMERICA and wrote its charter. He encouraged the founding and basic financing of the National Committee on Policies in Conservation Education which, its task complete, reorganized in 1953 into the Conservation Education Association. He was a leader against the "Great Land Grab" of the 1940s, an effort by the two national livestock organizations to obtain legislation that would permit federal grazing lands to pass into private ownership. In the same era, Reid also fought attempts by Wyoming-led groups, some connected with the livestock alliance, to have Jackson Hole National Monument abolished. To recognize his Jackson Hole work, the NATIONAL PARK SERVICE later named Mount Reid, in GRAND TETON NATIONAL PARK, in his honor. An indication of Reid's stature among his contemporaries is suggested by his role during the September 1948 Inter-American Conference on Natural Resources, held in Denver under the auspices of the Department of State. Reid alone among the six chosen as section chairmen was not an official representative of any of the participating governments.

Using a small Izaak Walton League Endowment, created at his suggestion in 1945, Reid began land acquisition efforts that helped round out and stabilize the Boundary Waters Canoe Area of Superior National Forest; he faithfully supported wilderness and a fair deal for the creatures of the wild. At various times, he was active in many conservation and related organizations, including the AMERICAN FORESTRY ASSOCIATION and the SOCIETY OF AMERICAN FORESTERS.

WILLIAM VOIGT, JR.

RESEARCH

See Forestry Research *and* Forest Products Research

RESOURCES FOR THE FUTURE

Resources for the Future (RFF) is a private nonprofit organization for research and education in the development, conservation, and use of natural resources and improvement of the quality of the environment. It was established in 1952 with the cooperation of the

Ford Foundation, and most of its work for the ensuing twenty-five years was supported by grants from that foundation. In recent years, substantial grants and contributions have been received from other foundations and corporations. RFF publishes a thrice-yearly journal called *Resources*.

Most of RFF's studies are in the social sciences and are broadly concerned with the relationships of people to the natural environment. Specific fields of interest embrace the basic resources of land, water, minerals, and air, and the goods and services derived from them. RFF pays special attention to environmental quality, including the relationship of population and economic growth to the environment and resource use in general. Because it is an important factor in every other area, energy is a particularly active concern.

In 1977, RFF established a special program of research in forest economics and forest policy. Close working relationships have been established with the SOCIETY OF AMERICAN FORESTERS, the AMERICAN FORESTRY ASSOCIATION, the U.S. FOREST SERVICE, several of the larger forest industry firms, and several of the conservation organizations. A number of books and special reports have been published and several conferences have been held. The senior staff in forest economics and policy includes Roger A. Sedjo, John V. Krutilla, and Marion Clawson. Financial support for the forest economics and forest policy program has come from the Ford Foundation, the Forest Service, and the Weyerhaeuser Company Foundation.

FURTHER READING: Resources for the Future, *The First 25 Years, 1952–1977* (1977).

RHODE ISLAND FORESTS

Much of Rhode Island was forested when Roger Williams and other dissenters began settlements in the colony during the 1630s. But it was the large treeless tracts, especially the meadows on the islands in Narragansett Bay, that attracted most of the emigrants from Massachusetts. By driving the wolves from the islands and clearing much of the timber, the colonists created havens for cattle, sheep, and horses that became the basis of an extensive coastal and foreign trade. Before the end of the seventeenth century, all the islands were heavily dependent on the mainland for firewood, fencing, and building timbers.

Timber resources along the mainland shores on the western side of Narragansett Bay were quite sparse in some areas, for the Indians had burned large tracts in the oak and chestnut forests. Thus, in the seventeenth century the islanders conducted many timber-poaching expeditions on the eastern shores and up the Taunton River into Massachusetts. By the eighteenth century, however, the Indians had been driven off, and a mixed agricultural, lumbering, manufacturing, and trading economy grew up in almost all mainland settlements where there was access to the backcountry. In Providence and other seaside communities, numerous craftsmen engaged in forest-related occupations. Coopers and tanners serviced the meat-packing industry, and leather goods, pails, barrels, and even furniture were prepared for export. Hardwood resources were sufficient to fuel rum distilleries, lime kilns, and brick and iron works. A number of sawmills were set up close to white pine tracts north of Pawtucket Falls. A small tar industry exploited the pine forests to supply shipwrights and also sheep raisers who used the gooey substance to mark sheep and dress cuts inflicted in shearing.

The pressure of a rapidly growing population on limited forest resources was already evident by the last quarter of the eighteenth century, and the state's wood-using industries began to decline. Many wooden handicraft industries and the well-established shipbuilding industry continued to be profitable, but the craftsmen relied heavily on imported timber. Likewise, the metal fabrication industry, which played an important part in subsequent industrial development, became wholly dependent on imported iron and coal. By the first decade of the nineteenth century, almost all the state's blast furnaces, which had consumed large quantities of CHARCOAL, had been shut down. Metal also replaced wood in textile machinery.

Those who remained on the poor and rocky soil in the hilly backcountry turned to dairying. Some subsistence farmers continued to engage in part-time woodland occupations, although many of the stunted trees in the backcountry were suitable only for firewood. By 1860, Rhode Island had become the most industrialized state in terms of population. Some wood-based industries such as carriage making, tanning, and shipbuilding survived amid the many base metal and precious metal firms, but they represented only a small percentage of the state's total economic activity.

Rhode Island's largest annual production of lumber came in 1902 with 32.9 million board feet reported cut by forty-one sawmills. Fifty-seven percent of the lumber produced was hardwood; chestnut alone provided 38 percent. Lumber production in more recent years has averaged only a small fraction of that peak amount.

State forestry efforts began in 1907 when a Forest Commission was created and the first forest commissioner, Jesse B. Mowry, was appointed. Mowry served until 1925 and initiated a fire warden law and a forest tax exemption incentive for tree plantations. Despite Mowry's repeated efforts, not until the early 1930s were two small state forests designated on donated lands; by the 1950s there were nine state forests totaling over 16,000 acres. Rhode Island's timber resources were devastated when the 1938 hurricane destroyed 85 million board feet, or nearly all of the state's merchantable softwood timber, and again in 1942 when 32,000 acres of timberland were burned. Much of the forest recovered in later years, and although it is the second most densely populated state in the Union, Rhode Island in 1977 was 60 percent forested. At that time, commercial forests constituted 98 percent of the 404,000 acres of woods. Private landowners controlled 92 percent of the commercial forest; state and local governments controlled 8 percent.

Rhode Island has provided for outdoor recreation with a small state park system which began in 1927 with R. H. I. Goddard's gift of 472 acres on Greenwich Bay. By the 1970s, there were eighty-five park and recreation areas totaling 12,000 acres, many of them forest covered.

FURTHER READING: Carl Bridenbaugh, *Fat Mutton and Liberty of Conscience: Society in Rhode Island, 1636–1680* (1974). Charles F. Carroll, *The Timber Economy of Puritan New England* (1975). Peter J. Coleman, *The Transformation of Rhode Island, 1790–1860* (1963).

CHARLES F. CARROLL

ROCKEFELLER, JOHN DAVISON, JR. (1874–1960), AND LAURANCE SPELMAN ROCKEFELLER (1910–)

Among American philanthropists who have contributed to conservation and national parks, the names of John D. Rockefeller, Jr., and his third son, Laurance S. Rockefeller, stand apart. John D., Jr., was born on January 29, 1874, in Cleveland, Ohio, where his father was in the process of building the family oil business to greatness. In 1893, John D., Jr., entered Brown University, where he was elected to Phi Beta Kappa. Following graduation, he went to work for his father, although he was never totally committed to pursuing a business career.

From an early age, his interests turned instead to cultural and philanthropic pursuits, which, following the death of his father, bore fruit in a variety of stunning projects. In HISTORIC PRESERVATION, his most famous achievement was the restoration of Colonial Williamsburg in Virginia to its former grandeur. In

conservation, his twenty-three-year battle to save Jackson Hole, Wyoming, from growing commercialism won him equal acclaim. The Jackson Hole campaign began in 1926 when Rockefeller, his wife, and their sons visited the valley with the superintendent of YELLOWSTONE NATIONAL PARK, Horace M. ALBRIGHT. Shortly afterward, Rockefeller agreed to begin purchasing private lands within Jackson Hole with the idea of donating them to the National Park Service. The formation of GRAND TETON NATIONAL PARK in 1929 brought most of the mountain range under federal protection; to Rockefeller fell the challenge of gaining control of the private farms and ranches within Jackson Hole before further encroachments could threaten its value as the Tetons' "frame." Moreover, the southern Yellowstone elk herd, which wintered in Jackson Hole, faced the possibility of extinction if the valley was not preserved.

Rockefeller's hopes of deeding these properties to the NATIONAL PARK SERVICE would not be fulfilled for another twenty years. Wyoming commercial interests enlisted the opposition of other Western ranchers, farmers, and agriculturists in condemning his project as outside interference in the commercial affairs of the state. Unable to get Congress to act, President Franklin D. ROOSEVELT over a storm of objections in 1943 established Jackson Hole National Monument. Not until 1950 did the antagonists reach a compromise and could Congress add Jackson Hole to Grand Teton National Park.

Meanwhile, Rockefeller engaged in myriad similar projects, both large and small. Chief among them was his contribution of $5 million, half the cost of purchasing property that would form the basis of GREAT SMOKY MOUNTAINS NATIONAL PARK on the Tennessee-North Carolina border. On the West Coast, Rockefeller aided in buying superlative groves of coast redwoods to be given to the California state park system. Added to his Williamsburg venture, his lifetime philanthropy on behalf of parks and historic preservation amounted to nearly $75 million by the time of his death on May 11, 1960.

His son, Laurance, had already won distinction as a philanthropist in his own right. Born on May 26, 1910, in New York City, he attended Princeton University and graduated with a B.A. in philosophy in 1932. In 1940, when his father established Jackson Hole Preserve, Inc., a nonprofit organization intended to oversee his philanthropic activities on behalf of national parks, Laurance became trustee and president.

The stage was set for a project uniquely Laurance's own. Through Jackson Hole Preserve, Inc., he began to acquire properties on St. Johns Island in the

Virgin Islands for donation to the National Park Service. These purchases, which began in 1954, led two years later to the dedication of Virgin Islands National Park.

Partly in response to this growing record of achievement, Laurance was appointed in 1958 by President Dwight D. Eisenhower to chair the OUTDOOR RECREATION RESOURCES REVIEW COMMISSION, an organization set up to assess the nation's growing need for parks and wilderness areas. As one example of Laurance's own commitment to bring parklands closer to major population centers, he purchased Dondenberg Mountain on the Hudson River and presented it to Palisades Interstate Park in October 1951. He later played a role as adviser to President Lyndon B. Johnson, exercising significant influence with regard to the redwoods in California and the Lyndon B. Johnson State Park in Texas. In 1965, Laurance served on the White House Conference on Natural Beauty.

Under the guidance of Laurance and Jackson Hole Preserve, Inc., the work of the Rockefeller family in conservation continues, not only in terms of additional purchases of parks and natural areas but also in applied research. Naturally, such large endeavors cannot fail to spark controversy, including charges that Jackson Hole Preserve, Inc., has in fact solidified the hold of the Rockefeller family over the years on national park concessions, most notably in Grand Teton National Park. In this, as in other issues, the Rockefeller legacy will form the basis of any final judgments.

FURTHER READING: Peter Collier and David Horowitz, *The Rockefellers: An American Dynasty* (1976). Nancy Newhall, ed., *A Contribution to the Heritage of Every American: The Conservation Activities of John D. Rockefeller, Jr.* (1957). Alfred Runte, *National Parks: The American Experience* (1979).

ALFRED RUNTE

ROCKY MOUNTAIN NATIONAL PARK

On January 16, 1915, President Woodrow Wilson signed the congressional act authorizing the establishment of Rocky Mountain National Park. This park after 1974 contained over 263,700 acres of land located in portions of three counties (Larimer, Grand, and Boulder) in north-central Colorado, about sixty-five miles northwest of Denver.

Enos A. Mills is generally considered to be the "Father of Rocky Mountain National Park." An avid outdoorsman, he operated a rustic inn near Longs Peak, the highest mountain in the park. Through countless speeches, several nature books, and articles in national periodicals, Mills generated interest in the establishment of a national park around his hostelry. After years of hard work and with the help of allies such as J. Horace MCFARLAND of the American Civic Association and Denver attorney James Grafton Rogers, Mills saw his dream come true in 1915.

Almost from the beginning, however, the park's history was characterized by controversy. The park's first superintendents, C. R. Trowbridge (1915–1916) and L. C. Way (1916–1921) had to deal with a public mainly ignorant of the "Park Idea" and often suspicious of the Washington bureaucracy. Way ran afoul of the National Park Service's policy of granting concession monopolies—this time to touring cars in the park—without advertisement or competitive bidding. The reaction from local hotel keepers, including Enos Mills, was for a time vocal and obstructive.

Way's successor, Roger W. Toll (1921–1929), labored to resolve a controversy concerning state or federal jurisdiction over the park's roads. A conclusion favorable to the park and the federal government was reached only after a legal struggle which eventually reached the United States Supreme Court. The fact that Arkansas, Oklahoma, Wyoming, Washington, and Oregon had already ceded jurisdiction over the roads in their national parks mattered little to the park's critics. Then too, the park service's threat to cut off road-building appropriations if ceding did not occur tended to inflame feelings.

The construction and maintenance of the park's roads and trails formed an important part of the administration of Edmund Rogers (1929–1936), the park's next superintendent. Under his watchful eye, the famous Trail Ridge Road was built, reaching an elevation of more than 12,100 feet and connecting Estes Park Village on the east with Grand Lake Village on the west. The construction of this road, in the face of its attendant hazards, captured the imagination of the public.

It was also the Rogers administration that welcomed the CIVILIAN CONSERVATION CORPS to the park. Enrollees in this New Deal program helped to build and maintain hundreds of miles of trails, constructed roads and parking lots, and manned information stations during the Depression years of the 1930s. Their presence was also a boon to the region's economy.

The economic needs of eastern plains farmers generated a philosophical crisis for the park's administration later in the 1930s. The building of the Colorado-Big Thompson diversion project by the BUREAU OF RECLAMATION pointed up the clash of two imperatives, the need for water on the eastern plains and restrictions imposed by park service philosophy. In this struggle, the economic imperative won. Despite the opposition of conservation societies, the NATIONAL PARK SERVICE, the secretary of the interior, and park officials, a water diversion tunnel was built through and under the park from the moist western slope to the drier eastern slope.

During the same period, the park staff confronted the increasingly serious problem of wildlife management. Officials discovered that they had been protecting the native animals too well. Vigorous predator control campaigns in the 1920s had all but eradicated the natural enemies of the deer and elk. By the 1930s, L. C. Way's earlier boasts of the plentifulness of wildlife had given way to the warnings of Edmund Rogers concerning the deterioration of the range. The park service undertook periodic reduction campaigns in the mid-1940s, but problems of wildlife management continued to exist in the park.

Park administrators also had problems managing the appetites of human as well as four-footed visitors. Many sports enthusiasts and businessmen wished to make the park into a winter skiing center, and they were aided and abetted by some official park service statements. Various park spokesmen had maintained that all outdoor sports, including winter sports, should be encouraged in national parks. The first director of the National Park Service, Steven MATHER, believed that he had to publicize the recreational potential of the park system in order to obtain appropriations from a parsimonious Congress. Mather's successor, Horace ALBRIGHT, contended that visitors should be allowed to use their parks to the fullest. As a result, ski lifts were eventually built in Mount Rainier, Sequoia, Yosemite, Lassen Volcanic, and Olympic national parks. To implement such a recreational policy in Rocky Mountain without marring the scenery became the special problem of more than one superintendent. The concern of superintendents Thomas J. Allen (1936–1937) and David Canfield (1937–1943 and 1946–1954) for the natural wonders of the area appeared to be vacillation to those eager to develop winter sports, while to purists the fact that a winter sports complex was built at all seemed evidence of park service appeasement of local political pressures.

As in several other parks, Rocky Mountain officials have been bothered by the presence of inholdings and campgrounds. The existence of both has been considered ecologically unsound, since the environment thereby became irrevocably altered. Thus it was a sound practice to buy out privately developed lands in the park. To replace them with campgrounds was, however, philosophically obtuse. Nevertheless, this policy was politically realistic. Pressures from politicians and chambers of commerce demanding more campgrounds, more roads, and more trails con-

tinued to be an ever present concern to Rocky Mountain administrators such as James V. Lloyd (1954–1961) and Allyn Hanks (1961–1964).

Still, the great majority of the visitors to the park had no interest in these administrative problems. Most visitor contacts have been with the park naturalists and park rangers, men and women dedicated to educating and protecting the tourists. The development of the park's department of interpretation has been one phase of policy that largely escaped controversy while receiving approval from visitors and local citizens from its inception in 1918.

FURTHER READING: Carl Abbott, "The Active Force: Enos A. Mills and the National Park Movement," *Colorado Magazine* 56 (Winter-Spring 1979): 56-73. Lloyd K. Musselman, *Rocky Mountain National Park: Administrative History, 1915–1965* (1971).

LLOYD K. MUSSELMAN

ROOSEVELT, FRANKLIN D. (1882–1945)

Franklin Delano Roosevelt was a lifelong conservationist. He was especially interested in forestry, scenic and wilderness preservation, soil conservation, and multiple-purpose river basin planning. As president from 1933 to 1945, he sparked a remarkable era of expansion and accomplishment in federal conservation programs.

Soon after moving into the White House, he launched the CIVILIAN CONSERVATION CORPS (CCC), which quickly became one of the most popular New Deal programs. It put more than 3 million unemployed young men, mostly from the big cities of the East and Middle West, to work in the national forests and parks fighting forest fires, planting trees, and building roads, trails, and structures. CCC funds were also used to add 8 million acres to the national forest system.

The NATIONAL PARK SERVICE expanded rapidly. Olympic and Kings Canyon national parks were established, both emphasizing scenic and wilderness values. Roosevelt created the Jackson Hole National Monument, a controversial but crucial step in the long fight to give the Jackson Hole region national park status. The parks attracted unprecedented numbers of visitors. By the end of the 1930s, the National Park Service was under fire from preservationists and wilderness advocates, who charged that it had abandoned preservationist values for the sake of attracting ever more visitors.

Other federal conservation agencies also flourished during Roosevelt's presidency. The BUREAU OF RECLAMATION built giant water conservation and hydroelectric power projects, including Grand Coulee

Dam in Washington and the Central Valley Project of California. The TENNESSEE VALLEY AUTHORITY took shape, a massive experiment in planning for an entire river basin that dealt with forest, water, soil, power, and human resources. The U. S. FOREST SERVICE did battle with the National Park Service to minimize conversion of national forestland into national parks. It also challenged the DEPARTMENT OF THE INTERIOR for leadership in managing public range lands and successfully resisted a concerted effort to be transferred to a proposed Department of Conservation.

The shelterbelt project, in which the CCC and other agencies planted millions of trees as 18,000 miles of windbreaks on the Great Plains, was another bold and popular experiment. The Soil Conservation Service replaced the Soil Erosion Service in 1935 and, under Hugh H. Bennett's dynamic leadership, inaugurated wide-ranging programs to curb devastating soil erosion, which was epitomized by the Dust Bowl in the nation's midlands.

Roosevelt recruited Harold ICKES, a devoted conservationist, as his secretary of the interior and gave him strong support. Ickes championed the conservation programs of his department with unusual stamina and skill and largely reversed its blighted conservation image. His ambition was to remake the Interior Department into a Department of Conservation and bring all the federal resource agencies under his control. He failed in this effort, but he helped Roosevelt make the 1930s into a golden age for the conservation of national resources and natural beauty.

FURTHER READING: Whitney R. Cross, "Ideas in Politics: The Conservation Policies of the Two Roosevelts," *Journal of the History of Ideas* 14 (June 1953): 421-438. Edgar B. Nixon, ed., *Franklin D. Roosevelt and Conservation, 1911–1945* (1957). Anna Lou Riesch, "Conservation under Franklin D. Roosevelt," Ph.D. dissertation, University of Wisconsin (1952). Donald C. Swain, "The Bureau of Reclamation and the New Deal, 1933–1940," *Pacific Northwest Quarterly* 61 (July 1970): 137–146, and "The National Park Service and the New Deal, 1933–1940," *Pacific Historical Review* 41 (Aug. 1972): 312-322.

DONALD C. SWAIN

ROOSEVELT, THEODORE (1858–1919)

The twenty-fifth president of the United States, Theodore Roosevelt, the son of Theodore Roosevelt, Sr., a banker, and Martha Bulloch Roosevelt, was born in New York City on October 27, 1858. He received most of his early education in travel with his parents, through private tutors, and through avid reading, and he developed an early interest in the study of natural

history. He graduated from Harvard University in 1880 and thereafter attended briefly the Columbia University Law School.

He was a Republican assemblyman for New York's twenty-first legislative district (1882–1884) and soon began to be considered an important member of the Republican party in the state. After the untimely deaths in 1884 of his wife and mother and a brief experience as a ranchman in Dakota Territory, he devoted much time to writing, an interest that had been shown as early as 1882 with the publication of his *Naval War of 1812.* In quick succession from 1885 to 1889, he wrote two books on ranch life and hunting, biographies of Thomas Hart Benton and Gouverneur Morris, and the first two volumes of *The Winning of the West.* In 1889, President Benjamin Harrison appointed him a member of the U. S. Civil Service Commission, and he served in this position until 1895 when he resigned to become president of the Board of Police Commissioners of New York City.

Roosevelt's support for the election of William McKinley to the presidency in 1896 brought his appointment as assistant secretary of the Navy, a post that he held until May 1898, when he entered active military service in the war against Spain. He returned from the war as a hero and was elected governor of New York and two years later vice-president of the United States. Anticipating a relatively inactive political life in the latter position, he was suddenly thrust into the office of president of the United States by the assassination of President McKinley in September 1901.

His presidency was notable for his interest and achievement in the conservation of natural resources. As an outdoor enthusiast and former ranchman, Roosevelt readily perceived the value of protecting forests, streams, and wildlife and of improving arid land. Hence early in his administration, he advocated the creation of additional forest reserves, and despite opposition in Congress he had nearly doubled the reserve acreage created by his predecessors by the end of his first presidential term through executive proclamation. He supported the convening of the American Forest Congress of 1905 to discuss the need for forest preservation and the efforts of the government's chief forester, Gifford PINCHOT, that led to the transfer of jurisdiction over federal forest preserves from the DEPARTMENT OF THE INTERIOR to the DEPARTMENT OF AGRICULTURE. He took steps to create more national parks and was instrumental in establishing important ones at Crater Lake and Mesa Verde. Meanwhile, under the Antiquities Act of 1906, he was able to set aside as NATIONAL MONUMENTS many historic and scenic land areas, such as the Petrified Forest and Grand Canyon of Arizona and the Natural Bridges of Utah. On the public domain he also withdrew from commercial exploitation several million acres of oil and coal lands to conserve these resources for public purposes.

Roosevelt supported passage of the Reclamation Act of 1902, and under his leadership the federal government in the following year embarked upon a major reclamation program through the irrigation of desert lands and the production of hydroelectric power in the western United States. During his presidency, some 3 million acres of arid land in a dozen states were irrigated under the reclamation program, which in 1907 was vested in the Reclamation Service, a new bureau in the Department of the Interior. His interest in conservation also extended to protection of wildlife, which was exemplified by his establishment of the first federal wildlife refuges. This federal action stimulated wildlife protection in the states. These several manifestations of Roosevelt's concern for conservation were widely publicized by the White House CONFERENCE OF GOVERNORS in May 1908, which dramatized conservation as a national objective and a considerable Rooseveltian achievement. Roosevelt died on January 6, 1919.

FURTHER READING: The principal books describing and evaluating in some detail Theodore Roosevelt's contribution to forestry and conservation are: Samuel Hays, *Conservation and the Gospel of Efficiency* (1959); E. Louise Peffer, *The Closing of the Public Domain: Disposal and Reservation Policies, 1900–50* (1951); and Elmo R. Richardson, *The Politics of Conservation: Crusades and Controversies, 1897–1913* (1962). Brief summaries of his contribution are given in George E. Mowry, *The Era of Theodore Roosevelt, 1900–1912* (1958); Henry F. Pringle, *Theodore Roosevelt* (1956); and Theodore Roosevelt, *Autobiography* (1913). Also of interest is Paul Russell Cutright, *Theodore Roosevelt, the Naturalist* (1956), and Farida A. Wiley, ed., *Theodore Roosevelt's America: Selections from the Writings of the Oyster Bay Naturalist* (1955).

HAROLD T. PINKETT

ROTHROCK, JOSEPH TRIMBLE (1839–1922)

Born in McVeytown, Pennsylvania, on April 9, 1839, Joseph Rothrock studied under Asa Gray at the Lawrence Scientific School at Harvard, interrupting his studies to serve in the Union Army during the Civil War. He was wounded at Fredericksburg and was later commissioned captain, 20th Pennsylvania Cavalry. He received a B.S. degree from Harvard in 1864 and an M.D. from the University of Pennsylvania in 1867.

For two years thereafter, Rothrock taught botany

at the Pennsylvania State Agricultural College, and in 1869 he began the practice of medicine in Wilkes-Barre. In 1873, he gave up his practice to serve two years as surgeon and botanist for the U. S. GEOLOGICAL SURVEY west of the 100th meridian. He was the author of the survey's *Catalog of Plants* published in its *Report*, vol. 6 (1878).

In 1877, Rothrock was designated a professor of botany in the auxiliary faculty of medicine at the University of Pennsylvania, where he served until 1904. Also in 1877 and more important, he was named Michaux lecturer on forestry by the American Philosophical Society of Philadelphia, an appointment made possible by a legacy from François André MICHAUX.

Following botanical study in Germany in 1880, where he observed well-managed forests, he wrote a prize-winning essay on "Forestry in Europe and America." Offered the chair of botany at Harvard, he declined it in order to devote his efforts to forest conservation, undertaking a strenuous campaign of lectures and public education throughout the Keystone State.

On November 30, 1886, the Pennsylvania Forestry Association was organized in Philadelphia with Rothrock as president. Henceforth, his lectures and educational work were continued under the auspices of the association, especially through its magazine *Forest Leaves* (later called *Pennsylvania Forests*).

As the botanist member of a commission authorized by the Pennsylvania legislature in 1893 to examine and report on forest conditions, Rothrock was largely responsible for its report (1895), which provided the first complete information on the extent of forest depletion in the state. When in 1895 the legislature created a Department of Agriculture with a Division of Forestry, Rothrock became the state's first commissioner of forestry. He held this post until 1904. Among his accomplishments was a law of 1897 providing for the acquisition of state forest reservations; the employment of Pennsylvania's first technically trained forester, George H. Wirt, in 1901; and the establishment of the State Forest Academy at Mont Alto in 1903. During Rothrock's tenure as forestry commissioner, the state forests expanded to the extent of 443,500 acres.

In retirement Rothrock continued to serve as secretary of the State Forestry Commission. Among his many writings was *Areas of Desolation in Pennsylvania* (1915) which alerted citizens to the urgency of forest and water conservation. The SOCIETY OF AMERICAN FORESTERS elected him an honorary member in 1915. He died June 2, 1922. He has been called the "Father of Forestry in Pennsylvania."

HENRY CLEPPER

S

SALVAGE

Headlines that proclaim "destruction" of vast forest tracts by fire or wind are usually an exaggeration, at least in a commercial sense. In fact, much of the "destroyed" timber can be and indeed is salvaged by prompt removal of the dead and down trees. Avoiding delay is crucial, lest insect infestations and additional fires in the drying material spread to surrounding stands, causing even greater losses of timber, watershed, wildlife habitat, and other uses of forested lands.

The salvage of damaged timber is usually more expensive than traditional logging, and there are other problems. First, fire-blackened trees are very dirty to work with, prompting loggers to be less than enthusiastic. The ash itself causes additional equipment wear. Second, storm-damaged timber is often strewn in jackstraw fashion, which makes bucking into log lengths, yarding, and loading much more difficult. Third, disasters strike at random, and the timing and location of the salvage operation may not be convenient to long-term logging plans or markets. Road engineering might not be available for the salvage area, causing expensive delays, and a depressed log market would not welcome a glut of fire or wind-damaged logs.

Salvage remains commonplace: decay-resistant cypress logs, long-sunken in southern swamps, are pulled to the surface; western redcedar trees, hardy remnants of the 1902 Yacolt Burn in Washington State, are still being bucked into shake bolts; and the 1981 eruption of Mount St. Helens launched a massive federal-state-private salvage operation.

The best-known and most comprehensive salvage program followed the 1938 hurricane that swept across New England. With 3 billion board feet of timber on the ground, the U. S. FOREST SERVICE coordinated cleanup efforts by 15,000 Works Progress Administration workers and manpower from fifty CIVILIAN CONSERVATION CORPS work camps. The Northeastern Timber Salvage Administration of the Federal Surplus Commodities Corporation looked to the sale of salvaged logs; $15 million in revenue greatly offset the $16 million effort, which included fireproofing the disaster area and reopening access roads.

Salvage operations will continue to follow disasters, greatly reducing potential commercial losses. Soil erosion, watershed deterioration, loss of wildlife and its habitat, and disruption of recreational activities are also attenuated by these efforts. Thus, the nearly routine operation of salvage greatly lessens the more or less catastrophic impacts of natural and man-caused disasters.

HAROLD K. STEEN

A 1962 windstorm damaged 10 billion board feet of Pacific Northwest timber. Much of this material, which also caused a severe fire hazard, was salvaged, despite difficulties caused by shattered or jack-strawed logs. American Forest Institute Photo.

Fire-blackened trees often contain valuable wood but present the logger with a dirty task. American Forest Institute Photo.

SARGENT, CHARLES SPRAGUE
(1841–1927)

Charles S. Sargent was born April 24, 1841, the son of a wealthy Boston merchant. He was an indifferent student at Harvard, graduating in 1862 near the bottom of his class. He served in the Union Army as a staff officer and invested three years in European travel. After his return to Boston in 1868, he developed his horticultural and agricultural interests. Appointed in 1873 as director of the Botanic Garden at Harvard University and as first director of the Arnold Arboretum at Jamaica Plain, Massachusetts, Sargent became a dedicated student of the arborescent species of America. His initial botanical learning was acquired informally from Asa Gray. Started on an abandoned farm, the arboretum was planned by Sargent and Frederick Law OLMSTED. As the arboretum developed, Sargent built up an elaborate network of botanists with whom he corresponded and whom he occasionally employed as collectors and taxonomists. During Sargent's half-century of vigorous and effective leadership, this institution and its library and herbarium became a center for the study of the nation's woody plants.

As the arboretum's financial base became more secure and as he gained confidence in his abilities, Sargent broadened his interests. After reading George Perkins MARSH's Man and Nature (1864), Sargent began to express an interest in conservation and in preserving the nation's forests. In 1880, he accepted the responsibility of preparing the section on forests that would appear in the Tenth Census. The aged George Engelmann and a number of other prominent botanical explorers aided Sargent in the collection of materials for this study, the Report on the Forests of North America (1884), which established its author's reputation as a talented forest scientist. Sargent's careful presentation of information on the distribution, habits, and taxonomy of 412 species of trees quickly made the Report a standard reference work. The Report warned that, if timber management policies were not altered, the nation would experience a substantial loss in its forest resources.

In 1883, Sargent became involved in an effort to persuade New York State to assume responsibility for maintaining the forests and watersheds of the Adirondacks. He chaired the state commission whose report led to the establishment of the Adirondack Forest Preserve in 1885.

In 1881, Sargent had assumed the task of collecting and preparing for display examples of American trees for the American Museum of Natural History. After great expense and frequent conflict, the Morris

K. Jesup Collection of North American Woods was displayed to the public in 1885. In addition to his other responsibilities, Sargent edited Garden and Forest (1887–1897), a weekly that discussed issues of taxonomy, morphology, geology, ecology, agriculture, and horticulture for the general public.

From 1891 to 1902, Sargent supervised the publication of the fourteen-volume Silva of North America, which served as a long-needed replacement for François André MICHAUX's classic, North American Sylva (1818–1819), and further enhanced Sargent's reputation as a silviculturist. Sargent also wrote the shorter Manual of the Trees of North America (1905). He developed an interest in the flora of China and Japan and in 1892 traveled to Japan to examine the variety of its plant life. In 1906, he employed E. H. Wilson as a plant collector in China, beginning Wilson's long career with the Arnold Arboretum.

More and more dismayed by the nation's forest management practices, Sargent agreed in 1896 to chair a commission of the National Academy of Sciences to examine the government's policy for the nation's timberlands. The commission's initial recommendation for establishment of thirteen additional forest reserves aroused an alarmed outcry in the West. The final report, calling for conservation and the establishment of wise forest harvesting policies, was presented too late to have an effect on the wording of the FOREST MANAGEMENT ACT of 1897. Nevertheless, in focusing public attention on the issue and by emphasizing the support of the prestigious National Academy of Sciences for conservation, the forestry commission made a significant contribution to the development of forest policy.

In 1920, the Garden Club of America recognized Sargent's services to horticulture by awarding him its first medal of honor. In 1923, he received the Frank N. Meyer horticultural medal from the American Genetics Association for work in plant introduction. By his death on March 22, 1927, Sargent had firmly inscribed both his name and that of the Arnold Arboretum upon the history of American silviculture.

FURTHER READING: Charles Sprague Sargent, "The First Fifty Years of the Arnold Arboretum," Journal of the Arnold Arboretum 3 (1922): 127–171. S. B. Sutton, Charles Sprague Sargent and the Arnold Arboretum (1970). William Trelease, "A Biographical Memoir of Charles Sprague Sargent," National Academy of Sciences Biographical Memoirs 12 (1929): 247–248.

PHILLIP DRENNON THOMAS

SAVE-THE-REDWOODS LEAGUE

One of the most active and effective of the regional conservation groups, the Save-the-Redwoods League

(SRL), was founded in 1918 to preserve the *Sequoia sempervirens* or redwood of the north coast of California. The league's principal founders were Henry Fairfield Osborn, president of the American Museum of Natural History; Madison Grant, chairman of the New York Zoological Society; and John C. Merriam, a University of California paleontology professor who had just become president of the Carnegie Institute in Washington, D.C. SRL's original objectives, drafted by Newton DRURY, the league's first executive secretary, were to save from destruction, representative areas of primeval forests, to cooperate with federal and state governments in establishing a national redwood park and a state redwood park, to purchase redwood groves by private subscription, to cooperate with state and county governments in obtaining the protection of timber along highways, and to support reforestation and forest conservation.

SRL took the lead in securing legislation, creating the California State Park Commission in 1927, and in promoting passage by referendum of the first California State Park Bonds Act in 1928. SRL had by 1933 either purchased or assisted the state in acquiring 30,000 acres of redwood forest in Mendocino, Humboldt, and Del Norte counties at a cost of $3 million of its own funds. By that time, it had deleted the establishment of a national redwood park from its statement of objectives.

The acquisition of first-growth redwood from private ownership remained SRL's principal activity until the 1960s. Although its primary project was the establishment and expansion of the Jedediah Smith, Del Norte Coast, Prairie Creek, Humboldt, and Big Basin redwood state parks, the league also participated in the movements to preserve under state ownership the sequoia (*Sequoiadendron giganteum*) in the North Calaveras Grove and the Point Lobos Monterey cypress (*Cupressus macrocarpa*). After some hesitation, the league also supported the establishment in 1968 of the REDWOOD NATIONAL PARK.

During the 1970s, SRL contributed half the funds ($31 million) toward the purchase of 9,043 acres of land added to state parks. Of about 135,000 acres of first-growth redwood still surviving in 1980, about 75,000 were in protected areas. After destructive floods in Humboldt State Park in 1955 and especially in 1964, the league concentrated its efforts on expanding the redwood parks to include their complete watersheds.

Governed by a self-perpetuating council and board of directors, SRL showed a remarkable continuity of leadership and policy from the 1920s through the 1970s. Throughout this period, SRL pursued a cooperative rather than adversarial approach in dealing with logging companies and government agencies, a method that sometimes drew criticism from more militant environmentalists during the 1960s and 1970s. Nevertheless, the league worked with the SIERRA CLUB in expanding the Redwood National Park in 1978. In 1980, the league's main objective was the acquisition of the Mill Creek watershed, a large tract between the Smith and Del Norte parks east of Crescent City.

League membership stood at about 7,000 through the 1930s, rose to 15,000 by 1950, then soared to 55,000 by 1980. SRL headquarters are in San Francisco, California.

FURTHER READING: Susan R. Schrepfer, "A Conservative Reform: Saving the Redwoods, 1917 to 1940," Ph.D. dissertation, University of California, Riverside (1971), and "Conflict in Preservation: The Sierra Club, Save-the-Redwoods League, and Redwood National Park," *Journal of Forest History* 24 (Apr. 1980): 60-77.

SAWDUST AND WOOD FLOUR

Until the late nineteenth century, the mountains of sawdust heaped up by sawmills represented serious waste and pollution problems. As recently as 1937, when many uses for sawdust had been discovered, the equivalent of 4 billion board feet of lumber was still being burned as waste or dumped into streams, a practice soon forbidden by most states.

The first use of sawdust was as fuel. Mills stoked their boilers with it and sold (or sometimes gave) it to nearby factories, heating plants, and private homes. However, where sawdust was abundant so was cordwood, and the low value of sawdust made shipping over any distance impractical. Nevertheless, as late as the 1930s some parts of the United States needed sawdust fuel, which could not be purchased at a reasonable price because of transportation costs, while other regions continued to dispose of it in waste burners. Sawdust as a domestic fuel became especially popular in the Pacific Northwest until it was superseded by natural gas in the 1960s. The sawdust was mostly unseasoned Douglas-fir, usually mixed with larger hogged mill refuse fragments and burned in modified coal furnaces. More than 7,000 such furnaces were said to have been in use in Portland and 5,000 in Seattle in the 1930s. The development by a Weyerhaeuser subsidiary at Lewiston, Idaho, of machines for pressing briquettes in the 1930s made available a more convenient form of sawdust, shavings, and other mill waste for use in domestic heating.

To some extent, sawdust was used as packing in the nineteenth century but, because of its weight, it was quickly displaced by EXCELSIOR and mosses. Sawdust

Under high pressure, sawdust is compressed into fireplace logs. American Forest Institute Photo.

was also traditionally employed as an absorbent in stables, slaughterhouses, and butcher shops. However, the dust produced by local carpenters and cabinet makers seems to have more than met this demand; there is no indication that such universal uses helped sawmills with their disposal problems.

Agriculturists have found sawdust useful both as a soil conditioner and as a mulch. It also makes an absorbent bedding for animals and poultry. Nursery plants are shipped in moist sawdust. The California grape industry, preferring spruce sawdust as a packing material because of its lack of odor and taste, is said to have thus employed 4,000 tons of it annually in the 1940s.

The perfection of dynamite in the late 1860s led to the process of converting sawdust into wood flour, which when combined with nitroglycerin produced Nobel's versatile explosive. Wood flour is milled in precisely the same manner as flour is ground from grain. It was strictly graded by type of wood, size, and uniformity. As the industry developed in the late nineteenth century, most wood flour was made from white pine but, at different periods and for various purposes, cottonwood, aspen, white birch, yellow-poplar, and willow were used. The finest and most uniform wood flour ("granularmetric wood flour") was extremely expensive to produce. Nevertheless, a host of applications were devised. In addition to dynamite, wood flour and

Fireplace logs made out of sawdust ready for shipment to market. Forest History Society Photo.

sawdust were used in the making of molded simulated carvings, synthetic woods of various kinds, linoleum, plastics, fabricated composition shingles, a concrete compound that could be sawed, and sweeping compounds. In the 1930s, the manufacture of linoleum employed more than 50 percent of the total production of wood flour.

In the 1930s, European researchers developed a way to incorporate sawdust into a cheap animal feed but, with grain remaining inexpensive in the United States, Americans took little interest in this application. Chemicals, especially alcohol, have also been made of sawdust.

As early as the late 1940s, some lumber mills had found enough uses for sawdust and other wood waste to abandon the use of refuse burners altogether; this was true, for example, of the Weyerhaeuser mills at

Longview and Everett, Washington, and at Springfield, Oregon.

SAWYER, PHILETUS (1816–1900)

Lumberman and politician, Philetus Sawyer was born on a hardscrabble farm in Rutland County, Vermont, on September 22, 1816. He was one of the seventh-generation of Sawyers in America, the first of whom had sailed from England to Massachusetts Bay in 1636. In 1817, the family moved to Crown Point, New York, on the western shore of Lake Champlain. There Philetus grew up, working on the family farm and attending a few brief sessions of school. He learned to read and write but never gained fluency in either writing or public speaking. When fourteen, he began to work at a local sawmill, and by the time he came of age he was renting and operating the mill on his own.

In 1847, Sawyer settled with his wife, née Melvina Hadley, and their son Edgar Philetus on a farm he had bought in Fond du Lac County, Wisconsin. After two discouraging years, he sold the farm and resettled in nearby Oshkosh, soon to be known as Sawdust City, the center of the Wolf River lumber trade. Here he rose rapidly from woodsman to millhand to lumber manufacturer, dealer, and pineland speculator. By the end of the Civil War, the firm of P. Sawyer & Son, with yards in both Oshkosh and Fond du Lac, was one of the largest in the area, and Sawyer himself was on the way to becoming one of the most important lumbermen in the state. Joining with others in collusive-bidding rings, he bought valuable Chippewa Valley pineland cheaply from the federal government. He became a partner in Chicago lumber companies having large investments in Wisconsin, Michigan, and elsewhere. As part owner, he helped to direct and to combine various railroads. He also invested in banks, boom companies, farm-implement manufacturing, the Texas cattle business, Canadian real estate, and a Maryland gold mine. Altogether, he realized $4 or $5 million, a small part of which he spent on philanthropy. He was a benefactor of Lawrence University and long an influential member of its board of trustees.

An early convert to the Republican party, Sawyer entered politics in 1856. Twice he served as a state assemblyman (1857 and 1861), as an Oshkosh alderman (1858–1859 and 1862–1863), and as the city's mayor (1863 and 1864). From 1865 to 1875, he was a congressman and from 1881 to 1893 a United States senator. In Congress he devoted himself to appropriations for river and harbor improvements for his area and to other legislation in the interest of lumber, railroad, and other corporations. By the 1880s, he was running the Wisconsin party as the senior of a three-man team of political bosses. In the 1890s, he faced an intraparty revolt under the leadership of Robert M. La Follette, who accused him of attempted bribery and who, soon after Sawyer's death on March 29, 1900, succeeded in capturing control of the party.

FURTHER READING: Richard N. Current, *Pine Logs and Politics: A Life of Philetus Sawyer, 1816–1900* (1950).

RICHARD N. CURRENT

SCHENCK, CARL ALWIN (1868–1955)

Carl Schenck was born in Darmstadt, Germany, March 26, 1868. Encouraged by his parents to go into forestry because of his poor health, he studied at the Institute of Technology in Darmstadt, the University of Tübingen, and the University of Giessen, where he was awarded a doctorate in 1895. He learned English and in the summers of 1889–1894 served as assistant, first to Sir Dietrich Brandis and then to Sir William Schlich, who successively brought students from England to tour forests of the continent.

In 1895, on the recommendation of Gifford PINCHOT, who had consulted with Brandis, Schenck was hired by George W. Vanderbilt to be the resident forester at his 100,000-acre Biltmore Estate in the mountains of North Carolina. Pinchot, who had become the estate's forest planner in 1892, continued to hold that position for three more years after Schenck arrived.

During the fourteen years Schenck spent at Biltmore, on what is now regarded as the first large tract of managed forestland in America, he made his most notable contributions to forestry. Under his supervision, roads were built to facilitate logging and fire prevention, fields were reforested, eroded slopes were terraced and planted, and a 7,500-acre area was placed under sustained-yield management. Trees personally selected by Schenck were cut and marketed for firewood, pulpwood, and lumber; bark was sold for its tannic acid.

On September 1, 1898, Schenck opened at the estate the Biltmore Forest School, the first forestry school in the United States, a month ahead of the New York State College of Forestry at Cornell. Biltmore offered a program in applied forestry that emphasized logging as well as SILVICULTURE. Schenck wrote most of the textbooks and taught most of the courses but brought in lecturers on such subjects as law, entomology, ornithology, and mycology. His strong convictions and high spirits encouraged an atmosphere of excitement and conviviality in the school. Among his students who became leaders in forestry were Coert duBois (1899), later U. S. FOREST SERVICE district forester in California, Inman F. Eldredge (1909), eventually director of the Forest Survey of the South, and Joseph S. Illick (1911), later dean of the College of Forestry, State University of New York at Syracuse.

The same traits that inspired students sometimes irritated colleagues. The friendship with Pinchot waned, partly because of Schenck's insistence on emphasizing lumbering in the study of forestry, partly because of his advocacy of a government-supported system of private forests in preference to government-owned forests.

When Vanderbilt lost heavily on several investments, he watched for opportunities to reduce his staff. Schenck was dismissed in 1909 after an argument with the head of the estate's landscape department and after signing a contract for the lease of hunting and fishing rights that displeased Vanderbilt. On the day of the dismissal, Schenck received a cablegram stating that a wealthy uncle had bequeathed him an annuity, one large enough to free him from the need for regular employment.

For five more years, 1909–1913, Schenck continued to operate the Biltmore Forest School, annually taking his students to locations in Germany, France, New York, North Carolina, Michigan, and Oregon. At the end of that time, discouraged by declining enrollments, he closed the school and returned to Darmstadt.

During World War I, Schenck served as an officer in the German army. In postwar Darmstadt, he raised funds for hungry children, worked as a forestry consultant, conducted tours for visiting forestry students, and continued to publish writings on forestry. From time to time, he returned to the United States to lecture and teach. After World War II, he was employed by the American government of occupation as chief forester for Greater Hesse. On a visit to the United States in 1951, he was honored and feted by admirers in education, government, and industry, who praised his contributions as teacher, author, and practitioner. In the following year, he received the honorary degree of Doctor of Forest Science from North Carolina State College. He died in Germany on May 15, 1955.

FURTHER READING: *The Biltmore Story: Recollections of the Beginning of Forestry in the United States* (1955), edited by Ovid Butler from Schenck's manuscript; reprinted as *The Birth of Forestry in America: Biltmore Forest School, 1898–1913* (1974). David A. Clary, "'Different Men from What We Were': Postwar Letters of Carl A. Schenck and Austin F. Cary," *Journal of Forest History* 22 (Oct. 1978): 228-234.

OLIVER H. ORR

SEQUOIA AND KINGS CANYON NATIONAL PARKS

Located contiguously in the southern Sierra Nevada of California, Sequoia and Kings Canyon National Parks together form one of the nation's largest and most scenic wilderness areas, incorporating major groves of giant sequoia or bigtree (*Sequoiadendron giganteum*), thousands of alpine lakes, deep glaciated valleys, and the highest part of the crest of the Sierra with its numerous 14,000-foot peaks. Sequoia National Park in particular has historic importance to American conservation since it became the nation's second national park in 1890, after Yellowstone (1872). The movement that led to its creation con-

stituted one of the first expressions of concern for the preservation of scenic and natural areas of national significance.

Following congressional action to set aside and protect the Mariposa Grove of *Sequoiadendron giganteum* near Yosemite in 1864, the large but scattered groves in the southern Sierra became known. These trees, the world's largest in terms of sheer bulk, are related botanically to the coastal redwood (*Sequoia sempervirens*). The tallest measured *Sequoiadendron giganteum* (in 1931) was 278 feet; the largest diameter was measured at over 33 feet. The greatest estimated age based on ring-count is 3,200 years, and no living specimen is believed to equal that age. In the nineteenth century, the *Sequoiadendron giganteum* became endangered because of logging operations as well as fires. Some of the largest specimens were cut and shipped east for exhibition, and many lesser giants became shakes, fence posts, and grape stakes.

John MUIR named the "Giant Forest" of bigtrees in what became Sequoia National Park following a lengthy trip in the Sierra in 1873, and he was among several people who expressed alarm at the destruction of the trees, which he believed to surpass an age of 4,000 years. However, Congress failed to act on a bill in 1881 that would have encompassed much of the Sierra Nevada, including many of the *Sequoiadendron giganteum*, in a national park.

In response to the filing of land claims in the Grant Grove and the Giant Forest, George W. Stewart, editor of the *Visalia Delta*, led a local effort that culminated in the creation of Sequoia National Park on September 25, 1890. Less than one week later, Congress passed a second bill that not only established YOSEMITE NATIONAL PARK to the north but also tripled the size of Sequoia and created the small General Grant National Park. Upon the urging of Muir, Stewart, and others, the higher elevations of the western slope of the Sierra, including the Kings and Kern rivers watershed, were set aside in 1893 as the Sierra Forest Reserve by proclamation of President Benjamin Harrison.

Until 1914, United States cavalry troops provided the principal protection for Sequoia and General Grant national parks, while the Sierra Forest Reserve lacked adequate protection until placed under the administration of the U. S. FOREST SERVICE in 1905. Nevertheless, the SIERRA CLUB and other park advocates wished to assure permanent preservation of outstanding scenic areas in the Sierra National Forest, as it now was called, and introduced a park bill in 1911 to incorporate the Kern and Kings rivers country into Sequoia National Park. Following blockage of this proposal by the

A park ranger describes the wonders of the General Sherman Tree in Sequoia National Park. Forest Service Photo.

Forest Service, which wished to continue to administer the area in question, and the creation of the NATIONAL PARK SERVICE in 1916, the two government bureaus negotiated a compromise. In 1926, the Kern Canyon and upper crest of the Sierra around Mount Whitney were added to Sequoia.

Because of objections by hydroelectric power company interests and irrigationists in the San Joaquin Valley as well as the Forest Service, Kings Canyon had been deleted from the Sequoia enlargement legislation. By another compromise in 1940, in which the key reservoir sites of Tehipite Valley and Cedar Grove were excluded from the park bill, and after a lengthy and heated debate in Congress, Kings Canyon National Park was established on March 4, 1940.

The small nearby General Grant National Park, administered jointly with Sequoia National Park since its creation in 1890, was converted into part of the new Kings Canyon park. After 1943, the two large parks, Sequoia and Kings Canyon, were administered jointly. In 1965, Congress added Cedar Grove and Tehipite Valley to Kings Canyon National Park after completion of dams downstream, outside the park. Following the addition to Sequoia in 1978 of the Mineral King area, once proposed by Walt Disney Productions as the site for an all-year resort, the two parks incorporated 863,159 acres of mountain landscape.

Recently, over 90 percent of the two parks has been managed de facto as wilderness. Only limited areas in lower elevations, particularly in the vicinity of several groves of *Sequoiadendron giganteum*, are accessible to automobiles. The park service's plan is to restore natural conditions and to prevent environmental deterioration from human activities as much as possible.

FURTHER READING: Oscar Berland, "Giant Forests' Reservation: The Legend and the Myth," *Sierra Club Bulletin* 47 (Dec. 1962): 68-82. Francis P. Farquhar, "Legislative History of Sequoia and Kings Canyon National Parks," *Sierra Club Bulletin* 26 (Feb. 1941): 42-58. Richard J. Hartesveldt, H. Thomas Harvey, Howard S. Shellhammer, and Ronald E. Stecker, *The Giant Sequoia of the Sierra Nevada* (1975). Douglas H. Strong, *Trees—or Timber? The Story of Sequoia and Kings Canyon National Parks* (1968). John R. White and Samuel J. Pusateri, *Sequoia and Kings Canyon National Parks* (1949).

DOUGLAS H. STRONG

SETON, ERNEST THOMPSON (1860–1946)

Artist, author, lecturer, traveler, and field naturalist, Ernest Thompson Seton led a career bathed in controversy, criticism, and acclaim. In more than 3,000 sketches, drawings, and paintings, he demonstrated the artistic skills with which he could capture the essence of animal life in the wilderness. In forty books and innumerable articles and pamphlets, he chronicled for both children and adults the nuances of the life of wild animals. Seton's *Studies in the Art Anatomy of Animals* (1896) demonstrated the diligence with which he mastered wildlife anatomy through dissection and observation. He was a skilled field ornithologist who developed identification charts for birds by sketching raptors in flight and profile portraits of birds at rest. This method of identification was later used in the field guides prepared by Roger Tory Peterson, and it has become the standard method for identifying waterfowl.

Seton was born in South Shields, England, on August 19, 1860. His family emigrated to Canada when he was five. Demonstrating a talent for art, Seton attended the Ontario Art School, and in 1880 he returned to England to study at the Royal Academy School of Painting and Sculpture in London. While in London, he also worked with the extensive natural history collections in the British Museum. Returning to Canada, he obtained a commission in 1885 from the Century Company in New York City to prepare a thousand wildlife drawings for their forthcoming *Century Dictionary*. His career as a wildlife artist had begun. To further improve his skills, he became a student in 1890 at the Julian Academy in Paris. While in France, he exhibit-

ed eighteen paintings of wolf subjects which received critical recognition.

In 1898, Seton published his first book, a collection of stories, *Wild Animals I Have Known*. The immediate success of this work launched his career as an author, and books for both children and adults soon followed from his pen. In his children's books, his stories of animals are always thrilling, romantic, and often highly anthropomorphic; but his *Life-Histories of Northern Animals* (1909) and his significant four-volume *Lives of Game Animals* (1925–1928) demonstrate his skills as a mature and serious student of animal life. Because of the romantic and anthropomorphic views of animals that were often found in his children's stories, Seton became involved with John Burroughs in 1904 in the "nature faker" controversy. Ultimately, Burroughs became convinced of Seton's abilities as a serious scientist, accepting some of Seton's views, and the two were reconciled.

Strongly believing in the morally redeeming qualities of nature, Seton in 1902 created the Woodcraft Indians (the later Woodcraft League) to improve the character of youth by teaching them the skills of woodcraft, outdoor living, natural history, and Indian lore. In 1910, Seton chaired a committee which established the Boy Scouts of America and not only authored the scouts' first handbook but also was the chief scout for five years. There is evidence to suggest that Lord Baden-Powell, who founded the Boy Scouts in England, patterned his organization after Seton's Woodcraft Indians.

Seton received the John Burroughs medal in 1928 for natural history writing. He died on October 23, 1946.

FURTHER READING: John G. Samson, ed., *The Worlds of Ernest Thompson Seton* (1976). Ernest Thompson Seton, *Trail of an Artist Naturalist* (1940). John Henry Wadland, *Ernest Thompson Seton, Man in Nature and the Progressive Era, 1880–1915* (1978).

PHILLIP DRENNON THOMAS

SHAKE AND SHINGLE INDUSTRY

The wooden shingle was developed perhaps as early as the Bronze Age; it was well established by 700 B.C. in the Iron Age Hallstatt culture of central Europe. By the end of the sixth century B.C., the shingle was being spread into western Europe and eastward to Asia. The use of shakes and shingles was introduced to America independently by different European colonists. As early as 1627, shingles were mentioned in Massachusetts, and early eighteenth-century accounts indicate the widespread use of shingles for roofing in the other English colonies along the Atlantic seaboard. Germans introduced shingles to Pennsylvania in the early eighteenth century, and they and Scots-Irish pioneers spread them westward with the frontier. The French introduced shingles throughout the Mississippi valley; and shingles, most likely of cypress, covered roofs in New Orleans in 1727. Shingles, known as *tejamanil* to the Spaniards, had been present in Mexico from the sixteenth century. They were used by the Spaniards in St. Augustine at least by the seventeenth century and in Texas in the early eighteenth century.

The word "shingle" derives from the Latin *scindula* and ultimately from the Greek *sciza*, which means "a cleft piece of wood." The word usually designates a piece of wood about eighteen inches long, five inches wide, and one-fourth to three-fourths inch in thickness. It was distinguished from a shake in the eighteenth century by the fact that the latter was longer, up to thirty-six inches in length. In the twentieth century, however, "shake" (or "split shingle") has referred to a product that has been rived on one or both faces, while a "shingle" has been sawed or milled on both sides. In the southern United States, the term "board" refers to long, crudely made shingles, perhaps up to one inch thick. This word is derived from the Indo-European *bherd*, meaning "to cut," which also is the root of one French word for shingle, *bardeau*.

Throughout the colonial period and the early nine-

In modern times, shakes are split but shingles are sawn. Here a western redcedar bolt is sawn into shingles. Forest History Society Photo.

teenth century and even late in the twentieth century, shingles were made by hand-splitting. A tall, even tree, with a desired diameter of about fifty inches, was cut down and then sawed into sections eighteen to twenty-four inches long, depending on the anticipated length of the shingles. These sections or "blocks" were halved thrice by splitting; the resultant wedgelike eighths were usually too wide for shingles and thus were "shaked" along the tree's growth lines to form "bolts," which were about five inches wide and of varying thicknesses. A froe, with a blade twelve to fifteen inches long and three-and-a-half inches wide and perpendicular to the handle, was then used. The blade was centered on top of the bolt and was struck with a wooden froe club or mallet to drive it into the bolt. This was repeated until shingle thicknesses were being split off. After riving, the shingles were each placed on a shingle horse, which held one end of the piece securely, and smoothed with a drawknife. A good shingle maker could rive some 1,000 shingles a day if he did not have to prepare the bolts. The introduction of shingle machines toward the middle of the nineteenth century led to the general replacement of the hand-rived shingle by the flat milled shingle. The 1950s saw a renaissance of the split shingle or shake, and by 1980 over half of the wood shingles manufactured were shakes.

The type of wood preferred for shingles reflected a considerable regional diversity. In New England and the Great Lakes states, Atlantic and northern white-cedar (*Chamaecyparis thyoides* and *Thuja occidentalis*) and eastern white pine (*Pinus strobus*) were most popular. Atlantic white-cedar was used southward along the coast into Virginia and North Carolina. In the South, yellow pine (*Pinus spp.*) and baldcypress (*Taxodium distichum*) were preferred materials; and in Washington and Oregon, the western redcedar (*Thuja plicata*) was the prime tree for shingle production. Hardwoods constituted a very small part of the shingle industry but they were important in the midwestern states and Kentucky and Tennessee. These included various types of oak, primarily the "shingle oak" (*Quercus imbricaria*), and the American chestnut (*Castanea dentata*).

Shingle production steadily increased through the nineteenth century. The introduction of various shingle machines in the 1850s and 1860s, which could produce up to 6,000 shingles per hour, contributed to the almost tenfold increase in the annual production of shingles to over 12 billion between 1860 and 1899. Annual production peaked at over 15 billion shingles in 1905, stabilized at about 7 billion through the 1920s, declined to about 3 billion in the 1940s, and in 1977 totaled about 2.5 billion. Like the lumber industry as a whole, shingle production has shifted regionally over time. During the colonial period, major production areas centered on northern New England and the James River area of Virginia and Maryland. An important dimension of the industry during this era was export to the West Indies. New England maintained its importance to 1850, when Maine accounted for almost 45 percent of all shingle production in the United States. By 1860, however, leadership had shifted to the Great Lakes states; and in 1870, Minnesota, Wisconsin, and Michigan accounted for about half of all shingle production in the country. Washington and Oregon had begun shingle production as early as the 1840s, primarily for the Pacific trade to California, Hawaii, and Alaska. By the 1880s, the arrival of the railroads turned western producers toward the domestic market, and by 1900 Washington and Oregon had eclipsed the Great Lakes states; in 1930, these two states accounted for some 93 percent of all United States production. Their almost complete dominance of shingle production and the importance of the western redcedar as the primary material persist into the present.

FURTHER READING: Marshall J. Becker, "Shingle-Making: An Aspect of Early American Carpentry," *Pennsylvania Folklife* 25 (1975–1976): 2–19. Edmund C. Burnett, "Shingle-Making on the Lesser Waters of the Big Creek of the French Broad River," *Agricultural History* 20 (1946): 225-235. John J. Winberry, "Origin and Dispersal of the Shingle Roof: A Preliminary Consideration," in R. L. Singh, ed., *Geographic Dimensions of Rural Settlement* (1976), pp. 190–198.

JOHN J. WINBERRY

SHELTERBELTS

The term shelterbelt refers generally to single belts or strips of trees (known also as field shelterbelts, windbreaks, or windbarriers) planted on agricultural lands in any locality to protect soils and crops from strong winds. Specifically, the word shelterbelt refers to the entire system of field protection belts planted under U. S. FOREST SERVICE direction in the years 1935 through 1942 on agricultural lands in the Great Plains of North Dakota, South Dakota, Nebraska, Kansas, Oklahoma, and northern Texas.

In the specific meaning, this activity was first known as the "Shelterbelt Project," and the individual tree strips planted in the delineated zone were called field shelterbelts. After the project got under way, its official name was changed to "Prairie States Forestry Project." The "shelterbelt zone" was delineated roughly by longitudes 97 to 100 degrees in the northern plains, and by 98 to 101 degrees in the southern plains.

The planting of trees for shelterbelts in the plains region was high on the recommended list of practices proposed by the Great Plains Agricultural Council during and after the dust storms of the early 1930s. Traditionally, the launching of the "Shelterbelt Project" is attributed to President Franklin D. ROOSEVELT, whose longtime concern for tree planting and proper land use spawned the idea. But one of Roosevelt's major aims for the project was also to provide employment to relieve the distress of economic conditions prevailing at that time.

The idea of tree planting to protect agricultural lands was not new, for Forest Service researchers had been involved in the study of the influences and values of windbreaks in the plains for a number of years beginning about 1908. Consequently, there was a considerable body of knowledge on which to draw when the shelterbelt project was proposed in 1934. Field shelterbelts could reduce wind velocities to leeward for distances of fifteen times the height of the tree barriers. By so doing, they created more favorable conditions for crop growth by affecting evaporation and temperatures; they helped stabilize soils, improved living conditions, protected livestock, and increased wildlife habitat.

The Forest Service was assigned the responsibility for organizing the project, which was directed by Paul H. Roberts from 1934 to 1942. The director and his staff were located at Lincoln, Nebraska. Each state was organized with a field director and local staff. The first task, truly monumental, was to obtain tree and shrub seed and to establish nurseries to produce the planting stock. During the peak year of 1939, thirteen nurseries produced over 60 million seedlings.

Beginning in the spring of 1935 and ending with the 1942 planting season, more than 200 million trees and shrubs were planted on 30,000 farms in the shelterbelt zone of the plains states. The total length of all tree strips planted during the project's eight years was 18,600 miles. Nearly all plantings were on private lands. Landowners undertook responsibility for cultivating and protecting the trees.

A survey of the shelterbelt plantings, made in 1944 while they were yet quite young, revealed that 80 percent were rated good or better as effective wind-protection barriers, although 10 percent had been removed or were seriously damaged by livestock use. Ten years later, another survey of the same plantings showed that 42 percent could still be rated good or better. Drought, disease, insects, and livestock use had taken considerable toll, but most of the well-estab-

Shelterbelts in Oklahoma. American Forest Institute Photo.

lished belts were functioning according to plan. Since the mid-1960s, however, many of the original shelterbelt plantings in some areas have been destroyed to provide space for large center-pivot irrigation systems.

Tree planting activities on farms in the Great Plains have since 1942 been carried out by the soil conservation districts in cooperation with the U. S. Soil Conservation Service. Tree and shrub planting stocks have been made available through the CLARKE-MCNARY ACT program of the Forest Service.

FURTHER READING: Carlos G. Bates, *Windbreaks: Their Influence and Value*, Forest Service Bulletin No. 86 (1911). Wilmon H. Droze, *Trees, Prairies, and People: A History*

of Tree Planting in the Plains States (1977). E. N. Munns
and J. H. Stoeckeler, "How Are the Great Plains Shelter-
belts?" *Journal of Forestry* 44 (Apr. 1946): 237-257. Ralph
A. Read, *The Great Plains Shelterbelt in 1954*, Great
Plains Agricultural Council Publication No. 16, Nebraska
Agricultural Experiment Station Bulletin No. 441 (1958).
U. S. Forest Service, *Possibilities of Shelterbelt Planting
in the Plains Region*, U. S. Forest Service, Lake States
Forest Experiment Station, Special Publication (1935).

RALPH A. READ

SHIPBUILDING

The ships that carried the early European settlers to
North America were built by craftsmen who had no
theoretical knowledge of hydrodynamics nor any interest in sophisticated models or plans. Yet in the age of
exploration and settlement, shipbuilding was the most
complex of all the woodworking crafts. A master ship-
wright possessed dexterity of hand, keenness of eye,
adeptness at creating three-dimensional images, and a
thorough knowledge of the behavioral characteristics
of many species of wood that had to survive attacks by
fungi and marine worms, tremendous impacts, and
great torsional stresses. The need for waterline timbers with high resistance to dry rot; masts, yards, and
spars with strength and resilience; knees, futtocks,
and floor pieces shaped from naturally carved timbers;
and pitch, tar, and other sealants derived from coniferous trees also meant that shipbuilding required commercial and organizational skills. For these materials
the industry was dependent on an extensive water-
borne trade in forest products. Until the mid-nineteenth century, forests were the basis of sea power in
all its military and commercial aspects, and each nation
strove to maintain its independence by protecting timber-supply routes that often extended over great distances.

The exploration and settlement of North America
opened up vast new sources of timber for shipbuilding. The British, who were running short of high-
quality oak timber and (save for Scotland) lacked
coniferous trees, were particularly eager to encourage shipbuilding in the colonies. All of the navigation
acts passed by Parliament in the seventeenth century
encouraged this activity directly or indirectly. The
British were not disappointed, for by 1700 their
colonial merchant marine was approaching 400 vessels and 25,000 tons. Because the average life of a
vessel was less than twenty-five years, this meant
that well over a thousand vessels were launched in
British North America during the seventeenth century. After 1700, the shipbuilding boom continued at

a more rapid pace. By 1775, 2,343 colonial-built trading vessels were plying the open seas. These ships,
representing only a fraction of the number built in
North America during the century, comprised one-
third of the total British registry.

Access to relatively cheap timber supplies was the
most important factor in the success of the colonial
shipbuilding industry. During the early years, small
vessels were launched in almost every forested bay
and inlet in the settled regions. In the seventeenth century, however, the construction of seagoing vessels
was concentrated almost entirely in Massachusetts.
Boston, the major shipbuilding center, was the distributing point for most of the cedar, maple, white pine,
spruce, and oak timber cut in New England. The port's
growing coastal and overseas trade in bulky timber
products accounted for a significant portion of the new
shipping tonnage. By the early eighteenth century,
Philadelphia and New York also were becoming important shipbuilding centers, and by mid-century shipwrights were beginning to take advantage of the
magnificent stands of oak, mulberry, cedar, and laurel
in Delaware, Maryland, and Virginia to turn out large
numbers of vessels on the Delaware River and in
Chesapeake Bay.

In this era, shipwrights used increasing amounts
of iron for bracing, bolts, anchors, and ordinance.
About 1 ton of iron was required for each 100 tons of
shipping. Although shipwrights continued to import
some of this metal from Europe, a good deal of their
demands were met by the American charcoal iron
industry, which consumed eight cords of hardwood
for every ton of metal produced for the shipbuilding
industry.

Almost all of the early colonial vessels were patterned after English or Dutch national types, but a
number of distinct American forms began to appear in
the eighteenth century. Smuggling, blockade running,
privateering, and finally the entrance of an independent United States into the highly profitable tea and
opium trades in the Far East stimulated an interest in
increased speed under sail. The success of the sharp-
lined fishing schooners built at Essex and Marblehead
and the streamlined trading schooners launched on
Chesapeake Bay encouraged shipwrights to use more
of the lighter woods, such as cedar, in large, fast, full-
rigged ships. These new vessels eventually influenced
designs for the great clipper ships launched in Boston
and New York during the 1840s and 1850s. Americans
also pioneered the use of wooden lift and section models—models that allowed empirical designs to be transformed into full-sized vessels without complex
mathematical calculations or drafting skills. Practical

experience, highly developed visual intuition, and the use of species of wood unknown in the Old World also led to designs for stronger and more effective fighting ships.

The frigate *Constitution*, designed in Philadelphia and launched in Boston in 1797, had a white oak keel from New Jersey, redcedar and live oak timbers from Georgia, and white pine masts from Maine. The warship reflected the changes in timber supply that were taking place in the American shipbuilding industry during the early national period. Despite the continued concentration of the craft in New England—and the tendency for a significant portion of the industry to move into Maine—specialty timbers, especially for large vessels of quality, were becoming scarce along some areas of the coast. Shipwrights began to hire agents to roam diverse sections of the North American forest in search of suitable trees. Carefully selected live oak and longleaf pine timbers were purchased in Mobile and New Orleans. After the opening of the Erie Canal in 1825, white oak cut in the Ohio Valley was distributed to shipyards along the Atlantic Coast, and the moist soils on the peninsulas of Delaware, Maryland, and Virginia nurtured great white oaks that also were transformed into ship frames in New York, Boston, and on the coast of Maine. By the 1850s, the northeast shipyards were also drawing on timber supplies from the Maritimes, the Ottawa Valley, and the Canadian and American shores of the Great Lakes. Some timbers moved more cheaply by water, but there was an increasing tendency to move valuable forest products over the many rail links that connected the distribution centers with the Atlantic ports.

Canada also developed an extensive shipbuilding industry during the first half of the nineteenth century. But the United States, because of its much larger population and greater internal development, attained world leadership in the production of wooden ships. Between 1815 and 1860, American shipbuilders sold nearly a million tons of wooden ships in foreign nations. The United States also carried almost all of its foreign trade in its own vessels. On the eve of the Civil War, this foreign commerce accounted for 2,545,000 tons of shipping. The coastal, river, and lake tonnage was even larger. The schooners of Maine dominated the coastal trades in cotton, grain, coal, and other bulky products. On the western rivers, thousands of flatboats were launched each year to carry lumber and foodstuffs to New Orleans. The building of wooden steamboats—equipped with dangerous high-pressure steam engines that consumed enormous amounts of FIREWOOD—was one of the major industries at Pitts-

burgh, Cincinnati, and Louisville. Buffalo, Detroit, and many smaller ports on the Great Lakes launched the more than 400,000 tons of sailing ships that carried grain, ore, and timber to the large distribution centers.

In 1860, only 10 percent of the Great Lakes fleet was powered by steam and only a small portion of America's oceangoing fleet was driven by coal or firewood. The British were much further advanced in the conversion to steam power on the open water. Their shipyards, located close to iron and coal supplies, were also beginning to produce iron hulls competitive with American wooden hulls. The cost of iron and coal also was decreasing in Britain at the very time that timber costs in America were beginning to increase sharply. Lumbering, the backbone of American shipbuilding, was emerging as the only significant extractive industry with rising unit costs and prices. There was also a growing shortage of the very large, curved, framing timbers that had allowed American shipwrights to build massive cargo carriers without recourse to expensive imported iron knees and longitudinal braces. In the 1870s, when the British began the large-scale production of hulls from open hearth steel, they gained an incontestable advantage over most American wooden hulls.

During the last four decades of the nineteenth century, the United States lost much of its prominence in shipbuilding. Between 1860 and 1879, Canada launched a greater wooden shipping tonnage than her southern neighbor, but after that time Canadian production declined at an even faster rate than that of the United States. In these years of decline and transition to a new technology, the wooden ship maintained a competitive advantage in some carrying trades. Builders continued to launch thousands of tons of wooden bulk carriers on the Great Lakes until steel vessels finally became more economical in the 1890s. Almost all the vessels that brought fresh fish to port in New England were built of wood and driven by sail until the early twentieth century. On the coast of Maine, a lack of alternative employment forced many men to accept long hours and low wages in shipyards. Some of the broad-beamed "Down-Easters" they produced in the 1880s and 1890s—framed with Virginia oak, covered in with southern longleaf and Canadian pine, and sporting five, or even six, masts of "Oregon pine" (Douglas-fir)—exceeded 3,000 tons. Some of these ships sailed for California to carry grain along a 14,000-mile route to Europe; others entered the West Coast timber trades. In the Pacific Northwest, they met competition from the great timber schooners launched on Puget Sound. These four- and five-masted vessels, built with a newly discovered shipbuilding timber, the Douglas-

Wooden ship under construction at Standier Clarkson Yards, Portland, Oregon. Forest Service Photo.

fir, carried timber to South America, Australia, and the Far East. They continued to make such long-distance voyages in the twentieth century long after the metal tramp steamers came to monopolize most of the bulk trades.

At the outbreak of World War I, most of the foreign trade of the United States was carried in steel vessels registered in foreign nations. Between 1914 and 1917, however, millions of tons of this shipping was destroyed by German submarines. Consequently, when Congress finally declared war on Germany in April 1917 there was a pressing need for ships for trade, troop transport, and the maintenance of supply lines. Congress had anticipated the emergency by creating the Shipping Board in 1916, and by February 1917 that agency had formulated plans to augment a large steel vessel construction program with a proposal to build 800 to 1,000 large wooden steamships. The wooden steamers designed by Theodore E. Ferris, the chief architect of the Shipping Board's Emergency Fleet Corporation, were 281 1/2 feet long, had a deadweight of 3,500 long tons, and required 1.5 million board feet of yellow pine or 1.7

million board feet of Douglas-fir. Some other steam vessels approached 5,000 long tons. Shipbuilding firms working under contract for the Fleet Corporation also launched experimental vessels with steel frames and wooden plating, wooden sailing vessels, barges, tugs, and even a tanker. Federal shipping officials were criticized for reviving an obsolete technology, failing to supervise contractors, and continually submitting design changes. Difficulties in procuring large timbers, locating appropriate dockyards, and recruiting skilled workers also seriously hampered production. Builders delivered only eighty-seven wooden steamships to the government by Armistice Day, and criticism of the program then intensified in Congress as shipyards launched 200 more wooden vessels. The Fleet Corporation canceled many contracts, and scores of builders who had not been able to amortize their investments in woodworking equipment went bankrupt. Some wooden steamships were used in commercial service on European, Latin American, and Hawaiian runs, but the postwar decline in world commerce, advances in turbines, and the transition to engines fueled by oil quickly diminished their value. During the early 1920s, most wooden vessels were sold to salvage firms that removed their machinery and burned the hulls to the waterline.

FURTHER READING: Robert Greenhalgh Albion, *Forests and Sea Power: The Timber Problem of the Royal Navy, 1652–1862* (1926). Bernard Bailyn and Lotte Bailyn, *Massachusetts Shipping, 1897–1914: A Statistical Study* (1959). Howard I. Chapelle, *History of American Sailing Ships* (1935). Thomas R. Cox, "Single Decks and Flat Bottoms: Building the West Coast's Lumber Fleet, 1850–1929," *Journal of the West* 20 (July 1981): 65-74. Joseph A. Goldenberg, *Shipbuilding in Colonial America* (1976). Henry Hall, *Report on the Ship-building Industry of the United States*, Tenth Census of the United States, 1880, vol. 8 (1884). Louis C. Hunter, *Steamboats on the Western Rivers: An Economic and Technological History* (1949). William Joe Webb, "The United States Wooden Steamship Program during World War I," *American Neptune* 35 (Oct. 1975): 275-288.

CHARLES F. CARROLL

SIERRA CLUB

From a small local organization formed in 1892 to protect California's Sierra Nevada, the Sierra Club developed in the twentieth century into a powerful national citizens' group. This growth has owed much to the uniqueness of the club's leadership and structure.

The Sierra Club was formed largely under the influence of John MUIR, who had begun advocating wilderness protection for the Sierra Nevada lands through government ownership in the 1870s. He was influential in the establishment in 1890 of YOSEMITE NATIONAL PARK, designed to protect the watershed surrounding Yosemite Valley, which had been administered by the State of California as a park since 1864. Shortly thereafter, Muir and fellow campaigners in the East began discussing a citizens' group to protect the Sierra Nevada. Meanwhile, students and faculty at the University of California in Berkeley were planning an alpine club. Merging the two impulses, twenty-seven men on June 4, 1892, signed the club's articles of incorporation in San Francisco. As its first president, Muir perceived that those who enjoy wilderness would be its most avid defenders. Hence the club was dedicated to "exploring, enjoying, and rendering accessible the mountain regions of the Pacific Coast," as well as to enlisting "the support and cooperation of the people and the government in preserving the forests and other features of the Sierra Nevada."

To improve the protection afforded Yosemite Valley, the club arranged its transfer from state jurisdiction to that of the federal government in 1906. The club's first major campaign in defense of wilderness—indeed the nation's first such battle—involved Yosemite National Park's Hetch Hetchy Valley, which the City of San Francisco proposed to convert into a reservoir. The fight was lost in 1913; Muir died the following year.

Among the club's most notable interwar leaders was William E. COLBY, Muir protégé, mining lawyer, club secretary (1900–1946), and club director (1900–1949). Shortly after Sequoia National Park had been established in 1890, Colby, Muir, and other club leaders had begun a campaign to enlarge the park and add the regions of the Kern and Kings rivers. In 1926, a bill was passed, but the club and the NATIONAL PARK SERVICE had been forced to exclude Kings Canyon. In 1940, however, the club and Secretary of the Interior Harold L. ICKES arranged establishment of Kings Canyon National Park. The club also blocked logging in Washington's OLYMPIC NATIONAL PARK in 1941 and 1947.

In line with Muir's belief that those who love the mountains will defend them, the club sponsored annual High Trips beginning in 1901, transporting some 200 members into the mountains each year. By the mid-1950s, the High Trips had expanded into a diverse outings program; in 1973, club guides led some 4,000 to 5,000 people on 462 trips. Club members made first ascents, improved climbing techniques, explored and mapped the mountains of the Pacific Coast, and helped develop skiing in California. During the interwar years, the Sierra Club helped the State of California construct the John Muir Trail from Yosemite through the southern Sierra. The club maintained a system of ski lodges and huts and the LeConte lodge in Yosemite Valley as a visitor center.

With little pressure on western space and resources, club relations with public land agencies were cordial during the interwar years. This situation began changing in the late 1940s and 1950s, however. In 1947, as the popularity of outdoor RECREATION grew, the club dropped from its by-laws the clause to "render accessible" the mountains and increasingly opposed road construction throughout California. In the 1950s, club leaders criticized recreational developments in the national parks. They clashed with the U.S. FOREST SERVICE over logging in the national forests of the Sierra Nevada and over wilderness protection in the northern Cascades. In 1956, the club began agitating for a Scenic Resources Review requiring public and private agencies to catalog park, wilderness, and wildlife resources and their recreational potential. This proposal helped produce the Outdoor Recreation Resources Review Act in 1958. Also in

On an outing in 1909, members of the Sierra Club receive a lesson in natural history from the club's founder, John Muir. Forest History Society Photo.

1956, the club and the WILDERNESS SOCIETY began urging legislation to give federal wilderness areas congressional, not merely administrative, guarantees. The eventual result was the Wilderness Act of 1964, which established a National Wilderness Preservation System.

From its inception, the club had been an all-volunteer California organization. Its board of directors and officers were elected by the members, who were organized in local chapters beginning in 1911. In 1952, David R. BROWER, wilderness enthusiast and editor, became the club's first executive director. Shortly thereafter, he led the club in a successful campaign to defend Dinosaur National Monument on the Colorado-Utah border against a dam proposed by the U. S. BUREAU OF RECLAMATION. The club's defeat of the project signaled both growing public interest in wilderness and the club's maturing politics. Between 1952 and 1954, the club established an Atlantic chapter and one in the Pacific Northwest, the first steps in the transition into a national organization. In 1955, the club established a central council of representatives from the steadily increasing number of chapters. Following publication of Ansel Adams's *This Is the American Earth*, the club expanded its publication program to include its beautifully illustrated Exhibit Format books (1960–1968), designed by Brower to reinforce conservation campaigns. With its growing San Francisco-based staff, volunteers nationwide, and innovative publications and advertising, the club's influence grew during the 1960s.

In 1963, the Bureau of Reclamation announced its Pacific Southwest Plan to include hydroelectric dams at Bridge and Marble canyons in Arizona's Grand Canyon. These projects threatened to flood a portion of GRAND CANYON NATIONAL PARK. The club masterminded a public relations and congressional campaign, defeating the dams in 1968. That same year, the club's influence was paramount in the establishment of the Redwood and the North Cascades national parks and in the passage of the National Wild and Scenic Rivers and National Trails System acts.

In 1966, however, the club lost its tax-deductible status as a result of its lobbying. Due in part to this loss and to its expanded conservation and publications programs, the club's fiscal position deteriorated. Simultaneously, differences appeared within the club over administrative and conservation policies. In April 1969, Brower resigned; he was replaced by an attorney, Michael McCloskey. The effects of the financial and leadership crisis were partially ameliorated by the club's foresight in having established a nonprofit educational arm, the Sierra Club Foundation, in 1960.

Despite fiscal constraints and a decline from a peak 30 percent annual growth in membership from 1965 to 1971, the club continued its defense of the environment and wilderness in the 1970s. It maintained its national interests and expanded its scope to include the urban environment. The issues in which it became involved multiplied dramatically in number and complexity; they related to the national park system and its administration, wildlife, wilderness, other public lands policies, pollution, and energy. Perhaps the most important ongoing club battle in the 1970s was over Alaskan lands, but worldwide environmental problems also received increasing attention. Following the United Nations Conference on the Human Environment in 1972, the club established an office of international environmental affairs. Based in New York, this office became the Sierra Club Earthcare Center.

During the 1970s, club lawsuits helped establish precedents that expanded the definition of legal standing to include noneconomic bases and more liberal definitions of direct interest. In 1970, the Sierra Club Legal Defense Fund institutionalized the legal advocacy function. Between 1971 and 1982, the club grew from 70,000 to 260,000 members, with fifty-three chapters covering the United States and Canada.

FURTHER READING: Stephen Fox, *John Muir and His Legacy: The American Conservation Movement* (1981). Holway Jones, *John Muir and the Sierra Club: The Battle for Yosemite* (1965). Roderick Nash, *Wilderness and the American Mind* (rev. ed., 1982).

SUSAN R. SCHREPFER

SILCOX, FERDINAND AUGUSTUS (1882–1939)

Born in Columbus, Georgia, on December 25, 1882, Ferdinand A. Silcox grew up in Charleston, South Carolina. He graduated with honors in chemistry and sociology from the College of Charleston in 1903 and received an M.F. from the Yale School of Forestry in 1905. Silcox served as a ranger in the Leadville National Forest and as supervisor successively of the Holy Cross, San Juan, and Durango national forests, all in Colorado. In December 1908, he was appointed assistant district forester for the Northern District in Missoula, Montana. His success in organizing logistical support for the fire fighters battling the enormously destructive blazes through the northern Rockies in 1910 earned Silcox a promotion to district forester in the following year.

In the spring of 1917, an event occurred that was to redirect Silcox's career for the next sixteen years. His district urgently needed fire fighters. The lumber industry was willing to provide them as long as there were no dealings with the Industrial Workers of the World, which was organizing a strike of lumberjacks. Silcox chose to deal directly with the strikers. He earned their respect and got his fire fighters, thereby establishing his credentials as a labor negotiator.

During World War I, Silcox served briefly as a captain in the Twentieth (Forestry) Engineers. From 1918 to 1919, he worked for the Department of Labor to settle labor problems in the Seattle shipyards and in spruce production for aircraft. He then helped reorganize the U. S. Employment Service. After that he took a position with a printers' trade association. When he left to rejoin the U. S. FOREST SERVICE after a sixteen-year absence, many printing unions sent him letters deploring his departure because of the fairness he had shown in labor negotiations over the years.

His longtime friend, Assistant Secretary of Agriculture Rexford G. Tugwell, persuaded the reluctant Silcox that he was the best man to take over after the sudden death of Robert Y. STUART in 1933. Silcox was an enthusiastic supporter of Franklin ROOSEVELT's New Deal. As head of the Forest Service (the title was changed from forester to chief in 1935), Silcox oversaw many programs that attempted to ameliorate unemployment, reclaim denuded and eroded forest- and rangeland, and control floods. During his tenure, 3 million young men of the CIVILIAN CONSERVATION CORPS worked under Forest Service direction in fighting fires, planting and thinning trees, and building roads, trails, and recreation facilities. In 1935, the Forest Service took on the Prairie States Forestry Project to provide employment and lessen wind erosion by planting SHELTERBELTS of trees on the Great Plains. In 1938, the service, with state help, began managing the big New England Hurricane salvage job.

During the Depression of the 1930s, the timber industry's substantial failure to reforest land and practice sound forest management again became topics of debate. Silcox proposed increased public ownership, public cooperation with private owners, and state or federal regulation on private lands. More funds from Congress to purchase land permitted the Forest Service to enlarge the national forests, especially in the cutover regions of the Great Lake states and the South, while legislation such as the 1937 Norris-Doxey Farm Forestry Cooperative Act enlarged the scope of its aid to states and private owners. However, Silcox was unable to impose regulation on the timber industry.

Six years after taking office, the strain of directing the service through one of its most frenetic periods contributed to Silcox's death by heart attack on December 2, 1939.

FURTHER READING: Henry Clepper, "Chiefs of the Forest Service," *Journal of Forestry* 59 (Nov. 1961): 800-801. Harold K. Steen, *The U. S. Forest Service: A History* (1976).

DENNIS M. ROTH

SILVICULTURE

Silviculture is the theory and practice of controlling the regeneration, composition, and growth of stands of forest vegetation. It has also been defined as the art and science of cultivating forest crops based on knowledge of silvics, or study of the life history, characteristics, and ecology of forest trees.

Until the twentieth century, exploitation of the North American forests was almost universal and little thought was given to encouraging or manipulating regrowth on logged-over areas. Alarm over the speedy demolition of the forests of the Lake States by heavy cutting and catastrophic fires during the last half of the nineteenth century stimulated programs to encourage the planting of trees, the one silvicultural practice which the public has generally supported. The Timber Culture Act of 1873 envisioned the planting of trees on the Great Plains in the mistaken hope that the trees would increase rainfall and the real prospect that they would break the wind and make life more pleasant. More generally, there has long been willingness to plant trees on deforested burns and other treeless areas without much analysis of costs and prospective benefits.

Silviculture for the production of timber on a sustained-yield basis evolved in western Europe in the nineteenth century. The practice became established in clearcutting oak and beech forests in Germany and replacing them with plantations of Scotch pine and Norway spruce. The first crop of softwoods was bounteous, the trees were harvested, and another crop of pine and spruce was planted. Often, the second crop did well. Occasionally, the second generation grew slower, was more afflicted with insects and diseases, and produced less.

Out of the examination of such problems grew a naturalistic school of silviculture which argued for the growing of mixed forests of softwoods and hardwoods, guided by but not limited to the species of trees that were endemic to the region and to the forest site. Such a forest could be maintained by partial cuts designed not only to harvest the mature trees but also to develop a new crop underneath. Since clearcutting and planting continued to work well on other sites, however, advocates of the practice continued to be influential. Thus, when German-trained foresters, notably Bernhard E. FERNOW and Carl A. SCHENCK, imported ideas about silviculture early in the nineteenth century, they brought the philosophies both of the clearcut-and-plant system of tree farming and of the ecologically sensitive naturalistic school. The partly ideological argument over the relative merits of the alternative silvicultural strategies has continued unabated ever since. However, until the 1930s it was largely academic. Silviculture was a subject which foresters studied but seldom were able to practice.

Most of what could be done during the first four decades of the twentieth century took the form of some modest improvements upon the kinds of harvesting practices that heretofore had been applied without real plans for the future. Earlier practices had involved cutting only those trees that were biggest, best, or most useful, and either leaving the others standing or casually allowing their destruction. The early foresters, in-

Reforestation is a key element of silvicultural practices. Here a two-man team uses the dibble to plant a southern pine seedling. American Forest Institute Photo.

cluding both the German émigrés and such Americans as Gifford PINCHOT and Henry S. GRAVES, recognized that their initial efforts had to be built mostly around crude kinds of partial, selective cutting which they viewed as temporary expedients later to be replaced by more intensive silviculture.

As the campaign for conscious forest management progressed, an increasing number of public and private owners were willing to reserve trees for future cuts but not to spend money on growing or regenerating forests. This trend called forth many techniques of "no investment silviculture," limited largely to things that could be done during the course of immediately profitable harvests. For example, it was argued that if owners could be shown that it was unprofitable to harvest small trees, they could be induced to leave them for a future harvest. Furthermore, the residual stand could be augmented if it could be demonstrated that somewhat larger trees would earn more if left to grow than if immediately harvested.

The result in many cases was "high grading," the removal of the large valuable trees and the leaving of crooked, rotten, and deformed trees and small-crowned trees unable to respond to release. Yet, because the partial cut bore some resemblance to those made to create and sustain uneven-aged stands of high quality in parts of Europe, the practice was termed "selective cutting" in parallel to the European "selection system."

The alternative was equally bad. Large-area clear-cutting, such as that induced by the exigencies of railroad logging in the South and West and often followed by fire, frequently left no growing stock and no sources of seed for natural regneration to form a new crop. Either these areas had to be planted or they remained unstocked for a decade or more.

The first major applications of silviculture were

made possible by the CIVILIAN CONSERVATION CORPS program of the 1930s. Some existing public forests were rehabilitated through planting and improvement cutting, but the time had not yet arrived for much control over timber-harvesting practices. By the end of World War II, however, the depletion of the national timber supply and the burgeoning demand finally caused silvicultural practices to appear in the woods on an ever growing scale. Although there had been isolated programs of silvicultural practice on industrial holdings before then, it was at this time that many of the large forest industry corporations embarked on long-term management. Also, for the first time, more of the burden of timber harvesting began to shift to the national forests, many of which had previously been in the status of rather remote storehouses for surplus trees.

During the early 1950s, there was a quiet and rather general departure from "selective" timber management. It was widely perceived that such cutting was sometimes degenerative and probably overdone. Perhaps more important, the owners of large private forests and public forest managers were finally able to spend money on regeneration so that it was no longer so necessary to use partial cutting as a holding action.

The shift of the 1950s and 1960s was to even-aged silviculture with a tendency for the practice to become more intensive as the owners of large holdings concluded that it was desirable to increase their long-term investments. One first step was commonly the reservation of scattered seed trees, coupled with the seed-bed preparation and vegetational control that is ordinarily necessary to make small amounts of seed effective. Usually, the next step, given the cost of the site preparation, was the substitution of artificial seeding for that from seed trees.

Typically, soon after this, intensive silvicultural practices are introduced. For example, nursery-grown trees are planted in plowed soil at well-chosen spacings, protected from weeds and pests with pesticides, fertilized, thinned, and finally harvested in highly mechanized operations. These practices were evolved to restock cutover forestlands in the South and to replace decrepit old-growth stands in the West with new, vigorous even-aged stands, often using seed of superior genetic strains developed through cooperative tree improvement programs. For many foresters, silviculture became a routine of clearcutting old stands and using heavy machinery, fire, or herbicides to prepare soils for planting.

Although these procedures work well, except for exposure-sensitive species, the heavy cutting associated with them makes the typical unsightliness of logging operations highly visible. Around 1970, there was a popular revulsion against these practices, coupled with growing conflicts over allocations of public forestland to various primary uses. The result has been a reduction of emphasis on the more mechanistic and heavy-handed approaches, particularly on public forestlands. Clearcut areas have been made smaller. Somewhat less reliance has been placed on regeneration by planting and use of pesticides. Especially on public lands, more use came to be made of the shelterwood methods of regenerating even-aged stands by two or more harvest cuts made at intervals of a decade or more, creating in the interval a shelter under which a new stand seeds in and becomes established. This method had formerly been little used because it necessitated cutting the smaller and poorer trees first and leaving fairly large numbers of the best trees in stands until the final harvest cuttings.

By the end of the 1970s, many American foresters had learned that there was no one ideal mode of silviculture but that each had its place for a given set of circumstances.

FURTHER READING: Frederick S. Baker, "Silviculture," in Robert K. Winters, ed., *Fifty Years of Forestry in the U. S. A.* (1950), pp. 65-77. Bernhard E. Fernow, *A Brief History of Forestry* (1907, rev. 1911). Henry S. Graves, *Principles of Handling Woodlands* (1911). Carl A. Schenck, *Biltmore Lectures on Silviculture* (1907). Stephen H. Spurr, "Progress in Silviculture," in Henry Clepper and Arthur B. Meyer, eds., *American Forestry: Six Decades of Growth* (1960), pp. 65-82. Stephen H. Spurr, "Silviculture," *Scientific American* 240 (Feb. 1979): 76-82, 87-91.

DAVID M. SMITH
STEPHEN H. SPURR

SMOKEY BEAR

"Smokey" is the name of a nationally famous fictional bear, who works for the prevention of man-caused forest and range fires.

During World War II, the problem of forest fire had become particularly severe due to the wartime demand for forest products as well as curtailments in the manpower available to fight fires. Approximately 30 million acres of forest- and rangeland had burned each year between 1937 and 1942. Nine out of ten fires were man-caused and thus preventable. State and federal forestry agencies organized the Cooperative Forest Fire Prevention Campaign (CFFPC), a nationwide program to educate citizens. The CFFPC appealed for help from the newly organized Wartime Advertising Council (later called The Advertising

Council, Inc.), a group that would direct such projects as the scrap metal and scrap lumber collection drives. Slogans such as "Careless Matches Aid the Axis" and "Our Carelessness, Their Secret Weapon" were used in the 1942 and 1943 campaigns. Walt Disney's Bambi provided a popular exponent of forest fire prevention for 1944 posters.

In 1945, the advertisers portrayed a bear in ranger's hat and fire fighter's dungarees: a blend of the emotional appeal of an animal with the ruggedness of a fire fighter. The Foote, Cone, and Belding Agency of Los Angeles contributed its facilities to help the campaign. The bear was named Smokey. His best-known slogan, "Only You Can Prevent Forest Fires," was introduced about 1947. The artists for Smokey Bear posters were first Albert Staehle and later Rudy Wendelin.

In 1950, more zest was added to the campaign when a badly burned bear cub, a real live Smokey, was rescued from a forest fire in New Mexico and taken to the National Zoological Park in Washington, D.C., to become the living symbol of forest fire prevention. Such entertainment figures as Bob Hope, Bing Crosby, and William ("Hopalong Cassidy") Boyd contributed time on radio and the screen to support the CFFPC. A 1952 act of Congress protected the Smokey symbol from unauthorized use. By 1968, over fifty manufacturers had been licensed to produce Smokey Bear commercial items, the royalties from which supported the formation of the "Smokey Bear Junior Forest Rangers," a group eventually including 4 million school children. In 1958, a Smokey Bear float participated in the Tournament of Roses New Year's Day parade in Pasadena, California, and in 1966 a fifty-nine-foot balloon image of Smokey appeared in the Macy's Thanksgiving Day parade in New York. Both parades have seen Smokey several times since. Smokey's fan mail in the 1970s averaged 1,000 letters and postcards a day.

Smokey found a partner in 1971 when the U. S. FOREST SERVICE designed Woodsy Owl as the symbol for its antipollution work. Woodsy's slogan was "Give a Hoot—Don't Pollute!"

Forestry, civic and youth organizations, Keep Green associations, conservation societies, and sportsmen's and garden clubs are only a few of the many groups that have supported the Smokey Bear Campaign. Advertising agencies worked voluntarily with the CFFPC, which determined the campaign

Forest Service Chief Lyle F. Watts looks on as Homer Pickens, assistant game warden of New Mexico, readies Smokey for the Washington, D.C., Zoo, 1950. Forest Service Photo.

theme from year to year. The Advertising Council lined up free space and time with the news media. Over $10 million worth of advertising was donated to the campaign each year. Although public use of forestlands increased fourfold between 1950 and 1980, the number of man-caused fires fell by more than half. The public response to Smokey's challenge helped save America more than $15 billion in losses that did not occur.

Smokey died on November 8, 1976.

MICHAEL E. MOON

SOCIAL ORIGINS OF LUMBERMEN

Because of the large number of individuals involved, their independence, and their geographical dispersion, it is hazardous to generalize about the men who made it to the top in the lumber industry. Nevertheless, there were some distinctive patterns in family backgrounds, nationality, religion, education, work experience, character, outlook, paths to business leadership, and acceptance of social responsibility. William Miller, Irene Neu, and other scholars, in studies of the social origins and careers of the late nineteenth- and early twentieth-century elite in such industries as textiles, railroads, steel, oil, commerce, and banking, questioned the reality of social mobility in American society. In contrast, a statistical analysis by this author in 1956 found a "conventional pattern of humble origins and homely virtues" among leading northern pine lumbermen from Maine to Minnesota over a century.

A few, such as Isaac STEPHENSON, Philetus SAW-YER, Henry Sage, and Edward HINES, gained prominence through political activity. T. B. Walker became a noted art collector. But even Frederick Weyerhaeuser (see WEYERHAEUSER FAMILY), who exercised hegemony over a large galaxy of associates along the Mississippi River, was not sufficiently prominent to merit mention in the *Dictionary of American Biography*. For the most part, lumbermen evidently "said little and sawed wood" and were unknown outside of their community or occupation.

Of the 131 men selected for analysis, nearly all were born between 1810 and 1850 and over 80 percent were children of English-speaking parents in Northeastern states or adjoining regions in Canada. Only ten were immigrants, mostly from Germany and Sweden. The parents of over half the industry leaders were farmers, some of whom doubled as storekeeper, harness maker, blacksmith, butcher, clergyman, logger, or sawmill operator. Only sixteen fathers had been employed full time in lumbering. Ten were storekeepers, nine were laborers, and a like number were professional men, ar-

tisans, or seafarers. Several of the 131 were orphans.

The majority evidently had no pronounced religious or political convictions. Of forty-nine individuals about whom information on religious preference is available, forty-seven were of Methodist, Presbyterian, or other Protestant affiliation, one was Catholic, and one an agnostic. As to politics, forty-five were Republican, four Democrat, and two Prohibitionist.

Eighty percent of these future leaders had only elementary school education, and thirty-two attended only a few winter terms. However, nine studied law books, surveyors' handbooks, or bookkeeping manuals on their own. Ten served apprenticeships in carpentry and other trades. Less than a fifth had high school or college educations, and of those, few completed their course of study. All had such occupational experience as farmhand, lumberjack, sawmill worker, carpenter, surveyor, or soldier in the Civil War. Clerking in a general store seems to have been ideal training for a career in business. The country storekeeper bought and sold every kind of produce and merchandise and engaged in barter and credit transactions. City boys might start by working for a lumber dealer.

Twenty of the future leaders launched their first business enterprise before the age of twenty-one, and seventy-nine ran their own businesses by the time they were twenty-six. T. B. Walker, when a teenager, supported himself and his widowed mother by working as a traveling salesman of grindstones. Nearly half accumulated modest capital in some activity other than lumbering. For over half, their first contact with lumbering consisted of woods or sawmill labor; twenty-two began in lumber marketing; sixteen entered the industry in managerial capacities, either in a family firm or by investing capital in a partnership; six began as bookkeepers; four as timberland dealers.

For ninety-seven men the first independent venture was with a partner in logging or sawmilling. A little capital, like a little education, went a long way. Weyerhaeuser and his brother-in-law had $3,000 cash when they purchased a sawmill in Rock Island in 1860. John H. Knapp came into an inheritance of $1,000 when he reached his twenty-first birthday, promptly went into partnership with a logger of no capital, and purchased a half interest in a Wisconsin sawmill. For a quarter-century, from 1875 to 1900, Knapp, Stout, and Company was the nation's largest lumber manufacturer.

Successful lumbermen created their own capital and reinvested profits. They devised or adopted improved techniques and continuously expanded the scale of their operations in collaboration with partners. They acquired their own stumpage, often buying timberlands to the limit of their financial ability. As local forests became depleted, lumbermen transplanted their operations to other frontiers. Only 3 of the 131 lumbermen studied made no major shift in location. Nearly all migrated not only once but a second and a third time.

The lumber industry did not conform to the organizational pattern observed by Alfred D. Chandler, Jr., in his study of the evolution of the corporate structures of duPont, General Motors, Standard Oil, and Sears, but followed its own unique historical pattern. Family firms and partnerships dominated, typically in numerous small, decentralized operations. New companies were organized for each new venture, with congeries of partners or shareholders. In 1936, F. K. Weyerhaeuser, grandson of the founder, lamented the amorphous nature of the various so-called Weyerhaeuser enterprises (he counted ninety-eight) "resembling a deep-sea invertebrate which did not seem to be actuated by a single brain." Typically, the younger generation, with new sets of partners, headed new and far-flung ventures while their fathers held the purse strings.

Most lumbermen grew deep roots in the communities in which they lived during their prime. They were devoted to family and gave time and money for civic improvement. For most, in later life, their only personal extravagances were building an imposing mansion and taking a then fashionable European tour. Their humble origins and the stern circumstances of their youth undoubtedly molded traits of character conducive to business success. Their frugal habits and simple personal tastes were reflected in a policy of rigid economy in business, the steady accumulation of capital, cautious investment, and shrewd bargaining.

Lumbermen took pride in their achievements, regarding themselves as good stewards whose lifetime efforts had made a positive contribution to the progress of mankind. In their old age, many lumbermen bitterly pondered the muckraker attitude that condemned them as exploiters of public wealth for their private enrichment.

Yet few of them had given much thought to the question of what their social responsibilities might be. Neither had most of their contemporaries. They simply accepted conditions as they were. If life and labor in the logging camps were harsh, so was life anywhere on the frontier. If hours in the sawmills were long or conditions bad, they were no worse than in other industries nor more than what they themselves had endured. Nor had there seemed any impelling need for conservation. The abundance of trees, the low price of lumber, market competition, and tax policies made reforestation unthinkable. The lumbermen of the nineteenth century supplied the nation abundantly with high-quality lumber and never doubted their contribution to the building of a great civilization.

What of the twentieth-century successors to these entrepreneurs? What kind of backgrounds did they come from and what kind of men were they? Analysis of twenty-five forest industry leaders of the mid-twentieth century—identified primarily by membership on the board of directors of the NATIONAL LUMBER MANUFACTURERS ASSOCIATION—suggests some of the changes that had taken place. The members of this group were born between 1860 and 1900 and achieved leadership positions between 1930 and 1950.

A cursory analysis reveals a composite profile not significantly different from that of their forebears. Their personal values and outlook were cast essentially in the same mold. In contrast to the nineteenth-century lumber pioneers, most of this second group perpetuated established businesses, but they matched their predecessors in adapting themselves to changing conditions, particularly the more complicated business and social environment. One important difference was the fact that the new generation of industry leaders was geographically dispersed, representing the exploitation of Southern and Western forests and also the utilization of hardwoods and manufacture of paper pulp. Northern pine lumbermen no longer dominated the scene.

Sixteen of the twenty-five individuals were of English or Scottish descent; five were German, two Irish. In most instances, their fathers had been in the lumber business, and for the remainder their fathers were storekeepers, lawyers, or in some other business or profession. Of nineteen whose religious affiliation could be ascertained, fifteen were members of the Presbyterian and other long-established English Protestant denominations. Two were Catholic, one Christian Scientist, and one Jewish. Most were active members of the Republican party; however, E. L. Kurth of Texas called himself a Conservative Democrat.

Their parents evidently valued education and had the means to send their children to college. With few exceptions, the twenty-five leaders attained a remarkably high level of education—far above the earlier generation and above the average education of their time. All except two went beyond high school. Six had some college training. Seventeen were university graduates and, of these, seven went beyond the baccalaureate to receive additional training in such fields as law, forestry, and accounting. Four had law degrees. John W. Watzek, Jr., went on from Yale to earn a master's degree from Cornell. J. E. McGaffrey received a degree in forestry, and Corydon Wagner took one year of postgraduate forestry training at Yale. Three others were Yale graduates; two graduated from the Massachusetts Institute of Technology. Others were university alumni of California, Chicago, Columbia, Harvard, Michigan, Notre Dame, and Princeton.

For seventeen, their first full-time employment was in the lumber business, starting in office work or managerial capacities at ages from twenty to twenty-three, often in family firms. One, H. E. Hardtner, worked in his father's shoe store at age sixteen, and two were woods and sawmill workers at age eighteen. Only four started their own business in logging, sawmilling, and lumber wholesaling—always with partners—between the ages of twenty-one and thirty-one. The rest worked their way through various executive echelons, a process which in four instances was accelerated by marriage into lumber families.

By mid-century, the former pattern became virtually unrecognizable. One observes a distinct break with the past—a discontinuity in managerial policies and decisions. Descendants of families that founded lumber enterprises now often were minor stockholders. In some cases, the identities of once illustrious companies as well as the founding-family names vanished in the wake of corporate mergers. A formerly independent lumber company could now be part of a conglomerate such as the Continental Group or Champion International, its destiny shaped by remote control. The new breed of managers and their ambitious and sophisticated goals ushered in a new era in the history of the forest products industry.

FURTHER READING: Alfred D. Chandler, Jr., *Strategy and Structure: Chapters in the History of Industrial Enterprise* (1962). Robert E. Ficken, *Lumber and Politics: The Career of Mark E. Reed* (1980). Fred W. Kohlmeyer, "Northern Pine Lumbermen: A Study in Origins and Migrations," *Journal of Economic History* 16 (Dec. 1956): 529-538. William Miller, ed., *Men in Business: Essays in the History of Entrepreneurship* (1952).

FRED W. KOHLMEYER

SOCIETY OF AMERICAN FORESTERS

Gifford PINCHOT convened the organizational meeting of the Society of American Foresters (SAF) on November 30, 1900. Two weeks later, the seven charter members met again to adopt a constitution, formalize its name, admit eight additional members, and elect Pinchot as president, a position he held until 1909 and again in 1910–1911. Subsequent presidents have served from one- to three-year terms.

The primary purpose of SAF has been to advance the profession of forestry in the United States. It has pursued this goal through its publications, by standardizing forestry TERMINOLOGY, and by setting standards for forestry education.

In 1917, SAF merged its *Proceedings* with Bernhard E. FERNOW's *Forestry Quarterly*, which began publication in 1902, to form the *Journal of Forestry*. Thus, the *Journal* began with volume XV. The monthly *Journal* carries technical and professional articles, editorials, book reviews, and news of the society. The *Journal's* editorial affairs have been guided by such distinguished foresters as Bernhard Fernow, Raphael ZON, Henry Clepper, Samuel Trask DANA, Henry Schmitz, Arthur B. Meyer, Hardin R. Glascock, Clyde M. Walker, and N. H. Sand. In 1955, the society began *Forest Science*, a quarterly publication that carries highly technical and scientific articles of special interest to those engaged in research. More recently, SAF has also sponsored regional publications.

Accurate communications between practitioners required standard terminology. The SAF Committee on Terminology was established in 1919 and reported through the *Journal of Forestry*. In 1944, the first in the series of *Forestry Terminology* appeared, and in 1955, the 1,200-page *Forestry Handbook* made methods, techniques, formulas, tables, and conversion factors conveniently available. This first edition of the *Handbook* carried contributions from over 200 experts in twenty-three specialties.

It is logical that an organization committed to the advancement of forestry would monitor education. Since 1933, SAF has examined the nation's forestry schools and accredited those meeting basic standards. Initially, fourteen schools received accreditation, and by 1980, there were forty-four with full credentials. SAF has also accredited fifty-two two-year technical programs. At first, only forestry graduates of accredited four-year schools could be full members of SAF; more recently, a baccalaureate degree and working in fields "closely allied to forestry" met membership requirements. Graduates of two-year technical programs have been admitted to membership, but without voting rights or the opportunity to hold office. This and other restricted categories of membership have been contentious issues. However, a general easing of membership requirements in recent years has reversed an earlier trend, when the definition of forestry was narrowed to discourage or exclude range management and other related specialties.

Professional conduct or ethics were of interest to SAF since its inception, but for nearly five decades the society had only informal guidelines to deal with these issues. In 1930, when the first forester was actually expelled from membership because of unethical conduct, interest in developing precise standards was renewed. But it was not until 1948 that members approved a referendum that established a Code of Ethics and a formal procedure for reviewing reports of misconduct.

Over the years, SAF has had to deal with another controversy: the degree to which political activism is appropriate.

During the tumultuous years of the New Deal, foresters debated with intensity whether they should participate in programs that had overtones of social reform or political bias or whether they should "stick to forestry." This narrow view that forestry is "above politics" has remained strong, allowing others a clearer field to influence significantly the course of forestry events through legislation and adjudication, much to the dismay of SAF.

SAF is governed by a council of regional delegates who are elected for three-year, staggered terms. An executive vice-president, appointed by the council for two-year terms, is SAF's executive officer. The House of Society Delegates, comprised of regional chairmen, has in recent years grown in stature and influence within the organization. Following a formal procedure, the council adopts policies on important issues, which become the official SAF position.

Membership in SAF has steadily expanded. Beginning with seven members in 1900, the ranks had grown to approximately 4,600 by 1940 and to more than 21,000 by 1980. The organization has also decentralized from its Washington, D.C., base; the first regional section was formed in 1913, and by 1975, there were twenty-four sections with 150 chapters nationwide. During the early 1980s, section boundaries were being shifted to coincide more nearly with state boundaries rather than with timber types. Since 1975, SAF national headquarters has been at Wildacres, a thirty-five-acre campus in Bethesda, Maryland, which also houses many other natural resource organizations.

FURTHER READING: Ralph S. Hosmer, "The Society of American Foresters: An Historical Summary," *Journal of Forestry* 38 (Nov. 1940): 837-854. Henry Clepper and Arthur B. Meyer, eds., *American Forestry: Six Decades of Growth* (1960).

HAROLD K. STEEN

SOILS

See Forest Soils

SOUTH CAROLINA FORESTS

Geographically, South Carolina has four major regions: mountains, piedmont, sandhills, and coastal plain. The composition of the state's forests tends to parallel these regions. The warm climate, with long summers, mild winters, and rainfall varying from forty-five inches on the coast to over sixty-five inches in the mountains, aided the original forest growth, which covered about 87 percent of the state. In the 1970s, forestland included about 62 percent of the state, or about 12.5 million acres of a total land area of almost 19.9 million acres. Commercial forest acreage had increased steadily since the 1930s but was expected to decline slightly over the next several decades.

Tree species common to the mountain region in the extreme western part of the state at the higher elevation (1,500 feet) are northern red and chestnut oaks, hickory, and eastern white and pitch pines. Mixed oaks, shortleaf pine, hickory, yellow-poplar, and hemlock predominate at lower elevations. The piedmont forests are composed of loblolly, shortleaf, and Virginia pines, with oaks, hickory, and yellow-poplar. Longleaf pine and blackjack oak dominate the sandhills. The major species on the drier sites in the coastal plain are loblolly, slash, and pond pines and mixed oaks. Associated with floodplains in both the coastal plain and lower piedmont are the "bottom forests" of baldcypress, tupelo, gum, bay, ash, water oak, willow, and swamp cottonwood. Palmettoes, magnolias, and live oaks on the coastal plain and a rich understory of flowering trees and shrubs in the upper piedmont and mountains contribute to the state's scenery.

Forest ownership is typical of most Southern states. More than 123,000 acres are held in four forests by the State Commission of Forestry, which was established in 1927. These state forests largely derived from lands purchased by the federal government during the 1930s and later transferred to the state. In addition to the administration of state forests, the commission has prepared management plans for over 68,000 acres owned by nine other state agencies. Two national forests were established in 1936: the Francis Marion near Charleston and the Sumter in three separate parcels in the northwest. The national forests of South Carolina contain almost 600,000 acres of federal land acquired under the WEEKS ACT of 1911 and the CLARKE-MCNARY ACT of 1924. About 18 percent of the state and national forests have been removed from multiple-use forest

A steam donkey engine supplied power for loading logs in South Carolina. Mules were used to pull loaded flatcars along the primitive rail system. Forest History Society Lantern Slide Collection.

management in order to protect wilderness, wildlife, or recreational-cultural values.

The bulk of the commercial forest is privately owned, largely in small holdings. More than 63 percent is held in parcels of 500 acres or smaller, 36 percent by farmers alone. About 20 percent of the value of farm products is derived from forest resources. South Carolina ranks fifth nationally in this regard.

Exploitation began in the colonial period with the exportation of NAVAL STORES to the British West Indies and England. A major industry until late in the nineteenth century, naval stores production dwindled into insignificance in the 1900s. Production of lumber peaked at 897.6 million board feet in 1909, and following improvements in transportation it peaked again at just over 1 billion board feet in 1923. Yellow pine provided over 85 percent of this lumber. Since World War II, lumber production has averaged over 800 million board feet a year. Pulpwood became a significant product after about 1937. Products of South Carolina's forests include pulp, saw timber, plywood, poles, fine furniture and veneer woods, and FIREWOOD.

South Carolina's forests also contribute to the protection of watersheds and to the recreation and tourist industry. Hunting and fishing are increasing.

Hunting centers on small game, white-tail deer, and turkey. Recently, a major controversy has dealt with the potential decline in wildlife habitat resulting from the conversion of hardwood forests into pine plantations. Surveys, however, have consistently shown that hardwood forests are increasing.

Fire, insects, disease, ice, and competition with less desirable tree species significantly reduce productivity in South Carolina's forests. Major insect and disease infestations in recent years have included the southern pine beetle, fusiform on loblolly pine, and littleleaf on shortleaf pine. Southern pine beetle infestation achieves dramatic proportions at periodic intervals. Ice storms sufficient to damage standing timber by glazing occur, on the average, about every five years. One such storm in 1969 did over $60 million damage. Wildfire reached its most damaging level in 1923, shortly before the creation of the State Commission of Forestry. More than 7,000 fires damaged or destroyed about 4 million acres. Invasion by kudzu and Japanese honeysuckle preempts growing space, prevents natural seeding, and smothers adjacent tree growth.

Clemson University is now the major provider of trained foresters and of extension and research in forest-related problems in South Carolina. Its experimental forest of some 17,000 acres is an outgrowth of federal Agricultural Adjustment Administration projects in the late 1930s.

G. WESLEY BURNETT

SOUTH DAKOTA FORESTS

In South Dakota, the only significant forest is in the Black Hills, a geological uplift of approximately 4,500 square miles within the Great Plains. Forests constitute only about 4 percent of the 48,611,000 acres of land in South Dakota; 1,367,000 are in the western Black Hills area and 335,000 acres are scattered throughout the eastern portion of the state. Ponderosa pine is the dominant tree species, but elements of the eastern deciduous, northern spruce, and Rocky Mountain forest and desert vegetation are present. Mixed prairie plant associations cover the interior meadows.

Mining and ranching interests brought rapid settlement after the land was opened by the federal government in 1875. Since then, man has had a profound effect on the presettlement forest that had been kept open by natural fires, which created ideal habitat for elk, grizzly bears, cougars, and other wildlife. Those relatively cool-burning natural fires also favored growth of magnificent pine stands by periodically eliminating overabundant seedlings. After settle-

ment, large areas of the forest were devastated by lumbering operations and by man-caused fires.

To protect this forest resource, President Grover Cleveland proclaimed the Black Hills Forest Reserve in 1897. The reserve became a national forest in 1907, as part of a renaming of all forest reserves; the first commercial harvest of timber on any federal forest was made there in 1899. Nearly two million acres of land in the Black Hills are suitable for producing commercial timber. Management of the forest, primarily through U. S. FOREST SERVICE programs, reestablished tree stands on devastated areas. Much of the Black Hills are now covered with mature pine forest maintained for timber and water production, for wildlife habitat, and for many kinds of RECREATION that attract several million visitors the year around.

Although the national forest now extends over 90 percent of the Black Hills, other portions are in private ownerships or public entities, including Custer State Park (72,000 acres), Wind Cave National Park (28,292 acres), and Mount Rushmore (1,278 acres) and Jewell Cave (1,274 acres) national monuments. Custer State Park was originally established as a state forest in 1912 but was redesignated as a park in 1919. Wind Cave National Park was established in 1903; Jewell Cave and Mount Rushmore national monuments were proclaimed in 1908 and 1925 respectively. South

Small, portable sawmills fit well the forest conditions of South Dakota. Forest History Society Lantern Slide Collection.

Dakota also contains 73,529 acres of the Custer National Forest and five national wildlife refuges totaling 19,069 acres of land and water. Badlands National Park was originally declared as a national monument in 1929 but redesignated as a park in 1978. It encompasses 243,302 acres, 152,689 of which are federal. Indian forestlands total 321,145 acres.

The South Dakota Department of Game, Fish, and Parks, which includes the division of forestry, was established in 1945. At that time, there was only Custer State Park, but by 1975, South Dakota had forty-five park and recreation areas totaling 90,000 acres. The forestry division administers the farm and forestry program, fire protection, and tree distribution.

There are scattered patches of locally significant forest growing in other areas of the state. Ponderosa pine with mixed hardwoods are on tablelands of the Cave Hills, Slim Buttes, and Pine Ridge in the northwest and southwest sectors. Eastern hardwoods grow along some water courses and in a few isolated areas in the eastern part of the state.

FURTHER READING: O. E. Guthe, "The Black Hills of South Dakota and Wyoming," *Papers of Michigan Academy of Science, Arts, and Letters* 20 (1955): 343-376. A. C. McIntosh, "A Botanical Survey of the Black Hills of South Dakota," *Black Hills Engineer* 25 (1931): 3-74. Carl A. Newport, *Forest Service Policies in Timber Management and Silviculture as They Affect the Lumber Industry: A Case Study of the Black Hills* (1956). D. R. Progulske, *Yellow Ore, Yellow Hair, Yellow Pine* (1974).

DONALD R. PROGULSKE

SOUTHERN FORESTRY CONGRESS

Forestry and a commitment to conservation were slower to develop in the South than in the other timber regions of the United States. Southeastern states lagged behind the Northeast, the Lake States, and the Pacific Northwest in establishing forestry agencies, and even federal forestry activities were established in other sections before, in the 1920s, the U. S. FOREST SERVICE began giving much attention to the South.

In part this was due to the generally retarded economic development of the former Confederacy and the states' rights provincialism of Southern congressmen. As a result, the Southern pinewoods and hardwood forests were the worst managed and most depleted in the nation. In order to remedy this, the AMERICAN FORESTRY ASSOCIATION (AFA) and the SOCIETY OF AMERICAN FORESTERS sponsored the first Southern Forestry Congress (SFC) in July 1916 in Asheville, under the auspices of the North Carolina Geological and Economic Survey. Joseph Hyde Pratt

served as principal executive officer through most of the life of the congress.

Designed to be a permanent membership organization meeting annually, the congress was suspended during the war years and did not meet again until 1920 (in New Orleans). Subsequently, congresses were held annually. During the 1920s, largely because of SFC efforts and the anxious cooperation of the Forest Service, numerous state forests were established throughout the South and state forestry agencies were founded in South Carolina, Georgia, Florida, Alabama, Mississippi, and Arkansas.

The congress also collaborated in organizing the American Forestry Association's Southern Forestry Educational Project. The project's "Dixie Crusaders" launched a propaganda campaign that eventually reached people in 8,000 remote towns. Its chief target was the regional tradition of woods burning in order to green them for grazing. Through film and lectures, this largest of forestry education programs was, according to the young state forestry agencies in the South, immensely successful.

The SFC last met in 1930 and was inactive thereafter. Industrial conditions during the Great Depression delayed further meetings, and with the New Deal's accelerated federal and state programs, the peculiar sectional problems that had resulted in the formation of the SFC were submerged into national policy. Considering that its major objectives had been accomplished or substantially advanced, the SFC formally dissolved in 1939 after turning its small assets over to the AFA.

SPANISH AND MEXICAN FOREST POLICIES IN CALIFORNIA

By 1777, Indian crews directed by padres and soldiers were chopping and pit-sawing redwood rafter and lintel beams in the forests of the San Francisco peninsula for the adobe missions of Santa Clara and Dolores. Soon, cargoes of lumber were being shipped from Monterey along the coast to Santa Barbara and San Diego for use in the construction of missions and forts. As early as 1815, Indian crews were sent into the Marin woods to obtain redwood beams for the Presidio of San Francisco; later, the same woods provided lumber for the building of Yerba Buena near the presidio.

A decree of the Spanish court dated June 23, 1813, ordered the local *ayuntamientos* (essentially township governments) to conserve and replant the "woods and plantations" of their communities. But such rules meant little where the users were so few, the virgin forests so vast, and lumber not yet an important object of commerce.

Under the unstable governments of the Mexican Republic after 1822, remote Upper California seemed a thinly settled province cast adrift. Large grants of land, including former mission lands, passed into private hands. Cattle hides and tallow were shipped out in great quantity. Hand-sawed lumber and hand-split shakes also became an export as well as an internal article of commerce. This newly important industry was directly related to the gradual immigration of Americans and Europeans who slipped in through the mountain passes or deserted their ships. Generally lumped as *Anglos* by the Mexican population, these foreigners were a rough lot of no particular allegiance, but a few were able craftsmen experienced in the harvesting and utilization of wood.

Joseph Chapman, a native of Maine, constructed California's first waterpowered sawmill at Mission San Gabriel between 1823 and 1825. In the 1830s, other *Anglos* operated a number of sawpits in the Santa Cruz Mountains and south of Monterey on the Sur River. American merchant Thomas Larkin was a principal exporter of lumber products as early as 1834. Near Santa Rosa that year, Larkin's half-brother John Cooper, a California citizen, built the first commercial waterpowered sawmill in the province. Steam equipment was not employed until Stephen Smith brought an engine around the Horn in 1843 and set up a grain and lumber mill at Bodega.

The economic activities of these foreigners threatened the political stability of the Mexican province. So did Russians from Alaska who from 1812 until 1841 maintained a colony at Bodega Bay and Fort Ross, a short distance north of San Francisco. Also disturbing were the actions of the Swiss John Sutter, recipient of a land grant in the Sacramento Valley, who welcomed American overland pioneers. The Russians logged nearby redwoods, while Sutter obtained pine timber from the Sierra Nevada.

The *Californios* had little need of government since they were so few and so isolated. Not until August 7, 1830, did the Provincial Assembly or *Diputacion* at Monterey enact a *reglamento* pertaining to trade in lumber and fuelwood. This regulation set prices for wood by the size of pieces or volume, forbade waste, and warned that no large piece of wood should be destroyed in order to secure a small piece. Apparently in recognition of the role of sea commerce, buyers were to be responsible for payment and for transportation of lumber to the beach or other destination. The regulation granted inhabitants the privilege of the trade and required that cutting fees be paid into the local municipal fund.

In response to reports that foreigners (no doubt meaning the *Anglos* concentrated around Santa Cruz) were destroying the forests near San Francisco, Governor Jose Figueroa issued a decree in November 1834 that ordered each *ayuntamiento* to enforce the decree of 1813, made captains of vessels responsible for the legality of their cargoes, and provided legal means for ships to acquire repair material. Surprisingly, Figueroa's decree included a clause providing that "exportation of timber from the territory is forbidden." In practice the prohibition was ignored or circumvented by the *Anglos*, who often were slow to pay their cutting fees as well.

In 1839, the Mexican minister of the interior warned of soil erosion, floods, and droughts due to careless destruction of the forests and recommended legislation to restrict cutting and encourage the replanting of forests. These advanced ideas produced meager results in California, however. The municipal council at Santa Barbara that year forbade nearby cutting of timber without official permit, and in 1841 the *Diputacion* reminded sawyers, "Mexican as well as foreigners," that they must pay their cutting fees.

The last measure of California's Mexican government in respect to forest conservation came with an order of the *Diputacion* signed by Governor Pio Pico on May 23, 1845. This act prohibited lumber harvesting without permission of landowners, permitted cutting of lumber for public service on private land, provided for common use (with compensation) of fuel and other wood from private lands, and reiterated established rules relating to firewood. A year later, American military forces occupied California, and the languid Spanish-Mexican era came to an end. With it began several decades of official indifference for the protection of forests.

FURTHER READING: Alan K. Brown, *Sawpits in the Spanish Red Woods 1787–1849* (1966). Sherwood D. Burgess, "Lumbering in Hispanic California," *California Historical Society Quarterly* 41 (Sept. 1962): 237-248. C. Raymond Clar, *California Government and Forestry*, vol. 1 (1959), pp.3-52, and *Harvesting and Use of Lumber in Hispanic California* (1971).

C. RAYMOND CLAR

SPANISH MOSS

An epiphytic, that is, air-growing, plant, *Tillandsia usneoides* is native to the southeastern United States and is known variously as Spanish moss, Florida moss, New Orleans moss, long moss, black moss, and vegetable moss. It was extensively used by the Muskogean-speaking Indians who originally occupied the area. The Creek, Choctaw, Apalachee, Chickasaw,

Live oak forest in South Carolina festooned with moss. Forest History Society Photo, Robert K. Winters Collection.

and Seminole peoples braided the hairlike strands of the moss and fashioned baskets, hats, mats, clothing, and lines from the braids. Spanish, French, and English pioneers in Atlantic and Gulf colonies adopted these crafts in order to meet household needs in isolated settlements. However, although specimens were shipped to Europe, no substantial commerce developed.

In the early nineteenth century, a device patterned on the cotton gin was developed for cleaning the fibers of the moss, and marginal farmers and slaves gathered it for sale as furniture stuffing and packing. Locally manufactured mattresses, pillows, saddles, horse collars, and saddle blankets were padded with Spanish moss. Because it reproduces easily and ranges from northern North Carolina into eastern Texas, it was readily available throughout much of the plantation South.

By the 1930s, the moss was gathered on a large scale. The picking season, involving as many as 18,000 people a year by 1940, ran from November through April. Most of the workers were poor farmers or sharecroppers, black and white, augmenting their income off season. Typically, they worked in family groups.

By the end of the 1940s, Spanish moss brought as much as $3 million a year into Louisiana and Florida and somewhat smaller amounts into Mississippi and Alabama. Although the demand flagged somewhat in the 1950s, the crop continued large, and working the harvest could be lucrative. An industrious picker could gather about 500 pounds of moss a day at about 1-3/4 to 3 cents a pound. An added inducement was the discovery by several Southern agriculturists that the moss was a favorite wintering place of the boll weevil; moss harvest aided the cotton industry.

Although none predicted the possible extinction of the rapidly reproducing plant (it is not a parasite—the host is simply a means of support, and Spanish moss grows on telephone wires and fences as well as on trees), by the 1970s, the gathering of Spanish moss was reduced to a minor affair. Depletion of the most accessible fields, higher wages in other less seasonal work, decreased demand for the moss as a result of the development of synthetic fillers and packing, and the general tenor of the environmentalist movement all contributed to this reduction. In some state and national forests in the region, commercial picking was forbidden by 1980.

FURTHER READING: A. J. Panshin et al., *Forest Products* (1962).

SPRUCE PRODUCTION DIVISION, U. S. ARMY SIGNAL CORPS

Sitka spruce (*Picea sitchensis*) grows abundantly on the coasts of the Pacific Northwest, but until 1917 it was of relatively little interest to lumbermen. The market for the wood was limited and, to the extent that it was harvested, it was taken as a by-product of fir operations.

American entry into the World War in the spring of 1917 created a huge market for the previously neglected wood. In the early days of aviation, Sitka spruce was the best and for a time the only lumber used in the construction of strut-and-canvas aircraft. The American aircraft industry had lagged behind Europe's and could make do with the region's incidental production. However, the nation's new allies wanted 7 to 8 million board feet a month.

Even with attractive terms, Pacific Northwest lumbermen were, by the fall of 1917, able to provide only 3 million board feet and, according to Colonel, later Brigadier General, Bryce P. Disque, only about half of that was suitable for AIRCRAFT CONSTRUCTION. There were several problems. A chaotic competitive situation discouraged the extensive capital outlays required to tap the isolated spruce stands, and labor relations in the region were in a turmoil as a result of the efforts of the militant Industrial Workers of the World (IWW) to organize and lead strikes of the previously nonunion loggers.

In October, Disque was under orders to sail for France when he was suddenly assigned to go to Portland and take over the critical spruce industry. It is difficult to imagine a better choice for the job of trebling production within a few months. Disque's love of order was virtually a fetish. He was all soldier. "In my opinion," he later wrote, "all citizens of the nation should go on the same status in time of war." If he had had his way, capital would have been conscripted as well as men. However, and somewhat unjustly to him, circumstances were to make him a hero of the lumbermen and, to many industry workers, something of a villain.

Disque's dynamic personality immediately awed the lumbermen he met in Portland, especially when he announced that his first task would be to resolve the labor crisis in the region. His solution was twofold. He organized and led a new service unit, the Spruce Production Division (SPD), 30,000 men strong, its enlisted ranks consisting of soldiers and inductees with woods experience, who were put to work in the lumber industry at civilian wages. He also organized the LOYAL LEGION OF LOGGERS AND LUMBERMEN (4L), a kind of industrywide company union in which employers and workers were brought together under the aegis of patriotism into a civilian auxiliary which would provide labor and managerial skills supplemental to the SPD. Together, the SPD and the 4L undercut the IWW by radically improving wages, hours,

and working conditions in the woods, by localizing in the Pacific Northwest any IWW infestation in the army, and by providing in the SPD a potential police unit in the event of any radical outbreaks.

The SPD was a great anomaly in the history of American business, not to mention of the lumber industry, and of the American military. The U. S. Army directly and officially took over a huge and essentially new industry, provided about 30 percent of the labor force for it, and pioneered both the opening of new forestlands to exploitation and the new milling technology required by aircraft manufacture. Disque directed the construction of railroads, seasoning kilns, new kinds of mills, and even marketing procedures. The SPD was

Members of the Spruce Production Division use a ratchet jack to split a Sitka spruce log for easier handling. Forest Service Photo.

immensely successful; by the armistice, it had increased production seventeen times. Most of the lumber was efficiently dispatched to England, France, and Italy by way of the Panama Canal.

It was expensive, however. The SPD was criticized for paying soldiers civilian wages which, by the end of the war, were quite high, and for the government's total expenditure of $45.5 million. But, as Disque somewhat peevishly replied, the employers, not the government, paid the "khaki loggers," and to have permitted a soldier-civilian differential would have created resentments in both parts of the labor force. As for the total cost of the operation, much of it was essential capital investment in roads, railways, and mills which were sold, albeit at salvage prices, to various private operators. The short, queer history of the SPD was unsettling to every interest group involved. The lumbermen were pleased with their huge profits, the settlement of their labor difficulties, and the improvements which they purchased at bargain prices. In retrospect, however, they were disturbed by the totality of army management. The workers saw their union, seemingly on the verge of job control, undercut and effectively destroyed. There would not be an effective unionism among loggers until the late 1930s but, although he crippled the IWW, Disque also improved wages and living conditions in the forests to unprecedented levels. Except in small GYPPO logging operations, the logger would never again be the sorely exploited and abused "timber beast" of prewar times. Political progressives liked to point to the SPD's example of rational government management of an industry as proof in their campaign against unbridled capitalism. But they were disturbed that it was the army employing strict military discipline that did the job.

FURTHER READING: U. S. Army, Spruce Production Division, *History of the Spruce Production Division, United States Army, and United States Spruce Production Corporation* (1920).

STATE FORESTRY

The role of state governments in forestry has followed two paths—the management of forests on state-owned lands and the protection and then regulation of privately owned forestlands within the respective states. Federal programs have looked to federal lands, with the important exceptions of encouragement and cooperation, and until recently have not been otherwise involved with state and private lands. Thus, his-

torically, jurisdiction of private land has been at the state or local level.

Some states have retained portions of their various and substantial federal land grants received when admitted to the union. Land exchanges, purchases, and gifts have added to state-owned forest domains. Resources on these lands of course have value, and state forestry agencies sell or lease their resources to generate revenue for specific programs, often in education or road construction and maintenance. The lands also gave states an opportunity to demonstrate good forestry techniques, as examples for private landowners to follow. The success of these demonstration forests has not been measured.

Less understood and philosophically more complex than management of state lands are state responsibilities for privately owned forestland. Collection of statistics, unification of commerce, and protection of water and forest resources were primary justifications for the initial efforts. California and New York began forestry programs in 1885, making them among the first states to do so. Impetus came from farmers concerned about water supply, lumbermen with valuable holdings vulnerable to fire, politicians seeking ways to safeguard their state's economic base, and private citizens of influence whom history would later describe as early conservationists.

At the beginning of the twentieth century, many legislatures authorized the creation of agencies that were responsible for the protection of forests held by the state and also those in private ownership. It is not clear whether these concurrent programs were only coincidental, whether the states were prompted by events on the national scene, or whether states were following the lead of other states, but nonetheless, early in the twentieth century, state forestry began to gain momentum. These generally small agencies received a substantial boost from the WEEKS ACT of 1911, which made up to $10,000 in federal money available every year to support each state protection program that qualified. The 1924 CLARKE-MCNARY ACT added still more federal assistance and in fact quickly became the financial mainstay of nonfederal fire protection and suppression efforts. Clarke-McNary also provided a comprehensive study of forestland TAXATION, a topic of continual interest to all sectors of the forest community. The Cooperative Farm Forestry Act of 1937, the Forest Pest Control Act of 1947, and the Cooperative Forest Management Act of 1950 were other important federal laws that enabled state agencies to increase substantially their ability to protect and improve forested lands within their jurisdiction. The bulk of this cooperative federal–state effort has been administered by the Division of State and Private Forestry of the U. S. FOREST SERVICE.

The issue of property taxation had been discussed at forestry gatherings since the 1880s and 1890s, when the psychological impact of taxes on investment decisions began to be articulated. Subsequent studies and especially the decade-long Clarke-McNary tax inquiry helped to clarify the issues and to present options. The chief stumbling block was that states, through county assessors, levied property taxes, and most state constitutions prohibited assessing land in ways favoring a specific category of land, such as forestland. Thus, when in the 1920s and 1930s states looked for ways to modify the basis of taxing forestland as a means to encourage voluntary conservation measures, many found that the first step was a constitutional amendment. This done, the way was clear for legislation to make properly classified forestland eligible to be taxed by methods that would spur reforestation following logging, usually by deferring the bulk of taxes until there was income from the next timber harvest. More recently, open space, greenbelt, and agricultural preserve legislation have added other tax options for forestland owners.

In 1920, Pennsylvania State Forester Gifford PINCHOT invited all state foresters to a conference in Harrisburg. The delegates agreed that coordinated efforts were needed and formed the Association of State Foresters. The group selected William T. Cox of Minnesota as its first president. The organization grew in numbers and scope and since 1963 has been known as the NATIONAL ASSOCIATION OF STATE FORESTERS, addressing the myriad issues that state foresters face in modern times.

States have made other less direct but still influential impacts on their forests. Beginning with Cornell University in 1898, formal education in forestry was offered by state colleges and universities as well as by private institutions. Today, there are more than fifty four-year forestry programs with forty-four accredited by the SOCIETY OF AMERICAN FORESTERS. Graduates of these programs have brought advanced skills to public agencies and to the industrial sector. As the conservation movement evolved throughout the twentieth century, forestry school graduates have played leadership roles in the implementation and enforcement of the lengthening list of management options and legislative mandates.

The topic of legislative mandates has been very controversial in forestry circles for more than three-quarters of a century, and the emergence of state authority in the 1940s resulted from compromises between extreme views. Earlier campaigns to impose federal regulation on private forestlands were deflected in favor of cooperation and incentive programs. When regulation of some sort seemed inevitable, supporters of state authority outweighed advocates of federal rules. By the end of the 1940s, state forest-practice acts provided a degree of regulation for most of the nation's privately owned forestlands.

Generally, these earlier forest-practice acts were not stringent. Lumbermen had to take reasonable precautions to prevent fire and in some cases were required to make provisions for reforestation following logging; in a few instances, logging itself was regulated. However mild these rules now seem, they were challenged in the courts. In 1949, the U. S. Supreme Court upheld the Washington State Supreme Court decision that the 1945 forest-practice act in that state was constitutional. The plaintiffs had claimed that to place restrictions on the use of private property constituted "taking" without compensation, an apparent violation of the Constitution's Fifth Amendment. When the high court ruled that regulation was a legitimate use of police power, its landmark decision validated the underlying premise of all state forest-practice acts.

The 1970s saw many states revising their forestland legislation in response to a nationwide wave of environmental concern. The original legislation which had required only that the operator provide for fire protection and perhaps reforestation, now often mandated harvesting practices and reforestation. Further, the earlier focus on timber production was augmented by broader considerations of soil, water, wildlife, and recreation values.

The 1970s also saw an attempt to set federal standards for state forest-practice laws. The Environmental Protection Agency (EPA) in 1973 proposed a model for state forestry legislation that drew heavily on the California law enacted that same year. EPA rationalized its venture into forest practices in terms of a broader mandate to achieve specific levels of water quality. Another justification for uniform standards could have been a need to attenuate the impact of diverse requirements on companies operating in several states. Whatever the rationale, the proposal failed to attract adequate support, and EPA looked to other means to carry out its responsibilities.

Even though federal environmental legislation, which included setting goals for water quality, brought the force of the national government directly onto private forestlands, state regulations have retained their dominance. In fact, in 1977, Congress exempted forest practices from the most important of these federal constraints, assuring that state forest-practice acts would continue to be the nation's primary means of regulating forestry activities on private land.

FURTHER READING: Jay P Kinney, *The Development of Forest Law in America* (1917). Ralph R. Widner, ed., *Forests and Forestry in the American States* (1968).

HAROLD K. STEEN

STATE PARKS MOVEMENT

There were state parks in the United States long before there was a state parks movement. The latter did not appear until about 1920, but the former have been present at least in embryonic form since colonial times.

Historically, state parks have embraced a multitude of types of areas dedicated to a host of different uses. The emergence of the state parks movement brought some uniformity, but diversity has continued. As Robert Y. STUART, then secretary of the Pennsylvania Department of Forests and Waters, said in 1924, "Practically every State is working out a policy and program along its own lines. The public finds that the 'State Park' in one state may be quite different in conception, administration, and purpose from the State Park in another state." State parks have encompassed developed and undeveloped areas; sites primarily cherished for their historic, scenic, or recreational value; tracts both large and small; and lands administered by a wide variety of agencies. Sometimes they have been called preserves, waysides, or monuments rather than parks. As Harlean James, an authority on parks and land-use planning, succinctly put it in 1926: "The term park has become a *generic* designation which includes a number of highly differentiated *species.*" This variation inevitably complicates discussion of state parks and of the state parks movement.

Massachusetts Bay Colony has been credited with the first action leading to state parks (or the equivalent). In 1641, its authorities set aside its "Great Ponds" as reserves for fishing and hunting. Included were all bodies of fresh water ten acres or more in size: some 2,000 lakes, totaling approximately 90,000 acres. However, this legislation was soon largely forgotten; not until 1898 did Massachusetts acquire Mount Greylock, its first area actually to be administered as a park.

The real vanguard of state parks came in the nineteenth century. In 1820, Governor DeWitt Clinton urged New York's legislature to halt sales of state land in the Adirondack Mountains. In 1885, the legislature finally acted, stopping sales and authorizing the NEW YORK STATE FOREST PRESERVE, which was to evolve into the nation's largest state park (embracing over 2.25 million acres of public land). Also in 1885, New York established Niagara State Reservation at the falls of the Niagara River. It was from the beginning a full-fledged state park. In the meantime, Congress in 1864 authorized, and California two years later accepted, Yosemite Valley and the nearby Mariposa Grove of giant sequoias as a state park. However, after prolonged controversy, this land was re-ceded to the federal government in 1906 to be incorporated into YOSEMITE NATIONAL PARK. In 1875, Congress created Mackinac National Park on Mackinac Island, Michigan. In 1895, reversing the process followed with Yosemite Valley, this land was ceded to Michigan and became Mackinac Island State Park. Wisconsin also acted early. In 1878, it set aside several tracts of state-owned timber as a "park." The reason for the action is not clear, although its primary purpose was probably watershed protection for flood control. The land was never administered as a park—indeed, it was simply neglected until disposed of beginning in 1897.

Out of all this has come a welter of claims to the first state park. Sites in Massachusetts, California, and New York have all been accorded the honor, and others could easily be added to the list of candidates. The best claim to primacy is that made in behalf of Niagara. No state park still in existence became one at an earlier date; none of the Great Ponds of Massachusetts were actually treated as parks until long after Niagara.

Around the turn of the century, more states began setting aside historic, scenic, and recreational sites as parks. In 1893, Minnesota acquired two parks: Birch Coulee, location of a battle between whites and Sioux, and Itasca State Park on the headwaters of the Mississippi River. In 1895 the nucleus of Palisades Interstate Park, along the Hudson River in New York and New Jersey, was acquired, and in 1900 Big Basin Redwoods State Park was launched in California. Growing interest in national parks and the activities of nature lovers and outdoor organizations lent indirect support and momentum to state and local efforts in behalf of parks.

Out of this amorphous, disconnected activity, a nationwide campaign for state parks gradually emerged. Stephen T. MATHER, first director of the National Park Service, believed that only the finest sites deserved national park status and that, since funds were limited, parks duplicating types of scenery already represented in the system should not be added. Mather recognized that this meant that numerous deserving locations would have to be protected in some other way. As early as 1919, he was traveling widely, trying to encourage efforts toward scenery preservation at the state and local levels. At the time, only twenty states had parks of their own; Mather hoped to encourage more. He helped create the SAVE-THE-REDWOODS LEAGUE, whose activities were to result in state parks among California's coastal redwoods, parks that became the heart of the REDWOOD NATIONAL PARK when it was created in 1968. In addition, with the support of Secretary of the Interior John Barton Payne and Governor W. L. Harding of Iowa, Mather arranged for a conference on state parks in Des Moines in 1921. Two hundred delegates from twenty-five states attended; most were private citizens. A permanent organization, the NATIONAL CONFERENCE ON STATE PARKS (NCSP), resulted. Payne became chairman, but the NCSP was administered from the office of vice-chairman Mather, who contributed considerable sums from his personal fortune to underwrite its efforts. Mather became chairman in 1927 and was succeeded after his death by Richard Lieber, director of the Indiana Department of Conservation. Under Payne, Mather, and Lieber, the NCSP became the driving force behind the burgeoning state parks movement.

Mather and the NCSP were so successful because interest was already present among key figures at the state and local levels. Many early parks, such as Baxter in Maine (established 1931) and Moran in Washington (1921), resulted from donations by private citizens; numerous others, including Cook Forest in Pennsylvania (1927) and Custer in South Dakota (1919) came into being as a result of pressure on government agencies by individuals and groups.

Efforts on behalf of state parks were unevenly spread during the 1920s. Activity was strong from Maine to South Dakota and on the Pacific Coast, but little was under way in the South or the Rocky Mountain-Intermountain Basin states. The pattern is understandable. In the South, poverty, the plantation-pastoral ideal, and the weakness of the transcendentalist tradition (with its New England, abolitionist overtones) combined to lessen the appreciation of unsullied natural scenes that undergirded the state parks movement. In the Rocky Mountain states, on the other hand, advocates of state parks found themselves repeatedly stymied: the large percentage of land still in federal hands, together with attitudes honed during struggles against the "locking up" of resources by the federal government in forest reserves and national parks, had created a local climate of opinion hostile to any additional withdrawals of land from commercial use. Governor W. P. Hunt of Arizona reflected regional sentiments: when invited to send delegates to the NCSP meetings in 1928, he refused, saying that all land in Arizona fit for parks was under federal control and that plenty of land in the state had already been set aside for parks anyway. Efforts to get park systems established in Nevada and Utah died aborning, while promising campaigns in Texas and Florida soon bogged down. Heyburn State Park in Idaho (1911) and Mount Mitchell State Park in North Carolina (1915) remained the only significant parks in the two regions.

The National Park Service continued to be supportive of state efforts after Mather's retirement, but friction developed when Senator Charles MCNARY of Oregon proposed legislation for federal aid to state parks. The NCSP at first endorsed the proposal but then backed off in 1931 under pressure from National Park Service officials, who were worried by the threat to their programs from the diversion of federal funds for parks to state use.

The Great Depression was a turning point for state parks. The NCSP was hit hard by a dearth of financial support. It cut back, combining its offices (and many of its activities) with those of the American Civic Association, which itself merged with the National Conference on City Planning to form the American Planning and Civic Association (APCA). Herbert Evison, who had been serving as executive secretary of the NCSP, moved over to the National Park Service to serve as liaison between the federal service and state parks departments; Harlean James served from 1935 to 1957 as executive secretary for both the APCA and the NCSP.

The Depression brought a tremendous windfall to state parks: the CIVILIAN CONSERVATION CORPS (CCC). By 1935, there were some 600 CCC camps carrying on work in parks in practically every state. Some states that had never had park systems, such as New Mexico, were now able to build them, and states long active in parks could push ahead at an unprecedented pace. Samuel H. Boardman, superintendent of Oregon's parks, estimated that CCC work put the parks in his charge twenty-five years ahead of where they would otherwise have been. D. E. Colp, chairman of the Texas State Parks Board, credited the impressive amount of CCC work in state parks to the efforts of the NCSP, without which "very little, if any, Emergency Conservation Work would have been done" in them.

The National Park Service oversaw CCC work in

state parks and had to approve all plans. Friction between state and federal officials sometimes resulted. Boardman, who wished to keep Oregon's parks natural, complained that federal planners wanted to "festoon the stars and moon"; he struggled steadily to blunt such tendencies in Oregon's parks. With a combination of relief and pride, he once reported to an associate that he had kept the federal planners from doing "any damage." But most state officials were not the purist that Boardman was. They scrambled for more and more CCC work in their parks and were delighted when they got it.

The Park, Parkway, and Recreation Area Act of 1936 also furthered state parks work. Under this act, the National Park Service, the U. S. FOREST SERVICE, and other agencies, state and federal, carried out regional surveys of recreational sites, facilities, and demand, both present and projected. These surveys made possible a level of sophistication in the planning and management of state parks that had never before been attained. In 1928, California had hired Frederick Law OLMSTED, Jr., to survey the state's parks and potential park sites and to recommend policies and a long-range program, but that action had stood out as the exception to the norm until the Park, Parkway, and Recreation Area Act encouraged the same sort of thing elsewhere.

Tastes in scenery were changing during the period. Deserts and other types of areas that had at first been overlooked—or disdained—slowly came to be embraced within state parks. Anza-Borrego Desert State Park in California, established in 1933, exceeded in size all but New York's Adirondack State Park. Historic preservation was also being more frequently included in state parks work. The same shifting interests that were affecting the national parks were at work shaping state parks too.

Parks activity came to a virtual halt during World War II. The annual meetings of the NCSP, which had long served as both rallying points and clearinghouses, were discontinued for the duration. But state parks work expanded rapidly after the war, especially with the boom in tourism that came in the 1950s. Under the leadership of Governor Robert Smylie, Idaho at last moved to create a Department of Parks and Recreation and to give it sufficient funds to build a real system of parks. Other laggards began to move as well, especially after the passage of the Land and Water Conservation Fund Act by Congress in 1964. Through the fund created by this act, federal aid to state parks at last became a reality.

Much that was taking place in postwar parks activity was essentially new. Earlier, well-to-do citizens, middle class civic organizations, local boosters, and dedicated amateurs had been the backbone of the state parks movement, providing invaluable support to the relative handful of park administrators and the workers under them. Many of the older park administrators, including Lieber and Boardman, had lacked professional training for their jobs. Gradually, such people were replaced by those with professional training in recreation or some related field. Meanwhile, the attention of amateur conservationists was turning away from the state parks; WILDERNESS PRESERVATION, WILD AND SCENIC RIVERS, endangered species, and other issues now absorbed their time. The old state parks movement was coming to an end.

The professionalization of state parks work led to organizational changes. Much of what the NCSP had once done was now handled by the American Institute of Park Executives (AIPE) and then by the National Association of State Park Directors, founded in 1962. In 1965, the NCSP and the AIPE merged into the NATIONAL RECREATION AND PARK ASSOCIATION, a group serving the needs of federal, state, and local parks.

Bigger budgets and a new level of expert management came to the state parks, but as crusading amateurs turned to other concerns there was an attendant loss of activist interest in and support of parks, even as the number of people using them continued to rise. The state parks movement was an important part of American social history during the period between the two world wars. It was in this social movement and its forerunners, not in the work of parks professionals, that the state parks systems of today were spawned.

FURTHER READING: Thomas R. Cox, "From Hot Springs to Gateway: The Evolving Concept of Public Parks, 1832–1976," *Environmental Review* 5 (1981): 14-26. Herbert Evison, ed., *A State Park Anthology* (National Conference on State Parks, 1930). Phillip O. Foss, *Recreation* (1971), pp. 223-290. Beatrice Ward Nelson, *State Recreation: Parks, Forests, and Game Preserves* (National Conference on State Parks, 1928). Freeman Tilden, *The State Parks: Their Meaning in American Life* (1962).

THOMAS R. COX

STEPHENSON, ISAAC (1829–1918)

Isaac Stephenson was born on June 18, 1829, in Maugerville, New Brunswick, of Scotch-Irish ancestry. As a youth, he learned the "practical side of lumbering" under the tutelage of a Maine lumberman, Jefferson Sinclair. At the age of sixteen, Stephenson left Maine for southern Wisconsin, working for a year on a farm near Janesville. The following year, in 1847, he began work as a timber cruiser in Michigan's Upper Peninsula.

Retaining his boyhood love of the outdoors, Stephenson explored and later bought pinelands in Michigan's Upper Peninsula and in northeastern Wisconsin. These lands became the basis of one of the great lumbering fortunes, ultimately estimated at about $5 million. Both his knowledge as a timber cruiser and his skill in managing mills and handling people were undoubtedly instrumental in the selection of Stephenson to manage the Nelson-Ludington mill in Marinette at the age of twenty-nine. He secured a quarter interest in this mill, and Marinette remained his home for the rest of his life.

In the aftermath of the panic of 1857, credit was scarce and Stephenson was forced to practice sharp economies in order to keep his firm's mill solvent. But a major turning point in the lumbering history of Green Bay and Stephenson's career occurred in 1863 when a drought in western Wisconsin put the pineries of the state's major western rivers at a disadvantage because lumbermen there could not float their logs and lumber rafts downriver to market on the Mississippi. However, Stephenson and his partners were able to ship lumber directly to the Chicago market, and from Chicago westward on railroads to the growing farm communities beyond the Mississippi, places formerly supplied from western Wisconsin. This opportunity established a pattern for the Green Bay pinery for much of the rest of the nineteenth century, helping to secure for Stephenson and the lumber companies with which he was associated both wealth and success. By 1870, Stephenson was Marinette's wealthiest citizen.

Stephenson excelled in his knowledge of the woods, his ability to control and direct the flow of logs downriver, his possession of the technical skills to keep sawmill machinery running, and his aptitude in handling logging gangs and sawmill crews. Although he had no formal education as an engineer, Stephenson built over sixty-seven dams on the tributaries of Green Bay, including twenty-seven on the Peshtigo River alone.

In 1867, he organized the Menominee River Boom Company to sort logs on the Menominee River for the mills of Marinette, Wisconsin, and Menominee, Michigan. In the 1870s, he constructed the Sturgeon Bay ship canal, greatly shortening the distance of shipping lumber from the ports of Green Bay to Chicago. He later helped negotiate the construction of the Chicago and North Western Railway to Green Bay and then secured competition for the North Western by helping to organize the Wisconsin-Michigan Railroad in 1893. He also revolutionized the shipment of lumber on Lake Michigan by converting old schooners to lumber barges and using tug boats to pull them efficiently and inexpensively from Marinette-Menominee, Escanaba, and Peshtigo Harbor to Chicago.

Stephenson served in the State Assembly of Wisconsin from 1866 to 1870, and in Congress from 1882 to 1888. In the local community, Stephenson was an economic and social leader and he dominated politics. He was a justice of the peace during his early years in Marinette and had an active hand in the city's incorporation in 1887. His principal political rival was his fellow Green Bay lumberman Philetus SAWYER, "boss" of Wisconsin's Republican party, who blocked Stephenson's ambition to be elected United States senator. Subsequently, Stephenson joined Progressive Republican Robert La Follette to challenge Sawyer's leadership of the party's stalwart faction. La Follette was elected governor of Wisconsin in 1900, and Stephenson, although La Follette did not actively support him, eventually secured the United States Senate seat, serving from 1908 to 1914.

Stephenson, married three times, was survived by six of his eight children. He died in 1918, a year after the last log drive on the Menominee.

FURTHER READING: Carl Krog, "Marinette Lumbermen: A Research Note," *Journal of Forest History* 21 (Apr. 1977): 97–100. Isaac Stephenson, *Recollections of a Long Life, 1829–1915* (1915).

CARL KROG

STREAMFLOW CONTROVERSY

One article of faith among conservationists in the first decade of the twentieth century was the belief that forests had an enormous influence upon streamflow and runoff. The theory had three major facets: forests retain rainfall and streamflow in their beds of humus and expend it gradually to equalize the runoff; forests retard the melting of snow in the spring and prolong the runoff from snow; and forests prevent erosion. The evidence for this set of propositions was drawn from both history and direct observation.

Streamflow proponents contended that once prosperous civilizations in China, North Africa, and the Middle East had decayed because their inhabitants had destroyed the forests. The principal early supporter of this historical theory was George Perkins MARSH, who had included it in his *Man and Nature; or, Physical Geography as Modified by Human Action* (1864). Others, including President Theodore ROOSEVELT, had given it wide currency in addresses and writings.

Many persons, including government scientists

During the early decades of the twentieth century, the Forest Service argued strenuously that there was a direct relationship between forest cover and the severity of floods, as this aftermath of the 1910 fires in Idaho suggests. Subsequent research revealed that the agency had overstated the case. Forest Service Photo.

working in Illinois, Texas, and the Appalachian Mountains, believed that their contemporary observations had confirmed the theory, while still others validated it by deduction or common sense. There were no quantitative studies to support it. Nevertheless, in spite of the paucity of scientific evidence, the streamflow theory was widely accepted by men such as Roosevelt, Gifford PINCHOT, W J McGee, and other prominent conservationists.

The streamflow theory came to have great political significance because of several developments beginning in 1907. The great flooding of the Ohio River in that year was attributed to deforestation of the watersheds of the river and its tributaries. In the same year, Pinchot, McGee, and Marshall O. Leighton pro-

claimed the doctrine of multiple-purpose resource use. Their unit for applying this seminal concept was the river basin. Also in 1907, Senator Francis G. Newlands of Nevada introduced a bill to establish a single federal department with responsibility for all waterways improvements. Both the multiple-purpose theorists and the advocates of the Newlands bill (often the same persons) stressed the direct relationship between deforestation and flooding. Finally, in 1908 a bill sponsored by Representative John W. Weeks of Massachusetts to create an Appalachian National Forest reached a crucial stage. To overcome objections that it was unconstitutional for the national government to acquire lands for forests, the bill was amended to permit the purchase of forested land if it could be shown that this land contributed to the navigability of a river by equalizing streamflow. Such a connection would shelter the bill within Congress's unquestioned power to regulate interstate commerce.

Although it had wide currency, the streamflow thesis also had many opponents. Chief among them were the officers of the ARMY CORPS OF ENGINEERS, whose traditional means of flood control was levee construction. They feared the loss of their river-control prerogatives under the Newlands bill; they were advocates of quantitative, not qualitative, proof through their engineering training; and some of them were fearful of declining corps prestige because of a notorious scandal in a project at Savannah, Georgia. Most serious of all was widespread talk in engineering circles that, because it was too small in numbers, the corps should be relieved of its rivers and harbors work in favor of a civilian Department of Public Works.

The corps struck back at its opponents by pointing out that there was very little quantitative evidence for the streamflow theory. The major architect of this attack was Hiram Martin Chittenden (1858–1917), who wrote an influential paper published in 1908 in the *Proceedings* of the American Society of Civil Engineers. Chittenden, an 1884 graduate of the United States Military Academy, had served in the corps in many stations throughout his professional career. In his essay he discounted the streamflow theory by drawing upon all the published records of river stages for the Connecticut, Mississippi, Ohio, and Tennessee rivers and upon selected data from foreign countries. But in his massive essay, Chittenden could present no accurate information on the amount of land logged on any of the watersheds he studied nor was he aware of any other possible variables in the watersheds.

Chittenden's paper was widely discussed by engineers and politicians. President Roosevelt attacked it in his message to Congress in December 1908. In the next three years, the corps published similar studies of other watersheds and acquired some allies in opposing the streamflow theory, including Charles F. Scott, the chairman of the U. S. House of Representatives' Committee on Agriculture, and Willis Moore, the chief of the United States Weather Bureau. But their opposition was insufficient to defeat the Weeks bill, which finally became law on March 1, 1911 (see WEEKS ACT).

The law required, however, that a connection between forests and streamflow be proved. The first quantitative test of the relationship was made by the U.S. GEOLOGICAL SURVEY in 1912 on two small New Hampshire watersheds, Burnt Brook and Shoal Pond Brook. The survey held that the evidence gathered on these two watersheds justified the acquisition of land for the Appalachian National Forest. The first long-range scientific attempt to assess the streamflow theory began in 1910 at Wagon Wheel Gap in Colorado under the joint supervision of the U. S. FOREST SERVICE and the Weather Bureau and continued for a decade and a half. While its results were awaited, the streamflow theory declined in influence. The Wagon Wheel Gap experiments never proved the accuracy of the streamflow theory. In 1927, after that year's great floods on the Mississippi River, the Geological Survey abandoned the theory and the Forest Service, although unrepentant, began to assess the more limited hypothesis that vegetation helped to prevent erosion. At the present time, scientists still remain uncertain about the specific roles of the variables involved in the relationship between forestry and streamflow.

FURTHER READING: Gordon B. Dodds, *Hiram Martin Chittenden: His Public Career* (1973), pp. 155–185, and "The Stream-Flow Controversy: A Conservation Turning Point," *Journal of American History* 56 (June 1969): 59-69. Ashley L. Schiff, *Fire and Water: Scientific Heresy in the Forest Service* (1962).

GORDON B. DODDS

STUART, ROBERT YOUNG (1883–1933)

Born in Cumberland County, Pennsylvania, on February 13, 1883, Robert Y. Stuart entered the U. S. FOREST SERVICE in July 1906 upon receiving his M.F. degree from Yale University. He began work in the northern Rocky Mountains where in 1910 he became assistant district forester, first in charge of operation and then in charge of SILVICULTURE, which included timber sales and planting. He served there under both William B. GREELEY and Ferdinand A. SILCOX. In November 1912, he followed Greeley to Washington to serve under him again as assistant chief of silviculture. After two years overseas in the tenth and twentieth (Forestry) Engineer Regiments in France during World War I, Stuart returned to the Forest Service. After only a year, he resigned to become deputy commissioner of forestry in Pennsylvania under Gifford PINCHOT in 1920. Two years later, when Pinchot became governor, Stuart became commissioner of forestry in Pennsylvania and, after 1923, secretary of forests and waters. Early in 1927, Stuart rejoined the Forest Service as assistant forester in charge of public relations, and a year later he succeeded Greeley as head of the service.

Stuart, like Greeley, favored encouragement of fire control and good forestry practices on private land rather than regulatory action. He advocated enlarging federal forest holdings in the East, the West, and Alaska to promote practical education by example, and he urged cooperative study and action to insure orderly marketing of timber to prevent overcutting and forest depletion. He recognized that some restraint of private cutting practices might be needed, but he preferred to leave that to the states.

Stuart's term as forester saw forestry research greatly stimulated and a nationwide timber survey begun following enactment of the MCSWEENEY-MCNARY ACT. Reforestation and stand improvement in national forests boosted by the Knutson-Vandenberg Act of 1930, the implementation of a system of primitive and natural areas under the L-20 regulation of 1929, and the revision of grazing fees to reflect livestock prices also took place during his tenure. The Depression and the New Deal resulted in greatly increased responsibilities for the Forest Service. In March 1933, the service issued a two-volume report to Congress, *A National Plan for American Forestry* (the COPELAND REPORT), calling for more intensive management and expansion of public forests. A few weeks later, appropriations were expanded for forest conservation and improvement, research, and land acquisition, while the establishment of the CIVILIAN CONSERVATION CORPS provided new manpower. Stuart and his assistants worked at top speed to get the first camps established and forestry work there underway. Many new national forests were established during his term of office, and field work began for the later establishment of national forests throughout the South and southern Midwest. Overwork must certainly have contributed to Stuart's death on October 23, 1933.

FURTHER READING: Henry Clepper, "Robert Y. Stuart, Indefatigable Worker," *Journal of Forestry* 59 (Nov. 1961): 800. Harold K. Steen, *The U. S. Forest Service: A History* (1976).

FRANK J. HARMON

SWEDISH IMMIGRANTS AND AMERICAN FORESTS

The first important wave of Swedish immigration to America arrived in the 1850s and 1860s; the immigrants were largely farmers and rural workers who headed for the Midwest, especially Illinois and Minnesota. Both the place of residence and the choice of occupation in America were determined to a high degree by the place of birth in Sweden. Many natives of Smaland and Blekinge, for instance, settled in Chisago County in Minnesota, while mainly Dalecarlians came to Isanti County. To a great extent, they found employment in the lumber industry.

The first widely known lumberman of Swedish birth in Minnesota was Charles Alton Smith from Ostergötland. He came to America in 1867 and in 1878 started a lumberyard at Herman in western Minnesota, eventually becoming one of the "lumber kings" of the Midwest. In Minneapolis in 1893, his firm erected a giant lumber-manufacturing establishment, while his subsidiaries bought vast timbered tracts in Oregon and California. Most of Smith's employees were Swedes.

The major Swedish immigration to America began about 1870 and lasted until the Great Depression of the 1930s. During the first two decades, a rapidly rising population together with economic depression and underemployment in their homeland prompted a half-million Swedes to leave for America. Thereafter, the large American Swedish population itself served as an attraction, and Swedes crossed the ocean in search of opportunity. Census statistics in the year 1900 showed that 26,000 Swedes of the first and second generation in the United States were carpenters, joiners, or sawmill workers.

In the late nineteenth and early twentieth centuries, skills learned in Sweden's forests and sawmills benefited the developing forest industries of the Pacific Northwest. Many natives of Värmland, Dalecarlia, and Norrland were to be found in the lumber camps there. In 1919, Ossian Anderson from Skelleftea and two of his brothers bought a modest sawmill in Washington above Tumwater Falls which was the beginning of the far-flung Anderson Brothers organization. In 1922, they began the production of prefabricated houses, known as Tumwater Ready-Cut Homes, which were sold all over the United States and also shipped abroad. In the 1920s, the brothers helped develop the rapidly growing cellulose industry in the Pacific Northwest, becoming the first producers of chemical wood pulp on the West Coast to use waste wood and also the first to ship pulp out of the Northwest. In 1936, Ossian Anderson built the first bleached-kraft mill at Tacoma and, in 1937, a new sulfite mill at Bellingham. By 1940, the plants built under his leadership produced 45 percent of the pulp production of Washington State. Importing equipment from Sweden, the Anderson Brothers in 1928 built the first gang-saw mill in the Northwest. The Swedish gang-saw equipment was gradually adopted by many mills in the American Northwest as well as in British Columbia. Such saws made it profitable to process logs that formerly were either left to rot on the ground or were burned as scrap. Also prominent in forest industry was Carl Magnus Hanson, an immigrant from Västergötland. With his three sons, Hanson in 1898 founded the White River Lumber Company, which became one of the largest lumber concerns in the State of Washington. Another prominent Swede was Edvard Emil Westman of Sundsvall, who settled in Olympia in 1921 and helped build the plywood industry. In the proportion of Swedes in its population, Washington ranked second among the states in 1930, a position it has held ever since.

FURTHER READING: Ulf Beijbom, "Swedes," in *Harvard Encyclopedia of American Ethnic Groups* (1980). Allan Kastrup, *The Swedish Heritage in America* (1975).

LEIF CARLSSON

T

TANNINS

The processing or tanning of skins and hides with extracts of plants to yield leather may be the oldest manufacturing industry of mankind. New World colonists quickly learned to use black oak (*Quercus velutina*) and eastern hemlock (*Tsuga canadensis*) bark for this purpose. Tannin was leached from the bark with water. The relatively weak solution produced required soaking heavy hides up to twelve to fifteen months.

Until the Revolutionary War, tanning was essentially a cottage industry, but with the industrial revolution and the expansion of the United States to the west in the middle 1800s, demand for leather increased exponentially. Leather belting drove the nation's factories, and leather for harnesses and saddles was needed for farming and transportation. Small tanneries sprung up all over the central eastern states. Following the Civil War, production was consolidated into larger factories. In Pennsylvania, for example, there were about 120 large tanneries, 65 of them in 1893 forming themselves into the United States Leather Company, which soon controlled 75 percent of the hemlock stumpage in the state. After pine lumbering opened up the state, vast acreages of hemlock, unwanted by lumbermen, became available to tanners. The bark was peeled into four-foot lengths during the spring or early summer

and quickly transported to the tannery. Here, it was stored in sheds or stacked in piles twenty or thirty feet high.

When ready for use, the bark was ground and then leached with hot water in a series of tanks. The spent bark was dried and used as fuel to generate steam for heating the leach tanks. Two and a half cords of bark were required to produce sufficient tannin for 100 hides. At the peak of the industry in the early 1900s, hemlock was being cut from more than a million acres in Pennsylvania. New England, West Virginia, Kentucky, North Carolina, Wisconsin, Michigan, and other central states also had tanning industries, but the focal point remained in Pennsylvania. Tabor (1974) points out that the Central Leather Company, successor to the United States Leather Company, was in 1910 one of the ten largest firms in the United States; it is also the only one of the ten no longer in existence.

In the early days of hemlock bark tanning, there does not seem to have been any record of the wood being used. Gradually, eastern hemlock lumber came to be marketed as a by-product of the tanning industry. In 1900, according to Brown (1919), nearly 1.2 million cords of hemlock bark were produced in the United States, yielding 72 percent of the total tannin manufactured from domestic sources. By the 1930s, hemlock supplied only 18 percent of the domestic tannins.

Chestnut oak (Q. prinus) bark was also widely used for the manufacture of tannins in the Appalachian region.

On the Pacific Coast, commercial tanning started soon after the Gold Rush; by the end of the nineteenth century, California ranked third in value of tanned hides produced. The chief source of tannins there was the bark of the tanoak (*Lithocarpus densiflorus*), which grew abundantly in the redwood region of the coast range. The state utilized 25,000 cords of tanoak bark in 1900; by that time, most of the accessible stands had been cut. As with eastern hemlock, most of the peeled tanoak logs were left to rot in the forest, only a small portion being used for mine timber or firewood. As eastern supplies of tanning materials were depleted, western hemlock (*T. heterophylla*) was used on a relatively small scale for tanbark in the Pacific Northwest early in the twentieth century.

As oak and hemlock bark became less available, tanners switched to the use of American chestnut (*Castanea dentata*) wood chips as a source of tannin. Chestnut extract produced a much lighter color of leather and was the principal domestic source of tannin after about 1910. However, by the middle 1930s, chestnut blight had destroyed the chestnut forests; for many years, extraction plants continued operating in Virginia, North Carolina, and Tennessee, utilizing wood from dead chestnut trees. Ten plants were still running as late as 1951. The spent chips were sometimes pulped for paper, fiberboard, or use as fuel.

The death of the chestnut essentially left the tanning industry without a source of domestic tanning material. Imported chestnut tannin from Europe, wattle tannin (extracted from acacia bark in South Africa), and quebracho tannin (from Paraguay, Uruguay, and Argentina) gradually supplanted domestic materials. There were only two producers of native tannins in the United States in 1955, and both ceased to operate before 1960.

Chemical investigations have shown that the bark extractives of western hemlock, Douglas-fir (*Pseudotsuga menziesii*), and redwood (*Sequoia sempervirens*) are useful for tanning. The Pacific Lumber Company at Scotia, California, built a plant in the early 1950s to produce a caustic extract of redwood bark, and Rayonier, Inc., built plants at Hoquiam, Washington, and Vancouver, British Columbia, in 1954 and 1956, respectively, to produce sulfonated tannins from hemlock. These tannin-containing extracts from redwood and hemlock bark were used for a time as a supplement to imported tannins, but mostly they were used as dispersants to control the viscosi-ty of oil well drilling fluids. Gradually, their use for this purpose was supplanted by oil-well dispersants produced from spent sulfite liquor, a by-product of the pulp industry, and all three plants shut down. Nevertheless, the study of the chemistry and utilization of tannins from native trees remains a popular subject for wood chemists. The main reason is that the tannin molecules are very reactive toward form-aldehyde and related chemicals and will produce strong thermoset resins under the right circum-stances. As the value of utilizing renewable resources becomes more recognized, the tannin extraction industry could once again become important in the United States.

FURTHER READING: Nelson Courtlandt Brown, *Forest Products: Their Manufacture and Use* (1919); *Timber Products and Industries* (1937); and *Forest Products* (1950). *California Tanbark Oak*, U. S. Forest Service Bulletin 75 (1911). James W. Cruikshank, George H. Hepting, E. Richard Toole, and Elmer R. Roth, *Chestnut Extract Production and the Timber Supply, 1951* (1951). F. W. Herrick and H. L. Hergert, "Utilization of Chemicals from Wood: Retrospect and Prospect," *Recent Advances in Phytochemistry* 2 (1977): 443-515. A. J. Panshin, E. S. Harrar, J. S. Bethel, and W. J. Baker, *Forest Products* (1950; rev. 1962). Thomas T. Taber, III, "Tanbark, Alcohol and Lumber," *Logging Railroad Era of Lumbering in Pennsylvania* 10 (1974): 1082–1091.

HERBERT L. HERGERT

TAXATION

Property Taxes

From colonial times to the present, property taxes have been a major source of local government revenue. Such taxes are levied at a certain percent of property value. In earlier times, taxable property often included many forms of wealth, but in recent decades, the property tax in most states has been restricted mainly to real estate, which in principle would include timber.

In practice, however, much timber value has historically escaped property taxation. Assessors have often not had adequate training to determine accurately timber values or the personnel to keep pace with changing markets and timber growth. Also, where full timber values were annually taxed, forest owners would often harvest timber prematurely to reduce taxes.

By the early 1900s, many foresters were concerned about possible adverse effects of property taxes upon forest management. On the other hand, some writers observed that the cut-and-run forestry of the early

1900s and before was less a result of tax policies than of economic conditions: timber prices were high enough to yield profitable harvest but far too low to promise favorable rates of return on reforestation investments. In the face of such economic odds, private forest management was unlikely to flourish, even without taxes.

Nevertheless, forest taxes remained a concern and were addressed in the 1909 report of the U. S. Conservation Commission. In 1926, the U. S. FOREST SERVICE established the Forest Taxation Inquiry, led by Fred R. Fairchild, which culminated in his monumental 1935 work, *Forest Taxation in the United States*. Fairchild found that tax delinquency on forestlands was widespread in certain states, particularly during the Depression. Although during periods of economic hardship one would generally expect such problems, tax delinquency rates were far higher on forests than on other lands—a fact that suggested a specific forest tax problem. In the early 1930s, it was not uncommon to find 10 to 20 percent of forested areas tax delinquent for two or more years. Much of this tax-delinquent land reverted to state ownership.

Fairchild maintained that the annual property tax was in theory biased against investments with deferred yields, such as reforestation, when compared to investments with shorter payoff periods or small income, such as agriculture. These theoretical arguments are still being debated in the literature, but there does seem to be agreement that the property tax, if levied annually on full market value of land and timber, would tend to be more discouraging to forestry than to most competing land uses, even if forestry values are assigned to the land. The problem becomes worse if forestlands are assessed at high development values where such higher uses are not feasible—a frequent occurrence in the history of forest taxation. This situation has led many states to allow managed forestlands to be taxed at current use values rather than higher development values—a policy that addresses taxes on land but not on timber.

Due to the foregoing problems, the property tax on American forests has been reduced or modified either by legislative design or inaccurate assessment procedures. Even with reduced assessments, however, the problem still remains that as trees become larger and more valuable, the annual property tax increases. This increase can stimulate premature harvest, especially for ownerships without annual income to offset the tax bill. Therefore, many states have been led either to abolish taxes on timber or to replace timber property taxes with levies that are independent of standing timber volumes.

Two of the most common taxes in lieu of a timber property tax are yield and productivity taxes, which are discussed below. Once the decision has been made to modify or replace the property tax on timber, one of the major unresolved questions is that of determining an equitable level of forest taxes. No consensus exists on the appropriate level or type of forest tax. From the early 1900s through the 1970s, forest tax laws in the states changed frequently. Table 1 shows the patchwork of different forest tax laws that existed in 1980. Many states have several types of timber taxes, mandatory and optional.

Yield Taxes

The yield tax is levied at a given percent of harvest value only when timber is cut. No taxes are paid on standing trees in the years before harvest, although usually some form of annual land tax is levied. In 1951, fourteen states had yield tax laws, most of which were optional and not widely applied. By the late 1970s, however, several states had adopted mandatory yield tax laws, including the major timber states of Washington, Oregon, and California. Most yield tax rates have been in the range of 5 percent to 12 percent of harvested timber value.

Yield tax proponents note that contrary to the property tax, the yield tax cannot stimulate premature cutting and does not impose costs upon owners of young timber without harvest income. Also, as compared to other levies of any given amount, the yield tax has the least discouraging impact on reforestation investment, because it is postponed the longest. These factors suggest that changing from a property tax to a yield tax might increase long-term wood output.

On the negative side, taxing authorities worry about uneven yield tax revenue flows in regions where forest taxes are major sources of local government financing. Under the usual fixed-rate yield tax, county timber tax revenues can fluctuate widely with stumpage price gyrations and changes in regional harvests. Although property tax levels are adjusted annually to meet local revenue needs, yield tax receipts are typically unrelated to county government plans. Elaborate yield tax revenue smoothing and redistribution schemes have been devised in states such as Oregon and Washington; however, resistance to the yield tax idea is still high in many areas. This resistance is especially strong among those who feel that local tax revenues raised in one county should not be redistributed to other counties. An added concern is that some owners not interested in timber income can escape timber taxes by never harvesting.

Classification of Forest Tax Laws by State and Type of Law, 1980

State	Exemption or Rebate	Modified Assessment	Modified Rate	Yield Tax	Severance Tax	Total
Alabama	X	X		X	X	4
Arkansas		X	X		X	3
California		X		X		2
Colorado	X					1
Connecticut		X		X		2
Florida		X				1
Hawaii	X	X		X		3
Idaho	X			X		2
Indiana		X				1
Iowa	X	X				2
Louisiana		X		X	X	3
Maine		XX				2
Maryland	X	X				2
Massachusetts		X		X		2
Michigan				XX		2
Minnesota			X	X		2
Mississippi				X		1
Missouri				X		1
Nevada		X				1
New Hampshire	X	X		X		3
New Jersey	X	X				2
New Mexico		X			XX	3
New York				XX		2
North Carolina	X	X				2
North Dakota			X			1
Ohio		X	X			2
Oregon		XX		XX	X	5
Pennsylvania		XX				2
Rhode Island	X	X				2
South Carolina		X				1
Tennessee	X	XX				3
Texas		X				1
Vermont		XX				2
Virginia		X			X	2
Washington		X		XX		3
West Virginia					X	1
Wisconsin			X	X		2
Total	11	32	5	20	8	76

Source: *Timber Tax Journal* 16 (1980), p. 211. Reprinted by permission.

Productivity Taxes

Under the productivity tax, annual taxes for a given quality of forestland are the same, regardless of timber stocking. Local property tax rates are applied annually to a taxable value, which increases with the land's capacity to produce timber. Examples of such tax laws are found in Florida, Maine, Virginia, and Texas.

Since the productivity tax is independent of timber stocking, proponents feel the tax will not discourage intensive timber management. In fact, some argue that it stimulates better management: since the annual tax is unavoidable, the owner might as well generate timber growth and harvest income to pay the tax. However, there are major disagreements on the method for determining taxable forest value. Some argue that the taxable value should be land value alone, but others suggest valuation formulas that include potential timber value in a sustained-yield forest. For owners of bare land or very young timber, the latter case could be more burdensome than an unmodified forest property tax. From an equity standpoint, some are concerned that, for any given size and quality land tract, the productivity tax would be the same, regardless of income or timber values.

Federal Income Taxes

Before the early 1900s, impacts of federal income taxes upon forests were minimal. Except for a temporary federal income tax between 1861 and 1872 and again in 1894–1895, continuous taxation of income did not begin until 1909 for corporations and 1913 for individuals.

Beginning in 1922, long-term capital gains were taxed at significantly lower rates than ordinary income. However, until 1944, timber harvesting income could receive such reduced tax treatment only if the timber was sold in a lump-sum transaction. Timber harvested by the landowner, or used in the ordinary course of his business, did not qualify for such taxation. This restriction effectively eliminated capital gains tax treatment for many industrial tree farms before 1944.

Federal income tax rates remained fairly stable between the two world wars. The ordinary corporate income tax rate was 15 percent in 1938 but rose to 40 percent by 1942, with an additional excess profits tax. These higher tax levels were accompanied by pressure to include all timber growers under the reduced capital gains tax umbrella, a proposal enacted in 1944. That law retained the previous requirement of "capitalizing" reforestation costs; that is, deducting them for timber capital gains tax purposes only when the timber was cut many decades later. Most other forestry costs could be "expensed" or deducted immediately for ordinary income tax purposes—a practice still allowed as of 1981.

In 1980, reforestation tax incentives were enacted by Congress to allow each landowner a 10 percent tax credit on one year's reforestation expenditures up to $10,000. Federal income taxes otherwise owed can thus be reduced by 10 percent of the reforestation costs up to a total credit of $1,000 in any one year. For reforestation costs up to $10,000 per year, the 1980 law also permits the forest owner effectively to deduct from taxable income one-seventh of the cost annually for seven years. These features were designed to encourage reforestation on nonindustrial private forests.

As of 1979, corporations paid federal income taxes at 46 percent of ordinary income over $100,000 and 28 percent of capital gains from assets held longer than one year. On such long-term capital gains, individuals at that time paid taxes at 40 percent of the ordinary income tax rate. The Economic Recovery Tax Act of 1981 reduced ordinary income tax rates for individuals and for corporations with annual earnings under $100,000.

Since 1944, when favorable capital gains tax rates were made available to all forest owners, there have been dramatic increases in private reforestation and funds spent on forest management and protection. Some observers feel that these increases have been the result of capital gains tax treatment of timber income. Others attribute most of the increased management intensity to the sharp rise in stumpage prices since World War II, as private old-growth timber supplies dwindled in the face of a burgeoning worldwide demand for wood fiber.

Favorable capital gains tax treatment of timber income is viewed by some as a forestry subsidy, while others point out that it is consistent with reduced income tax rates on all long-term capital gains, regardless of their source.

State Income Taxes

In relation to other forest taxes, state income taxes have not been a major factor in American forestry. By 1933, twenty states levied taxes on personal income and twenty-five on corporate income. Most maximum rates ranged from 3 to 7 percent. Today, most states levy personal and corporate income taxes, with maximum rates usually falling in the 5 to 10 percent range.

Death Taxes

Federal death taxes had been imposed intermittently between 1798 and 1916. Since then, the federal estate tax has remained in effect, with periodic changes in rates and exemptions. Death taxes apply only to noncorporate ownerships and thus present no problem for most of the large forest holdings. The chief concern for other ownerships is that high death taxes could force those who inherit forests to harvest or sell timberlands to pay taxes. The result could be premature cutting and fragmentation of timberlands into uneconomic units.

Through the first half of the 1900s, most observers have not considered death taxes to be a major forestry problem. Liberal exemptions and low rates for small estates (although sharply progressive) usually caused few problems for heirs of most small woodlands. However, rising timberland values led to increased concern about impacts of death taxes on forestry and to special timberland provisions in the 1976 Federal Tax Reform Act. The Economic Recovery Tax Act of 1981 substantially decreased the federal inheritance tax on timberlands.

Before 1976, no provisions of federal or state death tax laws related specifically to forests. For certain managed woodlands, the 1976 act allowed forest property valuation based on current rather than potential use for federal estate tax purposes and permitted delayed tax payment over periods of ten to fifteen years in certain cases. Several states have now enacted use valuation for death taxes, similar to the federal legislation.

State death taxes began with Pennsylvania's inheritance tax in 1825 but were not common until the 1900s. Today, all states except Nevada and California levy some form of death tax, but rates and exemptions vary widely. Beginning in 1924, federal death taxes on an estate have been reduced by the amount of state death taxes paid, up to certain limits which have changed periodically.

Other Taxes

Several states have enacted minor taxes in addition to, but not in lieu of, those mentioned above. Examples are severance taxes at a nominal fee per unit volume of timber harvested or fees per acre of forestland. These taxes are usually earmarked for purposes such as fire protection, forest research, and reforestation assistance.

Conclusions

Forestry interests have long sought the ideal combination of tax incentives that would stimulate output of needed wood products. However, others point out that the same argument can be made for stimulating production of all "needed" products. For any marketed good, consumer needs are expressed through higher product prices which in turn stimulate production. For this mechanism to work most efficiently, many economists have suggested neutral taxes that do not favor one industry over another. However, policymakers pursuing this argument must also recognize that many taxes are by nature nonneutral, the property tax being a prime example. Thus the neutrality argument allows tax adjustments to avoid biases against forestry but not to create a bias in favor thereof—except for the special cases where forestry may supply more nonmarket benefits than competing uses. In the final analysis, the goals of neutrality and equity that have permeated forest tax discussions over the years are at best elusive, given the nation's myriad overlapping and varied tax systems.

FURTHER READING: C. W. Briggs and W. K. Condrell, *Tax Treatment of Timber under Pertinent Sections of the Internal Revenue Code of 1954 as Amended* (1978). F. R. Fairchild, *Forest Taxation in the United States* (1935). Forest Industries Committee on Timber Valuation and Taxation, *Timber Tax Journal* 16 (1980): 1-330. W. D. Klemperer, "Unmodified Forest Property Tax—Is It Fair?," *Journal of Forestry* 75 (Oct. 1977): 650-652. R. W. Marquis, *Forest Yield Taxes* (1952). U. S. Advisory Commission on Intergovernmental Relations, *Tax Overlapping in the United States* (1964). E. T. Williams, *State Forest Tax Law Digest* (1968).

W. DAVID KLEMPERER

TAYLOR GRAZING ACT, 1934

The Taylor Grazing Act was approved June 28, 1934. The act with subsequent amendments effectively closed the public domain by creating grazing districts totaling 142 million acres. This acreage, added to that in national forests, parks, and other federal reserves, encompassed the bulk of commercially valuable public land.

The act established grazing districts that were to be administered by a Division of Grazing (renamed Grazing Service in 1939), with assistance from locally elected advisory boards. The original act authorized creation of 80 million acres of districts; an amendment in 1936 raised the total to 142 million acres. Twenty-five percent of grazing receipts was paid to the U. S. Treasury, 50 percent was paid to the states in which the districts lay, and 25 percent was earmarked for federal range improvement programs.

As with much landmark legislation, the Taylor Grazing Act grew out of controversy. Congressman Edward C. Taylor of Colorado had been philosophically opposed to increases in federal programs, but when local solutions to range problems continued to be inadequate, he became a champion of federal involvement. The U. S. FOREST SERVICE had deplored range conditions for decades and supported early drafts of the bill. However, amendments that increased local influence on administration caused the agency to oppose enactment vigorously. Following passage of the Taylor Grazing Act, the Forest Service produced *The Western Range* (1936), a lengthy study containing detailed

This experimental grazing plot on Arizona's Tonto National Forest contrasts the heavily grazed area right of the fence with the left side which has been allowed a few years to recuperate. Condition of the western range was of great importance to the supporters of the Taylor Grazing Act, as agencies of the Departments of Agriculture and the Interior vied for leadership during the 1930s. Forest Service Photo.

criticisms of the act and of its administration by the DEPARTMENT OF THE INTERIOR. Administration of the public range remained very controversial and at one point in the late 1940s was the rallying point for the emerging environmental movement. The FEDERAL LAND POLICY AND MANAGEMENT ACT of 1976 re-examined and redefined federal range policies and mandated close coordination of Forest Service and BUREAU OF LAND MANAGEMENT programs.

FURTHER READING: Wesley Calef, *Private Grazing and Public Lands: Studies of the Land Management of the Taylor Grazing Act* (1960). Phillip O. Foss, *Politics and Grass: The Administration of Grazing on the Public Domain* (1960).

TECHNICIAN TRAINING IN FORESTRY

Technician training is designed for those who plan to "handle or direct techniques of applying management plans on the ground and who will serve as the liaison between the professional forester (technologist) and the unskilled worker" (Dana and Johnson, 1963). Less appropriate titles sometimes used to describe this level of education are subprofessional, semiprofessional, and vocational. Some schools offering these forestry programs are called ranger schools, because of the desire of men so trained in the early days of American forestry to be rangers on the forest reserves and, later, the national forests. Eventually, ranger assignments were reserved for graduates of four-year professional schools; thus, recently established technician programs are not called ranger schools.

Technician training in the United States began in 1898 with the establishment of the Biltmore Forest School's one-year program in North Carolina. Carl A. SCHENCK, with academic and practical experience in Germany, initiated the program soon after his arrival from Europe and remained its leader until the school's demise in 1913. By most standards, the Biltmore School was producing technicians, even though many students had previously earned baccalaureate degrees, but the scarcity of professionally educated personnel resulted in its graduates assuming forester assignments throughout the nation.

The Pennsylvania State Forest Academy, near Mont Alto, began a two-year program in 1903. In 1921, it was made a four-year professional school and remained so until its merger with the Pennsylvania State College (now University) in 1929. In that year, a two-year ranger program was re-established, remaining viable until declining enrollment during World War II caused its closure in 1942.

The oldest continuing program is that of the New York State Ranger School in the Adirondacks. It began in 1912 and until the 1970s remained a one-year program.

Other institutions which have provided technician training are the University of Southern California (1899), North Dakota School of Forestry (1907–1923, 1925–), Wymans School of the Woods in Michigan (1909–c. 1920), Washington State College (now University) (1910–1916), Colorado College (1911–c. 1913), University of Missouri (1912), University of Wisconsin (1913–1915), University of Idaho (1916–1928), Lincoln Memorial University (1917–1922), Montana State University (1918–1925), and Louisiana State University (1921–1924).

Other field courses of study of a few weeks' to a few months' duration have been at Yale University (1901), Colorado A & M (now State University) (1907), Colorado College (c. 1908), University of Washington (1910), Washington State College (now University; 1910), and Montana State University (1910).

The beginning of the technician programs at the University of Florida (1935), West Virginia University (1935), and Lassen Junior College (1937) in California can be attributed to the need for leadership in the CIVILIAN CONSERVATION CORPS. Only the California school has continued to the present.

World War II's conclusion influenced the opening of schools in Arkansas (A & M), Michigan (Technological), New York (Paul Smith's), Massachusetts (University), and Florida (Lake City, as the Columbia Forest School). The five ranger schools in Canada also have come into being since 1943.

More recent programs (1950s) have been initiated at Nichols (Massachusetts) College of Business Administration, North Central School of Agriculture in Minnesota, and, in the 1960s, at eight other institutions. An additional seven two-year wood products programs now operate as well.

Graduates of technician schools serve subordinately to foresters as timber cruisers, surveyors, timber markers, timber buyers, planting foremen, game census takers, nursery managers, campground patrollers, trail and road foremen, and in fire suppression. Some pursue further education in professional schools.

FURTHER READING: Samuel Trask Dana and Evert W. Johnson, *Forestry Education in America Today and Tommorrow* (1963). "Forest Technician Training Programs in the United States," *Journal of Forestry* 65 (July 1967): 484-487. Laurence C. Walker, "Technician/Professional Bugaboo," *Journal of Forestry* 69 (Dec. 1971): 865.

LAURENCE C. WALKER

TENNESSEE FORESTS

Forests extend from the Appalachian Mountains westward over 400 miles of Tennessee to the Mississippi River bottomlands. Except for spruce-fir stands along the highest ridges, they contain largely mixed hardwoods with scattered areas of southern yellow pine, redcedar, white pine, and hemlock. Of the state's 27 million acres, 26 million were once covered with trees.

Settlers moving in from North Carolina and Virginia began cutting Tennessee forests in 1769. Within a century, they had cleared 7 million acres for some 82,000 farms. Peak production was in 1909 when 1.2 billion board feet were produced; over 1 billion board feet were hardwood, making Tennessee the leading hardwood producer for that year. Lowest production was 1932, when only 128,393,000 board feet were reported. By the 1930s, the forest covered less than half its original acreage. In the 1950s and early 1960s, significant areas were allowed to regain their forest cover, but since then the forest has once more receded —this time in favor of housing developments, shopping centers, superhighways, and powerlines. By 1980, some 13.1 million acres remained in forests, with about three-quarters of that in hardwoods.

More than 200 species of trees grow naturally in Tennessee, but only about 60 are of commercial importance. Early timber harvesting was a story of successive surges of demand for one wood at a time. First it was black walnut, then yellow-poplar, then white oak, followed by ash and other species. Besides sawtimber and pulp and paper, veneer, furniture, wood-treating, and cooperage are important forest product industries in Tennessee.

Commercial and industrial demands increased after the Civil War, and in 1874 the state secretary of agriculture called for laws to promote reforestation of abandoned fields. But the Tennessee Forest Association was not formed until 1901 to provide an effective voice for conservation. Legislation followed in 1907 to protect state and private forestlands from fire and trespass and to establish a Department of Game, Fish, and Forestry, but funds were not provided. In 1909–1910, the State Geological Survey and the U. S. FOREST SERVICE undertook a cooperative forest survey, but not until 1914 did the state hire its first professional forester, R. S. Maddox. By 1921, Maddox became state forester in a new Bureau of Forestry and began cooperation with the Forest Service for fire control and wasteland reclamation. After several organizational and name changes, the Bureau of

Red gum from Tennessee is converted to fine furniture at a factory in Memphis. Forest History Society Photo.

Forestry became the Division of Forestry under the Tennessee Department of Conservation in 1937. Since then, the division has been authorized to assist private owners in forest practices. Farm industry extension work began even earlier, under the CLARKE-MCNARY ACT of 1924. Forestry instruction at the University of the South in Sewanee dates from 1923 and at the University of Tennessee from 1936. The Division of Forestry manages 113,000 acres in eleven state forests.

The creation of a state park system was first suggested in 1919 by Wilbur A. Nelson, state geologist, but nothing was done until 1925 when the State Park and Forestry Commission was established and was authorized to purchase lands and accept gifts. In 1928, land acquired from the West Tennessee Land Company became Reelfoot Lake State Park. During the 1930s, the CIVILIAN CONSERVATION CORPS and the TENNESSEE VALLEY AUTHORITY (TVA) both contributed to park development in Tennessee. Between 1938 and 1951, the TVA leased five parks to the state, and it eventually gave a total of seven parks to the state. In 1978, there were thirty-eight park and recreation areas covering 276,000 acres.

The passage of the WEEKS ACT in 1911 was followed by federal acquisition of forestlands along the North Carolina border—the origin of the Cherokee National Forest, formally established in 1920 and containing 621,675 federal acres out of 1,204,520 in 1980. Federal involvement in Tennessee state forestry and parks increased with the Clarke-McNary Act and the Great Depression with its Civilian Conservation Corps program and projects aimed at the reclamation of submarginal farmland carried out by the Soil Conservation Service, the Agricultural Adjustment Administration, and the Tennessee Valley Authority. Under legislation passed in 1926, the federal government also began acquiring portions of the picturesque highland which became the GREAT SMOKY MOUNTAINS NATIONAL PARK, encompassing 517,368 acres, 241,206 of which are in Tennessee.

In 1980, Tennessee's hardwood timber supported an average annual lumber production of almost 500 million board feet. Since 1960, Tennessee had been one of the top five hardwood lumber producing states. Yet the state's most valuable tree species is a softwood, the eastern redcedar. Sixty percent of the commercial redcedar lands in the eastern United States are in middle Tennessee. Pines supply about 15 percent of the state's lumber produce as well as a large part of the pulpwood harvest. The PULP AND PAPER INDUSTRY moved into the state in the 1950s with the construction of the huge Bowaters plant. This new market increased the demand for pine seedlings, but softwoods are being used almost as quickly as they are being grown. In contrast, hardwoods are growing much faster than they are harvested. In general, on a statewide basis, tree quality is improving and the proportion of desirable commercial species is increasing. By 1960, over 96 percent of the state's forestland was under the protection of federal or state agencies. Tennessee Valley data, which should approximate state conditions, show that the average forest acre today contains twice as much above-ground tree material as it did in 1933 and that the annual rate of growth is about twice the 1933 rate.

Timber is not the only beneficiary of better forest management. As plant food and cover improve, wildlife populations grow. In west Tennessee, for example, the beaver comeback has been so successful that trapping is again being encouraged to protect forest and croplands from flood damage.

FURTHER READING: Bevley R. Coleman, "A History of State Parks in Tennessee," Ph.D. dissertation, George Peabody College for Teachers (1963). William Maughan, ed., *Guide to Forestry Activities in North Carolina, South Carolina, and Tennessee* (1939). Ralph R. Widner, ed., *Forests and Forestry in the American States* (1968).

ROBERT L. SCHNELL

TENNESSEE VALLEY AUTHORITY

Although a product of the Depression, the Tennessee Valley Authority (TVA) has roots in the earlier conservation movement of Theodore ROOSEVELT and Gifford PINCHOT. Shortly after the turn of the century, the Inland Waterways Commission advocated a program of coordinated resource utilization for the 26-million-acre Tennessee River basin, and Republican Congresses in 1928 and 1931 attempted more limited resource legislation, only to have it vetoed by Calvin Coolidge and Herbert Hoover. On May 18, 1933, Congress responded to Franklin D. ROOSEVELT's call for a "corporation clothed with the power of government but possessed of the flexibility and initiative of a private enterprise" by passing the Tennessee Valley Authority Act. The TVA has become the showcase for the New Deal, bringing resource managers and politicians from around the world to Knoxville to view the project's many activities: improved navigation, flood control, electric power and fertilizer production, soil stabilization, reforestation, and better transportation and recreational facilities.

An estimated 1 million acres of the area encompassed by the TVA needed erosion control. In 1933, TVA Chief Forester C. M. Richards, working cooperatively with local agencies, began a reforestation project. The effort received the benefit of thirty-eight CIVILIAN CONSERVATION CORPS (CCC) camps with a 7,600-man labor force available to combat erosion and forest fires. The momentum provided by the CCC continued after the Depression, for by 1950 landowners were reforesting some 15,000 acres annually at their own expense. The Soil Bank program added further encouragement, and in 1960, 7,000 landowners reforested 90,000 acres. To meet the demand for planting stock, the two TVA nurseries and those operated by the states produced 611 million seedlings in 1957 alone.

During the early 1930s, approximately 10,000 fires a year burned about 10 percent of the forested area of the Tennessee Valley basin. To reduce this loss, the CCC built fire towers and roads and provided manpower for suppression crews. TVA cooperated with state foresters and local newspaper editors to help spread the fire-prevention gospel. Local governments responded with increased appropriations for FIRE CONTROL, and judges began to treat incendiaries as criminals. By the 1960s, fully 98 percent of the TVA forested area received formal protection, and fire losses were generally well under 1 percent.

In addition to the Cherokee, Nantahala, Pisgah, and Chattahoochee national forests and the GREAT SMOKY MOUNTAINS NATIONAL PARK, there are over 11 million acres of private forestland in the Tennessee River basin owned by nearly 250,000 individuals, companies, and institutions. Large corporations complemented the multiple-use concept of the TVA, bringing capital and jobs to the region. After overcoming objections by the U. S. FOREST SERVICE, Bowaters Corporation in 1954 opened the world's largest paper mill near Calhoun, Tennessee. In 1967, U. S. Plywood-Champion Papers (now Champion International) began developing an 1,800-acre complex on the Tennessee River, near Courtland, Alabama. Furniture making, another important industry, accounted for 33 percent of forest products value in the 1960s. Lumber production in the basin peaked in 1946 with 1.4 billion board feet, leveling off in the 1960s to 700,000 feet per year.

TVA has not been without its critics, who label the project "socialistic" or "inefficient and costly." Its coal-fired generators have drawn criticism from environmentalists and the more recent addition of nuclear power plants has widened the controversy. In 1978, TVA received widespread publicity over its construction of the Tellico Dam on the Little Tennessee River, which allegedly threatened the snail darter, a small but officially designated endangered species of fish.

Proposals for programs similar to TVA, such as a Columbia Valley Authority, have not fared well in Congress. Nonetheless, FDR's eloquent justification for TVA, "It touches and gives life to all forms of human concerns," has been realized.

FURTHER READING: Willis M. Baker, "Reminiscing about the TVA," *American Forests* 75 (May 1969): 30-31, 56-60. Richard Kilbourne, "A Quarter-Century of Forestry Progress in the Tennessee Valley," *Southern Lumberman* 195 (Dec. 15, 1957): 100–105. Kenneth J. Seigworth, "Forestry Plus—In the Tennessee Valley," *Journal of Forestry* 66 (Apr. 1968): 324-328.

TERMINOLOGY

Forest terminology may be classified into three divisions: the technical vocabulary of the professional forester, the argot of the logger, and the technical vocabulary of the forest products industry. Most of the specialized dictionaries and glossaries of forestry or forest-related words and expressions have concentrated on one or more of these divisions.

Technical Vocabulary of the Professional Forester

The first attempt to record the specialized words used in American forests was *Terms Used in Forestry and Logging*, published by the U. S. Bureau of Forestry in 1905 as its Bulletin 61. Prepared in cooperation with the new SOCIETY OF AMERICAN FORESTERS (SAF), Bulletin 61 stated the terminology which the bureau intended to follow in its work. The bulletin's author claimed to have had the "cooperation of many lumbermen, and of practically all the trained foresters in the United States." Nevertheless, when Bernard E. FERNOW reviewed the booklet in *Forestry Quarterly*, finding it "very useful and timely," he charged that it failed to cover the subject comprehensively and that it tried too hard to replace long-accepted usage. He challenged the term "clean cutting," for example, because "we do not see an advantage in replacing *Clear* by *Clean*, the former being well established, perfectly clear in meaning, with satisfactory term-quality . . . ." *Cleaning* was already established in other usages, while "nothing is better known than a *Clearing* as a place from which the timber has been entirely removed." Later that year, Ernest Bruncken also attacked Bulletin 61's newly coined terms in the *Forestry Quarterly*. "Deliberately to invent a barbarism is the reverse of praise-worthy," he said; the term "silvics," for example, Bruncken thought "an entirely impossible word," considering the Latin root and the Greek ending. (Ironically, Fernow had found "silvics" to be "one of the best terms invented.")

Eight years later, *Forestry Quarterly*, still under Fernow's editorship, returned to the attack with an article by Parish Storrs Lovejoy who gave further examples of Bulletin 61's "perversion of terms" and suggested the appointment of a standing committee in SAF to consider and revise current professional terminology and to recommend new terms. These proposals were taken up by SAF at a 1914 meeting at Cornell University. In accordance with a resolution of that meeting, Fernow, then SAF president, appointed a committee of twenty-one (later twenty-five) to "revise and standardize" the terms of the field. For three years, the committee labored under the leadership of Fernow. Its report appeared in two parts: "Terms used in general forestry and its branches with the exception of forest protection and utilization," published in the *Journal of Forestry* in 1917, and "Terms used in the lumber industry," printed in the journal the following year. An intended separate report on forest protection terminology was never published. Fernow described the report as "the mature judgment, laboriously arrived at, by representative men of the profession, who by their occupation are in position to use the terminology systematically." Nevertheless, he recognized that "omissions, discrepancies, and disagreements will remain," and the report recommended the appointment of a standing committee. The Fernow committee's report was a more comprehensive list of forestry terms than that provided in Bulletin 61. Most of the terms found objectionable to Fernow in 1905 were omitted, redefined, or indicated as secondary alternatives to Fernow's preferred terms. Hence "clear cutting" replaced "clean cutting"; "conservative lumbering" in reference to methods of reproduction was declared obsolete; "felling" trees had preference over "cutting" them; and "forest policy" was restricted in meaning to cover only the attitude of governments toward forests rather than forest management principles in a broad sense.

Over the next twenty years, the scope of forestry broadened and its practice became more specialized and intensive; new terms were needed and some older ones became obsolete. The Mather Field conference of fire executives in 1921 expressed a need for control of the new terms constantly being coined in fire control work. After circulation of mimeograph drafts and achieving "definitions based on majority opinion or most common usage," the U.S. FOREST SERVICE in 1930 issued a *Glossary of Terms Used in Fire Control* as Department of Agriculture Miscellaneous Publication No. 70. Revised in 1939, this glossary proved to be a valuable reference when SAF undertook to update its forest terminology. In the 1930s, SAF noted not only the need to keep pace with the changing forestry profession but also a trend toward the inaccurate use of technical terms, a result of foresters acting as educators of the public and hence having to express technical matters in simple language. In 1938, SAF established a new committee on forest terminology. Under the chairmanship of Ralph C. Hawley, this group completed *Forestry Terminology: A Glossary of Technical Terms Used in Forestry* (1944). It was compiled by ten subcommittees of subject specialists and a central collating committee responsible for final decisions on the terms and definitions to be accepted. This eighty-four-page publication, with its approximately 4,500 definitions and cross references, was the most ambitious effort yet made to promote the more accurate use of forestry technical terms. "Perhaps improvement in this respect is too much to hope for from some of the older members of the profession," *Forestry Terminology* noted, "but it should be expected from the younger men in the earlier years of their professional career and from students in schools of forestry."

The supply of *Forestry Terminology* was quickly exhausted, and in view of the rapid advance of technology and science, the SAF council decided upon a revision rather than a reprint. SAF appointed a collating committee under the chairmanship of E. A. Munns, which enlisted authors, specialists, teachers, researchers, and administrators to suggest revisions of the initial glossary. The second edition of *Forestry Terminology* was published in 1950.

The continued rapid growth of such fields as genetics, aerial photography, and wood utilization soon led SAF to undertake a third edition of *Forestry Terminology* (1958). The terms and definitions of the first and second editions had met widespread acceptance, and the third edition primarily sought to keep pace with new terms. Accordingly, the task was undertaken by SAF's editorial staff with the assistance of four subject-matter consultants. The Forest Service's *Glossary of Terms Used in Forest-Fire Control*, revised in 1956, again provided the model for words in its field.

While the second edition of *Forestry Terminology* was nearing completion, the collating committee learned of a comparable project under way in the British Commonwealth. A partial draft of the British glossary was borrowed and became the basis for some changes in the SAF terminology. During the compilation of the third edition, this international cooperation continued in the interest of "bringing about mutually worded definitions for mutually used terms in British and American terminology."

At the World Forestry Congress in Helsinki in 1949, compilation of a comprehensive Multilingual Terminology was proposed. For ten years starting in 1954, the Joint Committee on Forest Bibliography and Terminology of the United Nations Food and Agriculture Organization (FAO) and the International Union of Forest Research Organizations (IUFRO) did exploratory work from the base provided by the *British Commonwealth Forest Terminology* and the third edition of SAF's *Forestry Terminology*. In 1964, through the initiative of V. L. Harper, chairman of SAF's Committee on International Relations, the governments of the United States and Canada agreed to finance FAO and IUFRO compilation of the English-language portion of the Multilingual Terminology, while SAF agreed to administer these funds and to publish the completed work. Editorial work on the project began in Oxford, England, late in 1964. The text, compiled in England and reviewed by commonwealth foresters, was then considered by American specialists under the supervision of an SAF project expediter, a post held successively by Arthur B. Meyer, Ivan H. Sims, and Robert K. Winters. The text of an intended fourth edition of *Forestry Terminology* was drawn upon during the SAF review of commonwealth material. In some areas, where American foresters had developed a wider vocabulary (such as cableways, range, recreation, and wildlife), definitions were first determined in the United States and then forwarded to Oxford for review. The multilingual project did not aim at international standardization; commonwealth or American usage were both indicated in *Terminology of Forest Science, Technology, Practice, and Products, English-Language Version*, edited by F. C. Ford-Robertson (1971).

Although leaving out terms adequately defined for forestry purposes in common dictionaries, local terms, and those of "purely archaic interest," the new *Terminology* comprised 6,807 defined concepts in over 5,150 entries. A French translation with additional terms in common use by French foresters was published by the Association Française des Eaux et Forêts in 1975. The Accademia Italiana di Scienze Forestali provided the Italian-language version in 1980, while work proceeded on editions in Spanish, Russian, Hungarian, and German.

In 1977, SAF published *Addendum Number One* to the English-language version, edited by Robert K. Winters, with new terms and revised definitions. By that time, the *Terminology* was beginning to appear obsolescent in content and format. At the 1981 IUFRO World Congress, participants discussed the problems of revising the *Terminology* to provide the basis for subject indicator lists for use in computerized information retrieval; for multiple-language machine translation aids; and for preparation of a thesaurus of forestry terms.

Supplementing SAF's efforts to produce a comprehensive terminology, specialized dictionaries of forestry terms have continued to be produced. An example is Ronald W. Mifflin and Hilton H. Lysons, *Glossary of Forest Engineering Terms* (1979), published by the Pacific Northwest Forest and Range Experiment Station.

Vocabulary of the Logger

The Bureau of Forestry's Bulletin No. 61 published in 1905 had included a separate section on logging terms. The bureau excluded mill and trade terms, the language of other forest products industries, and slang (although a number of highly informal words were included, such as "jiboo," meaning, in the North woods and the Lake States, "to remove a dog from a log," and "ballhooter," an Appalachian term for "one who rolls logs down a hillside"). Logging terms in regional use were so identified. This section of Bulletin 61 apparently did not provoke the challenges that greeted the technical forestry vocabulary, and many of the entries were repeated in the much expanded "Terms Used in the Lumber Industry," the second part of the Fernow committee's report, published in the *Journal of Forestry* in January 1918. As Fernow remarked, these terms were "merely recorded without controversy." Despite its title, the report included not only logging and lumber words, identified by region where appropriate, but also NAVAL STORES terminology. These early efforts at defining the forest vocabulary were given wider circulation by Ralph Clement Bryant who reprinted the logging terms section of Bulletin 61 in an appendix to his textbook, *Logging* (1913). When he revised his text in 1923, Bryant included as an appendix the lumber industry terminology section of the Fernow committee's report.

The vocabulary of the woods has frequently attracted the attention of both buffs and scholars eager to preserve a record of a disappearing vernacular. They generally worked independently, recording and trying to understand the speech used by loggers, in contrast to the institutional projects which sought to systematize the vocabulary of professional forestry. Unlike the dictionaries of professional terminology, glossaries of woods language were often regional in orientation.

American Forests in December 1924 published J. M. Morrison's article on "Lumberjack Rhetoric," which lamented the passing of the French-Canadian logger of the old days in Maine and the Lake States, who had felt "more at home in the companionship of 'tall trees' than anywhere else." Morrison's article was largely a review of some of the colorful words and expressions of woods operations in the Lake States. James Stevens discussed "Logger Talk" of the Pacific Northwest in the December 1925 issue of *American Speech*. "Never call the worker in the woods of the Pacific Northwest 'lumberjack,'" he began; "... logger is the name he has made for himself." The word "lumberjack" applied only to "the worker in the 'toothpick' timber, the small second-growth pine and hemlock" in the Lake States. There were different physical conditions in the Pacific Northwest and new technology and techniques, as steam replaced animal power in the woods; most of the words used in woods work were also new. Some older terms, such as "skid-road" and "nose-bag" changed in meaning. Others simply became obsolete. According to Stevens, trees in the Northwest were "falled," not "felled," and to call a logger a "feller" was to provoke great laughter. Modern loggers earned good wages, owned cars, and could speak "the universal American jargon of the comics and sports pages." They could still "swear magnificently," however, although about the severest examples Stevens gave were "Holy old blue-bellied, bald-headed Jesus H. jumping old mackinaw Christ," and "Hi, you red-eyed son-of-a-bitch!" Another compilation of Pacific Northwest words was a pamphlet of thirty pages called *Logger-Talk* by Guy Williams (1930). *Logger-Talk* contained 228 terms with many general and debatable definitions.

In October 1931, a study of words and expressions of the Southern woods appeared in "Lumberjack Lingo" by J. W. Clark in the journal *American Speech*. Terms not found in other sections of the country included "four-up" for four-mule teams; "Jim Crow men" for the men who made ties; "fightin' the bear," meaning to separate the boards and strips after they had been cut in the mill at the rate of fifty a minute; "kitchen sweats," the dances in a lumber camp; and "walking the table," meaning to walk on the table in the mess hall and kick off inferior food in order to get rid of a poor cook. Almost every camp in the South had a Negro section, usually on one side of the main camp. Saturday night was called "nigger day" when the black workers would go into the woods, hang their lanterns, spread the canvas, and gamble with dice. Southern lumberjacks carried their clothes in "yannigan bags." A "didapper" was a man who worked on a log pond.

Orlo H. Misfeldt of Montana, in *American Speech*, October 1941, published "Timberland Terminology,"

a glossary of sixty-two "printable terms," which included the basic vocabulary. Misfeldt defined "logger" as "a man employed as a lumberjack," without mentioning the West Coast area.

Stewart Holbrook's *Holy Old Mackinaw* (1938) contained a basic "Loggers Dictionary" of 151 terms used in all parts of the country and 11 Chinook words used in logging camps of the Pacific Northwest, such as "kultus," meaning worthless, "skookum," for "strong"; and "tyee," or "big shot." In 1941, Holbrook's *Tall Timber* contained a shorter list of 105 loggers' terms and 9 Chinook words. In *Yankee Loggers*, published for the International Paper Company in 1961, Holbrook shortened his glossary to 88 terms.

Elrick Davis in December 1942 published a glossary of five pages in *American Speech* called "Paul Bunyan Talk." As sustained-yield forestry came to treat America's forests as a vast tree farm, the logger was rapidly becoming an ordinary citizen and spoke like everyone else. With increased mechanization, even the technical jargon in the woods was changing. Although the old-timers had "contrived for themselves a vocabulary so pithy and colorful that its memory stays alive in loggers' sentimental hearts," little of it had passed into the common language. "The obvious reason," Davis stated, "is that most of the loggers' lingo has been, through the years, semantically too high-test for print even in a scientific journal." The only item that Davis credited with having spread widely beyond the woods was "haywire," a "generic term of disparagement."

Wilbur A. Davis, in *Western Folklore* for April 1950, published "Logger and Splinter-Picker Talk" based on his experience of thirteen years in the woods and sawmills in the northwestern part of Oregon. Davis included separate lists of words heard in the woods and in the mills and a shorter list, handed down by his father, of terms used in team logging in 1892. Davis believed that the language of the woods was not passing out of use; loggers self-consciously kept it alive. "Loggers are as well aware of the distinctive qualities of their speech as any student of language, and they enjoy coining new figures of speech." On the opposite side of the country, Fred Simmons, a Forest Service employee who edited the *Northeastern Loggers Handbook* (1951), incorporated a short basic glossary not limited to his own region; in part, he relied on SAF's *Forestry Terminology*. Lynwood Carranco published the first glossaries of the redwood country of northwestern California in *American Speech* for May 1956, February 1959, and May 1962.

In 1958, Walter McCulloch, retired dean of the Oregon State University Forestry School, published *Woods Words,* a comprehensive lexicon based on the Pacific Northwest Douglas-fir country, which remains the best work on this general subject. McCulloch's 219-page volume was the most extensive coverage yet given to the logging language of any region. Like other students of the subject, McCulloch ascribed the distinctiveness of the regional vernacular to the problems encountered and solved in dealing with local geographical and timber conditions. He also traced the derivation of words from the Lake States woods and from railroading. He felt that a new generation was adding little to the richness of the vernacular, although some terms, such as "hydramatic" for a "shiftless logger," were clearly of recent origin. In *Forest History* (October 1972), McCulloch explained how since 1919 he had collected his glossary by interviewing woods workers and old-timers. Local trade journals, Pacific Logging Congress proceedings, and loggers' handbooks also helped. But he had to omit the colorful, blasphemous, and obscene words and used "euphemistic substitutes which loggers would understand and forgive me for," because of the publishing taboos in the 1950s.

L. G. Sorden and Isabel J. Ebert published a booklet entitled *Logger's Words of Yesteryears* (1956) including 1,200 terms collected, starting in the 1930s, for the logging museum in Rhinelander, Wisconsin. Sorden revised and expanded the list to over 2,500 terms for publication as *Lumberjack Lingo* in 1969, still the basic reference on the woods argot of the Lake States. "Lumberjack," which McCulloch had dismissed as "a genteel term used by fiction writers who should have said logger if they meant a man working in the western woods," was acceptable in the Lake States. There, "logger . . . more often referred to the man directly in charge of a logging operation, a contractor or subcontractor."

A number of shorter regional glossaries were published during the 1960s. John T. Labbe and Vernon Goe included 106 logging and logging railroad terms of the Pacific Northwest in their *Railroads in the Woods* (1961). *The Story of Logging the White Pine in the Saginaw Valley* (1964), by Harold M. Foehl and Irene M. Hargraves, contained a short glossary of fifty-two basic terms. *Tumult on the Mountains: Lumbering in West Virginia, 1770–1920* (1964), by Roy B. Clarkson, told how workers from Pennsylvania, New York, Maine, Canada, and Nova Scotia brought in their own language to be adopted, modified, and mixed with Southern jargon. Clarkson's glossary contained about 250 terms, including local terms such as "coon skinner" for "a subcontractor cutting timber" and "Arbuckles" for coffee (taken from a trade name). Robert E. Pike's *Tall Trees, Tough Men* (1967) was a history of logging and log-driving in New England. Here again the backgrounds of the woods workers were varied. Those from Nova Scotia were called "Herring Chokers," those from New Brunswick were "Blue Noses"; but the term "P.I.'s" (for Prince Edward Island) was often applied to everyone from north of the border. Among the sixty-five items in Pike's glossary were some new ones and some with different meanings, such as "jill-poke" for a log with one end stuck in the stream bank or an awkward person, and "ton timber" for logs cut or hewn square to take up less space for shipping in colonial days.

The *Journal of Forest History* (July 1974) published Lynwood Carranco's "Logger Language in Redwood Country," which demonstrated how woods terms emerged, consistent with traditional modes of word-making, from new inventions, abbreviations, derivatives, functional shifts, compounds, semantic shifts, proper names, and slang. Prejudices of millworkers and loggers were shown by words derived from minority groups, such as "nigger," a steam-powered device for turning logs in the mill; "portagee broom," a rake used to gather sawdust; and "Oklahoma hooktender," a poor whistle punk (a hooktender being a foreman and a whistle punk a beginning worker on a logging crew). This article was the first study of woods terminology to give uncensored treatment of the taboo words.

Technical Vocabulary of the Forest Products Industry

The vocabulary used in the forest products industry includes both technical forestry terminology and the language of the woods and mill workers as well as trade terms. Several attempts have been made to gain systematic control over defined portions of this diverse vocabulary and to train personnel in accepted usage. The Education and Training Committee of the Redwood Region Conservation Council published *Words of the Woods* (1962), a mixed glossary leaning heavily toward lumber trade terms used in the redwoods. This glossary was intended for commercial departments of local high schools to prepare students for employment. In 1978, the Potlatch Corporation of Lewiston, Idaho, published its *Glossary of Forestry Related Terms*, which provided definitions of words "as they are commonly used by qualified Potlatch personnel." A much more ambitious project, completed the same year and covering the vocabulary of the softwood lumber industry of the United States, was *Terms of the Trade*, edited by William Dean and David S. Evans (1978) for Random Lengths, a commercial publishing house specializing in the lumber trade. *Terms of the Trade* provided a standard reference work for its field, but the lumber industry still lacked a lexicon as comprehensive as, or with the institutional authority of, those attempted for the pulp and paper industry. During World War I, the War Industries Board encouraged the compilation of *Classification and Definitions of Paper*, edited by Clarence J. West (1924, revised 1928). In view of the obsolescence of West's volume, the American Paper and Pulp Association appointed a Committee on Classification and Definitions to work in cooperation with the Institute of Paper Chemistry toward the compilation of the *Dictionary of Paper*, which appeared in 1940. Revised editions were published in 1951 and 1965.

LYNWOOD CARRANCO

TEXAS FORESTS

The commercial forest region of Texas is concentrated in the eastern portion of the state, where early travelers found impressive stands of loblolly, longleaf, shortleaf, and slash pines and hardwoods such as gum, oak, elm, hickory, and beech. Bordering the eastern pine region are forests containing post oak, hackberry, elm, mesquite, pecan, ash, hickory, and cedar. Extreme southeastern Texas grows baldcypress, and in central Texas are cedar brakes that serve primarily as watershed protection and wildlife habitat. The mountain region supports pinyon pine, southern yellow pine, Douglas-fir, juniper, ash, Spanish walnut, mesquite, and oaks. Of the 23,279,000 forested acres in Texas in 1977, 12,513,000 acres were of commercial value.

Until after the Civil War, lumbering operations were largely for local consumption, the reported cut in 1870 being only 100 million board feet taken from an estimated stand of 67 billion board feet. Beginning about 1877, lumbermen from all sections of the United States and some from Europe rushed to share in the great bonanza that the east Texas forests offered. Among the major lumber manufacturers operating in Texas before 1900 were Henry J. Lutcher and G. Bedell Moore, Joseph H. Kurth and Simon Henderson, Thomas L. L. Temple, Robert A. Long, William Cameron, and E. A. Frost. The most prominent was John Henry Kirby, an energetic and flamboyant native son, who between 1885 and 1933 operated as many as fourteen sawmills and a great complex of related enterprises.

As the railroads pushed into the piney woods, lumbermen bought extensive acreages, often at bargain prices, and built lumber manufacturing plants, often complete with logging railroads and COMPANY TOWNS. It was a common practice to pay employees with merchandise checks, redeemable at face value only in the company store or at the company office. Although mill owners themselves banded together to form organizations such as the Southern Pine and the Southern Lumber Operators associations, they adamantly rejected any unionization efforts among their employees and were able to stifle all labor activity and break any strikes that developed. Not until the New Deal period were workers able to organize successfully.

Lumber production increased rapidly and reached an annual cut of 1 billion board feet by 1900. Three times before 1917, the industry reported a cut of more than 2 billion board feet. During World War I, an active wood shipbuilding industry developed on the Texas Gulf Coast at such centers as Orange, Beaumont, and Houston. However, the war ended before most of the "pine-built" vessels could be completed. The 1920s saw a steady decline in the Texas lumber industry, with many companies discontinuing operations. The Depression years brought more foreclosures, and the annual cut fell to less than 400 million board feet by 1932—the lowest figure since 1880. During this fifty-year heyday, Texas lumbermen had cut more than 55 billion board feet of virgin timber.

The Depression decade also brought a breakthrough in pine utilization, based on a process developed by Charles H. HERTY. By 1940, a group of east Texas lumbermen headed by Ernest Kurth and Arthur Temple had completed the first plant to produce newsprint from southern yellow pine. The opening of the Southland Paper Mill in Lufkin, Texas, marked the beginning of a great new industry in the South and a new market for southern pine timber.

The postwar years brought many advances in wood chemistry, technology, and wood-based products. As a result, many old lumber families, feeling ill-equipped to deal with these changes, sold their companies, plants, and timber holdings to large multipurpose corporations. By 1980, most of the productive Texas timberlands were no longer held by family companies but by industrial giants such as International Paper, Owen-Illinois, Boise Southern, Time-Life Corporation, the Sante Fe Railroad, and St. Regis Paper.

The intensive scientific forestry methods practiced in the east Texas timberlands today originated in the first decades of the twentieth century. By acclamation, the "father of Texas forestry" was W. Goodrich Jones. Educated in Europe and at Princeton, Jones was a banker by profession but an ardent conservationist and advocate of both public and private reforestation. Jones, who knew both Bernhard E. FERNOW and Gifford PINCHOT, attended the White House Governors Conference on conservation in 1908 and returned to Texas determined to promote forestry in the Southwest. In 1914, he founded the Texas Forestry Association, a voluntary organization dedicated to forest regeneration in the state. With this support, Jones successfully lobbied in 1915 for the establishment of a state department of forestry.

At a time when many lumbermen thought of the Texas forests as inexhaustible, Jones warned of coming timber depletion and urged landowners to adopt policies of selective cutting, sustained yield, and reforestation. Among the first large landowners to adopt sound forestry practices were J. Lewis Thompson, Ernest L. Kurth, and Thomas L. L. Temple. Under the direction of E. O. Siecke, state forester from 1918 to 1942, the Texas Forest Service (renamed in 1928) developed an efficient fire-fighting program, a series of state forests, and a pine seedling nursery to provide young trees for both public and private plantings.

From the beginning, the Texas Forestry Association and the Texas Forest Service have had the strong support of industry leaders, professional foresters, and the public. As a result, they have in large part been able to avoid the political tugs-of-war that have plagued many state conservation programs. Thus, in the sixty-five years of operation until 1980, the Texas Forest Service has had only five directors—all trained, professional foresters.

In 1936, the federal government, at the invitation of the Texas legislature, purchased cutover acreages from some eleven lumber companies and established the Texas National Forests in four units. Aided by the CIVILIAN CONSERVATION CORPS, which operated seventeen camps in east Texas, the U. S. FOREST SERVICE undertook a program dedicated to producing a profitable second-growth forest, providing recreational facilities for public use and enjoyment, protecting watersheds from further erosion, and demonstrating sound forestry practices by experiment and example. After more than forty years, the four forests—Angelina, Davy Crockett, Sabine, and Sam Houston—known collectively as the Texas National Forests, have become a valuable economic and cultural asset to the Piney Woods region. In 1980, the forests totaled 665,034 acres of federal lands in a land area of 1,730,936 acres.

Texas A & M University and Stephen F. Austin State University both train professional foresters. The law establishing the state Department of Forestry directed the state forester to teach courses at Texas A & M, but because of overwork, E. O. Siecke discontinued these duties and a forestry program was not resumed there until after World War II. Stephen F. Austin State University established a forestry department in 1946. It was expanded to the School of Forestry in 1965 and was fully accredited by the SOCIETY OF AMERICAN FORESTERS a year later. The Stephen F. Austin School of Forestry now offers a complete program, including the doctoral degree.

In 1974, after more than twenty years of agitation and controversy, Congress established the BIG THICKET NATIONAL PRESERVE in southeast Texas. This unique biological crossroads is home to a great variety of flora and fauna, including bear, deer, many waterbirds, and several species of woodpeckers. The region, containing 84,550 acres, of which 55,938 acres are federally owned, will be forever closed to logging, new highway construction, and other marks of civilization. In addition to Big Thicket National Preserve, Texas contains two national parks. Big Bend National Park was authorized in 1935 and established in 1944. By 1979, it encompassed 708,118 acres. Guadalupe National Park, authorized in 1966 and established in 1972, covers 76,293 acres, of which 46,480 acres were designated as wilderness in 1978.

The Texas state park system began in 1923 and by 1927 included twenty-four park units, although no funds were appropriated for their development at that time. In 1975, Texas boasted eighty-seven park and recreation areas covering 102,000 acres.

Cooperative efforts of the Texas Forestry Association, the Texas Forest Service, the U. S. Forest Service, and the forest products industry have provided a vigorous second-growth forest that is a continuing resource. It provides important quantities of wood products to a variety of enterprises as well as recreational facilities and a region of rare beauty for wildlife advocates and preservationists.

FURTHER READING: Francis E. Abernathy, *Tales from the Big Thicket* (1966). Robert S. Maxwell, "Lumbermen in the East Texas Frontier," *Forest History* 9 (Apr. 1965): 12–16, and "One Man's Legacy: W. Goodrich Jones and Texas Conservation," *Southwestern Historical Quarterly* 77 (Jan. 1974): 355-380. Robert S. Maxwell and James W. Martin, *A Short History of Forest Conservation in Texas, 1880–1940* (1970). George T. Morgan, Jr., "No Compromise —No Recognition: John Henry Kirby, the Southern Operators Association, and Unionism in the Piney Woods, 1906–1916," *Labor History* 10 (Spring 1969): 193-204. Jack P.

Oden, "Charles Holmes Herty and the Birth of the Southern Newsprint Paper Industry," 1927–1940, *Journal of Forest History* 21 (Apr. 1977): 76-89.

ROBERT S. MAXWELL

TIMBER CONSERVATION BOARD

Troubled by overproduction of timber in the early part of the Great Depression, a group of lumbermen and foresters asked President Herbert Hoover to appoint a commission to investigate the state of the industry and to make recommendations to him, to Congress, and to private companies on how to remedy the critical situation. On November 12, 1930, Hoover created the U. S. Timber Conservation Board (TCB) and appointed thirteen men to sit on it, including the secretaries of commerce, agriculture, and interior; lumbermen; foresters; and "others representing the public interest." Although the TCB operated under the auspices of the Commerce Department, it was privately financed. The board divided its work into seven projects, each of which was assigned to a subcommittee. These projects included the economies of the industry; privately owned forestlands; policies affecting publicly owned timberlands; timber marketing; and laws governing forestlands.

In July 1932, the board presented Hoover with a series of recommendations. It called for reorganization of all government agencies dealing with forests under one head; more stringent controls on cutting on public lands both as a conservation measure and to curb production; increased federal funding of fire, insect, and fungus control programs; government promotion of sustained-yield methods; and government support for forest production and marketing research.

The report was couched in very general terms; the TCB made few specific recommendations. Hoover had responded to a preliminary report on May 14, 1931, by curtailing sales of timber from the national forests. However, by the time the board made its final recommendations, Hoover was in the midst of a presidential campaign in which he was warning against massive government action, and he ignored the report.

Nevertheless, in Samuel Trask DANA's phrase, the TCB "performed a valuable service in analyzing the difficult economic and technical problems faced by industry and in close cooperation between public and private agencies in the solution of these problems." This latter bore fruit, albeit briefly, in the drafting of the Lumber Code adopted under the National Industrial Recovery Act in August 1933.

FURTHER READING: Samuel Trask Dana, *Forest and Range Policy: Its Development in the United States* (1956).

TIMBER PRODUCTION WAR PROJECT

Even after the overwhelming first wave of wartime construction abated in early 1943, it was obvious that government demands for timber were not only going to remain at unprecedented levels but would even increase. Wood production was described as "our most critical raw material production problem." Particularly discouraged by the competitive anarchy and waste among the several thousand small and medium-sized mills of the Southeast, the Lumber and Lumber Products Division of the War Production Board (WPB) requested the U. S. FOREST SERVICE to oversee the rationalization and coordination of the industry. On August 21, 1943, the WPB organized the Timber Production War Project (TPWP) with an initial appropriation of $1 million. It was staffed and managed by the Forest Service.

TPWP (commonly referred to as "Teepee Weepee") worked principally in the Southeastern states, involving state and local agencies as fully as possible. Pulpwood, EXCELSIOR, veneer, and NAVAL STORES were the most critical areas of concern and labor was the most serious problem. Wages were low compared to those in other war-stimulated industries, and considerable numbers of the marginally employed population which traditionally manned the small mills had been drawn north and west. Urging what increases it could on the small, often marginal, operators, TPWP also immediately arranged for the deferment of 5,000 draft-eligible employees in the industry.

In order to combat the chronic absenteeism of the region (the population of the pineys yet had only one foot in an industrialized society), TPWP dispatched a team of wounded soldiers who showed enemy films of captured American equipment made of lumber and other forest products. These programs were presented to 80,000 woods and mill workers and their families. When labor shortages continued to be the major obstacle to full production, TPWP recruited about 30,000 prisoners of war (up to 19,000 at one time) for employment in pulpwood production.

TPWP also mobilized equipment (a shortage of trucks was the industry's second most serious problem), made additional stumpage available, and consulted with the management of small firms on efficient cutting and administrative practices. Although it was unable to measure its effects with complete precision, TPWP estimated that its actions increased production by 8 billion board feet, at a cost to the government of approximately thirty-four cents per thousand feet.

One reason for TPWP's extraordinary success and economy was that it was largely a field operation. It maintained only a tiny central office and kept virtually all of its 200 full-time employees (mostly from the Forest Service) on the scene of operations. TPWP was terminated on October 31, 1945.

TIMBER RESOURCES REVIEW

Early in 1952, the U. S. FOREST SERVICE announced its intention to update its 1945 inventory of the nation's forest resources. Although only seven years had passed, a number of circumstances seemed to warrant the project: an increase in the body of data available; new methods of collecting information; the rapid growth of interest in forestry among private landowners; accelerating utilization of resources; and the cold war with the Soviet Union, unanticipated in 1945.

Forest Service Chief Richard MCARDLE gave responsibility for the Timber Resources Review (TRR) to his assistant, Edward Crafts, who organized an informal advisory board made up of representatives

of thirteen major forestry organizations, wood processing industry associations, and labor and agricultural organizations. Many local associations also cooperated, and the departments of Commerce and Interior contributed to the exhaustive investigations of inventory, growth, utilization, and productivity. With misgivings because of Crafts's reputation as the Forest Service's leading regulationist, the FOREST INDUSTRIES COUNCIL also participated.

Western lumbermen were not reassured by TRR's preliminary report. Although it lacked the calamitous temper of some previous surveys, the report leaned toward stricter government controls of forest resources, traditionally a bugbear in the West. Industry and Forest Service economists fenced over the possibility of accurately projecting future needs, predictions on which TRR's findings were based. They could not agree, but industry spokesmen prevailed on the Eisenhower administration to tone down the final report, published in January 1958 as *Timber Resources for America's Future.*

The final report was cautiously optimistic. There was no "timber famine" in the offing but there were some worrisome problems. TRR found that quality species of timber trees were in decline; that excessive cutting in Southern pinewoods was reducing that re-

In the 1950s, a timber famine was no longer considered likely. Logging of this Douglas-fir forest has been quickly followed by vigorous new growth. American Forest Institute Photo.

gion's reserves; and that standards of forest management among small forest owners were declining. The review recommended an immediate program under which 52 million acres of potential forestland would be planted.

TRR also reported having found surprisingly high productivity on recently cut lands owned by large companies. It projected that the United States, while placing an increasing demand on its own resources, could continue to rely on them. However, "the Nation has no surplus of commercial forestland" and was relying too heavily on a small number of species, especially Douglas-fir, ponderosa pine, and southern yellow pine. Even though timber growth was increasing, quality was declining, and waste was unnecessarily high, up to 25 percent of the wood cut. Production was projected to fall somewhat short of future needs, but the gap could be closed by new plantings.

The Timber Resources Review of 1952–1958 was the most thorough and most scientific survey of forest resources ever done. Politically, its final report was not completely satisfying to either extreme in the durable regulation controversy but a compromise. Indeed, *Timber Resources for America's Future* reflected the classic theme of the Eisenhower era: there were problems, but none were irremediable.

FURTHER READING: Harold K. Steen, *The U. S. Forest Service: A History* (1976).

TIMBER TRESPASS AND DEPREDATION ON PUBLIC LANDS

The earliest efforts of the United States government to prevent timber trespass were irrevocably tied to maintaining a steady supply for naval needs. Prior to such protective action, timber depredation was considered simply an accessory to trespassing on public lands. In 1821, the U. S. attorney general opined that "no act of Congress provides for the waste of timber on the public lands, separately considered." The 1807 Act to Prevent Settlements until Authorized gave the United States government "all the civil remedies which individuals possess." Criminal penalties and active enforcement, however, waited a concern for supplies of naval timber.

On March 2, 1817, Congress empowered the secretary of the navy, under presidential direction, to reserve tracts of live oak and redcedar. Agents were authorized to survey lands bearing timber and to pursue depredators. The latter were defined as trespassers cutting or removing live oak and/or redcedar timber from any public lands, or cutting/removing any timber from authorized reserves. Penalties ran to a maximum $500 fine and six months imprisonment. Should any shipmaster be arrested with stolen timber as cargo, he could find his ship seized and forfeited with all its accessories. An attempt to export would be tagged with an additional penalty "not exceeding one thousand dollars."

The secretary's power to appoint agents was rescinded in 1820; instead, the president was instructed to hire "surveyors of public lands," as needed. This change did not halt the employment of timber agents; individuals were appointed in 1821, 1822, and 1826. In 1827, the president was asked by Congress to reserve "live oak, or other naval timber"—a broader employment than was allowed by the 1817 act. This authority was extended further in 1831 in order to enhance "application to the lands subsequently acquired by the United States," especially the Florida coast. Penalties were increased; fines were raised to three times the value of the timber cut, and convictions for depredations became subject to a year in prison. Enforcement became more active as informants and captors were to be given half of the fines and forfeitures gathered. The entire southeastern coast was districted, and agents using three schooners were appointed to patrol the lands bearing naval timber.

Federal efforts to prevent the cutting of timber from public lands were significantly changed by the 1850 Supreme Court decision in *United States* v. *Ephraim Briggs.* Briggs, charged with cutting white oak and hickory trees in Michigan, argued that this was not naval timber; therefore, he was subject to civil trespass, but not the 1831 act. The court disagreed, refusing to draw a distinction between naval and other timbers. Less than three weeks later, in *Forsyth* v. *U. S.,* with the act of 1831 again at issue, the Supreme Court ruled that there was "no distinction made between the act of trespass in cutting the timber on lands reserved and not reserved for the use of the navy." In fact, the court ignored both the language and intent of the 1831 act, designed as it was to stop the cutting and removing of naval timber. This new doctrine meant that all public lands, carrying every type of timber, were to be administered under the provisions of the naval timber act of 1831.

The GENERAL LAND OFFICE (GLO), recently transferred to the newly formed Interior Department, assigned timber agents to the Midwest in 1851. Neither Congress, the president, nor the secretary of the navy were involved. The appointments were justified by reference to *U. S.* v. *Briggs.* By 1854, five agents were patrolling the heavily timbered territories of Michigan, Minnesota, Wisconsin, and Iowa. Overwhelming opposition from settlers frustrated their efforts to stop timber cutting on public lands. Resistance included refusal to purchase seized timber, "rescue" of individuals under arrest, and physical abuse. This opposition was echoed by western congressmen, who declared the agents guilty of abusing hapless settlers. Cries that the distribution system for public lands was being subverted (how could honest settlers improve the land without cutting timber?) caused a change in the system of preventing timber trespass.

On December 24, 1855, the new GLO commissioner dismissed all timber agents and gave enforcement duties to the already overworked land registrars and receivers. Though "no compromise" was allowed, the officials were to be "careful not to interfere" with settlers' rights. By 1860, the policy of no compromise with commercial trespassers was forgotten. The secretary of the interior told the GLO to settle with offenders, who were to purchase the territory cut, pay fifty cents per 1,000 board feet, and cover the costs incurred in prosecution. In time, this fine became "a reasonable stumpage according to the market value of the timber cut, at a minimum, in no case, of less than $2.50 per thousand feet and costs." Enforcement of this minimal policy was at best uncertain in the immense wilderness. In 1864, the GLO commissioner reported that his people would not "pursue the offenders in a vindictive spirit." Agents were, until 1872, paid from collected stumpage fees; after 1871, annual appropriations (usually $5,000) were made by Congress. By 1880, the GLO reported that agents of its Division P had recovered $294,000 since 1855. This system, despite optimistic reports filed annually by the GLO, was ineffective in controlling timber depredations.

In 1877, GLO Commissioner J. A. Williamson and Secretary of the Interior Carl Schurz examined public timber protection measures and found them wanting. Registrars and receivers were then instructed to report on the activities of existing agents and told not to employ others without authorization from the commissioner. Reports of complicity by local officials with trespassers caused Williamson to appoint timber agents. On May 22, he issued a circular, telling registrars they were "not hereafter to act as agents for the protection of the public timber." The commissioner was determined to take responsibility for timber protection. Schurz reinstated a policy of no compromise. Within a year, however, terms of federal timber protection were completely transformed.

In 1878, Congress created the first laws regulating the use of timber on public lands. The act, passed on April 30, emasculated GLO efforts to prevent timber depredation. The GLO was not allowed "to collect and charge for wood or timber cut on the [unsurveyed] public lands in the Territories." Only the export of such timber was prohibited. On June 3, two other measures became law. One, the Timber and Stone Act, offered surveyed land, unfit for agriculture, in California, Oregon, Nevada, and Washington Territory, in quantities not exceeding 160 acres, at the minimum price of $2.50 per acre. Penalties for timber trespass were reduced. In 1892, this regulation was extended to all public lands. The other, the Free Timber Act, allowed residents of Colorado and Nevada and the territories of Arizona, Dakota, Idaho, Montana, New Mexico, Utah, and Wyoming to cut timber on mineral lands for "agriculture, mining, or other domestic purposes." In 1892, this law was extended to allow domestic manufacturing of the public timber, though Arizona and New Mexico were excluded until 1893. In 1901, California, Oregon, and Washington were brought under the Free Timber Act.

In the wake of congressional action, GLO's Division P toughened trespass prosecution. In 1887, the commissioner reported a 90 percent work-load increase since 1885; agents had handled 9,137 cases, including 101 alleged timber thefts that led to 24 criminal suits filed. A decade later, in 1897, agents reported 310 cases of timber depredation but also issued 35 timber cutting permits. The ability to issue cutting permits reduced the "need" to steal public timber.

Prosecution of trespass varied with the personalities of GLO commissioners. The primary problem, however, shifted at the turn of the century from trespass to fraud. Large timber conglomerates, unable to purchase public timber land directly, hired men to enter claims under the Timber and Stone Act, thereby amassing huge tracts. At the same time, the federal government began to reserve timbered tracts for national forests. By the end of World War I, few tracts of commercial timberlands remained under the jurisdiction of the GLO. A major exception was in western Oregon, where in 1916 the GLO regained control of 2.5 million acres of timberland. GLO merged with the Grazing Service in 1946 to form the BUREAU OF LAND MANAGEMENT, which continues to protect and manage the many resources on public lands, including timber.

FURTHER READING: Jenks Cameron, *The Development of Government Forest Control in the United States* (1928). Ivan C. Doig, "John J. McGilvra and Timber Trespass: Seeking a Puget Sound Timber Policy, 1861–1865," *Forest History* 13 (Jan. 1970): 6–17. Paul Gates, *History of Public Land Law Development* (1968). Jay P Kinney, *The Development of Forest Law in America* (1917). Daniel R. Mandell, "Compelling a Public Timberlands Policy: *United*

States v. *Briggs*, 1850," *Journal of Forest History* 25 (July) 1982). S. A. D. Puter, *Looters of the Public Domain* (1908).

DANIEL R. MANDELL

TRADE AND PROMOTIONAL ASSOCIATIONS

The trade association movement emerged in the late nineteenth century as part of a concerted business and industrial effort to escape from the ravages of the excessive competitiveness of laissez-faire capitalism. Many of these associations originated in a period of accelerating business conditions in the 1880s, and in the next decade they began to assume the character of legal institutions with open and regular meetings, elected officials, and a broad range of cooperative programs. Members of trade organizations were interested in a wide array of activities including the standardization of products, reducing internal litigation, exchanging credit information, compiling statistics, stimulating demand for particular commodities, and encouraging the passage of legislation favorable to the industry. The movement expanded and proliferated rapidly, first on a local and regional basis and subsequently at the national level. Trade associations achieved a formal and institutional role in the nation's economy during World War I. These industrywide organizations were part of a broader transitional stage in the development of capitalism in which modern and farsighted leaders in the industrial world attempted to cope with economic instability and an increasingly integrated economy through cooperative efforts on a national scale. The trade group mechanism represented a voluntary and collective endeavor to alleviate the disruptive strains of competition and to stabilize the market process.

There were close parallels between association work in lumber and the formation of trade organizations in other industries. Indeed, the cooperative efforts of lumbermen probably gained more scholarly attention than comparable activity in other trades. The reasons are obvious—the excessive competitiveness of the business, its propensity to overproduce, and the continual entry of new competitors. Moreover, there were a wide variety of specialty groups involved—timberland owners, logging companies, manufacturers, wholesalers, retailers, and a number of box, shook, shingle, and paper and pulp dealers. From the beginning, associations worked to gain legislative and regulatory measures intended to resolve the industry's perplexing competitive difficulties and to placate the public's concern for conservation.

Most trade association work was a commitment to order and efficiency in place of competitive rivalry and waste—an emphasis on organized activity as a way to effect a rational and smoothly functioning economic environment. Progressive and forward-looking lumbermen, professional foresters, and a few academics led these organized maneuvers in an effort to direct economic relationships in a more positive and concerted fashion. Lumber associations shared and exchanged knowledge about business conditions, marketing prospects, pricing details, and other statistical information to assist in the conduct of predictable and profitable commercial ventures. The trade groups represented a historic phase in the growth and consolidation of American capitalism which also witnessed the emergence of the pool, the trust, the holding company, and the large corporation.

The first trade associations in lumber appeared concurrently with similar associations in other industries. A few small and local antebellum trade groups were organized on a very limited geographical scale, but these and other lumber trade organizations formed before 1890 did not last long. One disgruntled trade journal editor expressed dismay that the industry was "rapidly building for itself a national reputation as the parent of commercial organizations that never amount to anything." Despite repeated failure, lumbermen persisted in their efforts to resolve the uncertainties of the lumber trade.

The Southern Lumber Manufacturers Association, formed in 1890 out of several state associations, was one of the earliest and most aggressive of the regional lumber associations. From its inception the organization tried to establish standard grades and dimensions of lumber products and to implement inspection procedures to promote its standardization work. The first of the national trade associations among the forest products industries was the American Paper and Pulp Association, founded in 1878. The organization influenced legislative matters, especially tariff policy, and cooperated with the purely lumber-producing sector of the industry on common issues. Finally, the expanding activities of the stronger regional associations, the increasing volume of West Coast lumber being shipped to eastern markets, improvements in transportation and communication, and the need to lobby at the federal level led to the formation of the NATIONAL LUMBER MANUFACTURERS ASSOCIATION in December 1902.

Both the national and the regional lumber trade associations and the other specialty or distributive organizations in the forest products industries worked diligently to shape and direct their economic and political world through planning, mutual cooperation, self-regulation, and a friendly relationship with the federal government. Like other forms of business combination and consolidation, the associations used techniques that placed them in continual conflict with the antitrust laws. This was particularly true of the many regional lumber trade associations which periodically had to contend with the more rigid enforcement of the antitrust laws by state and federal attorneys who were suspicious of any form of industrial cartelization. The notoriety given to the lumber antitrust cases reached high points in the few years after 1906, during the early 1920s, and again in the second term of the administration of Franklin D. ROOSEVELT. The prosecutions and threats of prosecution of lumber associations produced more dust than substance and in most cases the groups continued their traditional practices, albeit sometimes through subterfuge.

World War I was an exhilarating and energizing experience for most trade associations, and the lumber industry was no exception. Lumber trade officials enjoyed generally positive relationships with the federal government during the war, and the mobilization of the national economy vastly accelerated the formation of new regional and specialty forest products associations. Moreover, the government granted concessions to trade groups to enable them to circumvent the Sherman Anti-Trust Act for the duration of the conflict. The military and civilian demands for lumber goods required centralized agencies and made it essential for the government to deal with the many thousands of lumbermen scattered across the country through organized trade groups.

Rapid price inflation led to a renewal of official suspicion of trade groups immediately following the war. U. S. Supreme Court decisions regarding lumber trade associations revealed the tone of changing public attitudes toward business organizations during the 1920s. In the American Column and Lumber Company case in 1921, the Court upheld the government's contention that "open price" competition, based on the exchange of information through trade associations, was illegal. That decision led to the reorganization of the American Hardwood Manufacturers Association, then the principal group of hardwood lumber producers. The decision was controversial as soon as it was handed down, however, for trade associations were being accorded increasing influence and respect in government circles. Only four years later, the Court apparently reflected the new outlook in its verdict in the Maple Flooring Manufacturers Association case when it found that the exchange of

statistical information was not a restraint of competition as long as prices and production were not controlled.

No other individual articulated the idea of industry-government cooperation more forcefully than did Herbert Hoover as secretary of commerce. His belief in the efficacy of friendly cooperation between government and industry and the notion that the interests of business and the national interest were identical struck responsive chords in progressive lumbermen. Hoover called the purposes of trade associations "a constructive contribution of public welfare" in collecting information on raw materials and stocks on hand—"all of which ... contribute to stability and the increasing efficiency of industry and to the protection both of the smaller manufacturers and the consumer." The great potential achievement of associational activity, Hoover believed, was its work in voluntary cooperation and its avoidance of regulatory legislation. On one occasion, Hoover praised the lumber industry as "Exhibit A" of government–industry cooperation.

When a plunging stock market precipitated a general and persistent contraction in virtually every sector of the American economy, the optimistic and energetic former commerce secretary, now in the presidency, initiated government-sponsored voluntary and cooperative efforts to slow economic decline and to restore industrial growth. Again, Hoover turned to trade associations—in this case the National Lumber Manufacturers Association (NLMA)—to draft and implement voluntary programs of production control and other forms of self-regulation to right a faltering economy. Lumber trade officials worked closely with the U. S. FOREST SERVICE and other related government agencies in the Hoover-appointed TIMBER CONSERVATION BOARD to slow the worsening economic situation—all to no avail, of course: Hoover's self-regulatory, cooperative system of industry and government programs failed to halt the economy's collapse.

Many industrial leaders, and lumbermen were prominent among them, sought more effective and efficient national programs to bring about industrial recovery. The election of Franklin D. Roosevelt in November 1932 offered, if nothing else, an optimistic change in mood from the gloom and despair that had settled on the last days of the Hoover administration. When the new administration decided to move in the direction of an all-embracing industrial recovery program, it represented a departure from previous federal policy. But this marked a new strategy only insofar as the New Deal program was an effort to institutionalize the influence of business and industry in government through the allocation of great power and decision making to trade associations. The National Recovery Administration (NRA) was intended to legitimize the effort of private interests to circumvent the antitrust laws and to engage in all sorts of cartellike arrangements and to use the force of the state to regulate corporate business activity.

Organized lumbermen were ready for the New Deal experiment in industrial self-regulation. Some of them viewed the Roosevelt recovery program as a continuation of the Hoover cooperative program of the 1920s, but this time with the formal sanction of the state. One lumber trade journal noted euphorically as the recovery administration was getting under way that "the trade association will be the voice of its industry." Most lumber association officials concurred that the new administration was headed in the right direction in its push for industrial recovery. The lumber trade press generally applauded "the new system of economic control" and praised the Roosevelt administration for recognizing that the trade association was the "natural and logical agency" for implementing industrial control. Many lumber trade leaders viewed the Lumber Code Authority under the NRA as a way to invoke the power of the federal government to limit production and to regulate prices.

The failure of the Lumber Code to achieve "self-regulation" can be attributed to the unwillingness of individual producers to comply with code regulations and the failure of the government to enforce compliance. Actually, the larger lumber manufacturers wrote the industrial codes which were subsequently adopted by the Lumber Code Authority. When the smaller manufacturers refused to go along, the system broke down. The initial effort, therefore, to implement a form of compulsory cartelization resulted in failure. Although the industrial codes under the NRA formally integrated and legitimized trade associations as policy-making partners in directing the nation's economy, the Supreme Court decision which declared the recovery act unconstitutional in 1935 legally ended the experiment. However, lumber trade associations survived this setback, as did most other industrial organizations, and continued to probe for federal support and assurance in their quest for industrial stabilization.

Despite a period of indecision and equivocation after the 1935 decision, trade associations continued to muddle through their conflicting ambitions and objectives and to assert their considerable influence in government affairs. The failure of the NRA did not deter organized trade activity. The general principle of allocating great influence to the private sector lived on without formal name and structure. Although the recovery administration was a conspicuous failure during its brief existence, it subsequently became a model for business–government relations.

World War II once again provided trade associations with the opportunity to fully assert themselves. Trade officials, many of them with experiences in the earlier war mobilization effort, trekked to Washington, D.C. The NLMA and its regional affiliates and the many other specialty forest products groups provided the professional expertise and organizational know-how to carry out the government's requests for lumber-related war materials. During the course of the war, the forest products industries achieved much of the legislative program they had sought for decades, and, as they had twenty-five years earlier, the associations emerged from the war with an expanded sense of confidence and prestige.

Since 1945, the pervasive influence of organized trade groups in national economic and political life has not diminished. Although many of these organizations have undergone a metamorphosis of structural change and geographic and institutional adjustment, they have remained thoroughly integrated as power brokers for their respective trades. The associations always were thoroughly political and their work since 1945 is no exception. Although sometimes describing themselves as dispassionate adjudicators of public policy, trade leaders always have been primarily concerned with the economic health of and future prospects for their respective industries. In this capacity, they are part of a long tradition that has accompanied the evolution of capitalist institutions from individual competing units to more centralized, monopolylike forms of industrial control. The evolution and influence of the NLMA and its successor, the NATIONAL FOREST PRODUCTS ASSOCIATION, are good examples. The latter organization speaks much more assertively and authoritatively for the forest products industry than did the former association during its long service to the lumber business. A decline in the number of individual corporate units, a greater degree of centralized control, and an effective influence in national politics account for part of this change.

Parallel to the growth and development of the trade association movement in the lumber industry were a number of companion, and usually subsidiary, promotional organizations. These groups devoted their energies to the promotion of wood products, to trade extension work, and, when trade associations expanded to a national scale, to public relations work to counter criticism of the lumber and wood manufacturing industries. Committees within the national and regional associations carried out many of these activities. The NLMA and its regional affiliates, beginning in the second decade of the twentieth century, made a concerted effort to influence newspaper and magazine editorial policy and otherwise to refurbish the industry's somewhat tarnished public image. These committees and subsidiary organizations sought to show that the industry was a responsible caretaker for the nation's timberlands. Even nonlumbering commercial bodies, such as the United States Chamber of Commerce, had committees that testified at congressional hearings and otherwise spoke for the collective view of organized lumbermen.

The most prominent of these subsidiary organizations was the American Forest Products Industries (AFPI), which was originally created as a subsidiary of the NLMA in 1932 to promote trade in lumber products and to encourage research in the manufacture and utilization of wood materials. The AFPI became a separate organization in 1946 and directed its efforts to promoting public knowledge about forestry practices and providing positive public information about the lumber industry. The Tree Farm Program, initiated in 1941, is one example of AFPI public relations work. In 1968, AFPI changed its name to the AMERICAN FOREST INSTITUTE (AFI). Since then, AFI has carried on an ever expanding and evidently successful public relations campaign for the forest products industries, which includes annual press tours to enlighten the media about its views on important issues in contemporary forest management.

FURTHER READING: Nelson C. Brown, *The American Lumber Industry, Embracing the Principal Features of the Resources, Production, Distribution, and Utilization of Lumber in the United States* (1923). M. Browning Carrott, "The Supreme Court and American Trade Associations, 1921–1925," *Business History Review* 44 (Autumn 1970): 320-338. Henry Clepper, *Professional Forestry in the United States* (1971). John H. Cox, "Trade Associations in the Lumber Industry of the Pacific Northwest, 1899–1914," *Pacific Northwest Quarterly* 41 (Oct. 1950): 285-311. James E. Fickle, *The New South and the "New Competition" Trade Association Development in the Southern Pine Industry* (1980). James W. Silver, "The Hardwood Producers Come of Age," *Journal of Southern History* 23 (Nov. 1957): 427-453. Harold K. Steen, *The U. S. Forest Service: A History* (1976).

WILLIAM G. ROBBINS

TREE FARMS

The American Tree Farm System is a nationwide conservation program sponsored and supported by the forest products industry to recognize and encourage good management of privately owned woodlands.

The idea of tree farming reflects the historical shift in attitudes of Americans toward their forest resources from "timber mine" to "tree farm." Tree farming in a general sense is synonymous with forest management practiced on privately owned timberland. M. L. Alexander, commissioner of the Louisiana Department of Conservation, advocated "timber farming" on CUTOVER LANDS in 1917. The term "tree farm" was employed by various writers thereafter; the best known use was perhaps Gifford PINCHOT's statement in 1935: "Wood is a crop. Forestry is tree farming."

The traditional honor of being "Tree Farm No. 1" has gone to a 120,000-acre tract owned by the Weyerhaeuser Timber Company in western Washington's Grays Harbor County. Heavy use by hunters, fishermen, berry pickers, and vacationers posed a fire hazard to the timber. The company appealed to the public for cooperation in fire prevention. Chapin Collins, editor of the local *Montaesano Vidette*, suggested naming the tract the "Clemons Tree Farm" in honor of pioneer logger Charles H. Clemons. That title caught the fancy of the public. Clemons Tree Farm was formally dedicated by Governor Arthur B. Langlie on June 12, 1941. Langlie prophesied: "The Clemons Tree Farm . . . may set the pace for millions of acres of such lands throughout the state." (Indeed, by 1981 there were 615 tree farms in Washington State covering 5.85 million acres, while nationally the system embraced 80.8 million acres belonging to 40,713 owners.)

The attention attracted by the Clemons Tree Farm spurred similar efforts elsewhere. On December 26, 1941, a West Coast Tree Farm Program was established for the Douglas-fir region of western Oregon and Washington by the Joint Committee on Forest Conservation. This group represented the West Coast Lumbermen's Association and the Pacific Northwest Loggers Association (now the INDUSTRIAL FORESTRY ASSOCIATION). The Joint Committee certified sixteen tree farms totaling 726,617 acres on January 20, 1942. The Clemons Tree Farm was not actually certified as a West Coast Tree Farm until September 28, 1942. The West Coast program delayed in issuing certificates until February 16, 1943, when an official American Tree Farm System insignia could be included; because of its role in sparking the program, the Clemons Tree Farm received Certificate No. 1. By that time, the Western Pine Association had developed a similar program, certifying its first tree farm, a 450,000-acre property in eastern Oregon, on September 24, 1942. In the South, Alabama led the way, its program (sponsored by the state chamber of commerce) certifying its first tree farm on April 4, 1942. The Arkansas Forestry Commission was close behind, certifying that state's first tree farm on June 6, 1942.

In November 1941, the NATIONAL LUMBER MANUFACTURERS ASSOCIATION (NLMA), at the urging of its western members, resolved that a national tree farm program should be established. In the following year, sponsorship of the American Tree Farm System was undertaken by the American Forest Products Industries (AFPI), then a subsidiary of NLMA. At first, AFPI simply registered all tree farms and publicized the activities of participants in the program. After AFPI became independent of NLMA in 1946, the tree farm program spread to half the remaining states, each developing its own organization and criteria for certification.

The early tree farm movement applied primarily to large landholdings of companies already practicing modern forestry. It was an inspired public relations program, but it met criticism from some quarters. U. S. FOREST SERVICE Chief Lyle WATTS in 1943 attacked it as an industrial attempt to obviate the necessity of government regulation of forest industry lands.

In order to provide a truly national system, the trustees of AFPI in 1954 approved the "Principles of the American Tree Farm System." Although revised

through the years, the major criteria for AFPI tree farm certification have remained essentially the same: the property must be privately owned, managed for the growth and harvest of forest crops, and adequately protected from fire, insects, disease, and destructive grazing. Harvesting practices must assure prompt restocking with desirable trees.

To implement these regulations, AFPI in the late 1950s took over the administration of the program, in addition to sponsorship, in states east of the Rocky Mountains. Local sponsorship was placed in the hands of new state forest industry committees, except in the West, particularly in the Douglas-fir region of Oregon and Washington where the Industrial Forestry Association continued to sponsor and administer the tree farm movement. Under AFPI leadership, the system expanded to every state in the nation. When in the mid-1960s AFPI was reorganized as the AMERICAN FOREST INSTITUTE (AFI), its old state forest industries committees were dissolved and local tree farm sponsorship shifted back to independent state timber associations.

The reorganization of AFPI had a traumatic effect on its national tree farm system. The record-keeping system nearly collapsed until, during the early 1970s, AFI computerized its tree farm records. The new tabulation showed some 36,000 members of the system; but records for 6,000 of them could not be locat-

Tree planting machines, Pearl River County, Mississippi. Forest History Society Photo.

American Tree Farm System

Year	Number of Tree Farms	Total Acreage
1941	1	120,000
1945	945	11,134,950
1950	2,935	22,933,130
1955	7,534	37,838,910
1960	19,341	54,524,830
1965	27,309	65,345,574
1970	33,688	74,637,297
1975	31,667	76,343,741
1980	38,926	79,606,485

Figures are for December 31 for years 1941–1960, and for January 1 for years 1965–1980.

ed, and more than 20,000 had not been inspected for five years or more. If the credibility of other AFI programs was to be maintained, the tree farm system had to undergo a thorough renovation.

AFI began a massive campaign to reinspect every tree farm in the nation. Tree farms that no longer met the criteria were decertified. Only about ten states still had functioning tree farm committees, so AFI efforts were concentrated on revitalizing the structure of committees representing forestry-related companies, consulting firms, government agencies, and state and regional associations.

By the mid-1970s, the integrity of the national system had been reestablished and it was again growing. Whereas the primary efforts during the early days had been to add new members, the focus now shifted to forestry performance. Each tree farm would be reinspected by local sponsors approximately every five years, giving landowners continued contact with foresters and good forestry practices. An "Outstanding Tree Farmer" competition was initiated in several states, becoming national in scope by 1976.

The tree farm program was originally developed to demonstrate that privately owned forestlands could be managed in the public interest. Virtually all of the early tree farms were industry-owned, but subsequently the program was extended to nonindustrial forest in recognition of its importance in helping to meet the nation's wood needs. In 1980, 59 percent of the nation's commercial forestlands were in nonindustrial private ownership. These 283 million acres were held by perhaps 4 million Americans, and the Tree Farm Program proved to be a useful tool to encourage productive management of these small tracts. Indeed, in 1980, 52 percent of the certified tree farmers owned woodlots of 100 acres or less.

The program by that time had forty-eight active tree farm committees and there were tree farms in every state. About 8,000 foresters—employed by government, industry, or consulting firms—volunteered time to operate the program. The green and white diamond-shaped tree farm sign was a nationally recognized symbol of good private forestry. It offered a visible declaration by owners that they believed in forest management and that they were growing trees for the future.

FURTHER READING: William D. Hagenstein, "Tree Farms: How They Started," *Western Conservation Journal* 14 (July-Aug. 1957): 7-9, 56, 58, and *Tree Farms: Greener Every Year*, an H. R. MacMillan Lectureship Address delivered at the University of British Columbia, March 17, 1977. Paul F. Sharp, "The Tree Farm Movement: Its Origin and Development," *Agricultural History* 23 (Jan. 1949): 41-45.

RICHARD LEWIS

TREE NURSERIES AND TREE SEED COLLECTION

Records of forest tree planting in America date as far back as the 1820s, when attempts were made in Florida and in Massachusetts to grow oaks for ship timbers. At various times in the nineteenth century, small areas in New England were reforested by planting, and AFFORESTATION was attempted on the Great Plains under the Timber Culture Act of 1873. However, systematic planting on an extensive scale awaited the establishment of national and state forests around the beginning of the twentieth century. The U. S. Division of Forestry had engaged in experimental planting of conifers in the sandhills of Nebraska in the 1890s, using stock from a nursery at Lincoln. In 1903, the agency established a 240-acre tree nursery near Halsey, Nebraska, for afforestation of the Dismal River Forest Reserve, and in the same year it set up a nursery at Pasadena, California (later moved to Henninger's Flat), for planting on the San Gabriel Reserve. When administration of the forest reserves was transferred to the U. S. FOREST SERVICE in 1905, reforestation boomed, and by the end of 1908 the service could count twenty-four nurseries on the forests in the Great Plains, Rocky Mountains, the Southwest, and California, with a combined annual productive capacity of 8.8 million trees. In 1915, federal nurseries across the country inventoried 34 million seedlings. Most Forest Service nursery stock went for planting on national forests, although a federal nursery in Mandan, North Dakota, was giving away trees for windbreaks in 1916.

The earliest state nurseries began to enter the reforestation picture in the nineteenth century, but

Douglas-fir seedlings grow at the Nisqually Nursery near Olympia, Washington. American Forest Institute Photo.

for a long time they played a minor role. States in which timber harvesting had been heavy and forest fires extensive became concerned about the need to restock state and private lands; several passed laws establishing bounties or tax relief for tree planting. The California Board of Forestry in 1887 established two nurseries, one at Santa Monica in southern California and one at Chico in the northern part of the state, but the trees produced were mostly used for experimental reforestation and contributed little to regenerating denuded land.

It was not until about 1920 that there was a serious interest in state nurseries for large-scale operations. Section 4 of the CLARKE-MCNARY ACT of 1924 permitted the federal government to cooperate with states to pro-

duce and distribute nursery stock; Congress initially authorized the expenditure of $100,000 a year. California quickly took advantage of this cooperation, and in 1926 it received support for its production nursery established four years earlier near Davis in central California. As other states took advantage of the Clarke-McNary funds, state nurseries furnished stock to farmers and other owners of small forest holdings. Particularly in the South, there was rapid expansion of nursery production. Between 1935 and 1942, eight state and Soil Conservation District nurseries in the Great Plains assisted in producing massive numbers of trees for SHELTERBELTS.

Private nurseries have also played an important role in the development of reforestation. Private industrial forest owners were never able to purchase planting stock directly from Forest Service nurseries, and when demand began to exceed state nurseries' capacities, industrial nurseries began to spring up. Two of the most notable were in Louisiana; one of them produced stock for the Urania Lumber Company which reforested 25,000 acres in 1913, and the other was the Great Southern Lumber Company venture at Bogalusa, where stock was produced to plant 13,000 acres between 1920 and 1926. Between 1922 and 1932, two California lumber companies, Union and Hammond, produced and planted 12 million seedlings on 26,400 acres in the redwood region. Some forest trade associations established nurseries to produce stock for members. The West Coast Lumbermen's Association's Nisqually Nursery near Olympia, Washington, opened in the early 1940s and by the end of the decade produced 9 million seedlings annually.

Commercial nurseries operated by individuals or small companies have come into being more recently. In the Prairie States between 1935 and 1942, there were ten commercial nurseries producing stock for shelterbelt plantings. Since World War II, increased knowledge of the biological processes necessary to produce high-quality stock has reduced the risks of investment in forest nurseries, and more commercial ones have been established.

The largest increase in numbers of industrial nurseries has occurred in the Southern and Pacific Coast States. Private nurseries were more numerous in Kansas and Pennsylvania in 1950, but by 1976 most of them were in the Pacific Coast States.

Seeds are the backbone of nursery production. Local seed was probably the mainstay of early operations. The genetic quality of trees from which cones were collected, however, may have left something to be desired, since limby "wolf" trees and squirrel caches made the easiest collecting. However, some good-looking, well-formed plantations have resulted from the early seed.

The earliest processing of cones and seeds was a simple operation. Collected cones were spread on tarps in the sun to dry and open. After opening, the cones were tumbled in a hand-turned revolving drum covered with wire mesh to extract the seed. Detaching seed wings required another hand operation. Seeds could be placed in burlap bags and flailed or rubbed until the wings were removed. Winnowing in the wind cleaned out the chaff.

These hand methods gradually gave way to the use of sophisticated mechanical devices. Kilns took the place of solar drying, and machines were developed for detaching wings. Tumblers were power driven, and

TABLE 1. Forest Nurseries

	1949	1980
Federal	32	24
State	83	88
Industry	9	61
Commercial	14	125

various kinds of agricultural cleaners were used to separate seed and chaff and upgrade the seed. Processing became largely a continuous-flow operation.

Research begun in 1914 had shown that climate and soil conditions in the area where seed is being collected should match those where the seedlings from that seed source are going to be planted. Thus some control over source identification became necessary; instances of mislabeled seed became troublesome. In 1939, the Forest Service issued guidelines for seed selection for national forest plantings; only seed of known origins should be used.

New York was one of the first states to include provisions for tree seed in its seed law of 1939. Eventually, about a third of the states developed "truth of labeling" requirements for tree seed. Members of the tree seed trade set up voluntary certification systems in a number of states, following the lines of grain and vegetable crop certification. The first tree seed certification system was originated in Georgia in 1959 by the Georgia Crop Improvement Association and the Georgia Chapter of the SOCIETY OF AMERICAN FORESTERS. Since then, South Dakota, the Pacific Coast states, and most of the Southern states have developed certification programs. In the South, seeds are certified for tested genetic superiority, but in the West certification remains only an identification of the seed source.

FURTHER READING: C. Raymond Clar, *California Government and Forestry*, vol. 1 (1959). Ernest J. George, *Thirty-one Year Results in Growing Shelterbelts in the Northern Great Plains*, U. S. Department of Agriculture Circular No. 924 (1953). Julius F. Kummel, Charles A. Rindt, and Thornton T. Munger, *Forest Planting in the Douglas-fir Region* (1944). Ralph A. Read, *Tree Windbreaks for the Central Plains*, Agriculture Handbook No. 250 (1964). Gilbert H. Schubert and Ronald S. Adams, *Reforestation Practices for Conifers in California* (1971). C. H. Shinn, "The Forestry Stations," in University of California Experiment Stations, *Biennial Report* (1893), pp. 425-439. J. H. Stoeckeler and C. W. Jones, *Forest Nursery Practice in the Lake States*, Agriculture Handbook No. 110 (1957). C. S. Schopmeyer, *Seeds of Woody Plants in the United States*, Agriculture Handbook No. 450 (1974). James W. Toumey and Clarence F. Korstian, *Seeding and Planting in the Practice of Forestry* (3rd ed. 1942). U.S.D.A. Forest Service, "Forest Tree Nurseries of the

United States," *Tree Planters' Notes*, No. 1 (1950). Philip C. Wakeley, *Planting the Southern Pines*, Agriculture Monograph No. 18 (1954).

RONALD S. ADAMS

TREE RING RESEARCH

Research in the annual growth rings of trees has two general purposes. One is simply botanical. Detailed studies of the way the annual growth rings are created, their widths, the relationship of wood produced in winter and that in summer, variation between and among the rings of a species from different locations enable botanists to know much about how trees grow. By extension, they are able to provide guidelines for foresters and plant specialists to improve the species toward better usage. In this botanical effort, the individual cell structures are studied in relationship to

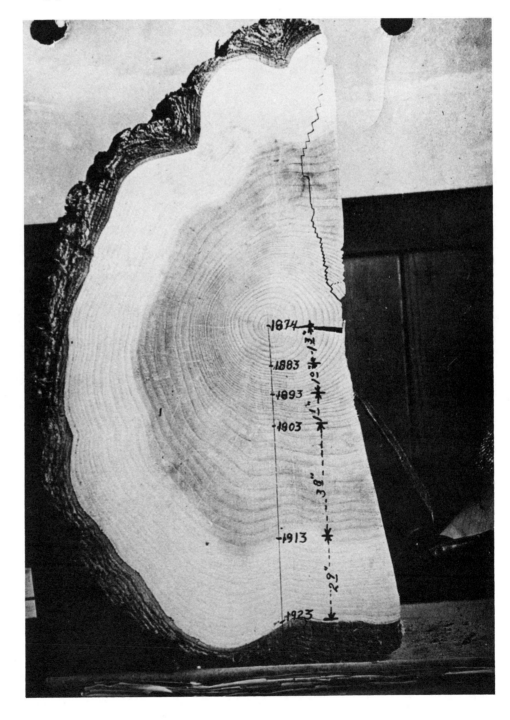

This cross-section of a Douglas-fir log cut in 1923 clearly shows that the tree did not grow at an even rate during the fifty years of its life. One can surmise that in 1903 neighboring trees were removed allowing growth to spurt for a decade. By 1913, canopies and root systems began to compete again for light and water, and the growth rate slowed. Forest History Society Lantern Slide Collection.

their counterparts and the results are applied to the annual rings and ultimately to the growth of the tree itself.

The second usage of these techniques primarily involves studying the rings over time. The width of the rings is a rough indicator of the type of climatic season experienced by the tree. As climatologists and geologists became interested in extending climate records back beyond those available from instrumental records, many individuals felt that an analysis of the width of tree rings would produce a good proxy record of climate in that area.

The first to do this work was Alfred E. Douglass, who began studying tree rings in the Southwest before World War I. Douglass was interested in learning about past rainfalls through the study of the rings and hoped to combine knowledge of ring width with knowledge of sun spot cycles, then also coming under scientific study. The geographer Ellsworth Huntington was also interested in rainfall and dessication, because he believed that the great human migrations could be tied to these phenomena. He traveled to the Southwest, and he and Douglass compared research notes. They extended their studies to the ancient sequoia and published several provocative articles urging further research.

Douglass continued his work, founding the Tree Ring Laboratory at the University of Arizona in 1937. This laboratory has become a world center for these studies. Douglass and his successors, most notably Harold C. Fritts, have extended the studies in a number of ways.

New species have been used, especially the very long-lived bristlecone pine. After analysis of both live and dead specimens, a chronology of the past 6,000 years has been achieved. This dendrochronology is used in dendroclimatology to analyze the deep past from a climate point of view—both to determine what occurred and to find cycles in the long climate experience.

New areas other than the Southwest have been brought into focus. By analogy with the known climate of these long chronologies, models of climate through much of the northern hemisphere have been proposed and are now being tested through tree ring methods, as well as other proxy and instrumental techniques. The rings of trees used to make lumber in very ancient structures are a source. The rings of trees buried in natural disasters such as mudslides, floods, and glacier action are also used. High-speed computers have provided considerable aid in the modeling of past climates derived from these sources, because they are able to absorb and digest the immense amounts of data generated.

Specialty techniques, most notably X-ray densitometry, have enabled researchers to combine the two usages of tree rings to produce not only a gross yearly statement but also one that can provide knowledge of seasonal climatological change, especially reflecting temperature and precipitation. Although the techniques work best on plants in a climatologically stressful situation, recently the techniques have been refined to provide good data in more typical and more stable regimes. Work thus far has concentrated in the northern hemisphere, especially in Europe and North America. In recent years, the work has been extended to other regions in the hope that these long-range climate records will be of great use in understanding the past.

FURTHER READING: Harold C. Fritts, *Tree Rings and Climate* (1976). *Tree-Ring Bulletin* (1940 to present). A. E. Douglass, *Climatic Cycles and Tree Growth* (1936).

DAVID C. SMITH

TREES AS EMBLEMS

American flags and coins have prominently displayed trees since before the Revolution, reflecting the important role that the forests played in the emerging nation. The Massachusetts General Court ordered tree coins made in 1652. A willow, an oak, and a white pine were displayed on three separate series of coins. Although the series was minted as late as 1683, nearly all of the coins are dated 1652, because the English had ordered its colony to stop making coins in 1652. The false date was a subterfuge.

Early Americans often saw individual trees as symbols of democracy. For example, the Sons of Liberty, a patriotic organization in Boston, met under a large elm. When British soldiers felled the elm in 1776, the Liberty Tree became a symbol of American defiance. One of the most famous tree emblems, the New England flag, used a pine as a banner of democratic independence. The flag shows a white pine with the slogan, "Appeal to Heaven." In still another example, Americans were angered that the British Crown had reserved the choicest pines to use as masts under the so-called Broad Arrow acts, and a pine tree flag was defiantly flown by the Revolutionary navy in 1775.

Another famous Revolutionary banner was the Bunker Hill flag of 1775, which contained a replica of the British admirals' flag with a pine tree superimposed in the corner—a symbol of democracy set in the midst of an English heritage. To this day, images of trees adorn several state flags: Florida since 1889, South Carolina since 1861, Maine since 1903, and Vermont since 1923. From 1861 to 1894, the Mississippi flag bore a magnolia, and since 1917, the Territory of Guam has used a palm tree on its flag.

In recent times, trees have been widely used as company logos and institutional symbols. Banks often incorporate trees in their company trademarks, as symbols of steady growth and strength. Some of these banks—most of which use an abstract portrayal of a tree—include the Savings Bank Association of New York State, the Citizens Fidelity Bank and Trust Company, and the Orange Savings Bank of Orange, New Jersey.

Trees are used in symbols for educational institutions, perhaps because of the original Tree of Knowledge that tempted Adam and Eve in the Garden of Eden. The New School of Social Research in New York City, the Rehabilitation Institute of Chicago, and the U. S. Department of Education use trees in their logos.

The U. S. Postal Service has often commemorated conservation efforts by displaying trees on stamps. Four-cent stamps celebrated the one-hundredth anniversary of the birth of president and conservationist Theodore ROOSEVELT by showing trees and the words "Forest Conservation." The Fifth World Forestry Congress was recognized in four-cent stamps in 1960, with a painting of a woodland setting. In 1964, Christmas stamps portrayed branches of a holly and a conifer along with the poinsettia and a mistletoe. Another Christmas stamp, the first stamp ever designed in needlepoint, showed a Christmas tree in 1973. And in 1978, a block of four stamps was dedicated at the annual meeting of the AMERICAN FORESTRY ASSOCIATION.

The best-known trees in Washington, D.C.—cherries donated by the Japanese government—have been the subject of two issues of stamps. In 1960, the one-hundredth anniversary of the goodwill treaty between the United States and Japan was commemorated by a stamp showing the Washington Monument with a blooming cherry branch in the foreground. In 1966, a five-cent stamp showed the Jefferson Memorial surrounded by cherry trees.

FURTHER READING: Henry Clepper, "America's Tree Flags," *American Forests* 82 (Mar. 1976): 22-25, 67. David D. Crouthers, *Flags of American History* (1973). Kent Dannen, "Postage Stamp Forest," *American Forests* 82 (Jan. 1976): 46-48. Whitney Smith, *The Flag Book of the United States* (1975).

DOROTHY HEINRICHS

JAY HEINRICHS

TREES FOR TOMORROW, INC.

An industry-sponsored conservation program, Trees for Tomorrow, Inc., was organized in 1944 by nine pulp and paper mill companies in the Wisconsin and Flambeau River valleys. It was funded by assessments based on the quantity of pulpwood each consumed annually.

A regional organization, its activities were and remain restricted to Wisconsin and the Upper Peninsula of Michigan. However, membership was expanded within a few years of its founding to include power companies, other business related to the paper industry, and private individuals. By 1980, over 300 corporate and individual members participated in the program.

One of Trees for Tomorrow's first programs was to distribute seedlings to private landowners. Over 23 million trees were planted under its auspices by 1960. The organization designed forest management plans for woodland owners and supervised the harvesting of forest products for small operators. The association also granted scholarships to forestry students.

Trees for Tomorrow's principal ongoing project is its conservation education program at its Resources Education Center at Eagle River, Wisconsin. By the late 1970s, the association sponsored over 100 workshops each year for interested groups, including camp programs for schoolchildren and educators. By 1980, an estimated 130,000 people had studied conservation at Eagle River.

FURTHER READING: Folke Becker, "Trees for Tomorrow," *Wisconsin Magazine of History* 36 (Autumn 1952): 43-47.

TREES IN LANDSCAPE DESIGN

Trees fulfill essential roles in landscape design. They define, articulate, enframe, join, and screen both architectural and natural settings. They provide visual canopies for streets and other passageways. They establish height and volume relationships among themselves and surrounding objects, thereby structuring the scene in human scale. Their shade creates patterns and contrasts. Considering trees in this way is an arbitrary intellectual exercise. Few people evaluate trees as landscape-aesthetic objects without also referring to their environmental attributes. Trees have significant environmental functions. They cool through shade and transpiration, dry low ground, absorb pollution, create oxygen, buffer the wind, and baffle noise.

Early American colonists considered trees very little, except as fuel, construction material, and nuisances to farming and settlement. The colonists stripped the land of its plant covering before building. They left the surrounding woods to provide a backdrop, by default rather than by design. As the seventeenth century gave way to the eighteenth, trees began to appear in urban settings. Views from the 1730s show Savannah with a few forest survivals, and New York with plantings along Broadway. By the end of the eighteenth century, saving the forest overstory, and planting or transplanting trees, were common practices. No articulated theory accompanied this planting, but it probably reflected a desire for shade and cooling, European influence, the preserving of "old country" memories among immigrants, and a cluster of socioreligious impulses having various origins.

A desire for beauty influenced urban planting as well, for it is otherwise impossible to explain the thousands of American elms once gracing the greens, squares, and streets of hundreds of cities and towns. Insect pests riddle the American elm. Its shallow roots play havoc with nearby paving. The youthful tree is somewhat ragged and spindly, its graceful vase shape and magnificent spreading crown becoming apparent only near maturity. Its purely aesthetic virtues assured for the American elm the role of urban landscape cliché from the mid-nineteenth to the mid-twentieth century. In the 1940s and after, the Dutch elm disease devastated the American elm population. Urban dwellers also planted maples, sycamores, and other large varieties.

Trees were also essential to nonurban landscapes. Wealthy colonists incorporated trees in estate designs. Trees helped to define sight lines on Southern plantations such as Westover, Virginia (1730s). They embellished a few New England gardens, including the Nichols garden of Salem, Massachusetts. Pastoral-romantic planting had developed on a few estate grounds by the 1830s, but received its great impetus from Andrew Jackson Downing's *A Treatise on the Theory and Practice of Landscape Gardening* (1841). Downing counseled against adopting the earlier, baroque "geometric" forms in favor of more natural expression. He argued that naturalistic scenes were equally adaptable to rural cottage plots where formalism would be ludicrous. Romantic landscape gardening dominated estate practice until the late nineteenth century, when trees again accented more formal gardens, as at Biltmore, North Carolina (opened 1895), and later at Ormston, Long Island (1922). Many estate designs used trees in formalistic and naturalistic settings on separate parts of their grounds. Topiary work and diminutive-tubbed varieties bespoke the affluence of the estate owners and the modest salaries of the corps of gardeners required for maintenance. Developments in estate landscape design all but ended during and after the Great Depression.

Twentieth-century promoters of upper middle and middle class garden suburbs such as Roland Park (begun 1891) near Baltimore, and Kansas City's Country Club District (begun 1907), continued the tradition of Riverside, Illinois (begun 1869), by incorporating trees into a landscape pattern that included generous setbacks and curvilinear streets. After the end of World War II, developers of cheap housing ignored most of the lessons of the garden suburbs. In their haste to satisfy the desire for single-family housing, they bulldozed the plant cover, built a house, then stuck a tree in the yard, almost as an afterthought. The Levittowns (begun 1947) were far better suburbs than their critics allowed, though they too followed the scrape-and-plant routine. At mass-produced but somewhat higher-priced Levittown, Pennsylvania (begun 1951), the standard planting was well above average. There, each bare yard received six evergreens, a pear, peach, and apple tree, and a grape vine. Back in the city, the general lack of sidewalks in post-World War II subdivisions inhibited street tree planting. Older streets ravaged by the Dutch elm or other diseases often were not replanted or were restocked with substitute varieties less aesthetically pleasing than the American elm. Shopping centers sprouted in the midst of paved expanses devoid of trees.

In the early 1960s, urban-suburban dwellers appeared to rediscover the tree. Landscape architects dotted the grounds of the newer shopping malls with hardy varieties, often clumped or in planters. Urban foresters replanted streets, sometimes in small trees or in clusters of large varieties designed to screen or enhance the buildings. Developers began siting houses among native trees carefully saved from the bulldozer's blade.

These changes seemed to indicate a growing awareness of the environmental-aesthetic qualities of trees, but critics of the 1970s argued against such an assumption. They pointed out that tree roots in planters suffered from severe cooling, heating, and drought unless the planters were carefully designed. Trees spotted around shopping malls, they claimed, represented a superficial deference to environmentalism, not an awareness of the place of trees in an integrated design. Saving forest giants in a new suburb often proved futile, they wrote, unless the developer paid equal attention to the drainage, wind, and pavement conditions affecting the survivors. They revealed that dead native trees were not replaced with saplings of the same type. Turning to street trees, they argued for a return to large, regularly spaced varieties whose branches would leave the foreground view uncluttered and restore a sense of rhythm to the street. Whatever the ultimate resolution of these arguments, it was clear that trees continued to play a significant role in landscape design.

FURTHER READING: Henry F. Arnold, *Trees in Urban Design* (1980). Norman T. Newton, *Design on the Land: The Development of Landscape Architecture* (1971). James A. Schmid, *Urban Vegetation: A Review and Chicago Case Study* (1975). Robert L. Zion, *Trees for Architecture and the Landscape* (1968).

WILLIAM H. WILSON

TROPICAL FORESTRY

Between the Tropics of Cancer and Capricorn grow about half of the world's forests. They are sufficiently distinct from those of the temperate zone to make their management and use a special branch of forestry. Historical and contemporary American interest in tropical forestry includes the Philippines, Hawaii, Puerto Rico, and the Virgin Islands. Also, there are many tropical nations with U. S. forest industry overseas investments and others receiving technical aid.

The distinctions of tropical and temperate forests that affect their management and utilization are not all absolutes. Many differences are merely matters of degree. Among them are floristic richness and heterogeneity, multistoried structure, and the preponderance of nutrient storage in the biomass rather than in the soil. Associated with these forest characteristics is the greater intensity of insolation, storms, weathering, biodegradation, and leaching that is typical of tropical environments.

Tom Gill, left, one of the first Americans to specialize in tropical forestry, searching for mahogany in Chiapas, Mexico, 1927. Forest History Society Photo.

Attempts to control indiscriminate tropical forest exploitation began in India in the early 1880s. The practice of forestry in the tropics apparently began with the appointment of a scientifically trained forester as superintendent of forests in Pegu, Burma, in 1856. Forest departments were subsequently established in most of the colonies of the tropics and are to be found now in virtually every independent tropical country.

The practice of forest management in the tropics was both assisted and handicapped by prior development of the state of the art in the temperate zone. A primary initial obstacle of much greater tropical significance than in the temperate zone has been the complexity of the mixture of species. One result was the discovery of first-class woods, such as teak, sal, the mahoganies, and the dipterocarps, which are readily acceptable in temperate zone markets. Another result, of corollary significance, is the presence of a great many woods of lesser utility, some of them too dense to be worked easily and mostly unmarketable in the past. Temperate-zone forestry deals with no problems of this complexity.

Highly mixed tropical forests (of unknown age) have not proven easy to manage for timber. Commercial harvesting leaves the worst trees to grow in the subsequent stand. The huge crowns that characterize mature tropical emergents may cause felling damage to most of the immature stand. Natural regeneration of preferred species is seldom satisfactory for a new crop.

The complexities of utilization and silviculture of native forests have led to artificial regeneration, either to enrich existing forests or to reforest bare lands. Plantation yields under favorable conditions have substantially exceeded those of the temperate zone. Enough native timber species have been produced successively in plantations to make it possible to meet most local and some export requirements for veneer, construction lumber, and cellulose. Plantations, because of their high yields, are particularly appropriate for tropical countries, where population pressures, actual or prospective, are great.

The social importance of tropical forestry is becoming more important as local populations grow. Water from forested areas supply most tropical cities and irrigated regions. The richness of tropical forests in both plant and animal species has become recognized as a resource for new crops and for medical research. Tourism in scenic tropical forests, particularly those with spectacular wildlife, is as yet in its infancy but promises to become important socially as well as economically. Accordingly, multiple-use forest management in the tropics can be expected to become as necessary as in the temperate zone.

The main technical problems that lie ahead of tropical foresters include the selection of tree species for reforestation and timber production on diverse sites, reduced costs of plantation establishment, increased yields and natural regeneration in secondary forests, closer utilization, the conservation of nutrients and site productivity, the reduction of logging damage, and the integration of tree production as a factor of diversity in stabilizing tropical agriculture.

FURTHER READING: Tom Gill, *Tropical Forests of the Caribbean* (1931). Ralph C. Hosmer, "The Beginning Five Days of Forestry in Hawaii," *Journal of Forestry* 57 (Feb. 1959): 83-89. *Proceedings of the Duke University Tropical Forestry Symposium* (1965). Elizabeth O. Rothra, ed., *On Preserving Tropical Florida* (1972). Lawrence Rakestraw, "George Patrick Ahern and the Philippines Bureau of Forestry, 1906–1914," *Pacific Northwest Quarterly* 58 (July 1967): 142–150. Frank H. Wadsworth, "The Development of the Forest Land Resources of the Luquillo Mountains, Puerto Rico," Ph.D. dissertation, University of Michigan (1949).

FRANK H. WADSWORTH

U

UDALL, STEWART LEE (1920–   )

Stewart L. Udall was born on January 31, 1920, in St. Johns, Arizona. His youthful experiences in a Western environment and in a Mormon family dedicated to principles of land stewardship left a distinct imprint. He interrupted his college studies to work for two years as a Mormon missionary and then served in World War II with the Army Air Forces. In 1948, Udall earned a law degree from the University of Arizona and practiced in Tucson with his younger brother, Morris. In 1954, he was elected to the first of three successive terms in the House of Representatives. As a congressman, Udall served as a member of the Committee on Interior and Insular Affairs where he became recognized as a member of the "conservation bloc."

Udall was appointed secretary of the interior in 1961 by President John F. Kennedy, and he continued in this position under President Lyndon B. Johnson. Secretary Udall emphasized water development, the protection of water qualities, protection for public lands, and the expansion of park and recreation areas. He supported passage of the major water quality legislation of the early 1960s. His DEPARTMENT OF THE INTERIOR received responsibility for water pollution control in 1966, and the BUREAU OF LAND MANAGEMENT developed a program to improve management of public domain land.

More parkland and more irreplaceable natural re-sources were reserved for public use during Udall's term of office than under any other interior secretary until Cecil D. Andrus's exceptional Alaskan set asides in the late 1970s. The National Park System acquired 246,000 acres during the Kennedy years and 3.6 million acres during the Lyndon Johnson administration. The major and most controversial units added under Udall's administration were the Redwood and North Cascades national parks, both created in 1968. Johnson said of the additions to the park system: "the person mainly responsible for it all is Secretary Udall."

In 1961, Udall created the Bureau of Outdoor Recreation in his department. In the Land and Water Conservation Fund enacted by Congress in 1964, Udall devised a self-financing system for the purchase of park and recreational areas by charging admission and user fees, a radical departure from the traditional free access. Sixty percent of the proceeds from the fund went to the states and 40 percent to the federal government. Udall also encouraged the passage of the Wilderness Act in the same year and subsequently encouraged Congress to extend the wilderness principle to the preservation of wildlife and to the nation's undeveloped rivers. The results were the Endangered Species Preservation Act of 1966 and the Wild and Scenic Rivers Act of 1968. The National Trails System Act followed later in the year. When water development and scenic preservation conflicted, however, Westerner Udall received his severest criticism. At first, he favored proposed hydro-electric dams which would disturb GRAND CANYON NATIONAL PARK. Later, he reversed his position and secured the establishment of Marble Canyon National Monument to include one of the sites.

Udall's *The Quiet Crisis* (1963) revealed his conception of conservation which included not only nature but also man, his welfare, and the dignity of his spirit. Udall encouraged conservationists to broaden their interests and to demand beautiful cities, tasteful architecture, efficient mass transportation, and clean water. Before leaving office, Udall wrote another book, *1976: Agenda for Tomorrow* (1968), which urged the development of a sense of ethical responsibility that encompassed the entire relationship of man to his environment and that stressed the unity and quality of all resources.

The Department of the Interior's primary concerns were the federal lands largely in the western United States. Udall, however, with his interests in water quality and urban environments, gave his department a national image. With the aid of Mrs. Lyndon Johnson, Udall convened the White House Conference on Natural Beauty in 1965 and promoted the subsequent Highway Beautification Act.

For his efforts in aesthetic conservation, the WILD-LIFE SOCIETY honored Udall with the Aldo Leopold Medal and the NATIONAL AUDUBON SOCIETY awarded him the Audubon Medal. In 1969, Udall organized Overview, an international environmental consulting firm, to continue the work in conservation.

FURTHER READING: Barbara Le Unes, "The Conservation Philosophy of Stewart L. Udall, 1961–1968," Ph.D. dissertation, Texas A & M University (1977).

BARBARA LE UNES

URBAN FORESTRY

See Municipal Parks and Urban Forestry

U. S. BIOLOGICAL SURVEY

See Biological Survey

U. S. DEPARTMENT OF AGRICULTURE

See Department of Agriculture

U. S. DEPARTMENT OF THE INTERIOR

See Department of the Interior

U. S. GEOLOGICAL SURVEY

See Geological Survey

UTAH FORESTS

Compared to most of the United States, Utah is only sparsely forested, a legacy of the state's arid climate. Of Utah's 52,541,000 acres, only 15,557,000 are forestlands, and of these, only 3,405,000 acres are considered commercial forest.

Some varieties of conifers, including ponderosa pine, spruce, and fir, are found in the mountains where annual rainfall is above twenty-five inches. Pinyon pine and juniper thrive in lower elevations, and boxelder and several varieties of poplar prosper along mountain creeks, following the streams into the valleys, where willows also thrive. Since the season for precipitation does not coincide with the growing season, mountain conifers are found mostly on the wetter north slopes and along the streams. Although Utah's mountains are primarily grassland, sparse tree growth helps protect the soil mantle, which holds water from winter snow until summer, when it is gradually released into aquifers or streams and runs into the valleys.

Before 1900, exploitation of watershed areas was excessive. Timber cutters looking for railroad ties and house logs overcut and burned many of the few timber stands available, and a few small sawmills, mostly along the Wasatch Front, cut lumber to meet local building needs. In 1899, Utah's 46 mills cut 17.5 million board feet yearly, a figure that dropped to 3.6 million feet by 1905 and remains relatively insignificant to the present. Apart from lumber production, junipers were cut for fence posts and fuel. Stockmen overgrazed grassland until erosion by wind and water forced local resource users to seek help managing the land.

At the turn of the century, national conferences on conservation problems peculiar to grassland erosion and flood control led to improved timber cutting and grazing patterns. Between 1897 and 1905, the Uinta, Fishlake, Manti, Cache, and Wasatch forest reserves were established and were managed to protect valuable watersheds. In 1911, the Utah Experiment Station was established in Ephraim Canyon on the Manti Forest to investigate mountain and desert grassland ecology. The facility, which in 1918 became the Great Basin Experiment Station, drew students from around the world seeking information applicable to similar problems in their own lands. During the 1920s and early 1930s, destructive flooding in Davis County resulted in pioneering rehabilitation and rangeland management efforts on local watersheds. Resistance

A band of sheep is moved on Utah's Cache National Forest, 1953. Forest Service Photo.

to regulation developed as grazing permits on the national forests were reduced, but gradually land users and the U. S. FOREST SERVICE reached an accommodation based on commitment to long-term use and maintenance of the forest and grazing lands. By the 1980s, with Forest Service help, users managed Utah's important forestlands for everyone.

Forestry at the state level focused on fire control. The state's first fire law was enacted in 1917, making it the duty of the sheriff to suppress fires. In 1927, watersheds were designated fire districts under the jurisdiction of county commissioners, and in 1941, in response to the CLARKE-MCNARY ACT, the State Board of Forestry and Fire Control was established. Subsequent years saw increased fire and disease control, the promotion of reforestation and AFFORESTATION, and public education for the protection of watersheds.

Utah boasts five national parks: Arches, estab-

lished as a monument in 1929 and as a park in 1971; Bryce Canyon, established as a monument in 1923 and as a park in the following year; Canyonlands, established in 1964; Capitol Reef, established as a monument in 1937 and as a park in 1971; and Zion, established as a monument in 1909 and as a park in 1919. The national parks encompass a total of 835,233 acres, 805,030 of which are federally owned. Although Utah has no state forests, the State Park and Recreation Commission, founded in 1925 as the State Board of Park Commissioners, oversees forty-three parks and recreation areas covering 56,000 acres.

FURTHER READING: Charles S. Peterson, *Look to the Mountains: Southeast Utah and the La Sal National Forest* (1975), and "Small Holding Land Patterns in Utah and the Problems of Forest Watershed Management," *Forest History* 17 (July 1973): 4–13.

JAY M. HAYMOND

VENEER

See Plywood and Veneer Industries

VERMONT FORESTS

"Voilà les verts monts," proclaimed Champlain when he first came upon Vermont. The state's 5.9 million acres were almost entirely forested at the time of the initial penetration by white settlers. Succeeding generations derived livelihood, shelter, and fuel from these abundant forests dominated by northern hardwoods—beech, birch, and maple—and associated softwoods—spruce and balsam fir. White pine, which often grew to a height of 150 feet in the river valleys, was the first commercially important species to be harvested from the region. Once the pine had been cut, lumbermen returned for the spruce, which after 1850 became the most important source of lumber in the state. Especially after 1880 with the advent of band mills and logging railroads, spruce was the dominant tree for lumber. Other products, especially potash, pearlash, charcoal, cordwood, cooperage, hemlock bark for tanneries, and, more recently, wood pulp were also important. By the 1930s, with the expansion of the furniture and veneer industries, hardwoods, which had grown up on the hillsides after the spruce was cut, were commercially prominent. Vermont has long been the nation's leading producer of maple syrup and maple sugar. Sugar maple, which made up 23 percent of the growing volume of the forest in 1973, is Vermont's most abundant tree species.

Within Vermont, over 1,000 sawmills, including small village mills, were recorded in the 1840 census. Lumbering increased until 1889, when 430 million board feet were produced. Production gradually declined in the early twentieth century and reached a low of 30 million board feet in 1933.

Lake Champlain had been an avenue for the export of timber to Quebec since the colonial period. Then, with the opening of the Champlain Canal in 1822 and the development of railroads after 1849, Burlington on the shore of the lake became a major lumber marketing and distribution center. Railroads brought timber from throughout the state as well as from New York and Quebec for resawing and planing at the busy mills of Burlington, while the Connecticut River, on the east side of the state, transported lumber and logs to cities in Connecticut and Massachusetts. In 1868, Burlington was the third largest lumber port in the United States. Later in the nineteenth century, Burlington as a lumber trading center faced crippling competition from Western forests. The duties placed on Canadian lumber by the Dingley Tariff of 1897 struck a mortal blow at the Vermont city.

In the nineteenth century, lumbering, land clear-

669

ing, and devastating fires reduced Vermont's forest cover to a fraction of its original extent. By 1880, nearly 80 percent of the state had been cleared for farming purposes. What remained of the Vermont forest was largely restricted to a small corner of the state—the "Northeast Kingdom"—and the steep slopes of the Green Mountains. Concern for the forests mounted and in 1884 the first general report on Vermont forest conditions was presented to the state legislature. In the same year, an act to encourage the planting of shade trees was passed into law, and Vermont celebrated its first ARBOR DAY in 1888. In that year, the scope of the Vermont agriculture department was broadened to include forestry. In 1905, the position of forest commissioner was created; the office was dedicated to fire prevention, reforestation,

white pine blister rust control, forestry education, and marketing. That same year, the state purchased a demonstration forest, and by 1925 it managed fifteen state forests, covering 32,238 acres. The movement to broaden state responsibility for forest resource management culminated in the establishment of the Vermont Forest Service in 1923. The Forest Service was reorganized in 1955 as the Department of Forests and Parks.

Despite the many public conservation efforts since the late nineteenth century, broader social forces, especially the demise of the "hill farm," have had the greatest impact upon the state's forests. As these farms were abandoned, forests reclaimed the fields and pastures. By 1970, the pattern of forest loss had been reversed to the point that 73 percent of all land in

Workers at a plant in Bradford, Vermont, roll yellow birch logs into a hot pond for steam treatment. The logs will then be cut into four-foot lengths and sliced into veneer. American Forest Institute Photo.

Vermont was in commercial forest. Significantly, forest ownership in the state is not dominated by large landowners. In 1968, only 16 percent of Vermont's commercial forestlands were owned by forest products industries. Small owners, many of whom hold their lands for amenity values, such as wildlife and recreation, predominate. This ownership pattern makes systematic timberland management planning difficult.

The initial impetus for public involvement in forestry has carried through to the present day. The Forest Service encourages proper management in a number of ways, although Vermont does not have a formal forest practices act as do many other states. Voluntary guidelines for timber harvesting have evolved, and forestry activities above 2,500 feet are strictly regulated through the state's landmark land use law, Act 250, passed in 1970. A use-value tax assessment on forestland provides incentives for forest management. In addition, an extensive system of public education, advisement, and research has been created through the Vermont Department of Forests, Parks, and Recreation and the University of Vermont. The state's first park, Mount Philo, was donated to the state in 1924. By 1975, there were forty-one park and recreation areas covering 35,000 acres. The state's twenty-nine state forests cover an area of 110,000 acres. Federal forest management has focused on the 290,000-acre Green Mountain National Forest, established in 1932, and on the George D. Aiken Maple Syrup Laboratory, which conducts significant research on one of the state's most famous and important forest products.

Although forestry and wood products have always been the foundation of the state's economy, it was the rediscovery of wood as an energy source that triggered renewed interest in Vermont's forest resources. By 1980, an estimated 45 percent of all Vermonters used wood as an important source of residential and commercial heating. This growing interest in the forests of Vermont, together with the state's long-standing tradition of environmental concern, is likely to sustain Vermont's commitment to its forest resource system.

FURTHER READING: William Gove, "Burlington, the Former Lumber Capital," *Northern Logger and Timber Processor* 20 (Oct. 1971): 10–13, 26-29. Perry H. Merrill, *History of Forestry in Vermont, 1909–1959* (1959).

MARK B. LAPPING

VIRGINIA FORESTS

Over 97 percent of the 25.5 million land acres now part of the State of Virginia were once wooded. The original forests were mixed hardwoods and pine. Occasional pure, sun-requiring pine stands occurred as a result of fires or insects destroying the preceding stand. These early forests were a vast resource for ship timbers, lumber, tar, and other products. These forest products were important exports to England and the Caribbean during the colonial period. The census of 1840 credited Virginia (exclusive of the counties which later formed West Virginia) with 782 sawmills producing a product annually valued at $437,397, surpassed among the states only by the production of New York, Maine, Pennsylvania, and North and South Carolina. Farmland abandonment starting just before the Civil War increased the forested acres that would be available during the twentieth century. Virginia reached its peak lumber production in 1909 when over 2.1 billion board feet were reported cut, more than two-thirds of it softwood, and most of that being yellow pine. In that year, Virginia still ranked sixth among the states as a lumber producer. Production rapidly declined, however, and reached a low of 450 million board feet in 1932 during the Great Depression. Since World War II, annual production has fluctuated somewhat above 1 billion board feet. As Virginia's softwood lumber industry declined, hardwood lumber production, principally in the mountainous part of the state, increased. In 1962 and after, production of hardwood lumber, largely oak and poplar, surpassed that of softwood.

The Chesapeake Pulp and Paper Company (later named the Chesapeake Corporation of Virginia) started its operations at West Point in 1914, making kraft sulfate pulp from the state's pine. A paperboard machine was installed in 1917. Expansion of the pulpwood industry subsequently alarmed those who feared depletion of Virginia's timber resources. Pulpwood production increased fairly steadily from about 167,000 cords in 1920 to 2.4 million cords in 1965, when Virginia reached its peak share, 4 percent, of the national pulpwood market. Pine pulpwood production in Virginia reached its height about that time, while hardwood continued to increase its proportion of the state's pulpwood output. After 1960, chips and mill residues became an increasingly important source of wood pulp, providing almost 40 percent of the state's pulp production by 1975. At that time, paperboard accounted for about 44 percent of the value of production of pulp and paper products.

Until 1914, the state's only concern for forestry had consisted of ineffective fire laws. In that year, the general assembly created the office of state forester (later the Virginia Division of Forestry). Still, citizens, women's clubs, and industry had made slow progress in promoting forest fire prevention and control, reforestation, and the application of modern forestry practices. These interests in 1943 established Virginia

This splash dam on Virginia's Big Sandy River stored water, which was released to provide a "flood" to float logs to the mill. Forest History Society Photo.

Forests, Inc. (later known as the Virginia Forestry Assocation) as an educational and informational agency. The following year, legislation was enacted to provide for annual collection of one cent per forested acre from each county, to be used specifically for forest fire protection and suppression. In 1946, the legislature enacted the Forest Management Assistance Act which was designed to step up forestry programs in the state with funds appropriated by the general assembly. An act creating a forest products tax was passed in 1948 to provide a fund for general forest management pro- grams including fire protection and suppression. This tax on the initial processor of forest products was matched from the state general fund.

Federal programs of the Great Depression, especially the work of the CIVILIAN CONSERVATION CORPS (CCC) from 1932 to 1942, drew public attention to the protection and development of forest resources. The Resettlement Administration acquired some 50,000 acres of worn-out farmlands in Virginia's southern piedmont. About 1955, title to these now reforested federal lands was transferred to the State Division of

Forestry. These state forests thereafter provided an annual revenue to local counties and demonstrated the profitability of modern forestry practices. The forest section of the Federal Agriculture Conservation Program, administered by the State Division of Forestry, permitted cost-sharing with small landowners in preparing CUTOVER LAND for planting, reforesting of open lands, improvement of poor-quality timber stands, and other forestry practices.

Lands acquired by the federal government under the WEEKS ACT formed the core of the Shenandoah National Forest, established in 1918, and the Unaka National Forest, established in 1920. These units have grown into the present George Washington and Jefferson national forests covering over 1.6 million acres of federal lands. The state's only national park, the Shenandoah, was dedicated in 1936 on land largely acquired by the state and presented to the federal government under legislation passed in 1926. The park straddles the Blue Ridge and offers recreation to the nearby Washington metropolitan area. Also in 1936, Virginia formally inaugurated its state park system, taking advantage of the presence of CCC workers and other federal assistance available in the Depression era.

By the late 1970s, 16,339,000 acres, approximately 64 percent of the land in Virginia, was in some type of forest cover. This included over 15.8 million acres of commercial forestland and 503,000 acres, approximately 3 percent of the land in the state, in reserved and noncommercial forestland. About 14 percent (1.65 million acres) of the commercial forest was in public ownership; almost the same amount (1.6 million) was owned by the forest industry; and 75 percent (nearly 12 million) was owned by persons holding less than 5,000 acres each.

These tracts owned by small forestland owners grew less than half the timber volume of which they were capable and were the focus of efforts to solve the state's timber drain problem. Legislation in 1970 imposed a special tax on pine forest products to assist the small landowner in reforestation by cost-sharing up to 50 percent. In 1980, allowable cost sharing was increased up to 75 percent. This Reforestation of Timberlands Act of 1970 was the first such legislation enacted in the United States. Two years later, the U. S. Congress passed similar legislation. North Carolina and Mississippi have also enacted "RT" programs. During the 1970s, Virginia replanted an average of 80,000 acres annually. This, along with an effective fire prevention and control organization, the state's New Kent and Augusta tree nurseries, orchards to produce genetically improved seed, laws requiring the leaving of seed trees or replanting after harvesting, and professional management of the state forests, produced substantial progress toward closing the gap between annual growth of tree volume and the annual drain, with the expectation of achieving an even balance by 1986.

GEORGE W. DEAN

VIRGIN ISLANDS FORESTS

See Puerto Rico and American Virgin Islands Forests

WASHINGTON FORESTS

The State of Washington contains two distinct geographical zones. "The land west of the Cascade Mountains is very wooded," noted an early white visitor to the region; "to the east, on the other hand, it has very little wood but is excellent for growing grain and for raising cattle." Heavy precipitation and dense timber typify western Washington, while scattered pine forests and arid, relatively treeless lands characterize the eastern portion of the state. A little less than 23.2 million acres, 54 percent of Washington's land area, remained forested in 1977. The forest of commercial value then covered 17.25 million acres.

The westside forest, between the Cascade crest and water's edge, contained around 90 percent of the state's commercially exploitable timber. The most important of the trees there is the majestic Douglas-fir. Pioneer botanist David Douglas thought his namesake tree to be "one of the most striking and truly graceful objects in Nature." Concentrated in the lowland regions of the state, Douglas-fir normally grows to a height of 200 feet. Highly sensitive to shade, the tree retains branches only on the upper portions of the trunk and normally grows only in extensive pure stands.

The development of large-scale lumber manufacturing in the state focused on exploitation of Douglas-fir.

The great strength of lumber produced from the tree made it especially suited for use in construction. In the mid-nineteenth century, western Washington became the principal supplier of lumber for use in the construction of buildings and wharves in California and Hawaii and of mining timber for Australia, Peru, and Chile.

Other westside commercial species became valuable with the development of new varieties of forest products and the increase in the price of timber during the early years of the twentieth century. Western hemlock, for instance, grows heavily along the coast. It normally reaches a height between 150 and 175 feet on good sites. Hemlock grows with great rapidity in this rain-drenched region, its seeds often sprouting from the rotting carcasses of fallen trees. With its rapid growth and thick foliage, hemlock often drives out other species on logged-off or burned-over tracts.

Lumbermen found hemlock to be a most difficult tree. Popular suspicion of its suitability for lumber because of the poor reputation of eastern hemlock limited the demand and timber companies engaged in repeated efforts to devise a new name for the species so as to disguise its identity from customers. Eventually, the expansion of pulp and paper manufacturing in the region created a profitable market for hemlock. That industry required a cheap supply of raw material and developed chemical processes for the breaking down of hemlock fibers.

Unlike hemlock, Sitka spruce is largely restricted to moist regions along the Pacific Coast. Trees occasionally grow to heights in excess of 250 feet but are normally much smaller. Because of its straight grain, lightness, and strength, spruce has always served a specialized market, focusing on such items as boxes, musical instruments, and racing shells. During World War I, and to a lesser extent in World War II, spruce enjoyed a major demand because of its suitability for use in the construction of airplanes.

Unlike hemlock and spruce, western redcedar has been used throughout the era of human existence in the region west of the mountains. Growing for the most part in damp and well-shaded areas, cedar is light and can easily be worked, even with primitive technology. Moreover, it is resistant to decay, an important consideration because of the soggy climate of the Pacific Northwest. Cedar was exploited by the Indians for the making of canoes and lodges and for many other purposes. It was adopted by the first white settlers for the construction of cabins and became the basis for the region's highly important shingle industry.

To the east of the mountains, the principal species is ponderosa pine. Concentrated in the northeastern corner of the state, ponderosa pine is found in heavy stands at altitudes between 300 and 6,000 feet. Normally growing to only around 125 feet in height, the species features a distinctive scaly and rough bark that is often ripped off in squares by strong winds. The wood is light and soft. In the early twentieth century, pine became the focus of a major Inland Empire lumbering industry, stretching from eastern Washington across the Idaho Panhandle. This industry, though, never became as important as that on the west side, in large part because of the differing forest environment in the two sections of the state. Washington's pine forests are an adjunct to the main activity of the inhabitants, commercial agriculture. West of the Cascades, forests are at the center of all life. They support a vast population of animals—from bear, deer, and elk to birds, beaver, and squirrels—and protect the essential watersheds. Human inhabitants, from the earliest Indians gnawing away at great cedars with crude tools to the modern corporate executive, have depended on the forest for their livelihood.

Systematic exploitation of the forests within what would later become Washington State began with the construction of the Hudson Bay Company's sawmill on the Columbia in 1827, but not until the California gold rush after 1849 did the lumber industry of the Northwest receive any real impetus. In 1889, the year in which Washington became a state, its annual lumber production exceeded 1 billion board feet, placing it fifth among the United States. From 1905 to 1913, and then from 1915 to 1938, Washington was the nation's leading lumber producer. The peak year of 1926 saw 7.46 billion board feet of lumber manufactured. Over 99 percent of that was softwood. Douglas-fir alone accounted for nearly 72 percent. Hemlock followed with about 21 percent while ponderosa pine provided under 6 percent. Small amounts of cedar, spruce, white pine, larch, white fir, and lodgepole pine made up the remainder. Washington's lumber production plunged to a Depression low of 2.26 billion board feet in 1932, recovered to a wartime high of 5.2 billion in 1941, and since 1945 has remained at slightly under 4 billion board feet annually. Washington was also the leading producer of softwood plywood from the early twentieth century until passed by Oregon in the early 1950s, and it led in production of wood pulp after 1930. The state's first paper mill, built at Camas in 1883, in the following year introduced to the Pacific Coast the manufacture of paper exclusively from wood. Wood pulp used more and more lumber mill residues—by the middle 1950s, one third of the total volume of wood consumption by the industry was material that otherwise would have gone to waste. In the mid-1960s, the state produced well over 3 million tons of wood pulp annually. At that time, forest industries provided a third of the manufacturing employment in the state and a quarter of the manufacturing payroll.

In the mid-twentieth century, forest landownership in Washington was about equally divided between government and private sectors. Reservation of forests from the public domain began in 1893 when President Grover Cleveland set aside the Pacific Forest Reserve of 967,680 acres. During the closing days of his second administration five years later, Cleveland expanded the reserved forestlands in the state to 7.9 million acres when he established the Olympic, Washington, and Mount Rainier forest reserves. Together with the nearly 1.3 million additional acres proclaimed by President Theodore ROOSEVELT as the Colville National Forest in 1907 and the Kaniksu National Forest in 1908, these tracts formed the basis of the eight national forests which covered 9,070,000 acres of federally owned land in the state in 1978. The NATIONAL PARK SERVICE controls an additional 1,279,000 acres of forestland in three units, the Mount Rainier National Park established in 1899, the Olympic, established first as a national monument in 1909, and the North Cascades, established in 1968. There are another 1.5 million acres of federally controlled forest on Indian reservations within the state.

Washington owns nearly 2 million acres of state forests and parks. State forest conservation activity be-

Douglas-fir remains Washington State's most important commercial species. Weyerhaeuser Company Photo.

gan following fires which devastated much of the Northwest's timber in 1902. The Yacolt Burn in Washington alone covered 240,000 acres. The Washington legislature enacted the state's first fire laws in the following year. In 1905, the state provided its first forestry appropriations and established the office of state fire warden and forester and the Board of Forestry Commissioners. Appropriations were so small that the new agency by its second season was relying on voluntary contributions from private industry in order to employ fire wardens. Still dissatisfied with the protection offered by these arrangements, lumbermen led by George S. LONG, manager of the Weyerhaeuser Timber Company, banded together to form the Washington Forest Fire Association in 1908, assessing themselves for the cost of fire patrols on members' lands. Prompted by another disastrous fire season in 1910 and by the availability of federal assistance under the WEEKS ACT, Washington abolished its old board in 1921 and established an effective forestry program under a new Department of Conservation and Development which included a Division of Forestry. Reacting to antagonism against national forest land acquisitions, the state authorized the Department of Conservation and Development to purchase cutover lands for reforestation purposes. In 1936, the state embarked upon a "Keep Washington Green" public relations campaign aimed at reducing the frequency of forest fires. Originally directed by Stewart Holbrook and sponsored by the State Division of Forestry, the U. S. FOREST SERVICE, and private industry, this campaign served as a model for other "Keep Green" programs throughout the United States.

Washington inaugurated a system of small state parks along public highways in 1919. With the gift of Moran State Park in 1921—5,000 acres on Orcas Island in Puget Sound—the state was prompted to form a park agency. The system grew to cover 79,000 acres in 171 units by 1975.

Forestry education in Washington has been offered since 1907 by both the University of Washington College of Forestry in Seattle and the Department of Forestry and Range Management at the State College of Washington (now Washington State University) in Pullman.

FURTHER READING: Edwin Truman Coman and Helen M. Gibbs, *Time, Tide, and Timber: A Century of Pope and Talbot* (1949). Thomas R. Cox, *Mills and Markets: A History of the Pacific Coast Lumber Industry to 1900* (1974). Robert E. Ficken, *Lumber and Politics: The Career of Mark E. Reed* (1979). Ralph Hidy, Frank Ernest Hill, and Allan Nevins, *Timber and Men: The Weyerhaeuser Story* (1963). Harold K. Steen, "Forestry in Washington to 1925,"

Ph.D. dissertation, University of Washington (1969). Richard White, *Land Use, Environment, and Social Change: The Shaping of Island County, Washington* (1980). Frederick J. Yonce, "Lumbering and the Public Timberlands in Washington: The Era of Disposal," *Journal of Forest History* 22 (Jan. 1978): 4–17.

ROBERT E. FICKEN

WASHINGTON STATE FORESTRY

In 1902, a major forest fire swept across south-central Washington State, one of many that dry year, causing extensive damage and providing graphic evidence that protection efforts were needed. As the ashes of the Yacolt Burn cooled, owners of forestland turned toward Olympia, for enabling legislation was required before the state could officially be involved in fire-protection programs. The legislature moved quickly and with near unanimity. On March 16, 1903, Governor Henry McBride signed into law a bill that designated the state land commissioner as ex-officio forest fire warden with authority to close the forests during hazardous periods. With strong support from the forest industries, whose efforts were coordinated by George S. LONG of the Weyerhaeuser Timber Company, the legislature two years later enacted a law creating a Board of Forest Commissioners and providing state funding specifically for fire protection; J. R. Whelty was appointed state fire warden. Industrial support for this action continued to be strong, and individual companies contributed $8,133 to bolster the meager $7,500 state appropriation. On another front, the state's role in forestry advanced further when in 1907 the University of Washington inaugurated a four-year degree program in forestry.

Fire protection remained at the center of forestry efforts in both the public and private sectors. In 1909, lumbermen formed the WESTERN FORESTRY AND CONSERVATION ASSOCIATION and asked E. T. Allen to head this private organization. Whereas the state appropriated $33,000 for fire prevention in 1911, the industry had allocated $207,000 for the same purpose. With the federal WEEKS ACT now providing up to $10,000 to match state protection appropriations, the public effort grew, and numerous statutes were enacted that were aimed at reducing the number of fires, such as the requirement of spark arresters on logging equipment. In the heavily timbered western third of the state, lumbermen lobbied effectively, and in 1917, the legislature passed into law a mandatory annual assessment of five cents per acre of privately owned timberland, this revenue to be used in support of the state fire warden.

Fire was not the only forestry issue, despite its center-stage role. The state had received federal land grants totaling more than 3 million acres when it entered the union in 1889. Unlike many western states, Washington retained the bulk of this federal largess, and as one of the major landowners, the state began to manage the resources on these lands to generate revenue. By 1980, sale of state-owned timber yielded an annual income in excess of $160 million.

By the 1920s, as county assessors increased existing valuations and brought more and more of the state's forestlands to the tax roles for the first time, property tax joined fire as an important forestry issue. Burgeoning interest in "equitable" taxation for forestland was a national phenomenon, as evidenced

in Section 3 of the 1924 CLARKE-MCNARY ACT, which launched a decade-long tax study by Fred R. Fairchild. But the Washington State constitution required that all lands be taxed on the same basis; thus any tax program that made allowance for the long-term nature of forestry enterprises would require a constitutional amendment. In 1930, the state's voters amended the constitution to permit classified forestlands to be taxed on a deferred basis, an advantage aimed at encouraging lumbermen to retain and reforest their logged-off lands. Effects of other elements of the conservation movement and the gross disruptions brought about by the Great Depression make assessment of this tax program difficult. It must be assumed, however, that at least some forestlands re-

More than a half-century later, portions of Washington's 1902 Yacolt Burn remained desolate. American Forest Institute Photo.

ceived better care because of it, for the process of LAND CLASSIFICATION included the notion of permanent ownership, a welcome alternative to "cut out and get out."

On the national scene, during the 1930s, the U. S. FOREST SERVICE was mounting an energetic campaign for legislation to regulate lumbering practices on private land. Owners collectively decided that if regulation of their activities was inevitable, then it was preferable to report to a state, rather than a federal, agency. The political effort in Washington was typical of many states at the time, and with well-coordinated industrial support, in 1945, the legislature adopted a forest practice act.

The 1945 act proclaimed that keeping forestland "continuously and fully productive" was in the public interest and thus could be regulated. Henceforth, cutting permits had to be obtained from state authority before logging; the application had to include a map of the logging area, its legal description, and acreage. The operator also had to take "adequate precautions" to assure future growth and protect the area from fire. This law was challenged because its requirements allegedly constituted a "taking" of private property without compensation, a violation of the Fifth Amendment of the Constitution. In 1949, the U. S. Supreme Court affirmed the constitutionality of the Washington State law, setting a landmark precedent that validated similar statutes in other states. The administration of this statute was better coordinated with other forest and land programs in 1957, when the State Department of Natural Resources was created and was given responsibility for all natural resources.

In 1974, a new forest-practices act superseded the original law, which had emphasized reforestation of cutover land. The more recent law reflected increased concern for environmental quality and addressed soil, water, air, recreation, and scenic beauty, in addition to the traditional focus on timber production. In accordance with a nationwide tendency, informing and involving the general public is routinely incorporated in forest-policy decisions.

FURTHER READING: Ralph R. Widner, ed., *Forests and Forestry in the American States* (1968). Harold K. Steen, "Forestry in Washington to 1925," Ph.D. dissertation, University of Washington (1969).

HAROLD K. STEEN

WATERSHED MANAGEMENT

From the earliest beginnings of forestry in the United States, the belief that forests benefited streamflow

has been assumed, debated, and argued. In 1897, Congress determined that a primary reason for setting aside the forest reserves was "for the purpose of securing favorable conditions of water flows." In 1911, the WEEKS ACT authorized the purchase of lands for national forests in the East "for the protection of the watersheds of navigable streams." Indeed, in the early years of the conservation movement, the forest–streamflow relationship was "the peg upon which to hang the conservation hat." The "forest influence," as it was then known, became a part of the forester's philosophy, an article of faith.

Controversy erupted early in the century when proponents of the forest influence claimed that forest cutting caused floods and that, conversely, reforesting watersheds would reduce floods. Thus was sparked a flood control controversy that pitted foresters and others against engineers and dam builders for more than fifty years. The dispute evolved into a powerful political force during the developmental years of the fledgling U. S. FOREST SERVICE.

Watershed management means managing land to decrease floods and siltation, or to increase the quantity and quality of streamflow or groundwater for water supply purposes. Because these "products" have values that are difficult to measure monetarily, watershed management is normally practiced only on public lands, except where mandated by law. Therefore, the history of watershed management in the United States is largely the history of the arguments and legislation that revolved around the forest influence, and of the research that followed.

Congress first recognized the idea that forests or tree planting might affect water in 1873 with the passage of the Timber Culture Act, which allowed tree planting as a substitute for the residence requirements of the Homestead Act. It was thought then that establishing new forests would increase rainfall on the prairies. After all, wherever there were forests there was rain, and the logic of the times saw forests bringing rain rather than the reverse. The authority for these early claims for the forest influence was George Perkins MARSH's *Man and Nature* (1864), written after his extensive study of the European scientific literature. Twenty years later, Bernhard E. FERNOW, chief of the Division of Forestry, acknowledged that the relation of forests to climate had been exaggerated and that more information was needed on their relation to streamflow. Even so, the FOREST MANAGEMENT ACT of 1897, which gave criteria for the forest reserves, gave streamflow control as their primary purpose.

The forest–streamflow hypothesis gained additional support with the passage of the Newlands Act and the creation of the Reclamation Service in 1902. Afforestation was now officially important for irrigation as well as for navigation and flood control. The disastrous flooding of the Ohio River in 1907 was linked to logging in the watersheds of the Allegheny and Monongahela rivers, making the controversy a national issue.

One of the calmer voices in the argument came not from a forester but from an engineer. Hiram Martin Chittenden, who as a young officer began a distinguished career with the ARMY CORPS OF ENGINEERS by surveying and building the primary road system in YELLOWSTONE NATIONAL PARK, at first had supported the forestry viewpoint. But after witnessing raging torrents from pristine Yellowstone watersheds, he concluded that forests indeed did not prevent floods. In his scholarly "Forests and Reservoirs in Their Relation to Streamflow with Particular Reference to Navigable Streams," he presented his modified views at the 1908 annual meeting of the American Society of Civil Engineers. The main benefit of the forest, he said, was to protect the soil from erosion. Simply cutting the trees did not lead to erosion, because natural regrowth soon took over the land. However, he said that road building, which removed and totally destroyed the forest, did cause serious erosion. These conclusions, based only on his observation, would be corroborated by scientific research fifty years later.

Chittenden's position on the forest–streamflow controversy was forcefully opposed by Forest Service Chief Gifford PINCHOT, who in 1910 remarked that "the connection between forests and rivers is like that between father and son. No forests, no rivers." Both arguments were used to their fullest in the prolonged and heated debate that led to the passage of the 1911 WEEKS ACT. Indeed, the controversy was fueled by the legislation because the standard interpretation of the Constitution limited such purchase "for the protection of the watersheds of navigable streams."

Although the law was passed before any factual evidence became available, the controversy over its passage did spur the first on-the-ground studies of forest–water relations in the United States: the Wagon Wheel Gap study, a joint endeavor by the Forest Service and the Weather Bureau in Colorado, which began in 1910; and the Burnt Brook-Shoal Pond study by the Geological Survey in New Hampshire, begun in 1911. In both studies, streamflow from two small mountain watersheds—one essentially forested and the other cutover or burned—was actually measured and compared.

The Wagon Wheel Gap study, although financed by the two agencies, was essentially a Forest Service project. The Weather Bureau went along with the study only reluctantly, Bureau Chief Willis L. Moore having bitterly disputed all the claimed beneficial effects of forests on streamflow. The study ran for sixteen years, but for various reasons its findings were largely inconclusive. The Forest Service man-in-charge and prime mover from its inception to the final report was Carlos G. Bates, who was to become the nation's first real authority on the forest–streamflow question.

Although the Burnt Brook-Shoal Pond streams were measured for only a year, some conclusions were drawn from the study: "The removal of forest growth must be expected to decrease the natural steadiness of dependent streams during the spring months at least"; the study also showed "ample evidence for the purposes of the NATIONAL FOREST RESERVATION COMMISSION that a direct relationship exists between forest cover and stream regulation."

So began scientific research on the forest–streamflow relationship in the United States. In 1915, a Branch of Research was established in the Forest Service with Earle CLAPP in charge. By the end of the 1920s, the agency had established twelve regional experiment stations, and during the 1930s, watershed programs were begun at three of them. Even so, the controversy would still continue for many years, though muted in some quarters. By 1927, the Forest Service had begun to downplay its position on the role of forests in flood prevention and to emphasize instead their role in erosion prevention.

Forest Service Chief William B. GREELEY, commenting on the alleged effect of forest removal on the disastrous Mississippi River floods of 1927, remarked that the first thing needed in trying to stop floods by tree growth was to "drop all exaggeration about it." Similarly, Herbert Hoover noted that "the floods of the Mississippi . . . cannot wait for trees to grow up even if they were a contributory remedy. But in any event, I am for trees." A few years later, J. C. Stevens, in 1934, referring to the requirements of the Weeks Act, dryly commented that "everyone loves the forests; everyone is glad they are in the hands of the Government. . . . If it was necessary once to attribute to them properties they do not possess in order to 'kid' the people and Congress into doing the thing that everybody wanted done anyway, that necessity has passed . . . . Is there any further necessity to keep up the farce?"

Congress apparently was not listening too closely, however, because in 1936 it passed the Omnibus Flood Control Act. This legislation gave the DEPARTMENT OF AGRICULTURE responsibility for conducting flood-control surveys on watersheds for "runoff and waterflow retardation and soil erosion prevention." The Forest Service was assigned primary responsibility on watersheds that were mostly forested, and the Soil Conservation Service was given primary responsibility on watersheds that were mostly agricultural. The law required a detailed survey report and a favorable cost–benefit ratio before an actual plan of improvement could be considered on a specific watershed. Thus, foresters were for the first time actually forced into quantifying the forest's influence on floods. Since sufficient research data did not yet exist, various empirical methods were devised, such as determining the average depth of the forest humus layer under forests of different ages and densities and then assigning water storage values that could be used in an analysis of river runoff from a "design storm."

Started under the New Deal, the program was dropped during the war years but was soon reactivated. To justify its participation, the Forest Service had to dust off some of the old rhetoric: "If each drop of water were held at the place where it first reaches the ground, there would be no floods."

Although hundreds of watersheds across the country were authorized for survey and flood control survey teams were organized at several Forest Service experiment stations, actual improvement projects were ultimately approved and implemented for only a handful of watersheds. Dissatisfaction with the program finally led to the Watershed Protection and Flood Prevention Act of 1954, which added engineering works to the "land treatment measures" originally authorized by the 1936 act. The Flood Control Act of 1950 and the Water Resources Planning Act of 1965 both authorized comprehensive surveys of major river basins under the Corps of Engineers' leadership, with the Forest Service playing a relatively minor role.

Meanwhile, the Forest Service had established watershed management research projects at all of its regional experiment stations, staffed partly by scientists who had started out on flood control surveys. Therefore, the scientific basis for management of forest watersheds was to be written in effect by streamflow gauges on experimental watersheds ("catchments") throughout the forest regions of the country. Before catchment studies began, however, research data on the presumed benefits of forests as flood preventers began trickling in. That the forest was an insatiable sponge was a widely held bit of folklore in the early years. Indeed, Pinchot had demonstrated this "fact" to congressional committees hearing testimony on the Weeks Act by pouring a small amount of water on a sloping blotter. This notion was finally put to rest by studies in California in the 1920s, when

Walter Lowdermilk found that forest litter did not hold much water, although it was, he found, important in shielding the mineral soil from rainfall impact, thus promoting water intake and preventing erosion. Later research for flood control surveys showed that forest litter and humus normally do not accumulate in thick enough layers to absorb significant amounts of flood-producing rainfall, corroborating at last what Chittenden and later Bates had concluded from their observations years before.

Public works programs of the 1930s finally gave the Forest Service an opportunity for full-blown research on that elusive forest–streamflow relationship. Experimental forests were established in North Carolina, Arizona, and California, when CIVILIAN CONSERVATION CORPS (CCC) labor became available for building roads, houses, and stream-gauging stations. In the postwar era, other major projects were started in New Hampshire, West Virginia, northern Minnesota, the Colorado Rockies, and in the Cascade Ranges of Oregon and Washington. Although watershed management (also called forest hydrology) research was and still is primarily a Forest Service activity, some universities, notably Pennsylvania State and Oregon State, have made important contributions in recent years.

In addition to catchment studies—in which streamflow is actually measured before and after logging or otherwise altering the vegetative cover on small, experimental catchments—research includes basic studies on all the various elements of the water cycle that might determine what happens to the rain or snow that falls on the forest. These basic studies help interpret streamflow changes measured on experimental catchments and also provide a basis for applying the results to other watersheds.

One of the earlier and more significant findings from catchment research came from the Coweeta Hydrologic Laboratory in the Appalachian Mountains of North Carolina. At Coweeta, cutting all the trees and leaving them where they fell substantially increased streamflow, without erosion or flooding. Later studies at Coweeta and elsewhere showed that clearcutting entire watersheds could increase annual streamflow by as much as 50 percent, depending upon the amount of precipitation and the water storage capacity of the watershed soil. The increase in waterflow resulted largely from reducing the amount of water transpired into the air by the trees. These studies also showed that cutting the trees does not in itself result in erosion or muddy streams. However, building roads and skidding logs may erode soil and muddy streams, if the roads are not properly located and constructed and the skidding system used is not compatible with the soil type. Studies in the mountains of the West showed that logging may damage streams in geologically unstable areas, even without road building. Areas too unstable for road construction, however, may be safely logged by helicopter, balloon, or aerial cable systems that lift the logs as they are carried to the awaiting truck.

Although simply cutting the trees does not reduce the capacity of the forest soil to absorb rain, logging followed by land use change can indeed increase the potential for floods. Changing a forest to farm fields or urban developments has a much different impact than cutting the trees and letting the forest regrow. Failure to recognize this difference helped spark the early controversy and spawned the myth that logging dries up springs.

A basic study by John Hewlett in 1960 answered the puzzling question, "Why do streams keep flowing without rain?" Using a model designed to simulate a soil mass on steep slopes, he found that water continued to seep from the eighteen-inch deep model for seventy-one days after water had been applied. Hewlett concluded that slow percolation from the soil of mountain watersheds could indeed account for sustained flow of streams during rainless periods. Carlos Bates had made the same deduction from observing the Wagon Wheel Gap streams fifty years earlier.

Until the 1960s, forest hydrology research dealt mainly with how forests and forest management practices affected the amount and timing of stream-flow and soil erosion. The objectives were to find out either how forest products could be harvested without damaging the water resource, or how water supplies could be increased by changing the forest (or other vegetative cover) on the watershed. In the late 1960s, a study at the Hubbard Brook Experimental Forest in the White Mountains of New Hampshire showed that logging could also affect water quality by accelerating the flushing of soil nutrients into streams draining the logged area. Known as "stream eutrophication," the phenomenon also depletes minerals from the soil that might be important for tree growth. The greatest increases were found in concentrations of nitrate and calcium ions. The Hubbard Brook results added fuel to a swelling outcry by environmentalist organizations against clearcutting on national forests and prompted similar research elsewhere. However, these studies showed only a minimal increase of nutrients in streams after logging.

Despite the language of the Forest Management Act of 1897 and passage of the MULTIPLE USE-SUSTAINED YIELD ACT of 1960, under which Congress mandated for the first time that the national forests "shall be administered for outdoor recreation, range, timber, watershed, and wildlife and fish purposes," the actual practice of watershed management (except for barring logging on watersheds used to supply water) was slow in coming. This tardiness was in part due to the need for the research branch first to develop the techniques, but

Watershed experiment in the Colorado Rockies to determine the effect of logging patterns on water runoff. Forest Service Photo.

also because the Forest Service was traditionally timber oriented.

Although watershed management in a formal sense was not widely practiced until the 1950s, some notable success stories were written in the 1930s. Planting pines and constructing erosion-control devices on worn-out and gullied cotton lands dramatically reduced floods and siltation on the Yazoo-Little Tallahatchie watersheds in Mississippi. Eliminating grazing by sheep and constructing bench terraces on overgrazed forest rangelands removed the threat of mud-rock floods in Utah; watershed management in many areas is akin to range management. Special methods for controlling erosion on unstable slopes were devised and put into use on mountain roads in California's chaparral region. The recognition that critical flood-erosion problems in the chaparral region resulted from destruction of the vegetation by wild fires prompted institution of intensive fire control programs. Forestry agencies began the immediate seeding of burned chaparral watersheds with fast-growing herbaceous plants.

In today's management of the national forests, watershed management is given high priority, particularly with respect to controlling erosion and siltation. Because these normally occur only on disturbed areas —roads, log-skidding trails, strip mines, and other sites where the forest has been destroyed—most practices that are strictly for watershed management are concentrated here. However, since logging, burning, and grazing the forest may also affect the water resource, their impact must also be considered in watershed management planning.

Among the most important federal statutes enacted during the 1970s that affected forest and range management were the Federal Water Pollution Act of 1972 and the Clean Water Act of 1977. This immensely complex legislation was crafted to curb urban and industrial pollution; their application to forestlands was restrained pending refinement of definitions. The 1972 act mandated state programs to meet water quality standards set by the Environmental Protection Agency (EPA). The Clean Water Act exempted "normal" silvicultural practices and gave EPA broader discretion. Cooperative cost-sharing programs are carried out by local agencies.

The newest and perhaps potentially the most serious problem facing watershed management is acid rain, caused by fallout of sulfuric and nitric acids created by the burning of fossil fuels. Acid rain (or snow melt) has already destroyed trout and other game fish in many Adirondack lakes and is recognized as a growing threat to fishing waters of other northeastern and north central states. One remedial measure being tried by the New York Department of Environmental Conservation is spreading lime on affected lakes. It remains to be seen whether such stopgap measures are effective or whether trout as a natural resource must end up on the sacrificial altar of the industrial age.

FURTHER READING: Henry W. Anderson, Marvin D. Hoover, and Kenneth G. Reinhart, *Forests and Water: Effects of Forest Management on Floods, Sedimentation and Water Supply* (1976). E. A. Colman, *Vegetation and Watershed Management* (1953). Howard W. Lull and Kenneth G. Reinhart, *Forests and Floods in the Eastern United States* (1972). Ashley L. Schiff, *Fire and Water: Scientific Heresy in the Forest Service* (1962).

RICHARD S. SARTZ

WATTS, LYLE FORD (1890–1962)

Lyle Watts, seventh chief of the U. S. FOREST SERVICE (1943–1952), was born November 18, 1890, near Clear Lake, Iowa. He studied forestry at Iowa State College, Ames, earning his B.S. degree in 1913. He later received M.S.F. and honorary D.Sc. degrees there. As a student he held two summer jobs with the Forest Service. Upon graduation, Watts joined the service and he was to remain with it for most of thirty-eight years.

Early in his career, Watts had charge of timber survey work in Wyoming and Utah, then directed nursery tree planting in Idaho. He served as supervisor of three national forests in Idaho between 1918 and 1926. He was assistant chief for forest management in the Intermountain Region from 1926 to 1928. Then for fifteen months, he organized and headed the department of forestry at Utah State Agricultural College, Logan, before returning to the Forest Service as senior silviculturist for the experiment station at Ogden, Utah, where he directed watershed studies. In 1931, he became director of the experiment station at Missoula, Montana.

In February 1936, Watts was appointed North Central regional forester at Milwaukee, Wisconsin, during a period of establishment and expansion of national forests in that region. Three years later, he took the same post for the heavily forested Pacific Northwest Region. In the fall of 1942, he was special assistant to Secretary of Agriculture Claude Wickard for farm labor activities. On January 1, 1943, he became chief of the Forest Service, serving during the war and postwar period when many special forest product and planning projects were undertaken.

Watts was an earnest advocate of state, private, and federal cooperation to assure more efficient and less wasteful timber-harvesting methods by operators on privately owned land, backed up by federal regulation. However, federal regulation never became law, and in this respect Watts was unsuccessful as had been his likeminded predecessors, Gifford PINCHOT, Henry GRAVES, Ferdinand SILCOX, and Earle CLAPP. Nevertheless, conditions gradually improved through state laws and the good examples of some major firms. Watts also helped get much important cooperative legislation passed that advanced forestry nationwide, particularly technical services to landowners. Watts regarded as his major accomplishments as chief a more than 20 percent reduction in cattle grazing on national forest lands in ten years despite fierce opposition, a balanced increase in timber cut up to sustained-yield levels to meet greatly increased postwar demands, and a policy of selecting vigorous and capable young men for leadership positions aimed at retaining the agency's forward-looking, aggressive tradition. Watts also helped start international forestry work under the United Nations Food and Agriculture Organization, for which he received the *Croix du Chevalier de la Mérite Agricole* from the French government and the Distinguished Service Award from the U. S. DEPARTMENT OF AGRICULTURE.

In 1953, after retiring from federal service, Watts accepted the appointment as chairman of Oregon's Water Resources Committee, a group instrumental in securing reform of the state's water law two years later. He was prominent in other conservation causes, particularly in the affairs of the IZAAK WALTON LEAGUE. He served as conservation adviser to Richard L. Neuberger during the latter's successful campaign for election as United States Senator from Oregon in 1954. Watts continued as counsel on conservation issues to Senator Neuberger and to his wife, Maureen Neuberger, after she succeeded him in office in 1960. In 1956, Watts served on the national executive board of Conservationists for Stevenson-Kefauver, and in 1960 he was on the natural resources advisory committee for the Kennedy-Johnson campaign. Lyle Watts died June 15, 1962, in Portland, Oregon.

FRANK J. HARMON

WEEKS ACT, 1911

The Weeks Act of March 1, 1911, resulted from a decade of debate in and out of Congress that addressed basic constitutional and conservation issues. Named for Congressman John W. Weeks of Massachusetts, the act authorized federal purchase of forestlands in the headwaters of navigable streams, established the NATIONAL FOREST RESERVATION COMMISSION, gave consent for states to enter into compacts for the purpose of conserving forests and water supplies, and authorized federal matching funds for approved state agencies to protect forested watersheds of navigable streams.

The Constitution does not contain explicit authority for federal purchase of forestlands. In fact, the whole of federal land policy until 1891 had been to sell or grant the vast public domain as quickly as the administrative machinery would allow. The Forest Reserve Act of 1891 authorized retention of certain forested public lands; only two decades later, in 1911, Congress authorized additions to the public land base through purchase. Even though disposal continued apace, this major shift in policy paralleled the growth of the conservation movement. By 1980, over 22 million acres of land had been added, through purchase, to the national forest system in the eastern United States.

Most of the debate centered on the purchase clause of the act; of equal importance but of little controversy was the authorization of matching funds. At a time when states were only beginning to develop forestry agencies with traditional timidity or skepticism on the part of legislatures, this federal incentive of up to $10,000 per year for each state provided an important impetus to the conservation movement. Some writers have linked the passage of the Weeks Act to the devastating forest fires in Idaho ("The Big Blowup"), which occurred a year earlier and attracted national headlines, but there is little evidence to support this view. In fact, the section of the act that was instrumental in bolstering state-level forestry received little attention at the time; opponents and proponents focused on the land purchase section instead.

The National Forest Reservation Commission was comprised of the secretaries of war (now defense), agriculture, interior, and two members each from the House of Representatives and the Senate. (The commission was abolished by the FEDERAL LAND POLICY AND MANAGEMENT ACT of 1976, and its functions were transferred to the secretary of agriculture.) The commission appraised and selected land for purchase on the basis of protecting watersheds of navigable streams. All purchased lands became a permanent part of the national forest system.

The CLARKE-MCNARY ACT of 1924 eliminated the purchase restriction to watersheds of navigable streams and increased the matching funds for state forestry agencies. The Woodruff-McNary Act of 1928 greatly increased authorization for purchase.

FURTHER READING: William Shands and Robert Healy, *The Lands Nobody Wanted* (1977). Harold K. Steen, *The U. S. Forest Service: A History* (1976).

WENTWORTH, BENNING (1696–1770), AND JOHN WENTWORTH (1737–1820)

Benning Wentworth and his able nephew, John Wentworth, served not only as successive royal governors of New Hampshire but also concurrently as surveyors-general of the woods. Each was significant in the shaping of British policies concerning the very important and abundant pine trees that were suitable for masts. However, it was the younger Wentworth who, despite the loss of his governorship during the Revolutionary crisis, devised a workable plan which, inaugurated in the Canadian maritime provinces, guaranteed supplies of masts for the Royal Navy.

Benning Wentworth amassed a large fortune through his twin offices (1741–1766) by using his political power to maintain a monopoly of the lumber industry in New Hampshire. Wentworth made few attempts to enforce the provisions of the so-called Broad-Arrow acts of 1711 and 1729, which required that all trees in the public domain and many on private property more than twenty-four inches in diameter be reserved as masts for the Royal Navy. At issue was compensation for the trees, which the Crown refused to consider. In the face of protests from owners of "private" property, such as the proprietors of the Kennebeck Purchase Company, Wentworth retreated. He managed most efficiently by supplying mast trees from his own seemingly inexhaustible forestlands. As mast contractor, he arranged for shaping the trees in his own lumberyards as well as for their delivery to London, where prime specimens brought him up to 100 pounds each.

John Wentworth became royal governor and surveyor-general of the woods in 1767. A conscientious and honest administrator, he immediately announced his intention to enforce the much neglected broad-arrow acts. Although he filed lawsuits against those he regarded as poachers, he still felt sympathy for the private owners who not only lost their most valuable timber to his agents but also suffered much damage to the smaller trees growing amidst those marked by the infamous broad arrow. Most owners were unable to prove that their titles antedated 1690, the date required by the law for exemptions. Wentworth met a direct challenge from the Kennebeck proprietors, however, who went so far as to petition the Admiralty for compensation for their losses. In 1773, they even won a case involving trespass in the Massachusetts Admiralty Court.

The complicated question of ownership of the Kennebeck tract was still pending when the American Revolution erupted, and John Wentworth was forced to flee to the safety of the British lines. Although no longer royal governor of New Hampshire, he retained his position of surveyor-general of the woods in the Canadian maritime provinces. He had undoubtedly learned much from his quarrel with the Kennebeck Company, for in 1778, Wentworth submitted a five-point program to the Admiralty that he believed would create effective controls for a new royal mast policy. His plan provided for the establishment in Canada of six-mile-square "parishes," with timberland to be reserved for the use of the Royal Navy and property owners to be paid a bounty for felled mast trees. Wentworth's comprehensive proposal was introduced in parts of Nova Scotia and New Brunswick.

FURTHER READING: Robert G. Albion, *Forests and Sea Power* (1926). Gordon E. Kershaw, *The Kennebeck Proprietors* (1975). Lawrence S. Mayo, *John Wentworth, Governor of New Hampshire* (1921). Joseph J. Malone, *Pine Trees and Politics* (1964).

GORDON E. KERSHAW

WESTERN FORESTRY AND CONSERVATION ASSOCIATION

After the disastrous forest fire season of 1902, a number of forestry associations were founded in the Pacific Northwest. In January 1909, several of these local groups from Idaho and Washington met in Spokane to coordinate their antifire campaigns. Out of this convention emerged the Pacific Northwest Protection and Conservation Association which, when similar local groups from California and British Columbia expressed an interest in joining, was renamed the Western Forestry and Conservation Association (WFCA). E. T. Allen led the organization until 1932. By 1980, 800 local forestry agencies in eleven western states and Canadian provinces belonged to the organization under the motto, "One Forest under Two Flags."

WFCA has been an active organization with a series of campaigns closely paralleling the general development of utilitarian conservation in the United States. Initially, it concentrated its efforts on forest fire prevention, urging the western state governments to pass laws requiring compulsory disposal of highly flammable logging slash. It also advocated state sponsorship of educational campaigns on the dangers of forest fires and the means of preventing them.

In the 1920s and 1930s, the association emphasized reforestation and contributed to the studies that led to the CLARKE-MCNARY ACT of 1924 as well as to several state and provincial programs. In the 1940s, in cooperation with the U. S. FOREST SERVICE and other federal and state agencies, WFCA sponsored research into forest pest control, one result of which was the Forest Pest Control Act of 1947 and similar legislation in Canada.

While maintaining these programs, the association in the 1960s and 1970s actively worked to halt further government acquisition of private forests for purely cultural or recreational purposes. WFCA advocates multiple use of forests, except in special cases. In addition to its annual Western Forestry Conference, one of the largest forestry conferences in North America, WFCA maintained an active publishing program, issuing many pamphlets, research reports, and some books.

FURTHER READING: Eloise Hamilton, *Forty Years of Western Forestry: A History of the Movement to Conserve Forest Resources by Cooperative Effort, 1909–1949* (1949). Clyde S. Martin, "History and Influence of the Western Forestry and Conservation Association in Cooperative Forestry in the West," *Journal of Forestry* 43 (Mar. 1945): 167–170.

WEST VIRGINIA FORESTS

Originally, West Virginia's 15,405 million acres were almost entirely covered with forests. Hardwoods, particularly oaks, poplars, walnut, cherry, ash, chestnut, and locust, predominated, but white pine, spruce, and hemlock were also common along the high ridges of the Allegheny Mountains. Although the pioneers were notoriously wasteful, about 10 million acres, or nearly two-thirds of the state, remained in virgin forest in 1870. A century later, West Virginia forests covered about three-quarters of the land area and included 11.5 million acres of commercial forest.

Before World War I, West Virginia forests were exploited mercilessly. Sawlogs and crossties were rafted down numerous streams, and lumber, barrel staves, poles, and tanbark were sent on small barges down Middle Island Creek and the Little Kanawha, Elk, Guyandotte, and Big Sandy rivers. The use of booms in other streams, such as the Greenbrier and Cherry rivers, was common. In the late nineteenth century, the coal mining industry became one of the largest forestland owners in West Virginia, consuming timber for mine props, headers, wedges, ties, cars, and houses. Beginning in the 1880s, with the introduction of band saws in the mills and logging railroads in the Allegheny Mountains, lumber companies, chiefly from New York, Pennsylvania, Michigan, and Wisconsin, entered the state and swept the forests before

them. Lumber production peaked in 1909 at 1.5 billion board feet and then declined to a Depression low of 135 million board feet in 1932. By 1920, the virgin forests were gone.

Floods along the Monongahela River caused by denuded watersheds prompted the West Virginia Reform Law of 1909, which provided for a state forest, game and fish wardens, two deputies, and as many county wardens as needed. The law also gave wardens authority to require individuals to fight forest fires. In addition, the 1909 legislation provided for federal acquisition of lands in the state for conservation purposes. It was under this provision that in 1920 the Monongahela National Forest was created. During the 1930s, the CIVILIAN CONSERVATION CORPS stimulated conservation in the state, particularly through reforestation and fire-fighting programs. In 1933, the legislature created a conservation commission with authority over forests, soils, water, and wildlife. The commission became part of a new Department of Natural Resources in 1961.

In the 1970s, the successfully reforested Monongahela watershed became the center of a national controversy over clearcutting on national forest lands. On May 14, 1973, the IZAAK WALTON LEAGUE, in concert with the SIERRA CLUB, the Natural Resources Defense Council, and other groups, brought suit against Secretary of Agriculture Earl Butz to halt clearcutting in the national forest, claiming that this method of timber harvesting violated the 1897 FOREST MANAGEMENT ACT. This law authorized cutting of only dead, mature, or large-growth trees, which had also been marked, in national forests. The plaintiffs won the case and a later appeal. Although the decision was specific to the states under the jurisdiction of the Fourth Circuit Court, its possible application was nationwide and led to the 1976 NATIONAL FOREST MANAGEMENT ACT, which amended the 1897 statute to permit more flexible silvicultural practices on national forest lands.

The transition from deep mining to strip- and auger-mining after World War II created another conflict between mining companies and residents seeking to preserve their environment. Tensions, which developed particularly after the energy crisis of the 1970s, prompted the 1977 Surface Mining Control and Reclamation Act, which established nationwide control over stripmining and required, among other things, reclamation of mined-over lands.

Out-of-state coal, petroleum, railroad, and steel corporations in 1968 owned 61 percent of the privately held commercial forestland in the state. These firms have had a significant impact on the direction of private forestry measures. For several decades, mining companies have cooperated with lumber concerns to prevent forest fires, and today most mining companies manage their timberlands to ensure continuous supplies of mine timbers and set aside quality timber for production of lumber.

In 1974, West Virginia's 365 lumber mills produced 381 million board feet of lumber, 95 percent of it from hardwoods such as oaks, poplars, and beeches. As a result of state and private conservation efforts, 308 million cubic feet of wood were grown in 1977, in contrast to the 119 million cut. Forest fires continued to be a threat, and in 1978–1979 the state suffered 1,953 fires, 63 percent of them in its southern counties. The state nursery, however, provided 5.1 million seedlings, and 5,994 of the 37,884 burned acres were replanted.

West Virginia has nine state forests, totaling 79,308 acres, all with recreational facilities. In 1975, there were thirty-three park and recreational areas covering 66,000 acres. In addition, three national forests lie wholly or partially within the state: the Monongahela, with 1,647,146 acres (842,106 acres federally owned); portions of the George Washington, which totals 157,568 acres; and portions of the Jefferson, with 29,651 acres.

FURTHER READING: Roy B. Clarkson, *Tumult on the Mountains: Lumbering in West Virginia, 1770–1920* (1964). C. R. McKim, *50 Year History of the Monongahela National Forest* (1970). Ralph R. Widner, ed., *Forests and Forestry in the American States* (1968).

OTIS K. RICE

WEYERHAEUSER FAMILY

The prominence of a single individual in the development of an American industry is not unusual. As oil had its Rockefeller and steel its Carnegie, lumber had Frederick Weyerhaeuser. The lumber industry is unique, however, in that four generations later it continues to be led by a direct descendant of its dominant figure.

There is no question that Frederick Weyerhaeuser (1834–1914) exploited the forest resource in Wisconsin and Minnesota at least as thoroughly as did his contemporaries, yet he kept one eye focused on the future. The organizations he founded reflected this vision. Although his operations grew ever larger, forcing increased delegation of authority, this did not mean a lessening of his personal attention. The certainty that Frederick cared and the likelihood of Frederick inspecting provided continual encouragement to personnel throughout the Wisconsin pinery. Still, decentralization, reflecting the assumption that those closest to the questions were likely to have the best answers, has been a characteristic of the Weyerhaeuser organization throughout its history. Such an assumption has sometimes been the source of frustration in the short term, but over time decentralization has contributed to efficiency and has provided a reservoir of experienced managerial personnel from within the organization.

The Weyerhaeuser family has never held a controlling interest in the Weyerhaeuser Company. Some of the leaders of the organization had been competitors originally, but tough competitors often had the makings of valued partners. As the pineland of the upper Mississippi diminished in extent and increased in value, Weyerhaeuser allies came to include such lumbering families as the Longs, Lairds, Nortons, Ingrams, Mussers, Bells, Irvines, Carsons, McCormicks, and many others. These associations, continuing to the present, have been vital to the growth and success of the Weyerhaeuser organization; the associates became members of the family in effect, and sometimes in fact. By 1981, the Weyerhaeuser Company was a corporation owned by nearly 35,000 stockholders, although the Weyerhaeusers continue their traditional leadership role.

Many of their associates were involved in the initial move to the Pacific Northwest at the turn of the twentieth century. Of greatest importance was George S. LONG who assumed the responsibilities of resident agent (or general manager) for the original 900,000-acre investment of the Weyerhaeuser Timber Company, all of which had been purchased from the Northern Pacific Railway Company. In this new endeavor, the early emphasis was on timberland acquisition, sale, and management, and it was not until the 1920s that large-scale manufacturing efforts were begun. Although John Philip Weyerhaeuser (1858–1935) had succeeded his father as president of the Weyerhaeuser Timber Company in 1914, Long supervised the consolidation of the vast timber holdings into what would become strategic operating units and oversaw the commencement of production at Everett and Longview, Washington, and Klamath Falls, Oregon.

J. P. Weyerhaeuser resigned as Timber Company president in 1928 and was succeeded by Frederick Somers Bell, who served until 1934 when Frederick Edward Weyerhaeuser (1872–1945), youngest son of Frederick, assumed the office. F. E.'s greatest contribution was the coordination of the widespread divisions and departments of the rapidly growing organization. In addition, he was committed to the importance of research and development, instituting the first forestry research program within an industrial

In 1924, Frederick E. (right) and J. P. Weyerhaeuser (middle) discuss company holdings near Klamath Falls, Oregon, with C. A. Barton, manager of the Boise-Payette Lumber Company. Members of the Weyerhaeuser family had a major interest in Boise-Payette. Forest History Society Photo.

company. Working out of offices in Saint Paul, Minnesota, F. E. patiently bridged the miles and the differences in cooperation with his nephew, J. P. Weyerhaeuser, Jr., in Tacoma.

J. P. "Phil" Weyerhaeuser, Jr. (1899–1956) had been appointed executive vice president in 1933, a new office responsible for production and the properties of the Timber Company. Under Phil's management, the modernization of milling went forward at an unprecedented rate as rising costs of production encouraged efforts to measure as exactly as possible how best to utilize each sawlog. This concern was evidenced in a variety of ways, from an increased emphasis on advanced accounting procedures to the host of new products that were developed from what had previously been waste. Phil became president in 1947 and served in that capacity for the remainder of his life.

The most significant changes during Phil's administration took place in the woods, when Weyerhaeuser assumed leadership in what became known as sustained-yield forestry. The firm's dedication of the Clemons Tree Farm in western Washington in June 1941, officially designated as the nation's first, symbolized the evolution of logging, traditionally simply the

exploitation of the forest resource, into the harvesting of a timber crop. Weyerhaeuser began calling itself "the tree growing company."

Phil was succeeded in office by his older brother, Frederick King Weyerhaeuser (1895–1978), who became president after long experience directing the work of the Weyerhaeuser Sales Company. During the term of F. K., Weyerhaeuser Timber Company became simply the Weyerhaeuser Company, the shortened designation more accurately reflecting its enlarging involvements, many of which were no longer woods related.

F. K.'s successor in 1960 was Norton Clapp, who served ably as president until 1966 when he was succeeded by F. K.'s nephew, George Hunt Weyerhaeuser (1926–), elected to the presidency after having served seventeen years with the company, including two years as executive vice president for operations. His administration featured a fundamental reorganization of the firm into fourteen geographic regions and six business groups. In part, this was in recognition of an expansion into such distant timber areas of Oklahoma, Arkansas, North Carolina, Mississippi, and Alabama, where holdings came to comprise more than half of the nearly 6 million acres of domestic ownership. The company also expanded its timber resource base to include more than 10 million acres in Canada and elsewhere abroad. In addition, tree farming has become high-yield forestry, or intensive forest management.

Such terms would have had little meaning to the first Frederick, but he would likely understand the continuing acceptance of decentralization, the continuing emphasis upon an expanded resource base, and the continuing concern of the company for the future.

FURTHER READING: Ralph W. Hidy, Frank Ernest Hill, and Allan Nevins, *Timber and Men: The Weyerhaeuser Story* (1963).

CHARLES E. TWINING

WILD AND SCENIC RIVERS

In the early 1960s, in response to the recommendation of a Senate Select Committee on National Water Resources, the departments of Agriculture and the Interior undertook a joint study of rivers or river segments suitable for preservation in a free-flowing condition. With the support of the Lyndon B. Johnson administration, Senator Frank Church of Idaho sponsored enabling legislation in 1965. Debate in the Senate focused on demands for inclusion or exclusion of particular rivers. In concept, the wild rivers system met little opposition, and the Senate twice passed Church's bills before the House would act. In the House, consideration of wild rivers legislation was delayed both by the opposition of Wayne Aspinall, chairman of the Interior Committee, and by the insistence of the bill's primary sponsor, John Saylor of Pennsylvania, that the selection of rivers for preservation be based on a more rational scheme than had prevailed in the Senate.

The Wild and Scenic Rivers Act of 1968 supplemented the long-standing national policy of building dams and otherwise developing major rivers; the new act provided "that certain selected rivers . . . which, with their immediate environments, possess outstandingly remarkable scenic, recreational, geologic, fish and wildlife, historic, cultural, or other similar values, shall be preserved in free-flowing condition . . . for the benefit and enjoyment of present and future generations." Rivers and river segments could be added to the National Wild and Scenic Rivers System in two ways: they might be designated by Congress or be designated by state legislatures and accepted by the secretary of the interior. Recommendations made to Congress by the executive agencies were to include comment from state governors, the Federal Power

Commission, the ARMY CORPS OF ENGINEERS, and other concerned federal bureaus. Protected zones along the rivers were to include not more than a quarter-mile strip on each bank. Three classes of rivers were to be protected: wild river areas, "free of impoundments and generally inaccessible except by trail; . . . vestiges of primitive America"; scenic river areas, free of impoundments and with shores undeveloped but occasionally accessible by roads; and recreational river areas, readily reached by road or railroad, with some shoreline development and past impoundment or diversion of waters. Although Congress dictated the rivers to be included within the system, the executive branch could determine the suitable categories for particular rivers.

The act designated portions of eight rivers and adjacent lands as immediate members of the National Wild and Scenic River System: the middle fork of the Clearwater, Idaho; the Eleven Point, Missouri; middle fork of the Feather, California; the Rio Grande, New Mexico; the Rogue, Oregon; the Upper Saint Croix, between Minnesota and Wisconsin; middle fork of the Salmon, Idaho; and the Wolf, Wisconsin. These river segments had a combined length of 392 miles. The act named twenty-seven other rivers for study within ten years by the departments of the Interior and Agriculture as potential additions to the system. Others have been added to the study list since then.

The two federal departments established a joint steering committee to implement the act. Initially, the Bureau of Outdoor Recreation provided staff support to this committee. The U.S. FOREST SERVICE, the NATIONAL PARK SERVICE, the BUREAU OF LAND MANAGEMENT, and in some cases other federal agencies retained responsibility for administering designated areas and making required studies. Rivers added to the system through state designation were to be administered by state or local agencies.

By 1980, twenty-eight river segments had been accepted into the system. They covered 719,000 acres of land and water surface and had a combined length of 2,300 miles, 841 of which were in the "wild" category. The Alaska National Interest Lands Conservation Act, passed in that year, expanded the system enormously, adding twenty-six new segments and a land and water area of 1.3 million acres.

Senator Church had advanced wild rivers legislation as a "working partner" of the National Wilderness Preservation System established by the Wilderness Act of 1964. Wild and scenic rivers provide protection against dams and other water development projects which may be allowed in wilderness, if judged by the president to be in the public interest.

Canoeists enjoy the Allagash Wilderness Waterway, administered by the State of Maine. Forest History Society Photo.

Wild and scenic rivers classification prohibits power transmission lines, provides for the condemnation of inholdings under certain circumstances, and forbids mineral entry within one quarter mile of the bank of any river designated under the "wild" category. Thus, where wilderness and wild rivers overlap, the protection afforded by the Wilderness Act is considerably strengthened.

Beginning with Tennessee in 1968, twenty-four states created their own wild and scenic river systems. Not all of the waterways classified under state systems could qualify under national standards, but five additions to the National Wild and Scenic Rivers System came through the action of state governments. The first of these, in 1970, was the Allagash of Maine, which the state had already protected under the Allagash Wilderness Waterway Act of 1966. The others included the Little Miami and Little Beaver of Ohio, the New in North Carolina, and the Obed in Tennessee.

WILDERNESS CONFERENCES

In 1949, the SIERRA CLUB began sponsoring a series of conferences for the exchange of ideas relating to the preservation and management of wilderness. The first

conference, held in Oakland, California, saw the exchange of views among representatives of CONSERVATION ORGANIZATIONS, public agencies, commercial outfitters, and naturalists concerned with keeping the human impact to a minimum in the high mountain country of the West, particularly in California's Sierra Nevada. Held biennially thereafter, the conference gradually broadened to consider more general themes, such as expansion of the designated wilderness system; philosophical, literary, and artistic implications of wilderness; scientific study and wilderness; the behavior of wilderness visitors; wildlife and wilderness; protection of the seacoast and the oceans; air pollution; education for conservation; population overgrowth, wilderness, and mental health; and wilderness protection in deserts and in the arctic.

The wilderness conferences provided forums for the discussion of particular problems in preservation, such as the Echo Park controversy of the 1950s and the enactment of legislation for a National Wilderness Preservation System. The conferences were largely a forum for the exchange of ideas, until the twelfth conference held in 1971 in Washington, D.C. —the first outside the San Francisco area. In response to the slow pace with which Congress and the executive branch were fulfilling the purposes of the Wilderness Act, the twelfth conference became an activist training session. In particular, the conference was a planning session for a public relations and congressional campaign launched by the Sierra Club and other conservation organizations to challenge the U. S. FOREST SERVICE's interpretation of the Wilderness Act and to force the expansion of the National Wilderness Preservation System into the roadless lands of the national forests.

The sixth conference in 1959 on "The Meaning of Wilderness for Science" had seen the participation of natural scientists from around the world. International participation culminated in the fourteenth conference, held in New York City in 1975 and jointly sponsored by the NATIONAL AUDUBON SOCIETY. With the theme "Earthcare," this session saw the participation of specialists from fifteen countries on five continents in an assessment of the conditions and prospects of the world's natural systems.

WILDERNESS MANAGEMENT

During the 1960s and 1970s, administration of wilderness lands emerged as a distinct field of forest management. The goal was to maintain natural wilderness qualities and to minimize the impact of wilderness users on the landscape. Perhaps the most controversial problem to be faced was the return of fire to its natural influence in park and forest ecosystems.

Having determined that the complete fire elimination policies followed by almost all land management agencies since the late nineteenth century were gradually changing the composition and character of American forests, the NATIONAL PARK SERVICE established a natural fire management zone in the backcountry of SEQUOIA AND KINGS CANYON NATIONAL PARKS in 1968. Within this zone, fires resulting from natural causes such as lightning would be allowed to burn freely. Similar zones were designated in Yosemite and Yellowstone National Parks in 1972 and 1973, and the U. S. FOREST SERVICE instituted parallel policies in the Selway-Bitterroot Wilderness in 1970. These new fire plans met opposition from both conservative land managers and recreationists, but they found support among CONSERVATION ORGANIZATIONS and fitted into the ecological enthusiasm of the 1970s.

The numbers of recreational visitors to wilderness areas is generally thought to have increased rapidly since the end of World War II. Forest Service figures indicate 1.8 million "man-days" use of its wilderness and wild areas in 1959. By 1979, the agency reported 9.6 million "visitor-days" annual use of classified wilderness, primitive areas, and wilderness study areas. In both national forests and national parks, ever growing numbers of visitors traveled over trail systems that had been built largely for administrative transportation in the 1920s and 1930s and was little expanded thereafter. Before the 1940s, wilderness recreational use had been of little concern, unless it posed a fire or sanitation hazard.

The traditional way of managing the wilderness areas of the national forests had been to "draw a line around it and leave it alone." William B. GREELEY, chief of the Forest Service during the 1920s, was very explicit that no limitations should be set on the numbers of visitors. When the primitive areas were established under Regulation L-20 (L Lands), management plans drawn up for each area largely consisted of lists of prohibited and permitted economic activities. The U-regulations (U Uses) of 1939 eliminated most of the commercial use but placed no restrictions on wilderness recreation.

Some foresters thought that the impact of increasing use should be alleviated by limiting the numbers of visitors. As early as 1935, the supervisor of the Santa Barbara National Forest in California proposed restricting the numbers of campers in primitive areas. Writing in *American Forests* in 1940, J. V. K. Wagar, then a professor of forestry at Colorado State College, suggested that wilderness use be restricted to outdoorsmen certified by responsible agencies as competent to take care of themselves in the backcountry without harm to their environment; in 1953, Wagar proposed the actual rationing of wilderness use where solitude was threatened, but federal agencies were not yet ready to go that far.

In the later 1950s, the Forest Service began a formal study of user impact upon the High Sierra Primitive Area. Its conclusion: "the philosophy of living off the land in wilderness must be dispelled." The Forest Service saw the Wilderness Act of 1964 as a legal mandate supporting this point of view. The new law did supply a formal definition of wilderness, but it was not really the primary source of the wilderness regulations promulgated in 1966. These new rules derived instead from the agency's general authority to regulate forest use, as well as from its four decades of experience in administering wilderness.

In 1966, the Forest Service began requiring entry permits for the Boundary Waters Canoe Area in Minnesota. In 1971, a permit system was imposed in all national forest wilderness and primitive areas in California, and in the following year, similar systems were set up in the Pacific Northwest. The most heavily used wilderness areas in California saw the first actual rationing starting in 1973, as restrictions were placed on the number of persons allowed to enter a given area at one time.

The National Park Service developed a parallel permit and rationing policy. ROCKY MOUNTAIN NATIONAL PARK required permits for overnight camping in its backcountry in 1968, and within five years, permits had been required and restrictions imposed for backcountry camping in Sequoia and Kings Canyon, Yellowstone, Grand Canyon, Great Smoky Mountains, Yosemite, and North Cascades national parks, although Congress had not yet approved the addition of any of these areas to the National Wilderness Preservation System. In some cases, National Park Service restrictions were even more rigorous than those imposed by the Forest Service; in Rocky Mountain National Park, for example, backcountry hikers were required to keep to predetermined itineraries. By the late 1970s, most national parks with classified wilderness or backcountry and over half of the national forests with wilderness required entry permits, although fewer units actually restricted numbers of visitors.

The principal conservation organizations supported these permit and rationing policies, and the administrative agencies claimed they had found favor with the majority of wilderness users, even those who had been turned away by the quotas. Yet criticism was loud. One writer in the *Journal of Forestry* denounced "police state wilderness" and suggested that the permits were desired less for the protection of wilderness than for the convenience of administrators. Some foresters feared that widespread opposition to the permit system might become a focal point for opposition to wilderness. Most of the criticism, however, came from wilderness users, and some old-time backpackers, missing their former freedom, found a new sport in the evasion of the new regulations.

WILDERNESS PRESERVATION

Although an aesthetic appreciation for the American wilderness dates from colonial times, it was not until the mid-nineteenth century that Americans began to propose that some tracts of wilderness be deliberately left unchanged. Early proponents of the idea of wilderness preserves included artists such as George Catlin and Thomas Cole, journalists Horace Greeley and Samuel Bowles, philosopher Henry David Thoreau, and diplomat George Perkins MARSH. The woods of Maine and New York were frequently mentioned as suitable for perpetual wilderness. The first such public program was implemented in the Adirondacks in 1885,

when the NEW YORK STATE FOREST PRESERVE was set aside to be "forever kept as wild forest lands." By then, YELLOWSTONE NATIONAL PARK, which had been created by Congress in Wyoming Territory in 1872, came to be regarded as a preserved wilderness.

Other national parks established in the nineteenth century were set aside from the public domain in large part to protect the forests. However, except for the fact that they were established by acts of Congress, there was little legal basis for distinction between park units and the early forest reserves proclaimed by the president under authority of the FOREST RESERVE ACT passed in 1891. The national parks and the forest reserves both consisted largely of wild lands, but in either case it was merely lack of development that determined the extent of wilderness preservation. Preservation was the only form of forest conservation on federal lands before passage of the FOREST MANAGEMENT ACT of 1897, which specified protection of waterflow and timber supply as the purposes of the presidentially designated reserves. After passage of the Forest Management Act, wilderness enthusiasts, such as John MUIR, endeavored to awaken the nation to the threat that improper forest management posed to the federal wilderness.

National Forest Wilderness

The Forest Management Act of 1897 made clear the utilitarian purposes of the forest reserves; Congress had intended the reserves for the protection of watershed and timber resources. However, both western residents and visitors were already using the forests for hunting, camping, mountaineering, and other forms of RECREATION. In 1901, *Forest and Stream* called for game preserves on the forest reserves. The U. S. FOREST SERVICE, however, regarded game protection and hunting as relatively minor forest uses and generally limited its efforts in these fields to cooperating with the states, especially after 1911 when a number of states began establishing game refuges on the national forests.

The government, in fact, had no intention that its forests should remain a wilderness. As early as 1907, Congress began making annual appropriations for improvements. In 1909, the Forest Service and the Bureau of Public Roads drafted plans for a comprehensive system of roads and trails, and an ongoing source of funding was secured in 1913 when Congress gave permanent authorization to allocate 10 percent of all receipts from national forests for road and trail construction. The Federal Aid Road Act of 1916 approved $11 million a year over the next decade for forest road construction in cooperation with local governmental units. By 1917, the national forests still contained fewer than 2,000 miles of improved roads, but Forest Service proposals included a primary road system for each forest to provide for protection and administration, and a secondary system intended to assist in the development of resources. Under the 1921 Federal Highway Act, the Forest Service drew up plans for a 39,000-mile forest road and highway network. The Forest Service expressed confidence that "the public will doubtless demand a larger mileage as more intensive use is made of the forests."

Although appearing to conflict at times with the utilitarian mission assigned to forest administration under the Forest Management Act, recreational provisions gained importance after the turn of the century. The first Forest Service manual (1905) included instructions on the issuance of occupancy permits for summer residences. By 1910, the Forest Service claimed that its lands had 400,000 recreational visitors a year. Recreation, encouraged by the expanding road network, was rapidly becoming the third major use of the forests by World War I.

As recreational interest developed, the wilderness aspects of the national forest lands gained supporters. Members of the Forest Service attributed the loss of wild country less to industrial exploitation than to the increased recreational accessibility. Aldo LEOPOLD, then assistant district forester in the Southwest, was particularly concerned with the threat to wildlife and the dwindling opportunities for pack trips in pursuit of game in remote country. About 1918, Leopold suggested measures to exclude a portion of the Gila National Forest in New Mexico from road extensions. Soon after that, Arthur Carhart, a landscape architect, proposed that an area around Trappers Lake in the White River National Forest of Colorado and portions of Minnesota's Superior National Forest be closed to summer home permit applications.

The district forester in 1920 approved Carhart's plan to keep Trappers Lake roadless and undeveloped. In 1926, Carhart's Superior proposal, supported by the IZAAK WALTON LEAGUE OF AMERICA and the State of Minnesota, resulted in a national forest management plan "retaining as much as possible of the Forest area in a wilderness condition." In 1930, the Shipstead-Nolan Act sanctioned the unique QUETICO-SUPERIOR wilderness on the national forest lands.

Leopold's Gila plans were also successful, leading by 1924 to a provisional ten-year restriction on development for more than a half-million acres of the Gila National Forest. By then, Leopold's concept of a nationwide wilderness system had already taken shape. Alarmed by the implications of the 1921 Federal Highway Act, he wrote articles for both the *Journal of Forestry* and *American Forests*, intending to acquaint his fellow professionals with the wilderness problem.

The Forest Service's annual report for 1923 for the first time referred to the "overgrowth of recreational visits." The number of visitors had doubled in six years (from the first comprehensive estimate of 2.37 million in 1916 to 6.17 million in 1922). The agency proposed to encourage growth by providing recreational facilities. At the same time, Chief William B. Greeley felt that the movement to preserve portions of national forests, not as parks but as "stretches of untrammeled wilderness," represented a contribution to the "physical and social health of the American people. It is a wholesome reaction from the multiplication of improved roads and automobiles."

The Forest Service was initially cautious about getting ahead of public opinion on the subject of wilderness. By 1925, district foresters in Wyoming, Montana, and Idaho had designated roadless areas. When the NATIONAL CONFERENCE ON OUTDOOR RECREATION (NCOR) asked the AMERICAN FORESTRY ASSOCIATION (AFA) and the National Parks Association (NPA) to form a joint committee to study the recreational uses of federal lands, the Forest Service listed twenty-one western candidates for wilderness protection, ranging from 2 million acres down to 30,000 acres each, and totaling 12.5 million acres. Aldo Leopold spoke eloquently before the second general session of NCOR in 1926 and worked with the AFA-NPA joint committee to ensure extensive consideration of wilderness in its report.

In October 1926, Greeley laid out his thoughts on wilderness in the *Service Bulletin*: such preservation was "highly important, if not dominant," he thought, but it would not normally interfere with economic use of timber, forage, and water. In December, Greeley issued instructions to review development and special use plans to make sure that wilderness was not unnecessarily precluded. By 1928, the districts had designated over 5 million acres as wilderness. The agency's annual reports for 1927 and 1928 endeavored to alleviate the fear that the policy meant locking up needed economic resources; it was, rather, directed more against the unlimited expansion of other forms of recreational use, such as tourist roads, resorts, and other developments that would compromise the protected areas' "major values."

After much consultation with personnel in the field, the Washington office in the summer of 1929 issued its first regulation concerning wilderness. Regulation L-20 requested the districts to nominate tracts for in-

Fishermen are waiting for a bite in Colorado's White River National Forest, 1919. Forest Service Photo.

clusion in a system of "primitive areas," within which "will be maintained primitive conditions of environment, transportation, habitation, and subsistence, with a view toward conserving the value of such areas for purposes of public education, inspiration, and recreation." (In the following year the word "inspira-

tion" was deleted.) The accompanying instructions made it clear to staff (if not to the public) that the establishment of primitive areas was not incompatible with industrial use of timber, forage, or water resources.

District nomination and Washington approval of primitive areas established a basic system by 1933, with sixty-three areas totaling almost 8.7 million acres, all but 3 percent of which were in federal ownership. Management plans for twenty-three areas allowed logging, and plans for only eight areas definitely precluded it. Commercial grazing was permissible in all but ten areas. Clearly, the L-20 areas were not closed to economic exploitation, but they did serve as holding action to slow up unessential development, while the public demand for wilderness recreation could be further assessed.

Not everyone was satisfied with the Forest Service program for primitive areas; for one thing, many areas were relatively small—fine for day hikes and overnight trips, but hardly suitable for two-week pack trips as Leopold had envisioned. In the New Deal planning study, *National Plan for American Forestry* (1933), Robert MARSHALL, author of the recreation section, proposed a system of "wilderness areas," each at least 200,000 acres in size, supplemented by a number of "outing areas," less restricted in size and use. Marshall's ideas did not prevail, but a year and a half later, Chief Ferdinand SILCOX brought Marshall into the Forest Service as chief of recreation and lands, where he served until his death in late 1939. By this time, Marshall had succeeded Leopold as the most prominent spokesman for the preservation of wilderness. Marshall sought both to expand the national forest wilderness acreage and to impose more rigid protective regulations. His first objective saw little success. Primitive areas, totaling about 14 million acres in seventy-three units in 1937, remained nearly stable until the end of the 1950s.

Marshall's second aim had a greater impact. In September 1939, the secretary of agriculture approved the "U" regulations that established sizes and designations of wilderness units. Regulation U-1 classified certain tracts over 100,000 acres as wilderness areas, while U-2 granted parcels of 5,000 to 100,000 acres status as wild areas—areas without roads but too small for wilderness classification. U-3(b) authorized recreation areas where substantial improvements would be required. Areas once established under U-1 and U-2 could not be modified thereafter without a public hearing if protest was made; this safeguard did not apply to areas designated under U-3. The decade of the 1940s saw reclassifications and adjustments; the 1950s would usher in an era of increasing controversy.

The Pacific Northwest, where timber was of paramount importance to the local economy, saw some of the most bitter contests over national forest wilderness policy in the 1950s. In addition to 1.7 million acres of wilderness, wild, and primitive areas, the Pacific Northwest Region also contained another seventeen areas, comprising nearly 1.3 million acres, which had been designated as "limited areas" by authority of the regional forester in the early 1940s. A classification unique to the Pacific Northwest, limited areas were protected until such time as they could be studied to determine their resources and suitability for classification under U-1 and U-2. In 1957, the Forest Service proposed classifying the largest of them, the Glacier Peak Limited Area, under regulation U-1, expanding the original area, but deleting some of the best timber. Preservationist groups such as the SIERRA CLUB and the Mountaineers responded with a plan for a NORTH CASCADES NATIONAL PARK that would be three times as large as the area the Forest Service proposed for wilderness. Compromise resulted in the 458,505-acre Glacier Peak Wilderness Area, created in 1960, and the establishment of the North Cascades National Park and two recreation areas in 1968.

The Glacier Peak imbroglio demonstrated the growing breach between wilderness advocates and the Forest Service. But despite some deletions in timberland acreage, the agency managed to keep the total acreage of its classified wilderness system more or less even and in the early 1960s increased it slightly. Also, beginning about 1950, the Forest Service made earnest efforts to place its primitive areas under the more protective U-regulations. In that year, only about 16 percent of the system was so classified, but on the eve of the passage of the Wilderness Act in 1964, the proportion was over 50 percent. All of these reclassifications followed upon public hearings, and all reflected support voiced by local communities.

Wilderness in the Department of the Interior

The thrust of the NATIONAL PARK SERVICE policy, following agency establishment in 1916, often appeared to be contrary to the concept of wilderness preservation. Park Service Director Stephen T. MATHER campaigned energetically for road building in the parks, and Congress approved his ambitions in 1924. Beginning in 1929, Congress expanded this program with a ten-year appropriation of $51 million for park roads and trails. Like the national forest roads, the national park network expanded rapidly with the unemployment relief programs and emergency funds available in the 1930s.

With park roadbuilding and other tourist-related development increasing in the late 1920s and 1930s, so too did criticism from preservationists. However, following the example of the Forest Service, the Park Service experimented with a series of restrictive land classifications. It first used the term "primitive areas" in 1927 to designate relatively small tracts reserved for scientific study, similar to those known on the national forests as "natural areas." In the following year, Mather established a "wilderness area" of some 50,000 acres in MOUNT RAINIER NATIONAL PARK. Then in 1933, the Park Service adopted new regulations which would permit the parks to be divided into "developed areas," "sacred areas," and "research reserves," the latter being the new name for the former primitive areas. Sacred areas guarded unique features and were to contain no buildings or roads. Park custodians remained uncomfortable with the concept of segregating specific areas, since special classifications did not fit easily into the traditional concept of parks as overall protected units.

In 1936 and 1937, preservation groups, still suspicious of Park Service developmentalism, suggested the creation of district "National Primeval Parks." Secretary of the Interior Harold ICKES himself proposed in 1939 that Congress "define and set standards for wilderness national parks…." Later that year, Ickes had the Park Service draft a bill to authorize the president to proclaim wilderness areas in national parks and monuments. This proposal won favor with the WILDERNESS SOCIETY and the Izaak Walton League, but its wisdom was questioned by the National Parks Association, which preferred to see the parks as units and feared that special status for some areas might encourage the assumption that the remainder of the parks was not subject to the strictest standards of preservation.

Up to 90 percent of the 22 million acres of the park system remained wild into the 1960s, if only because the agency had as yet made no plans for their development. Unlike the Forest Service areas designated under the U-regulations, there was no presumption that any park land would be kept undeveloped in perpetuity, nor was there any provision for consulting public opinion should the service's plans change. Preservationists wondered what to make of the policies of an agency whose head, Conrad Wirth, could tell the Fifth Biennial Wilderness Conference in 1957 that when the National Park Service constructed a new road into an undeveloped region, "the road is a wilderness road, to bring people into the wilderness."

The only other federal agency to designate wilderness-type areas on its lands before the passage of the Wilderness Act was the Bureau of Indian Affairs (BIA). In 1937, an order issued by the Indian commissioner John Collier established sixteen areas, totaling 4.8 million acres, to provide a last frontier beyond which the Indian might retreat from contact with whites; also, the areas were to provide Indians opportunity for employment as wilderness guides. The Ei-

senhower administration promptly eliminated most of the designated areas on the grounds that the tribes had not been consulted when the areas were set aside. Some Indians favored the wilderness idea, however, and in 1982 there remained three areas so designated by tribal authority on reservations in Wyoming, Montana, and Arizona.

The Wilderness Act of 1964

Starting with the recommendations of the NCOR's AFA-NPA joint committee in 1926, proposals for congressional recognition of wilderness preservation were made recurrently without drawing the support of the federal land-holding agencies. By the mid-1950s, however, a well-organized lobby of citizen organizations was becoming increasingly sensitive to various proposals for logging and mining operations or recreational development within the wilderness areas. The Wilderness Society, Izaak Walton League, National Parks Association, NATIONAL WILDLIFE FEDERATION, National Council of State Garden Clubs, and outing groups such as the Sierra Club and other regional organizations banded together into the FEDERATION OF WESTERN OUTDOOR CLUBS and developed a number of methods of communication which provided common grounds for action.

A single incident can be taken as a turning point in the crusade to protect America's scenic resources. It centered in the tiny, almost unknown Dinosaur National Monument in Utah, where the U. S. BUREAU OF RECLAMATION had planned to construct a dam as part of its Colorado River Storage Project. Extending over some seven years, the Dinosaur controversy was the largest confrontation between utilitarian and preservationist branches of the CONSERVATION MOVEMENT since the argument over damming Hetch Hetchy Valley in YOSEMITE NATIONAL PARK in the 1910s. When Congress decided in 1956 that Dinosaur should remain inviolate, preservationists became convinced that if a wilderness preservation system could be established in law, encroachments could be opposed on the principle of defense of the system, rather than on the merits of the particular tract of land involved.

Howard ZAHNISER, executive secretary of the Wilderness Society, drafted a bill to establish a National Wilderness Preservation System (NWPS), created at least initially out of lands already under some restriction from development. When the Wilderness Bill had its first hearings in 1957, opposition came both from the DEPARTMENT OF THE INTERIOR, which proposed an area-by-area study, and from the DEPARTMENT OF AGRICULTURE, which proposed substitute language, mandating multiple use on the national forests but in-

Campers in Idaho's Salmon National Forest, 1952. Forest Service Photo.

cluding a provision for wilderness. Both departments rejected the concept of a wilderness system. Private opposition had also emerged. Less formally organized than the proponents, the opponents included such groups as the American Mining Congress, the Western Oil and Gas Association, the FOREST INDUSTRIES COUNCIL, the INDUSTRIAL FORESTRY ASSOCIATION, the Western Forest Industries Association, the American National Cattlemen's Association, the National Reclamation Association, and the United States Chamber of Commerce. The only general membership conservation organization opposing the bill was the American Forestry Association. In succeeding sessions of Congress, the wilderness lobby accepted one compromise after another and gradually reduced the membership of the opposition.

In 1961, John F. Kennedy became president of the United States, and Clinton Anderson of New Mexico became chairman of the Senate Interior Committee. Both were personally interested in wilderness preservation. Before the Senate Interior Committee, both Secretary of the Interior Stewart L. UDALL and Secretary of Agriculture Orville Freeman testified without reservation in favor of a wilderness bill, and for the

first time a bill was reported favorably by the committee. By 1962, when stock interests dropped their opposition, once assured that existing grazing privileges would continue indefinitely, the burden of opposition was carried by mining interests.

Negotiations and compromises continued for two more years. The Wilderness Act, as passed and signed by President Lyndon B. Johnson on September 3, 1964, gave legal recognition only to those wilderness and wild areas already established. Thus, the NWPS in 1964 consisted of 9.1 million national forest acres in fifty-four units. Among them were eighteen wilderness areas, thirty-five smaller wild areas, and one canoe area classified under U-3. Another 5.4 million acres of primitive areas (thirty-four units) were to be reviewed within ten years.

The lands of the NWPS were to "be administered for the use and enjoyment of the American people in such manner as will leave them unimpaired for future use and enjoyment as wilderness." They would remain under the administrative jurisdictions of the agencies that had previously managed them. Wilderness was defined as "an area where the earth and its community of life are untrammeled by man, where man himself is a visitor who does not remain." The system was to retain "its primeval character and influence, without permanent improvements or human habitation," while additions would have to demonstrate "outstanding opportunities for solitude or a primitive and unconfined type of recreation."

Mandated Reviews under the Wilderness Act

The Forest Service promptly began field studies of the nearly 5.5 million acres in its thirty-four primitive areas, holding its first public hearings under the act in November 1965 on the San Rafael Primitive Area in California. By 1974, the agency completed its review as scheduled by the Wilderness Act. Congress, however, did not begin its approval of any of these proposals until 1968, when it passed separate bills adding to the NWPS four primitive areas totaling 784,000 acres. In 1969, it passed two more primitive area bills for 159,000 acres, and in 1970, it enacted the first of the omnibus wilderness bills, approving four Forest Service areas as well as nineteen wildlife refuges and the first two national park units, a total of over 200,000 acres. Seven more areas, with 632,000 acres of forest, park, and refuge, were added in 1972.

The Wilderness Act also required the Department of the Interior to review the suitability for wilderness classification of every roadless area over 5,000 contiguous acres in the national parks, wildlife refuges, game ranges, and larger islands in the wildlife refuges. The national parks and monuments contained an estimated 22.7 million roadless acres in fifty-seven areas. The Park Service created a controversy by planning the construction of new roads into existing wildlands and in proposing semiwild buffer or "threshold" zones up to two miles wide around its proposed wilderness areas. Although the plans followed traditional Park Service policies and met the approval of some preservationists, there was no basis for such policies under the terms of the Wilderness Act of 1964. During a Senate Interior Committee hearing in 1972, Senator Church bluntly informed Assistant Secretary of the Interior Nathaniel Reed that the National Park Service wilderness policies were incorrect under the law. Thereafter, under new departmental guidelines, Park Service wilderness reviews improved somewhat in the eyes of the preservationists.

Review of the estimated 29 million acres of potential wilderness within the jurisdiction of the Fish and Wildlife Service began with nineteen public hearings in 1967. A year later, the 3,750-acre Great Swamp Wilderness in the Great Swamp National Wildlife Refuge in New Jersey, previously threatened by plans for an airport, became the first area to be established under the Wilderness Act on lands administered by the Department of the Interior. Most other National Wildlife Refuge wilderness proposals involved relatively small uncontroversial areas.

Congressional approval often followed years behind Department of the Interior wilderness recommendations. By mid-1978, seventeen national park areas (over 1.1 million acres) had been added to the NWPS, but thirty-one proposals (14.6 million acres) still waited for Congress to act. In the national wildlife refuges the situation was similar. The truly enormous expansion of classified wilderness on Department of the Interior lands came a few years later, although it did little to reduce the backlog of areas awaiting congressional approval.

Roadless Lands on National Forests

The Wilderness Act neither specifically required nor prohibited review of the wilderness qualities of roadless national forest land not contiguous to any primitive area. However, the Forest Service assumed that it could anticipate demands for extension of the NWPS into such "de facto wilderness," and in 1964 it began drafting regulations requiring the identification, but not formal designation, of potential new wilderness areas. This initiative failed to earn for the Forest Service the goodwill of preservationists, nor did it enable the agency to control the review process free from interference from Congress and from the wilderness lobby.

The Forest Service study of the wilderness recommendations submitted by the regional foresters in 1972 was designated as the Roadless Area Review and Evaluation (RARE). Conducting the "biggest public involvement program ever attempted by the federal government," the Forest Service inventoried a total of 1,449 roadless tracts totaling 56.2 million acres and conducted 300 hearings attracting 25,000 people and drawing more than 50,000 oral and written comments.

The wilderness lobby, however, charged that the Forest Service, like the Interior Department, limited the extent of lands under study by interpreting management criteria specified in the Wilderness Act as standards for entry into the NWPS. Urged by the Nixon administration to hasten identification of potential wilderness in the East where it would better serve the larger part of the American population, the Forest Service conceived of a new "wild areas" system parallel to the NWPS but not required to meet the same standards in regard to the appearance of human impact. The Eastern Wilderness Areas Act of 1974 added sixteen eastern areas (207,000 acres) to the NWPS and designated seventeen other tracts (125,000 acres) as wilderness study areas.

To end the stalemate over RARE I, the Carter administration launched RARE II to examine all roadless and undeveloped areas on the national forests and divide them into three classes: those recommended for addition to the NWPS, those opened to other use, and those needing further study. In July and August 1977, the Forest Service conducted 227 workshops around the country and gathered written comments from 50,000 other citizens. RARE II covered not only all the lands previously examined in RARE I but also the national grasslands and the eastern national forests. RARE II displeased both preservationists and developers. The SOCIETY OF AMERICAN FORESTERS complained of "too little study time and too little recognition of economic tradeoffs." The Sierra Club expressed concern "about the poor quality of the processes involved." The NATIONAL FOREST PRODUCTS ASSOCIATION feared that RARE II, like its predecessor, would "keep the timber supply uncertain."

While RARE II progressed, Congress continued its consideration of other wilderness proposals. Between 1976 and 1979, it added over 3.3 million acres to the system. In 1980, it established the River of No Return Wilderness in Idaho, with 2.2 million acres; the area became the largest unit of the national forest wilderness system. By the beginning of 1981, 25.8 million acres of national forest lands had been classified as wilderness, providing 86 percent of the entire NWPS outside of Alaska.

Wilderness on Bureau of Land Management Lands

The Wilderness Act of 1964 made no reference to the public lands administered by the Department of the Interior's BUREAU OF LAND MANAGEMENT (BLM). With more than 450 million acres (175 million outside of Alaska), BLM was responsible for two-thirds of all federal lands. The Classification and Multiple Use Act of 1964 (CMU) directed the secretary of the interior to determine which of those lands should be disposed of and which retained in federal ownership. By 1966, the BLM had initiated an inventory of sixty-one tracts of undeveloped lands covering over 5 million acres.

Because they would be protected by administrative order and would not be part of the NWPS, BLM chose the term "primitive areas" for its wildernesses. The first primitive areas to be established were Aravaipa and Paria canyons in Arizona, recommended by the BLM state office after public hearings and approved by Secretary of the Interior Stewart Udall. By 1976, despite some pressure from the Sierra Club, only eleven BLM primitive areas totaling just over 234,000 acres had been established in six western states.

The FEDERAL LAND POLICY AND MANAGEMENT ACT (FLPMA), passed in 1976, provided for a review of roadless areas of 5,000 acres or more and roadless islands having wilderness characteristics. Although the secretary of the interior was to report to the president upon their suitability for preservation by 1991, as of mid-1982 no BLM wilderness proposal had yet reached Congress.

Alaska Wilderness

With passage of the Wilderness Act, Alaska's 7.5 million acres in national parks and 22 million acres in national wildlife refuges and ranges presented a huge opportunity for mandated reviews. Designation of wilderness in Alaska was to present special difficulties, however. The Alaska Native Claims Settlement Act of 1971 (ANCSA) allocated 40 million acres to native villages and corporations subject, under its clause d-2, to withdrawal by the secretary of the interior of 80 million acres as potential additions to the national park, national wildlife refuge, national forest, and wild and scenic rivers systems. Alaska witnessed one of the most bitter quarrels in the history of wilderness legislation. Preservationists, banded together as the Alaska Coalition, initially asked that 146 million acres be classified as wilderness, while opposing interests, led primarily by the Alaska state government and its congressional delegation, wished to minimize wilderness and other amenity classifications.

In 1977, Interior Secretary Cecil Andrus withdrew 110 million acres for three years under the emergency provisions of FLPMA. Two weeks later, President Carter followed up under authority of the 1906 Antiquities Act by proclaiming 56 million acres of the withdrawn lands as seventeen national monuments. Legislation that would permit designation of some portion of the withdrawn lands as wilderness, however, remained stalled in the Senate. In early 1980, Andrus prodded Congress again by withdrawing 40 million new acres. Facing the prospect of continuing executive withdrawals, Congress eventually agreed upon terms for the Alaska National Interest Lands Conservation Act of 1980, increasing both the national park system and the national wildlife refuge system by about 150 percent. National park wilderness gained 32 million acres, nearly ten times the total existing in the lower forty-eight states; more than 18.5 million acres were added to the NWPS within the national wildlife refuge system, twenty-three times the area existing in the lower states; and over 5 million acres were added to the national forest wilderness in the Tongass National Forest, equaling about 30 percent of the previous total area of national forest wilderness. Altogether, Alaska had provided over 55.5 million acres to the NWPS, or 56 percent of the national total.

Mineral Resources in Wilderness

Ever since the Forest Management Act of 1897, forest reserves created out of the public domain have been open to entry under the Mining Law of 1872, without consideration given to any competing values. By 1960, thirty-two wilderness and large primitive areas contained 225 patented mineral properties covering almost 11,000 acres, and nearly 7,500 unpatented claims containing another 140,000 acres. In its final stages, the passage of the Wilderness Act had depended upon compromises between preservationists and mining interests. The act left undisturbed those mineral rights already established, but new claims or mineral leases were outlawed in designated wilderness after 1983. The act also placed restrictions on the rights gained by miners on claims filed in wilderness between 1964 and 1983.

State Wilderness

In 1933, Robert Marshall predicted that state parks, more subject to political whims than federal lands, would prove less satisfactory as guardians of wilderness. He has been proved largely correct, although some state governments have made significant contributions to the preservation movement. Some state wilderness areas have been established on public lands while other states have reserved lands in roadless, undeveloped condition under a variety of other designations. However, much nominal state wilderness has consisted of tracts too small to minimize external influences, or insufficiently primeval to have met standards equivalent to those required for federal wilderness. Some states have cooperated with federal wilderness programs by protecting intermingled state lands with comparable standards.

Among the most significant state wilderness preserves are: New York State Forest Preserve (1885), Maine's Baxter State Park (1931), and Michigan's Porcupine Mountain State Park (1946). Both California (1974) and Michigan (1972) have created wilderness systems.

FURTHER READING: Craig W. Allin, *The Politics of Wilderness Preservation* (1982). Donald N. Baldwin, *The Quiet Revolution: Grass Roots of Today's Wilderness Preservation Movement* (1972). James P. Gilligan, "The Development of Policy and Administration of Forest Service Primitive and Wilderness Areas in the Western United States," Ph.D. dissertation, University of Michigan (1954).

John C. Hendee, George H. Stankey, and Robert C. Lucas, *Wilderness Management* (1978). Roderick Nash, *Wilderness and the American Mind* (rev. ed., 1982). ORRRC, *Wilderness and Recreation: A Report on Resources, Values, and Problems* (1962).

WILDERNESS SOCIETY

In the *Scientific Monthly* for February 1930, Robert MARSHALL proposed that the "one hope" to accomplish such a program as that recommended at the NATIONAL CONFERENCE ON OUTDOOR RECREATION to retain wilderness areas in various parts of the country would be the formation of an "organization of spirited people who will fight for the freedom of the wilderness." Four years later, Marshall's article was recalled by a group of individuals concerned about road building along the scenic crests of the Appalachians. Benton MACKAYE had proposed an Appalachian Trail from Maine to Georgia in 1921, but no sooner had construction started than parts of the trail were obliterated by new highways. At the Knoxville convention of the AMERICAN FORESTRY ASSOCIATION in 1934, MacKaye and Harvey Broome, a Tennessee attorney and outdoorsman, met with Marshall and Bernard Frank, a forester with the TENNESSEE VALLEY AUTHORITY. The four men agreed on the need for an organization to promote wilderness nationally. They asked the help of Harold Anderson, founder of the Potomac Appalachian Trail Club; Ernest OBERHOLTZER, principal proponent of the QUETICO-SUPERIOR wilderness; Aldo LEOPOLD, originator of the U.S. FOREST SERVICE's wilderness program; and Robert Sterling YARD, one of the architects of the national parks movement. In January 1935, the eight formed the Wilderness Society in Washington, D.C.

The society soon involved itself in a number of disputes over the use of undeveloped and scenic lands, arguing that as much as possible of the wilderness should be preserved for its emotional, intellectual, and scientific values. Wilderness, as Leopold wrote in the first issue of the society's magazine, *The Living Wilderness* (September 1935), "gives significance to civilization." The society opposed the penetration of ROCKY MOUNTAIN NATIONAL PARK by an aqueduct tunnel, denounced plans for the riddling of the Adirondacks by CIVILIAN CONSERVATION CORPS truck trails, and stirred up a local movement to stop construction of a skyline parkway in the Green Mountains of Vermont.

The founding of a national organization with the sole purpose of imposing a wilderness condition permanently on a large part of the undeveloped resources of the country smacked of "loose thinking" to some professional foresters; Herbert A. Smith, editor of the *Journal of Forestry*, denounced this new "cult of the wilderness," composed of "urbanites in easy circumstances." The public wanted development and easy access to resources and recreation, Smith asserted.

The founders of the Wilderness Society thought membership should be kept small and committed. The society started not as an educational organization but as an action organization of believers. Membership conferred little more than a subscription to *The Living Wilderness*, members voted on neither issues nor directors. Yet membership grew, despite the oligarchical nature of the organization. Whereas at first members were largely easterners, by the late 1940s, as park and wilderness controversies spread throughout the United States, most of the membership lived in the West, with California providing the largest contingent. The society had about 5,000 members in 1952. By 1982, it claimed a membership of 60,000.

The eight founders constituted themselves as the Organizing Committee in 1935. When incorporation papers were filed in 1937, the governing board was styled the council, and its number was increased to thirteen, among whom were the eight founders. Since 1941, the council has consisted of fifteen members. It has always been self-perpetuating. Decisions have been made by consensus. When agreement could not be reached, decisions were usually deferred.

Yard was the principal official of the society in the early years; from 1935 to 1937 he served as editor of *The Living Wilderness* and as secretary-treasurer; thereafter until his death in 1945, he combined the offices of president, permanent secretary, and editor. He was succeeded as president by Olaus J. MURIE; the secretariat and editorship went to Howard ZAHNISER. Murie and Zahniser led the society and the wilderness movement during the lobbying and public relations struggle against the Echo Park Dam in the 1950s and then on behalf of the Wilderness Act. Robert Marshall, although the dominant figure in the society's founding, held no office other than membership on the council and its executive committee, but his leadership was assured both by his personality and his contribution of the major portion of the society's income until his death in 1939, and thereafter by a substantial bequest to the society.

After passage of the Wilderness Act in 1964, the society continued to find a mission in urging agency and congressional expansion of the National Wilderness Preservation System and particularly in successfully urging new legislation safeguarding Alaska's wilderness. With the advent of the Reagan administration in 1981, the society renewed its crusading spirit as it attacked the administration's developmental programs. These concerns were reflected in staff expansion as the society provided itself with departments of economic policy analysis and forest management. These new departments were to study conflicts between WILDERNESS PRESERVATION and resource development, and monitor and influence the administration of both wilderness and nonwilderness forestlands.

FURTHER READING: Lewis Mumford et al., "Benton MacKaye: A Tribute," *Living Wilderness* 39 (Jan./Mar. 1976): 6-34.

WILDLIFE CONSERVATION

Early observers estimated that America's wildlife resources included some 40 million pronghorn antelope, 30 to 40 million bison, 5 billion of the now extinct passenger pigeon, and 40 million whitetailed deer. The grizzly bear ranged from the Mississippi Valley to the Pacific Coast. The abundance of fish, sea mammals, birds, and other wildlife attracted European fishermen and hunters long before the colonies were settled. During the early 1500s, Portuguese, Spanish, French, and English fishermen plied the waters off Newfoundland for cod; by 1624, William Bradford of the Plymouth Plantation was already complaining about the scarcity of fish, due to the number of foreign vessels that came every year. The colonists saw this abundance of wildlife as a source of food and clothing and as a trade commodity. The history of wildlife conservation traces the shift in America's attitude toward wildlife from a food source to a source of recreational, aesthetic, ecological, scientific, and symbolic values.

Early regulation of wildlife was limited mainly to bounties for predators. Massachusetts, for instance, passed a bounty law in 1630 for eagles, bears, mountain lions, wolves, and coyotes. In general, bounties were paid for any animal that killed livestock, fowl, or game. This list included wolves, cougars, foxes, bobcats, bears, hawks, eagles, and owls. As early as 1646, however, Rhode Island passed a deer protection act that prohibited hunting from May to November. Other colonies adopted similar restrictions by 1720. Virginia prohibited the use of jack lights for fishing in 1678, Massachusetts appointed deer wardens in 1739, and Maine employed fish wardens in 1843 and moose wardens in 1852.

The question, "who owns the wildlife?," was first addressed by the Supreme Court in 1842. The issue in *Martin* v. *Waddell* involved property rights to the oysters in the Raritan River in New Jersey. The plaintiff claimed that his property along the riverbank gave him title to the river bottom as well. Chief Justice Roger Taney, applying the English common law principle that game is held in trust by the king, declared that the oysters were public property, entrusted to the states. Taney's judgment that the people's right to fish was paramount over individual property rights introduced the doctrine of the public trust into American jurisprudence.

While *Martin* v. *Waddell* established the relation between state and individual in wildlife matters, the 1896 *Geer* v. *Connecticut* decision determined the state's jurisdiction in relation to the federal government. Geer was charged with possessing game birds with intent to ship them across state lines. Although Geer shot the birds legally, out-of-state shipment violated Connecticut law. Geer charged that the Connecticut law interfered with the federal government's authority over interstate commerce. Justice Edward White declared that it was "the duty of the State to preserve for its people a valuable food supply" and authorized the state's power, so long as interstate commerce was only "remotely and indirectly affected." This decision became the bulwark for states' rights in future cases involving authority over wildlife. Only after wildlife took on values other than food did the federal government assert its powers, using regulation of interstate commerce, property rights, and treaty making as its legal basis.

Between 1865 and 1900, game protection systems were set up in each state. Closed seasons, especially in the East, protected the heath hen and deer. State fish and game commissions were encouraged by early sportsmen's clubs and associations. The commissions regulated hunting and fishing seasons, enforced laws, stocked streams, and managed preserves. They also provided public education programs.

Nevertheless, by 1890, deer had been virtually eliminated in the East, except in northern Maine and southeastern Massachusetts. South of Canada, bighorn sheep existed only in scattered bands; moose also had been reduced to remnant herds roaming the northern Rockies, northern Minnesota, and northern Maine. The woodland caribou were gone from northern New England, and the nearly extinct bison and elk survived only in protected herds in YELLOWSTONE NATIONAL PARK. Extermination of the passenger pigeon later became a symbol of man's thoughtlessness; the last of the species died in the Cincinnati Zoological Garden in 1914. Naturalist John Audubon had realized that the pigeons were doomed, not only by excessive hunting, but by loss of the forests required for their dense roosting habits.

The decline of fresh-water and marine fish became noticeable between 1900 and 1910. Logging activities,

High fashion through the years has threatened various species. The millinery industry has been particularly destructive. The American beaver population was decimated to provide felt to make hats for English men during the nineteenth century, and whole birds adorned women's hats. Forest History Society Photo.

reclamation projects, and dams for waterpower were in part responsible. Fish in inland waters are affected by the temperature of the water, speed of the current, fluctuations in the water levels, availability of food, nature of the bottom, and the amount of shade and shelter provided by vegetation on the banks and in the water. Dams created conditions unsuitable for some species, and reclamation projects drained wetlands, destroying habitats for others. Streams and rivers were cleared and splash dams built for log drives. Rapid deforestation in the nineteenth century created erosion and runoff problems that increased sedimentation in the streams. During the first 150 years of the nation's history, some 200,000 miles of waterways were altered either to drain land, control floods, or provide transport. Water pollution, a result of rapid industrial expansion, also took its toll on fish habitat. At the same time, overfishing created shortages of several commercial species. The sturgeon catch reached its peak in 1890, yielding 18 million pounds. It declined to 6 million pounds in 1900 and dropped steadily thereafter. Pacific salmon fishing peaked in the Sacramento River in 1880 and again in 1910 at 10 million pounds. By 1927, the catch had been reduced to 800,000 pounds. The Puget Sound stocks experienced a similar decline due to overfishing and the construction of dams that hindered spawning. Herring in Lake Erie declined from a catch of about 28.5 million pounds in 1919 to about 4.5 million in 1926.

Awareness of the decline of fish and wildlife increased due to publicity surrounding the bison and passenger pigeon. However, no public pressure was brought to bear on the states to enforce their game laws. Rather, it was the growing antipathy of the sportsman to the market hunter that stimulated enforcement. The distinction between the sportsman and the market hunter had become apparent as early as 1850. Although the sportsman hunted for his table, he also hunted for recreational and aesthetic enjoyment. The market hunter, on the other hand, conducted mass killings and was motivated solely by economic demand for food and hides. In addition, women's hat styles in the late 1800s used plumage from exotic birds; many species, such as the snowy egret, were nearly eliminated by hunters killing for this market.

Sportsmen concerned about the perpetuation of their favorite species found voice in publications such as *American Sportsman* (1871), *Forest and Stream* (1873), *Field and Stream* (1874), *American Angler* (1881), and *Outdoor Life* (1898). Sportsmen also formed clubs and tried to conserve game by buying land for private preserves. The New York Sportsman's Club, formed in 1844 by eighty sports hunters, was the first of this type. They set out to stop the sale of game for market, to eliminate spring shooting, and to stimulate enforcement of game laws. The club sued apprehended violators as a way to gain public attention, and its efforts resulted in the formation of similar groups before the Civil War in major eastern cities. Other groups active against the market hunter were the BOONE AND CROCKETT CLUB (1887), the League of American Sportsmen (1898), and the NATIONAL AUDUBON SOCIETY (1905). The sportsmen's efforts to protect their own preserves from market hunters were extended to a concern for wildlife conservation in general.

The national park movement complemented the sportsmen's concern for wildlife. The 1872 act establishing Yellowstone National Park provided for the preservation of all timber, mineral deposits, natural curiosities, and wonders within the park "in their natural condition." However, Congress failed to appropriate money to fulfill these conditions, and timber rustling and poaching continued. The last bison herd of a few hundred head were constantly plundered. Even when poachers were caught, the army personnel who administered the park had no authority to prosecute. The Boone and Crockett Club along with other citizen groups and individuals lobbied to strengthen the park's jurisdiction over its wildlife. In 1894, the Yellowstone Park Protection Act was signed by President Cleveland, making the park the first inviolate refuge in the country and establishing a precedent for prohibiting hunting in the national parks.

Aside from a few Alaska fish and wildlife measures, the Yellowstone Protection Act was the first federal wildlife legislation. The first federal legislation of a national scope was the 1900 Preservation of Game Birds and Other Wild Birds Act, known as the Lacey Act for Congressman John F. LACEY of Iowa, who had also been a sponsor of the Yellowstone bill. Enforcement of the Lacey Act was based on the powers of the federal government to regulate interstate commerce, and it prohibited the transport over state lines of any wild animals or birds taken in violation of state or territorial law. The Lacey Act also prohibited the importation of wildlife determined to be injurious to agriculture or horticulture. The U. S. Bureau of BIOLOGICAL SURVEY, heretofore a purely scientific agency involved in studies of animals and birds in relation to agriculture, was called upon to implement the act. Simply put, the Lacey Act upheld the states' right to regulate the use of wildlife within their borders, as established in *Geer* v. *Connecticut*.

Protection of migratory birds was bolstered in 1913 by the passage of the Migratory Bird Act. Its uncertain constitutionality led in 1918 to the Migratory Bird Treaty Act between the United States and Great Britain, acting for Canada. The treaty prohibited the sale of specified game birds, abolished spring and night shooting, and protected plume, song, and insectivorous bird species. Daily bag limits were imposed on all game birds, and closed seasons were announced for some species. Hunters were limited to shotguns of ten-gauge or smaller.

A 1920 Supreme Court decision upheld the treaty. A federal game warden named Ray Holland had arrested the attorney general of Missouri for violating the treaty, and the state sued to have it declared unconstitutional. In *Missouri* v. *Holland*, Justice Oliver Wendell Holmes declared that although the state had the power to regulate hunting, wild birds were not the possession of any one state. He further stated that the states could not be relied upon to protect a food supply. After this court decision, the states cooperated with the federal government and adopted laws and regulations similar to those contained in the treaty.

National forest reserves, first established by presidential proclamation in 1891, provided a certain amount of protection for wildlife habitat. By 1901, when Theodore ROOSEVELT assumed the presidency, reserved forestlands totaled 47 million acres. To this land base Roosevelt added another 148 million acres. The Bureau of Forestry (later the FOREST SERVICE) interpreted its responsibilities toward wildlife on the reserves in terms of predator control to protect livestock and game animals. In other respects, rangers simply cooperated with state game laws and state officials. In 1906, Chief Forester Gifford PINCHOT allowed rangers to serve as deputy state game wardens, but he resisted efforts to designate the national forests as game refuges. However, beginning in 1911, some states were allowed to establish refuges on national forest land, and by 1925, there were 130 such refuges.

Historically, the Forest Service has managed the land under its administration, but the wildlife has fallen under the jurisdiction of the state. It was not until 1936 that the Forest Service established its Division of Wildlife Management. Forest wildlife benefited nonetheless from such Forest Service practices as fire control, nonexploitative cutting practices, and tree planting. The agency also cooperated with the Bureau of Biological Survey by conducting annual game surveys on the forests. However, efficient and profitable timber production includes practices sometimes detrimental to wildlife. Forestry practices such as even-age management, short rotation, monotypic silviculture, and the use of pesticides such as DDT have been injurious to wildlife. In order to maintain a spectrum of animals and birds, wildlife conservationists recognized that areas with all stages of forest succession must be retained. The MULTIPLE USE-SUSTAINED YIELD ACT of 1960 specifically lists wildlife and fish among the resources of national forest land. The act requires maintenance of a reasonable representation of native animals on all major soil and vegetation types. The FOREST AND RANGELAND RENEWABLE RESOURCES PLANNING ACT of 1974 and the 1976 NATIONAL FOREST MANAGEMENT ACT have reiterated this policy.

Like the Forest Service, the BUREAU OF LAND MANAGEMENT (BLM) traditionally left wildlife management on lands under its jurisdiction to the states and concerned itself mainly with grazing and mining. The 1934 TAYLOR GRAZING ACT stated specifically, however,

Wildlife biologists install a wood duck "nest" in California to encourage hatching and rearing. Forest History Society Photo.

that the Grazing Service (now BLM) cooperate with state conservation and wildlife agencies. Consistent with the Taylor Act, the BLM was instructed by the Classification and Multiple Use Act of 1964 to manage its lands under principles of multiple use and sustained yield. In practice, grazing district managers had discretionary powers to determine suitable ranges and the number of wild game animals a given range could support in common with livestock. The 1969 NATIONAL ENVIRONMENTAL POLICY ACT narrowed these discretionary powers. Subsequently, the BLM operated under greater public scrutiny. The 1976 FEDERAL LAND POLICY AND MANAGEMENT ACT (the BLM Organic Act) opened the agency to even more public involvement by requiring public participation at all stages of planning and implementation of land management plans. The act further required that one half of the grazing fees be spent on "range betterment," including "fish and wildlife enhancement."

National forests, BLM lands, and other public lands also provided the base for a growing system of federal bird and game preserves. In 1892, President Harrison proclaimed Alaska's Afognak Forest and Fish Culture Reserve to protect and preserve "salmon and other fish and sea animals, and other animals and birds." Eleven years later, using the 1891 FOREST RESERVE ACT, President Theodore Roosevelt created by executive order the first federal bird preserve on Pelican Island off Florida, as a sanctuary for egrets, terns, and pelicans. In 1905, he established the Wichita Game Preserve from the Wichita National Forest to protect bison, elk, antelope, and deer, and in 1906 the Grand Canyon National Game Preserve on the Kaibab Plateau was created to protect mule deer. By the end of his term of office, Roosevelt had created fifty-one wildlife and bird refuges under the authority of the 1891 act and the 1906 Antiquities Act.

The various "game ranges," "wildlife ranges," "wildlife management areas," "waterfowl refuges," and "wildlife refuges" added to this system were initially placed under the management of the Biological Survey (later, the FISH AND WILDLIFE SERVICE) jointly with the BLM. The refuge system was consolidated under the Fish and Wildlife Service as the National Wildlife Refuge System in 1966 to be managed as "dominant use" lands.

In the early 1900s, conservationists turned their efforts to restocking areas depleted of certain wildlife species. Whitetail deer had been practically eliminated east of the Mississippi, but it made a comeback between 1900 and 1920 due to restocking and to farm abandonment in the Northeast, which left open clearings that favored deer. The introduction of the ring-necked pheasant in Oregon was especially successful. Brought from China in 1881, the pheasant adapted so well that an open season was declared only ten years later. State game agencies across the country bought birds to stock their area. For the most part, however, the introduction of a game bird has not been successful.

Nearly thirty years before turning its attention to wildlife restocking, Congress appropriated funds for fish propagation. The U. S. Fish Commission was established in 1871, the result of successful lobbying by the American Fisheries Society, founded a year earlier. Although initially concerned with shad and salmon stocks, the commission (which in 1903 became the Bu-

reau of Fisheries in the Department of Commerce) extended its interests to other species. In 1873, Congress provided the commission with funds for propagating fish, and stocking became the predominant management tool. In 1928, the Bureau of Fisheries operated thirty-eight fish cultural stations and thirty-five substations, and distributed 7 billion eggs, fry, and fingerlings. The states maintained 414 hatcheries. Private fish hatcheries were devoted primarily to raising trout for market, but they also sold eggs to federal or state agencies and fry and fingerlings to private clubs. Species were stocked throughout the United States; California's rainbow trout were transplanted to all other states; bass, pike, and perch were distributed through the United States; shad and striped bass, originally an East Coast species, were established on the Pacific Coast. Propagation was not always successful. In 1928, for example, the Bureau of Fisheries estimated that 90 percent of the 80 to 90 million salmon fry released in the Columbia River were lost in irrigation ditches. After 1930, conservationists began promoting habitat improvement as well.

Federal propagation of wildlife began with the Yellowstone bison herd. Although protected in the national park, herds continued to dwindle, and in 1902 Congress appropriated $15,000 to restore their numbers. A breeding program was initiated and continued until 1952. The Wichita Game Preserve, along with the National Bison Range in Montana (1908) and the Wind Cave National Game Preserve in South Dakota (1912), protected the bison while the breeding program was carried forward. Between 1905 and 1975, the bison increased from 970 animals to a stabilized population of around 25,000.

In contrast to the controlled bison breeding program, the deer population in the Kaibab Plateau preserve, protected in 1906, increased to such an extent that they were destroying their own habitat. In 1906, there were 4,000 deer; by 1924, there were 100,000; but by 1933 the starved population had plummeted to 15,000. In order to protect the habitat and reduce deaths by starvation, the Forest Service attempted to control the population by eliminating surplus deer. The state of Arizona, however, objected and sought to enforce its state game laws by preventing federal officials from killing and transporting Kaibab deer across state lines. In *Hunt* v. *United States* (1928), the Supreme Court determined that the federal government had the right to protect its property and preserve the habitat.

Despite such experiences with uncontrolled population increases, federal wildlife management continued to emphasize propagation and protection, a policy that included extensive programs for predator eradication.

A beaver dam in South Dakota. The beaver works tirelessly to construct and maintain a favorable habitat for itself and at the same time alters water regimes. In some areas, beavers cause serious flooding and are trapped out. American Forest Institute Photo.

Predator control was undertaken by both the Forest Service and the Bureau of Biological Survey. Congress first authorized funds for this purpose in 1915 and hired professional trappers and hunters to exterminate wolves, coyotes, mountain lions, and other predators harmful to livestock and game. Wolves were a special target. Some conservationists and sportsmen had criticized the idea of total elimination of certain species rather than control, but the need for a program of some kind was not questioned. By 1930, however, a few people were questioning the use of poisons and traps that affected wildlife in addition to the target species.

In 1930, Aldo LEOPOLD, generally acknowledged as the father of professional wildlife management and author of the classic *Game Management* (1933), chaired the American Game Policy Committee for the Seventeenth American Game Conference. The game policy he wrote for the conference differed from the previous approaches to game management, which had been characterized by artificial restocking and protection in reserves. Addressing both public and private landowners, Leopold advocated management of the total habitat, which he felt would result in natural propagation. Leopold also recognized the positive role of predators in a scientific wildlife management program. Decades later, a 1973 report by Durward L. Allen for the WILDLIFE SOCIETY noted the changes in public attitude toward predators and recommended management and relocation rather than poisoning and eradication. Disagreement over trapping and poisoning continues, especially in the western states where sheep and cattle ranchers still view the coyote as their primary enemy.

Predatory birds, on the other hand, have received some legal protection. The bald eagle was protected in 1940 and the golden eagle in 1962. The Snake River Birds of Prey Natural Area was created in 1971 under the administration of the Bureau of Land Management. Many states have adopted the National Audubon Society's Model Predatory Bird Protection Law, which places hawks and owls under full protection.

Despite earlier gains, game birds and their decline were the primary concern of wildlife conservationists during the 1920s and 1930s. The Migratory Bird Treaty Act of 1918 brought hunting under regulation, but nesting grounds were being reduced by agricultural development and wetlands reclamation. The long drought during the 1930s also affected the wetlands, causing grave concern. Disputes over the allowed federal bag limit continued through the decade. The Migratory Bird Conservation Act (Norbeck-Andresen Act), passed in 1929, provided funds for federal acquisition of migratory bird habitat and ensured that the preserves would be operated as inviolate sanctuaries.

In 1934, Congress enacted three important wildlife and fish measures. The Fish and Wildlife Coordination Act aimed to coordinate the development of a nationwide program of wildlife conservation and rehabilitation and mandated that all federal water control projects consult appropriate fishery and wildlife agencies. Provisions for enforcement of the act, however, proved inadequate. The Migratory Bird Hunting Stamp Act, the so-called Duck Stamp Act, authorized that receipts from hunting permits could be used to purchase and develop wetlands for the national refuge system. The Cooperative Wildlife Research Unit Program was inaugurated at ten land grant colleges. The program was supported by the state wildlife agency, the participating college, and the American Wildlife Institute, which was formed in 1935. Since 1934, twenty-two other units have been added, in addition to twenty-five fishery units.

However, the 1937 Federal Aid in Wildlife Restoration Act (Pittman-Robertson Act) has had the most far-reaching results for wildlife. This act specified that the 10 percent excise tax on sporting arms and ammunition be allotted to the states for approved projects in wildlife research and land acquisition, development, and maintenance. In order to qualify for the funds, each state had to earmark their hunting license fees specifically for wildlife protection. The states were also required to employ trained personnel for their programs, which promoted the professionalization of wildlife management. During the 1940s, the states used the Pittman-Robertson Act to develop and restock wildlife populations. Between 1938 and 1948, thirty-eight states acquired almost 900,000 acres of refuges and management areas. During the same period, the states restocked deer, pronghorn antelope, elk, mountain goats, mountain sheep, bears, wild turkeys, moose, and beaver. By 1974, 3.5 million acres of land and water had been acquired and $435

million had been spent to improve 7 million acres of state-owned fish and wildlife habitat. In 1950, the Federal Aid in Fish Restoration Act (Dingell-Johnson) was passed, giving sport fisheries protection and management similar to that which the Pittman-Robertson Act provided for wildlife.

During the 1930s, several citizen groups concerned with wildlife were formed: the NATIONAL WILDLIFE FEDERATION (1935), the Wildlife Society (1937), Ducks Unlimited (1937), the FEDERATION OF WESTERN OUTDOOR CLUBS (1932), the American Wildlife Institute (1935, later to become the Wildlife Management Institute in 1946), and the North American Wildlife Foundation (1935). In varying degrees these groups engaged in education programs, political lobbying, and fundraising to buy land for wildlife, sponsor research, and help fight local battles to save habitats.

By the end of World War II, habitat for 34 percent of the country's larger mammals had been placed in the care of the national forests, national parks, and national refuges, a jurisdiction that included some 184 million acres. During the 1950s, this habitat was jeopardized when Secretary of the Interior Douglas McKay proposed opening refuges to gas and mineral exploration and expressed his willingness to accede to requests by the military to build on or use refuge and park system lands. McKay resigned in 1956 and was replaced by Frederick A. Seaton, a more conservation-minded secretary. At the same time, America was experiencing the postwar population boom that led to the rise of suburbia, the industrialization of agriculture, and the increased use of chemical pesticides. The cumulative chemical impact on the environment and wildlife was publicized by Rachel CARSON in *Silent Spring* (1962), which became the touchstone of the modern ENVIRONMENTAL MOVEMENT.

Increased public awareness and concern for the environment resulted in passage of legislation that affected wildlife. In 1964, the Wilderness Act created a national wilderness preservation system, which included vast areas of fish and wildlife habitat. The Land and Water Conservation Fund was also created in 1964, providing a revenue-sharing program for state and federal agencies to preserve and develop outdoor recreation resources. It was amended in 1976 explicitly to allow the Fish and Wildlife Service to acquire undeveloped refuge lands.

In 1966, the first Endangered Species Preservation Act was enacted, which obliged the government to protect native wild species threatened with extinction. The definition of eligible species was extended to all vertebrates, mollusks, and crustaceans by the

1969 Endangered Species Conservation Act which was itself superseded by the Endangered Species Act of 1973. The latter act, which included all animal and plant life, established the distinction between threatened and endangered species and introduced the concept of critical habitat. The act went far beyond the nineteenth-century definition of wildlife, which recognized only those species used for survival or commercial purposes. Animals and plants, according to the 1973 act, were of "aesthetic, ecological, educational, historical, recreational, and scientific value to the Nation and its people." By 1982, the Department of the Interior listed 288 endangered domestic species. An important aspect of the 1973 law was the section 7 provision that the secretary of the interior must insure that federal activities do not jeopardize an endangered or threatened species or damage or modify a critical habitat. The act acknowledged the need to protect the ecosystem upon which endangered and threatened species depend and directed management activities toward this end. Section 7 has prompted several court cases, the best known being *Hill* v. *TVA* in 1976 regarding the Tellico Dam and the snail darter, an endangered fish.

Although it does not specifically mention the word "wildlife," the National Environmental Policy Act of 1969 (NEPA) may be among the most important federal laws for the protection of wildlife. The broad environmental policies of NEPA recognized the "responsibilities of each generation as trustee of the environment for succeeding generations," and "the profound impact of man's activity on the interrelations of all components of the national environment."

In 1976, the states managed 5,236 wildlife habitat areas totaling 11.3 million acres. Other state-owned areas, such as forests and parks that support wildlife, covered 28 million acres. The federal systems in 1981 included over 80 million acres of wilderness and natural areas, 83.7 million acres of national wildlife refuges, 44.5 million acres of national parks, and 7.8 million acres of national recreation areas and national monuments. These federally owned lands—about half of which are located in Alaska—provide habitat for America's wildlife. In addition, the Forest Service administers 191 million acres and the Bureau of Land Management around 470 million acres, upon which wildlife has been an increasingly important management consideration.

The 1842 Supreme Court enunciation of the principle that wildlife belongs to all the people and is a public trust has been basic in the development of the state and federal laws and regulations. Public perception of the meaning of wildlife has changed from one of economic commodity to one of recreational and symbolic value. Federal and state governments have accordingly shifted their perspective from particular species and problems to comprehensive programs based on the concept of maintaining the ecosystems necessary for all forms of wildlife.

FURTHER READING: Howard P. Brokaw, ed., *Wildlife and America* (1978). Theodore W. Cart, "'New Deal' for Wildlife: A Perspective on Federal Conservation Policy, 1933–40," *Pacific Northwest Quarterly* 63 (July 1972): 113–120. Environmental Law Institute, *The Evolution of National Wildlife Law* (1977). Susan L. Flader, *Thinking Like a Mountain: Aldo Leopold and the Evolution of an Ecological Attitude toward Deer, Wolves, and Forests* (1974). John F. Reiger, *American Sportsmen and the Origins of Conservation* (1975). Donald C. Swain, *Federal Conservation Policy, 1921–1933* (1963). James A. Tober, *Who Owns the Wildlife? The Political Economy of Conservation in Nineteenth-Century America* (1981). James B. Trefethen, *An American Crusade for Wildlife* (1975).

MARY ELIZABETH JOHNSON

WILDLIFE MANAGEMENT INSTITUTE

The Wildlife Management Institute (WMI) is a private, nonprofit foundation that promotes "better use of natural resources for the welfare of the nation." Its forerunner was formed in New York City in 1911 as the American Game Protective and Propagation Association by a group of wealthy sportsmen and interested conservationists. A major interest was the widespread importation of exotic game birds. In 1915, it began to sponsor the annual American Game Conference, which was eventually renamed the American Game Association. For a time, it was named American Wildlife Institute, and in 1946 it was reorganized as the Wildlife Management Institute.

Supported by individual donors, conservation groups of various stripe, and business organizations, WMI generally espoused traditional conservationist policies, that is, with an eye to future use. However, it placed particular emphasis on wildlife as a resource and monitored the effects of timber operations on wildlife habitat. Where these effects were found destructive, the institute supported the establishment of protected wilderness areas. WMI supports research and publishes *Outdoor News Bulletin*. By its sponsorship of the annual North American Wildlife and Natural Resources Conference, WMI serves as a coordinating group for various conservationist, naturalist, and environmentalist associations. It is headquartered in Washington, D. C.

WILDLIFE SOCIETY

Founded in Washington, D.C., at the first North American Wildlife Conference, February 3-7, 1936, the Wildlife Society fulfilled a need for professional organization in the growing field of wildlife management. The society, under the chairmanship of Ralph T. King of the Minnesota Agricultural Experiment Station, was initially known as the Society of Wildlife Specialists. The Second North American Wildlife Conference in 1937 established the society's current name, defined its purposes and organizational structure, and provided for publication of the *Journal of Wildlife Management*, under the editorship of W. L. McAtee. Within six months, the society had drawn more than 500 members, mostly wildlife educators, technicians, and administrators.

The Wildlife Society serves as an organizational clearinghouse, a means for disseminating professional and scientific information, and a source for statistics on wildlife-related matters. The society promotes "the wise management and conservation of the wildlife resources of the world" by issuing publications and position papers on conservation issues and testifying before congressional committees. It pursues its goals in a growing variety of ways, such as cooperating with international, national, and local wildlife organizations, collecting and disseminating information on educational programs and wildlife curricula, publishing scientific papers, issuing employment statistics, upholding professional standards, and granting awards. The Wildlife Society certifies, but does not accredit, biologists specializing in wildlife resources.

Increased activity since 1960 led the society to hold semiannual rather than annual meetings, and in 1962 it established chapter units to encourage local participation. During the conservation controversies of the 1960s and 1970s, the society generally took a moderate position, advocating a "non-manipulative policy for plant and animal resources . . . when practicable" and the application of professional land and water management standards where human interference was necessary. In a May 1979 position paper on forest management, the society called for strict enforcement of wildlife protection laws on government-owned forestlands and "encouraged" private owners to manage their properties "with full consideration to wildlife as a product of these lands." But the society did not advocate expanded government authority in the private sector. Rather, it encouraged forest owners to hire qualified wildlife biologists to work with foresters in order to guarantee diversity of tree species and a range of age classes, stand densities, and other conditions required by forest animal life.

Membership in the society grew from 539 in 1937 to 6,918 in 1968 and 7,500 in 1980. The society publishes three periodicals: *Journal of Wildlife Management*, the *Wildlife Society Bulletin*, and *Wildlife Monographs*.

FURTHER READING: P. F. English, "The Wildlife Society," *Journal of Forestry* 44 (May 1946): 345-346. Daniel L. Leedy, "The Wildlife Society," *Journal of Forestry* 54 (Dec. 1956): 821-823.

WISCONSIN FORESTS

The Wisconsin forest was part of a vast boreal woodland that stretched from New York and New England to northern Michigan, Wisconsin, and Minnesota. Forests once covered 85 percent of Wisconsin's 35 million acres. In the northern part of the state, white and red pines predominated, interspersed with jack pine, spruce, balsam fir, and hardwood. Stands of white pine grew intermixed with deciduous forests on sandy loams and more fertile sands, while jack pine grew on the least fertile sands and well-drained acid soils. Sugar maple could be found on rich soil built up by previous generations of pioneer tree species. In southern Wisconsin, the dominant species were hardwood—primarily oak, elm, sugar maple, basswood, and, in the east, beech. Southwestern portions of the state contained prairies and oak openings characterized by widely scattered, broad-crowned burr oaks growing above a luxuriant blanket of prairie plants and grasses. The northern margin of this deciduous forest stretched across Wisconsin, trending northwest from Sheboygan County on Lake Michigan to Polk County on the Minnesota border. The predominantly coniferous and deciduous forest regions were separated by a mixed belt sometimes called the Lake Forest.

Throughout geologic time, southern Wisconsin has been alternately forest and prairie. As each of the major ice sheets approached, the coniferous forest (especially the spruce-fir type) increased, only to be replaced during interglacial periods by hardwood forests or prairie. When the forests again encroached upon the prairie, black oaks, best fitted to start on dry open lands, were first to emerge. Maturing black oaks created shade in which white and red oak seedlings grew. Finally, sugar maple and basswood replaced the oaks. Fires also destroyed forests, favoring the expansion of prairie lands. Tough-barked burr oaks survived the fires to become the ancient sentinels of the prairies and oak openings.

Wisconsin's Indians used birch and cedar bark for shelter, for woven mats, and for canoes. Dyes were made from woodland plants, and sugar and syrup from

Pulpwood is being loaded at Green Bay, Wisconsin. American Forest Institute Photo.

maple sap. Fur trading, introduced by French voyageurs, dominated the Indian way of life by 1700. The first lumber mill in the state was erected on the Devil River in 1809, but for several decades lumbering was hampered by disputes over Indian lands, limited markets, and the high cost of transporting supplies. By the 1830s, small mills were established on the Red Cedar River, the Chippewa, and the Menominee. In 1851, the St. Croix Boom Company was chartered, giving the company the right to erect a boom at Osceola. Wisconsin was providing lumber to Chicago and to ports on the lower Mississippi River by 1854, and after the Civil War the state's lumber output increased rapidly.

By 1869, more than 1 billion feet of lumber were produced annually, ranking Wisconsin fourth among the lumber-producing states. Mills on the eastern shore of Lake Michigan, particularly in the Green Bay region, shipped lumber on steam barges to Chicago. Rafts of lumber were also floated through the Great Lakes to eastern markets and mills. Lumber manufactured in southern and western Wisconsin was collected in huge rafts, floated to points along the Mississippi, and distributed from these ports to western prairie towns. Whole logs were similarly made into rafts and exported downriver. After the mid-1860s, the Mississippi rafts were propelled by steamboats. In 1892, Wisconsin mills sawed a record 4.1 billion board feet of lumber, and between 1900 and 1904 the state led the nation in lumber production. During this period, white pine supplied 60 to 70 percent of Wisconsin's lumber manufacture, hemlock 11 to 26 percent, and hardwoods most of the remainder. In the twentieth century, however, lumber output decreased steadily and by 1920 Wisconsin, manufacturing 1.1 billion board feet, ranked tenth among the states in lumber production. Annual output reached a low of 180 million board feet in 1932 and has increased at a moderate rate since then.

Harvesting patterns also changed at the end of the nineteenth century. With stocks of good pine largely depleted, production of hemlock and cedar, along with hardwoods such as basswood, elm, and ash, increased. Northern hardwoods were cut as early as the 1870s, but the big harvest occurred between 1910 and 1930. In 1925, Wisconsin produced an estimated 626 million board feet of hardwood and only 467 million board feet of softwood. Hardwoods dominated the state's lumber trade after that.

Pulpwood production in Wisconsin began in 1871 when a paper mill at Appleton began supplying itself with groundwood pulp from aspen unwanted by nearby lumber mills. Thereafter, the PULP AND PAPER INDUSTRY in Wisconsin expanded as the use of wood pulp spread, with mills locating wherever they could find sites with waterpower near a wood supply. Spruce supplied the bulk of the pulp for a time. By the early twentieth century, pulpwood production was becoming the state's leading forest industry. From 1899 to 1929, while lumber production plummeted, pulpwood consumption gained by 560 percent. New pulping processes increased the variety of usable woods. After the sulfite process was introduced in 1887, hemlock became important, and in 1911 Wisconsin mills began producing sulfate pulp from pine. After 1948, semichemical pulp was made from mixed hardwoods. By 1956, hardwoods, mainly aspen, supplied 72 percent of the pulpwood harvest. Sawmill residues became important pulp sources after 1960.

Initially, all the pulp made by Wisconsin mills had come from wood harvested within the state, but pulpwood imports gradually grew to 69 percent of the total in 1950; thereafter, the proportion of domestic pulpwood increased to reach 70 percent of the total of 2.6 million cords consumed in 1977. As a pulpwood consumer Wisconsin ranked second among the states during the 1920s and 1930s but, despite a continually increasing total consumption, the state had fallen to thirteenth place in 1977. In the production of paper, however, Wisconsin has been the leading state for most of the twentieth century, generally supplying 10 to 11 percent of the national total.

Fire may have destroyed more good pine than ever reached the mills in Wisconsin. During the heyday of the lumbering industry, as many as twenty forest fires could be found burning simultaneously in a single county. The Peshtigo fire of 1871 was the worst single fire in Wisconsin history, taking as many as 1,500 lives and consuming 1.3 million acres of forestland. By 1923, fires, along with unrestrained cutting, left less than 2 million acres of merchantable timber standing in Wisconsin.

Conservation had not been popular in the frontier lumbering region, but as early as 1867 Wisconsin established a Special Commission on Forestry, which recommended regulating timber cutting in the interests of fire and flood control and soil conservation. Forest fire prevention services began in 1895 when the legislature authorized a system of town fire wardens, financed and largely controlled at the local level. In the next three decades, the legislature provided limited state supervision and finally, in 1927, gave major responsibility for forest protection to the state.

In 1904, E. M. Griffith became Wisconsin's first state forester. While concentrating on building a state forest reserve, controlling forest fires, and protecting watersheds, Griffith promoted reforestation as a goal for the future. Initial forestry efforts were directed at fire suppression, but in later years concern shifted to fire prevention and early detection, and by the 1950s destruction by forest fires had been reduced to 3,400 acres a year.

In 1927, nearly 25 percent of the land in Wisconsin's seventeen northern counties was tax delinquent. Although the state offered these largely CUTOVER LANDS for sale, there were few buyers. To remedy the situation, the legislature in that year passed the Forest Crop Law, which provided an option for TAXATION of immature growing forests as a crop. The law also authorized counties to adopt zoning ordinances that would regulate areas within which agriculture, forestry, and recreation could be conducted. Counties were also permitted to acquire land for tax deeds and to exchange these lands for other parcels. As tax delinquency increased during the Depression years, Wisconsin counties under the Forest Crop Law developed a system of public forests, county-owned and managed with financial aid and technical assistance from the state. Wisconsin counties thus set a nationwide precedent for land use zoning, and by 1960 the state had established twenty-seven forests, totaling over 2 million acres. In addition, the state managed nine forests covering 366,409 acres and thirty parks and recreation areas with 22,391 acres. By 1977, over 2.9 million acres of commercial timberland were in state, county, or municipal ownership, accounting for almost 20 percent of the total forest area of the state.

Reforestation was first proposed by Increase Lapham in 1854 and was promoted by State Forester Griffith between 1904 and 1915; during the latter's term, the state established a forest nursery at Trout Lake in Vilas County. By the end of the Depression, the obvious unsuitability of the northern lands for farming and the resulting tax forfeitures had ended the farm-it-all dream, and reforestation was accepted by state and county governments as a program for millions of acres of cutovers. By 1973, the state's four nurseries had grown more than 900 million seedlings to support this program and continued to distribute about 18 million trees a year.

In 1967, the State Conservation Department merged with the Department of Resource Development to form the Department of Natural Resources.

This reorganization brought together traditional conservation and newer environmental protection responsibilities at the state level. In order to insure continued protection of natural resources, the state created the office of Public Intervenor, a watchdog agency authorized to sue other agencies within the department and to initiate any legal proceedings needed to protect public rights regarding natural resources.

In 1956, the University of Wisconsin established a department of forestry and wildlife management in Madison; forestry, offering graduate work only, became an independent department in 1962. Later, the university started a second forestry program on its Stevens Point campus.

In 1977, there were almost 15 million acres of forestland in Wisconsin, comprising 43 percent of the total land area. Private forest ownership amounted to 9.8 million acres. Nearly 1.8 million acres were managed by the federal government. Wisconsin's national forests are the result of a 1925 state act which authorized the federal government to acquire tax delinquent lands in the state under the WEEKS ACT. The Nicolet and Chequamegon national forests were established in 1933 and then comprised 328,000 federal acres. By 1980, they totaled almost 1.5 million acres of federally owned land.

The Menominee Indian Reservation, established by the 1854 Treaty of Wolf Rivers, contained another 276,480 acres, of which 175,000, including the largest block of northern hardwood sawtimber in the state, was commercial forest. In 1956 reservation timberlands formerly held in trust by the Bureau of Indian Affairs were transferred to Menominee Enterprises, a corporation owned by tribal members. The Menominee mill, sawing over 20 million board feet annually, was the largest in the state.

FURTHER READING: Vernon Carstensen, *Farms or Forests: Evolution of a State Land Policy for Northern Wisconsin, 1850–1932* (1958). John C. Curtis, *The Vegetation of Wisconsin: An Ordination of Plant Communities* (1959). Robert W. Finley, *Geography of Wisconsin: A Content Outline* (1970). Robert F. Fries, *Empire in Pine: The Story of Lumbering in Wisconsin, 1830–1900* (1951). Raymond R. Hernandez, ed., *Some Events in Wisconsin's Forest History*, Forest History Association of Wisconsin, Proceedings of the Fourth Annual Meeting (Sept. 28-29, 1979). James A. Larson, *Wisconsin's Renewable Resources: A Report on Research at the University of Wisconsin into the Renewable Resources of Field, Forest, Lake, and Stream* (1957). Erling D. Solberg, *New Laws for New Forests: Wisconsin's Forest-Fire, Tax, Zoning and County-Forest Laws in Operation* (1961).

GEORGE W. SIEBER

WOMEN'S CLUBS AND FORESTRY

Although it dated back several decades, the American women's club movement mushroomed in the early 1900s, a reflection of Progressive movement activism and the final stages of the female suffrage campaign. Looking beyond the tea-and-cookies character of its origins, the movement turned to public issues and was quickly attracted to conservation. In part because leading conservationists were more active than their adversaries in searching out supporters, the General Federation of Women's Clubs (founded in 1890) favored the cause of forestry from the beginning. In 1896, it adopted resolutions pledging to study forestry needs and conditions and to promote forestry interests, and it established a committee on forestry.

The General Federation lobbied for passage of bills protecting watersheds and forest fire prevention measures on both state and national levels. In the early 1900s, it demanded that Congress establish national forests in the East. The General Federation joined with the District of Columbia Federation of Women's Clubs, the National Society of the Daughters of the American Revolution, and the Woman's National Rivers and Harbors Congress in 1908 to support the conservation policies of President Theodore ROOSEVELT. Although it emphasized the utilitarian in preference to the aesthetic, the General Federation lobbied against the proposed dam at Hetch Hetchy Valley in YOSEMITE NATIONAL PARK, and it encouraged such projects as the establishment of ROCKY MOUNTAIN NATIONAL PARK in 1915. During the 1910s and early 1920s, women's state federations promoted reforestation, fire control, and the establishment of community forests in Connecticut, New York, Massachusetts, Louisiana, and Florida; demanded legislation setting up state forestry commissions in Alabama, Kentucky, Louisiana, Texas, and Florida; supported the efforts of the SAVE-THE-REDWOODS LEAGUE to acquire groves in California; planted trees in Nebraska and North Dakota; and favored reforestation projects in Minnesota and Mississippi. However, just as the World War caused a suspension of the conservation movement in the nation generally, it also distracted the women's clubs, which devoted their energies to scrap drives, bandage rolling, loyalty campaigns, and programs to promote soldier morale. After the war, the culmination of the long fight for woman suffrage preoccupied most groups although it was often divisive.

By the mid-1920s, the General Federation was searching for an issue on which all could agree and draw together. Although the energies of the movement ran in a dozen directions, it was the cause of forest conservation to which the clubs turned. Beginning about 1930, forestry was the movement's most important single project in terms of both the militance of the commitment and the extent of support for the program. Since it was not a divisive issue, it enabled the clubs to show tangible, progressive accomplishments. In addition to those groups associated with the General Federation, the Woman's National Farm and Garden Association (founded in 1914, with a mostly rural membership) began to offer scholarships to female students in forestry as well as agriculture and horticulture.

The women's club forestry campaign centered on the Washington Bicentennial observance of 1932. In order to commemorate it, the General Federation launched a series of tree-planting campaigns, the first of which was in the Nicolet National Forest in Wisconsin. In these projects the federation collaborated with the NATIONAL PARK SERVICE, the U.S. FOREST SERVICE, many state park systems, and private conservation groups such as the AMERICAN TREE ASSOCIATION (whose founder, Charles Lathrop PACK, had been instrumental in enlisting the clubs' support for the endeavor). Women's clubs were responsible for the planting of 2.5 million trees during the year. In addition, the California Federation of Women's Clubs purchased 1,500 acres of first-growth redwood forest, which it donated to the state park system, and the Florida federation established and administered the 4,000-acre Royal Palm State Park from 1915 until 1947, when it became a part of Everglades National Park.

Although at a lesser pace, the clubs continued to sponsor tree-planting programs until the 1950s. In 1941, the General Federation also adopted a comprehensive forestry policy that called for an expanded federal and state government interest in practices designed "to strengthen our national defense and to better social and economic conditions generally." For its part, the federation resolved to purchase and maintain a "federation forest" in every state and a "community forest" in every town and city having a women's club; to beautify roadsides with "trails of indigenous plantings"; to campaign against illegal cutting of Christmas trees; and to carry on a forestry study program for members.

Even though these ambitious objectives were not fully realized, the federation and many local clubs played prominent roles in the Wartime Forest Fire Prevention Campaign—second, perhaps, only to the Forest Service. In one patriotic radio transcript, which the clubs distributed throughout the country,

Mrs. John L. Whitehurst inadvertently struck a discouraging note when she concluded, "Today, wood flies and floats and shoots. Let's plan and work now, so that a hundred years hence there will be plenty of wood, if necessary, to fly and float and shoot to keep America free."

The women's clubs' interest in forestry and conservation was always receptive to aesthetic arguments. In 1948, for example, the General Federation was one of the strongest sources of opposition to threatened commercial exploitation in OLYMPIC NATIONAL PARK. The clubs were just as frequently concerned with the economic use of the forests, however. As a result, the unifying theme proved divisive in the environmental controversies of the late 1960s and 1970s. Some local organizations (which were always autonomous) supported extreme environmentalist positions, while others turned to other subjects. As of 1980, the General Federation and some state groups still sponsored regular symposia and other educational programs having to do with forestry, and they maintained conservation departments.

WOOD DENSIFICATION

Although the process of wood densification derives from nineteenth-century experiments and even older accidental discoveries, the modern process was developed in England and, to a lesser extent, the United States during the 1930s. The impetus for its perfection came from military needs.

By compression under heat, with or without impregnation with resins, the voids in the wood's cellular structure are closed and sealed, the result being increased hardness, durability, and dimensional stability.

Under a variety of brand names (Compreg, Pregwood, Pluswood, Jicwood or, when paper was used, Formica, Panelite), densified wood proved useful where usage was rough or where moisture and frequent cleaning were a problem for soft, porous surfaces. In addition to military construction, densified wood was adapted to paneling and wainscoting, table tops and legs, in making shuttles and other moving wood parts, golf heads, flooring, toys, and other specialties.

Until the 1950s, densified wood was comparatively expensive. Then, with improvements in the methods of manufacture and the growing scarcity of hardwoods, it became an inexpensive alternative to veneers and natural lumber. By the 1970s, densified wood products were more common in some construction than untreated wood. Perhaps ironically, consid-

Golf head stock produced by laminating many pieces of densified wood. American Forest Institute Photo.

ering its earlier status, densified wood is often associated with cheapness and vulgarity, like plastics.

FURTHER READING: Erle Kauffman, "House of Wood Magic (part three)," *American Forests* 52 (Mar. 1946): 125–126, 142. A. J. Panshin et al., *Forest Products* (2nd ed., 1962).

WOOD PRESERVATION

Although wood preservation was practiced by ancient Greeks and Romans, it was not of much importance in the United States until late in the nineteenth century. Abundant American supplies of wood, particularly of such durable types as chestnut, white oak, redcedar, and baldcypress, delayed concern for preservative treatments, and such work as was done in this field borrowed heavily from European experience. The first wood-treating plant in the United States was built in Lowell, Massachusetts, in 1848 to soak timbers for locks, canals, and bridges for the Merrimack River. Various water-soluble salts were used, such as zinc chloride, mercuric chloride, and copper sulfate. The first pressure-treatment plant was at West Pascagoula, Mississippi, in 1875 to treat timbers and piling for bridges of the New Orleans and Mobile Railroad with creosote.

Although it had long been recognized that shipworms destroyed wood in salt water, the causes of much wood decay were unknown until Robert Hartig in Germany in the early 1870s recognized the effects of fungi. This realization put the wood preservation industry on a firmer foundation.

Octave Chanute, chairman of an American Society of Civil Engineers committee on the preservation of timber, presented a report, five years in preparation, in June 1885. Chanute's recommendations on preservatives, preparation of wood for treatment, and methods of application guided a fledgling industry. The committee proposed treatment by mercuric chloride ("kyanizing") in dry climates where the preservative would not be leached out of the wood; the costlier creosote was found more appropriate for piling in marine waters; the use of zinc chloride (the "Burnett" process), because of its relative cheapness, was recommended for railroad crossties. Although timber still seemed plentiful and cheap, the decay of untreated crossties in particular was a huge drain on forests. The increased life of treated crossties more than made up for cost of treatment. Between 1890 and 1940, 2.39 billion crossties were saved by preservation, the equivalent of 543,000 acres of timber.

The other leading pioneer of the American wood preservation industry was Hermann von Schrenk, who worked first for the U. S. DEPARTMENT OF AGRICULTURE and then as a consultant to several major railroads. During the Louisiana Purchase Exposi-

Poles at right have been treated with creosote to fend off rot and insects and thus markedly increase their life expectancy. The poles on the left are being readied for treatment. American Forest Institute Photo.

tion in St. Louis in 1904, while an employee of the government, von Schrenk supervised experimental treatments with creosote, which despite its expense attracted much attention. Von Schrenk's exhibit prompted railroaders and timber producers to organize the American Wood Preservers Association (AWPA) in 1904. Incorporated early in the following year, AWPA became the body responsible for industry standards and provided a vehicle for dissemination of research results.

From the beginning of the twentieth century until about 1930, railroad use of treated wood continued to dominate the wood-preserving industry. About 75 million crossties were treated in 1927; the number declined to about 30 million annually by the late 1970s. Most ties were treated with zinc chloride until the 1920s when creosote and mixtures of creosote with coal tar or petroleum were applied more and more (see RAILROADS AND FORESTS). Before 1922, poles constituted a small part of wood treated in the United States, but expansion in use of electricity and telephones changed this. Fifty years later, about 2.7 million poles were treated

per year, mostly by pressure processes. The adoption of pressure treatment led to the replacement of cedars by southern pine as the predominant pole wood, especially in shorter lengths (see POLES AND PILING). Other major items treated were piling, lumber and construction timbers, cross arms, and fence posts. At one time, wooden street-paving blocks were a major item, and some blocks continued to be treated for factory flooring (see PLANK ROADS AND WOOD BLOCK PAVEMENTS; FENCING).

After zinc chloride was largely replaced by creosote and its mixtures for crosstie treatment, the latter was the most widely used preservative by far. But by 1980, although creosote was still employed for 47 percent of all treated wood, others were challenging it for leadership. Pentachlorophenol, the first solvent-soluble synthetic chemical to find use in large quantities for wood preservation, gained a foothold after World War II when creosote was scarce. Depending on the solvent, penta could replace creosote for poles (where it became the most widely used preservative) and timbers, or it could protect clean, paintable wood products.

Extensive experiments abroad and in the United States with chemical mixtures introduced into wood in water solutions led to the preservatives containing arsenates, copper, and chromates, or binary mixtures of chromium and copper or copper and arsenic, all widely used for lumber and plywood. Until the "arsenicals" appeared, treated wood had not been readily available to the small consumer, although starting about 1935 lumber treated with chromated zinc chloride was sold through local yards in California. Another impetus to wider distribution was the invention of pole barns and buildings. Such buildings are supported on treated poles embedded in the soil, much like utility poles, instead of on a concrete foundation. Originally, round poles were used; later, square or rectangular timbers were adopted as well, particularly in the Midwest. Since these buildings were popular on farms, retail lumber yards stocked timbers and the treated planking used around the lower parts of the structure.

Early patents were concerned with the method of application of preservatives to wood. The full-cell or Bethell process using an initial vacuum followed by pressure began with zinc chloride and creosote and later was employed with water-borne preservatives and creosote. Because of the relatively high cost of creosote, ways were found to obtain adequate penetration with less preservative being left in the wood. The Rueping and Lowry empty cell processes used higher than atmospheric and atmospheric pressure respectively to achieve penetration with less retention. The thermal process is used primarily to treat western redcedar poles and, to a lesser extent, poles of other species such as lodgepole pine. Most wood millwork is treated by a short immersion in preservative, a treatment first used in the 1930s.

Research in wood preservation was given a push with the establishment of the U. S. Forest Products Laboratory (FPL) in Madison, Wisconsin, in 1910. Scientists such as Clyde H. Teesdale, G. M. Hunt, J. D. MacLean, E. Bateman, C. A. Richards, C. G. Duncan, T. C. Scheffer, R. D. Baechler, and J. O. Blew, Jr., furthered knowledge in toxicity of preservatives, effect on wood, testing of treated wood, heat transfer, and penetration. Other agencies also contributed through the efforts of Arthur Verrall, Henry Schmitz, R. H. Colley, M. S. Hudson, and many others.

Wood preservation by the 1970s was a mature industry concentrated in the Southeast and the South and on the West Coast with little change from year to year in total wood treated. New preservatives and processes continued to be developed, however, and markets continued to change. Government maintained a large role in the regulation of the industry, primarily through the cooperation of FPL with AWPA in the development and adoption of standards, and later through the activities of the Environmental Protection Agency and the Occupational Safety and Health Administration. The importance of the wood preservation industry to forest conservation lies in its reduction of the annual timber harvest needed to replace wood that would otherwise be destroyed by insects, marine borers, decay, or fire.

FURTHER READING: J. Bethell, Samuel Boulton, and Octave Chanute, *Pioneer Work in Modern Wood Preservation* (1929). James E. Cronin, *Hermann von Schrenk: A Biography* (1959). Robert D. Graham, "History of Wood Preservation," in *Wood Deterioration and Its Prevention by Preservative Treatments*, ed. by Darrel D. Nicholas (1973). George M. Hunt and George A. Garratt, *Wood Preservation* (3rd ed., 1967). H. Broese VanGroenou, H. W. L. Rischen, and J. Van DenBerg, *Wood Preservation during the Last 50 Years* (1951). Howard F. Weiss, *The Preservation of Structural Timber* (1916).

ELDON A. BEHR

WOOD PRODUCTS EXPORTS

Wood products have been exported from North America since the beginning of European settlement on the continent. Vikings dispatched timber from Vinland to their settlements in Greenland during the eleventh and twelfth centuries, while Englishmen began shipping wood from Jamestown to their mother country almost immediately after arrival. By 1609, shipments of masts and spars, "divers sorts of wood for wainscot and other uses, soapashes, some pitch and tar," and other products of the North American forest were arriving in England. Settlers in the Massachusetts Bay and Plymouth colonies followed suit, sending clapboards and deals soon after their arrival. By 1705, the British government was encouraging such shipments, for masts and NAVAL STORES were vital to the Royal Navy.

Overseas shipments made good sense. The American colonies desperately needed exports if they were to survive; their rich stores of timber provided a ready source of raw material that could be tapped even with limited labor and capital; and they provided materials that were becoming more and more scarce and costly in Britain. Demand was always ample. As residents of a resource-abundant society, Americans would be major exporters of forest products from that time on.

At first, settlers focused their attention on erecting shelters, clearing land, and doing other tasks directly related to survival. Shipments of wood products were

At Coos Bay, Oregon, a ship flying the German flag loads plywood destined for Sydney, Australia. Georgia-Pacific Photo.

encouraged by the empty cargo space of eastbound vessels and the need for earnings to help underwrite the costs of colony building, but they were a decidedly secondary matter.

In time, such shipments became more important. As the colonial societies grew, the production of forest products rose too; and as colonial economies developed, becoming increasingly intertwined in the complex web of the North Atlantic commercial world, the demand for exports assumed a larger place. Fortunately, the initial demands of colony building were by this time over, and there was a growing surplus of goods to ship abroad. As a result, in the mid-eighteenth century, exports of woodstuffs rose rapidly in both size and importance.

The extent of exportation during the colonial period is difficult to establish with precision. Early records are incomplete and often vague. Much of the trade was intentionally hidden: it was tied to the outlawed commerce with the French West Indies, and much of the lumber was sawn illegally from large white pines re-

served under the Crown's Broad Arrow policy to provide masts for the Royal Navy. In New Hampshire in particular, friction between royal authorities seeking to save the pines for the navy and colonists wanting to fell them for lumber to sell in the West Indies was intense. The dispute contributed to the growing sentiment for independence in the years before 1776.

Despite the inadequacies of the data, it is evident that exports grew rapidly during the late colonial period. In 1731, Virginia and Maryland shipped a reported total of $15,000 worth of timber abroad; by 1770, records show their shipments as being worth $686,588. In 1765, Philadelphia sent 783,000 feet of boards and scantling overseas; by 1773, shipments had increased to over 4 million feet. Increases were also occurring elsewhere in the colonies. They continued at an even high rate after independence.

Pine masts, lumber, and naval stores were the most frequently mentioned exports of forest products, but there were other items of importance, too. Early in the nineteenth century, large quantities of hickory hoops, used in making casts and barrels, went to the West Indies. Huge numbers of oak staves also went to the West Indies, as well as to Britain, Madeira, and the Canary Islands. Responding to the increased domestic and foreign demand, prices rose steadily. In 1720, staves sold in Philadelphia for $3 per thousand, in 1798 for $18, in 1807 for $55, and in 1808 for $100. Most of the white oak staves shipped to England from Quebec came in fact from around Lake Champlain in the United States. The sale abroad of wood-built American merchant vessels also constituted an exportation of forest products. Sales of ships were frequent during the eighteenth and nineteenth centuries and were a significant source of income, especially for the Northeast.

The Embargo Act of 1808 and the War of 1812 each interrupted the steady growth of exports of forest products from the United States. Lumber shipments plummeted from 79.4 million board feet in 1807 to 25.8 million in 1808. The timber and mast trades declined even more precipitously. By 1811, lumber exports had recovered to a new high of 85.3 million board feet, but the War of 1812 soon eroded the gains; by 1814, the last year of the war, lumber shipments from the United States totaled only 11.1 million board feet. Again, shipments of timbers and masts suffered even more than shipments of lumber, no doubt because the main overseas markets for the former were in Great Britain.

Exports were desperately needed by the newly independent United States, with its overseas debts and shortage of foreign exchange, but large shipments of live oak became a source of concern. This shipbuilding wood of unparalleled quality was vital in maintaining a navy adequate for national defense. Appalled by the rate at which it was being cut, François André MI-CHAUX warned shortly after 1800 that the live oak's "disappearance throughout the United States within fifty years . . . is nearly certain." Congress agreed; its earliest acts dealing with the forest were all aimed at protecting this species. Exportation of live oak continued, however, and in time the United States did find its naval construction programs hampered by a scarcity of live oak.

Data on the exportation of forest products after 1817 are more complete. The picture revealed is one of a relatively steady increase in both volume and value, but with forest products making up a fairly constant percentage of all exports. From 1817 to 1905, forest products normally constituted about 3 to 4 percent of all exports from the United States. The high points were 6 percent in 1820 and 13 percent in 1865 (the latter figure reflecting, in large part, the general distortion of foreign trade caused by the cutting off of cotton shipments during the Civil War); the low point reached during the nineteenth century was 2 percent in 1878. The depression years of 1873 to 1877 also stand out, since exports of wood products rose sharply as Americans cultivated overseas markets to make up for the drop in domestic demand.

Products of the forest remained a fairly steady portion in the export trade of the United States, but changes were taking place in the makeup of shipments. In 1884, approximately 40 percent of the timbers shipped abroad were hand-hewn; from 1886 to 1893, the percent fluctuated around 25 percent; from 1894 to 1898, around 18 percent; and from 1899 to 1905, around 10 percent. Thereafter hewn timbers were an insignificant item. Forest products for both domestic use and export more and more were goods of machine manufacture. POTASH AND PEARLASH by-products of agricultural land clearing were major exports until the last half of the nineteenth century, when they ceased to be significant because of changing forest and agricultural patterns and discoveries of mineral substitutes.

At first, furniture was the only manufactured wood product listed separately in the government's data on commerce. The rest was lumped together as "other manufactures" of wood. In 1864, woodenware, hogsheads, and barrels were placed in a category of their own. In 1884, two additional listings appeared: "mouldings, trimmings and other house furnishings" and "doors, sashes, and blinds." In 1898, wood pulp was separated even though the United States still imported ten times more pulp than it exported. Of course, shipments of these products did not begin in the years in which they first appeared in the commercial reports; they had by those dates simply reached a level sufficient to justify segregating the data on them. Their appearance reveals a growing diversification of trade as surely as it does greater precision in the collection and dissemination of information.

The increasing importance of machine manufactures and the growing diversity of exports reflected the basic change that came to the utilization of America's forests in the mid-nineteenth century. Until that time, primarily small farmers tapped the forests with preindustrial methods to supplement their other sources of income; other primitive resource gatherers had more in common with fur trappers than with the industrial lumbermen of a later age. After that time, production was dominated by industrial operations. The change took place somewhat earlier in Maine, but for most areas the transition period was around 1850.

Since commercial timber stands were located in sparsely settled hinterlands and since logs were too bulky to be shipped far before undergoing at least the primary stages of manufacturing, then as now lumbering was of necessity an undertaking that had to export from the point of production to distant markets. Most shipments, however, did not go abroad. American lumbermen always found their primary outlets at home. From 1880 to 1916, over 97 percent of the lumber produced in the United States was used inside the country. The percentage was probably slightly lower in earlier years, but even then domestic consumption clearly dominated.

But foreign markets had an importance greater than their size would seem to suggest. Individual lumber-producing centers—such as Bangor, Maine; Wilmington, North Carolina; Savannah, Georgia; and Grays Harbor and Puget Sound, Washington—found an important share of their markets overseas. Moreover, foreign demand was often complementary to the domestic trade, taking grades and items for which there was little market at home and thereby reducing costs for all. Overseas sales also provided lumbermen with some protection against the wide fluctuations to which domestic demand was subject. Indeed, when plantation agriculture boomed in the Caribbean or Hawaii, when railroad construction burgeoned in Latin America or China, and when mining discoveries occurred in Australia or South Africa, many an American lumberman soon enjoyed increased demand and improved prices for his products. Isolated as it long was from the main national markets, the West Coast was especially influenced by overseas demand. A similar pattern existed for Wilmington, Savannah, Pensacola, and Mobile during the antebellum period. Cotton may have been king in the South, but lumbermen in these centers had to follow developments in the sugar-producing islands of the Caribbean as closely as they did those in the cotton centers if they hoped to prosper. Lumber shipments were especially important to Pensacola, which had little else to dispatch, and to Charleston, South Carolina, whose overworked hinterlands no longer produced cotton so abundantly as they once had and which found in lumber an export to take up some of the resulting economic slack.

In the twentieth century, the United States has continued to be an exporter of forest products, although the patterns of trade again have altered. The rise of steamships and the opening of the Panama Canal gave West Coast producers greater access to European markets. Japan's rising demand, coupled with depletion of its own stands, made this one-time exporter a major importer of forest products—at first mostly squared timbers that were resawn in Japan, but later large quantities of pulp, chips, and logs as well. Shipments of lumber and plywood to Japan from the United States have remained disappointingly small, partly because Japanese authorities have sought to increase their domestic employment by carrying out as many of the manufacturing processes as possible within their own country.

From the 1930s on, exports have been less important to the nation's lumber industry than they once were. Improved internal transportation made domestic markets easier to reach from once isolated ports; the increasing scarcity of sawlogs priced American lumber out of many markets in developing nations; and the increasing sophistication of the nation's economy combined with the country's new-found creditor status to lessen the importance of resource-intensive exports.

Still, the United States has remained an exporter of forest products. Indeed, the diversification noted in the nineteenth century has continued into the twentieth. Items such as plywood, veneer, chips, and wood pulp have become important exports since World War II. Species once unimportant, most notably hemlock from the Pacific Northwest and spruce from Alaska, now contribute significantly to the commercial flow. Rapidly growing and oil-rich nations that once took little have become important buyers; larger and larger shipments have gone to Mexico and the Middle East since the 1950s. Alaska, long an insignificant source, has become a major shipper of wood products exports, thanks in part to sizable Japanese investments in pulping plants and other facilities designed to use wood from Alaska's forests. And nations that have long been buyers now take wood products for new purposes; plywood goes for concrete forms, housing, and packaging and cardboard (or the pulp or chips to make it) is used for boxes. As a result of all this, three of the fifty largest exporters in the United States in 1979 were firms dealing in forest products: Weyerhaeuser, International Paper, and Louisiana Pacific.

Like the shipments of live oak during the early nineteenth century, shipments of forest products have stirred concern and controversy during the twentieth century as well. In fact, since the 1950s, no single ongoing issue has been debated so often and heatedly in the Pacific Northwest as that of log exports to Japan. They are blamed for mill closures, unemployment, high lumber (and housing) costs, and more. At the same time, they are lauded for bringing higher prices for the region's major resource, providing important earnings to help improve the nation's chronically unfavorable balance of trade (thus helping dampen inflation), and furnishing jobs for ports such as Coos Bay, Oregon, and Grays Harbor, Washington. It has been a debate with ramifications for Americans far distant from the shipping centers in the Pacific Northwest. As earlier, the importance of forest products exports looms much larger than the mere value and quantity of the shipments involved would seem to indicate. For all the changes, much remains the same.

FURTHER READING: Thomas R. Cox, *Mills and Markets: A History of the Pacific Coast Lumber Industry to 1900* (1974). James Elliott Defebaugh, *History of the Lumber Industry of America* (1906), vol. I, pp. 527-549. John A. Eisterhold, "Lumber and Trade in the Seaboard Cities of the Old South, 1607-1860," Ph.D. dissertation, University of Mississippi (1970). Ivan M. Elchibegoff, *United States International Timber Trade in the Pacific Area* (1949). Edward E. Pratt, *The Export Lumber Trade of the United States*, U. S. Bureau of Foreign and Domestic Commerce, Miscellaneous Series, No. 67 (1918).

THOMAS R. COX

WOOD SCIENCE AND TECHNOLOGY

Wood science is concerned with knowledge of wood as a material, including its origin, structure, properties, and characteristics. It embraces knowledge pertaining or applicable to wood in a number of separate fields—primarily in biology, chemistry, physics, engineering, and mathematics. Wood technology is the application of wood science in the conversion and processing of wood for use.

In modern technological society, wood is used in vast quantities and in innumerable ways. Annual production of timber in the United States in the 1970s was on the order of 250 million tons, exceeding the combined total for steel, copper, aluminum, plastics, and cement. The efficient conversion of raw timber to a multitude of established products and their application to end use—not to mention the development of new products—is dependent upon the quality of decisions based in wood science and technology. Solution of typical problems in wood products development, production, and application involves proper identification of each wood and knowledge of its structure and the extent of its quality variability. Proper wood utilization demands understanding of wood-moisture reactions, methods of seasoning, and causes and prevention of wood deterioration. Other technical problems in wood utilization deal with wood machining, structural design principles, and the efficient use of mechanical fasteners, adhesives, and finishes. In some lines of processing (such as pulp and paper or fiberboard production), chemical properties or fiber

behavior are dominant. Although incomplete, this listing of problem areas suggests the scope of wood science and technology which provides the technical underpinning to one of America's major industries.

Professional programs of study in wood science and technology, at the graduate or undergraduate level, are offered today at twenty-eight universities in the United States and Canada, primarily within the ad-

A photomicrograph provides a cross-sectional view of an annual ring of post oak, magnified fifty times. The large vessels are plugged by growths called tyloses, making the wood nearly impermeable—a quality of special significance to the cooperage and wood preservation industries. Impermeable wood is good for making barrels but is difficult to impregnate with preservative chemicals. Forest Service Photo.

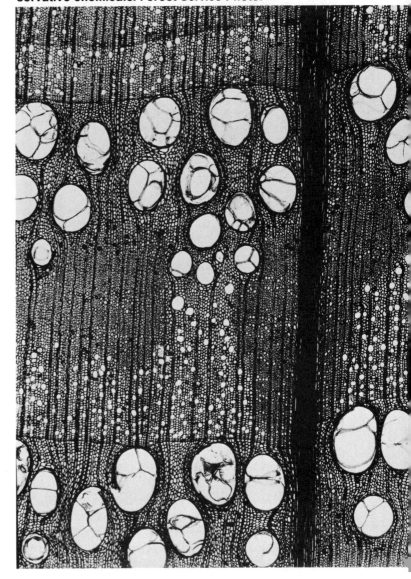

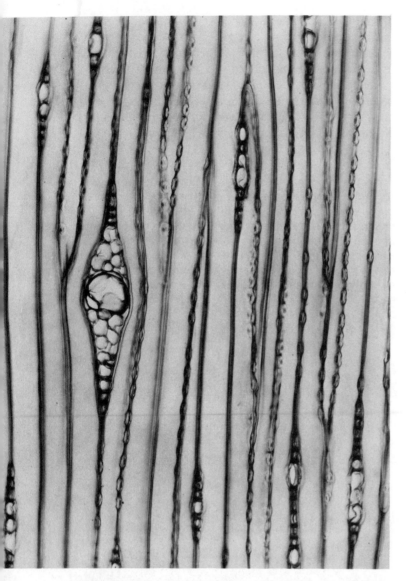

This photomicrograph gives a tangential view of short-leaf pine, magnified twenty-five times. Shown are end views of resin ducts, which radiate out from the center of the tree. The systematic wounding of the tree yields the basic raw material for the naval stores industry. Forest Service Photo.

ministrative structure of a forestry school or college. In addition, certain aspects of wood science and technology are included in a number of educational programs in materials science, engineering, and pulp and paper technology.

The FOREST PRODUCTS RESEARCH SOCIETY (FPRS), a technical association founded in 1947, and the Society of Wood Science and Technology, a professional society founded in 1958, have provided channels for communication on developments in wood science and technology through international and regional meetings, frequent conferences, symposia, and similar events. The field has been served by a number of journals. FPRS has published the *Forest Products Journal* since 1947 and *Wood Science* since 1968, while the Society of Wood Science and Technology began publishing *Wood and Fiber* in 1969. Other important periodicals in this field are the Technical Association of the Pulp and Paper Industry's *TAPPI*, started in 1949, and *Wood Science and Technology*, published by the International Academy of Wood Science since 1966. A computerized information retrieval service (AIDS) sponsored by FPRS regularly abstracts more than 300 periodicals and other publication series from the worldwide literature on wood science and technology.

Preceded by more than 175 years of studies of wood in Europe, the beginnings of scientific inquiry in the United States into the properties of American woods were recorded in the Tenth Census (1884). In the following year, the results of tests of full-size timbers conducted at the Watertown Arsenal in Massachusetts provided the first values for some American woods that could be used in structural design. Nevertheless, engineers well into the first decade of the present century used very conservative working stresses for timber, ranging from 900 to 1200 pounds per square inch in bending with no variation for grade. By contrast, engineers of the later twentieth century could select from an array of stepped grades of structural lumber with machine-stress ratings for extreme fiber in bending ranging from 900 to 3300 pounds per square inch.

In the later 1880s, research in forest products assumed high priority in planning within the new Division of Forestry in the U. S. DEPARTMENT OF AGRICULTURE. Recognition of the importance of efficient wood utilization as a partner of SILVICULTURE and forest management in the conservation of a threatened timber resource underlay that planning. The inception of a worldwide pattern of governmental involvement in forest products research can be traced to the research program set forth in 1892 by Bernhard E. FERNOW in U. S. Division of Forestry Bulletin No. 6, *Timber Physics*. Division of Forestry—later U. S. FOREST SERVICE—studies were to provide the principal data base in the development of wood science and technology.

Laboratories for the strength testing of timber were established cooperatively by the Division of Forestry at a number of universities as well as in Washington, D.C. Research was also conducted in pulp and paper and in WOOD PRESERVATION. One outcome of these investigations was the publication in 1895 of a treatise by

Filibert Roth on work started while he was still a student at the University of Michigan. Entitled *Timber: An Elementary Discussion of the Characteristics and Properties of Wood* and published as Bulletin No. 10 of the Division of Forestry, this text incorporated the results of work done at some of these laboratories with Roth's own studies of the anatomy and physical properties of wood. It was to serve as the first American textbook in the area we now know as wood science and technology. A few years later, Harry D. Tiemann at the Forest Service cooperative laboratory at Yale University did important work leading to publication as Forest Service Bulletin No. 70 of his *Effect of Moisture upon the Strength and Stiffness of Wood* (1906), which elucidated the concept of "fiber saturation point."

Despite their productivity, the activities of these widely dispersed federal research laboratories were difficult to coordinate. The obvious advantages of a central integrated facility led the Forest Service in cooperation with the University of Wisconsin in 1910 to establish the Forest Products Laboratory (FPL) in Madison under the direction of McGarvey Cline. FPL, with its charter to deal with all aspects of wood research including structure, properties, treatments, and use of wood in the United States, achieved worldwide recognition for its leadership and accomplishments. Through this research it contributed in many ways to the development, diversification, and growth of American forest products industries and, in fact, to the founding of the discipline of wood science and technology. Its *Wood Handbook*, most recently revised in 1974, became one of the most widely used books of its kind; but it was only one of many published by the FPL. Wood research has also been carried on at several of the Forest Service's experiment stations, notably at the Southern station in Louisiana, where one of the results was the publication of Peter Koch's *Utilization of the Southern Pines* (Agriculture Handbook No. 420, 1972).

Early in the twentieth century, the older forestry schools in the United States were established. The availability of a significant body of literature, deriving to a considerable extent from the work of the FPL and its predecessors, inspired and encouraged many of these schools to incorporate into their curricula individual courses, and later complete programs, in forest products utilization and wood technology. The first curriculum entitled "Wood Technology" came into being in 1929. Development of this new subject proceeded rather slowly before World War II. Textbooks written by faculty members supplemented and interpreted the growing number of technical publications. Authors of widely used publications of that era—many of them revised and still consulted—include figures well known in the forestry profession, among them H. P. Brown, Nelson C. Brown, Ralph C. Bryant, C. C. Forsaith, George A. Garratt, Lee Fred Hawley, R. B. Hough, George M. Hunt, Edward C. Jeffrey, Royal S. Kellogg, Arthur Koehler, Lorraine J. Markwardt, Alexis J. Panshin, Samuel J. Record, Arlie W. Schorger, A. J. Stamm, Harry D. Tiemann, Thomas R. Truax, T. R. C. Wilson, and Louis E. Wise.

The war years 1942 to 1945 emptied the colleges but witnessed intense wood research and development activity by the military agencies and the FPL. The immediate postwar period was characterized by a deluge of veterans returning to the schools, by the rebuilding of teaching staffs, and by a spate of activity in the development of educational programs, in research, and in publication—all stimulated by wartime developments in technology. The increasing complexity of the forest products industries demanded more technical personnel in the industrial establishment, and the schools responded. This was an era of growth under the leadership of a second generation of teachers and researchers, some of whom remained active in the 1980s.

As late as 1955, college-level programs in this area continued to be designated under such names as wood utilization, forest products, and wood technology. Wood science, by that name, was yet to be born. Not even among the "insiders" was the term wood science well recognized. At a meeting called to found a new professional society in 1958, the name selected was American Institute of Wood Engineering. Not until two years later did this group adopt the name Society of Wood Science and Technology.

As the schools extended their degree programs to the graduate level, their research programs, consisting primarily of thesis research, grew accordingly, often subsidized by grants from government or industry. Research results from graduate student projects have greatly contributed to knowledge in wood science. Total annual enrollment in the late 1970s was on the order of 1200 in baccalaureate programs, 160 in programs at the master's level, and 70 at the level of the doctorate. Among the schools which developed extensive research facilities were the New York, North Carolina, Mississippi, Washington, and Oregon state universities, and the universities of Washington and California.

By the late 1970s, a third generation of teachers and authors—possibly better grounded in the underlying disciplines of wood science and technology than their predecessors and certainly better equipped with modern tools of investigation—were directing wood science and technology toward a more basic understanding of wood properties in relation to wood structure and away from the empiricism of an earlier day. This new generation tended to approach wood science and technology in the pattern applied to other materials under the general heading of materials science and engineering. Nevertheless, the discipline has continued to confirm the faith of the American founding fathers of forestry—in ways that they could hardly have foreseen—in its contributions to forest conservation through more complete and efficient utilization of America's renewable timber resource.

FURTHER READING: Samuel Trask Dana and Evert W. Johnson, *Forestry Education in America Today and Tomorrow* (1963). Everett L. Ellis, *Education in Wood Science and Technology* (1964).

FREDERICK F. WANGAARD

WOODWORKING MACHINES

In the past 200 years, machines have been developed to perform every operation needed to convert rough logs into finished products. The principal operations are sawing, planing, boring, turning, and chipping.

The process of replacing or augmenting muscle power with waterpower and wind power had been going on for centuries when James Watt's steam engine came together with newly invented machines to create an industrial revolution. Woodworking machines were among the earliest to be highly developed. Using the new machines, relatively unskilled labor could outproduce skilled craftsmen using hand tools by a factor of ten or more.

Revolutionary advances in woodworking took place in the Royal Navy dockyards of England in the 1790s and early 1800s, when Sir Samuel Bentham and Sir Marc Isambard Brunel were able to develop machines to mass-produce ships' block pulleys. Since large sailing vessels of the time often required as many as 1,000 blocks and the Royal Navy used 130,000 blocks a year, a means of speeding production had obvious military and economic significance. By 1808, 10 unskilled laborers, using steam-powered machines, had replaced 110 skilled block-makers at the Portsmouth dockyard, resulting in an annual saving of 17,000 pounds. Circular saws with a pendulum motion were an important improvement in this operation.

Bentham applied steam power to a score of other important machines before 1800. He produced working prototypes of nearly every basic woodworking machine used in the nineteenth century: circular saws, planers, mortisers, dovetailing machines, lathes, screw-threading machines with rotary cutters, and others.

Sawing

Among the oldest of human inventions, the saw is the basic wood-cutting tool. Saws of obsidian were used by prehistoric man, and saws of hardened copper were used as early as 4900 B.C. Since the invention of steel in the nineteenth century, saws have improved steadily, but such basic practices as raking the teeth to cut in one direction, setting the teeth to make the cut wider than the back of the saw, and mounting the blade in a frame to keep it taut, are very old.

Sawmills powered by waterwheels and windmills, using saws set in wooden frames, date from the Middle Ages. The frame kept the soft iron blade from buckling, and a drive rod connected eccentrically to the power wheel produced a reciprocating up-and-down motion much like that of the primitive pit saw operated by two men. Pit sawyers could produce 200 board feet of lumber per day, but ganging reciprocating frame saws allowed a log to be cut into several rough boards at once and production could approach 4,000 board feet per day. Typically, these boards varied greatly in thickness, and there was much waste due to the thickness of the kerf, a quarter or more of the wood being converted into sawdust.

The perfection of the circular saw in the late eighteenth century permitted continuous action of the cutting edge on the wood, resulting in greater speed and efficiency and in straighter cuts and smoother edges. The earliest English patent was that of Samuel Miller in 1777, but the earliest important commercial use of the circular saw was by Walter Taylor for the Royal Navy in 1781. Circular saws were introduced to North America in the very early nineteenth century. In an 1824 report of a circular sawmill invented by Captain William Kendall, Jr., of Waterville, Maine, the *New England Farmer* of Boston observed that "circular saws have long been in use." Robert Eastman, of Brunswick, Maine, in 1824 patented a circular saw with inserted replaceable teeth, which he had invented at least two years earlier. Replaceable teeth prevented the reduction of disc diameter by repeated sharpenings and also made repair easy if any teeth broke off. Circular saws were in widespread use in America in the 1820s and 1830s for the production of shingles, clapboards, and common lumber. Eastman advertised in 1835 that he was renewing his patent on a circular-saw clapboard machine, and others claimed to have improved upon his invention. Circular saws imported from England during this period ranged in size from three to thirty-six inches in diameter.

Inside and outside of wooden gutter are being formed in one pass through of woodworking machine. Forest History Society Photo.

In New England, the building of woodworking machines became an industry in itself. At least fourteen such shops are known to have been in operation before 1840. Within a generation there were factories producing woodworking machinery in most parts of the country. Woodworking factories increased dramatically in number in the same period and were widely distributed: in 1810, there were 2,541 sawmills in the United States, and in 1860 there were 10,658. Other kinds of wood-conversion plants multiplied proportionately.

Warren Miller of Brooklyn, New York, in 1878 patented an inserted-tooth circular saw that has been called the first really successful one of the kind. The patent was sold to the Robert Hoe Company, which manufactured and marketed it widely. George Simonds of Fitchburg, Massachusetts, in 1885 made further improvements that have not been surpassed significantly since. Extra large circular saws were developed after the lumber industry shifted to the big trees of the Pacific Coast. Double circular mills, the lower blades of which were six feet in diameter, were used in Oregon and Washington to saw Douglas-fir logs.

The band saw, last of the major innovations in saw blades, was patented in England by William Newberry in 1808. Like the circular saw, the band saw had the advantage of continous cutting action. The early efforts to make band saws practical centered on two problems: finding a steel tough and flexible enough, and finding an effective way of joining the ends of the band together. Although an 1858 patent for running the band over a spring wheel at one end helped reduce breakage by equalizing tension, it was not until about 1870, when Swedish steel became available in America, that the band mill became important. J. A. Fay & Company of Cincinnati, perhaps the largest American manufacturer of woodworking machinery at the time, listed eleven different models of band saws in its 1885 catalog. A band mill with nine-foot wheels is reported to have been in action that year.

Planing

Sir Samuel Bentham must again be credited with the pioneering work in developing machines for smoothing the surface of lumber. His planing machine was the first in the long series of successful powered tools he developed before 1800.

Fixed-blade planers, into which lumber was fed over rollers, were patented and used early, but the most efficient and effective—developed in the eighteenth century and still the standard—used cylindrical steel cutter heads rotating at high speed. Chipping, a common problem of hand planing against the grain, was virtually eliminated if the blades were sharp and ground at the proper angle and if the feed rate was regulated.

Bentham's planer could dress two sides of a board at once, although the principle was not fully perfected for another half-century. The high-speed cutter head was also adapted to the production of moldings in the shop Bentham had set up in the house and extensive outbuildings near London owned by his brother Jeremy, the utilitarian philosopher.

John Richards, in his classic *A Treatise on the Construction and Operation of Woodworking Machines* (1872), noted that American planing practice differed from British in that in American mills green rough lumber was rapidly surfaced directly as it came from the sawmill. This made the roller feed more important than it had been in England, where lumber was seasoned before planing. The practical planing of all four surfaces of a board at once depended upon power feeding on roller beds that could control thick-

ness. Completely enclosing planing and molding machines made possible a vacuum effect for the removal of chips and sawdust—a contribution to the health and safety in woodworking plants as well as to their efficiency.

Sanding machines have proven to be an effective substitute for rotating cylinder planers. Successively finer grit on cylindrical drums was used on an endless-bed triple drum machine patented in 1900. Flint, emery, and garnet sand were eventually replaced by silicon carbide and aluminum oxide. The multiple wide-belt sander appeared in the United States in about 1955 and is able to give a smoother finish at higher speed than drum sanders.

Chipping headings, introduced in the early 1960s, produce cants from logs and convert outer portions directly into pulp chips for papermaking or flakes for structural flakeboard.

Boring and Mortising

Since wood had been joined for more than 2,000 years by drilling and pegging, or by mortise and tenon, it was natural that machines for joinery that could make precision holes at high speed should be developed. Like so much else, these were developed by Bentham in London in the 1790s. His achievements included tubular boring instruments for core boring, reciprocating and rotary mortising machines, and forked or double mortise chisels.

Power Sources

It has been observed by Peter Koch that "the history of wood machining is closely tied to advances in metallurgy and power sources." Bentham's machines were powered by steam engines, but sawmills and woodworking shops in both England and America continued to be run by waterwheels as well. The line-shaft system, for transmitting power to individual machines through belts and pulleys, was standard in woodworking factories well into the twentieth century. Richards's 1872 *Treatise* included a chapter on the proportions for pulleys to achieve proper speeds for various machines and their specializing operations. The trade catalogs of American woodworking-machine manufacturers also contained practical directions to aid mechanics in making such computations. Another chapter in Richards was devoted to bearings for shafts and spindles.

Woodworking machines did not begin to use ball bearings until the twentieth century, and the first electrically powered sawmill did not begin operation until 1896. Direct-current electric motors, belted to individual machines, began to replace line shafts powered by steam in about 1906. Line shafts and steam engines had all but disappeared by 1950, replaced by individual electric motors.

Turning

Lathes for turning wood were known to the Greeks more than 3,000 years ago and to the Egyptians even earlier. In Africa and other regions of the world, ingenious lathes were operated with foot treadles, bows, flexible saplings, or arm power. Lathes rotate a piece of wood mounted lengthwise between two chucks. Pressure of a cutting tool, usually resting on a surface parallel to the axis of rotation, shapes the wood into variations of cylindrical forms such as table legs, spindles, spokes, rungs, and bowls. Wooden decorative forms, such as urns, often resemble products made in similar fashion on a potter's wheel.

Lathes for copying irregular forms were developed in the eighteenth century. These follow a model set up parallel to the blank; the cutting tool is controlled by a stylus that follows the contours of the model, reproducing the form desired. Copying lathes were developed by Bentham and Brunel for finishing ships' blocks. The American Thomas Blanchard in 1819 patented an improved lathe for turning out gunstocks.

The lathe also proved to be a superior machine for making veneer, largely replacing various slicing tools used earlier. John Dresser of Stockbridge, Massachusetts, patented a veneer lathe in 1840. By advancing a knife at a controlled rate into the turning log, a veneer lathe can "peel" it into a continuous thin sheet of wood.

Wood Fiber

As the supply of large logs has steadily decreased or become more expensive to harvest, machines have been developed for utilizing most of what was once regarded as waste material. Increasing demand for fiber for paper and other pulp products has led to improved machinery for converting wood to this use. Particleboard is another product that uses wood fiber.

Stone grinding—a standard process for converting cordwood into pulp—is a century old. Today, chipping machines are used, followed by disc-refining of the fiber under high pressure. Debarking machinery has been perfected as part of a processing cycle which recognizes that waste material needs to be bark-free for optimum use in papermaking. High-pressure water jets were widely used in the West for debarking logs until about 1950, when a rotating-ring mechanical barker was invented simultaneously by T. W. Nicholson of Seattle and Söderhamn of Sweden, greatly increasing efficiency in keeping bark out of wood pulp.

Woodworking Specialties

The development of woodworking machines has followed other historic developments that created new demands and opportunities for specialized wood conversion. For example, the rise of the railroads as a significant transportation network after 1850 led to improved machines for building railway cars. These included railway cut-off saws, multiple-spindle borers, hollow-chisel mortisers, and combination machines that could perform more than one operation at once or in rapid sequence. Also in the nineteenth century, parts of wagons, carriages, and stagecoaches were shaped by special machines and assembled by hand; in the early twentieth century, spoke-turning and mitering machines, spoke-turning lathes of the Blanchard type, felly-sawing machines, and hub-boring machines were used in preparing wooden parts for automobile manufacture. J. A. Fay & Company's 1885 catalog listed thirty-six machines for making wooden wheels, and the 1910 catalog of the Defiance Machine Works of Defiance, Ohio, one of the largest woodworking-machine makers of the time, still listed thirty-two machines for the production of wooden automobile wheels.

As John Richards observed in 1872, the high cost of American skilled labor dictated the production of machines that could produce the maximum amount of work in the shortest possible time. English woodworking machines, by contrast, were produced for a world market where ignorant and unskilled labor was the rule and therefore had to be stronger and better made to survive abuse. American machines, operated by skilled workers, could be crude by comparison and still astonish foreign observers by their productivity. European machines were framed in cast iron, but most American machines were framed in wood until late in the nineteenth century.

Electronics

Hiram Hallock has observed that there was little advance in American sawmill practice between 1880 and World War II; most of the equipment in use in 1900 was still running in 1950, but dramatic changes lay just ahead. During the following decade, increasing labor costs prompted more mechanization in American mills and woodworking plants. By the 1960s, the cost of timber further spurred the development of new technology. The industry had to shift from large old-growth timber to sustained-yield TREE FARMS that produce smaller logs in cycles of thirty to fifty years, depending upon species and region. The higher cost of logs and labor made reduction of waste in wood conversion a high priority of the industry.

By the 1960s, electronic scanning equipment could analyze the characteristics of individual logs and feed the data into computers programmed to select the cutting pattern that would yield the greatest value. The equipment positions logs accurately with respect to taper, sweep, and selected patterns. Scanners can detect the water content in individual pieces of wood, as well as their diameters, profiles, knots, and other physical characteristics. In veneer plants, logs can be rotated 360 degrees while 120 scan readings are taken at multiple points from end to end. The computer instantly selects the ideal axis and makes independent adjustments at each end of the log to position it for peeling. In 1980, more than 100 companies were producing electronic equipment for forest products mills.

FURTHER READING: Hiram Hallock, "Sawmilling Roots," in *Electronics in the Sawmill: Proceedings of the Electronics Workshop—Sawmill and Plywood Clinic* (1979). Peter Koch, "History of Wood Machining," *Wood Science and Technology* 1 (1967): 180–183. Rodney C. Loehr, "Saving the Kerf: The Introduction of the Band Saw Mill," *Agricultural History* 23 (July 1949): 168–172. Judson H. Mansfield, "History of the Development of Woodworking Machinery from 1852 to 1952," in *Proceedings of Wood Symposium* (1952). Nathan Rosenberg, "America's Rise to Woodworking Leadership," in Brooke Hindle, ed., *America's Wooden Age: Aspects of Its Early Technology* (1975), pp. 37-62.

ARTHUR A. HART

WORLD WAR I AND AMERICAN FORESTS AND FOREST INDUSTRY

World War I was a turning point for the forests of America and the industries and professions dependent upon them. The demands of mobilization helped to convert the timber industry from a series of migratory swaths through virgin forests to a network of stable regional enterprises engaged in long-term production. For the forests, the experience of war helped to show that, even in the demands of emergency, they did not face inevitable and irreversible destruction; second-growth timber established its place in the market, and forests and forest industries bid fair at war's end to continue together for a long future. The war also helped to reduce old tensions between timber industries and professional foresters. The wartime experience abated the force of arguments for federal regulation of the industry, promoted those favoring cooperation between the private and public sectors, and provided precedents for later national management of the economy.

When war broke out in Europe in 1914, its effects on the American forest products industry were at first negative, as European purchase orders were canceled. Within a few months, however, the industry fell upon prosperity, as Allied orders for forest products increased astronomically. The Allies turned to America because European forest resources were inaccessible. The forests of the Central Powers now belonged to the enemy, while the Allied nations lacked the manpower required to exploit their own woodlands.

Production, employment, and profits in the American forest products industries increased dramatically. That growth placed these industries on a sound footing to support the campaign for "Preparedness," and, ultimately, American entry into the war. The demands made against the nation's forests were unprecedented. Millions of board feet of lumber were required for the construction of training camps and other facilities, railroad cars, war materiel, crates and containers, and a shipbuilding program calling for 1,000 wooden cargo ships.

The timber industry came under increasing federal economic control during the war, as did nearly every other sector of the economy. The experience presaged the federal management of the economy which has increased in the decades since. It also strengthened industry trade associations and increased the industrywide cooperation necessary to allow lumbermen to deal with the government on more equal terms. At the same time, despite frequent accusations that it placed profits before patriotism, the industry emerged from the war with an improved public image. No longer were timbermen decried uniformly as heartless plunderers of public resources; they had proven as cooperative and patriotic as any other citizens. And national economic management had led to familiarity between people in industry and those in the government. As a result, the federal forest conservation campaign after the war eschewed demands for federal control of the timber industry and turned more and more to the development of cooperative programs.

Within the industry, there were other changes. To continue the prosperity of wartime, the industry launched programs to promote residential construction, especially single-family houses which provided a long-term market for lumber. Because of wartime labor shortages, blacks, Mexican-Americans, and women entered the industry labor force in growing numbers, and—despite some temporary union busting—unionization became firmly established in the forest products industries. The demands of the war helped to further trends in the FURNITURE INDUSTRY away from handcrafted hardwood pieces and toward the use of softwood and veneer and the adoption of mass production.

Although the war showed that conservation was possible in American forests with industry cooperation, other resources did not fare so happily. In particular, wartime requirements for meat and wool led to increases in grazing in the national forests and on lands of the public domain. The public rangelands—already suffering from the effects of long-term overgrazing despite efforts to reduce the numbers of stock—were severely loaded with cattle and sheep. To make matters worse, much of the Western range experienced drought during the war years. By the end of the war, the inevitable decline in demand and prices plunged the livestock industry into hard times. Federal land managers were forced to retard their stock-reduction efforts in the postwar years, prolonging the overgrazing.

The effects of wartime were dramatic, for the range and for the livestock industry, but they occurred within a context of decades of private and public abuse of the public range. Nonetheless, the errors of World War I became a focus of public debate over federal range management. They strengthened the arguments of conservationists favoring stock-reduction policies and led to more restrained responses to the demands of World War II.

The national parks during World War I also came under pressure, from friends and foes alike. The isolationism that accompanied the outbreak of hostilities, combined with the growing popularity of the automobile and the appeals of the "See America First" campaign, led to dramatic increases in park visitation. Most of the parks, initially developed for the carriage trade and indifferently managed by a variety of agencies, were overwhelmed. Affronted by this situation, a wide public supported the administrative reform realized in the creation of the NATIONAL PARK SERVICE in 1916.

No sooner was the park service established than it faced demands that the resources in its charge be opened to exploitation for the war effort. Through adroit political footwork and insignificant compromises, the service and the parks managed to emerge from the war intact. But it was only after the war that appropriations and personnel became available to develop and operate the parks at a higher standard.

The most dramatic event of World War I for American forest history was the direct participation of foresters and woodsmen in the conflict. When the United States entered the war in 1917, the Allies projected a steady buildup of forces for a war of attrition expected to last for years. The effort demanded prodi-

Packaging military supplies required enormous quantities of wood during World War I. Here a revolving drum at the Forest Products Laboratory in Madison, Wisconsin, puts a wooden crate through its paces to test the effectiveness of its design. Forest Service Photo.

gious quantities of timber. Nearly the entire trench system of the Western Front was constructed of wood shielded by earth. In addition, millions of feet of wood were required for entanglement stakes, buildings, road and bridge construction, containers, docks and warehouses, and other uses, as well as firewood for heating and cooking.

The Allies, their manpower committed to armed service, could not meet their own requirements for forest products. Although they would have preferred to import all their lumber from America, limited shipping space made that impossible. Therefore, forestry units were established in the American and Canadian armies

The Army organized fire crews of rather unmilitary appearance to protect vital timber supplies in the Pacific Northwest. Forest Service Photo.

for service in the forests of France. Eventually, over 30,000 American foresters, woodsmen, and millmen served in Europe and were organized by July 1918 into the 20th Engineers (Forestry), the largest regiment in the American Army. Back home, another large group of logging units produced aircraft material in the SPRUCE PRODUCTION DIVISION of the Signal Corps's Aviation Section.

Veterans of military forestry returned to America with a strong sense of shared experience and contribution to the war effort, which had a subtle influence on growing cooperation between industry and gov-

ernment. The government foresters—among them U. S. FOREST SERVICE Chief Henry S. GRAVES and his immediate successor William B. GREELEY had gained an appreciation of industry's perspective on regulation, for they had felt the frustration of trying to increase production in the face of controls by the French government foresters. The punitive attitude toward industry that had formerly characterized much of the Forest Service campaign for federal regulation moderated after the war.

That change of attitude sparked a division in conservation circles between the pragmatic foresters and industrialists, suspicious of federal control, and the hard-line reformers, ever suspicious of industry. Ironically, the former, even though they became a growing presence in the forestry profession, were deprived of some of their strongest arguments and spokesmen as German perspectives on conservation were discredited. Nonetheless, foresters were no longer of one mind on ideological and political questions.

FURTHER READING: See the topical issue of the *Journal of Forest History* 22 (Oct. 1978).

DAVID A. CLARY

WORLD WAR II AND AMERICAN FORESTS AND FOREST INDUSTRY

The American entry into World War II found existing lumber inventories at 17 billion board feet. In addition to this apparently adequate reserve, total lumber production of all grades and species stood at 36 billion board feet in 1941 and matched that level in 1942. For at least the first five months of the war, these figures fed a false optimism as the government sought to allocate lumber among competing war mobilization and civilian demands.

The war effort consumed lumber in three distinct categories: as integral components for materiel such as tool handles, small naval craft, truck bodies, and airplanes; as the chief structural material for new defense plants, troop cantonments, and housing in defense centers; and as crating and dunnage for the vast tonnages of materiel shipped domestically and overseas. In each of these areas, the expanding mobilization increased demand, and shortages of other materials such as metals led to the use of wood as a substitute, often in new and ingenious applications. The first year of the war saw the lumber inventory drawn down to 11 billion board feet. As American and allied forces took the offensive in North Africa and the Pacific, crating and dunnage ran to 9.5 billion board feet, 4 billion more than in 1941.

On a par with lumber supply, manpower remained a concern of the industry and the war agencies. The draft drew experienced loggers out of the woods almost as fast as the war industries which offered higher wages to traditionally lower-paid woodsmen. The industry, consisting of some 31,000 mills, including many hand-to-mouth operations, was paradoxically facing insolvency in the midst of dramatically increasing demand for cut timber. Mid-1943 found the industry short of some 60,000 hands. Wartime controls, furthermore, added to the pinch by freezing loggers' and sawmill hands' wage rates much below those of designated de-

fense industries. Operators and loggers alike resisted the forty-eight-hour week. Farm workers, a traditional source of extra seasonal woods labor, stayed in their fields as the war raised commodity prices and expanded demand for foodstuffs.

The principal agency established to control military and civilian lumber allocation was the Lumber and Lumber Products Division of the War Production Board (WPB). Its charter made it supreme in lumber distribution for the duration of the war. Its officials identified stands of timber critical for war materiel and encouraged owners to harvest them. It influenced appropriations for building access roads into national forests, and sought out machinery, spare parts, and supplies to help the lumber industry maintain production. The office of WPB's Western Log and Lumber Administrator in Portland, Oregon, procured most of the high-grade spruce used principally for Canadian and British aircraft production. The Lumber and Lumber Products Division's Log and Lumber Policy Committee included members from the War and Agriculture departments, the War Manpower Commission, the Office of Price Administration, the War Labor Board, and the Smaller War Plants Corporation. This committee attempted solutions to stumpage, manpower, and equipment problems. The War Manpower Commission gave first priority to woods labor, especially in the West, and imposed the forty-eight-hour workweek on woods and mill operators. The WPB arranged for Selective Service deferments for loggers, but this failed to prevent the shortage of men in the industry from reaching 108,000 in September 1943.

Bottlenecks in labor and other needs particularly hurt production in the eastern United States where most lumber was produced by small mills. The TIMBER PRODUCTION WAR PROJECT (TPWP), administered for the WPB by the U. S. FOREST SERVICE in cooperation with state forestry departments and extension services from August 1943 to October 1945, undertook to stimulate output of lumber and veneer logs, and later of pulpwood, NAVAL STORES, EXCELSIOR, and veneer in the major forested areas east of the Great Plains. The TPWP tackled the "small mill problem" with technical advice, training, morale-building programs, and assistance in securing draft deferments and obtaining needed equipment. TPWP also trained most of the prisoners of war who were employed to supplement native labor in American forest industries beginning in January 1944. By war's end, 18,300 German prisoners were in the American woods.

Lumber controls were ineffective until relatively late in the war but developed as the crisis in distribu-

The charcoal used for gas mask filters during World War II had to be of a very high density. Charcoal produced from coconut shells and fruit pits was preferred, but wartime scarcities prompted a search for substitutes. At the Forest Products Laboratory in Madison, Wisconsin, a satisfactory product was obtained by compressing sawdust under very high pressure. These briquettes were then distilled, still under pressure, to produce gas mask quality charcoal. Forest Service Photo.

tion grew. When cantonment construction began straining the system in May 1942, the WPB's Lumber and Lumber Products Division issued Limitation Order L-121 giving overall softwood lumber priority to army and navy requirements, complete figures for which neither service could provide. Forest Service forecasts, based on peacetime consumption, proved largely inaccurate. Later orders through the summer

of 1942 relaxed the first priority given the military, but made no headway toward true national control. In September 1942, military purchasing was consolidated in the Central Procurement Agency under the ARMY CORPS OF ENGINEERS, which bought all the stock needed by the army, the navy, and the Maritime Commission. The Central Procurement Agency eliminated some artificial shortages arising from separate competitive bidding among military branches, but it became itself a competitor to the Lumber and Lumber Products Division. Only in the aircraft industry, a fairly discrete entity using only the best grades of Sitka spruce, Douglas-fir, and noble fir, was lumber supply and demand balanced by late 1943 through stringent controls imposed by the Western Log and Lumber Administrator.

Despite this limited success, the WPB's lumber division remained the victim of its own unwillingness to control unrestricted military procurement and even abetted it with orders affecting softwood and hardwood lumber, plywood, and imported species, notably balsa and mahogany. By early 1944, wartime lumber administration had "progressed from disorder through confusion to chaos." Attempts to apply principles derived from the WPB's Controlled Materials Program of November 1942, which dealt chiefly in scarce metals, were partially useful, but only in March 1944 did the Lumber and Lumber Products Division accede to its intended position as the United States lumber czar of World War II.

Through WPB Order L-335, the division finally imposed its will upon the allocation process, reversing the dominant role of the Central Procurement Agency. Using quarterly applications for specific amounts and types of wood from all users, the division allocated the total national supply for the last eleven months of the war.

Other governmental forest-management agencies contributed heavily to the war effort. The Forest Service released some 500,000 acres of national forest land for military purposes in 1942 and supplemented timber production by selecting national forest stands for cutting. The service continued and expanded its normal statistical, research, and protection activities. Enemy recognition of the strategic economic importance of American forests was revealed by the unsuccessful attempt in September 1942 of a small Japanese submarine-launched seaplane to drop fire bombs in the western Oregon woods near Brookings. From November 1944 to March 1945, the Japanese attempted, also unsuccessfully, to set fires in American forests with hydrogen-filled balloons carried across the Pacific by high-altitude air currents. To meet this incendiary threat, the "Firefly Project" supplemented the work of regular "smoke jumpers" (largely drawn during the war from Civilian Public Service Camps) with the cooperative loan of paratroopers, army ground forces, and military aerial reconnaissance.

Ongoing disputes over forest policies continued during the war. While the Forest Service, accusing industry of complacency and destructive cutting practices, advocated public regulation of timber harvest on private lands, industrial spokesmen asserted that the needs of the war were being met by overcutting of private timber and undercutting of national forest timber. The Forest Service reappraisal of the nation's timber resource in 1945–1946 was to support the latter claim, as it found that 32 percent of the sawtimber volume on commercial forestlands stood in national forests, while all private ownership together totaled 57 percent. Yet in 1944, the peak year of wartime production, national forests had supplied only 10 percent of the total timber cut, virtually all the rest coming from private lands. Industry proposed that in meeting the expected postwar housing demands government timber should redress the balance. The national forests' contribution to the total timber harvest had already doubled, from 5 percent in the late 1930s to 10 percent in 1944, and the Sustained-Yield Forest Management Act of that year authorized the Forest Service to offer long-term guarantees of public timber to local mills with the object of maintaining community stability.

Also affected by the war was the NATIONAL PARK SERVICE. Despite its isolation in Chicago, where service headquarters were located from 1942 until 1947 in order to make room in Washington for war agencies, the park service, with the support of Secretary of the Interior Harold L. ICKES, was able to avoid major wartime development of the resources contained in the parks. Livestock grazing remained within prewar limits in the major parks and the WPB failed to obtain approval for logging of aircraft-grade Sitka spruce in OLYMPIC NATIONAL PARK. Some mining occurred in the parks, particularly of tungsten in Yosemite and of sand and gravel on lands which had been acquired for addition to Olympic. With tourist visitation reduced to below half of the prewar levels, some park areas proved useful for the training of troops and for the testing of mountain and arctic equipment. Among the units thus affected were Mount Rainier, Mount McKinley, Shenandoah, Yosemite, Hawaii, and Grand Canyon. Hotels in Yosemite and Mount McKinley were used for military convalescent and recreation centers. More serious was the withdrawal by Congress of 6,400 acres of Hawaii National Park as a bombing range in 1940.

The nation's wood resources met the demands of the war but not without residual effect. Of a total of 184 billion board feet consumed during the conflict, 70.1 billion, or 38 percent of the total, went to purely military use. At no time, according to postwar Forest Service analyses, did military use exceed aggregate civilian use from 1941 to 1945, even though the heavy demand for shipping containers in 1943 made for shortages in civilian supply. The lumber inventory had shrunk to 4.5 billion board feet by 1945, and the annual harvest and production had declined by 1.4 billion feet each year through the last three years of the war. In construction softwoods, the United States had become a net importer during the war, with nearly all imports coming from Canada. More telling was the serious depletion of high-quality standing timber and the suspension of most reforestation and other conservation programs during the war. Even though the crisis was surmounted with an eventually successful management program, it served as a reminder of the conservation principle that the American timber resource was a finite one requiring husbanding and careful renewal.

FURTHER READING: David Novick, Melvin Anshen, and W. C. Truppener, *Wartime Production Controls* (1949). U. S. Civilian Production Administration, Bureau of Demobilization, *Industrial Mobilization for War: History of the War Production Board and Predecessor Agencies, 1940–1945* (1947). U. S. Department of Agriculture, Forest Service, *Report of the Chief of the Forest Service* (1940–1946).

ALFRED M. BECK

WYOMING FORESTS

Forests cover 10 million acres of Wyoming, about one-sixth of its area. Nearly all of Wyoming's forests lie within mountainous regions, which are concentrated in the northwestern section of the state. Engelmann spruce and subalpine fir are found at the highest elevations. Lodgepole pine predominates in the middle ranges, and ponderosa pine and Douglas-fir grow in the lower elevations. The U. S. FOREST SERVICE administers 9 million acres of forestland in ten national forests and another 572,000 acres in the Thunder Basin National Grassland. The NATIONAL PARK SERVICE manages Grand Teton and Yellowstone national parks, totaling 2.3 million acres in Wyoming. In addition, the BUREAU OF LAND MANAGEMENT oversees approximately 18 million acres of range- and forestlands; Indian reservations contain another 1.3 million acres.

Early settlers used Wyoming's forests for fuel and building purposes. Railroad ties became an important forest product after the Union Pacific crossed the southern end of the state in the late 1860s. Often these ties came from lands owned and logged by the Union Pacific itself. Nineteenth-century lumber production in Wyoming remained under 20 million board feet annually and increased by 1911 to 33 million feet. Since 1935, lumber output has expanded gradually, and by 1962, Wyoming sawmills produced 116 million board feet, lodgepole pine being the principal sawtimber. In recent years, wood and wood products have ranked among the state's five leading industries. Grazing and recreational opportunities afforded by Wyoming's forests contribute to agriculture and tourism, two of the state's other leading industries.

Wyoming played a significant role in the early conservation movement. Yellowstone became the world's first national park in 1872. The national forest system began with the creation of Yellowstone Timberland Reserve in 1891. The Wapati Ranger Station, established near Cody in 1903, was the first facility of its kind. Devil's Tower, the first national monument, was established in 1906, and in 1912 the National Elk Refuge near Jackson became the first federal wildlife preserve.

Like most Westerners, the people of Wyoming were initially hostile toward the conservation movement, but through the years they have come to accept the principles of sustained yield and multiple use in regard to their forestlands. Wyoming's first state forester was appointed in 1952. Although there are no designated state forests in Wyoming, the State Forestry Division manages state-owned timberlands and cooperates with private owners and the Forest Service on fire and pest control projects. The Wyoming State Parks Commission was created in 1953 and in 1975 managed forty-eight parks and recreation areas totaling 157,000 acres.

BILL BRYANS

YARD, ROBERT STERLING (1861–1945)

Robert S. Yard gave a facile pen and a zealous conscience to America's early national park movement. Born in New York State on February 1, 1861, a Princeton graduate and a veteran of thirty-six years in journalism, Yard was asked by Stephen MATHER, a personal friend of long standing, to join the DEPARTMENT OF THE INTERIOR in 1914 as national park publicity chief. Yard's publicity helped establish the NATIONAL PARK SERVICE (where he became chief of the Educational Division) and expand the park system. Yard advertised the parks in a number of illustrated volumes, including *The National Parks Portfolio* (1916), *The Top of the Continent* (1917), *The Book of the National Parks* (1919), and *Our Federal Lands* (1928).

In 1919, Yard left the National Park Service and with Mather's financial backing established the National Parks Association in Washington, D.C. As general secretary and editor of the *National Parks Bulletin*, Yard defended the parks against commercial assaults until his retirement in 1936. He served on federal advisory boards (1925–1932). He was a founder of the WILDERNESS SOCIETY and served as its secretary and president until 1945. He was also editor of *Living Wilderness*.

Yard insisted that overuse was destroying the parks' wilderness character. Their mission should be educational, scientific, and inspirational, not recreational. He fought to bar from the National Park System areas unsuitable either for reasons of previous development, preexisting use rights, or inferior scenic quality. He argued that careless expansion made it harder to defend the system against exploitation.

Yard's purism brought him into conflict with the National Park Service, but preservationists in private organizations often agreed with his aversion to recreational developments. Since the 1930s, lay environmentalists and Park Service officials have increasingly shared his concern about overuse, but they have rendered a less favorable verdict on his opposition to the inclusion in the National Park System of such areas as the Everglades, Jackson Hole, and Kings Canyon.

Yard died on May 17, 1945, but the National Parks Association, renamed the NATIONAL PARKS AND CONSERVATION ASSOCIATION, still defends the parks.

FURTHER READING: Stephen Fox, *John Muir and His Legacy: The American Conservation Movement* (1981).

SUSAN R. SCHREPFER

YELLOWSTONE NATIONAL PARK

The Yellowstone National Park comprises more than 2.2 million acres, mostly in northwest Wyoming with slight overlaps into Montana and Idaho. The region had been the subject of rumors since mountain

An early-day visitor views tourist facilities and a peculiar rock formation in Yellowstone National Park. Forest History Society Lantern Slide Collection.

man John Colter's return from the northern Rockies in 1810. Thermal phenomena, a beautiful mountain lake, and a magnificent canyon entered into the unconfirmed reports. In 1870, the Washburn-Langford-Doane expedition of Montana residents entered the region and in the following year the Hayden Survey explored Yellowstone. Shortly thereafter, a combination of interests, including members of these expeditions and Northern Pacific Railroad officials, prompted the campaign to make the region into a national park.

On March 1, 1872, President Ulysses S. Grant signed the act of Congress creating Yellowstone National Park. Precedent had been established eight years before when Congress gave Yosemite and the Mariposa Big Tree Grove to California. However, Yellowstone became the first *national* park because it was surrounded by the federally administered territories of Idaho, Montana, and Wyoming and would be administered by the federal government. Yosemite was within the boundaries of a state and was given initially to California to administer.

The act creating the park placed Yellowstone under jurisdiction of the DEPARTMENT OF THE INTERIOR but failed to provide funds for administering it. Nathaniel P. Langford, the park's first superintendent, did not reside there. Poachers killed game, tourists damaged the thermal formations, and careless campers started forest fires. Gradually, Interior Department officials began to grapple with these threats to park integrity.

Philetus W. Norris, the second superintendent (1887–1882), posted hundreds of muslin signs listing the rules and regulations, thus beginning the never ending process of educating the public to fire prevention, game protection, and the inviolability of the thermal formations. The trouble was that no penalties existed for violations.

The situation in Yellowstone deteriorated until 1886 when the army assumed the task of policing the reservation although the Department of the Interior continued to fix policy. In 1894, Congress passed an Act to Protect the Birds and Other Animals in Yellowstone National Park (the Yellowstone National Park Protection Act) which enunciated violations and provided for a resident United States commissioner empowered to arrest violators and impose punishment. In that same year, Congress passed an act clarifying government policies toward concessionaires.

In these years, fish and wildlife policy began to concern Yellowstone's officials. Steps were taken to infuse new blood into the Yellowstone buffalo herd. Open season was held on predators, and not until 1934 were such animals as coyotes, wolves, and mountain lions protected. Control of the elk, which propagated so rapidly that they faced starvation in winter and damaged the browse and grass cover, posed a problem for park officials from the turn of the century on; it is not yet satisfactorily solved.

In the 1880s and 1890s, Yellowstone Park was the object of a long campaign to allow railroads into the park. In particular, a right-of-way was desired through the northeast quarter (unless it could be separated and returned to the public domain) to the mining camp of Cooke City. Such organizations as the BOONE AND CROCKETT CLUB and such conservationists as George Bird GRINNELL and Senator George Graham Vest of Missouri successfully fought off these raids.

Another park defender was Arnold Hague of the United States GEOLOGICAL SURVEY. In the course of his professional activities in the park, Hague became convinced that Yellowstone and its environs, most especially on the south and east, must be retained in their pristine wilderness state because of their heavy forest cover which, he explained, held back the water, releasing it steadily and gently into such rivers as the Yellowstone, Snake, and Green. He influenced the climate of opinion in Washington, D.C., that made possible the FOREST RESERVE ACT of 1891. An immediate result of this act was the removal from the public domain of extensive timberlands south and east of the park; ultimately these became national forests.

From 1886 until 1918, the army policed Yellowstone while the ARMY CORPS OF ENGINEERS constructed the park's excellent road system. In 1915, automobiles were allowed in the park. The following year, President Woodrow Wilson signed the bill creating the NATIONAL PARK SERVICE, and by 1918 the Service was entrenched in the park. In 1919, energetic, dedicated Horace ALBRIGHT became superintendent. He sought to bring as many visitors to the park as possible. He adjusted Yellowstone's services to the automobile tourists, most of whom at that time were also campers. An educational program including evening fireside lectures was inaugurated. The road system was improved; after 1925, much of this work was done by the Bureau of Public Roads.

Shortly after World War I, the park was threatened by reclamation interests. One plan was to segregate the southwest corner of the park and there construct a dam and reservoir, giving the farmers of central Idaho a steady source of water. Hardly had this plan been defeated before a new one called for damming Yellowstone Lake to divert its waters through tunnels south and southwest of the lake into the Snake River drainage. Then Montana interests decided that a dam at Fishing Bridge would stabilize the flow in the Yellowstone River, thus improving the prosperity of the Yellowstone Valley's inhabitants. All of these plans were defeated, but for nearly two decades they kept Yellowstone officials on their toes.

During World War II, Yellowstone received a respite from the increasing visitation, but following the conflict the park was deluged. Visitor facilities were hopelessly inadequate. The Mission 66 program, designed in 1955 with the intention of upgrading national park facilities by the service's fiftieth anniversary, resulted in the building of Canyon Village and Grant Village, better roads, new bridges, and other improved visitor services. Still, as Yellowstone National Park approached its twelfth decade, constantly increasing visitation posed major problems for authorities, problems that needed to be solved if the service was to succeed in retaining the park in something at least approaching the "natural condition" specified by the Act of 1872.

FURTHER READING: Richard A. Bartlett, *Nature's Yellowstone* (1974). Aubrey L. Haines, *The Yellowstone Story*, 2 vols. (1977). H. Duane Hampton, *How the U.S. Cavalry Saved the National Parks* (1971). Donald C. Swain, *Wilderness Defender: Horace M. Albright and Conservation* (1970).

RICHARD A. BARTLETT

YOSEMITE NATIONAL PARK

From Horace Greeley, who pronounced Yosemite Valley "the greatest marvel of the continent," to the millions of tourists who threatened to love the park to death in the 1970s, Yosemite National Park has always inspired ardor in its admirers. It is not more spectacular than the Grand Canyon nor more startling than Yellowstone, yet it epitomizes the wonders of the Sierra Nevada of California, John MUIR's "range of light," so splendidly that it claims a special place in the hearts of many park lovers.

Its centerpiece is the great Yosemite Valley, a seven-mile-long, mile-wide, U-shaped valley, gouged more than 2,000 feet deep out of solid granite by river and glacier. Down its cliffs plunge thundering falls of sparkling water and along the valley floor the icy Merced River meanders through meadows and forests. Discovered in 1851 by the Indian-hunters of California's Mariposa Battalion, the valley's sheer, glacier-polished cliffs, spectacular domes, and incomparable waterfalls drew national interest. Although the battalion's commander, despairing of ever capturing Chief Tenaya and his Yosemite (meaning "great grizzly bear") Indians among the cliffs and canyons, called the valley "a hell of a place," another expedition member described a more common emotion when he wrote that the valley's grandeur moved him to tears. Congress was impressed by such reports, and in 1864 it turned over to the state of California about forty square miles covering the valley and the nearby

Mariposa Grove of sequoia for "public use, resort, and recreation."

Yosemite Valley did not prosper as a state park. Not wishing to spend money on it, the state allowed settlers in, and their fields, fences, and buildings altered its character and made access difficult for visitors, despite the efforts of Acting Superintendent Galen Clark. In 1890, pioneer conservationists John Muir, Frederick Law OLMSTED, Sr., Robert Underwood Johnson, and others persuaded Congress to create a 1,512 square-mile Yosemite National Park, with the result that the neglected state park was surrounded by a neglected national park. Unsatisfactory from every standpoint, the double-park situation nevertheless lasted until 1906, when a pragmatic alliance of conservationists and railroaders eager to build a passenger line to the valley worked out arrangements for the state to return the valley to the federal government for inclusion in the national park.

Jagged granite peaks, tumbling streams, and forests of pine and groves of giant sequoia (*Sequoiadendron giganteum*) made the park seem more serene and secure than was actually the case. Its only security lay in its uselessness to the entrepreneurs of a growing American economy. Sometimes, business interests worked for the park, as when the railroaders supported inclusion of the valley in the national park, but more often private interests conflicted with the park's purposes. Farmers in the valley and sheepherders, lumbermen, and hunters in the high country were gradually brought under control by an undermanned and underfinanced park administration, but it was nearly impossible to do anything about the legal poachers whose activities were supported by Congress. In 1905, for example, Congress removed from the national park over 400 square miles including several choice areas sought by lumber and mining interests.

The worst attack on the park, however, came not from private interests but from the City of San Francisco. In 1901, the city staked a claim to the park's Hetch Hetchy Valley, often described as a smaller Yosemite, for a reservoir. After a twelve-year national battle that split the young CONSERVATION MOVEMENT into "utilitarian" and "preservationist" wings, Congress in 1913 passed the Raker Act giving the city what it wanted. Muir and others who demanded the protection of the valley as a natural cathedral were denounced on the Senate floor as monsters who "would rather have the babes of the community suffering anguish and perishing for want of sufficient water than destroy something that they may go once in many years and gaze

upon in order to satisfy their aesthetic and exquisite taste for natural beauty."

The point thus colorfully stated was indeed central. The preservationist argument *was* elitist and intangible; that of the city fitted the prevailing definition of conservation as planned development. Unable to defend the inaccessible valley as a tourist attraction, Muir and his friends were defeated by the argument that the greatest good of the greatest number would be served by making it a reservoir.

As the Hetch Hetchy issue demonstrates, man's relationship to the wilderness has been a central theme of Yosemite's history. The 1890 Yosemite Act directs the secretary of the interior to preserve "in their natural condition" all of the "timber, mineral deposits, natural curiosities, or wonders" of the park so that they can be enjoyed by the tourists who come, in the words of the 1864 act, for "public use, resort and recreation." In short, the park is to be a wilderness accessible to tourists. Over the years, it has become more and more clear that these two goals are in conflict.

In the early years, the park's rugged terrain and primitive accommodations discouraged all but the most hardy visitors. Until the Yosemite Valley Railroad was completed in 1907, the only access to the valley was by foot, horseback, or stagecoach over primitive toll roads, and hotel facilities ranged from bad to awful. Thereafter, however, things changed rapidly. The first automobiles were admitted in 1913, the Tioga Road giving access to the high country was acquired by the park in 1915, and an all-weather road up the Merced Canyon was completed in 1926. Other tourist facilities developed along with improved transportation. When David A. Curry and his wife began renting tent cabins to visitors in 1899, there were almost two dozen concessionaires operating in the valley alone. Over the years, Curry gradually bought out most of these others, and by 1925, when the Curry Company merged with its last major competitor to form the Yosemite Park and Curry Company, he had achieved a near-monopoly. The NATIONAL PARK SERVICE, created in 1916, encouraged this process on the theory that it was easier to regulate one company than several.

Improved transportation and facilities brought an influx of tourists who overcrowded Yosemite Valley as early as the 1930s. By 1979, the park had thirty miles of paved roads, more than 1,300 buildings, a golf course, and many other facilities catering to almost 3 million annual visitors. Advance reservations were necessary even to camp in the valley, and other areas of the park, previously less popular, were becoming crowded as well. The National Park Service tried to reduce man's impact on the park by halting the feeding of the bears in 1941, by stopping the nightly "firefall" from Glacier Point to the valley floor in 1968, and by banning private cars and developing a shuttlebus system in the valley in 1970–1971, but the struggle was a losing one.

Just how far the pendulum had swung toward development rather than wilderness became clear in 1974, when the National Park Service and the Music Corporation of America, successor to the Yosemite Park and Curry Company, announced a master plan for the park that included a convention complex and other "improvements." Outraged by this violation of the park's purposes, the NATIONAL PARKS AND CONSERVATION ASSOCIATION led a strong campaign against the proposed plan and compelled the park service to withdraw it and to begin a five-year process of developing a new plan based largely on public hearings and questionnaires. The new plan, announced in December 1979, recommended a major effort to reduce man's impact while still keeping the park accessible to visitors. Although still critical of some features of the new proposal, most conservation organizations welcomed it as a definite improvement over both the 1974 plan and current practices.

Like its past, the future of Yosemite lies in the ability of its guardians to find viable compromises between the wilderness and the tourists. Difficult though this is, it is in reality only a microcosm of the even broader problem faced by American society as a whole: whether man can learn to live in his world without so altering it as to make it uninhabitable.

FURTHER READING: Francis P. Farquhar, *History of the Sierra Nevada* (1965). John Ise, *Our National Park Policy: A Critical History* (1961). Holway R. Jones, *John Muir and the Sierra Club: The Battle for Yosemite* (1965). Alfred Runte, *National Parks: The American Experience* (1979). Carl P. Russell, *One Hundred Years in Yosemite: The Story of a Great Park and Its Friends* (rev. ed., 1947).

KENDRICK A. CLEMENTS

Z

ZAHNISER, HOWARD CLINTON
(1906–1964)

Howard Zahniser was born on February 25, 1906, in Franklin, Pennsylvania. A minister's son, he grew up in the Allegheny River valley where he developed what were to be lifelong interests in nature and linguistic expression. With a degree in the humanities from Greenville College, Illinois, he began a brief career as teacher and newspaper reporter. Then in 1930, he entered government service with the U. S. BIOLOGICAL SURVEY. For twelve years, his dual interests in nature and writing found expression in the bureau's information division where his duties included research, writing, and editing. In 1942, he moved to the U. S. Department of Agriculture's Bureau of Plant Industry, Soils, and Agricultural Engineering as director of its publication and research-reporting program. Zahniser refined his literary skills on the job, regularly contributing essays and reviews to conservation-oriented journals. He became more and more concerned with North American wilderness issues in particular. This growing concern drew Zahniser to the crystallizing ideas of Robert MARSHALL, Olaus Johan MURIE, Benton MACKAYE, and Harvey Broome, the driving forces behind the newly formed WILDERNESS SOCIETY.

In 1945, Zahniser left government service to become executive secretary (later executive director) of the society and editor of its journal, *The Living Wilderness.* Under Zahniser's direction, *The Living Wilderness* assumed an ever growing role in publicizing wilderness issues and supporting an emerging national consensus for wildland protection, an effort perhaps best reflected in the successful, decade-long effort to block hydroelectric power development in Dinosaur National Monument. With the protracted Dinosaur debate, Zahniser emerged as an important spokesman for conservationists in Washington, effectively stating his case in both formal public hearings and informal congressional contacts. He was soon a major strategist for wildlands preservation. His attention focused more and more on the need for a National Wilderness Preservation System protected by statute. From the resolution of the Dinosaur controversy in 1956 until his death in 1964, Zahniser labored relentlessly for passage of a Wilderness Act. Through writings and addresses to citizens' groups, he sought to rally public opinion. Through seemingly endless congressional testimony and close cooperation with environmentally oriented political leaders, he helped keep the idea alive in Washington. When in 1964 Congress passed the Wilderness Act, both the law's conceptual framework and much of its specific language were directly attributable to Zahniser. Unfortunately, Zahniser died on May 5, 1964, shortly

741

before final passage of the act. This important legislation stands in tribute to his many contributions to American conservation, and he has often been called the "Father of the Wilderness Act."

To Zahniser, wilderness politics lay at the core of broader literary and conservation interests. He was an organizer of the Natural Resources Council of America in 1946 (serving as chairman in 1948–1949), president of the Thoreau Society in 1956, a member of the secretary of the interior's Advisory Committee on Conservation from 1951 to 1954, vice-chairman of the Citizen's Committee for Natural Resources in 1955, and honorary vice-president of the SIERRA CLUB after 1952. He maintained membership in many other outdoor and conservation organizations. He received a Litt.D. from Greenville College in 1957.

CRANDALL BAY

ZON, RAPHAEL (1874–1956)

Raphael Zon was born in Simbirsk, Russia, on December 1, 1874. While a student in medical and natural sciences at the University of Kazan he was arrested for political activity but escaped before the sentence could be carried out. He resided briefly in Germany and Belgium before finding employment in the British Museum, London. In the late 1890s, he came to the United States. In his newly adopted nation, Zon developed his formidable talents to become one of America's premier forest researchers. His marriage to Anna Puziriskaya, a fellow student at Kazan University, produced two sons, Leo and Henry.

Zon studied forestry at Cornell University under Bernhard E. FERNOW and Filibert Roth. Fernow's recommendation helped Zon gain a student assistantship in the Special Investigations Section of the U. S. Bureau of Forestry. Gifford PINCHOT, chief of the bureau, became one of the important influences upon Zon's career. Promoted to assistant forest expert and forest assistant, Zon advocated the appointment of trained researchers to each national forest staff in order to place management on a scientific basis.

As head of the Office of Silvics from 1907 to 1914 and of the Office of Forest Investigations from 1914 to 1923, Zon called for freeing research investigation from administrative snarls. Zon played a leading role in the establishment of a system of forest experiment stations beginning with that at Coconino National Forest at Fort Valley, Arizona, in 1908. The stations provided useful information on the improvement of tree growth, the disposal of slash, and the relationship between forests and streamflow. Zon was also a prime mover in the creation of the Forest Products Laboratory in Madison, Wisconsin. He aided in the writing of the "Capper Report" (1920) calling for a comprehensive national forest policy. He served as editor of the *Proceedings* of the SOCIETY OF AMERICAN FORESTERS and in 1923 succeeded Bernhard Fernow as editor of the *Journal of Forestry*.

From 1923 to 1944, Zon was director of the Lake States Forest Experiment Station in St. Paul, Minnesota. He devoted himself to the task of planning and overseeing federal forest research in the geographic region including the states of Michigan, Wisconsin, and Minnesota. The station staff under Zon's leadership amassed an impressive record of practical research projects and publications ranging in content from forest protection and forest economics to forest management. These investigations often stimulated state forest activity. One of the most significant investigative projects led to the creation of a shelterbelt of trees along the 99th meridian from Texas to the Canadian border.

After his retirement from the U. S. FOREST SERVICE, Zon pursued a number of writing projects in connection with the United Nations Relief and Rehabilitation Administration, the Food and Agricultural Organization, and the journal *Unasylva*. Zon died on October 27, 1956. Through articles in both scholarly and popular media, through correspondence with other friends of forestry, and through his influence with Forest Service associates, Zon consistently championed forestland policies that combined a humane concern for the public good with a tough-minded insistence on rational management principles.

FURTHER READING: Norman J. Schmaltz, "Raphael Zon: Forest Researcher," *Journal of Forest History* 24 (Jan. 1980): 24-39; (Apr. 1980): 86-97. Among Zon's key writings are: "The Future Use of Land in the United States," United States Department of Agriculture, Forest Service *Circular* 159 (1909): 1-15; "Toward Fuller Use of All Land," *Land Policy Review* 7 (Fall 1944): 17-21; "Research Methods in the Study of the Forest Environment" (with Carlos G. Bates), United States Department of Agriculture *Bulletin* No. 1059 (1922): 1-209; *Forest Resources of the World* (with William N. Sparhawk) (2 vols., 1923); "Forest Research in the United States Department of Agriculture," Food and Agricultural Organization *Preliminary Report* (1951): 1-65; *Forests and Water in the Light of Scientific Investigation* (1927); "The Human Side of Land Use," *Journal of Forestry* 37 (Sept. 1939): 735-737; "The Search for Forest Facts," *American Forests and Forest Life* 36 (July 1930): 421-423, 482.

NORMAN J. SCHMALTZ

APPENDIX I

The National Forests of the United States

The following listing has been compiled from the *Establishment and Modification of National Forest Boundaries: A Chronologic Record, 1891–1973*, by S. Lo Jacono (U. S. Forest Service, Division of Engineering, 1973); the U. S. Forest Service's *National Forest Areas* (1905–1966) and its sequel, *National Forest System*, published annually since 1966; annual reports of the chief, U. S. Forest Service and its predecessors, the Division of Forestry (1886–1901) and the Bureau of Forestry (1902–1904); the U. S. Geological Survey's *Annual Reports* (1897–1900); and from information supplied by the Office of Administrative Management, U. S. Forest Service, Washington, D.C.

The listing shows the establishment, change of name, or discontinuation of every forest reserve and national forest created since 1891, along with the legal citation for each action and the effective date of each proclamation, executive order, public law, or other order. In 1907, an act of Congress redesignated forest reserves as national forests.

The acreage for each forest is given at the time of establishment and on September 30, 1981. Until 1913, only the gross acreage is documented even though private and state lands were within forest boundaries. After 1913, all lands except those administered by the Forest Service are noted under "other." Purchase units are not included. Only changes in the name of the forest or its discontinuation either as a name or as a forest due to consolidation, transfer, or abolishment are shown. Thus the name of a forest can be traced but not necessarily its boundaries, which in any case were usually subject to numerous minor modifications. Details of such boundary adjustments, additions, and eliminations may be found in Jacono's publication.

There are four levels of organization within the Forest Service: national headquarters, regional offices, forest supervisor's offices, and ranger districts. Since 1960, the supervisor's offices have been the basic long-range planning unit. They also provide supervisory, administrative, training, and specialist assistance to the ranger districts. The size of the supervisory administrative units has often been adjusted for efficiency and effectiveness. In most cases, two or more forests are administratively combined and assigned to one supervisor's office. Only one forest, the Tongass in Alaska, has been split; it is presently administered by three supervisory units. Since these combinations do not change the formal individual names of the forests, or their boundaries, or the goods and services produced, there has been no need for congressional action regarding them. The twenty-four administrative combinations listed here are those in effect as of 1981. Previous adjustments are not listed unless they involved presidential or congressional action.

In 1981, there were a total of 155 national forests administered from 121 supervisors' offices. These forests totaled 223,378,106 acres, 186,441,602 acres of which were national forest lands.

Definitions

EO   Executive Order. A presidential order having the force of law, usually dealing with the administrative details of the activities and services of the executive departments and independent establishments.

FR   *Federal Register*. Created by the Federal Register Act of 1935 and consisting of daily publication containing executive orders and proclamations and the rules and regulations of the executive agencies that have general applicability and legal effect.

PLO Public Land Order. An order regarding public lands made by the secretary of the interior under the authority of EO 9146 (1942), EO 9337 (1943), EO 10355 (1952), and the Federal Land Policy and Management Act of 1976.

Proc Proclamation. A presidential order with the force of law usually dealing with matters of general interest.

Stat *U. S. Statutes at Large*. Includes acts and resolutions of Congress as well as presidential proclamations and agreements. The first number refers to the volume and the second to the page. Thus, 36 Stat 2729 reads volume 36, page 2729.

Name, Date Established, History	Citation	Acreage When Established or Earliest Documentation			Acreage as of September 1981		
		NF Land	Other	Total	NF Land	Other	Total
Absaroka, Montana							
1902 Sept 4 Established.	Proc 32 Stat 2027			1,311,600			
1903 Jan 29 Consolidated with Yellowstone; name discontinued.	Proc 32 Stat 2030						
1908 July 1 Reestablished from part of Yellowstone and all of Crazy Mountain.	EO 875			980,440			
1932 Feb 17 Part of Beartooth added.	EO 5800						
1945 July 1 Entire forest divided between Gallatin and Lewis and Clark.	PLO 305 11-FR 249						
Afognak Forest and Fish Culture, Alaska							
1892 Dec 24 Established.	Proc 27 Stat 1052	"Acreage unknown at time of establishment" (1893 Chief's Report); 403,640 in 1905					
1908 July 1 Combined with Chugach; name discontinued.	EO 908						
Alabama, Alabama							
1918 Jan 15 Established.	Proc 1423 40 Stat 1740	36,418	29,590	66,008			
1936 June 19 Name changed to Black Warrior.	Proc 2178 49 Stat 3526 1-FR 645						
Alamo, New Mexico							
1908 July 1 Established by consolidation of Guadalupe and Sacramento	EO 908			1,164,906			
1919 July 1 Entire forest transferred to Lincoln; name discontinued.	EO 2633						

Name, Date Established, History	Citation	Acreage When Established or Earliest Documentation			Acreage as of September 1981		
		NF Land	Other	Total	NF Land	Other	Total
Alexander Archipelago, Alaska							
1902 Aug 20 Established.	Proc 32 Stat 2025			4,506,240			
1908 July 1 Combined with Tongass; name discontinued.	EO 908						
Allegheny, Pennsylvania							
1923 Sept 24 Established.	Proc 1675 43 Stat 1925	73,019	666,258	739,277	509,163	233,530	742,693
Angeles, California							
1908 July 1 Established from entire San Bernardino and parts of Santa Barbara and San Gabriel.	EO 846			1,350,900	653,846	39,821	693,667
Angelina, Texas							
1936 Oct 13 Established.	Proc 2202 50 Stat 1780 1-FR 1601	134,917	253,783	388,700			
1936 Combined administratively with Davy Crockett, Sabine, and Sam Houston, known as National Forests in Texas.					154,916	247,315	402,231
Apache, Arizona							
1908 July 1 Established from portion of the Black Mesa.	EO 876			1,302,711			
1974 Combined administratively, with Sitgreaves, known as Apache-Sitgreaves.			Ariz. N. Mex.	1,187,478 614,202 1,801,680	39,208 36,017 75,225	1,226,686 650,219 1,876,905	
Apalachicola, Florida							
1936 May 13 Established.	Proc 2169 49 Stat 3516 1-FR 408	198,750	107,645	306,395	558,871	73,129	632,000
1936 Combined administratively with Ocala and Osceola, known as National Forests in Florida.							
Aquarius, Utah							
1903 Oct 24 Established.	Proc 33 Stat 2320			639,000			
1908 July 1 Name changed to Powell.	EO 908						
Arapaho, Colorado							
1908 July 1 Established from part of Medicine Bow, Pikes Peak, and Leadville.	EO 893			796,815			
1930 May 26 Part of Leadville added.	Proc 1906 46 Stat 3021						
1975 Combined administratively with Roosevelt, known as Arapaho-Roosevelt.					1,025,065	131,948	1,157,013
Arkansas, Arkansas							
1907 Dec 18 Established.	Proc 786 35 Stat 2167			1,073,955			
1926 Apr 29 Name changed to Ouachita.	EO 4436						

Name, Date Established, History		Citation	Acreage When Established or Earliest Documentation			Acreage as of September 1981		
			NF Land	Other	Total	NF Land	Other	Total
Ashland, Oregon								
1893 Sept 28	Established.	Proc 28 Stat 1243			18,560			
1908 July 1	Entire forest combined with other forestlands to establish the Crater; name discontinued.	EO 867						
Ashley, Utah and Wyoming						Utah		
1908 July 1	Established from part of the Uinta.	EO 884	Utah		947,490	1,288,422	12,486	1,300,908
			Wyo.		4,596	Wyo. 96,277	8,424	104,701
					952,086	1,384,699	20,910	1,405,609
Baboquivari, Arizona								
1906 Nov 5	Established.	Proc 34 Stat 3251			126,720			
1908 July 1	Combined with Huachuca and Tumacacori to establish the Garces; name discontinued.	EO 908						
Baker City, Oregon								
1904 Feb 5	Established.	Proc 33 Stat 2331			52,480			
1906 Mar 15	Portions combined with Blue Mountains; remainder restored to public domain; name discontinued.	Proc 34 Stat 3194						
Battlement, Colorado								
1908 July 1	Established from part of Battlement Mesa.	EO 894			753,720			
1924 Mar 11	Name changed to Grand Mesa.	EO 3970						
Battlement Mesa, Colorado								
1892 Dec 24	Established.	Proc 27 Stat 1053			858,240			
1908 July 1	Part combined with Holy Cross; part established as Battlement; name discontinued.	EO 870, 894						
Bear Lodge, Wyoming								
1907 Mar 1	Established.	Proc 34 Stat 3287			136,784			
1908 July 1	Combined with part of Black Hills to establish Sundance; name discontinued.	EO 850						
Bear River, Utah								
1906 May 28	Established by combining Logan and other lands.	Proc 34 Stat 3206			267,920			
1908 July 1	Part combined with Pocatello, remainder to establish Cache; name discontinued.	EO 801, 802						
Beartooth, Montana								
1908 July 1	Established from part of Yellowstone and entire Pryor Mountains.	EO 896			685,293			
1932 Feb 17	Entire forest divided between Absaroka and Custer.	EO 5800, 5801						

Name, Date Established, History	Citation	Acreage When Established or Earliest Documentation			Acreage as of September 1981		
		NF Land	Other	Total	NF Land	Other	Total
Beaver, Utah							
1906 Jan 24 Established.	Proc 34 Stat 3189			261,593			
1908 July 1 Combined with Fillmore; name discontinued.	EO 826						
Beaverhead, Montana							
1908 July 1 Established from parts of Big Hole, Bitter Root, and Hell Gate.	EO 877		Mont. Ida.	1,506,680 304,140 1,810,820			
1931 Dec 16 Land added from Madison.	EO 5757				2,120,464	77,745	2,198,209
Bellevue-Savanna, Illinois							
1926 June 15 Name changed from Savanna.	EO 4458	10,710		10,710			
1954 July 15 Abolished.	PLO 982 19-FR 4499						
Benning, Georgia							
1924 Oct 3 Established from part of Fort Benning Military Reservation	EO 4081	78,560		78,560			
1927 Dec 2 EO 4081 rescinded.	EO 4776						
Bienville, Mississippi							
1936 June 15 Established.	Proc 2175 49 Stat 3521 1-FR 606	99,679	283,141	382,820			
1936 Combined administratively with DeSoto, Holly Springs, Homochitto, known as National Forests in Mississippi.					178,403	204,418	382,821
Big Belt, Montana							
1905 Oct 3 Established.	Proc 34 Stat 3153			630,260			
1908 July 1 Part combined with Gallatin; remainder to Helena; name discontinued.	EO 879, 881						
Big Burros, New Mexico							
1907 Feb 6 Established.	Proc 34 Stat 3274			156,780			
1908 June 18 Combined with Gila; name discontinued.	Proc 811 35 Stat 2190						
Big Hole, Montana and Idaho							
1906 Nov 5 Established.	Proc 34 Stat 3254		Mont. Ida.	1,612,960 304,140 1,917,100			
1908 July 1 Lands divided among Beaverhead, Deerlodge, and Bitterroot; name discontinued.	EO 877, 880, 883						
Big Horn, Wyoming							
1897 Feb 22 Established, effective March 1, 1898.	Proc 29 Stat 909			1,198,080			
1908 July 1 Name changed to Bighorn.	EO 908						
Bighorn, Wyoming							
1908 July 1 Name changed from Big Horn.	EO 908			1,151,680	1,107,670	7,501	1,115,171

Name, Date Established, History	Citation	Acreage When Established or Earliest Documentation			Acreage as of September 1981		
		NF Land	Other	Total	NF Land	Other	Total
Bitter Root, Idaho and Montana							
1897 Feb 22 Established, effective March 1, 1898.	Proc 29 Stat 899			4,147,200			
1908 July 1 Name changed to Bitterroot; lands added from Big Hole and Hell Gate; lands transferred to Beaverhead, Clearwater, Nezperce, and Salmon.	EO 883						
Bitterroot, Idaho and Montana							
1908 July 1 Name changed from Bitter Root; lands added from Big Hole and Hell Gate.	EO 883			1,180,900			
1934 Oct 29 Part of Selway added.	EO 6889				Ida.		
					464,165	52	464,217
					Mont.		
					1,113,718	74,502	1,188,220
					1,577,883	74,554	1,652,437
Black Hills, South Dakota and Wyoming							
1897 Feb 22 Established, effective March 1, 1898.	Proc 29 Stat 902			967,680			
1915 July 1 Entire Sundance added.	EO 2161				S.D.		
1954 July 1 Entire Harney added.	PLO 1016 19-FR 6500				1,061,104	266,930	1,328,034
					Wyo.		
					174,743	26,388	201,131
					1,235,847	293,318	1,529,165
Black Mesa, Arizona							
1898 Aug 17 Established.	Proc 30 Stat 1782			1,658,880			
1908 July 1 Land divided among Sitgreaves, Tonto, Apache, and Coconino; name discontinued.	Proc 818 EO 868, 869, 876						
Black Warrior, Alabama							
1936 June 19 Name changed from Alabama.	Proc 2178 49 Stat 3526 1-FR 645	149,392	411,212	560,604			
1936 Combined administratively with Conecuh and Talladega, known as National Forests in Alabama.							
1942 June 6 Name changed to William B. Bankhead	56 Stat 327						
Blackfeet, Montana							
1908 July 1 Established from part of Lewis and Clark.	EO 834			1,956,340			
1935 June 22 Entire forest divided between Flathead and Kootenai; name discontinued.	EO 7082						

Name, Date Established, History	Citation	Acreage When Established or Earliest Documentation			Acreage as of September 1981		
		NF Land	Other	Total	NF Land	Other	Total
Blue Mountains, Oregon							
1906 Mar 15 Established from part of Baker City plus other lands.	Proc 34 Stat 3194			2,675,620			
1907 Mar 2 Maury Mountain added.	Proc 34 Stat 3302						
1908 July 1 Land distributed among Whitman, Malheur, Umatilla, and Deschutes; name discontinued.	EO 813, 814, 815, 816						
Boise, Idaho							
1908 July 1 Established from part of Sawtooth.	EO 857			1,147,360			
1944 April 1 Payette (old) added.	PLO 217 9-FR 3655				2,645,967	313,752	2,959,719
Bonneville, Wyoming							
1908 July 1 Established from part of Yellowstone.	EO 874			1,627,840			
1916 July 1 Entire forest transferred to Washakie; name discontinued.	Proc 1338 39 Stat 1784						
Boone, North Carolina							
1920 Jan 16 Established.	Proc 1553 41 Stat 1784	95,394	396,946	492,340			
1921 Mar 25 Entire forest transferred to Pisgah; name discontinued.	Proc 1591 42 Stat 2234						
Bridger, Wyoming							
1911 July 1 Established from part of Bonneville.	Proc 1164 37 Stat 1713			577,850			
1923 May 14 Entire forest transferred to Wyoming; name discontinued.	EO 3842						
1941 Mar 10 Name changed from Wyoming.	EO 8709 6-FR 1400	1,699,095	11,127	1,710,222			
1973 Combined administratively with Teton, known as Bridger-Teton.					1,733,575	11,151	1,744,726
Bull Run, Oregon							
1892 June 17 Established.	Proc 27 Stat 1028			142,080			
1908 July 1 Entire forest combined with part of Cascade to establish Oregon; name discontinued.	EO 864						
Cabinet, Idaho and Montana							
1907 Mar 2 Established.	Proc 34 Stat 3295		Ida. Mont.	494,560 1,566,000 2,060,960			
1954 July 1 Entire forest divided among Kaniksu, Kootenai, and Lolo.	PLO 965 19-FR 3007						

Name, Date Established, History	Citation	Acreage When Established or Earliest Documentation			Acreage as of September 1981		
		NF Land	Other	Total	NF Land	Other	Total
Cache, Idaho and Utah							
1908 July 1 Established from part of Bear River.	EO 802		Ida. Utah	276,640 257,200 533,840			
1915 July 1 Entire Pocatello added.	EO 2179				Ida.		
1973 Idaho portion combined administratively with Caribou, known as Caribou. Utah portion combined with Wasatch, known as Wasatch-Cache.					263,941 Utah 416,045 679,986	500 538,019 538,519	264,441 954,064 1,218,505
Calaveras Bigtree, California							
1954 May 11 Established as authorized in P.L. 237, approved Feb 18, 1909; administratively combined with Stanislaus.	35 Stat 626	379		379	380	0	380
California, California							
1908 July 1 Established from parts of Trinity and Stony Creek.	EO 907			976,949			
1932 July 12 Name changed to Mendocino.	EO 5885						
Caribbean, Puerto Rico							
1935 June 4 Name changed from Luquillo.	EO 7059-A	13,483	52,467	65,950	27,846	27,819	55,665
Caribou, Idaho, Wyoming, and Utah							
1907 Jan 15 Established.	Proc 34 Stat 3267		Ida. Wyo.	733,000 7,740 740,740			
1973 Combined administratively with Idaho portion of Cache, known as Caribou.					Ida. 972,855 Utah 6,955 Wyo. 7,913 987,723	94,548 1,985 1,701 98,234	1,067,403 8,940 9,614 1,085,957
Carson, New Mexico							
1908 July 1 Established from entire Taos and part of Jemez.	EO 848			946,480	1,391,722	98,872	1,490,594
Cascade, Oregon							
1907 Mar 2 Name changed from Cascade Range.	Proc 34 Stat 3300			5,886,840			
1933 July 1 Entire forest combined with Santiam to establish the Willamette.	EO 6104						
Cascade Range, Oregon							
1893 Sept 28 Established.	Proc 28 Stat 1240			4,492,800			
1907 Mar 2 Name changed to Cascade and land added.	Proc 34 Stat 3300						

Name, Date Established, History	Citation	Acreage When Established or Earliest Documentation			Acreage as of September 1981		
		NF Land	Other	Total	NF Land	Other	Total

Cassia, Idaho

1905 June 12 Established.	Proc 34 Stat 3099			326,160			
1908 July 1 Combined with Raft River to establish the Minidoka; name discontinued.	EO 908						

Cave Hills, South Dakota

1904 Mar 5 Established.	Proc 33 Stat 2335			23,360			
1908 July 1 Added to Sioux; name discontinued.	EO 908						

Challis, Idaho

1908 July 1 Established from parts of Salmon River and Sawtooth.	EO 840			1,161,040			
1938 Oct 8 Part of Lemhi added.	EO 7986 3-FR 2435				2,463,719	19,936	2,483,655

Charleston, Nevada

1906 Nov 5 Established.	Proc 34 Stat 3252			149,165			
1908 July 1 Added to Moapa; name discontinued.	EO 908						

Chattahoochee, Georgia

1936 July 9 Established from parts of Cherokee, Nantahala, and other lands.	Proc 2184 50 Stat 1739 1-FR 776	514,894	650,106	1,165,000			
1971 Combined administratively with Oconee, known as Chattahoochee and Oconee.					746,158	825,632	1,571,790

Chelan, Washington

1908 July 1 Established from part of Washington.	EO 823			2,492,500			
1921 July 1 Entire Okanogan added.	EO 3380						
1955 Mar 23 Name changed to Okanogan.	PLO 1101 20-FR 1890						

Chequamegon, Wisconsin

1933 Nov 13 Established; Moquach and Flambeau units of the Nicolet included.	Proc 2061 48 Stat 1716	223,043	408,399	631,442	844,641	204,705	1,049,346

Cherokee, Tennessee and North Carolina

1920 June 14 Established.	Proc 1568 41 Stat 1798	Tenn. 113,724	252,868	366,592	N.C. 327		327
		Ga. 60,234	356,022	416,256	Tenn. 633,215	581,305	1,204,520
		N.C.	44,851	44,851	623,542	581,305	1,204,847
		173,958	653,741	827,699			

Name, Date Established, History	Citation	Acreage When Established or Earliest Documentation			Acreage as of September 1981		
		NF Land	Other	Total	NF Land	Other	Total
Chesnimnus, Oregon							
1905 May 12 Established.	Proc 34 Stat 3022			220,320			
1907 Mar 1 Combined with the Wallowa to create the Imnaha; name discontinued.	Proc 34 Stat 3284						
Cheyenne, Wyoming							
1908 July 1 Established from part of Medicine Bow and entire Crow Creek.	EO 861			617,932			
1910 July 1 Portion eliminated; name of remainder changed to Medicine Bow.	Proc 1067 36 Stat 2726						
Chippewa, Minnesota							
1928 June 22 Name changed from Minnesota.	EO 4913	191,785	120,874	312,659	661,161	938,488	1,599,649
Chiricahua, Arizona							
1902 July 30 Established.	Proc 32 Stat 2019			169,600			
1908 July 1 Entire Peloncillo added.	EO 908						
1917 July 1 Entire forest transferred to Coronado; name discontinued.	EO 2630						
Choctawhatchee, Florida							
1908 Nov 27 Established.	Proc 825 35 Stat 2208			467,606			
1911 July 1 Combined with Ocala to establish Florida; name discontinued.	Proc 1122 37 Stat 1678						
1927 Nov 10 Name changed from Florida.	EO 4756	184,449	183,599	368,048			
1940 June 27 Entire forest transferred to War Department.	54 Stat 655						
1980 June 19 Lands returned to Forest Service.	PLO 5730	632		632	675		675
Chugach, Alaska							
1907 July 23 Established.	Proc 35 Stat 2149			4,960,000			
1908 July 1 Afognak added.	EO 908				6,236,040	341,261	6,577,301
Cibola, New Mexico							
1931 Dec 3 Name changed from Manzano.	EO 5752	1,651,031	638,069	2,289,100	1,634,112	474,706	2,108,818
Clark, Missouri							
1939 Sept 11 Established.	Proc 2363 54 Stat 2657 4-FR 3908	824,118	1,147,767	1,971,885			
1973 July 1 Combined administratively with Mark Twain, known as Clark and Mark Twain.							
1976 Feb 17 Name changed to Mark Twain.	Proc 4415						
Clearwater, Idaho							
1908 July 1 Established from parts of Coeur d'Alene and Bitter Root.	EO 842			2,687,860			
1934 Oct 29 Part of Selway added.	EO 6889				1,688,687	76,858	1,765,545

Name, Date Established, History	Citation	Acreage When Established or Earliest Documentation			Acreage as of September 1981		
		NF Land	Other	Total	NF Land	Other	Total
Cleveland, California							
1908 July 1 Established by consolidation of San Jacinto and Trabuco Canyon.	EO 908			1,904,826	420,033	146,748	566,781
Cochetopa, Colorado							
1908 July 1 Name changed from Cochetopah.	EO 892			932,890			
1930 May 26 Land from Leadville added.	Proc 1907 46 Stat 3021						
1944 July 1 Entire forest distributed among Gunnison, Rio Grande, and San Isabel.	PLO 258 10-FR 1243						
Cochetopah, Colorado							
1905 June 13 Established.	Proc 34 Stat 3101			1,133,330			
1908 July 1 Name changed to Cochetopa; land added from Leadville; lands transferred to Rio Grande, Leadville, and Gunnison.	EO 892						
Coconino, Arizona							
1908 July 1 Established from parts of Tonto, Black Mesa, and Grand Canyon, and from entire San Francisco Mountains.	Proc 818 35 Stat 2196			3,689,982	1,835,930	174,819	2,010,749
Coeur d'Alene, Idaho							
1906 Nov 6 Established.	Proc 34 Stat 3256			2,331,280			
1908 July 1 Palouse added.	EO 843						
1933 Sept 30 Portion of Pend Oreille added.	EO 6303						
1973 Combined administratively with Kaniksu and St. Joe, called the Idaho Panhandle National Forests.					722,691	86,056	808,747
Colorado, Colorado							
1919 July 1 Name changed from Medicine Bow.	Proc 1062 36 Stat 2720			659,780			
1932 Mar 28 Name changed to Roosevelt.	EO 5826						
Columbia, Washington							
1908 July 1 Established from part of Rainier.	EO 820			941,440			
1949 June 15 Name changed to Gifford Pinchot.	Proc 2845 63 Stat 1277 14-FR 3273						
Colville, Washington							
1907 Mar 1 Established.	Proc 34 Stat 3288			869,520	944,434	76,188	1,020,622
Conecuh, Alabama							
1936 July 17 Established.	Proc 2189 50 Stat 1754 1-FR 859	67,846	271,727	339,573	82,790	88,387	171,177
1936 Combined administratively with Black Warrior and Talladega, known as National Forests in Alabama.							

Name, Date Established, History	Citation	Acreage When Established or Earliest Documentation			Acreage as of September 1981		
		NF Land	Other	Total	NF Land	Other	Total

Coquille, Oregon

| 1907 Mar 2 | Established. | Proc   34 Stat 3299 | | | 148,317 | | | |
| 1908 July 1 | Entire forest combined with Siskiyou; name discontinued. | EO 866 | | | | | | |

Coronado, Arizona and New Mexico

1908 July 1	Established by consolidation of Dragoon, Santa Catalina, and Santa Rita.	EO 908			966,368			
1911 July 1	Entire Garces added.	Proc 1121						
1917 July 1	Entire Chiricahua added.	EO 2630						
1953 July 1	Part of Crook added.	PLO 924 18-FR 6823			Ariz. N. Mex.	1,713,258 68,936 1,782,194	70,994 2,605 73,599	1,784,252 71,541 1,855,793

Crater, California and Oregon

1908 July 1	Established from parts of Cascade, Klamath, Siskiyou, and entire Ashland.	EO 867		Calif. Ore.	58,614 1,061,220 1,119,834			
1915 July 19	Part of Paulina added.	Proc 1302 39 Stat 1735						
1932 July 9	Name changed to Rogue.	EO 5882						

Crazy Mountain, Montana

| 1906 Aug 10 | Established. | Proc   34 Stat 3224 | | | 234,760 | | | |
| 1908 July 1 | Combined with part of Yellowstone to reestablish the Absaroka; name discontinued. | EO 875 | | | | | | |

Croatan, North Carolina

| 1936 July 29 | Established. | Proc 2192   50 Stat 1759   1-FR 909 | 112,966 | 193,334 | 306,300 | | | |
| 1954 | Combined administratively with Nantahala and Pisgah, known as National Forests in North Carolina | | | | | 157,075 | 151,151 | 308,226 |

Crook, Arizona

| 1908 July 1 | Established from part of Tonto, Mount Graham, and other lands. | Proc 816   35 Stat 2194 | | | 788,624 | | | |
| 1953 July 1 | Entire forest divided among Coronado, Gila, and Tonto. | PLO 924   18-FR 6823 | | | | | | |

Crow Creek, Wyoming

| 1900 Oct 10 | Established. | Proc   31 Stat 1981 | | | 56,320 | | | |
| 1908 July 1 | Entire forest combined with part of Medicine Bow to establish the Cheyenne; name discontinued. | EO 861 | | | | | | |

Cumberland, Kentucky

| 1937 Feb 23 | Established. | Proc 2227   50 Stat 1818   2-FR 361 | 385,656 | 952,558 | 1,338,214 | | | |
| 1966 Apr 11 | Name changed to Daniel Boone. | Proc 3715   31-FR 5807 | | | | | | |

Name, Date Established, History	Citation	Acreage When Established or Earliest Documentation			Acreage as of September 1981		
		NF Land	Other	Total	NF Land	Other	Total
Custer, Montana and South Dakota							
1908 July 1 Name changed from Otter.	EO 908			590,720			
1920 Jan 13 Entire Sioux added.	EO 3216						
1932 Feb 17 Part of Beartooth and other lands added.	EO 5801				Mont. 1,112,153	88,272	1,200,425
					S.D. 73,529	4,298	77,827
					1,185,682	92,570	1,278,252
Dakota, North Dakota							
1908 Nov 24 Established.	Proc 824 35 Stat 2207			13,940			
1917 July 30 Abolished.	Proc 1387 40 Stat 1685						
Daniel Boone, Kentucky							
1966 Apr 11 Name changed from Cumberland.	Proc 3715 31-FR 5807	462,281	894,808	1,357,089	527,037	833,691	1,360,728
Datil, New Mexico							
1908 June 18 Established from part of Gila and other lands.	Proc 812 35 Stat 2191			1,255,883			
1909 Feb 23 Magdalena and other land added.	Proc 851 35 Stat 2230						
1931 Dec 24 Entire forest transferred to Gila; name discontinued.	EO 5765						
Davy Crockett, Texas							
1936 Oct 13 Established.	Proc 2203 50 Stat 1782 1-FR 1603	165,030	229,170	394,200			
1936 Combined administratively with Angelina, Sabine, and Sam Houston, known as National Forests in Texas.					161,497	232,703	394,200
Deerlodge, Montana							
1908 July 1 Established from parts of Big Hole and Hell Gate.	EO 880			1,080,220			
1931 Dec 16 Land from Madison and Missoula added.	EO 5759				1,195,754	159,233	1,354,987
Delta, Mississippi							
1961 Jan 12 Established; added administratively to Bienville, Desoto, Holly Springs, Homochitto, Tombigbee, known as National Forests in Mississippi.	Secretary of Agriculture Order 26-FR 627	58,956	59,278	118,234	59,518	58,616	118,134
Deschutes, Oregon							
1908 July 1 Established from part of Blue Mountains, Cascade, and Fremont.	EO 816			1,504,207			
1915 July 19 Part of Paulina added.	Proc 1303 39 Stat 1736				1,602,680	249,602	1,852,282

Name, Date Established, History	Citation	Acreage When Established or Earliest Documentation			Acreage as of September 1981		
		NF Land	Other	Total	NF Land	Other	Total
DeSoto, Mississippi							
1936 June 17 Established.	Proc 2174 49 Stat 3526 1-FR 609	385,896	826,924	1,212,820			
1936 Combined administratively with Bienville, Holly Springs, Homochitto, known as National Forests in Mississippi.					500,356	295,716	796,072
Diamond Mountain, California							
1905 July 14 Established.	Proc 34 Stat 3113			626,724			
1908 July 1 Portion transferred to Plumas; remainder combined with Lassen; name discontinued.	EO 905, 906						
Dismal River, Nebraska							
1902 Apr 16 Established.	Proc 32 Stat 1995			85,123			
1908 July 1 Transferred to Nebraska.	EO 908						
Dix, New Jersey							
1925 Apr 10 Established from part of Dix Military Reservation.	EO 4199	6,785		6,785			
1928 Apr 6 EO 4199 rescinded.	EO 4852						
Dixie, Utah							
1905 Sept 25 Established.	Proc 34 Stat 3147			465,920			
1922 July 1 Western part of Sevier added.	EO 3636						
1944 Oct 1 Entire Powell added.	PLO 260 10-FR 1244				1,883,745	83,443	1,967,188
Dragoon, Arizona							
1907 May 25 Established.	Proc 35 Stat 2135			69,120			
1908 July 1 Combined with Santa Catalina and Santa Rita to establish Coronado; name discontinued.	EO 908						
Durango, Colorado							
1911 July 1 Established from part of San Juan.	Proc 1142 37 Stat 1697			704,000			
1920 Nov 21 Entire forest transferred to San Juan; name discontinued.	EO 3357						
Ekalaka, Montana							
1906 Nov 5 Established.	Proc 34 Stat 3245			33,808			
1908 July 1 Added to Sioux; name discontinued.	EO 908						
Eldorado, California and Nevada					Calif.		
1910 July 28 Established from part of Tahoe and other lands.	Proc 1070 36 Stat 2729	Calif. 841,211			671,021	213,678	884,699
		Nev. 400			Nev. 53		53
		841,611			671,074	213,678	884,752
Elkhorn, Montana							
1905 May 12 Established.	Proc 34 Stat 3024			186,240			
1908 July 1 Entire forest combined with Helena; name discontinued.	EO 881						

Name, Date Established, History	Citation	Acreage When Established or Earliest Documentation			Acreage as of September 1981		
		NF Land	Other	Total	NF Land	Other	Total
Eustis, Virginia							
1925 Apr 10 Established from part of Fort Eustis Military Reservation.	EO 4197	4,220		4,220			
1927 Dec 2 EO 4197 rescinded.	EO 4776						
Fillmore, Utah							
1906 May 19 Established.	Proc 34 Stat 3200			399,600			
1908 July 1 Entire Beaver added.	EO 826						
1923 Sept 24 Entire forest transferred to Fishlake; name discontinued.	EO 3908						
Fish Lake, Utah							
1899 Feb 10 Established.	Proc 30 Stat 1787			67,840			
1908 July 1 Name changed to Fishlake. Glenwood added.	EO 908						
Fishlake, Utah							
1908 July 1 Name changed from Fish Lake.	EO 908			537,233			
1923 Sept 24 Entire Fillmore added.	EO 3908				1,424,159	101,509	1,525,668
Flathead, Montana							
1897 Feb 22 Established effective March 1, 1898.	Proc 29 Stat 911			1,382,400			
1903 June 9 Consolidated with Lewis and Clarke; name discontinued.	Proc 33 Stat 2311						
1908 July 1 Reestablished from part of Lewis and Clark.	EO 835			2,092,785			
1935 June 22 Part of Blackfeet added.	EO 7082				2,349,932	278,740	2,628,672
Florida, Florida							
1911 July 1 Established by combining Ocala and Choctawhatchee.	Proc 1122 37 Stat 1678			674,970			
1927 Oct 17 Ocala Division excluded to reestablish Ocala.	Proc 1816 45 Stat 2927						
1927 Nov 10 Name changed to Choctawhatchee.	EO 4756						
Francis Marion, South Carolina							
1936 July 10 Established.	Proc 2186 50 Stat 1744 1-FR 792	244,228	170,472	414,700			
1969 Combined administratively with Sumter, known as Francis Marion and Sumter.					249,987	164,713	414,700
Fremont, Oregon							
1906 Sept 17 Established.	Proc 34 Stat 3231			1,235,720			
1908 July 1 Goose Lake added; other lands transferred.	EO 817						
1915 July 19 Part of Paulina added.	Proc 1304 39 Stat 1737				1,198,308	512,282	1,710,590
Fruita, Colorado							
1906 Feb 24 Established.	Proc 34 Stat 3191			7,680			
1908 July 1 Combined with Uncompahgre; name discontinued.	EO 885						

Name, Date Established, History	Citation	Acreage When Established or Earliest Documentation			Acreage as of September 1981		
		NF Land	Other	Total	NF Land	Other	Total
Gallatin, Montana							
1899 Feb 10 Established.	Proc 30 Stat 1788			40,320			
1908 July 1 Part of Big Belt added.	EO 879						
1931 Dec 16 Part of Madison added.	EO 5760						
1945 July 1 Part of Absaroka added.	PLO 305 11-FR 249				1,735,409	415,301	2,150,710
Gallinas, New Mexico							
1906 Nov 5 Established.	Proc 34 Stat 3243			78,480			
1908 July 1 Entire forest transferred to Lincoln; name discontinued.	EO 908						
Garces, Arizona							
1908 July 1 Established by consolidation of the Baboquivari, Huachuca, and Tumacacori.	EO 908			644,395			
1911 July 1 Combined with Coronado; name discontinued.	Proc 1121						
Garden City, Kansas							
1905 July 25 Established.	Proc 34 Stat 3131			97,280			
1908 May 15 Name changed to Kansas.	Proc 808 35 Stat 2188						
George Washington, Virginia and West Virginia							
1932 June 28 Name changed from Shenandoah.	EO 5867 Va. W. Va.	374,337 66,537 440,874	275,163 86,663 361,826	649,500 153,200 802,700			
1933 July 22 Natural Bridge added.	EO 6210			Va. W. Va.	954,116 100,806 1,054,922	684,458 56,762 741,220	1,638,574 157,568 1,796,142
Gifford Pinchot, Washington							
1949 June 15 Named changed from Columbia.	Proc 2854 63 Stat 1277 14-FR 3273	1,263,342	158,220	1,421,562	1,250,840	114,392	1,365,232
Gila, New Mexico							
1905 July 21 Named changed from Gila River.	Proc 34 Stat 3123			2,327,040			
1908 June 18 Big Burros and other lands added.	Proc 811 35 Stat 2190						
1931 Dec 24 Datil added.	EO 5765						
1953 July 1 Part of Crook added.	PLO 924 18-FR 6823				2,705,572	92,059	2,797,631
Gila River, New Mexico							
1899 Mar 2 Established.	Proc 34 Stat 3126			2,327,040			
1905 July 21 Name changed to Gila.	Proc 34 Stat 3123						
Glenwood, Utah							
1907 Feb 6 Established.	Proc 34 Stat 3275			173,896			
1908 July 1 Entire forest added to Fishlake; name discontinued.	EO 908						

Name, Date Established, History	Citation	Acreage When Established or Earliest Documentation			Acreage as of September 1981		
		NF Land	Other	Total	NF Land	Other	Total
Goose Lake, Oregon							
1906 Aug 21 Established.	Proc 34 Stat 3226	630,000		630,000			
1908 July 1 Entire forest combined with Fremont; name discontinued.	EO 817						
Grand Cañon, Arizona							
1893 Feb 20 Established.	Proc 27 Stat 1064			1,851,520			
1906 Aug 8 Name changed to Grand Canyon.	Proc 34 Stat 3223						
Grand Canyon, Arizona							
1906 Aug 8 Name changed from Grand Cañon.	Proc 34 Stat 3223			2,267,300			
1908 July 1 Part combined with Coconino; part taken to create Kaibab; part restored to public domain; name discontinued.	EO 909 Proc 818 35 Stat 2196						
Grand Mesa, Colorado							
1924 Mar 11 Name changed from Battlement.	EO 3970	659,264	20,535	679,799			
1976 Combined administratively with Gunnison and Uncompahgre.					346,141	5,485	351,626
Grantsville, Utah							
1904 May 7 Established.	Proc 33 Stat 2352			68,960			
1908 July 1 Combined with Wasatch; name discontinued.	EO 908						
Green Mountain, Vermont							
1932 Apr 25 Established.	Proc 1997 47 Stat 2509	1,842	100,258	102,100	289,839	339,180	629,019
Guadalupe, New Mexico							
1907 Apr 19 Established.	Proc 35 Stat 2124			283,065			
1908 July 1 Combined with Alamo; name discontinued.	EO 908						
Gunnison, Colorado							
1905 May 12 Established.	Proc 34 Stat 3025			901,270			
1944 July 1 Land from Cochetopa added.	PLO 258 10-FR 1243						
1976 Combined administratively with Grand Mesa and Uncompahgre.					1,662,813	104,943	1,767,756
Harney, South Dakota and Wyoming							
1911 July 1 Established from part of Black Hills and other lands.	Proc 1124 37 Stat 1680			642,550			
1954 July 1 Entire forest transferred to Black Hills.	PLO 1016 19-FR 6500						

Name, Date Established, History	Citation	Acreage When Established or Earliest Documentation			Acreage as of September 1981		
		NF Land	Other	Total	NF Land	Other	Total
Hayden, Colorado and Wyoming							
1908 July 1 Established from entire Sierra Madre and part of Park Range.	EO 839		Colo. Wyo.	84,000 370,911 454,911			
1929 Aug 2 Entire forest transferred to Medicine Bow and Routt; name discontinued.	Proc 1888 46 Stat 3003						
Helena, Montana							
1906 Apr 12 Established.	Proc 34 Stat 3196			782,160			
1908 July 1 Part of Big Belt and entire Elkhorn added.	EO 881				975,125	187,477	1,162,602
Hell Gate, Montana							
1905 Oct 3 Established.	Proc 34 Stat 3168			1,581,120			
1908 July 1 Lands divided among Beaverhead, Deerlodge, Missoula, and Bitterroot; name discontinued.	EO 877, 880, 882, 883						
Henrys Lake, Idaho							
1905 May 23 Established.	Proc 34 Stat 3052			798,720			
1908 July 1 Combined with portion of Yellowstone to establish the Targhee; name discontinued.	EO 871						
Heppner, Oregon							
1906 July 18 Established.	Proc 34 Stat 3222	292,176		292,176			
1908 July 1 Combined with part of the Blue Mountains to establish the Umatilla; name discontinued.	EO 815						
Hiawatha, Michigan							
1931 Jan 16 Established.	Proc 1931 46 Stat 3043	56,635	214,379	271,014			
1962 Feb 9 Marquette added.	EO 10993 27-FR 3712				881,461	400,207	1,281,668
Highwood Mountains, Montana							
1903 Dec 12 Established.	Proc 33 Stat 2325			45,080			
1908 July 1 Combined with Little Belt, Snowy Mountains, and Little Rockies to establish Jefferson; name discontinued.	EO 908						
Holly Springs, Mississippi							
1936 June 15 Established.	Proc 2176 49 Stat 3522 1-FR 606	46,743	415,297	462,040			
1936 Combined administratively with Bienville, DeSoto, Homochitto, known as National Forests in Mississippi.					147,304	372,639	519,943

Name, Date Established, History	Citation	Acreage When Established or Earliest Documentation			Acreage as of September 1981		
		NF Land	Other	Total	NF Land	Other	Total
Holy Cross, Colorado							
1905 Aug 25 Established.	Proc 34 Stat 3144			990,720			
1920 Aug 7 Sopris added.	EO 3317						
1945 Jan 1 Entire forest transferred to White River; name discontinued.	PLO 263 10-FR 2251						
Homochitto, Mississippi							
1936 July 20 Established.	Proc 2191 50 Stat 1758 1-FR 872	190,170	183,290	373,460			
1936 Combined administratively with Bienville, DeSoto, Holly Springs, known as National Forests in Mississippi.					188,995	184,502	373,497
Hoosier, Indiana							
1951 Oct 1 Established.	Administrative Order 4 by Secretary of Agriculture 16-FR 9174	113,926	667,541	781,467			
1952 Combined administratively with Wayne, known as Wayne-Hoosier.					186,961	457,178	644,139
Huachuca, Arizona							
1906 Nov 6 Established.	Proc 34 Stat 3255			314,125			
1908 July 1 Combined with Baboquivari and Tumacacori to establish Garces; name discontinued.	EO 908						
Humboldt, Nevada							
1908 July 1 Established by consolidation of Independence and Ruby Mountains.	EO 908			558,679			
1917 July 1 Entire Ruby and Santa Rosa added.	EO 2631						
1957 Oct 1 Part of Nevada added.	PLO 1487 22-FR 7309				2,527,929	152,511	2,680,440
Humphreys, Virginia							
1925 Apr 10 Established from part of the Humphreys Military Reservation	EO 4198	3,184		3,184			
1928 Aug 11 EO 4198 rescinded.	EO 4946						
Huron, Michigan							
1928 July 30 Established from part of Michigan and other lands.	Proc 1844 45 Stat 2959	237,135	316,306	553,441			
1955 Combined administratively with Manistee, known as Huron-Manistee.					425,301	268,796	694,097

Name, Date Established, History	Citation	Acreage When Established or Earliest Documentation			Acreage as of September 1981		
		NF Land	Other	Total	NF Land	Other	Total
Idaho, Idaho							
1908 July 1 Established from part of Payette.	EO 855			1,293,280			
1944 Apr 1 Entire forest combined with Weiser to establish the Payette (new); name discontinued.	PLO 218 9-FR 3655						
Imnaha, Oregon							
1907 Mar 1 Established by consolidation of the Chesnimnus and Wallowa.	Proc 34 Stat 3284			1,750,240			
1908 July 1 Name changed to Wallowa.	EO 908						
Independence, Nevada							
1906 Nov 5 Established.	Proc 34 Stat 3251			135,019			
1908 July 1 Combined with Humboldt; name discontinued.	EO 908						
Inyo, California and Nevada					Calif.		
1907 May 25 Established.	Proc 35 Stat 2134			221,324	1,800,302	43,289	1,843,591
					Nev.		
1945 July 1 Land from Mono added.	PLO 307 11-FR 250				60,576	1,772	62,348
					1,860,878	45,061	1,905,939
Jackson, South Carolina							
1924 Dec 22 Established from part of Jackson Military Reservation.	EO 4115	20,225		20,225			
1928 May 17 EO 4115 rescinded.	EO 4884						
Jefferson, Montana							
1908 July 1 Established by consolidation of Little Belt, Little Rockies, Snowy Mountains, and Highwood Mountains.	EO 908			1,255,320			
1932 Apr 8 Entire forest transferred to Lewis and Clark; name discontinued.	EO 5834						
Jefferson, Virginia, West Virginia, and Kentucky					Kent.		
1936 Apr 21 Established from parts of Unaka, George Washington, and other lands.	Proc 2165 49 Stat 3506	136,845	2,283,824	2,420,669	961	53,653	54,614
					Va.		
					672,966	912,930	1,585,896
					W. Va.		
					18,196	11,586	29,782
					692,123	978,169	1,670,292
Jemez, New Mexico							
1905 Oct 12 Established.	Proc 34 Stat 3182			1,237,205			
1915 July 1 Combined with Pecos to establish the Santa Fe; name discontinued.	EO 2160						
Kaibab, Arizona							
1908 July 1 Established from the northern portion of the Grand Canyon.	EO 909			1,080,000	1,556,467	43,608	1,600,075

Name, Date Established, History	Citation	Acreage When Established or Earliest Documentation			Acreage as of September 1981		
		NF Land	Other	Total	NF Land	Other	Total
Kaniksu, Idaho, Montana, and Washington							
1908 July 1 Established from part of Priest River.	EO 845		Ida. Wash.	544,220 406,520 950,740			
1933 Sept 30 Part of Pend Oreille added.	EO 6303						
1954 July 1 Part of Cabinet added.	PLO 965 19-FR 3007				Ida.		
1973 July 1 Combined administratively with Coeur d'Alene and St. Joe, known as Idaho Panhandle National Forests.					894,313 Mont. 446,092 Wash. 269,982 1,610,387	167,607 43,660 23,317 234,584	1,061,920 489,752 293,299 1,844,971
Kansas, Kansas							
1908 May 15 Name changed from Garden City.	Proc 808 35 Stat 2188			302,387			
1915 Dec 1 Abolished.	Proc 1314 39 Stat 1752						
Kern, California							
1910 July 1 Established from portion of Sequoia and other lands.	Proc 1061 36 Stat 2720			1,951,191			
1915 July 1 Entire forest transferred to Sequoia; name discontinued.	EO 2169						
Kisatchie, Louisiana							
1930 June 10 Land purchased and forest established by authority of Weeks Act, 1911.	Secretary of Agriculture Order.	9,613		9,613			
1936 June 3 Established by presidential proclamation.	Proc 2173 49 Stat 3520 1-FR 637	413,020	464,046	877,066	597,672	425,031	1,022,703
Klamath, California and Oregon					Calif.		
1905 May 6 Established.	Proc 34 Stat 3001			1,896,313	1,670,695 Ore. 26,334 1,697,029	216,063 205 216,268	1,886,758 26,539 1,913,297
Knox, Kentucky							
1925 June 5 Established from part of Camp Knox Military Reservation.	EO 4248	22,660		22,660			
1928 Apr 6 EO 4248 rescinded.	EO 4852						
Kootenai, Montana and Idaho							
1906 Aug 13 Established.	Proc 34 Stat 3225		Mont.	887,360			
1935 June 22 Land from Blackfeet added.	EO 7082						
1954 July 1 Land from Cabinet added.	PLO 965 19-FR 3007				Ida. 46,480 Mont. 1,778,739 1,825,219	319,246 319,246	46,480 2,097,985 2,144,465
Lake Tahoe, California and Nevada							
1899 Apr 13 Established.	Proc 31 Stat 1953			136,335			
1905 Oct 3 Name changed to Tahoe; boundary redescribed.	Proc 34 Stat 3163						

Name, Date Established, History	Citation	Acreage When Established or Earliest Documentation			Acreage as of September 1981		
		NF Land	Other	Total	NF Land	Other	Total
La Sal, Colorado and Utah							
1906 Jan 25 Established.	Proc 34 Stat 3190		Colo. Utah	29,502 128,960 158,462			
1908 July 1 Combined with Monticello and renamed La Salle.	EO 908						
1909 Mar 16 Name changed back to La Sal.	EO 1051		Colo. Utah	29,502 444,628 474,130			
1949 Nov 28 Entire forest transferred to Manti.	PLO 618 14-FR 7271						
La Salle, Utah							
1908 July 1 Established by combination of La Sal and Monticello.	EO 908		Colo. Utah	29,502 444,628 474,130			
1909 Mar 16 Name changed to La Sal.	EO 1051						
Las Animas, Colorado and New Mexico							
1907 Mar 1 Established.	Proc 34 Stat 3288		Colo. N. Mex.	196,140 480 196,620			
1910 May 27 Part transferred to San Isabel; remainder restored to public domain; name discontinued.	Proc 1040 36 Stat 2701						
Lassen, California							
1908 July 1 Name changed from Lassen Peak.	EO 906			1,209,298	1,060,003	314,944	1,374,947
Lassen Peak, California							
1905 June 2 Established.	Proc 34 Stat 3063			897,115			
1908 July 1 Lands transferred to and from Plumas, Shasta, and Diamond Mountain; name changed to Lassen.	EO 906						
Leadville, Colorado							
1905 May 12 Established.	Proc 34 Stat 3013			1,219,947			
1930 May 26 Entire forest distributed among Arapaho, Cochetopa, and Pike.	Proc 1906, 1907, 1909 46 Stat 3021, 3022						
Lee, Virginia							
1925 Apr 10 Established from part of Lee Reservation.	EO 4196	7,177		7,177			
1928 June 23 EO 4196 rescinded.	EO 4916						
Lemhi, Idaho							
1906 Nov 5 Established.	Proc 34 Stat 3248			1,344,800			
1938 Oct 8 Entire forest divided between Challis and Salmon; name discontinued.	EO 7986 3-FR 2435						

Name, Date Established, History	Citation	Acreage When Established or Earliest Documentation			Acreage as of September 1981		
		NF Land	Other	Total	NF Land	Other	Total
Lewis and Clark, Montana							
1907 Mar 2 Name changed from Lewis and Clarke; land added.	Proc 34 Stat 3304			5,541,180			
1932 Apr 8 Entire Jefferson added.	EO 5834						
1945 July 1 Part of Absaroka added.	PLO 305 11-FR 249				1,843,397	155,625	1,999,022
Lewis and Clarke, Montana							
1897 Feb 22 Established, effective March 1, 1898.	Proc 29 Stat 907			2,926,000			
1903 June 9 Flathead added.	Proc 33 Stat 2311						
1907 Mar 2 Spelling changed to Lewis and Clark; land added.	Proc 34 Stat 3304						
Lincoln, New Mexico							
1902 July 26 Established.	Proc 32 Stat 2018			500,000			
1908 July 1 Entire Gallinas added.	EO 908						
1917 July 1 Entire Alamo added.	EO 2633				1,103,339	167,730	1,271,069
Little Belt, Montana							
1905 Oct 3 Name changed from Little Belt Mountains.	Proc 34 Stat 3180			583,560			
1908 July 1 Combined with Little Rockies, Snowy Mountains, and Highwood to establish Jefferson; name discontinued.	EO 908						
Little Belt Mountains, Montana							
1902 Aug 16 Established.	Proc 32 Stat 2022			501,000			
1905 Oct 3 Name changed to Little Belt; boundary redescribed.	Proc 34 Stat 3180						
Little Rockies, Montana							
1907 Mar 2 Established.	Proc 34 Stat 3290			31,000			
1908 July 1 Combined with Little Belt, Snowy Mountains, and Highwood to establish Jefferson; name discontinued.	EO 908						
Logan, Utah							
1903 May 29 Established.	Proc 33 Stat 2307			182,080			
1906 May 28 Combined with other lands to establish Bear River; name discontinued.	Proc 34 Stat 3206						
Lolo, Montana							
1906 Sept 20 Established.	Proc 34 Stat 3234			1,211,680			
1931 Dec 16 Part of Missoula added.	EO 5761						
1934 Oct 29 Part of Selway added.	EO 6889						
1954 July 1 Part of Cabinet added.	PLO 965 19-FR 3007				2,091,950	522,899	2,614,849
Long Pine, Montana							
1906 Sept 24 Established.	Proc 34 Stat 3235			111,445			
1908 July 1 Combined with Sioux; name discontinued.	EO 908						

Name, Date Established, History	Citation	Acreage When Established or Earliest Documentation			Acreage as of September 1981		
		NF Land	Other	Total	NF Land	Other	Total
Los Padres, California							
1936 Dec 3 Name changed from Santa Barbara.	EO 7501 1-FR 2141	1,773,942	242,135	2,016,077	1,752,218	211,031	1,963,249
Luquillo, Puerto Rico							
1903 Jan 17 Established.	Proc 32 Stat 2029			65,950			
1935 June 4 Name changed to Caribbean.	EO 7059-A						
McClellan, Alabama							
1924 Dec 22 Established from part of Camp McClellan Military Reservation.	EO 4114	15,350		15,350			
1928 May 4 EO 4114 rescinded.	EO 4877						
Madison, Montana							
1902 Aug 16 Established.	Proc 32 Stat 2024			736,000			
1931 Dec 16 Entire forest distributed among Beaverhead, Deerlodge, and Gallatin.	EO 5757, 5759, 5760						
Magdalena, New Mexico							
1906 Nov 5 Established.	Proc 34 Stat 3245			153,781			
1908 July 1 San Mateo added.	EO 908						
1909 Feb 23 Combined with Datil; name discontinued.	Proc 851 35 Stat 2230						
Malheur, Oregon							
1908 July 1 Established from part of Blue Mountains.	EO 814			1,167,400	1,459,422	81,332	1,540,754
Manistee, Michigan							
1938 Oct 25 Established.	Proc 2306 53 Stat 2492 3-FR 2577	238,796	1,018,017	1,256,813			
1955 Combined administratively with Huron, known as Huron-Manistee.					520,662	811,010	1,331,672
Manti, Utah							
1903 May 29 Established.	Proc 33 Stat 2308			584,640			
1915 July 1 Nebo added.	EO 2153						
1949 Nov 11 La Sal added.	PLO 618 14-FR 7271						
1950 Aug 28 Name changed to Manti-La Sal.	PLO 667 15-FR 5957						
Manti-La Sal, Colorado and Utah		Colo.			Colo.		
1950 Aug 28 Name changed from Manti.	PLO 667 15-FR 5957	26,631	43	26,674	27,105	40	27,145
		Utah			Utah		
		1,235,721	77,053	1,312,774	1,238,149	72,496	1,310,645
		1,262,352	77,096	1,339,448	1,265,254	72,536	1,337,790
Manzano, New Mexico							
1906 Nov 6 Established.	Proc 34 Stat 3257			459,726			
1908 Apr 16 Mount Taylor and other lands added.	Proc 803 35 Stat 2184						
1914 Sept 10 Zuni added.	EO 2045						
1931 Dec 3 Name changed to Cibola; lands added.	EO 5752						

Name, Date Established, History	Citation	Acreage When Established or Earliest Documentation			Acreage as of September 1981		
		NF Land	Other	Total	NF Land	Other	Total
Mark Twain, Missouri							
1939 Sept 11 Established.	Proc 2362 54 Stat 2655 4-FR 3907	391,702	957,926	1,349,628			
1973 July 1 Combined administratively with Clark, known as Clark-Mark Twain.							
1976 Feb 17 Total forest named Mark Twain.	Proc 4415	1,439,669	1,504,127	2,943,796	1,450,206	1,493,674	2,943,880
Marquette, Michigan							
1909 Feb 10 Established.	Proc 838 35 Stat 2220			30,603			
1915 July 1 Entire forest transferred to Michigan; name discontinued.	EO 2163						
1931 Feb 12 Reestablished. Name changed from Michigan.	Proc 1938 46 Stat 3050	67,644	207,266	274,910			
1962 Feb 9 Entire forest transferred to Hiawatha; name discontinued.	EO 10993 27-FR 1312						
Maury Mountain, Oregon							
1905 June 2 Established.	Proc 34 Stat 3066			54,220			
1907 Mar 2 Combined with Blue Mountains; name discontinued.	Proc 34 Stat 3302						
Meade, Maryland							
1925 Apr 10 Established from part of Camp Meade Military Reservation.	EO 4200	4,725		4,725			
1927 Dec 2 EO 4200 rescinded.	EO 4776						
Medicine Bow, Wyoming							
1902 May 22 Established.	Proc 32 Stat 2003			400,051			
1910 July 1 Changed name to Colorado.	Proc 1062 36 Stat 2720						
1910 July 1 Reestablished. Name changed from Cheyenne.	Proc 1067 36 Stat 2726			521,747			
1929 Aug 2 Added part of Hayden.	Proc 1888 46 Stat 3003				1,093,517	308,635	1,402,152
Mendocino, California							
1932 July 12 Name changed from California.	EO 5885	829,459	232,913	1,062,372	882,617	196,866	1,079,483
Michigan, Michigan							
1909 Feb 11 Established.	Proc 841 35 Stat 2222			132,770			
1915 July 1 Marquette added.	EO 2163						
1931 Feb 12 Name changed to Marquette.	Proc 1938 46 Stat 3050						
Minam, Oregon							
1911 July 1 Established from part of Wallowa.	Proc 1128 37 Stat 1683			448,330			
1920 June 20 Entire forest transferred to Whitman; name discontinued.	EO 3286						

Name, Date Established, History	Citation	Acreage When Established or Earliest Documentation			Acreage as of September 1981		
		NF Land	Other	Total	NF Land	Other	Total
Minidoka, Idaho and Utah							
1908 July 1 Established by consolidation of Cassia and Raft River.	EO 908		Ida. Utah	619,204 117,203 736,407			
1953 July 1 Entire forest transferred to Sawtooth.	PLO 923 18-FR 6822						
Minnesota, Minnesota							
1908 May 23 Established.	35 Stat 268			294,752			
1928 June 22 Name changed to Chippewa.	EO 4913						
Missoula, Montana							
1906 Nov 6 Established.	Proc 34 Stat 3259			194,430			
1908 July 1 Part of Hell Gate and other lands added.	EO 882						
1931 Dec 16 Entire forest divided between Deerlodge and Lolo.	EO 5759, 5761						
Moapa, Nevada							
1908 July 1 Established by consolidation of Charleston and Vegas.	EO 908			345,005			
1915 July 1 Entire forest transferred to Toiyabe.	EO 2162						
Modoc, California							
1904 Nov 29 Established.	Proc 33 Stat 2380			288,218			
1908 July 1 Warner Mountains added.	EO 908				1,651,630	327,777	1,979,407
Monitor, Nevada							
1907 Apr 15 Established.	Proc 35 Stat 2123			572,640			
1908 July 1 Entire forest added to Toiyabe; name discontinued.	EO 908						
Mono, California and Nevada							
1908 July 1 Established from parts of Inyo, Sierra, Stanislaus, and Tahoe.	EO 898		Calif. Nev.	658,106 1,440 659,546			
1945 July 1 Entire forest divided between Inyo and Toiyabe.	PLO 307 11-FR 250						
Monongahela, West Virginia		W. Va.					
1920 Apr 28 Established.	Proc 1561 41 Stat 1792	53,335 Va. ——— 53,335	600,386 23,245 623,631	653,721 23,245 676,966	843,748	807,203	1,650,951
Monterey, California							
1906 June 25 Established.	Proc 34 Stat 3218			335,195			
1908 July 1 Pinnacles and San Benito added.	EO 908						
1919 Aug 18 Entire forest transferred to Santa Barbara; name discontinued.							

Name, Date Established, History	Citation	Acreage When Established or Earliest Documentation			Acreage as of September 1981		
		NF Land	Other	Total	NF Land	Other	Total
Montezuma, Colorado							
1905 June 13 Established.	Proc 34 Stat 3106			576,719			
1908 July 1 Part of Ourey added.	EO 889						
1947 July 1 Entire forest divided between San Juan and Uncompahgre.	PLO 400 12-FR 5849						
Monticello, Utah							
1907 Feb 6 Established.	Proc 34 Stat 3272			214,270			
1908 July 1 Combined with La Sal and renamed La Salle.	EO 908						
Mount Baker, Washington							
1924 Jan 21 Name changed from Washington.	EO 3943	1,459,491	30,488	1,489,979			
1974 Combined administratively with Snoqualmie, known as Mount Baker-Snoqualmie.					1,281,063	31,057	1,312,120
Mount Graham, Arizona							
1902 July 22 Established.	Proc 32 Stat 2017			118,600			
1908 July 1 Part combined with Crook; remainder restored to public domain; name discontinued.	Proc 816 35 Stat 2194						
Mount Hood, Oregon							
1924 Jan 21 Name changed from Oregon.	EO 3944	1,054,459	104,750	1,159,209	1,060,289	48,239	1,108,528
Mount Rainier, Washington							
1897 Feb 22 Established from Pacific and other lands effective March 1, 1898.	Proc 29 Stat 896			2,234,880			
1907 Mar 2 Name changed to Rainier; lands added.	Proc 34 Stat 3296						
Mount Taylor, New Mexico							
1906 Oct 5 Established.	Proc 34 Stat 3239			110,525			
1908 Apr 16 Combined with Manzano; name discontinued.	Proc 803 35 Stat 2184						
Nantahala, North Carolina		Ga.					
1920 Jan 29 Established.	Proc 1554 41 Stat 1785	47,511	216,783	264,294			
		N.C. 72,255	338,369	410,624			
		S.C. 18,454	118,762	137,216			
		138,220	673,914	812,134			
1954 Combined administratively with Croatan and Pisgah, known as National Forests in North Carolina.					N.C. 514,479	834,521	1,349,000

Name, Date Established, History	Citation	Acreage When Established or Earliest Documentation			Acreage as of September 1981		
		NF Land	Other	Total	NF Land	Other	Total

Natural Bridge, Virginia

1918 May 16 Established.	Proc 1450 40 Stat 1780	77,401	29,637	107,038			
1933 July 22 Entire forest transferred to George Washington; name discontinued.	EO 6210						

Nebo, Utah

1908 July 1 Established by consolidation of Payson, Vernon, and part of Fillmore.	EO 827			343,920			
1915 July 1 Entire forest transferred to Manti; name discontinued.	EO 2153						

Nebraska, Nebraska

1908 July 1 Established by consolidation of Dismal River, Niobrara, and North Platte.	EO 908			556,072			
1971 Administered with Samuel R. McKelvie, known as Nebraska National Forests.					141,558	88,039	229,597

Nevada, Nevada

1909 Feb 10 Established.	Proc 839 35 Stat 2220			1,222,312			
1932 July 1 Entire Toiyabe added.	EO 5863						
1957 Oct 1 Entire forest divided between Humboldt and Toiyabe; name discontinued.	PLO 1487 22-FR 7309						

Nezperce, Idaho

1908 July 1 Established from parts of Bitter Root and Weiser.	EO 854			1,946,340			
1934 Oct 29 Part of Selway added.	EO 6889				2,218,333	28,749	2,247,082

Nicolet, Wisconsin

1933 Mar 2 Established.	Proc 2035 47 Stat 2561	219,428	246,826	466,254	654,777	318,627	973,404

Niobrara, Nebraska

1902 Apr 16 Established.	Proc 32 Stat 1993			123,779			
1908 July 1 Added to Nebraska; name discontinued.	EO 908						

North Platte, Nebraska

1906 Mar 10 Established.	Proc 34 Stat 3193			347,170			
1908 July 1 Added to Nebraska; name discontinued.	EO 908						

Name, Date Established, History	Citation	Acreage When Established or Earliest Documentation			Acreage as of September 1981		
		NF Land	Other	Total	NF Land	Other	Total
Ocala, Florida							
1908 Nov 24 Established.	Proc 823 35 Stat 2206	207,285					
1911 July 1 Combined with Choctawhatchee to establish Florida; name discontinued.	Proc 1122 37 Stat 1678						
1927 Oct 17 Reestablished from Florida, Ocala Division.	Proc 1816 45 Stat 2927	158,731	93,449	252,180			
1936 Combined administratively with Apalachicola and Osceola, known as National Forests in Florida.					381,297	48,825	430,122
Ochoco, Oregon							
1911 July 1 Established from parts of Deschutes and Malheur.	Proc 1165 37 Stat 1713			819,030	843,676	134,826	978,502
Oconee, Georgia							
1959 Nov 27 Established; combined administratively with Chattahoochee and known as Chattahochee and Oconee.	Proc 3326 24-FR 9651	96,066	173,649	269,715	108,738	152,095	260,833
Okanogan, Washington							
1911 July 1 Established from part of Chelan.	Proc 1150 37 Stat 1701			1,732,820			
1921 July 1 Entire forest transferred to Chelan; name discontinued.	EO 3380						
1955 Mar 23 Reestablished; name changed from Chelan.	PLO 1101 20-FR 1890	2,042,126	48,504	2,090,630	1,499,512	37,497	1,537,009
Olympic, Washington							
1897 Feb 22 Established, effective March 1, 1898.	Proc 29 Stat 901			2,188,800	649,975	65,776	715,751
Oregon, Oregon							
1908 July 1 Established from part of Cascade and entire Bull Run.	EO 864		1,787,280				
1924 Jan 21 Name changed to Mount Hood.	EO 3944						
Osceola, Florida							
1931 July 10 Established.	Proc 1961 47 Stat 2465	145,403	16,410	161,813			
1936 Combined administratively with Apalachicola and Ocala, known as National Forests in Florida.					157,218	4,596	161,814
Ottawa, Michigan							
1931 Jan 27 Established.	Proc 1932 46 Stat 3044	38,749	213,802	252,551	924,951	634,941	1,559,892

Name, Date Established, History	Citation	Acreage When Established or Earliest Documentation			Acreage as of September 1981		
		NF Land	Other	Total	NF Land	Other	Total
Otter, Montana							
1907 Mar 2 Established.	Proc 34 Stat 3305			590,720			
1908 July 1 Name changed to Custer.	EO 908						
Ouachita, Arkansas						Ark.		
1926 Apr 29 Name changed from Arkansas.	EO 4436	663,987	294,790	958,777	1,336,834	624,601	1,961,435
					Okla.		
					247,585	165,327	412,912
					1,584,419	789,928	2,374,347
Ouray, Colorado							
1907 Feb 22 Established.	Proc 34 Stat 3271			273,175			
1908 July 1 Land divided between Montezuma and Uncompahgre; name discontinued.	EO 885, 889						
Ozark, Arkansas							
1908 Mar 6 Established.	Proc 802 35 Stat 2182			917,944			
1963 Combined administratively with St. Francis, known as Ozark-St. Francis.					1,118,170	378,750	1,496,920
Pacific, Washington							
1893 Feb 20 Established.	Proc 27 Stat 1063			967,680			
1897 Feb 22 Combined with other lands to establish Mount Rainier, effective March 1, 1898; name discontinued.	Proc 29 Stat 896						
Palisade, Idaho and Wyoming							
1910 July 1 Established from southern portion of Targhee.	Proc 1053 36 Stat 2712		Ida. Wyo.	293,770 289,880			
				583,650			
1917 July 1 Entire forest transferred to Targhee; name discontinued.	EO 2632						
Palouse, Idaho							
1907 Mar 2 Established.	Proc 34 Stat 3293			194,404			
1908 July 1 Entire forest combined with Coeur d'Alene; name discontinued.	EO 843						
Park Range, Colorado							
1905 June 12 Established.	Proc 34 Stat 3079			757,116			
1908 July 1 Divided between Routt and Hayden; name discontinued.	EO 837, 839						
Paulina, Oregon							
1911 July 1 Established from parts of Cascade, Crater, Deschutes, Fremont, and Umpqua.	Proc 1155 37 Stat 1705			1,333,360			
1915 July 19 Part transferred to Crater, Deschutes, and Fremont; remainder eliminated; name discontinued.	Proc 1305 39 Stat 1738						

Name, Date Established, History	Citation	Acreage When Established or Earliest Documentation			Acreage as of September 1981		
		NF Land	Other	Total	NF Land	Other	Total
Payette (New), Idaho							
1944 April 1 Reestablished by combining Idaho and Weiser.	PLO 218 9-FR 3655	2,300,103	111,536	2,411,639	2,314,436	111,337	2,425,773
Payette (Old), Idaho							
1905 June 3 Established.	Proc 34 Stat 3067			1,460,960			
1944 Apr 1 Entire forest transferred to Boise.	PLO 217 9-FR 3655						
Payson, Utah							
1901 Aug 3 Established.	Proc 32 Stat 1985			86,400			
1908 July 1 Combined with Vernon and part of Fillmore to establish Nebo; name discontinued.	EO 827						
Pecos, New Mexico							
1908 July 1 Established; name changed from Pecos River.	EO 908			430,880			
1915 July 1 Combined with Jemez to establish Santa Fe; name discontinued.	EO 2160						
Pecos River, New Mexico							
1892 Jan 11 Established.	Proc 27 Stat 998			311,040			
1908 July 1 Name changed to Pecos.	EO 908						
Peloncillo, New Mexico							
1906 Nov 5 Established.	Proc 34 Stat 3248			178,977			
1908 July 1 Combined with Chiricahua; name discontinued.	EO 908						
Pend d'Oreille, Idaho							
1908 July 1 Established from parts of Cabinet, Coeur d'Alene, Kootenai, and Priest River.	EO 844			913,364			
1910 May 6 Name changed to Pend Oreille.	Proc 1025 36 Stat 2688						
Pend Oreille, Idaho							
1910 May 6 Name changed from Pend d'Oreille.	Proc 1025 36 Stat 2688			911,764			
1933 Sept 30 Largest portion consolidated with Kaniksu; remainder transferred to Coeur d'Alene; name discontinued.	EO 6303						
Pike, Colorado							
1908 July 1 Name changed from Pikes Peak.	EO 888			1,457,524			
1930 May 26 Part of Leadville added.	Proc 1909 46 Stat 3022						
1975 Combined administratively with San Isabel, known as Pike-San Isabel.	Proc 1909 46 Stat 3022				1,106,870	176,464	1,283,334
Pikes Peak, Colorado							
1905 May 12 Name changed from Pikes Peak Timber Land Reserve.	Proc 34 Stat 3029			847,968			
1908 July 1 Name changed to Pike.	EO 888						

Name, Date Established, History	Citation	Acreage When Established or Earliest Documentation			Acreage as of September 1981		
		NF Land	Other	Total	NF Land	Other	Total
Pikes Peak Timber Land Reserve, Colorado							
1892 Feb 11 Established.	Proc 27 Stat 1006			184,320			
1905 May 12 Boundary redescribed; combined with Plum Creek and South Platte; name changed to Pikes Peak.	Proc 34 Stat 3029						
Pinal Mountains, Arizona							
1905 Mar 20 Established.	Proc 34 Stat 2991			45,760			
1908 Jan 13 Combined with Tonto; name discontinued.	Proc 795 35 Stat 2176						
Pine Mountain and Zaka Lake, California							
1898 Mar 2 Established.	Proc 30 Stat 1767			1,644,594			
1903 Dec 22 Combined with Santa Ynez to create Santa Barbara; name discontinued.	Proc 33 Stat 2327						
Pine Plains, New York							
1925 Apr 10 Established from part of Pine Plains Military Reservation.	EO 4193	9,800		9,800			
1927 Dec 2 EO 4193 rescinded.	EO 4776						
Pinnacles, California							
1906 July 18 Established.	Proc 34 Stat 3221			14,108			
1908 July 1 Added to Monterey; name discontinued.	EO 908						
Pisgah, North Carolina							
1916 Oct 17 Established.	Proc 1349 39 Stat 1811			53,810			
1921 Mar 25 Boone and other lands added.	Proc 1591 42 Stat 2234						
1936 July 10 Unaka and other lands added.	Proc 2187 50 Stat 1745 1-FR 792						
1954 Combined administratively with Croatan and Nantahala, known as National Forests in					493,582	582,929	1,076,511
Plum Creek Timber Land, Colorado							
1892 June 23 Established.	Proc 27 Stat 1029			179,200			
1905 May 12 Consolidated with Pikes Peak; name discontinued.	Proc 34 Stat 3029						
Plumas, California							
1905 Mar 27 Established.	Proc 34 Stat 2992			579,520			
1908 July 1 Part of Diamond Mountains added.	EO 905				1,163,658	247,871	1,411,529
Pocatello, Idaho and Utah							
1903 Sept 5 Established.	Proc 33 Stat 2318			49,920			
1908 July 1 Port Neuf and part of Bear River added.	EO 801						
1915 July 1 Entire forest transferred to Cache; name discontinued.	EO 2179						

Name, Date Established, History		Citation	Acreage When Established or Earliest Documentation			Acreage as of September 1981		
			NF Land	Other	Total	NF Land	Other	Total
Portales, New Mexico								
1905 Oct 3	Established.	Proc 34 Stat 3178			172,680			
1907 Mar 16	Proclamation revoked; land restored to public domain.	Proc 35 Stat 2120						
Port Neuf, Idaho								
1907 Mar 2	Established.	Proc 34 Stat 3292			99,508			
1908 July 1	Combined with Pocatello; name discontinued.	EO 801						
Powell, Utah								
1908 July 1	Name changed from Aquarius.	EO 908			726,159			
1922 July 1	Eastern division of Sevier added.	EO 3635						
1944 Oct 1	Entire forest transferred to Dixie.	PLO 260 10-FR 1244						
Prescott, Arizona								
1898 May 10	Established.	Proc 30 Stat 1771			10,240			
1908 July 1	Verde added.	EO 908						
1934 Oct 22	Tusayan added.	EO 6882				1,237,076	170,526	1,407,602
Priest River, Idaho and Washington								
1897 Feb 22	Established, effective 3/1/1898.	Proc 29 Stat 903			645,120			
1908 July 1	Divided to establish Pend d'Oreille and Kaniksu; name discontinued.	EO 844, 845.						
Pryor Mountains, Montana								
1906 Nov 6	Established.	Proc 34 Stat 3258			78,732			
1908 July 1	Combined with part of Yellowstone to establish Beartooth; name discontinued.	EO 896						
Raft River, Utah and Idaho								
1906 Nov 5	Established.	Proc 34 Stat 3247	Utah Ida.	117,203 293,044 410,247				
1908 July 1	Combined with Cassia to establish Minidoka; name discontinued.	EO 908						
Rainier, Washington								
1907 Mar 2	Name changed from Mount Rainier.	Proc 34 Stat 3296			2,565,760			
1933 Oct 13	Entire forest divided among Columbia, Snoqualmie, and Wenatchee.	EO 6333, 6334, 6335, 6336						
Rio Grande, Colorado								
1908 July 1	Established from parts of San Juan and Cochetopa.	EO 887			1,262,158			
1944 July 1	Land from Cochetopa added.	PLO 258 10-FR 1243				1,851,792	109,292	1,961,084

Name, Date Established, History		Citation	Acreage When Established or Earliest Documentation			Acreage as of September 1981		
			NF Land	Other	Total	NF Land	Other	Total
Rogue River, California and Oregon			Calif.			Calif.		
1932 July 9	Name changed from Crater.	EO 5882	47,401	8,805	56,206	53,826	7,205	61,031
			Ore.			Ore.		
			811,642	290,082	1,101,724	584,244	49,488	633,732
			859,043	298,887	1,157,930	638,070	56,693	694,763
Roosevelt, Colorado								
1932 Mar 28	Name changed from Colorado.	EO 5826	785,522	316,436	1,101,958			
1975	Combined administratively with Arapaho, known as Arapaho-Roosevelt.					788,333	294,327	1,082,660
Routt, Colorado								
1908 July 1	Established from part of Park Range.	EO 837			1,049,686			
1929 Aug 2	Part of Hayden added.	Proc 1888 46 Stat 3003				1,126,622	121,033	1,247,655
Ruby, Nevada								
1912 June 19	Established from portion of Humboldt and other lands.	Proc 1202 37 Stat 1747			433,570			
1917 July 1	Entire forest transferred to Humboldt; name discontinued.	EO 2631						
Ruby Mountains, Nevada								
1906 May 3	Established.	Proc 34 Stat 3198			423,660			
1908 July 1	Added to Humboldt; name discontinued.	EO 908						
Sabine, Texas								
1936 Oct 13	Established.	Proc 2204 50 Stat 1787 1-FR 1606	183,571	256,029	439,600			
1936	Combined administratively with Angelina, Davy Crockett, and Sam Houston, known as National Forests in Texas.					188,220	254,485	442,705
Sacramento, New Mexico								
1907 Apr 24	Established from part of Lincoln and other lands.	Proc 35 Stat 2127			881,841			
1908 July 1	Combined with Guadalupe to establish Alamo; name discontinued.	EO 908						
St. Francis, Arkansas								
1960 Nov 8	Established; combined administratively with Ozark, known as Ozark-St. Francis.	Proc 3379 25-FR 10863	20,611	9,269	29,880	20,946	8,783	29,729
St. Joe, Idaho								
1911 July 1	Established from parts of Clearwater and Coeur d'Alene.	Proc 1143 37 Stat 1697			1,033,500			
1973 July 1	Combined administratively with Kaniksu and Coeur d'Alene, known as Idaho Panhandle National Forests.					865,068	209,832	1,074,900

Name, Date Established, History	Citation	Acreage When Established or Earliest Documentation			Acreage as of September 1981		
		NF Land	Other	Total	NF Land	Other	Total
Salmon, Idaho							
1908 July 1 Established from parts of Bitter Root, Lemhi, and Salmon River.	EO 841			1,762,472			
1938 Oct 8 Part of Lemhi and other lands added.	EO 7986 3-FR 2435				1,771,029	23,090	1,794,119
Salmon River, Idaho							
1906 Nov 5 Established.	Proc 34 Stat 3250			1,879,680			
1908 July 1 Part combined with Challis and part with Salmon; name discontinued.	EO 840, 841						
Salt Lake, Utah							
1904 May 26 Established.	Proc 33 Stat 2364			95,440			
1908 July 1 Combined with Wasatch; name discontinued.	EO 908						
Sam Houston, Texas							
1936 Oct 13 Established.	Proc 2205 50 Stat 1789 1-FR 1608	147,833	343,967	491,800			
1936 Combined administratively with Angelina, Davy Crockett, and Sabine, known as National Forests in Texas.					160,437	331,363	491,800
Samuel R. McKelvie, Nebraska							
1971 Oct 15 Established from part of Nebraska. Administered with Nebraska, known as Nebraska National Forests.	85 Stat 383	115,703	1,116	116,819	115,703	1,116	116,819
San Benito, California							
1907 Oct 26 Established.	Proc 779 35 Stat 2159			140,069			
1908 July 1 Added to Monterey; name discontinued.	EO 908						
San Bernardino, California							
1893 Feb 25 Established.	Proc 27 Stat 1068			737,280			
1908 July 1 Entire forest combined with parts of Santa Barbara and San Gabriel to establish Angeles; name discontinued.	EO 846						
1925 Sept 30 Reestablished from parts of Angeles and Cleveland.	Proc 1750 44 Stat 2586	597,301	206,824	804,125	635,620	174,667	810,287
San Francisco Mountains, Arizona							
1898 Aug 17 Established.	Proc 30 Stat 1780			975,360			
1908 July 1 Entire forest combined with other lands to establish Coconino; name discontinued.	Proc 818 35 Stat 2196						
San Gabriel, California							
1892 Dec 20 Established.	Proc 27 Stat 1049			555,520			
1908 July 1 Part combined with Angeles and remainder with Santa Barbara; name discontinued.	EO 846, 852						

Name, Date Established, History	Citation	Acreage When Established or Earliest Documentation			Acreage as of September 1981		
		NF Land	Other	Total	NF Land	Other	Total
San Isabel, Colorado							
1902 Apr 11 Established.	Proc 32 Stat 1988			77,980			
1908 July 1 Entire Wet Mountains added.	EO 908						
1910 May 27 Part of Las Animas added; land eliminated.	Proc 1040 36 Stat 2701						
1944 July 1 Part of Cochetopa added.	PLO 258 10-FR 1243						
1975 Combined administratively with Pike, known as Pike-San Isabel.					1,110,576	130,874	1,241,450
San Jacinto, California							
1897 Feb 22 Established.	Proc 29 Stat 893			740,000			
1908 July 1 Combined with Trabuco Canyon to establish Cleveland; name discontinued.	EO 908						
San Juan, Colorado							
1905 June 3 Established.	Proc 34 Stat 3070			1,437,406			
1920 Nov 21 Durango added.	EO 3357						
1947 July 1 Part of Montezuma added.	PLO 400 12-FR 5849				1,867,782	233,679	2,101,461
San Luis, California							
1908 July 1 Established from part of San Luis Obispo.	EO 847			355,990			
1910 July 1 Consolidated with Santa Barbara; name discontinued.	EO 1209						
San Luis Obispo, California							
1906 June 25 Established.	Proc 34 Stat 3217			363,350			
1908 July 1 Part combined with Santa Barbara; remainder used to establish San Luis; name discontinued.	EO 847, 852						
San Mateo, New Mexico							
1906 Nov 5 Established.	Proc 34 Stat 3249			424,663			
1908 July 1 Entire forest added to Magdalena; name discontinued.	EO908						
Santa Barbara, California							
1903 Dec 22 Established by consolidation of Pine Mountain and Zaca Lake, and Santa Ynez.	Proc 33 Stat 2327			1,838,323			
1908 July 1 Part of San Gabriel and San Luis Obispo added.	EO 852						
1910 July 1 San Luis added.	EO 1209						
1919 Aug 18 Monterey added.	EO 3153						
1936 Dec 3 Name changed to Los Padres.	EO 7501 1-FR 2141						

Name, Date Established, History	Citation	Acreage When Established or Earliest Documentation			Acreage as of September 1981		
		NF Land	Other	Total	NF Land	Other	Total
Santa Catalina, Arizona							
1902 July 2 Established.	Proc 32 Stat 2012			155,520			
1908 July 1 Combined with Santa Rita and Dragoon to establish Coronado; name discontinued.	EO 908						
Santa Fe, New Mexico							
1915 July 1 Established by combining Jemez and Pecos.	EO 2160			1,357,210	1,587,550	146,985	1,734,535
Santa Rita, Arizona							
1902 Apr 11 Established.	Proc 32 Stat 1989			337,300			
1908 July 1 Combined with Santa Catalina and Dragoon to establish Coronado; name discontinued.	EO 908						
Santa Rosa, Nevada							
1911 Apr 11 Established.	Proc 1120 37 Stat 1678			299,960			
1917 July 1 Entire forest transferred to Humboldt; name discontinued.	EO 2631						
Santa Ynez, California							
1899 Oct 2 Established.	Proc 31 Stat 1954			145,280			
1903 Dec 22 Combined with Pine Mountain and Zaca Lake to create Santa Barbara; name discontinued.	Proc 33 Stat 2327						
Santiam, Oregon							
1911 July 1 Established from parts of Cascade and Oregon.	Proc 1163 37 Stat 1712			710,170			
1933 July 1 Entire forest combined with Cascade to establish Willamette.	EO 6104						
Savanna, Illinois							
1925 June 5 Established from part of Savanna Military Reservation.	EO 4247	10,710		10,710			
1926 June 15 Name changed to Bellevue-Savanna.	EO 4458						
Sawtooth, Idaho and Utah							
1905 May 29 Established.	Proc 34 Stat 3058			1,947,520			
1953 July 1 Minidoka added.	PLO 923 18-FR 6822				Ida. 1,731,504 Utah 71,183 1,802,687	74,150 21,221 95,371	1,805,654 92,404 1,898,058
Selway, Idaho							
1911 July 1 Established from parts of Clearwater and Nezperce.	Proc 1140 37 Stat 1695			1,802,000			
1934 Oct 29 Entire forest divided among Bitterroot, Clearwater, Lolo, and Nezperce; name discontinued.	EO 6889						

Name, Date Established, History	Citation	Acreage When Established or Earliest Documentation			Acreage as of September 1981		
		NF Land	Other	Total	NF Land	Other	Total
Sequoia, California							
1908 July 1 Established from portion of Sierra.	EO 904			3,051,782			
1915 July 1 Kern added.	EO 2169				1,125,533	54,509	1,180,042
Sevier, Utah							
1905 May 12 Established.	Proc 34 Stat 3020			357,000			
1922 July 1 Entire forest transferred to Dixie and Powell; name discontinued.	EO 3634, 3636						
Shasta, California							
1905 Oct 3 Established.	Proc 34 Stat 3157			1,377,126			
1954 Combined administratively with Trinity, known as Shasta-Trinity.					1,099,001	536,054	1,635,055
Shawnee, Illinois							
1939 Sept 6 Established.	Proc 2357 54 Stat 2649 4-FR 3860	186,627	615,317	801,944	253,440	461,202	714,642
Shenandoah, Virginia and West Virginia		Va.					
1918 May 16 Established.	Proc 1448 40 Stat 1779	132,256	21,980	154,236			
		W. Va.					
		13,318	383	13,701			
		145,574	22,363	167,937			
1932 June 28 Name changed to George Washington.	EO 5867						
Short Pine, South Dakota							
1905 July 22 Established.	Proc 34 Stat 3129			19,040			
1908 July 1 Transferred to Sioux; name discontinued.	EO 908						
Shoshone, Wyoming							
1908 July 1 Established from part of Yellowstone.	EO 895			1,689,680			
1945 July 1 Washakie added.	PLO 296 10-FR 13077				2,433,236	32,779	2,466,015
Sierra, California							
1893 Feb 14 Established.	Proc 27 Stat 1059			4,096,000	1,303,112	109,529	1,412,641
Sierra Madre, Wyoming							
1906 Nov 5 Established.	Proc 34 Stat 3242			370,911			
1908 July 1 Combined with part of Park Range to establish Hayden; name discontinued.	EO 839						
Sioux, Montana and South Dakota							
1908 July 1 Established by consolidation of Cave Hills, Ekalaka, Long Pine, Short Pine, and Slim Butte.	EO 908		Mont.	145,253			
			S. Dak.	104,400			
				249,653			
1920 Jan 13 Entire forest transferred to Custer; name discontinued.	EO 3216						

Name, Date Established, History	Citation	Acreage When Established or Earliest Documentation			Acreage as of September 1981		
		NF Land	Other	Total	NF Land	Other	Total
Siskiyou, Oregon and California							
1906 Oct 5 Established.	Proc 34 Stat 3239			1,132,582			
1908 July 1 Coquille and other lands added.	EO 866				Calif.		
					33,354	6,314	39,668
					Ore.		
					1,060,175	64,121	1,124,296
					1,093,529	70,435	1,163,964
Sitgreaves, Arizona							
1908 July 1 Established from parts of Black Mesa and Tonto.	EO 868			749,084			
1974 Combined administratively with Apache, known as Apache-Sitgreaves.					815,343	69,138	884,481
Siuslaw, Oregon							
1908 July 1 Established from parts of Tillamook and Umpqua.	EO 860			821,794	628,237	207,112	835,349
Six Rivers, California							
1947 June 3 Established from parts of Klamath, Siskiyou, and Trinity.	Proc 2733 61 Stat 1070 12-FR 3647	926,105	167,771	1,093,876	980,416	137,750	1,118,166
Slim Buttes, South Dakota							
1904 Mar 5 Established.	Proc 33 Stat 2337			58,160			
1908 July 1 Transferred to Sioux; name discontinued.	EO 908						
Snoqualmie, Washington							
1908 July 1 Established from part of Washington.	EO 824			961,120			
1933 Oct 13 Part of Rainier added.	EO 6334						
1974 Combined administratively with Mount Baker, known as Mount Baker-Snoqualmie.					1,227,582	330,311	1,557,893
Snowy Mountains, Montana							
1906 Nov 5 Established.	Proc 34 Stat 3246			126,080			
1908 July 1 Combined with Little Belt, Highwood Mountains, and Little Rockies to establish Jefferson; name discontinued.	EO 908						
Sopris, Colorado							
1909 Apr 26 Established from portion of Holy Cross.	EO 1069			655,360			
1920 Aug 7 Entire forest transferred to Holy Cross; name discontinued.	EO 3317						
South Platte, Colorado							
1892 Dec 9 Established.	Proc 27 Stat 1044			683,520			
1905 May 12 Consolidated with Pikes Peak; name discontinued.	Proc 34 Stat 3029						

Name, Date Established, History	Citation	Acreage When Established or Earliest Documentation			Acreage as of September 1981		
		NF Land	Other	Total	NF Land	Other	Total
Stanislaus, California							
1897 Feb 22 Established.	Proc 29 Stat 898	691,200					
1954 Combined administratively with Calaveras Big Tree.					898,248	192,295	1,090,543
Stony Creek, California							
1907 Feb 6 Established.	Proc 34 Stat 3273			937,569			
1908 July 1 Transferred to Trinity; portion used to establish California; name discontinued.	EO 900, 907						
Sumter, South Carolina							
1936 July 13 Established.	Proc 2188 50 Stat 1750 1-FR 799	251,433	756,467	1,007,900			
1969 Combined administratively with Francis Marion, known as Francis Marion and Sumter.					358,589	607,173	965,762
Sundance, Wyoming							
1908 July 1 Established from entire Bear Lodge and part of Black Hills.	EO 850			183,224			
1915 July 1 Entire forest transferred to Black Hills; name discontinued.	EO 2161						
Superior, Minnesota							
1909 Feb 13 Established.	Proc 848 35 Stat 2223			909,734	2,048,937	1,211,906	3,260,843
Tahoe, California							
1905 Oct 3 Name changed from Lake Tahoe; boundary redescribed.	Proc 34 Stat 3163			838,837			
1906 Sept 17 Yuba and other lands added.	Proc 34 Stat 3232				813,233	395,693	1,208,926
Talladega, Alabama							
1936 July 17 Established.	Proc 2190 50 Stat 1755 1-FR 860	232,601	488,764	721,365			
1936 Combined administratively with Black Warrior and Conecuh, known as National Forests in Alabama.					371,139	356,015	727,154
Taos, New Mexico							
1906 Nov 7 Established.	Proc 34 Stat 3262			233,200			
1908 July 1 Entire forest combined with part of Jemez to establish Carson; name discontinued.	EO 848						
Targhee, Idaho and Wyoming							
1908 July 1 Established from portion of Yellowstone and entire Henrys Lake.	EO 871			Ida. 1,101,720 Wyo. 377,600 1,479,320			
1917 July 1 Palisade added.	EO 2632				Ida. 1,311,737 Wyo. 330,783 1,642,520	43,682 2,421 46,103	1,355,419 333,204 1,688,623

Name, Date Established, History	Citation	Acreage When Established or Earliest Documentation			Acreage as of September 1981		
		NF Land	Other	Total	NF Land	Other	Total
Teton, Wyoming							
1897 Feb 22 Established, effective March 1, 1898.	Proc 29 Stat 906			829,440			
1903 Jan 29 Consolidated with Yellowstone; name discontinued.	Proc 32 Stat 2030						
1908 July 1 Reestablished from portion of Yellowstone.	EO 872			1,991,200			
1973 Combined administratively with Bridger, known as Bridger-Teton.					1,666,694	28,389	1,695,083
Tillamook, Oregon							
1907 Mar 2 Established.	Proc 34 Stat 3310			175,518			
1908 July 1 Portion combined with part of Umpqua to establish Siuslaw; remainder restored to public domain; name discontinued.	EO 860						
Tobyhanna, Pennsylvania							
1925 Apr 10 Established from part of Tobyhanna Military Reservation.	EO 4194	20,870		20,870			
1928 Oct 10 EO 4194 rescinded.	EO 4976						
Toiyabe, Nevada and California							
1907 Mar 1 Established.	Proc 34 Stat 3278			625,040			
1908 July 1 Monitor and Toquima added.	EO 908						
1915 July 15 Moapa added.	EO 2162						
1932 July 1 Entire forest transferred to Nevada; name discontinued.	EO 5863						
1938 May 9 Reestablished from parts of Humboldt and Nevada.	EO 7884 3-FR 913	2,152,231	46,268	2,198,499			
1945 July 1 Part of Mono added.	PLO 307 11-FR 250						
1957 Oct 1 Part of Nevada added.	PLO 1487 22-FR 7309			Nev. Calif.	2,558,450 633,891	133,249 61,096	2,691,699 694,987
					3,192,341	194,345	3,386,686
Tombigbee, Mississippi							
1959 Nov 27 Established; added administratively to Bienville, DeSoto, Holly Springs, Homochitto; known as National Forests in Mississippi.	Proc 3326 24-FR 9654	65,232	53,901	119,133	66,341	52,814	119,155
Tongass, Alaska							
1907 Sept 10 Established.	Proc 35 Stat 2152			2,262,624			
1908 July 1 Alexander Archipelago added.	EO 908						
1974 Divided administratively into three units: Chatham, Ketchikan, and Sitka.					16,931,502	509,612	17,441,114

Name, Date Established, History	Citation	Acreage When Established or Earliest Documentation			Acreage as of September 1981		
		NF Land	Other	Total	NF Land	Other	Total

Tonto, Arizona

1905 Oct 3	Established.	Proc 34 Stat 3166			1,115,200			
1908 Jan 13	Pinal Mountains and other lands added.	Proc 795 35 Stat 2176						
1908 July 1	Part of Black Mesa added. Other lands transferred.	EO 869						
1953 July 1	Part of Crook added.	PLO 924 18-FR 6823				2,874,500	95,020	2,969,520

Toquima, Nevada

| 1907 Apr 15 | Established. | Proc   35 Stat 2121 | | | 368,000 | | | |
| 1908 July 1 | Entire forest added to Toiyabe; name discontinued. | EO 908 | | | | | | |

Trabuco Cañon, California

| 1893 Feb 25 | Established. | Proc   27 Stat 1066 | | | 49,920 | | | |
| 1907 July 6 | Name changed to Trabuco Canyon and land added. | Proc   35 Stat 2144 | | | | | | |

Trabuco Canyon, California

| 1907 July 6 | Spelling changed from Trabuco Cañon and land added. | Proc   35 Stat 2144 | | | 153,387 | | | |
| 1908 July 1 | Combined with San Jacinto to establish Cleveland; name discontinued. | EO 908 | | | | | | |

Trinity, California

| 1905 Apr 26 | Established. | Proc   34 Stat 2998 | | 1,243,042 | | | | |
| 1954 | Combined administratively with Shasta, known as Shasta-Trinity. | | | | 1,047,164 | 131,934 | 1,179,098 | |

Tumacacori, Arizona

| 1906 Nov 7 | Established. | Proc   34 Stat 3263 | | | 203,550 | | | |
| 1908 July 1 | Combined with Baboquivari and Huachuca to establish Garces; name discontinued. | EO 908 | | | | | | |

Tusayan, Arizona

| 1910 July 1 | Established from part of Coconino and other lands. | Proc 1049   36 Stat 2709 | | | 1,830,487 | | | |
| 1934 Oct 22 | Entire forest transferred to Prescott; name discontinued. | EO 6882 | | | | | | |

Tuskegee, Alabama

| 1959 Nov 27 | Established; added administratively with William B. Bankhead, Conecuh, and Talladega, known as National Forests in Alabama. | Proc 3326   24-FR 9651 | 10,777 | 4,850 | 15,627 | 10,795 | 4,833 | 15,628 |

Uinta, Utah

| 1906 Jan 16 | Name changed from Uintah. | Proc   34 Stat 3186 | | Utah Wyo. | 2,148,510 4,596 2,153,106 | 812,787 | 76,421 | 889,208 |

Name, Date Established, History	Citation	Acreage When Established or Earliest Documentation			Acreage as of September 1981		
		NF Land	Other	Total	NF Land	Other	Total
Uintah, Utah							
1897 Feb 22 Established, effective March 1, 1898.	Proc 29 Stat 895			875,520			
1906 Jan 16 Name changed to Uinta; land added.	Proc 34 Stat 3186						
Umatilla, Oregon and Washington							
1908 July 1 Established from part of Blue Mountains and all of Heppner.	EO 815			540,496			
1920 Nov 5 Wenaha added.	EO 3349				Ore.		
					1,088,158	101,589	1,189,747
					Wash.		
					311,209	8,152	319,361
					1,399,367	109,741	1,509,108
Umpqua, Oregon							
1907 Mar 2 Established.	Proc 34 Stat 3301			798,400	988,093	45,558	1,033,651
Unaka, North Carolina, Tennessee, Virginia							
1920 July 24 Established.	Proc 1571 41 Stat 1801	N.C.	123,289	123,289			
		Tenn.					
		95,135	420,036	515,171			
		Va.					
		22,404	180,132	202,536			
		117,539	723,457	840,996			
1936 July 10 Entire forest transferred to Pisgah; name discontinued.	Proc 2187 50 Stat 1745 1-FR 792						
Uncompahgre, Colorado							
1905 June 14 Established.	Proc 34 Stat 3109			478,111			
1908 July 1 Fruita and part of Ouray and other lands added.	EO 885						
1947 July 1 Part of Montezuma added.	PLO 400 12-FR 5849						
1976 Combined administratively with Grand Mesa and Gunnison.					944,237	99,789	1,044,026
Upton, New York							
1925 Apr 10 Established from part of Upton Military Reservation.	EO 4195	6,154		6,154			
1927 June 29 EO 4195 rescinded.	EO 4676						
Uwharrie, North Carolina							
1961 Jan 12 Established from part of the Uwharrie Purchase Unit; added administratively to Croatan, Nantahala and Pisgah, known as National Forests in North Carolina.	Secretary of Agriculture Order 26-FR 627 26-FR 628	43,391	176,948	220,339	46,655	173,102	219,757
Vegas, Nevada							
1907 Dec 12 Established.	Proc 784 35 Stat 2165			195,840			
1908 July 1 Transferred to Moapa; name discontinued.	EO 908						

Name, Date Established, History	Citation	Acreage When Established or Earliest Documentation			Acreage as of September 1981		
		NF Land	Other	Total	NF Land	Other	Total
Verde, Arizona							
1907 Dec 30 Established.	Proc 789 35 Stat 2170			721,780			
1908 July 1 Combined with Prescott; name discontinued.	EO 908						
Vernon, Utah							
1906 Apr 24 Established.	Proc 34 Stat 3197			68,800			
1908 July 1 Combined with Payson and part of Fillmore to establish Nebo; name discontinued.	EO 827						
Wallowa, Oregon							
1905 May 6 Established.	Proc 34 Stat 3004			747,200			
1907 Mar 1 Combined with Chesnimnus to create Imnaha; name discontinued.	Proc 34 Stat 3284						
1908 July 1 Reestablished; name changed from Imnaha.	EO 908			1,750,240			
1954 Combined administratively with Whitman, known as Wallowa-Whitman.					986,105	78,674	1,064,779
Warner Mountains, California							
1904 Nov 29 Established.	Proc 33 Stat 2375			306,518			
1908 July 1 Combined with Modoc; name discontinued.	EO 908						
Wasatch, Utah and Wyoming							
1906 Aug 16 Established.	Proc 34 Stat 3225			85,440			
1908 July 1 Entire Grantsville and Salt Lake added.	EO 908				Utah 848,716	175,604	1,024,320
					Wyo. 37,762	9,942	47,704
					886,478	185,546	1,072,024
Washakie, Wyoming							
1911 July 1 Established from part of Bonneville.	Proc 1147 37 Stat 1699			393,950			
1916 July 1 Bonneville added. Other lands transferred.	Proc 1338 39 Stat 1784						
1945 July 1 Entire forest transferred to Shoshone.	PLO 296 10-FR 13077						
Washington, Washington							
1897 Feb 22 Established, effective March 1, 1898.	Proc 29 Stat 904			3,594,240			
1924 Jan 21 Name changed to Mount Baker.	EO 3943						
Wayne, Ohio							
1951 Oct 1 Established.	Secretary of Agriculture Order No. 4 16-FR 9174	103,842	1,362,187	1,466,029			
1952 Combined administratively with Hoosier, known as Wayne-Hoosier.					176,071	656,882	832,953

Name, Date Established, History	Citation	Acreage When Established or Earliest Documentation			Acreage as of September 1981		
		NF Land	Other	Total	NF Land	Other	Total
Weiser, Idaho							
1905 May 25 Established.	Proc 34 Stat 3055			324,964			
1944 Apr 1 Entire forest combined with Idaho to establish Payette (New).	PLO 218 9-FR 3655						
Wenaha, Oregon and Washington							
1905 May 12 Established.	Proc 34 Stat 3010		Ore. Wash.	413,250 318,400 731,650			
1920 Nov 5 Entire forest transferred to Umatilla; name discontinued.	EO 3349						
Wenatchee, Washington							
1908 July 1 Established from part of Washington.	EO 825			1,421,120			
1933 Oct 13 Part of Rainier added.	EO 6335				1,618,329	284,186	1,902,515
Wet Mountains, Colorado							
1905 June 12 Established.	Proc 34 Stat 3096			239,621			
1908 July 1 Combined with San Isabel; name discontinued.	EO 908						
White Mountain, Maine and New Hampshire		Maine			Maine		
1918 May 16 Established.	Proc 1449 40 Stat 1779	27,860 N.H. 332,778 360,638	2,780 70,959 73,739	30,640 403,737 434,377	41,833 N.H. 686,432 728,265	11,728 111,631 123,359	53,561 798,063 851,624
White River, Colorado							
1902 June 28 Name changed from White River Plateau Timber Land Reserve.	Proc 32 Stat 2008			970,880			
1945 Jan 1 Entire Holy Cross added.	PLO 263 10-FR 2251				1,960,740	128,727	2,089,467
White River Plateau Timber Land Reserve, Colorado							
1891 Oct 16 Established.	Proc 27 Stat 993			1,198,080			
1902 June 28 Name changed to White River; boundary redescribed.	Proc 32 Stat 2008						
Whitman, Oregon							
1908 July 1 Established from part of Blue Mountains.	EO 813			1,234,020			
1920 June 20 Minam added.	EO 3286						
1954 Combined administratively with Wallowa, known as Wallowa-Whitman.					1,264,694	46,578	1,311,272
Wichita, Oklahoma							
1901 July 4 Established.	Proc 32 Stat 1973			57,120			
1936 Nov 27 Abolished.	Proc 2211 50 Stat 1797 1-FR 2148						
Willamette, Oregon							
1933 July 1 Established by combining Santiam and Cascade.	EO 6104	1,624,446	173,890	1,798,336	1,675,383	121,331	1,796,714

Name, Date Established, History	Citation	Acreage When Established or Earliest Documentation			Acreage as of September 1981		
		NF Land	Other	Total	NF Land	Other	Total
William B. Bankhead, Alabama							
1942 June 6 Name changed from Black Warrior. Combined administratively with Conecuh and Talladega, known as National Forests in Alabama.	56 Stat 327	177,936	382,668	560,604	179,608	169,309	348,917
Winema, Oregon							
1961 July 1 Established.	Proc 3423 26-FR 6799 26-FR 6802	908,985	57,880	966,865	1,043,179	51,952	1,095,131
Wyoming, Wyoming							
1908 July 1 Established from part of Yellowstone.	EO 873			976,320			
1923 May 14 Bridger added.	EO 3842						
1941 Mar 10 Name changed to Bridger.	EO 8709 6-FR 1400						
Yellowstone, Wyoming, Montana, and Idaho							
1902 May 22 Name changed from Yellowstone Park Timber Land Reserve.	Proc 32 Stat 1999			6,580,920			
1903 Jan 29 Absaroka and Teton added.	Proc 32 Stat 2030						
1908 July 1 Lands divided among Targhee, Teton, Wyoming, Bonneville, Absaroka, Shoshone, and Beartooth; name discontinued.	EO 871, 872, 873, 874, 875, 895, 896						
Yellowstone Park Timber Land Reserve, Wyoming							
1891 Mar 30 Established.	Proc 26 Stat 1565			1,239,040			
1902 May 22 Name changed to Yellowstone; lands added and eliminated.	Proc 32 Stat 1999						
Yuba, California							
1905 Nov 11 Established.	Proc 34 Stat 3184			524,287			
1906 Sept 17 Combined with Tahoe; name discontinued.	Proc 34 Stat 3232						
Zuni, Arizona and New Mexico							
1909 Mar 2 Established from parts of Zuni and Navajo Indian Reservations and other land.	Proc 864 35 Stat 2242		Ariz. N. Mex.	266,981 404,000 670,981			
1914 Sept 10 Entire forest transferred to Manzano; name discontinued.	EO 2045						

APPENDIX II

The National Parks of the United States

The following listing has been compiled from *Index: National Park System and Related Areas as of June 30, 1979* (GPO, 1979), *Our National Parks Policy: A Critical History* by John Ise (Johns Hopkins University Press, 1961), the *U.S. Statutes at Large*, and "National Park Service, Listing of Acreages, 12/31/81" (NPS, 1982).

Although the National Park Service was established in 1916, it was not until President Franklin Roosevelt signed Executive Order 6155 in 1933 that the national park system was formally created. The 1933 order brought areas administered by the secretary of agriculture and the secretary of war under the authority of the National Park Service in the Department of the Interior. It consolidated all national parks, monuments, historical areas, military parks, cemeteries, memorials, battlefields, and the National Capital Parks into one system. After 1933, national recreational areas, parkways, seashores, lakeshores, rivers, and trails were also added to the system. All of these areas were managed under a single administrative code until 1964 when Secretary of the Interior Stewart L. Udall reorganized the National Park Service. He named three categories of areas—natural, historical, and recreational. In 1968, National Park Service Director George B. Hartzog issued administrative policies for the categories, giving each appropriate principles of resource management, resource

use, and physical development. In 1970, President Nixon signed the General Authorities Act recognizing the three categories; almost all national parks fall into the "natural" category.

National parks are established by special acts of Congress. Most were created from the public domain, from national forests, or from other federal lands. A few, such as the Grand Canyon, Bryce Canyon, and, more recently, Gates of the Arctic and Kenai Fjords, were established from national monuments, which had previously been set aside by presidential proclamation under authority of the 1906 Antiquities Act. Once park boundaries had been established, Congress sometimes appropriated funds for the purchase of private inholdings. Parks such as the Shenandoah, Mammoth Cave, and Isle Royale were created from lands that had previously been largely in private ownership. To provide the secretary of the interior with greater latitude in dealing with the problems of inholdings, the Sundry Civil Appropriations Act of June 20, 1920, authorized the acquisition of parkland through private donations of land or money; in some cases, the state acquired the land and the secretary was authorized to accept title to it. Congress authorized all parks formed from private lands to be automatically established upon the federal acquisition of a specified minimum acreage. However, years often intervened between authorization and establishment of these parks, and Congress sometimes changed the minimum acreage during the interim.

Because park acreage at the time of establishment is at best a tentative figure, the following table provides only 1981 acreages. The parks are listed under their current names; however, their legal histories, including name changes, changes in status, accompanying dates, and legal citations are provided. Areas once established as parks but later redesignated or absorbed by other areas are also listed. No acreages are shown for parks that no longer exist.

As of December 1981, there were forty-eight park units with 44,470,322.54 acres of federal land and 2,392,321.95 acres of nonfederal inholdings.

Definitions

FR   *Federal Register*. Created by the Federal Register Act of 1935 and consisting of daily publication containing executive orders and proclamations and the rules and regulations of the executive agencies that have general applicability and legal effect. The first number refers to the volume, the second to the page.

Proc   Proclamation. A presidential order with the force of law, usually dealing with matters of general interest.

Stat   *U. S. Statutes at Large*. Includes acts and resolutions of Congress as well as presidential proclamations and agreements. The first number refers to the volume and the second to the page.

			Acreage as of December 1981		
Name and Date Established		Citation	Federal	Nonfederal	Total
Acadia, Maine					
1916 July 8	Established as Sieur de Monts National Monument.	Proc 39 Stat 1785			
1919 Feb 22	Lafayette National Park established from Sieur de Monts.	40 Stat 1178			
1929 Jan 19	Name changed to Acadia.	45 Stat 1083	38,462	594	39,056
Arches, Utah					
1929 Apr 12	Proclaimed as national monument.	Proc 1875			
1971 Nov 12	Established as park.	85 Stat 422	66,343	7,035	73,378
Badlands, South Dakota					
1929 Mar 4	Authorized as monument.	45 Stat 1553			
1939 Jan 25	Established as monument.	Proc 2320 4–FR 457 53 Stat 2521			
1978 Nov 10	Established as park.	92 Stat 3521	152,689	90,613	243,302
Big Bend, Texas					
1935 June 20	Authorized.	49 Stat 393			
1944 June 12	Established.	61 Stat 91	708,118	33,000	741,118
Biscayne, Florida					
1968 Oct 18	Authorized as monument.	82 Stat 1188			
1980 June 28	Established as park.	94 Stat 599	95,071	85,057	180,128

Name and Date Established		Citation	Acreage as of December 1981		
			Federal	Nonfederal	Total
Bryce Canyon, Utah					
1923 June 8	Proclaimed as monument.	Proc 1664 43 Stat 1914			
1924 June 7	Established as Utah National Park.	43 Stat 593			
1928 Feb 25	Name changed to Bryce Canyon.	45 Stat 147	35,833	2	35,835
Canyonlands, Utah					
1964 Sept 12	Established.	78 Stat 934	337,570		337,570
Capitol Reef, Utah					
1937 Aug 2	Established as monument.	Proc 2246 50 Stat 1856			
1971 Dec 18	Established as park.	85 Stat 739	222,753	19,151	241,904
Carlsbad Caverns, New Mexico					
1923 Oct 25	Established as Carlsbad Cave National Monument.	43 Stat 1929			
1930 May 14	Established as park; name changed to Carlsbad Caverns.	46 Stat 279	46,435	320	46,755
Channel Islands, California					
1938 Apr 26	Proclaimed as monument.	Proc 2281 3–FR 981			
1980 Mar 5	Established as park.	94 Stat 74	10,891	238,463	249,354
Crater Lake, Oregon					
1902 May 22	Established.	32 Stat 202	160,290		160,290
Denali, Alaska					
1917 Feb 26	Established as Mount McKinley National Park.	39 Stat 938			
1978 Dec 1	Denali National Monument proclaimed.	Proc 4616 43–FR 57035			
1980 Dec 2	Monument and park lands combined; name changed to Denali National Park.	94 Stat 2382	4,698,583		4,698,583
Everglades, Florida					
1934 May 30	Authorized.	48 Stat 816			
1947 June 20	Established as park.	12–FR 4189	1,397,921	879	1,398,800
Gates of the Arctic, Alaska					
1978 Dec 1	Proclaimed as monument.	Proc 4617 43–FR 57043			
1980 Dec 2	Established as park.	94 Stat 2378	7,008,673	489,393	7,498,066
General Grant, California					
1890 Oct 1	Established as park.	26 Stat 650			
1940 Mar 4	Abolished and added to Kings Canyon as General Grant Grove.	54 Stat 43			

Name and Date Established		Citation	Acreage as of December 1981		
			Federal	Nonfederal	Total
Glacier, Montana					
1910 May 11	Established as park.	36 Stat 354			
1932 May 2	Authorized as part of Waterton-Glacier International Peace Park.	47 Stat 145	1,012,712	883	1,013,595
1932 June 30	Proclaimed as part of Waterton-Glacier International Peace Park.	Proc 2003 47 Stat 2519			
Glacier Bay, Alaska					
1925 Feb 25	Proclaimed as monument.	43 Stat 1988			
1978 Dec 1	Enlarged.	Proc 4618 43–FR 57053			
1980 Dec 2	Established as park.	94 Stat 2382	3,020,198	198	3,020,396
Grand Canyon, Arizona					
1893 Feb 20	Grand Canyon Forest Reserve established by proclamation.	27 Stat 1064			
1906 June 29	Grand Canyon Game Preserve authorized by Congress.	34 Stat 607			
1906 Nov 28	Grand Canyon Game Preserve established by proclamation.	34 Stat 3263			
1908 Jan 11	Grand Canyon National Monument established.	35 Stat 2175			
1919 Feb 26	Established as park.	40 Stat 1175			
1932 Dec 22	Another Grand Canyon National Monument established.	47 Stat 2547			
1969 Jan 20	Marble Canyon National Monument established.	Proc 3889 34–FR 909			
1975 Jan 3	Park and the two monuments combined with portions of Glen Canyon and Lake Mead Recreational Areas and additional lands.	88 Stat 2089	1,189,743	28,632	1,218,375
Grand Teton, Wyoming					
1929 Feb 26	Established as park.	45 Stat 1314			
1943 Mar 15	Established Jackson Hole National Monument.	Proc 2578 57 Stat 731			
1950 Sept 14	45 Stat 1314 and Proc 2578 repealed; lands combined to create new park.	64 Stat 849	305,613	4,904	310,517
Great Smoky Mountains, Tennessee and North Carolina					
1926 May 22	Authorized.	44 Stat 616			
1934 June 15	Established.	48 Stat 964	517,660	2,609	520,269
Guadalupe Mountains, Texas					
1966 Oct 15	Authorized.	80 Stat 920			
1972 Sept 30	Established.	37–FR 21193 92 Stat 3490	76,292	1	76,293
Haleakala, Hawaii					
1916 Aug 1	Authorized as part of Hawaii.	39 Stat 432			
1960 Sept 13	Established from Hawaii, effective July 1, 1961.	74 Stat 881	27,456	1,199	28,655

Name and Date Established		Citation	Acreage as of December 1981		
			Federal	Nonfederal	Total
Hawaii Volcanoes, Hawaii					
1916 Aug 1	Established as Hawaii National Park.	39 Stat 432			
1961 Sept 22	Redesignated as Hawaii Volcanoes.	75 Stat 577	217,298	11,879	229,177
Hot Springs, Arkansas					
1832 Apr 20	Established as reservation.	4 Stat 505			
1880 June 16	Established as permanent reservation.	21 Stat 289			
1921 Mar 4	Established as park.	41 Stat 1407	4,778	1,047	5,825
Isle Royale, Michigan					
1931 Mar 3	Authorized.	46 Stat 1514			
1940 Apr 3	Established.	Secretary of the Interior accepts title to lands from state.			
1942 Mar 6	Congress confirms jurisdiction.	56 Stat 133	539,288	32,508	571,796
Katmai, Alaska					
1918 Sept 24	Proclaimed as monument.	Proc 1487			
1978 Dec 1	Enlarged.	Proc 4619 43–FR 57059			
1980 Dec 2	Established as park.	94 Stat 2392	3,544,900	134,029	3,678,929
Kenai Fjords, Alaska					
1978 Dec 1	Proclaimed as monument.	Proc 4620 43–FR 57067			
1980 Dec 2	Established as park.	94 Stat 2379	567,000	109,667	676,667
Kings Canyon, California					
1940 Mar 4	Established from General Grant and other lands.	54 Stat 41	460,079	57	460,136
Kobuk Valley, Alaska					
1978 Dec 1	Proclaimed as monument.	Proc 4621 43–FR 57073			
1980 Dec 2	Established as park.	94 Stat 2380	1,710,000	39,037	1,749,037
Lake Clark, Alaska					
1978 Dec 1	Proclaimed as monument.	Proc 4622 43–FR 57079			
1980 Dec 2	Established as park.	94 Stat 2380	2,617,513	16,420	2,633,933
Lassen Volcanic, California					
1907 May 6	Established as Lassen Peak and Cinder Cone National Monument.	Proc 35 Stat 2132			
1916 Aug 9	Established as park.	39 Stat 442	106,366	6	106,372
Mackinac Island, Michigan					
1875 Mar 3	Established.	18 Stat 517			
1895 Mar 2	Ceded to Michigan as a state park.	28 Stat 946			

Name and Date Established		Citation	Acreage as of December 1981		
			Federal	Nonfederal	Total
Mammoth Cave, Kentucky					
1926 May 25	Authorized.	44 Stat 635			
1941 July 1	Established.	Secretary of the Interior accepts lands from state.			
1942 June 5	Congress confirms jurisdiction.	56 Stat 317	51,543	827	52,370
Mesa Verde, Colorado					
1906 June 29	Established.	34 Stat 616	51,894	191	52,085
Mount McKinley, Alaska					
See Denali.					
Mount Rainier, Washington					
1899 Mar 2	Established from Pacific Forest Reserve.	30 Stat 993	235,239	165	235,404
North Cascades, Washington					
1968 Oct 2	Established.	82 Stat 926	504,478	302	504,780
Olympic, Washington					
1909 Mar 2	Established as Mount Olympus National Monument.	Proc 869 35 Stat 2247			
1938 June 29	Mount Olympus monument abolished; park created and renamed Olympic.	52 Stat 1241	902,840	12,586	915,426
Petrified Forest, Arizona					
1906 Dec 8	Established as monument.	Proc 34 Stat 3266			
1958 Mar 28	Authorized as park.	72 Stat 69			
1962 Dec 9	Established as park.	27–FR 10984	93,493		93,493
Platt, Oklahoma					
1902 July 1	Established as Sulphur Springs Reservation.	32 Stat 655			
1906 June 29	Redesignated as Platt National Park.	34 Stat 837			
1976 Mar 17	Repealed; established as Chickasaw National Recreation Area.	90 Stat 235 90 Stat 236			
Redwood, California					
1968 Oct 2	Established.	82 Stat 931			
1978 Mar 27	Enlarged.	92 Stat 163	74,314	34,942	109,256
Rocky Mountain, Colorado					
1915 Jan 26	Established.	38 Stat 798	256,999	9,944	266,943
Sequoia, California					
1890 Sept 25	Established.	26 Stat 478	401,770	718	402,488
Shenandoah, Virginia					
1926 May 22	Authorized.	44 Stat 616			
1935 Dec 26	Established.	Secretary of the Interior accepts titles to land.			
1937 Aug 19	Congress confirms jurisdiction.	50 Stat 700	195,032	25	195,057

Name and Date Established		Citation	Acreage as of December 1981		
			Federal	Nonfederal	Total
Sullys Hill, North Dakota					
1904 June 2	Established.	Proc			
1931 Mar 3	Changed to national game preserve; added lands.	46 Stat 1509			
Theodore Roosevelt, North Dakota					
1947 Apr 25	Established as Theodore Roosevelt Memorial Park.	61 Stat 52			
1978 Nov 10	Name changed to Theodore Roosevelt.	92 Stat 3521	69,675	741	70,416
Virgin Islands, Virgin Islands					
1956 Aug 2	Authorized.	70 Stat 940			
1956 Dec 1	Established.	21–FR 10521	12,631	2,064	14,695
Voyageurs, Minnesota					
1971 Jan 8	Authorized.	84 Stat 1970			
1975 Apr 8	Established.	40–FR 15921	129,225	89,903	219,128
Wind Cave, South Dakota					
1903 Jan 9	Established.	32 Stat 765			
1935 June 15	Wind Cave National Game Preserve, established August 10, 1912, added.	49 Stat 383	28,060	232	28,292
Wrangall-St. Elias, Alaska					
1978 Dec 1	Proclaimed as monument.	Proc 4625 43–FR 57101			
1980 Dec 2	Established as park.	94 Stat 2381	7,445,047	886,359	8,331,406
Yellowstone, Wyoming, Idaho, Montana					
1872 Mar 1	Established.	17 Stat 32	2,219,805	18	2,219,823
Yosemite, California					
1864 June 30	Valley ceded to State.	13 Stat 325			
1890 Oct 1	Park established as reserved forestlands surrounding Yosemite Valley.	26 Stat 650			
1905 Mar 3	California re-cedes Valley to federal government.	33 Stat 1286			
1906 June 11	Federal government accepts lands.	34 Stat 831	759,200	1,717	760,917
Zion, Utah					
1909 July 1	Established as Mukuntuweap National Monument.	Proc 36 Stat 2498			
1918 Mar 18	Name changed to Zion National Monument.	Proc 40 Stat 1760			
1919 Nov 19	Established as park.	41 Stat 356			
1937 Jan 22	Another Zion National Monument created.	50 Stat 1809			
1956 July 11	Monument added to park.	70 Stat 527	142,547	4,004	146,551

APPENDIX III

Chronology of Federal Legislation Cited

1783   Sept. 3 (8 Stat. 80) Treaty of Paris. End of Revolutionary War.

1789   July 4 (1 Stat. 24) First protective tariff.

1791   Feb. 25 (1 Stat. 191) First National Bank Act. Bank of the United States.

1802   Mar. 16 (2 Stat. 137) U. S. Military Academy at West Point established. Army Corps of Engineers authorized.

1803   Apr. 30 (8 Stat. 200) Louisiana Purchase. Added 828,000 square miles between Mississippi River and Rocky Mountains to public domain, but no exact boundaries were defined.

1807   Mar. 3 (2 Stat. 445) Act forbade settlement on public lands until authorized by law.

Dec. 22 (2 Stat. 451) Interdicted all land and seaborne commerce with foreign nations. Supplemented by Embargo Acts of Jan. 9 and Mar. 12, 1808.

1812   Apr. 25 (2 Stat. 716) General Land Office established in Treasury Department.

July 1 (2 Stat. 768) Tariff on furniture imports as well as on other articles.

1816   Apr. 10 (3 Stat. 266) Second National Bank Act. Bank of the United States Act.

1817   Mar. 1 (3 Stat. 347) Live oak and redcedar reserves set aside under administration of Navy Department.

1818   Oct. 20 (8 Stat. 249) Convention with Great Britain established boundary line along 49th parallel westward to Rocky Mountains and established title to the Red River Basin.

1819   Mar. 3 (3 Stat. 523) Florida purchase. Added 43 million acres to public domain.

1827   Mar. 3 (4 Stat. 242) Timber Reservation Act. President authorized to preserve live oak timber on public lands and to reserve such lands from sale.

1831   Mar. 2 (4 Stat. 472) Timber Trespass Act. Fines and imprisonment imposed on those unlawfully cutting any live oak, redcedar, or other timber from reserved lands.

1832   July 14 (4 Stat. 583) Tariff of 1832.

1833   Mar. 2 (4 Stat. 632) Compromise Tariff. Revision of the "Tariff of Abominations of 1828"; lowered duties.

1841   Sept. 4 (5 Stat. 453) Preemption Act. Allowed settlers to purchase surveyed public land before auction.

1842   Aug. 9 (8 Stat. 572) Webster-Ashburton Treaty. Established northeastern boundary of U. S.

Aug. 30 (5 Stat. 548) Tariff of 1842. Returned duties to levels of 1832.

1846   June 15 (9 Stat. 869) Treaty with Great Britain confirming U. S. possession of 181 million acres in Oregon Territory.

July 30 (9 Stat. 42) Walker Tariff. Reduction of

duties imposed in the Compromise Tariff.

1848　Feb. 2 (9 Stat. 922, 926) Treaty of Guadalupe Hidalgo. Mexican Session. Mexico gave up all claims to Texas above the Rio Grande and ceded New Mexico and California. Added 335 million acres to public domain.

1849　Mar. 3 (9 Stat. 395) Department of the Interior established with responsibility for the public lands, the General Land Office, and the Bureau of Indian Affairs.

1850　Sept. 9–20 (9 Stat. 446, 452, 453, 462, 467) Compromise of 1850. Phrase used to describe five statutes enacted to resolve slavery issue in the territories and newly admitted states.

1853　Dec. 30 (10 Stat. 1031) Gadsden Purchase. Settled boundary dispute arising from Treaty of Guadalupe Hidalgo. For $10 million, the U. S. gained 45,535 square miles of territory in what now comprises southern Arizona and New Mexico.

1854　June 5 (10 Stat. 1089) Canadian Reciprocity Treaty. Elgin-Marcy Reciprocity Treaty. Settled fishing rights disputes and allowed free entry for agricultural commodities. U. S. abrogated March 17, 1866.

Aug. 4 (10 Stat. 574) Graduation Act. Reduced the price of public land according to the duration it had been on the market, not to go below 12.5 cents per acre after thirty years.

1862　May 15 (12 Stat. 387) Department of Agriculture established without cabinet status.

May 20 (12 Stat. 392) Homestead Act. Allowed settlers to acquire 160 acres of public land by living on it for five years.

July 1 (12 Stat. 489) Transcontinental Railroad Act. Granted to Union Pacific and Central Railroad alternate odd-numbered sections of land for ten miles on each side of the road and other benefits.

July 2 (12 Stat. 503) Morrill Act. Lands granted to each state for colleges of agriculture and mechanic arts on basis of congressional representation.

1864　July 2 (13 Stat. 365) Granted Northern Pacific Railroad alternate, odd-numbered sections of nonmineral land for forty miles on each side of the right-of-way in territories, and for twenty miles in the states, and other benefits.

1866　July 25 (14 Stat. 239) Oregon & California Railroad Company granted alternate, odd-numbered sections of nonmineral public land to a distance of twenty miles on each side of the road.

July 26 (14 Stat. 251) Lode Law. Mineral Patent Law. Mineral lands of the public domain, surveyed and unsurveyed, declared free and open to exploration and occupation.

1867　Mar. 30 (15 Stat. 539) Alaska purchased from Russia for $7.2 million, adding 365 million acres to the public domain.

1870　July 9 (16 Stat. 217) Placer Act. Provided for sale of placer mines at $2.50 per acre not to exceed 160 acres.

1871　Feb. 9 (16 Stat. 593) President authorized to appoint a commissioner of fish and fisheries.

1872　May 10 (17 Stat. 91) General Mining Law. Mineral lands designated a distinct class; provided for their survey and sale.

June 6 (17 Stat. 230) Tariff of 1872. Reduced rates on manufactured goods.

1873　Mar. 3 (17 Stat. 605) Timber Culture Act. Offered to donate 160 acres of public land to any person who would plant forty acres to trees and keep them growing in a healthy condition for ten years.

1876　July 4 (19 Stat. 73) Opened public lands in South to homesteaders.

Aug. 15 (19 Stat. 143, 167) Appropriations Act. Provided $2,000 for an expert to study and report on forest conditions. Franklin B. Hough was appointed.

1877　Mar. 3 (19 Stat. 377) Desert Land Act. Offered for sale 640 acres of nontimber, nonmineral, uncultivable land to any settler who would irrigate it within three years after filing.

1878　June 3 (20 Stat. 88) Free Timber Act. Provided that residents in the several western states might cut timber on public mineral lands.

June 3 (20 Stat. 89) Timber and Stone Act. Provided 160 acres of surveyed, nonmineral land for sale in Washington, Oregon, California, and Nevada. The land was to be chiefly valuable for timber or stone and unfit for cultivation.

1879　Mar. 3 (20 Stat. 377) Sundry Civil Appropriations Act. Created the Geological Survey.

Mar. 3 (20 Stat. 394) Sundry Civil Appropriations Act. Created the Public Land Commission.

1885　Mar. 3 (23 Stat. 353, 354) Agricultural Appropriations Act. Provided funds for economic ornithology in the Entomological Division of the Department of Agriculture.

1886　June 30 (24 Stat. 100, 101) Agricultural Appropriations Act. Division of Economic Ornithology and Mammalogy established.

June 30 (24 Stat. 100, 103) Division of Forestry

permanently established in Department of Agriculture. Bernhard E. Fernow, chief.

1887	Feb. 4 (24 Stat. 379) Interstate Commerce Act. Created the Interstate Commerce Commission, the first regulatory agency with the power to inquire into and regulate the railroads. Subsequent acts extended its authority.

Feb. 8 (24 Stat. 388) Dawes Severalty Act. General Allotment Act. Provided for the dissolution of Indian tribes as legal entities and the division of tribal lands among individual members.

Mar. 2 (24 Stat. 440) Hatch Act. Provided for financial assistance to states to establish agricultural experiment stations.

1888	Oct. 2 (25 Stat. 505, 526) Survey of public lands suitable for irrigation, to be withdrawn from entry.

1889	Feb. 16 (25 Stat. 673) President authorized to permit Indians to cut and sell dead timber on Indian reservations.

Mar. 2 (25 Stat. 835) Granted cabinet status to Department of Agriculture.

Mar. 2 (25 Stat. 854) Discontinued private sale of timberlands in South.

1890	June 12 (26 Stat. 146) Secretary of the interior authorized to employ Indians to cut green timber on Menominee Indian Reservation.

July 2 (26 Stat. 209) Sherman Antitrust Act. Provided for regulation of trusts.

Oct. 1 (26 Stat. 567) McKinley Tariff. Raised average level of duties to 49.5 percent.

1891	Mar. 3 (26 Stat. 1095) Forest Reserve Act. General Revision Act. Repealed the Timber Culture Act of 1873, the Preemption Act of 1841, and empowered the president to set aside forest reserves from public lands covered with timber or undergrowth.

1892	Aug. 4 (27 Stat. 348) Timber and Stone Act of 1878 extended to all of the public-land states.

1894	May 7 (28 Stat. 73) Act to Protect the Birds and Other Animals in Yellowstone National Park. Yellowstone National Park Protection Act. Established principle that no hunting would be allowed in national parks.

Aug. 3 (28 Stat. 222) National Park Concessionaires Act. Leases in Yellowstone National Park. Secretary of the interior may grant specific leases within park, not including natural wonders.

Aug. 18 (28 Stat. 372, 422) Carey Act. Sundry Civil Appropriations Act. Authorized the president to grant to each state not more than 1 million acres of public lands to be sold in support of irrigation and settlement.

Aug. 27 (28 Stat. 509) Wilson-Gorman Tariff. Placed wool, copper, and lumber on free list, and lowered duties to an average of 39.9 percent.

1896	Apr. 25 (29 Stat. 99, 100) Agricultural Appropriations Act. Established Division of Biological Survey in the Department of Agriculture.

1897	June 4 (30 Stat. 11, 34–36) Forest Management Act. Sundry Civil Appropriations Act. Organic Act. Forest Lieu Act. Pettigrew Act. Specified the purposes for which forest reserves might be established and provided for their protection and administration.

July 24 (30 Stat. 151) Dingley Tariff. Raised rates to an average of 57 percent.

1898	July 1 (30 Stat. 597, 618) Sundry Civil Appropriations Act. First appropriation ($75,000) for protection and administration of forest reserves.

1899	Mar. 3 (30 Stat. 1121, 1152) Rivers and Harbors Act. Refuse Act. Forbade discharge or deposit of refuse into waterways that would be hazardous to navigation.

1900	May 25 (31 Stat. 187) Lacey Game and Wild Birds Preservation and Disposition Act. Lacey Act. Prohibited interstate transport of wild animals or birds taken in violation of state law; prohibited importation of any animal or bird injurious to agriculture or horticulture.

1901	Feb. 15 (31 Stat. 790) Right-of-Way Act. Authorized the secretary of the interior to grant rights-of-way through forest reserves.

Mar. 2 (31 Stat. 922, 929) Changed Division of Forestry to Bureau of Forestry.

1902	June 7 (32 Stat. 327) Alaska Game Act. Provided for protection of certain game animals in Alaska.

June 17 (32 Stat. 388) Newlands Act. Reclamation Act. Created the reclamation fund; authorized the secretary of the interior to construct irrigation works and to withdraw irrigable lands from entry.

1905	Feb. 1 (33 Stat. 628) Forest Transfer Act. Transferred the administration of the forest reserves from the secretary of the interior to the secretary of agriculture.

Mar. 3 (33 Stat. 861, 872–873) Bureau of Forestry became Forest Service.

Mar. 3 (33 Stat. 861, 877) Division of Biological Survey became Bureau of Biological Survey.

Mar. 3 (33 Stat. 1264) Repealed Forest Lieu provision of Forest Management Act of 1897.

1906 June 8 (34 Stat. 225) American Antiquities Act. Antiquities Act. Authorized the president to establish by proclamation national monuments for the preservation of features of historic, prehistoric, and scientific interest; forbade anyone without proper authority to injure objects of antiquity.

June 11 (34 Stat. 233) Forest Homestead Act. Opened agricultural lands for entry within forest reserves.

June 29 (34 Stat. 626) Burton Act. Provided study of Niagara Falls to determine acceptable degree of water diversion.

June 30 (34 Stat. 768) Pure Food and Drug Act. Forbade manufacture, sale, or transport of adulterated or fraudulently labeled foods and drugs sold in interstate commerce.

1907 Mar. 4 (34 Stat. 1256, 1269) Forest reserves renamed national forests; further creation or enlargement forbidden in six western states except by act of Congress.

1908 May 11 (35 Stat. 102) Act for the Protection of Game in Alaska. Amends the 1902 act, providing for protection, hunting regulations, and enforcement of the law.

1909 Feb. 19 (35 Stat. 639) Enlarged Homestead Act. Made it possible to acquire homesteads of 320 acres in several states.

Mar. 4 (35 Stat. 1051) Agriculture appropriation for experimentation and demonstration in destroying noxious animals.

Aug. 5 (36 Stat. 11) Payne-Aldrich Tariff. Lowered duties.

1910 June 25 (36 Stat. 847) Authorized president to withdraw public lands from entry and reserve them for specified purposes.

1911 Mar. 1 (36 Stat. 961) Weeks Act. Authorized federal purchase of lands in watersheds of navigable streams, matching funds for state forestry agencies, and for other purposes.

1912 June 6 (37 Stat. 123) Homestead residency requirement reduced.

Aug. 24 (37 Stat. 497) Added California to list of states within which the creation of national forests was prohibited, except by act of Congress; provided that all lands withdrawn by president under act of 1910 should be open to mineral exploration and occupation under U. S. mining laws.

1913 Mar. 4 (37 Stat. 828, 843) Authorized the secretary of agriculture to spend 10 percent of the gross receipts from national forests for the construction of roads and trails.

Mar. 4 (37 Stat. 878) Migratory Bird Act. Weeks-McLean Act. Appropriations Act for USDA. Declared all migratory game and insectivorous birds to be within the custody and protection of the federal government. Repealed in 1918 with Migratory Bird Treaty Act.

Oct. 3 (38 Stat. 114) Underwood-Simmons Tariff. Lowered duties and put iron, steel, raw wool on the free list.

Dec. 19 (38 Stat. 242) Raker Act. San Francisco given the right to construct a dam in Hetch Hetchy Valley in Yosemite National Park.

1914 May 8 (38 Stat. 372) Smith-Lever Act. Provided for cooperative agricultural extension work between the Department of Agriculture and the land-grant colleges.

1915 Mar. 4 (38 Stat. 1086, 1101) Special Use Permit Act. Agricultural Appropriations Act. Authorized the secretary of agriculture to grant permits for summer homes and other recreational structures in the national forests.

1916 June 9 (39 Stat. 218) Chamberlain-Ferris Act. Revested in the U. S. title to unsold lands from the Oregon & California Railroad Company grant.

July 11 (39 Stat. 355) Federal Aid Road Act. Appropriated $11 million a year for ten years for construction of roads and trails within national forests.

Aug. 25 (39 Stat. 535) National Park Service established.

Aug. 31 (39 Stat. 673) Standard Baskets and Containers Act. Standardized sizes of containers for a variety of agricultural products.

Sept. 7 (39 Stat. 728) Shipping Board Act. Established the U. S. Shipping Board to supervise the merchant marine.

1917 Feb. 23 (39 Stat. 929) Smith-Hughes Act. Federal grant-in-aid to be matched by state funds to promote agricultural and trade instruction.

1918 July 3 (40 Stat. 755) Migratory Bird Treaty Act. Confirmed the convention of August 16, 1916, with Great Britain for the protection of migratory birds.

1920 Feb. 25 (41 Stat. 437) Mineral Leasing Act. Provided for leasing of deposits of coal, phosphate, sodium, oil, oil shale, or gas on national forests created from the public domain.

June 5 (41 Stat. 988) Jones Act. Merchant Marine Act. Repealed emergency war legislation related to shipping, reorganized the Shipping Board, and provided that coastwise commerce was to be carried in U. S. vessels whenever practicable.

June 10 (41 Stat. 1063) Water Power Act. Created the Federal Power Commission and gave it authority to grant licenses for the development of power across, along, or in any part of the navigable waters of the United States, or on any part of the public lands.

1921 Nov. 9 (42 Stat. 212, 218) Federal Highway Act. Funds appropriated specifically for forest development roads and forest highways.

1922 Mar. 20 (42 Stat. 465) General Exchange Act. Secretary of agriculture authorized to exchange land in national forests for private land of equal value within national forest boundaries.

1923 Mar. 3 (42 Stat. 1435) Naval Stores Inspection Act. Specified minimum standards and required federal inspection of all exported naval stores.

1924 May 26 (43 Stat. 153) Immigration Act. Johnson Bill. Reduced the number of people allowed to immigrate to the U. S. and revised the quota system based on national origins.

June 7 (43 Stat. 653) Clarke-McNary Act. Authorized appropriations for cooperation with state agencies for fire control and other cooperative programs; purchase of forestlands no longer restricted to the watershed of navigable streams.

1926 June 15 (44 Stat. 745) Forbade further creation of or additions to national forests in Arizona and New Mexico, except by act of Congress.

July 13 (44 Stat. 915) Oregon & California Railroad Land. Provided for payment to counties of amount equal to taxes that would have been paid if land was held in private hands.

1927 Mar. 4 (44 Stat. 1422) National Arboretum established.

1928 Apr. 30 (45 Stat. 468) McNary-Woodruff Act. Authorized funds for purchase of land under the Weeks Act and the Clarke-McNary Act.

May 15 (45 Stat. 534–39) Mississippi Flood Control Act. Mississippi River and Tributaries Act.

May 21 (45 Stat. 685) Standard Baskets and Containers Act. Substantially reduced number of basket styles.

May 22 (45 Stat. 699) McSweeney-McNary Forest Research Act. Authorized a ten-year

program of forestry research, including a timber survey.

Dec. 21 (45 Stat. 1057) Boulder Canyon Project Act. Provided for the protection and development of Colorado River Basin and the Colorado River.

1929 Feb. 18 (45 Stat. 1222) Migratory Bird Conservation Act. Norbeck-Andresen Act. Authorized continuing program of inviolate bird refuges and established the Migratory Bird Conservation Commission.

1930 June 17 (46 Stat. 590) Smoot-Hawley Tariff. Raised rates on agricultural raw materials and other commodities.

July 10 (46 Stat. 1020) Shipstead-Nolan Act. Withdrew from entry all public land north of Township 60 in Minnesota; required the Forest Service to conserve for recreational use the lakes and streams of the region.

1931 Mar. 2 (46 Stat. 1468) Authorized a ten-year cooperative program for control of predatory and other wild animals on national forests and other areas of the public domain.

1932 June 6 (47 Stat. 169) Revenue Act. Added $3 per thousand board feet over and above existing lumber tariff.

1933 Mar. 31 (48 Stat. 22) Funds appropriated for relieving unemployment and for promoting conservation of natural resources.

May 18 (48 Stat. 58) Tennessee Valley Authority Act.

June 16 (48 Stat. 195) National Industrial Recovery Act. Authorized the National Recovery Administration, the Public Works Administration, and other measures to promote economic recovery.

1934 Feb. 15 (48 Stat. 351) Civil Works Emergency Relief Act. Authorized the Works Project Administration and the Resettlement Administration.

Mar. 10 (48 Stat. 400) Fish and Game Sanctuary Act. Authorized president to establish refuges on national forests.

Mar. 10 (48 Stat. 401) Fish and Wildlife Coordination Act. Authorized the secretary of agriculture and the secretary of commerce to cooperate with federal, state, and other agencies to develop nationwide program of wildlife conservation, study effect of water pollution on wildlife, and consult with construction agencies for effects of development on wildlife and fish.

Mar. 16 (48 Stat. 451) Migratory Bird Hunting Stamp Act. Duck Stamp Act. Required duck hunters to purchase a federal hunting stamp; proceeds to be made available for acquisition and development of land for refuges.

June 12 (48 Stat. 943) Reciprocal Trade Agreement. Encouraged American trade through series of reciprocal agreements; employed "most-favored-nation" concept.

June 18 (48 Stat. 984, 986) Indian Reorganization Act. Wheeler-Howard Act. Directed the secretary of the interior to make rules and regulations for Indian forestry units based on principle of sustained yield.

June 28 (48 Stat. 1269) Taylor Grazing Act. Grazing districts to be established on unreserved public domain by secretary of the interior.

1935   Apr. 27 (49 Stat. 163) Soil Conservation Act. Congress to provide permanently for the control and prevention of soil erosion. Soil Conservation Service established in Department of Agriculture.

July 5 (49 Stat. 449) National Labor Relations Act. Wagner-Connery Act. Created National Labor Relations Board.

Aug. 14 (49 Stat. 620) Social Security Act.

Aug. 21 (49 Stat. 666) Historic Sites and Buildings Act. Historic Sites Act. Transferred to the National Park Service the administration of historic sites, cemeteries, monuments, and other historical areas.

1936   Feb. 29 (49 Stat. 1148) Naval Stores Conservation Program. Funds to aid gum stores producers.

June 22 (49 Stat. 1570) Omnibus Flood Control Act. Flood Control Act. Recognized flood control on navigable rivers or their tributaries as a proper activity of the federal government.

June 23 (49 Stat. 1894) Park, Parkway, and Recreation Area Study Act. Authorized and directed National Park Service to study programs of the United States and the states.

1937   Feb. 11 (50 Stat. 19) Federal Disaster Act. Created a Disaster Loan Corporation to provide funds for relief from disasters; Northeastern Timber Salvage Administration would receive funds for the 1938 hurricane salvage program.

Apr. 6 (50 Stat. 57) Incipient or Emergency Insect or Plant Disease Control Act. Authorized funds for control of outbreaks.

May 18 (50 Stat. 188) Cooperative Farm Forestry Act. Norris-Doxey Act. Authorized funds for promotion of farm forestry.

June 28 (50 Stat. 319) Civilian Conservation Corps established as official successor to the Emergency Conservation Work.

July 22 (50 Stat. 522) Bankhead-Jones Farm Tenant Act. Provided funds for acquisition and rehabilitation of submarginal agricultural lands.

Aug. 28 (50 Stat. 874) Secretary of the interior authorized to establish sustained-yield forestry units on Oregon & California Railroad lands.

Sept. 2 (50 Stat. 917) Federal Aid in Wildlife Restoration Act. Pittman-Robertson Act. Tax on firearms and ammunition to be used in cooperation with states for wildlife restoration programs.

1938   June 25 (52 Stat. 1060) Fair Labor Standards Act. Established a minimum wage, the 40-hour work week, and forbade child labor for all business engaged in interstate commerce.

June 28 (52 Stat. 1215) Flood Control Act. Amended 1936 Omnibus Flood Control Act.

1939   May 9 (53 Stat. 1431) Reorganization Plan II. Transferred Bureau of Fisheries from the Department of Commerce and the Bureau of Biological Survey from the Department of Agriculture to the Department of the Interior.

July 20 (53 Stat. 1071) Restored to the president authority to establish national forests in Montana.

1940   Apr. 2 (54 Stat. 1231, 1232) Reorganization Plan No. III. Consolidated the Bureau of Fisheries and the Bureau of Biological Survey into the Fish and Wildlife Service.

June 8 (54 Stat. 250) American Eagle Protection Act. Bald Eagle Protection Act.

June 27 (54 Stat. 628) Second Deficiency Appropriations Act. Provided funds for financing agricultural and forestry experts in foreign countries.

July 16 (54 Stat. 761) Hawaii National Park Bombing Range. Lands for Air Corps bombing range transferred from jurisdiction of secretary of the interior to the secretary of war.

1944   Mar. 29 (58 Stat. 132) Sustained-Yield Forest Management Act. Authorized the secretary of agriculture and the secretary of the interior to establish cooperative sustained-yield forestry units.

1946   May 16 (60 Stat. 1097, 1099) Reorganization Plan No. 3. Consolidated the General Land Office and the Grazing Service to form the

Bureau of Land Management in the Department of the Interior.

Aug. 2 (60 Stat. 812) Legislative Reorganization Act. Reduced number of standing committees.

Aug. 14 (60 Stat. 1082) Agricultural Research and Marketing Act. Hope-Flannagan Act. Provided for further research into principles relating to agriculture and for improving the marketing and distribution of agricultural products.

1947 June 25 (61 Stat. 163) Federal Insecticide, Fungicide, and Pesticide Act. Designed to protect consumer from labeling fraud and also required a warning or caution statement.

June 25 (61 Stat. 177) Forest Pest Control Act. Declared it to be a federal policy to protect all forestlands from destructive insect pests and diseases.

July 31 (61 Stat. 681) Materials Disposal Act. Materials Act. Secretary of the interior authorized to sell timber, sand, stone, gravel, and other resources without transfer of title, exclusive of national forests, parks, monuments, or Indian lands.

Oct. 30 (61 Stat. A3) General Agreement on Tariffs and Trade. GATT. Held in Geneva with twenty-eight participating nations.

1948 June 22 (62 Stat. 568) Thye-Blatnick Act. Authorized the Forest Service to purchase lands within the Quetico-Superior wilderness for recreational purposes.

June 30 (62 Stat. 1155) Water Pollution Control Act. Taft-Barkley Act. Cooperative program for stream pollution abatement.

1950 Apr. 24 (64 Stat. 82) Granger-Thye Act. Broadened the authority of the secretary of agriculture to accept contributions for administration, protection, improvement, reforestation, and other work on nonfederal lands within or near national forests.

Aug. 9 (64 Stat. 430) Fish Restoration and Management Act. Dingell-Johnson Act. Revenue from tax on fishing equipment and baits and flies to be used in cooperation with states for fish restoration and management programs.

Aug. 25 (64 Stat. 473) Cooperative Forest Management Act. Provided funds enabling the secretary of agriculture to cooperate with state foresters to provide services to private forest landowners. Cooperative Farm Forestry Act of 1937 was repealed, effective June 30, 1951.

1952 May 23 (66 Stat. 92) Smokey Bear Act. Protected Smokey symbol from unauthorized use.

1953 Mar. 25 (67 Stat. 633) Reorganization Plan No. 2. Transferred to the secretary of agriculture, with certain exceptions, all functions of all agencies and employees of the department, and added two assistant secretaries. Abolished Bureau of Entomology and Plant Quarantine and set up the Division of Forest Insect Research and the Agricultural Research Service.

1954 Aug. 4 (68 Stat. 666) Watershed Protection and Flood Prevention Act. Authorized secretary of agriculture to cooperate with states and local agencies to prevent erosion, floodwater, and sediment damages and to promote conservation, development, and utilization of water.

1955 July 23 (69 Stat. 367, 375) Multiple-Use Mining Act. Returned surface rights from mining claims to the U. S., unless the claim is proven valid.

Aug. 1 (69 Stat. 434) Repealed provisions of Timber and Stone Act of 1878, as amended, providing for the sale of public lands chiefly valuable for timber or stone.

1958 June 28 (72 Stat. 238) National Outdoor Recreation Resources Review Act. Outdoor Recreation Resources Review Commission. To determine the outdoor recreation requirements of the American people and the resources needed to meet those needs in 1958, 1976, and 2000.

Aug. 28 (72 Stat. 988) Agriculture Act of 1958. To amend the Agriculture Trade Development and Assistance Act of 1954.

1960 June 12 (74 Stat. 215) Multiple Use-Sustained Yield Act. Directed the Forest Service to give equal consideration to outdoor recreation, range, timber, water, and wildlife and fish resources and to manage them on the basis of sustained yield.

June 27 (74 Stat. 220) Reservoir Salvage Act. Provided for recovery and preservation of significant scientific, prehistoric, historic, or archaeological data affected by construction of dams or reservoirs.

1962 Oct. 10 (76 Stat. 806) Forestry Research, State Plans, Assistance Act. McIntire-Stennis Cooperative Forestry Act. Authorized federal support for forestry research at land-grant colleges.

Oct. 24 (76 Stat. 1246) Golden eagle protected.

1963   May 28 (77 Stat. 49) Outdoor Recreation Act. Promoted coordination and development of programs related to outdoor recreation among eighteen federal agencies.

Dec. 17 (77 Stat. 392) Clean Air Act. Amends the 1955 act to provide for encouragement of uniform laws among states and local governments, research, enforcement, automobile emission control, and cooperation among federal agencies to control air pollution from federal facilities.

1964   Sept. 3 (78 Stat. 890) Wilderness Act. Provided for a ten-year congressional review program for wilderness designation; set up the National Wilderness Preservation System.

Sept. 3 (78 Stat. 897) Land and Water Conservation Fund Act. Authorized establishment of a fund to support acquisition and development of state parks and other outdoor recreation facilities. Amended in 1976, Sept. 28 (90 Stat. 1313).

Sept. 19 (78 Stat. 982) Public Land Law Review Commission Act.

Sept. 19 (78 Stat. 986) Classification and Multiple-Use Act. Classification of public land for purpose of disposal or interim management. First BLM authorization to inventory its lands.

Sept. 19 (78 Stat. 988) Public Land Sales Act. Companion to the Classification and Multiple-Use Act; gave the BLM interim authority to sell lands classified for disposal.

1965   July 9 (79 Stat. 213) Federal Water Project Recreation Act. Provided fund for recreation facilities at existing federal dams.

July 22 (79 Stat. 244–54) Water Resources Planning Act. Encouraged conservation, development, and utilization of water and water-related land resources.

Oct. 22 (79 Stat. 1028) Highway Beautification Act. Included measures for control of outdoor advertising and junkyards adjacent to highways; provided for scenic development.

1966   Oct. 15 (80 Stat. 915) National Historic Preservation Act. National Historic Policy. National Historic Properties Act. Established a program for preservation of historic properties.

Oct. 15 (80 Stat. 926) Endangered Species Preservation Act. First act to protect endangered species. Directed the secretary of the interior to carry out a program of conserving, protecting, restoring, and propagating selected species of native fish and wildlife. Funds from Land and Water Conservation Fund could be used to acquire habitat.

Oct. 15 (80 Stat. 927) Wildlife Refuge System Administration Act. Consolidated various refuge and protective areas into one system.

1967   Nov. 21 (81 Stat. 485) Air Quality Act. Further amended the Clean Air Act of 1955; added enforcement provisions for abatement of stationary sources of pollution and motor vehicle pollution.

1968   Aug. 1 (82 Stat. 476) National Housing Policy Act. Housing and Urban Development Act. Provided assistance for housing for low and moderate income families.

Oct. 2 (82 Stat. 906) Wild and Scenic Rivers Act. Provided for the preservation of selected rivers in their natural state.

Oct. 2 (82 Stat. 919) National Trails Systems Act. Established system of recreational and scenic trails.

1969   Dec. 5 (83 Stat. 275) Endangered Species Conservation Act. Authorized the secretary of the interior to promulgate a list of wildlife threatened with worldwide extinction and to prohibit their importation; expanded definition of fish or wildlife to include any wild mammal, fish, wild bird, amphibian, reptile, mollusk, or crustacean.

1970   Jan. 1 (83 Stat. 852) National Environmental Policy Act of 1969. Established Council on Environmental Quality and required evaluation of potential environmental impact of federal legislation and agency programs.

Aug. 18 (84 Stat. 825) General Authorities Act. To improve the administration of the national park system by the secretary of the interior and to clarify the authorities applicable to the system.

Dec. 29 (84 Stat. 1590) Occupational Safety and Health Act. Mandated that employers provide a work environment free from recognized hazards to employees; provided for federal establishment and enforcement of safety and health standards for workers.

Dec. 31 (84 Stat. 1676) Clean Air Act. Established a three-year comprehensive air pollution control program.

1971   Dec. 18 (85 Stat. 688) Alaska Native Claims Settlement Act. Granted Alaskan natives the right to select up to 44 million acres of public lands.

1972   Aug. 30 (86 Stat. 670) Rural Development Act.

Rural Community Fire Protection. Directed the secretary of agriculture to provide assistance to state foresters and other appropriate local officials for the prevention, control, and suppression of fires.

Oct. 18 (86 Stat. 816) Federal Water Pollution Control Act. Limited effluent discharges and set water quality standards.

Oct. 21 (86 Stat. 973) Federal Environmental Pesticide Control Act. Expanded federal authority over pesticides and their use.

1973 Aug. 10 (87 Stat. 242, 245) Agriculture and Consumer Protection Act. Directed secretary of agriculture to develop and execute forestry incentive programs to encourage the development, management, and protection of nonindustrial private forestlands.

Dec. 28 (87 Stat. 884) Endangered Species Act. Provided for the protection of ecosystems of endangered species, expanded definition of wildlife, established distinction of endangered and threatened species and the concept of critical habitat.

1974 Aug. 17 (88 Stat. 476) Forest and Rangeland Renewable Resources Planning Act. Humphrey-Rarick Act. Resources Planning Act. RPA. Directed the secretary of agriculture to assess all lands and prepare a management program to be updated every five years.

1975 Jan. 2 (88 Stat. 1924) Water Pollution Act. Extended the authorizations of the 1972 Federal Water Pollution Control Act.

Jan. 3 (88 Stat. 2096) Eastern Wilderness Act. Lands east of the 100th meridian to be identified, studied, and designated for inclusion in the National Wilderness Preservation System.

Jan. 4 (88 Stat. 2203) Indian Self-Determination and Education Assistance Act. Assures maximum Indian participation in direction of educational and other federal programs.

1976 Sept. 28 (90 Stat. 1342) National Park System-Mining Activity Act. Provided for regulation of mining within, and repealed the application of mining laws to, the National Park System.

Oct. 4 (90 Stat. 1520) Tax Reform Act.

Oct. 20 (90 Stat. 2662) Payments in Lieu of Taxes. Secretary of agriculture directed to pay local governments annually for public lands in their jurisdiction on the basis of a formula.

Oct. 21 (90 Stat. 2743) Federal Land Policy and Management Act. FLPMA. BLM Organic Act. Authorized multiple-use management of public lands administered by BLM and declared the government policy of retaining federal ownership of public lands.

Oct. 22 (90 Stat. 2949) National Forest Management Act. Amended RPA planning process, repealed litigated provisions in 1897 Forest Management Act, mandated greater public involvement in Forest Service decision making.

1977 Aug. 3 (91 Stat. 445) Surface Mining Control and Reclamation Act. Created Office of Strip Mining in Department of the Interior to oversee planning and review requirements.

Dec. 27 (91 Stat. 1566) Clean Water Act. Amended the BLM Organic Act relating to some forestry practices and provided for cost-sharing program with rural landowners to control nonpoint sources of pollution.

1978 Feb. 24 (92 Stat. 40) Endangered American Wilderness Act. Designated 1.3 million acres of wilderness in ten western states.

June 30 (92 Stat. 349) Renewable Resources Extension Act. Expanded the extension program to promote increased yields on private lands through education.

June 30 (92 Stat. 353) Forest and Rangeland Renewable Resources Research Act. Authorized a comprehensive research program and a continuing survey and analysis of renewable resources.

July 1 (92 Stat. 365) Cooperative Forestry Assistance Act. Brought together programs in cooperative forestry under one statutory authority; provided grants to states for programs in management and planning assistance.

Nov. 10 (92 Stat. 3467) National Parks and Recreation Act. Omnibus Parks Act. Tripled park wilderness acreage, tripled size of National Trails System, enlarged the National Wild and Scenic Rivers System, and authorized funds for an Urban Park and Recreation Recovery Program.

1979 Oct. 31 (93 Stat. 721) Archaeological Resources Protection Act. Prohibited organized destruction of archaeological sites and resources on federal system and Indian lands. Covered resources 100 years or older and set up a permit system for excavation or study.

1980 Dec. 2 (94 Stat. 2371) Alaska National Interest

Lands Conservation Act. D-2 Lands Act. Placed 97 million acres into new or expanded parks and refuges; protected twenty-five free-flowing rivers, and classified 56 million acres as wilderness.

1981   Aug. 13 (95 Stat. 172) Economic Recovery Tax Act. Amended Internal Revenue Code of 1954 to encourage growth through reduction of tax rates for individual taxpayers, acceleration of capital cost recovery of investment in plant, equipment, and real property; provided for incentives in savings.

APPENDIX IV

Chronology of Administrations

President	Term	Party	Secretary of the Interior[1]	Term	(General Land Office Commissioner) BLM Director[2]	Term
Madison, James	1809–1817	Republican			Tiffin, Edward Meigs, Josiah	1812–1814 1814–1822
Monroe, James	1817–1825	Republican			Meigs, Josiah McLean, John Graham, George	1822–1823 1823–1830
Adams, John Quincy	1825–1829	Federalist			Graham, George	
Jackson, Andrew	1829–1837	Democrat			Graham, George Hayward, Elijah Brown, Ethan Allen	1830–1835 1835–1836
Van Buren, Martin	1837–1841	Democrat			Whitcomb, James	1836–1841
Harrison, William Henry	1841	Whig			Huntington, Elisha	1841–1842
Tyler, John	1841–1845	Whig			Huntington, Elisha Blake, Thomas H.	1842–1846
Polk, James Knox	1845–1849	Democrat			Blake, Thomas H. Shields, James Young, Richard	1846–1847 1847–1849
Taylor, Zachary	1849–1850	Whig	Ewing, Thomas	1849–1850	Butterfield, Justin	1849–1852
Fillmore, Millard	1850–1853	Whig	McKennan, Thomas M. Stuart, Alexander H.	1850 1850–1853	Butterfield, Justin Wilson, John	1852–1855
Pierce, Franklin	1853–1857	Democrat	McClelland, Robert	1853–1857	Hendricks, Thomas A.	1855–1859
Buchanan, James	1857–1861	Republican	McClelland, Robert Thompson, Jacob	1857–1861	Hendricks, Thomas A. Smith, Samuel A. Wilson, Joseph S.	1859–1860 1860–1861
Lincoln, Abraham	1861–1865	Republican	Smith, Caleb B. Usher, John P.	1861–1863 1863–1865	Edmunds, James M.	1861–1866
Johnson, Andrew	1865–1869	Democrat	Harlan, James Browning, Orville H.	1865–1866 1866–1869	Edmunds, James. M. Wilson, Joseph S.	1866–1871
Grant, Ulysses S.	1869–1877	Republican	Cox, Jacob D. Delano, Columbus Chandler, Zachariah	1869–1870 1870–1875 1875–1877	Wilson, Joseph S. Drummond, Willis Burdett, Samuel Williamson, James	1871–1874 1874–1876 1876–1881
Hayes, Rutherford B.	1877–1881	Republican	Schurz, Carl	1877–1881	Williamson, James	
Garfield, James A.	1881	Republican	Kirkwood, Samuel J.	1881–1882	McFarland, Noah C.	1881–1885
Arthur, Chester A.	1881–1885	Republican	Kirkwood, Samuel J. Teller, Henry M.	1882–1885	McFarland, Noah C.	
Cleveland, Grover	1885–1889	Democrat	Lamar, Lucius Q. C. Vilas, William F.	1885–1888 1888–1889	Sparks, William A. J. Stockslager, Strocker M.	1885–1887 1888–1889
Harrison, Benjamin	1889–1893	Republican	Noble, John W.	1889–1893	Groff, Lewis Carter, Thomas Stone, William	1889–1891 1891–1892 1892–1893
Cleveland, Grover	1893–1897	Democrat	Smith, Hoke Francis, David R.	1893–1896 1896–1897	Lamoraux, Silas	1893–1897
McKinley, William	1897–1901	Republican	Bliss, Cornelius N. Hitchcock, Ethan A.	1897–1899 1899–1907	Hermann, Binger	1897–1903

National Park Service Director[3]	Term	Secretary of Agriculture[4]	Term	Forest Service Chief[5]	Term
		Newton, Isaac	1862–1867		
		Newton, Isaac Stokes, John W. (acting)	1867		
		Capron, Horace Watts, Frederick	1867–1871 1871–1877	Hough, Franklin B.	1876–1883
		Le Duc, William G.	1877–1881	Hough, Franklin B.	
		Loring, George B,	1881–1885	Hough, Franklin B.	
		Loring, George B.		Hough, Franklin B. Egleston, Nathaniel H.	1883–1886
		Colman, Norman J.	1885–1889	Egleston, Nathaniel H. Fernow, Bernhard E.	1886–1898
		Rusk, Jeremiah M.	1889–1893	Fernow, Bernhard E.	
		Morton, J. Sterling	1893–1897	Fernow, Bernhard E.	
		Wilson, James	1897–1913	Fernow, Bernhard E. Pinchot, Gifford	1898–1910

President	Term	Party	Secretary of the Interior[1]	Term	(General Land Office Commissioner) BLM Director[2]	Term
Roosevelt, Theodore	1901–1909	Republican	Hitchcock, Ethan A. Garfield, James R.	1907–1909	Hermann, Binger Richards, William A. Ballinger, Richard A. Dennett, Fred	1903–1907 1907–1908 1908–1913
Taft, William H.	1909–1913	Republican	Ballinger, Richard A. Fisher, Walter L.	1909–1911 1911–1913	Dennett, Fred	
Wilson, Woodrow	1913–1921	Democrat	Lane, Franklin K. Payne, John B.	1913–1920 1920–1921	Tallman, Clay	1913–1921
Harding, Warren G.	1921–1923	Republican	Fall, Albert B. Work, Hubert	1921–1923 1923–1928	Spry, William	1921–1929
Coolidge, Calvin	1923–1929	Republican	Work, Hubert West, Roy O.	1928–1929	Spry, William	
Hoover, Herbert C.	1929–1933	Republican	Wilbur, Ray L.	1929–1933	Moore, Charles	1929–1933
Roosevelt, Franklin D.	1933–1945	Democrat	Ickes, Harold L.	1933–1946	Johnson, Fred W.	1933–1948
Truman, Harry S	1945–1953	Democrat	Ickes, Harold L. Krug, Julius A. Chapman, Oscar L.	1946–1949 1950–1953	Johnson, Fred W. Clawson, Marion	1948–1953
Eisenhower, Dwight D.	1953–1961	Republican	McKay, Douglas J. Seaton, Frederick A.	1953–1956 1956–1961	Woozley, Edward	1953–1961
Kennedy, John F.	1961–1963	Democrat	Udall, Stewart L.	1961–1969	Landstrom, Karl S. Stoddard, Charles	1961–1963 1963–1966
Johnson, Lyndon B.	1963–1969	Democrat	Udall, Stewart L.		Stoddard, Charles Rasmussen, Boyd	1966–1971
Nixon, Richard M.	1969–1974	Republican	Hickel, Walter J. Morton, Rogers C. B.	1969–1970 1971–1975	Rasmussen, Boyd L. Silcock, Burton Berklund, Curt	1971–1973 1973–1977
Ford, Gerald R.	1974–1977	Republican	Morton, Rogers C. B. Hathaway, Stanley K. Kleppe, Thomas S.	1975 1975–1977	Berklund, Curt	
Carter, James E.	1977–1981	Democrat	Andrus, Cecil D.	1977–1981	Berklund, Curt Turcott, George L. (acting) Gregg, Frank	1978 1978–1981
Reagan, Ronald	1981–	Republican	Watt, James	1981–	Gregg, Frank Burford, Robert R.	1981–

National Park Service Director[3]	Term	Secretary of Agriculture[4]	Term	Forest Service Chief[5]	Term
		Wilson, James		Pinchot, Gifford	
		Wilson, James		Pinchot, Gifford Graves, Henry S.	1910–1920
Mather, Stephen T.	1917–1929	Houston, David F. Meredith, Edwin T.	1913–1920 1920–1921	Graves, Henry S. Greeley, William B.	1920–1928
Mather, Stephen T.		Wallace, Henry C.	1921–1924	Greeley, William B.	
Mather, Stephen T.		Wallace, Henry C. Gore, Howard M. Jardine, William M.	1924–1925 1925–1929	Stuart, Robert Y.	1928–1933
Albright, Horace M.	1929–1933	Hyde, Arthur M.	1929–1933	Stuart, Robert Y.	
Cammerer, Arno B. Drury, Newton B.	1933–1940 1940–1951	Wallace, Henry A. Wickard, Claude R.	1933–1940 1940–1945	Stuart, Robert Y. Silcox, Ferdinand A. Clapp, Earle H. (acting) Watts, Lyle F.	1933–1939 1939–1943 1943–1952
Drury, Newton B. Demaray, Arthur E. Wirth, Conrad L.	1951 1951–1964	Wickard, Claude R. Anderson, Clinton P. Brannan, Charles F.	1945–1948 1948–1953	Watts, Lyle F. McArdle, Richard E.	1952–1962
Wirth, Conrad L.		Benson, Ezra Taft	1953–1961	McArdle, Richard E.	
Wirth, Conrad L.		Freeman, Orville L.	1961–1969	McArdle, Richard E. Cliff, Edward P.	1962–1972
Wirth, Conrad L. Hartzog, George B., Jr.	1964–1972	Freeman, Orville L.		Cliff, Edward P.	
Hartzog, George B., Jr. Walker, Ronald H.	1973–1975	Hardin, Clifford M. Butz, Earl L.	1969–1971 1971–1976	Cliff, Edward P. McGuire, John R.	1972–1979
Walker, Ronald H. Everhardt, Gary	1975–1977	Butz, Earl L.		McGuire, John R.	
Everhardt, Gary Whalen, William J. Dickerson, Russell E.	1977–1980 1980–	Knebel, John A. Bergland, Robert	1976–1977 1977–1981	McGuire, John R. Peterson, R. Max	
Dickerson, Russell E.		Block, John R.	1981–		

1. The Department of the Interior was created in 1849.
2. The General Land Office (GLO) was created in 1812 as part of the Treasury Department; it was moved to the newly created Department of the Interior in 1849. The 1934 Taylor Grazing Act established a Division of Grazing, which was renamed Grazing Service in 1939. Farrington R. Carpenter served as director from 1934 to 1938, Richard H. Rutledge from 1939 to 1944, and Clarence L. Forsling from 1944 to 1946. In 1946, the GLO merged with the U. S. Grazing Service to become the Bureau of Land Management; Fred W. Johnson served both as GLO commissioner and as BLM director.
3. The National Park Service was established in 1916, but Congress failed to appropriate funds for its operation until April 17, 1917.
4. The Department of Agriculture was established in 1862 but did not receive cabinet status until 1889; until then, it was headed by the commissioner of agriculture.
5. The Division of Forestry was established in 1881, receiving permanence in 1886. In 1901, the agency's name was changed to Bureau of Forestry; in 1905, the name was changed again to Forest Service. Its head administrator was called forestry agent from 1876 to 1880, chief from 1881 to 1898, forester from 1898 to 1935, and again chief from 1935 until the present.

APPENDIX V

Atlas

MAP 1. Ecoregions of the United States

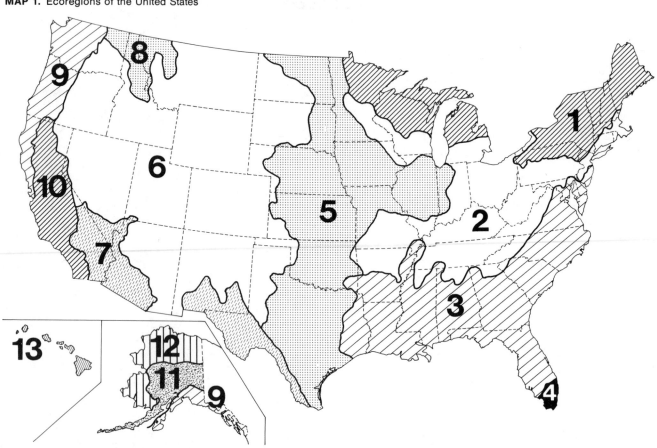

Western half of the United States:

6 Steppe
7 Desert
8 Warm Continental
9 Marine
10 Mediterranean
11 Subarctic
12 Tundra
13 Rainforest

Eastern half of the United States:

1 Warm Continental
2 Hot Continental
3 Subtropical
4 Savanna
5 Prairie

MAP 2. Major Forest Types of the United States, according to the 1949 *Yearbook of Agriculture*.

Forest Vegetation (Western)

Spruce-Fir (N. Coniferous Forest)

"Cedar"-Hemlock (N.W. Coniferous Forest)

Western Larch-Western White Pine

Pacific Douglas-Fir

Redwood

Pinyon-Juniper (S.W. Coniferous Woodland)

Chaparral (S.W. Broadleaved Woodland)

Ponderosa Pine-Douglas-Fir (Western Pine Forest)

Ponderosa Pine-Sugar Pine

Ponderosa Pine-Douglas-Fir

Lodgepole Pine

Forest Vegetation (Eastern)

Spruce-Fir (N. Coniferous Forest)

Jack, Red, and White Pines (Northeastern Pine Forest)

Birch-Beech-Maple-Hemlock (Northern Hardwoods)

Oak (S. Hardwood Forest)

Chestnut-Chestnut Oak-Yellow-Poplar

Oak-Hickory

Oak-Pine

Cypress-Tupelo-Sweetgum (River-Bottom Forest)

Longleaf-Loblolly-Slash P. (S. Eastern Pine Forest)

Mangrove (Subtropical Forest)

MAP 3. Lumber Regions of the United States, 1893, as compiled by Bernhard E. Fernow, chief of the Division of Forestry.

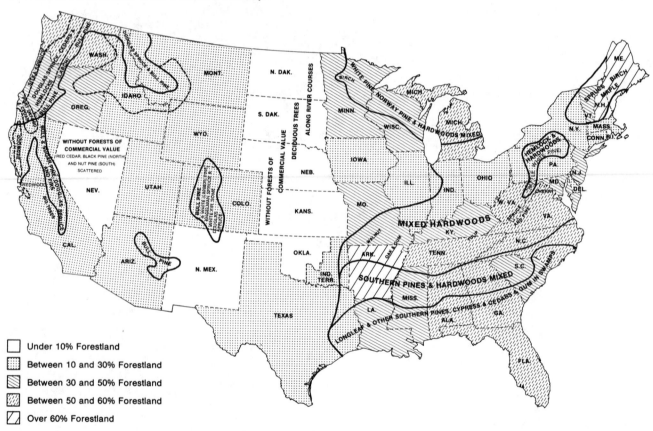

Under 10% Forestland

Between 10 and 30% Forestland

Between 30 and 50% Forestland

Between 50 and 60% Forestland

Over 60% Forestland

MAP 4. Forestland as a Percentage of Total Land Area

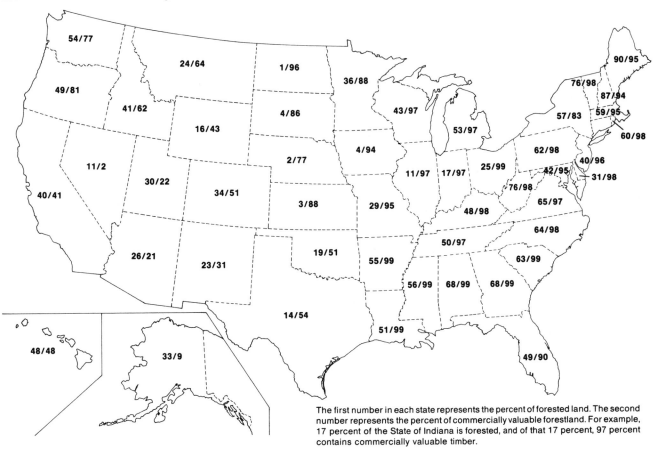

The first number in each state represents the percent of forested land. The second number represents the percent of commercially valuable forestland. For example, 17 percent of the State of Indiana is forested, and of that 17 percent, 97 percent contains commercially valuable timber.

MAP 5. Land Acquisitions of the United States

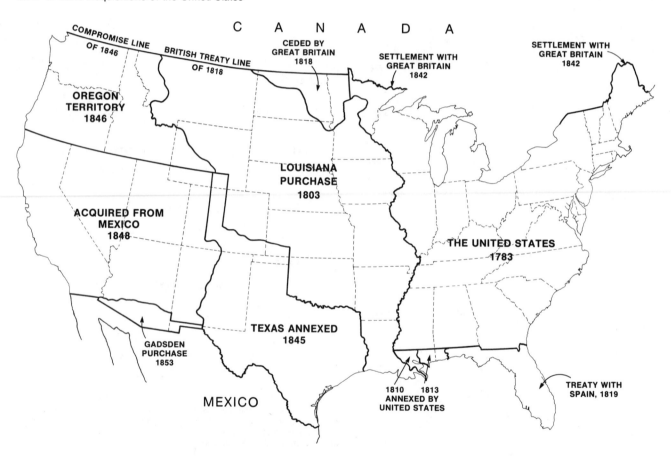

MAP 6. Railroad Land Grants.

Shaded areas are within railroad land grant zones established between 1850 and 1871; less than half of the zone area was actually granted. Because of myriad technicalities, the precise figures of the land grants are still debated, but a reasonable approximation would be some 190 million acres or between 9 and 10 percent of the nation's land.

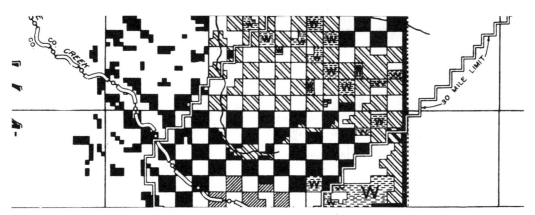

Railroad land grants formed checkerboard patterns, with the company receiving every other 640-acre section of land within the grant zone. Approximately half of the area remained in public ownership and subject to public land laws. This example shows a portion of the 2.5 million-acre Oregon and California Railroad land grant in western Oregon. The dark squares are railroad land. In 1916, three years after the Bureau of Corporations published this map, the federal government revested the grant because the railroad had violated its terms. These heavily timbered lands are administered by the Bureau of Land Management.

MAP 7. National Forest System

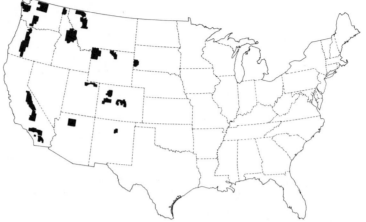

1898: The forest reserves (national forests) created by Presidents Benjamin Harrison and Grover Cleveland. In this year, Gifford Pinchot became chief of the Division of Forestry (Forest Service).

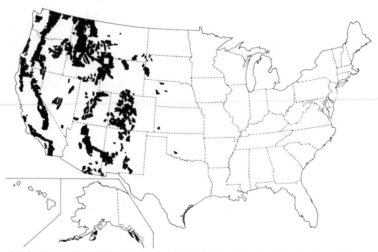

1907: Greatly expanded national forest system due to proclamations by President Theodore Roosevelt under the Forest Reserve Act of 1897.

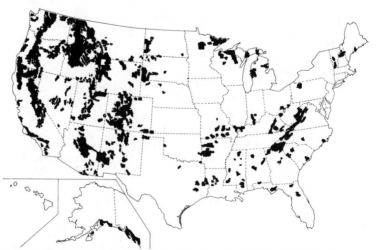

1980: The national forest system in the West shows little change from 1907. Forests in the East have been purchased since 1911 under the Weeks Act.

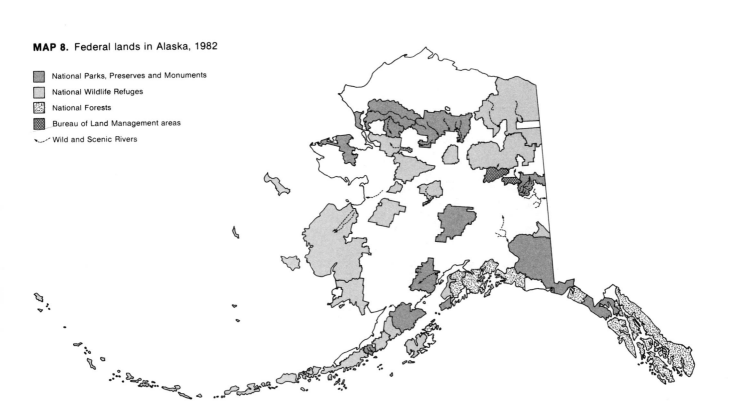

MAP 8. Federal lands in Alaska, 1982

National Parks, Preserves and Monuments
National Wildlife Refuges
National Forests
Bureau of Land Management areas
Wild and Scenic Rivers

MAP 9. Federal lands, 1968: Pacific Northwest Region

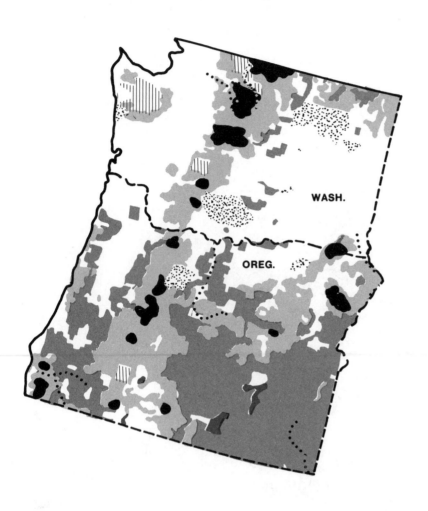

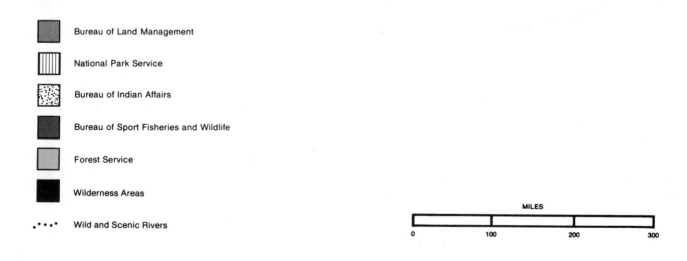

Bureau of Land Management

National Park Service

Bureau of Indian Affairs

Bureau of Sport Fisheries and Wildlife

Forest Service

Wilderness Areas

Wild and Scenic Rivers

MILES

0   100   200   300

MAP 10. California Region

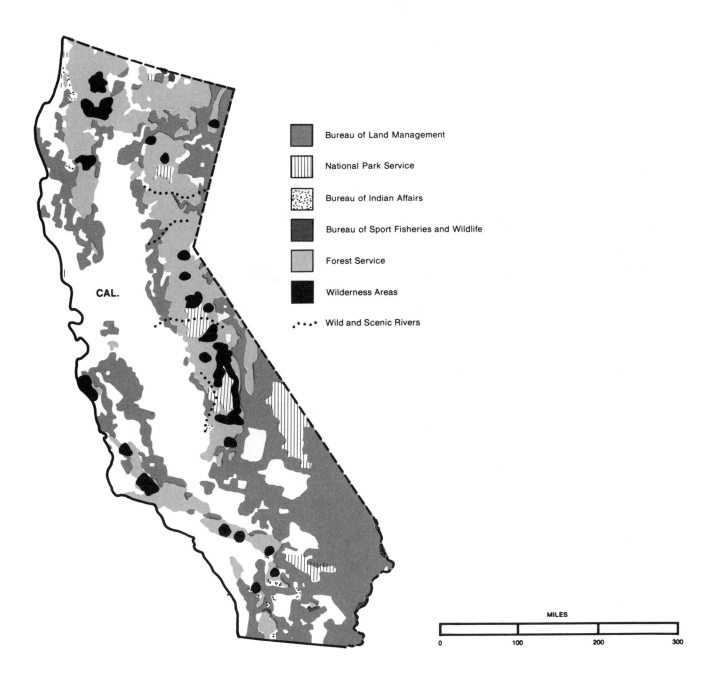

Bureau of Land Management

National Park Service

Bureau of Indian Affairs

Bureau of Sport Fisheries and Wildlife

Forest Service

Wilderness Areas

•••• Wild and Scenic Rivers

CAL.

MILES

0   100   200   300

MAP 11. Intermountain Region

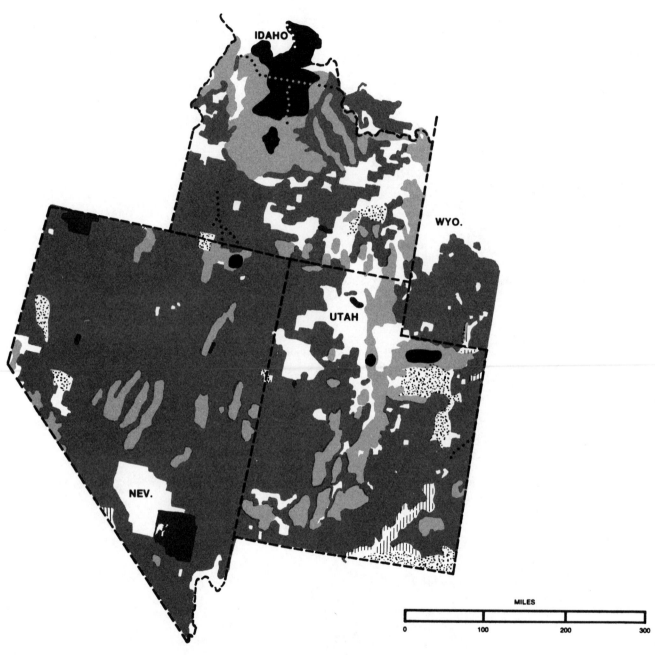

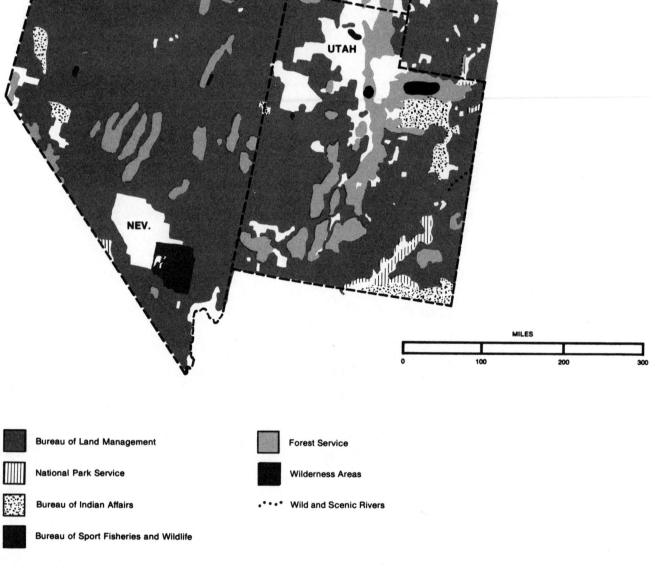

MILES

0 100 200 300

Bureau of Land Management

Forest Service

National Park Service

Wilderness Areas

Bureau of Indian Affairs

Wild and Scenic Rivers

Bureau of Sport Fisheries and Wildlife

MAP 12. Northern Region

IDAHO

MONT.

N. DAK.

Bureau of Land Management

National Park Service

Bureau of Indian Affairs

Bureau of Sport Fisheries and Wildlife

Forest Service

Wilderness Areas

Wild and Scenic Rivers

MILES

0   100   200   300

MAP 13. Rocky Mountain Region

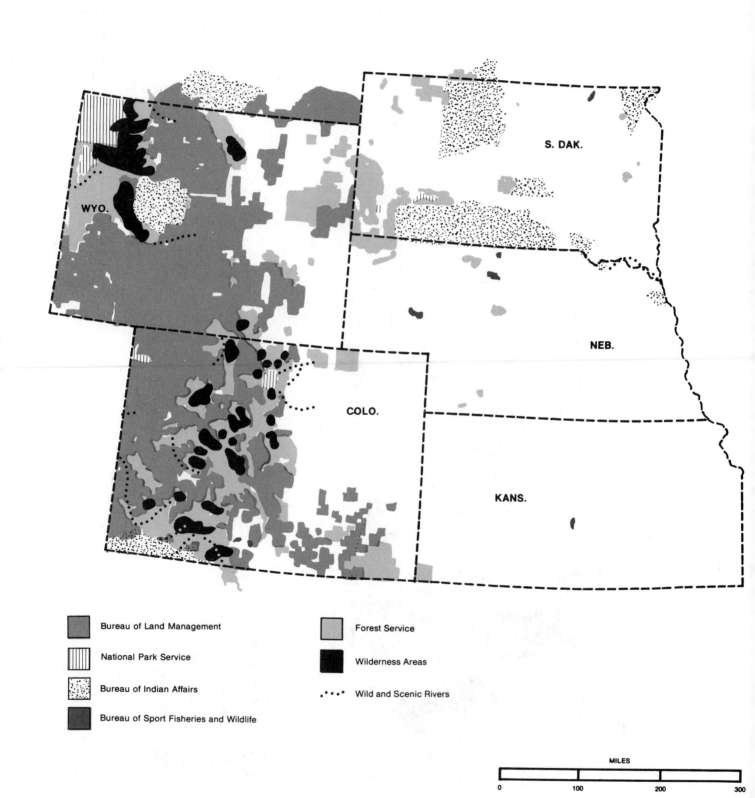

Bureau of Land Management

National Park Service

Bureau of Indian Affairs

Bureau of Sport Fisheries and Wildlife

Forest Service

Wilderness Areas

Wild and Scenic Rivers

MILES

0   100   200   300

MAP 14. Southwestern Region

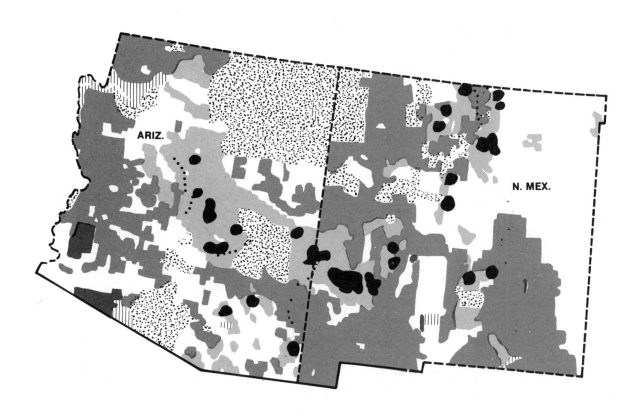

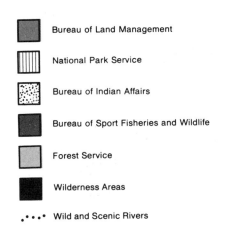

Bureau of Land Management

National Park Service

Bureau of Indian Affairs

Bureau of Sport Fisheries and Wildlife

Forest Service

Wilderness Areas

•••• Wild and Scenic Rivers

MILES

0   100   200   300

MAP 15. Eastern Region

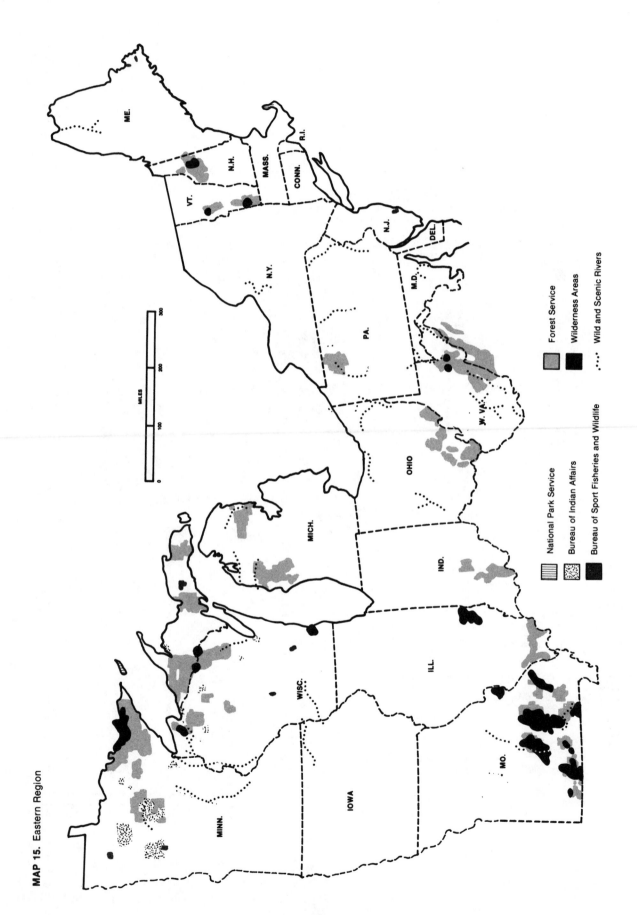

ME.

N.H.

VT.

MASS.

CONN.

R.I.

N.Y.

N.J.

DEL.

M.D.

PA.

W. VA.

OHIO

MICH.

IND.

ILL.

MINN.

WISC.

IOWA

MO.

MILES

0   100   200   300

National Park Service

Bureau of Indian Affairs

Bureau of Sport Fisheries and Wildlife

Forest Service

Wilderness Areas

Wild and Scenic Rivers

828

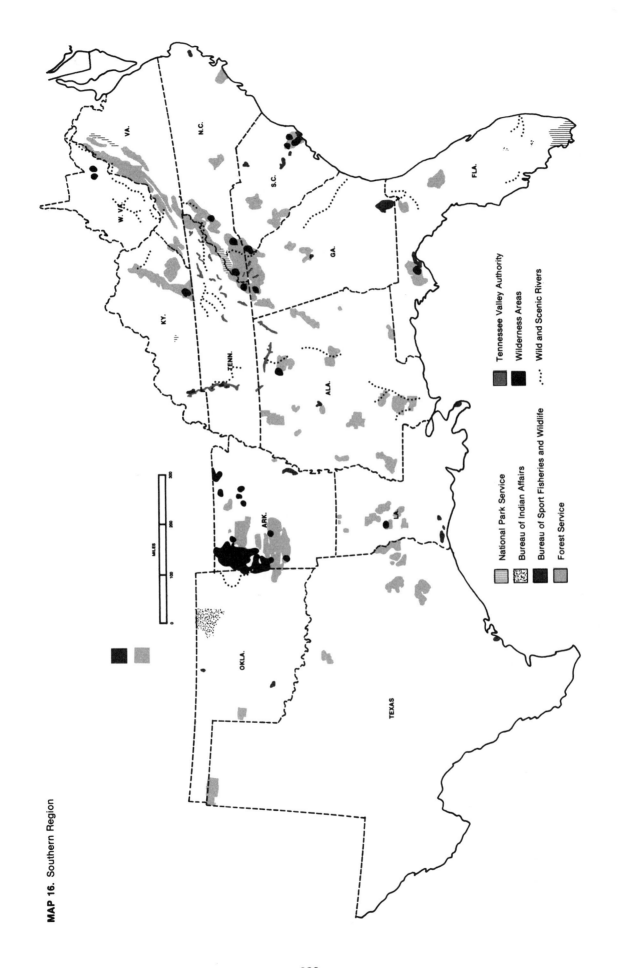

MAP 16. Southern Region

National Park Service

Bureau of Indian Affairs

Bureau of Sport Fisheries and Wildlife

Forest Service

Tennessee Valley Authority

Wilderness Areas

Wild and Scenic Rivers

MILES

0 100 200 300

VA.

N.C.

S.C.

W. VA.

KY.

TENN.

GA.

ALA.

FLA.

ARK.

OKLA.

LA.

TEXAS

MAP 17. Peaks of Lumber Production and Major Lumber Centers, 1923.

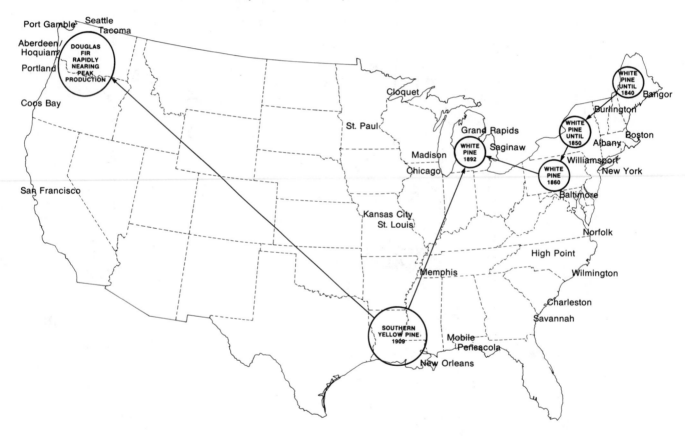

MAP 18. Tahoe Basin

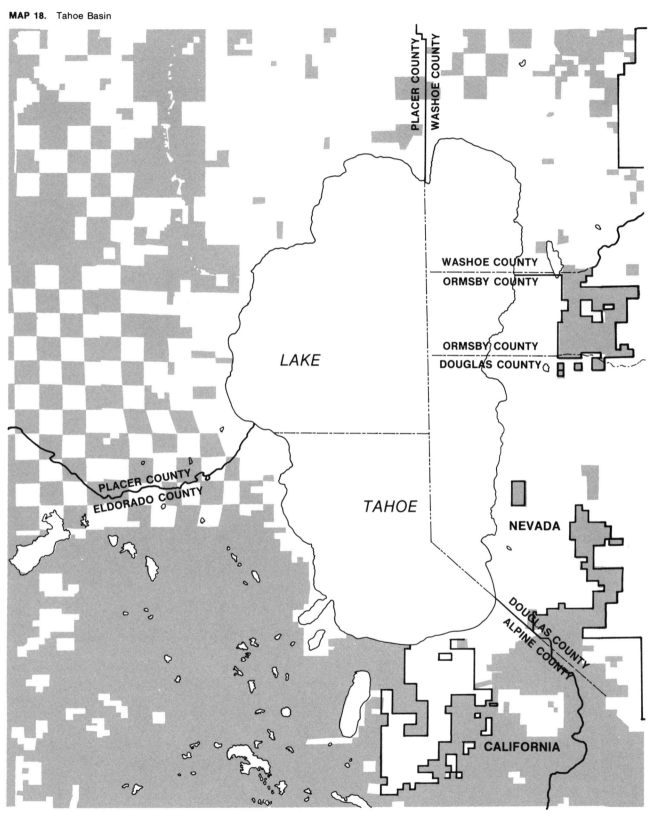

Conflicting jurisdictions and values have been important elements in the history of conservation. When political subdivisions are superimposed over a geographic region and are coupled with changing and competing values, very complex administrative conditions result. In the Tahoe Basin, two state governments, five county administrations, and many towns must work with the U.S. Forest Service and large number of private land owners to develop workable regional plans. The shaded areas are national forest lands administered according to federal law; the white areas are private lands under the jurisdiction of state and county governments. At issue are watershed protection, skiing, hiking, boating, fishing, lumbering, gambling, and vacation homes.

Directory of Contributors

Abbott, Carl
Portland (Oregon) State University
PLANK ROADS AND WOOD BLOCK
PAVEMENTS

Adams, Ronald S.
New Forests, Davis, California
TREE NURSERIES AND TREE SEED
COLLECTION

Adrosko, Rita J.
Smithsonian Institution
DYEWOODS

Allen, James B.
Brigham Young University
COMPANY TOWNS

Argow, Keith A.
*The American Resources Group,
Washington, D.C.*
FORESTRY AS A PROFESSION

Austin, Judith
Idaho State Historical Society
O & C LANDS

Baker, Andrew J.
*Forest Products Laboratory,
Madison, Wisconsin*
CHARCOAL

Baldwin, Henry I.
*New Hampshire Forestry
Commission*
NEW HAMPSHIRE FORESTS

Bartlett, Richard A.
Florida State University
GEOLOGICAL SURVEY; YELLOWSTONE
NATIONAL PARK

Bay, Crandall
University of California, Santa Cruz
MURIE, OLAUS JOHAN; ZAHNISER,
HOWARD CLINTON

Beck, Alfred M.
*U. S. Army Center of Military
History*
WORLD WAR II AND AMERICAN
FORESTS AND FOREST INDUSTRY

Beek, James
American Forest Institute
AMERICAN FOREST INSTITUTE

Behr, Eldon A.
Michigan State University
WOOD PRESERVATION

Bell, Rodney E.
South Dakota State University
ALGER, RUSSELL A.

Berge, Dennis E.
San Diego State University
NORWEGIAN IMMIGRANTS AND
AMERICAN FORESTS

Berkebile, Don H.
Smithsonian Institution
CARRIAGE AND WAGON BUILDING

Bethea, John M.
Florida Division of Forestry
FLORIDA FORESTS

Bethke, Robert D.
University of Delaware
BUNYAN, PAUL

Bofinger, Paul O.
*Society for the Protection of New
Hampshire Forests*
NEW HAMPSHIRE STATE FORESTRY

Boisfontaine, A. S.
Southern Pine Inspection Bureau
LUMBER STANDARDS AND GRADING

Brundage, Roy C.
Purdue University
INDIANA FORESTS

Bryans, Bill
University of Wyoming
WYOMING FORESTS

Buchholtz, C. W.
Arapahoe Community College, Littleton, Colorado
GLACIER NATIONAL PARK

Budy, Jerry D.
University of Nevada, Reno
NEVADA FORESTS

Burnett, G. Wesley
Clemson University
MONTANA FORESTS; SOUTH CAROLINA FORESTS

Burns, Anna C.
Louisiana State University, Alexandria
GOODYEAR, CHARLES WATERHOUSE; LOUISIANA FORESTS

Callison, Charles H.
Public Lands Institute
MINING CLAIMS ON NATIONAL FORESTS AND NATIONAL PARKS

Campbell, Dale C.
Forest Heritage Center, Oklahoma
OKLAHOMA FORESTS

Canham, Hugh O.
State University of New York, College of Environmental Science and Forestry
NEW YORK FORESTS

Carlsson, Leif
The House of Emigrants, Växjö, Sweden
SWEDISH IMMIGRANTS AND AMERICAN FORESTS

Carranco, Lynwood
College of the Redwoods, Eureka, California
TERMINOLOGY

Carroll, Charles F.
University of Lowell, Massachusetts
BRITISH COLONIAL FOREST POLICIES; MASSACHUSETTS FORESTS; RHODE ISLANL FORESTS; SHIPBUILDING

Carstensen, Vernon
University of Washington
CUTOVER LANDS

Cart, Theodore W.
Francis Marion College, South Carolina
LACEY, JOHN FLETCHER

Clar, C. Raymond
California Department of Forestry
CALIFORNIA STATE FORESTRY; SPANISH AND MEXICAN FOREST POLICIES IN CALIFORNIA

Clark, Thomas D.
University of Kentucky
KENTUCKY FORESTS; LUMBER INDUSTRY: SOUTHERN STATES

Clary, David A.
Historical, Cultural, and Environmental Consulting, Indiana
BUREAU OF OUTDOOR RECREATION AND HERITAGE CONSERVATION AND RECREATION SERVICE; HISTORIC PRESERVATION; WORLD WAR I AND AMERICAN FORESTS AND FOREST INDUSTRY

Clawson, Marion
Resources for the Future
FOREST DEPLETION AND GROWTH; LUMBER, PLYWOOD, AND PAPER PRICES; LUMBER PRODUCTION

Clements, Kendrick A.
University of South Carolina
YOSEMITE NATIONAL PARK

Clepper, Henry
American Forestry Association
AMERICAN FORESTRY ASSOCIATION; BUTLER, OVID MCQUAT; CHARLES LATHROP PACK FORESTRY FOUNDATION; DANA, SAMUEL TRASK; NATURAL RESOURCES COUNCIL OF AMERICA; PACK, CHARLES LATHROP; ROTHROCK, JOSEPH TRIMBLE

Cobb, Samuel S.
Pennsylvania Bureau of Forestry
PENNSYLVANIA FORESTS

Cockrell, Robert A.
University of California, Berkeley
CALIFORNIA FORESTS

Condit, Carl W.
Northwestern University
ARCHITECTURAL STYLES AND LUMBER UTILIZATION

Conlin, Joseph R.
California State University, Chico
CONGRESSIONAL COMMITTEES AND FEDERAL FORESTLANDS; FOOD FROM THE FOREST; FOOD IN LOGGING CAMPS

Cox, Thomas R.
San Diego State University
DUBOIS, JOHN; HAWAII FORESTS; LOGGING TECHNOLOGY AND TOOLS; LUMBER INDUSTRY: PACIFIC COAST; LUMBERMAN'S FRONTIER; LUMBER TARIFFS; ONTHANK, KARL WILLIAM; OREGON STATE PARKS; POLES AND PILING INDUSTRY; STATE PARKS MOVEMENT; WOOD PRODUCTS EXPORTS

Cozine, James
Lamar University, Beaumont, Texas
BIG THICKET NATIONAL PRESERVE

Current, Richard N.
University of North Carolina, Greensboro
CIVIL WAR AND AMERICAN FORESTS AND FOREST INDUSTRY; SAWYER, PHILETUS

Curry, Corliss C.
University of Arkansas, Monticello
ARKANSAS FORESTS

Daubenmire, Rexford
Washington State University
EVOLUTION AND DISTRIBUTION OF AMERICAN FORESTS

Dean, George W.
Virginia Forestry Association
VIRGINIA FORESTS

DeCoster, Lester A.
American Forest Institute
MAINE FORESTS

Devens, Carol
Rutgers University
INDIAN FOREST USE

Diller, Oliver D.
Ohio State University
OHIO FORESTS

Dodds, Gordon B.
Portland (Oregon) State University
STREAMFLOW CONTROVERSY

Dunlap, Thomas R.
*Virginia Polytechnic Institute and
    State University*
FOREST ENTOMOLOGY; PESTICIDES
    AND BIOLOGICAL CONTROL;
    PREDATOR AND RODENT CONTROL

Egerton, Frank N.
University of Wisconsin, Parkside
BARTRAM, JOHN, AND WILLIAM
    BARTRAM; ECOLOGY AND FORESTS;
    MARSH, GEORGE PERKINS

Fazio, James R.
University of Idaho
IDAHO FORESTS

Ficken, Robert E.
Forest History Society
LONG, GEORGE SMITH; MCNARY,
    CHARLES L.; MASON, DAVID T.;
    OLYMPIC NATIONAL PARK;
    WASHINGTON FORESTS

Fickle, James E.
Memphis State University
MISSISSIPPI FORESTS

Fisher, James G.
Oregon State Forestry Department
OREGON STATE FORESTRY

Flader, Susan L.
University of Missouri, Columbia
LEOPOLD, ALDO; MISSOURI FORESTS;
    NATIONAL AUDUBON SOCIETY

Fleischer, Herbert O.
*Forest Products Laboratory,
    Madison, Wisconsin*
FOREST PRODUCTS RESEARCH;
    PLYWOOD AND VENEER INDUSTRIES

Flynt, Wayne
Auburn University
ALABAMA FORESTS

Funigiello, Philip J.
College of William and Mary
ICKES, HAROLD LE CLAIRE

Fusonie, Alan E.
*USDA Science and Education
    Administration*
ARBORETUMS AND BOTANICAL
    GARDENS

Gabel, W. F.
*Forestry Section, Delaware
    Department of Agriculture*
DELAWARE FORESTS

Garratt, George A.
Yale University
CHAPMAN, HERMAN HAUPT; FOREST
    HISTORY SOCIETY

Gatewood, Willard B., Jr.
University of Arkansas
GREAT SMOKY MOUNTAINS NATIONAL
    PARK

Gray, Gary Craven
*Historical, Cultural, and
    Environmental Consulting,
    Indiana*
CONSERVATION MOVEMENT

Gwinner, G. Myron
Christmas Trees, Missouri
CHRISTMAS TREES

Hallion, Richard P.
Smithsonian Institution
AIRCRAFT CONSTRUCTION

Hargrove, Eugene C.
University of Georgia
PHILOSOPHY, RELIGION, AND
    AMERICAN FORESTS

Harmon, Frank J.
U. S. Forest Service
EGLESTON, NATHANIEL HILLYER;
    FERNOW, BERNHARD EDUARD;
    HOUGH, FRANKLIN BENJAMIN;
    MCARDLE, RICHARD EDWIN;
    STUART, ROBERT YOUNG; WATTS,
    LYLE FORD

Hart, Arthur A.
Idaho State Historical Society
MILLWORK INDUSTRY; WOODWORKING
    MACHINES

Haymond, Jay M.
Utah State Historical Society
LUMBER INDUSTRY: ROCKY
    MOUNTAIN REGION; UTAH FORESTS

Hays, Samuel P.
University of Pittsburgh
CONSERVATION ORGANIZATIONS;
    ENVIRONMENTAL MOVEMENT

Heinrichs, Dorothy
*American Farmland Trust,
    Washington, D.C.*
TREES AS EMBLEMS

Heinrichs, Jay
Society of American Foresters
TREES AS EMBLEMS

Hepting, George H.
U. S. Forest Service
FOREST PATHOLOGY

Hergert, Herbert L.
ITT Rayonier, Inc.
CHEMICALLY DERIVED WOOD
    PRODUCTS; TANNINS

Hibbard, John E.
*Connecticut Forest and Park
    Association*
CONNECTICUT FORESTS

Hoglund, A. William
University of Connecticut
FENCING; FIREWOOD

Holmes, Jack D. L.
*Louisiana Collection Series of Books
    and Documents on Colonial
    Louisiana*
FRENCH, SPANISH, AND MEXICAN
    FOREST POLICIES ON THE GULF
    COAST

Hughes, J. Donald
University of Denver
GRAND CANYON NATIONAL PARK

Hummasti, P. George
University of Oregon
FINNISH IMMIGRANTS AND AMERICAN
    FORESTS

Hyman, Harold M.
Rice University
LOYAL LEGION OF LOGGERS AND
    LUMBERMEN

Ives, Edward D.
University of Maine at Orono
FOLKLORE AND FOLK MUSIC

Izlar, Bob
American Pulpwood Association
AMERICAN PULPWOOD ASSOCIATION;
    GEORGIA FORESTS

Johnson, Mary Elizabeth
Forest History Society
ARBOR DAY; BOX AND CONTAINER
    INDUSTRY; WILDLIFE
    CONSERVATION

Jolley, Harley E.
Mars Hill College, North Carolina
NORTH CAROLINA FORESTS

Jordan, Terry G.
North Texas State University
LOG CONSTRUCTION

Judd, Richard W.
Forest History Society
COMMUNITY FORESTS;
    CONGRESSIONAL COMMITTEES AND
    FEDERAL FORESTLANDS

Kephart, George S.
Bureau of Indian Affairs
INDIAN FORESTRY; KINNEY, JAY P;
    NAVAL LIVE OAK RESERVES

Kershaw, Gordon E.
Frostburg (Maryland) State College
WENTWORTH, BENNING, AND JOHN
    WENTWORTH

Kilar, Jeremy W.
*Delta College, University Center,
    Michigan*
LAW AND ORDER IN LUMBER CAMPS
    AND TOWNS; POLISH IMMIGRANTS
    AND AMERICAN FORESTS

Kinch, P. Michael
Oregon State University
FOREST AND CONSERVATION
    PUBLICATIONS

King, Joseph E.
Texas Tech University
MINE TIMBER

Kirkpatrick, Dahl J.
U. S. Forest Service
ARIZONA FORESTS; NEW MEXICO
    FORESTS

Klemperer, W. David
*Virginia Polytechnic Institute and
    State University*
TAXATION

Knox, Richard L.
U. S. Forest Service
COOPERATIVE FORESTRY

Kohlmeyer, Fred W.
Illinois State University
HINES, EDWARD; ILLINOIS FORESTS;
    LUMBER DISTRIBUTION AND
    MARKETING; SOCIAL ORIGINS OF
    LUMBERMEN

Krog, Carl
*University of Wisconsin Center,
    Marinette*
STEPHENSON, ISAAC

Lapping, Mark B.
University of Guelph, Ontario
VERMONT FORESTS

Lee, Lawrence B.
San Jose State University
RECLAMATION AND WATERPOWER
    DEMANDS ON FORESTS

LeMaster, Dennis C.
Washington State University
FOREST INDUSTRIES STRUCTURE

Lendt, David L.
Iowa State University
DARLING, JAY NORWOOD

Le Unes, Barbara
Blinn College, Bryan, Texas
UDALL, STEWART LEE

Lewis, Richard
American Forest Institute
TREE FARMS

Littleton, Dowe
Auburn University
ALABAMA FORESTS

Lockmann, Ronald F.
University of Southern California
KINNEY, ABBOT

McCarthy, G. Michael
Community College of Denver
COLORADO FORESTS

McKinney, J. Gage
McKinney Hardwood Company
IMPORTED HARDWOODS

McLintock, Thomas F.
U. S. Forest Service
FORESTRY RESEARCH

Maloney, Thomas M.
Washington State University
COMPOSITION BOARD INDUSTRY

Mandell, Daniel R.
University of Virginia
TIMBER TRESPASS AND DEPREDATION
    ON PUBLIC LANDS

Martin, George L., Jr.
University of Wisconsin—Madison
FOREST INVENTORY AND VALUATION
    PRACTICES

Martinson, Arthur D.
*Pacific Lutheran University, Tacoma,
    Washington*
MOUNT RAINIER NATIONAL PARK;
    NORTH CASCADES NATIONAL PARK

Maxwell, Robert S.
*Stephen F. Austin State University,
    Nacogdoches, Texas*
KIRBY, JOHN HENRY; TEXAS FORESTS

Meeks, David M.
Bourbon Cooperage Company, Inc.
COOPERAGE INDUSTRY

Melendy, H. Brett
San Jose State University
ASIAN IMMIGRANTS AND AMERICAN
    FORESTS

Merriam, L. C., Jr.
University of Minnesota
RECREATION

Miller, Paul R.
U. S. Forest Service
AIR POLLUTION AND FORESTS

Moon, Gareth C.
Montana Division of Forestry
FARM FORESTRY; SMOKEY BEAR

Moon, Michael E.
Montana Division of Forestry
FARM FORESTRY; SMOKEY BEAR

Moore, John H.
Florida State University
MASON, WILLIAM HORATIO

Musselman, Lloyd K.
Oklahoma City University
ROCKY MOUNTAIN NATIONAL PARK

Newson, Harold P.
National Forest Products Association
FOREST INDUSTRIES ADVISORY
    COUNCIL; FOREST INDUSTRIES
    COUNCIL; NATIONAL FOREST
    PRODUCTS ASSOCIATION

Noonan, Patrick F.
The Nature Conservancy
NATURE CONSERVANCY

O'Callaghan, Jerry A.
Bureau of Land Management
BUREAU OF LAND MANAGEMENT;
    FOREST SERVICE PLACEMENT

Oden, Jack P.
*Enterprise (Alabama) State Junior
    College*
HERTY, CHARLES HOLMES

Orr, Oliver H.
Library of Congress
SCHENCK, CARL ALWIN

Overfield, Richard A.
University of Nebraska, Omaha
NEBRASKA FORESTS

Pablo, Jean M.
U. S. Forest Service
GRAVES, HENRY SOLON; POTTER,
    ALBERT FRANKLIN; PRICE,
    OVERTON WESTFELDT

Page, W. D.
American Plywood Association
AMERICAN PLYWOOD ASSOCIATION

Paige, John C.
National Park Service
EVERGLADES NATIONAL PARK AND
    BIG CYPRESS NATIONAL PRESERVE

Parr, William A.
Maryland Forest and Park Services
MARYLAND FORESTS

Penick, James Lal, Jr.
Loyola University of Chicago
BALLINGER-PINCHOT CONTROVERSY

Perry, Percival
Wake Forest University
NAVAL STORES

Pinkett, Harold T.
*National Archives and Records
    Service*
CONSULTING FORESTRY; GENERAL
    LAND OFFICE; HISTORICAL
    SOURCES; PINCHOT, GIFFORD;
    REGULATION OF FOREST
    PRACTICES; ROOSEVELT, THEODORE

Potter, Barrett G.
State University of New York, Alfred
CIVILIAN CONSERVATION CORPS

Progulske, Donald R.
University of Massachusetts
SOUTH DAKOTA FORESTS

Pyne, Stephen J.
University of Iowa
FIRE AND FOREST MANAGEMENT;
    FIRE CONTROL; FIREFIGHTING
    METHODS AND EQUIPMENT; FOREST
    FIRES

Rakestraw, Lawrence W.
Michigan Technological University
ALASKA FORESTS; HISTORIOGRAPHY;
    MICHIGAN FORESTS; NATIONAL
    MONUMENTS; OLMSTED,
    FREDERICK ERSKINE

Rasmussen, Wayne D.
USDA Economic Research Service
DEPARTMENT OF AGRICULTURE

Rathke, Ann
*State Historical Society of North
    Dakota*
NORTH DAKOTA FORESTS

Read, Ralph A.
U. S. Forest Service
AFFORESTATION; SHELTERBELTS

Rector, William G.
University of Wisconsin, Platteville
LOG TRANSPORTATION

Reiger, John F.
University of Miami
BOONE AND CROCKETT CLUB;
    GRINNELL, GEORGE BIRD

Reuss, Martin
Army Corps of Engineers
ARMY CORPS OF ENGINEERS

Rice, Otis K.
West Virginia Institute of Technology
WEST VIRGINIA FORESTS

Righter, Robert W.
University of Wyoming
GRAND TETON NATIONAL PARK

Roberts, William I., III
Pennsylvania State University
POTASH AND PEARLASH

Robbins, William G.
Oregon State University
COMPTON, WILSON MARTINDALE;
    TRADE AND PROMOTIONAL
    ASSOCIATIONS

Robinson, Michael C.
Public Works Historical Society
BUREAU OF RECLAMATION; MEAD,
    ELWOOD; NEWELL, FREDERICK
    HAYNES

Roth, Dennis M.
U. S. Forest Service
CLIFF, EDWARD PARLEY; GREELEY,
    WILLIAM BUCKHOUT; MCGUIRE,
    JOHN RICHARD; PETERSON, RALPH
    MAX; SILCOX, FERDINAND
    AUGUSTUS

Rowley, W. D.
University of Nevada, Reno
GRAZING ON FORESTLANDS

Runte, Alfred
University of Washington
MATHER, STEPHEN TYNG;
    MCFARLAND, JOHN HORACE;
    NATIONAL PARKS AND
    CONSERVATION ASSOCIATION;
    NATIONAL PARKS AND NATIONAL
    PARK SERVICE; NIAGARA FALLS;
    OLMSTED, FREDERICK LAW, SR.
    AND JR.; ROCKEFELLER, JOHN
    DAVISON, JR., AND LAURANCE
    SPELMAN ROCKEFELLER

Sartz, Richard S.
U. S. Forest Service
WATERSHED MANAGEMENT

Scheiber, Harry N.
University of California, Berkeley
LAW AND THE FOREST

Schmaltz, Norman J.
Concordia College, Ann Arbor, Michigan
CLAPP, EARLE HART; LAND
  CLASSIFICATION; ZON, RAPHAEL

Schnell, Robert L.
Tennessee Valley Authority
TENNESSEE FORESTS

Schrepfer, Susan R.
Rutgers University
BROWER, DAVID ROSS; DRURY,
  NEWTON B.; LEONARD, RICHARD
  MANNING; MERRIAM, JOHN
  CAMPBELL; REDWOOD NATIONAL
  PARK; SIERRA CLUB; YARD,
  ROBERT STERLING

Scott, Roy V.
Mississippi State University
RAILROADS AND FORESTS

Searle, R. Newell
St. Paul Area Chamber of Commerce
MINNESOTA FORESTS; OBERHOLTZER,
  ERNEST C.; OLSON, SIGURD
  FERDINAND; QUETICO-SUPERIOR

Self, Huber
Kansas State University
KANSAS FORESTS

Shanklin, John F.
Department of the Interior
NATURAL AREAS

Shofner, Jerrell H.
University of Central Florida
BLACKS AND AMERICAN FORESTS;
  CONVICT LABOR IN FOREST
  INDUSTRIES

Sieber, George W.
University of Wisconsin, Oshkosh
WISCONSIN FORESTS

Smith, David C.
University of Maine at Orono
CARY, AUSTIN; FRENCH-CANADIAN
  IMMIGRANTS AND AMERICAN
  FORESTS; LUMBER INDUSTRY:
  NORTHEAST; PULP AND PAPER
  INDUSTRY; TREE RING RESEARCH

Smith, David M.
Yale University
CONNECTICUT FORESTS;
  SILVICULTURE

Snyder, Glenn Q.
Hastings School of Law, California
DEVOTO, BERNARD AUGUSTINE

Spurr, Stephen H.
University of Texas, Austin
SILVICULTURE

Stannard, Jerry
University of Kansas
MEDICINAL PRODUCTS

Steen, Harold K.
Forest History Society
FOREST SERVICE; SALVAGE; SOCIETY
  OF AMERICAN FORESTERS; STATE
  FORESTRY; WASHINGTON STATE
  FORESTRY

Steinbrenner, Eugene C.
Weyerhaeuser Company
FOREST SOILS

Sterling, Keir
Pace University, New York City
BOTANICAL EXPLORATION AND THE
  DISCOVERY OF PRINCIPAL FOREST
  TREE SPECIES

Strong, Douglas H.
San Diego State University
COLBY, WILLIAM EDWARD; MUIR,
  JOHN; SEQUOIA AND KINGS CANYON
  NATIONAL PARKS

Swain, Donald C.
University of Louisville
ALBRIGHT, HORACE MARDEN;
  ROOSEVELT, FRANKLIN D.

Thomas, Phillip Drennon
University of Alaska, Anchorage
MICHAUX, ANDRÉ, AND FRANÇOIS
  ANDRÉ MICHAUX; NUTTALL,
  THOMAS; SARGENT, CHARLES
  SPRAGUE; SETON, ERNEST
  THOMPSON

Trani, Eugene P.
University of Missouri, Kansas City
DEPARTMENT OF THE INTERIOR

Twining, Charles E.
Northland College, Ashland, Wisconsin
CANADIAN-AMERICAN RELATIONS IN
  THE FOREST PRODUCTS INDUSTRIES;
  LUMBER INDUSTRY: LAKE STATES;
  WEYERHAEUSER FAMILY

Verner, William K.
Adirondack Mountain School, Inc., New York
ADIRONDACK PARK; CATSKILL PARK;
  NEW YORK STATE FOREST
  PRESERVE

Voigt, William, Jr.
Izaak Walton League
IZAAK WALTON LEAGUE OF AMERICA;
  PENFOLD, JOSEPH WELLER; REID,
  KENNETH ALEXANDER

Wacker, Peter O.
Rutgers University
NEW JERSEY FORESTS

Wadsworth, Frank H.
U. S. Forest Service
PUERTO RICO AND AMERICAN VIRGIN
  ISLANDS FORESTS; TROPICAL
  FORESTRY

Walker, Laurence C.
Stephen F. Austin State University, Nacogdoches, Texas
FOREST INFLUENCES; FORESTRY IN
  GENERAL EDUCATION; TECHNICIAN
  TRAINING IN FORESTRY

Walther, Robert G.
Smithsonian Institution
MUSEUMS OF FOREST HISTORY

Wangaard, Frederick F.
Colorado State University
WOOD SCIENCE AND TECHNOLOGY

White, Fred M.
*North Carolina Department of
    Natural Resources and Community
    Development*
DENDROLOGY

Wilkins, Austin H.
Maine Bureau of Forestry
MAINE STATE FORESTRY

Wilkins, Mira
Florida International University
MULTINATIONAL CORPORATIONS

Williams, Michael
University of Oxford
LUMBER INDUSTRY: CENTRAL STATES;
    PIONEER FARM LIFE AND FOREST
    USE

Williamson, David H.
*Portland (Oregon) Community
    College*
GYPPO LOGGING

Willins, Henry H.
*National Oak Flooring
    Manufacturers Association*
HARDWOOD FLOORING INDUSTRY

Wilson, William H.
North Texas State University
TREES IN LANDSCAPE DESIGN;
    MUNICIPAL PARKS AND URBAN
    FORESTRY

Winberry, John J.
University of South Carolina
SHAKE AND SHINGLE INDUSTRY

Winters, Robert K.
Society of American Foresters
INTERNATIONAL FORESTRY

Wisdom, Carmen Del Coro
Blacksburg, Virginia
FURNITURE INDUSTRY

Wisdom, Harold W.
*Virginia Polytechnic Institute and
    State University*
FURNITURE INDUSTRY

Wollner, Craig E.
Portland (Oregon) State University
OREGON FORESTS

Wright, Jonathan W.
Michigan State University
INTRODUCED FOREST TREES

Yonce, Frederick J.
Denver Public Library
FOREST OWNERSHIP

Zieger, Robert W.
Wayne State University
LABOR IN THE PULP AND PAPER
    INDUSTRY

Index

A

AFA. *See* American Forestry
    Association
AFI. *See* American Forest Institute
AFPI (American Forest Products
    Industries, Inc.). *See* American
    Forest Institute
AID. *See* Aid for International
    Development
Acadia National Park, 404
Acid rain, 7, 684
Act to Protect the Birds and Other
    Animals in Yellowstone
    National Park (1894), 42, 704,
    736
Adirondack Forest Preserve. *See*
    New York State Forest
    Preserve
Adirondack Park, **1–2**, 204, 491
    See also State parks
Aesthetics, nature, 444, 464, 466,
    527, 528, 662, 693
    and landscape design, 448, 662
    See also Scenic preservation;
    Wilderness preservation
Afforestation, **2–4**, 479, 498, 656
    See also Arbor Day;
    Reforestation; Shelterbelts;
    Tree planting
Agassiz, Louis, 141
Agricultural and Trade Assistance
    Act (1954), 314
Agricultural Research and
    Marketing Act (1946), 479

Agricultural Research Service, 135,
    201, 523
Agriculture Act (1958), 314
Agriculture and Consumer
    Protection Act (1973), 121
Aid for International Development
    (AID), 313–314, 315
Aircraft construction, **4–6**, 539, 619,
    732
Aircraft, uses
    fire detection, 179
    fire suppression, *178*, 180, *180*,
    181
    forest inventory, 221
    insect control, 201
    logging, *351*, 362, 683
Air pollution
    control, 7, 8, 80, 516, 557
    and forests, **6–8**
    from smoke, 172, 205, 516
Alabama, **8–9**, 829 (map)
    See also Lumber industry:
    Southern states
Alaska, **9–13**, 35, 388, 407, *527*, 821
    (map)
    and Bureau of Land Management,
    12, 54, 821 (map)
    "d-2 lands" controversy, 12
    and fires, 205
    and Japanese trade, 10, 446, 720
    Tongass National Forest, 10, 13,
    432, 701
Alaska National Interest Lands
    Conservation Act (1980), 12, 54,
    690, 700

Alaska Native Claims Settlement
    Act (1971), 12, 55, 700
Albright, Horace Marden, **13**, 274,
    414, 466
Alcohol (wood), 78, 79–80
Alger, Russell A., **14–15**
Allagash Wilderness Waterway, 691,
    691
Alliance for Environmental
    Education, 19
Allowable cut, 13, 54, 307, 381, 455
American Antiquities Act (1906), 12,
    294, 461
American Association for the
    Advancement of Science, 297
American Association for
    Conservation Information. *See*
    Association for Conservation
    Information
American Civic Association, 109,
    114, 415, 466, 583, 623, 624
American Fisheries Society, 113, 706
American Forest congresses, 17, 57,
    107
American Forest Institute (AFI),
    15–16, 207, 208, 460, 654, 655,
    656
    archives, 293
    See also National Lumber
    Manufacturers Association;
    Lumber trade associations;
    Trade associations
American Forest Products
    Industries, Inc. (AFPI). *See*
    American Forest Institute

⌈ Page numbers in **boldface** indicate main entries; page numbers in ⌉
⌊ *italics* refer to illustrations. Vol. I: pp. 1–400; Vol. II: pp. 401–839. ⌋

843

Page numbers in **boldface** indicate main entries; page numbers in
italics refer to illustrations. Vol. I: pp. 1–400; Vol. II: pp. 401–839.

National Parks Association. *See*
National Parks and
Conservation Association
National Parks and Recreation Act
(1978), 486
National Park Service, 114, 238, 249,
253, 299, 462, 463, **466–467,** 572,
584, 623, 665
Albright, Horace Marden, **13,** 274,
414, 466
concessionnaire policy, 271, 443,
583, 738, 739
congressional committees, 99
Drury, Newton P., **136**
establishment of, 13, 132, 249,
415, 464, 466, 572, 735, 737
fire policy, 172, 174, 175, 205,
692
historical sources, 291
historic preservation, 294
Mather, Stephen Tyng, 13, 114,
253, **414,** 463, 466, 573, 622–623,
696, 697
"Mission 66," 114, 443, 466, 737
recreation management, 56, 249,
414, 466, 573, 584, 693, 729, 735,
737, 739
roads, 696, 697, 699, 737, 738
wilderness, 114, 693, 696–697,
700, 737
wildlife management, 283, 584,
704, 706, 736
and World War I, 729
and World War II, 733
See also Aesthetics, nature; Scenic
preservation; Utilitarianism
National Park Service Act (1916),
13, 416, 509, 572
National Park System-Mining
Activity Act (1976), 432
National Plan for American
Forestry. *See* Copeland Report
National Plan for Outdoor
Recreation, 54, 55
National Planning Board, 112
National preserves
in Alaska, 12
Big Cypress, **149–150**
Big Thicket, **39–40**
National Recovery Administration
(NRA), 19, 369, 410, 460
See also New Deal programs
National Recreation and Park
Association, **467–468,** 624
National Register of Big Trees, 18

National Register of Historic Places,
294
National Resources Board, 112
National Resources Committee, 112
National Resources Planning Board,
112, 333
National Trails System Act (1968),
665
National Watershed Congress, 113
National Wildfire Coordinating
Group, 176, 205
National Wildlife Federation, 42,
113, 114–115, 128, 343, **468,**
697
Conservationist of the Year
Award recipient, 71
National Wood Promotion Program,
455
National Woodwork Manufacturers
Association, 427
Natural areas, **468–469,** 470
Natural history
artists, 596
collections, 589
descriptions by explorers and
early settlers, 42, 43, 44, 45,
139–141
Naturalists, 283, 444, 499, 500, 589,
596
See also Botanical explorations;
Botanists; Plant collectors and
collecting
Natural resources
history, 296
policy and legislation, 98–102, 105
research, 580–581
Natural Resources Council of
America, **469,** 520, 580, 742
Natural Resources Defense Council,
115, 147, 687
Nature Conservancy, 115, 468, **469–**
470
Naval live oak, 269, **471,** 649, 719
See also British colonial forest
policies; Shipbuilding
Naval stores, **471–479,** *722*
Alabama, 9
American colonial period, 48, 50,
185, 409, 471, 472–474
black workers in, 41
convict labor in, 116, 117
cup-and-gutter method, 289, 476
Florida, 185
Georgia, 268–269
medicinal uses, 419

North Carolina, 475, 494
Ohio, 504
Polish workers in, 543
South Carolina, 614
Naval Stores Act (1705), 48
Naval Stores Act (1729), 48, *49*
Naval Stores Conservation Program,
111, 113, 476, 477
Naval Stores Inspection Act (1923),
479
Naval Timber Act. *See* Timber
Trespass Act (1831)
Nebraska, **479–480,** 656, 826 (map)
founding of Arbor Day, 4, 21–23
Nevada, 382, **480–481,** 824 (map)
Comstock lode, 428, 429, 480
fires, 205
See also Lumber industry: Rocky
Mountain region
Newberry, John S., 45
New Deal programs
agricultural, 131
and the conservation movement,
13, 111–112, 131, 584, 585
and the Department of the
Interior, 132, 133, 299, 300
and the forest industries, 19, 20,
410, 553, 554, 555
and the Forest Service, 250, 606
and the lumber industry, 369, 460,
578, 579, 653
Tennessee Valley Authority, **639–**
640
water conservation and
waterpower, 56, 584, 585
See also Civilian Conservation
Corps; Copeland Report; Great
Depression; National Industrial
Recovery Act; National
Recovery Administration; state
entries
Newell, Frederick Haynes, 55, 97,
481, 569, 570
archives, 293
New England Salvage
Administration, 378
New Hampshire, 89, **481–483,** 627,
681, 683, 686, 828 (map)
state forestry, 482, **483–485**
See also Lumber industry:
Northeast
New Jersey, **485–487,** 828 (map)
fires, 205, 486
Great Swamp Wilderness, 699
Pine Barrens, 485, 486, 487